THE THEORY OF
PARSING, TRANSLATION,
AND COMPILING

Prentice-Hall
Series in Automatic Computation

George Forsythe, editor

MATHISON AND WALKER, *Computers and Telecommunications: Issues in Public Policy*
MCKEEMAN, et al., *A Compiler Generator*
MEYERS, *Time-Sharing Computation in the Social Sciences*
MINSKY, *Computation: Finite and Infinite Machines*
PLANE AND MCMILLAN, *Discrete Optimization: Integer Programming and Network Analysis for Management Decisions*
PRITSKER AND KIVIAT, *Simulation with GASP II: a FORTRAN-Based Simulation Language*
PYLYSHYN, editor, *Perspectives on the Computer Revolution*
RICH, *Internal Sorting Methods: Illustrated with PL/1 Program*
RUSTIN, editor, *Algorithm Specification*
RUSTIN, editor, *Computer Networks*
RUSTIN, editor, *Data Base Systems*
RUSTIN, editor, *Debugging Techniques in Large Systems*
RUSTIN, editor, *Design and Optimization of Compilers*
RUSTIN, editor, *Formal Semantics of Programming Languages*
SACKMAN AND CITRENBAUM, editors, *On-line Planning: Towards Creative Problem-Solving*
SALTON, editor, *The SMART Retrieval System: Experiments in Automatic Document Processing*
SAMMET, *Programming Languages: History and Fundamentals*
SCHAEFER, *A Mathematical Theory of Global Program Optimization*
SCHULTZ, *Digital Processing: A System Orientation*
SCHULTZ, *Spline Analysis*
SCHWARZ, et al., *Numerical Analysis of Symmetric Matrices*
SHERMAN, *Techniques in Computer Programming*
SIMON AND SIKLOSSY, *Representation and Meaning: Experiments with Information Processing Systems*
SNYDER, *Chebyshev Methods in Numerical Approximation*
STERLING AND POLLACK, *Introduction to Statistical Data Processing*
STOUTEMYER, *PL/1 Programming for Engineering and Science*
STRANG AND FIX, *An Analysis of the Finite Element Method*
STROUD, *Approximate Calculation of Multiple Integrals*
STROUD AND SECREST, *Gaussian Quadrature Formulas*
TAVISS, editor, *The Computer Impact*
TRAUB, *Iterative Methods for the Solution of Polynomial Equations*
UHR, *Pattern Recognition, Learning, and Thought*
VAN TASSEL, *Computer Security Management*
VARGA, *Matrix Iterative Analysis*
WAITE, *Implementing Software for Non-Numeric Application*
WILKINSON, *Rounding Errors in Algebraic Processes*
WIRTH, *Systematic Programming: An Introduction*

THE THEORY OF PARSING, TRANSLATION, AND COMPILING

VOLUME II: COMPILING

ALFRED V. AHO

Bell Telephone Laboratories, Inc.
Murray Hill, N.J.

JEFFREY D. ULLMAN

Department of Electrical Engineering
Princeton University

PRENTICE-HALL, INC.

ENGLEWOOD CLIFFS, N.J.

ISBN: 0-13-914564-8
Library of Congress Catalog Card No. 72-1073

Printed in the United States of America

PRENTICE-HALL INTERNATIONAL, INC., London
PRENTICE-HALL OF AUSTRALIA, PTY. LTD., Sydney
PRENTICE-HALL OF CANADA, LTD., Toronto
PRENTICE-HALL OF INDIA PRIVATE LIMITED, New Delhi
PRENTICE-HALL OF JAPAN, INC., Tokyo

PREFACE

Compiler design is one of the first major areas of systems programming for which a strong theoretical foundation is becoming available. Volume I of *The Theory of Parsing, Translation, and Compiling* developed the relevant parts of mathematics and language theory for this foundation and developed the principal methods of fast syntactic analysis. Volume II is a continuation of Volume I, but except for Chapters 7 and 8 it is oriented towards the non-syntactic aspects of compiler design.

The treatment of the material in Volume II is much the same as in Volume I, although proofs have become a little more sketchy. We have tried to make the discussion as readable as possible by providing numerous examples, each illustrating one or two concepts.

Since the text emphasizes concepts rather than language or machine details, a programming laboratory should accompany a course based on this book, so that a student can develop some facility in applying the concepts discussed to practical problems. The programming exercises appearing at the ends of sections can be used as recommended projects in such a laboratory. Part of the laboratory course should discuss the code to be generated for such programming language constructs as recursion, parameter passing, subroutine linkages, array references, loops, and so forth.

Use of the Book

The notes from which this book evolved were used in courses at Princeton University and Stevens Institute of Technology at both the senior and graduate levels. The material in Volume II was used at Stevens as a one semester course in compiler design following a one semester course based on Volume I.

As a text in compiler design, we feel, certain sections of the book are more important than others. On a first reading proofs can be omitted, along with Chapter 8 and Sections 7.4.3, 7.5.3, 9.3.3, 10.2.3, and 10.2.4.

As in Volume I, problems and bibliographic notes appear at the end of each section. We have coarsely graded problems, other than research and open problems, according to their level of difficulty, using stars. Unstarred problems test understanding of basic definitions. Singly starred problems require one significant insight for their solution. Doubly starred problems are considerably harder than singly starred problems.

Acknowledgments

In addition to the acknowledgments made in the Preface to Volume I, we would also like to thank Karel Culik, Amelia Fong, Mike Hammer, and Steve Johnson for helpful comments.

ALFRED V. AHO

JEFFREY D. ULLMAN

CONTENTS

8   THEORY OF DETERMINISTIC PARSING   666

9   TRANSLATION AND CODE GENERATION   720

10   BOOKKEEPING   788

11   CODE OPTIMIZATION   844

THE THEORY OF
PARSING, TRANSLATION,
AND COMPILING

7 TECHNIQUES FOR PARSER OPTIMIZATION

In this chapter we shall discuss various techniques that can be used to reduce the size and/or increase the speed of parsers.

First, we shall consider reducing storage requirements for precedence matrices. In certain cases, including many of practical interest, we shall show that an $m \times n$ precedence matrix can be replaced by two vectors of length m and n, respectively. We shall also discuss how a precedence matrix can be modified without affecting the shift–reduce parsing algorithm constructed from the matrix.

Next we shall show how a production language parser can be mechanically generated from a weak precedence grammar, and then we shall consider various techniques which can be used to reduce the size of the resulting parser.

Finally, we shall consider in some detail various transformations which can be used to reduce the size of an LR parser without adversely affecting its error-detecting ability. The "Simple LR" method of DeRemer and the grammar splitting method of Korenjak are discussed in detail.

The techniques presented in this chapter are indicative of the types of optimization that can be performed on all parsers constructed by the methods of Chapter 5 (in Volume I). Many more optimizations are possible, but a complete "catalogue" of these does not exist. The summary at the end of this chapter is recommended for those readers desiring merely an overview of parser optimization techniques.

7.1. LINEAR PRECEDENCE FUNCTIONS

A matrix whose entries are either -1, 0, $+1$, or "blank" will be called a *precedence matrix*. There are obvious applications for precedence matrices in the implementation of precedence-oriented parsing algorithms. For example, we can use a precedence matrix to represent the Wirth–Weber precedence relations for a precedence grammar by associating

$$-1 \quad \text{with} \quad \lessdot$$
$$0 \quad \text{with} \quad \doteq$$
$$+1 \quad \text{with} \quad \gtrdot$$
$$\text{blank} \quad \text{with} \quad \textbf{error}$$

Or we can use a precedence matrix to represent the parsing decisions of a shift–reduce parsing algorithm. One such representation would be to associate

$$-1 \quad \text{with} \quad \textbf{shift}$$
$$0 \quad \text{with} \quad \textbf{error}$$
$$+1 \quad \text{with} \quad \textbf{reduce}$$

In this section we shall show how a precedence matrix can often be concisely represented by a pair of vectors called linear precedence functions.

7.1.1. A Matrix Representation Theorem

Let M be an $m \times n$ precedence matrix. We say that a pair (f, g) of vectors of integers *represents* M if

(1) $f = (f_1, f_2, \ldots, f_m)$;
(2) $g = (g_1, g_2, \ldots, g_n)$; and
(3) $f_i < g_j$ whenever $M_{ij} = -1$,
    $f_i = g_j$ whenever $M_{ij} = 0$, and
    $f_i > g_j$ whenever $M_{ij} = +1$.

We can use f and g in place of M as follows. To determine M_{ij} we look up f_i and g_j. If $f_i < g_j$, $f_i = g_j$, or $f_i > g_j$, we shall assume that $M_{ij} = -1, 0$, or $+1$, respectively. Note that by using f and g in place of M in this manner, we do not recover the blank entries of M, because one of the relations $<, =$, or $>$ holds between each f_i and g_j.

We shall call the vectors f and g *linear precedence functions* for M. By using f and g to represent M, we can reduce the storage requirement for the precedence matrix from $m \times n$ entries to $m + n$ entries. We should point out, however, that linear precedence functions do not exist for every precedence matrix.

Example 7.1

Consider the simple precedence grammar G with productions

$$S \longrightarrow aSc \,|\, bSc \,|\, c$$

	S	a	b	c	$
S				$\doteq$	
a	$\doteq$	$\lessdot$	$\lessdot$	$\lessdot$	
b	$\doteq$	$\lessdot$	$\lessdot$	$\lessdot$	
c				$\gtrdot$	$\gtrdot$
$		$\lessdot$	$\lessdot$	$\lessdot$	

Fig. 7.1 Matrix of Wirth–Weber precedence relations.

The Wirth–Weber precedence relations for G are shown in the matrix in Fig. 7.1. We shall henceforth call this matrix the *matrix of Wirth–Weber precedence relations* to avoid confusion with the term precedence matrix. We can represent the precedence relations in Fig. 7.1 by the precedence matrix M shown in Fig. 7.2, associating

$$-1 \quad \text{with} \quad \lessdot$$
$$0 \quad \text{with} \quad \doteq$$
$$+1 \quad \text{with} \quad \gtrdot$$

and leaving blank entries unchanged. We can then represent this precedence matrix by the linear precedence functions

$$f = (1, 0, 0, 2, 0)$$
$$g = (0, 1, 1, 1, 0)$$

		1	2	3	4	5
		S	a	b	c	$
1	S				0	
2	a	0	−1	−1	−1	
3	b	0	−1	−1	−1	
4	c				+1	+1
5	$		−1	−1	−1	

Fig. 7.2 Precedence matrix M.

We can easily verify that these are linear precedence functions for M. For example, $f_4 = 2$ and $g_5 = 0$. Thus, since $f_4 > g_5$, f and g faithfully represent the $+1$ entry M_{45}.

The entry M_{41} in the precedence matrix is blank. However, $f_4 = 2$ and $g_1 = 0$. Thus, if we use f and g to represent M, we would reconstruct M_{41}

as $+1$ (since $f_4 > g_1$). Likewise, the blank entries M_{11}, M_{15}, M_{42} and M_{43} would all be represented by $+1$'s, and M_{12}, M_{13}, M_{25}, M_{35}, M_{51} and M_{55} would be represented by 0's.

The blank entries in the original precedence matrix represent error conditions. Thus, if we use linear precedence functions to represent the precedence relations in this fashion, we shall lose the ability to detect an error when none of the three precedence relations holds. However, this error will eventually be caught by attempting a reduction and discovering that there is no production whose right side is on top of the pushdown list. Nevertheless, this delay in error detection could be an unacceptable price to pay for the convenience of using precedence functions in place of precedence matrices, depending on how important early error detection is in the particular compiler involved. ☐

Example 7.2

We can overcome much of this loss of timely error detection by implementing a shift–reduce parsing algorithm for a precedence grammar in which we associate both the precedence relations $\lessdot$ and $\doteq$ with **shift** and $\gtrdot$ with **reduce**. Moreover, for the shift–reduce parsing action function we need only the precedence relations from $N \cup \Sigma \cup \{\$\}$ to $\Sigma \cup \{\$\}$. For example, we can associate $\lessdot$ and $\doteq$ with -1 and $\gtrdot$ with $+1$ and obtain the precedence

		1	2	3	4
		a	b	c	$\$$
1	S			-1	
2	a	-1	-1	-1	
3	b	-1	-1	-1	
4	c			$+1$	$+1$
5	$\$$	-1	-1	-1	

Fig. 7.3 Precedence matrix M'.

matrix M' in Fig. 7.3 from Fig. 7.1. The blank entries represent error conditions. We can show that

$$f = (0, 0, 0, 2, 0) \qquad \text{and} \qquad g = (1, 1, 1, 0)$$

are linear precedence functions for M'. These linear precedence functions have the advantage that they reproduce the blank entries M_{14}, M_{24}, M_{34}, and M_{54} as 0 (since $f_1 = f_2 = f_3 = f_5 = g_4$). We can thus use 0 to denote an error condition and in this way preserve error detection that was present in the original matrix M'. We shall consider this problem in greater detail in Section 7.1.3. ☐

We shall first present an algorithm which, given a precedence matrix M, will find precedence functions for M whenever they exist. In the next section we shall present a modification of this algorithm which when presented with a precedence matrix with -1, $+1$, and blank entries will find precedence functions for the matrix such that blank entries will be represented by 0's as often as possible.

We first observe that if two rows of a precedence matrix M have identical entries, then the two rows can be merged into a single row without affecting the existence of linear precedence functions for M. Likewise, identical columns can be merged. We shall call a precedence matrix in which all identical rows and identical columns have been merged a *reduced* precedence matrix. We can find precedence functions more efficiently if we first reduce the precedence matrix, of course.

ALGORITHM 7.1

Computation of linear precedence functions.

Input. An $m \times n$ matrix M whose entries are $-1, 0, +1$, and blank.

Output. Two vectors of integers $f = (f_1, \ldots, f_m)$ and $g = (g_1, \ldots, g_n)$ such that

$$\begin{aligned}
f_i < g_j & \quad \text{if } M_{ij} = -1 \\
f_i = g_j & \quad \text{if } M_{ij} = 0 \\
f_i > g_j & \quad \text{if } M_{ij} = +1
\end{aligned}$$

or the output "no" if no such vectors exist.

Method.

(1) Construct a directed graph with at most $m + n$ nodes, called the *linearization graph* for M. Initially, label m nodes $F_1, F_2, \ldots, F_m$ and the remaining n nodes $G_1, G_2, \ldots, G_n$. These nodes will be manipulated, and at all times there will be some node $\hat{F}_i$ representing F_i and a node $\hat{G}_j$ representing G_j. Initially, $\hat{F}_i = F_i$ and $\hat{G}_j = G_j$ for all i and j. Then do step (2) or (3), as appropriate, for each i and j.

(2) If $M_{ij} = 0$, create a new node N by merging $\hat{F}_i$ and $\hat{G}_j$. N now represents all those nodes previously represented by $\hat{F}_i$ and $\hat{G}_j$.

(3) If $M_{ij} = +1$, draw an edge from $\hat{F}_i$ to $\hat{G}_j$. If $M_{ij} = -1$, draw an edge from $\hat{G}_j$ to $\hat{F}_i$.

(4) If the resulting graph is cyclic, answer "no."

(5) If the linearization graph is acyclic, let f_i be the length of a longest path beginning at $\hat{F}_i$ and let g_j be the length of a longest path beginning at $\hat{G}_j$. □

In step (4) of Algorithm 7.1 we can use the following general technique to determine whether a directed graph G is cyclic or acyclic:

(1) Let G be the graph at hand initially.

(2) Find a node N in the graph at hand that has no descendants. If no such node exists, report that G is cyclic. Otherwise, remove N.

(3) If the resulting graph is empty, report that G is acyclic. Otherwise, repeat step (2).

Once we have determined that the graph is acyclic, we can use the following labeling technique in step (5) of Algorithm 7.1 to determine the length of a longest path extending from every node.

Let G be a directed acyclic graph (dag).

(1) Initially, label each node in G with 0.

(2) Repeat step (3) until no further changes can be made to the labels of G. At that time the label on each node gives the length of a longest path beginning at that node.

(3) Find a node N in G. Let N have direct descendants $N_1, N_2, \ldots, N_k$ with labels $l_1, l_2, \ldots, l_k$. Change the label of N to $\max\{l_1, l_2, \ldots, l_k\} + 1$. (If $k = 0$, the label of N remains 0.) Repeat this step for every node in G.

It should be clear that we shall repeat step (3) at most l times per node, where l is the length of a longest path in G.

Example 7.3

Consider the precedence matrix M of Fig. 7.4.

	1	2	3	4	5
1	-1	-1	0		-1
2			+1	-1	0
3	-1		+1	0	
4		-1	+1		
5				+1	+1

Fig. 7.4 Precedence matrix.

The linearization graph constructed from M is shown in Fig. 7.5. Note that in step (2) of Algorithm 7.1, three pairs of nodes are merged: (F_3, G_4), (F_2, G_5), and (F_1, G_3).

The linearization graph is acyclic. From step (5) of Algorithm 7.1 we obtain linear precedence functions $f = (0, 1, 2, 1, 3)$ and $g = (3, 2, 0, 2, 1)$. For example, f_5 is 3 since the longest path beginning at node F_5 is of length 3. □

THEOREM 7.1

A precedence matrix has linear precedence functions if and only if its linearization graph is acyclic.

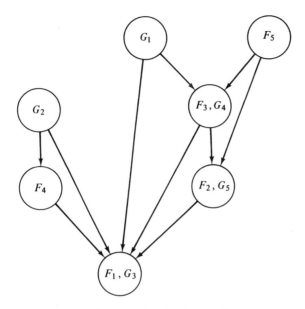

Fig. 7.5   Linearization graph.

Proof.

If: We first note that Algorithm 7.1 emits f and g only if the linearization graph is acyclic. It suffices to show that if f and g are computed by Algorithm 7.1, then

(1) $M_{ij} = 0$ implies that $f_i = g_j$,
(2) $M_{ij} = +1$ implies that $f_i > g_j$, and
(3) $M_{ij} = -1$ implies that $f_i < g_j$

Assertion (1) is immediate from step (2) of Algorithm 7.1. To prove assertion (2), we note that if $M_{ij} = +1$, then edge $(\hat{F}_i, \hat{G}_j)$ is added to the linearization graph. Hence, $f_i > g_j$, since the length of a longest path to a leaf from node $\hat{F}_i$ must be at least one more than the length of a longest path from $\hat{G}_j$, if the linearization graph is acyclic. Assertion (3) follows similarly.

Only if: Suppose that a linear precedence matrix M has linear precedence functions f and g but that the linearization graph for M has a cycle consisting of the sequence of nodes $N_1, N_2, \ldots, N_k, N_{k+1}$, where $N_{k+1} = N_1$ and $k \geq 1$. Then by step (3), for all i, $1 \leq i \leq k$, we can find nodes H_i and I_{i+1} such that

(1) H_i and I_{i+1} are original F's and G's;
(2) H_i and I_{i+1} are represented by N_i and N_{i+1}, respectively; and,
(3) Either H_i is F_m, I_{i+1} is G_n and $M_{mn} = +1$, or H_i is G_m, I_{i+1} is F_n and $M_{nm} = -1$.

We observe by rule (2) that if nodes F_m and G_n are represented by the same N_i, then f_m must equal g_n if f and g are to be linearizing functions for M.

Let f and g be the supposed linearizing functions for M. Let h_i be f_m if H_i is F_m and let h_i be g_m if H_i is G_m. Let h_i' be f_m if I_i is F_m and let h_i' be g_m if I_i is G_m. Then

$$h_1 > h_2' = h_2 > h_3' = \cdots = h_k > h_{k+1}'$$

But since N_{k+1} is N_1, we have $h_{k+1}' = h_1$. However, we just showed that $h_1 > h_{k+1}'$. Thus, a precedence matrix with a cyclic linearization graph cannot have linear precedence functions. □

COROLLARY

Algorithm 7.1 computes linear precedence functions for M whenever they exist and produces the answer "no" otherwise. □

7.1.2. Applications to Operator Precedence Parsing

We can try to find precedence functions for any matrix whose entries have at most three values. The applicability of this technique is not affected by what the entries represent. To illustrate this point, in this section we shall show how precedence functions can be applied to represent operator precedence relations.

Example 7.4

Consider our favorite grammar G_0 with productions

$$E \longrightarrow E + T \mid T$$
$$T \longrightarrow T * F \mid F$$
$$F \longrightarrow (E) \mid a$$

The matrix giving the operator precedence relations for G_0 is shown in Fig. 7.6.

	$	(	+	*	a	)
$		<·	<·	<·	<·	
(		<·	<·	<·	<·	≐
+	·>	<·	·>	<·	<·	·>
*	·>	<·	·>	·>	<·	·>
a	·>		·>	·>		·>
)	·>		·>	·>		·>

Fig. 7.6 Matrix of operator precedence relations for G_0.

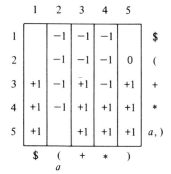

	1	2	3	4	5	
1		−1	−1	−1		\$
2		−1	−1	−1	0	(
3	+1	−1	+1	−1	+1	+
4	+1	−1	+1	+1	+1	*
5	+1		+1	+1	+1	a,)

$ \quad \$ \quad\quad (\quad\quad + \quad\quad * \quad\quad) $
$\qquad\qquad\quad a$

Fig. 7.7 Reduced precedence matrix M'.

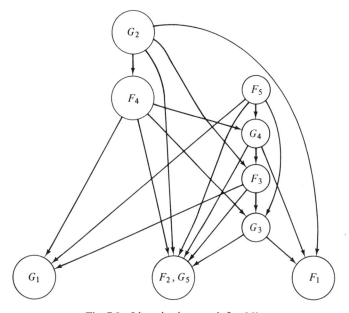

Fig. 7.8 Linearization graph for M'.

If we replace $\lessdot$ by -1, $\doteq$ by 0, and $\gtrdot$ by $+1$, we obtain the reduced precedence matrix M' shown in Fig. 7.7. Here we have combined the rows labeled a and) and the columns labeled (and a. The linearization graph for M' is shown in Fig. 7.8. From this graph we obtain the linear precedence functions $f' = (0, 0, 2, 4, 4)$ and $g' = (0, 5, 1, 3, 0)$ for M'. Hence, the linear precedence functions for the original matrix are $f = (0, 0, 2, 4, 4, 4)$ and $g = (0, 5, 1, 3, 5, 0)$. $\square$

7.1.3. Weak Precedence Functions

As pointed out previously, -1, 0, and $+1$ of the matrix of Algorithm 7.1 can be identified with the Wirth–Weber precedence relations $\lessdot$, $\doteq$, and

$\succ$, respectively. If linear precedence functions are found, then the precedence relation between X and Y is determined by applying the first function to X and the second to Y. In this case, all pairs X and Y will have some precedence relation between them, so error detection is delayed until either the end of the input is reached or an impossible reduction is called for.

However, the linear precedence function technique can be applied to the representation of shift–reduce parsing decisions with an opportunity of retaining some of the error-checking capability present in the blank entries of the original matrix of precedence relations. Let us define a *weak precedence matrix* as an $m \times n$ matrix M whose entries are -1, $+1$, and blank. The -1 entries generally denote shifts, the $+1$ entries reductions, and the blank entries errors. Such a matrix can be used to describe the shift–reduce function of a shift–reduce parsing algorithm for a weak precedence grammar, a $(1, 1)$-precedence grammar, or a simple mixed strategy precedence grammar.

We say that vectors f and g are *weak precedence functions* for a weak precedence matrix M if $f_i < g_j$ whenever $M_{ij} = -1$ and $f_i > g_j$ whenever $M_{ij} = +1$.

The condition $f_i = g_j$ can then be used to denote an error condition, represented by a blank entry M_{ij}. In general, we may not always be able to have $f_i = g_j$ wherever M_{ij} is blank, but we would like to retain as much of the error-detecting capability of the original matrix as possible.

Thus, we can view the problem of finding weak precedence functions for a weak precedence matrix M as one of finding functions which will produce as many 0's for the critical blank entries of M as possible. We choose not to fill in all blanks of the weak precedence matrix with 0's immediately, since this would restrict the number of useful weak precedence matrices that have weak precedence functions. Some blank entries may have to be changed to -1 or $+1$ in order for weak precedence functions to exist (Exercise 7.1.9). In addition, some blank entries may never be consulted by the parser, so these entries need not be represented by 0's.

The concept of independent nodes in a directed acyclic graph is of importance here. We say that two nodes N_1 and N_2 of a directed acyclic graph are *independent* if there is no path from N_1 to N_2 or from N_2 to N_1.

We could use Algorithm 7.1 directly to produce weak precedence functions for a weak precedence matrix M, but this algorithm as given did not attempt to maximize the number of 0's produced for blank entries. However, we shall use the first three steps of Algorithm 7.1 to produce a linearization graph for M.

From Theorem 7.1 we know that M has weak precedence functions if and only if the linearization graph for M is acyclic. The independent nodes of the linearization graph determine which blank entries of M can be preserved. That is, we can have $f_i = g_j$ if and only if F_i and G_j are independent nodes. Of course, if we choose to have $f_i = g_j$, then there may be other pairs of independent nodes whose corresponding numbers cannot be made equal.

Example 7.5

The matrix of Wirth–Weber precedence relations for the grammar G_0 is shown in Fig. 7.9. The columns corresponding to nonterminals have been deleted, since we shall use this matrix only for shift–reduce decisions. The corresponding reduced weak precedence matrix is shown in Fig. 7.10, and the linearization graph that results from this reduced matrix is shown in Fig. 7.11. In this graph the nodes labeled F_1 and G_4 are independent. Also, G_2 and G_4 are independent, but F_1 and G_3 are not. ☐

	a	$($	$)$	$+$	$*$	$\$$
E			$\doteq$	$\doteq$		
T			$\cdot >$	$\cdot >$	$\doteq$	$\cdot >$
F			$\cdot >$	$\cdot >$	$\cdot >$	$\cdot >$
a			$\cdot >$	$\cdot >$	$\cdot >$	$\cdot >$
$)$			$\cdot >$	$\cdot >$	$\cdot >$	$\cdot >$
$($	$<\cdot$	$<\cdot$				
$+$	$<\cdot$	$<\cdot$				
$*$	$<\cdot$	$<\cdot$				
$\$$	$<\cdot$	$<\cdot$				

Fig. 7.9 Precedence relations for G_0.

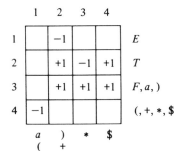

Fig. 7.10 Reduced weak precedence matrix.

We can generalize step (5) of Algorithm 7.1 to determine precedence functions which maximize the number of 0's produced for blank entries. We can view the determination of the components of the precedence vectors as an assignment of numbers to the nodes of the linearization graph. Any set of pairwise-independent nodes can be assigned the same number, but a node which is an ancestor of one or more nodes must be assigned a larger number than any of its descendants.

We shall assign numbers to the nodes as follows. First, we partition the nodes of the linearization graph into clusters of independent nodes such

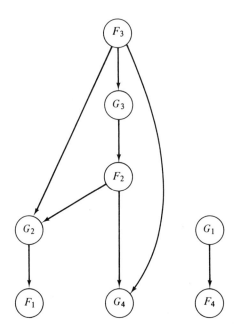

Fig. 7.11   Linearization graph.

that the total number of *F-G* pairs together in a cluster is as large as possible and no one cluster contains both descendents and ancestors of another cluster. In general there may be many different sets of clusters possible, and certain *F-G* pairs may be more desirable than others. This part of the process may well be a large combinatorial problem.

However, once we have partitioned the graph into a set of clusters, we can then find a linear order $<$ on the clusters such that, for clusters C and C', $C < C'$ if C contains a node that is a descendant of a node in C'. If $C_0, C_1, \ldots, C_k$ is the sequence of clusters in this linear order, we then assign 0 to all nodes in C_0, 1 to all nodes in C_1, and so forth.

Example 7.6

Consider the linearization graph for G_0 shown in Fig. 7.11. The set $\{F_1, F_4, G_4\}$ is an example of a cluster of independent nodes, and so are $\{F_4, G_2, G_4\}$, $\{F_2, G_1\}$, $\{G_1, G_3\}$, and $\{F_3, G_1\}$. However, the cluster $\{G_1, G_3\}$ is not desirable, since both nodes in this cluster are labeled by G's and thus it would not produce a 0 entry in the weak precedence matrix. The cluster $\{F_3, G_1\}$ might be more desirable than the cluster $\{F_2, G_1\}$, since $f_3 = g_1$ will detect errors whenever aa, $a($, $)a$, or $)($ appear in an input string, while $f_2 = g_1$ will detect errors only for the pairs Ta and $T($. Also, note that if we detect an error whenever aa appears, we shall not be able to reduce a to F, so the adjacencies Fa and Ta would never occur.

Thus, one possible clustering of nodes is $\{F_1\}$, $\{F_4, G_2, G_4\}$, $\{F_2\}$, $\{G_3\}$, $\{F_3, G_1\}$. Taking the linear order on clusters to be the left-to-right order shown, we obtain the weak precedence functions

$$f = (0, 2, 4, 1) \quad \text{and} \quad g = (4, 1, 3, 1)$$

These functions define the precedence matrix shown in Fig. 7.12. □

	a	(	)	+	*	$
E	−1	−1	−1	−1	−1	−1
T	−1	−1	+1	+1	−1	+1
F	0	0	+1	+1	+1	+1
a	0	0	+1	+1	+1	+1
)	0	0	+1	+1	+1	+1
(	−1	−1	0	0	−1	0
+	−1	−1	0	0	−1	0
*	−1	−1	0	0	−1	0
$	−1	−1	0	0	−1	0

Fig. 7.12 Resulting precedence matrix for G_0.

7.1.4. Modification of Precedence Matrices

Example 7.6 suggests that certain error entries in the matrix of Wirth–Weber precedence relations will never be consulted by the shift–reduce parsing algorithms for simple and weak precedence grammars (Algorithms 5.12 and 5.14). If we can isolate these entries and replace them by "don't cares," then we can ignore these entries when we are attempting to find weak precedence functions that cover as many error entries as possible.

To understand what modifications can be made to a matrix of precedence relations, we first define what we mean when we say two shift–reduce parsing algorithms are exactly equivalent. We shall use the notation for shift–reduce parsing algorithms that was given in Section 5.3 (Volume I).

DEFINITION

Let $\alpha_1 = (f_1, g_1)$† and $\alpha_2 = (f_2, g_2)$ be two shift–reduce parsing algorithms for a context-free grammar $G = (N, \Sigma, P, S)$. We say that α_1 and α_2 are *exactly equivalent* if their behavior on each input string is identical: that is, if an input string w is in $L(G)$, then both parsing algorithms accept w. If w is not in $L(G)$, then both parsers announce error after the same number of steps and in the same phase. If in the reduction phase, an error relation is found after scanning an equal number of symbols down the stack.

We shall determine which blank entries in the canonical matrix of Wirth–Weber precedence relations can be changed without affecting the parsing

†Here f_1 is the shift–reduce function and g_1 is the reduce function.

behavior of the shift–reduce parsing algorithm constructed from that matrix using Algorithm 5.12. The chief use of this analysis is in finding good clusters for weak precedence functions as discussed in the previous section. Blank entries which should not be changed will be called *essential blanks*. The theorem that follows identifies the essential blanks.

First, let us establish some notational conventions. Suppose that $G = (N, \Sigma, P, S)$ is a CFG. We let M_c be the matrix of canonical Wirth–Weber precedence relations for G. (These are the ones that are created by the definition.) We shall subscript these precedence relations with c. If no Wirth–Weber precedence relation holds between a pair of symbols X and Y, we shall write $X \ ?_c \ Y$.

We can also create an arbitrary matrix M of $\lessdot$'s, $\doteq$'s, $\gtrdot$'s, and blanks. If M has the same dimensions as M_c, then we shall call M a *matrix of precedence relations* for G. We shall write $X \ ? \ Y$ if the (X, Y) entry in M is blank.

We can use Algorithm 5.12 to construct the shift–reduce parsing algorithm $\mathcal{Q}_c = (f_c, g_c)$ for G using the Wirth–Weber precedence relations in M_c. We can also use Algorithm 5.12 to construct another shift–reduce parsing algorithm $\mathcal{Q} = (f, g)$ for G using the precedence relations in M. Theorem 5.15 guarantees that $\mathcal{Q}_c$ is a valid parsing algorithm for G, but there is no guarantee that $\mathcal{Q}$ will be a valid parsing algorithm for G. However, the following theorem states necessary and sufficient conditions for $\mathcal{Q}$ to be exactly equivalent to $\mathcal{Q}_c$.

THEOREM 7.2

$\mathcal{Q}$ is exactly equivalent to $\mathcal{Q}_c$ if and only if the following four conditions are satisfied for all X and Y in $N \cup \Sigma \cup \{\$\}$, a and b in $\Sigma \cup \{\$\}$, and A in N.

    (1) (a) If $X \lessdot_c Y$, then $X \lessdot Y$.
        (b) If $X \doteq_c Y$, then $X \doteq Y$.
        (c) If $X \gtrdot_c a$, then $X \gtrdot a$.
    (2) If $b \ ?_c \ a$, then $b \ ? \ a$.
    (3) If $A \ ?_c \ a$, then either
        (a) $A \ ? \ a$ or
        (b) For all Z in $N \cup \Sigma$ such that $A \rightarrow \alpha Z$ is a production in P the relation $Z \gtrdot_c a$ is false.
    (4) If $X \ ?_c \ A$, then either
        (a) $X \ ? \ A$ or
        (b) For all Z in $N \cup \Sigma$ such that $A \rightarrow Z\alpha$ is in P the relation $X \lessdot_c Z$ is false.

Proof.

If: By condition (1), the moves of $\mathcal{Q}$ and $\mathcal{Q}_c$ must agree until the latter detects an error. Therefore, it suffices to show that if the two parsing algorithms reach configuration $Q = (X_1 \cdots X_m, a_1 \cdots a_r, \pi)$ and we find $Q \mid_{\overline{a_c}}$ **error**, then $Q \mid_{\overline{a}}$ **error**, and, moreover, the mechanism of error detection is the same in both α and α_c.

Let us first assume that in configuration Q, $f_c(X_m, a_1) = $ **error** but $f(X_m, a_1) \neq$ **error**. We shall show that a contradiction arises. Thus, suppose that $X_m \ ?_c \ a_1$ but that $X_m \ ? \ a_1$ does not hold. By condition (2), X_m must be a nonterminal. By condition (3), for all Y such that $X_m \rightarrow \alpha Y$ is in P, $Y \gtrdot_c a_1$ is false.

Examination of the precedence parsing algorithm indicates that the only way for a nonterminal to be on top of the stack is for the previous move to have been a reduction. Then there is some production $X_m \rightarrow \alpha Y$ in P such that the move of both parsers before configuration Q was entered is $(X_1 \cdots X_{m-1} \alpha Y, a_1 \cdots a_r, \pi') \vdash Q$. But this implies that $Y \gtrdot_c a_1$, in contradiction.

The other possibility is that in configuration Q, $g_c(X_1 \cdots X_m, e) = $ **error** but $g(X_1 \cdots X_m, e) \neq$ **error**. The only case that needs to be considered here is that in which $X_m \gtrdot_c a_1$, $X_m \gtrdot a_1$ and there is some s such that $X_s \ ?_c \ X_{s+1}$, while $X_i \doteq_c X_{i+1}$ and $X_i \doteq X_{i+1}$ for $s < i < m$, but the relation $X_s \ ? \ X_{s+1}$ does not hold. We claim that X_{s+1} must be a nonterminal, because the only way α_c could place a terminal above X_s on the stack is if $X_s \lessdot_c X_{s+1}$ or $X_s \doteq_c X_{s+1}$.

By condition (4), we can not have $X_s \lessdot_c Y$ if $X_{s+1} \rightarrow Y\alpha$ is in P. But the only way that X_{s+1} could appear next to X_s on the stack is for a reduction of some $Y\alpha$ to X_{s+1} to occur. That is, there must be some configuration $(X_1 \cdots X_s Y\alpha, b_1 \cdots b_k, \pi'')$ leading to Q such that

$$(X_1 \cdots X_s Y\alpha, b_1 \cdots b_k, \pi'') \mid_{\overline{a_c}} (X_1 \cdots X_s X_{s+1}, b_1 \cdots b_k, \pi''i).$$

But then $X_s \lessdot_c Y$ in violation of condition (4).

Only if: It is straightforward to show that if condition (1) is violated, the parsers are not exactly equivalent. We therefore omit this portion of the proof and proceed to the more difficult portions.

Case 1: Suppose that condition (2) is violated. That is, for some $b \ ?_c \ a$, we do not have $b \ ? \ a$. Since G is a simple precedence grammar (and hence proper), there is some sentence wbx in $L(G)$. Consider the parsing of wba by α_c and α. Since wbx is in $L(G)$, neither parser can declare an error until the a in wba becomes the next input symbol. Thus, both parsers must enter some configuration $(\$\alpha, ba\$, \pi)$, at which time the b is shifted onto the stack, yielding configuration $(\$\alpha b, a\$, \pi)$. Since $b \ ?_c \ a$ but $b \ ? \ a$ is false, α_c and α are not exactly equivalent.

Case 2: Suppose that condition (3) is violated. That is, we have $A \ ?_c \ a$, $A \ ? \ a$ is false, and there is some $A \rightarrow \alpha X$ in P such that $X \gtrdot_c a$.

Since G is proper, there is some right-sentential form βAw of G and there is some x in Σ^* such that $A \underset{rm}{\Rightarrow} \alpha X \underset{rm}{\Rightarrow} \beta_1 \underset{rm}{\Rightarrow} \cdots \underset{rm}{\Rightarrow} \beta_n \underset{rm}{\Rightarrow} x$. Moreover, there exists y in Σ^* such that $\beta \overset{*}{\Rightarrow} y$. By Lemma 5.3, if Y is the last symbol of any of $\beta_1, \ldots, \beta_n$ or x, then $Y \gtrdot_c a$.

In the parsing of yxw, we note that the first symbol of w is not shifted until yx is reduced to βA. Therefore, the parsing of yxa will proceed exactly as that of yxw—until configuration $(\$\beta A, a\$, \pi')$ is reached. But $A ?_c a$ holds while $A ? a$ does not, so the two parsers are not exactly equivalent.

Case 3: Suppose that condition (4) is violated. That is, we have $X ?_c A$ and some production $A \rightarrow Y\alpha$ such that $X ? A$ is false and $X \lessdot_c Y$. Let βAw be a right-sentential form and $A \underset{rm}{\Rightarrow} Y\alpha \underset{rm}{\Rightarrow} \gamma_1 \underset{rm}{\Rightarrow} \cdots \underset{rm}{\Rightarrow} \gamma_n \Rightarrow x$. Also, let δXu be a right-sentential form such that $\delta \overset{*}{\Rightarrow} y$ and $X \overset{*}{\Rightarrow} z$. Then by Lemma 5.3, X is related by $\lessdot_c$ to every first symbol in each of $\gamma_1, \ldots, \gamma_n$ and x. Moreover, the last symbol of each right-sentential form in a derivation $X \underset{rm}{\overset{*}{\Rightarrow}} z$ is related by $\gtrdot_c$ to the first symbol of x.

Then when parsing $yzxw$, the configuration $(\$\delta X, xw\$, \pi)$ will be reached, and subsequently $(\$\delta XA, w\$, \pi')$ will be entered. The parsers will eventually attempt to reduce by the production that introduced A into βAw. If $X ?_c A$, but $X ? A$ is false, the exact equivalence of the two parsers is again contradicted. $\square$

Example 7.7

Consider the following simple precedence grammar G:

$$E \longrightarrow E + A \mid A$$
$$A \longrightarrow T$$
$$T \longrightarrow T * F \mid F$$
$$F \longrightarrow (B \mid a$$
$$B \longrightarrow E)$$

It should be evident that $L(G) = L(G_0)$. The matrix of canonical Wirth–Weber precedence relations for G is shown in Fig. 7.13. Let us consider which entries of Fig. 7.13 can be modified according to Theorem 7.2. Condition (1) states that no nonblank entries can be changed. Condition (2) states that all blank entries in the intersection of the last six rows and the last six columns are essential.

By condition (3), $(E, \$)$ is an essential blank since $E \rightarrow A$ is a production and $A \gtrdot \$$. The remaining blanks in the last six columns are not essential and thus can be changed arbitrarily.

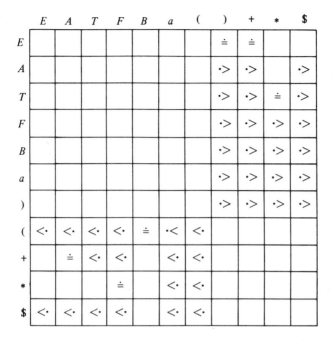

	E	A	T	F	B	a	(	)	+	*	$
E								$\doteq$	$\doteq$		
A								$\cdot>$	$\cdot>$		$\cdot>$
T								$\cdot>$	$\cdot>$	$\doteq$	$\cdot>$
F								$\cdot>$	$\cdot>$	$\cdot>$	$\cdot>$
B								$\cdot>$	$\cdot>$	$\cdot>$	$\cdot>$
a								$\cdot>$	$\cdot>$	$\cdot>$	$\cdot>$
)								$\cdot>$	$\cdot>$	$\cdot>$	$\cdot>$
(	$<\cdot$	$<\cdot$	$<\cdot$	$<\cdot$	$\doteq$	$\cdot<$	$<\cdot$				
+		$\doteq$	$<\cdot$	$<\cdot$		$<\cdot$	$<\cdot$				
*			$\doteq$			$<\cdot$	$<\cdot$				
$	$<\cdot$	$<\cdot$	$<\cdot$	$<\cdot$		$<\cdot$	$<\cdot$				

Fig. 7.13   Matrix of canonical Wirth–Weber precedence relations.

Condition (4) requires that the ($, B$) entry be an essential blank, because
$B \longrightarrow E$) is a production and $\$ < E$. The remaining blank entries in the first
five columns can be changed arbitrarily.   □

If we use Algorithm 5.14 to construct a shift–reduce parsing parsing
algorithm for a uniquely invertible weak precedence grammar, then we can
show that the analogous parsers $\mathcal{C}$ and $\mathcal{C}_c$ of Theorem 7.2 are exactly
equivalent if and only if the first three conditions of Theorem 7.2 are satisfied.†

Example 7.8

Using conditions (1)–(3) of Theorem 7.2 on the weak precedence relations
for G_0 shown in Fig. 7.9 (p. 553), we find that all the blanks in the last six
rows are essential. The only other essential blank is (E, $), since $E \longrightarrow T$ is a
production and $T \gg \$.
Examining the linearization graph of Fig. 7.11, we find that there are
no precedence functions such that every essential blank is represented by 0.

---

†Recall that reductions do not depend on the precedence matrix in a weak precedence
parser.

This would require, for example, that nodes F_4, G_2, G_3, and G_4 all be placed in one cluster.

At this point we might give up trying to use precedence functions to implement the parser. However, we can consider using a slightly weaker definition of equivalence between parsers.

Exact equivalence is very stringent. In practical situations we would be willing to say that two shift–reduce parsing algorithms are equivalent if they either both accept the same input strings or both announce error at the same position on erroneous input strings. Thus, one parser could announce error while the other made several reductions (but no shift moves) before announcing error. Under this definition, which we shall call simply *equivalence*, we can modify precedence relations even more drastically but still preserve equivalence. (See Exercise 7.1.13.)

With this weaker definition of equivalence we can show that a shift–reduce parsing algorithm using the precedence functions

	E	T	F	a	(	)	+	*	$
f	0	2	5	5	4	5	4	4	4
g				5	5	1	1	3	0

is equivalent to the parser constructed by Algorithm 5.14 from the weak precedence relations in Fig. 7.9. □

We shall explore this weaker form of equivalence in much greater detail in Sections 7.2, 7.3, and 7.4.

EXERCISES

7.1.1. Find linear weak precedence functions for the following grammars or prove that none exist:

(a) $S \longrightarrow SA \,|\, A$
$A \longrightarrow (S) \,|\, (\,)$

(b) $E \longrightarrow E + T \,|\, +T \,|\, T$
$T \longrightarrow T * F \,|\, F$
$F \longrightarrow (E) \,|\, a$

7.1.2. Show that if M' is a matrix formed from M by permuting some rows and/or columns, then the vectors f and g produced by Algorithm 7.1 for M' will be permutations of those produced for M.

7.1.3. Find linear precedence functions for the matrix of Fig. 7.14.

7.1.4. Find an algorithm to determine whether a matrix has linear precedence functions f and g such that $f = g$.

			+1	+1	+1
			+1	+1	+1
−1	−1		+1	+1	+1
−1	−1	−1	+1	+1	+1
−1	−1	−1	−1	+1	+1
−1	−1	−1	−1	−1	0

Fig. 7.14   Matrix.

*7.1.5. (a) Show that the technique given after Algorithm 7.1 for determining whether a directed graph is acyclic actually works.

(b) Show that this technique can be implemented to work in time $0(n) + 0(e)$, where n is the number of nodes and e is the number of edges in the given graph. *Hint:* Choose a node in the graph. Color all nodes on a path extending from this node until either a leaf or previously colored node is encountered. If a leaf is found, remove it, back up to its immediate ancestor, and then continue the coloring process.

7.1.6. (a) Show that the labeling technique given after Algorithm 7.1 will find the length of a longest path beginning at each node.

(b) Show that this technique can be implemented in time $0(n) + 0 (e)$, where n is the number of nodes and e the number of edges in the graph.

7.1.7. Give an algorithm which takes a matrix M with entries $-1, 0, +1$, and blank and a constant k and determines whether there exist vectors f and g such that

(1) If $M_{ij} = -1$, then $f_i + k < g_j$;
(2) If $M_{ij} = 0$, then $|f_i - g_j| \leq k$;
(3) If $M_{ij} = +1$, then $f_i > g_j + k$.

DEFINITION

Let M be a weak precedence matrix. We say a sequence of integers $i_1, i_2, \ldots, i_k$, where k is even and greater than 3, is a *cycle* of M if

(1) $M_{i_j i_{j+1}} = -1$ for odd j, $M_{i_{j+1} i_j} = +1$ for even j, and $M_{i_1 i_k} = +1$,

or

(2) $M_{i_j i_{j+1}} = +1$ for odd j, $M_{i_{j+1} i_j} = -1$ for even j, and $M_{i_1 i_k} = -1$.

7.1.8. Show that there exist weak precedence functions for a weak precedence matrix if and only if M contains no cycle.

7.1.9. Let M be a weak precedence matrix and let i, j, k, and l be indices such that either

(1) $M_{ik} = M_{jl} = -1$, $M_{jk} = +1$, and M_{il} is blank, or
(2) $M_{ik} = M_{jl} = +1$, $M_{jk} = -1$, and M_{il} is blank.

Let M' be M with M_{il} replaced by -1 in case (1) and by $+1$ in case (2).

Show that f and g are weak precedence functions for M if and only if f and g are weak precedence functions for M'.

DEFINITION

We say that two rows (columns) of a precedence matrix are *compatible* if whenever they differ one is blank. We can *merge* compatible rows (columns) by replacing them by a single row (column) which agrees with all their nonblank entries.

7.1.10. Show that the operations of row and column merger preserve the property of not having linearizing functions.

We can also use linear precedence functions to represent the $\lessdot$ and $\doteq$ relations used by the reduce function in the shift–reduce parsing algorithm constructed by Algorithm 5.12. First, we construct a weak precedence matrix M in which -1 represents $\lessdot$, $+1$ represents $\doteq$, and blanks represent both $\gtrdot$ and **error**. We then attempt to find linear precedence functions for M, again attempting to represent as many blanks as possible by 0's.

7.1.11. Represent the $\lessdot$ and $\doteq$ relations of Fig. 7.13 with linear precedence functions. Use Theorem 7.2 to locate the essential blanks and attempt to preserve these blanks.

*7.1.12. Show that under the definition of exact equivalence for weak precedence parsers a blank entry (X, Y) of the matrix of Wirth–Weber precedence relations is an essential blank if and only if one of the following conditions holds:

(1) X and Y are in $\Sigma \cup \{\$\}$; or
(2) X is in N, Y is in $\Sigma \cup \{\$\}$, and there is a production $X \longrightarrow \alpha Z$ such that $Z \gtrdot_c Y$.

In the following problems, "equivalent" is used in the sense of Example 7.8.

*7.1.13. Let $\mathcal{A}_c$ and $\mathcal{A}$ be shift–reduce parsing algorithms for a simple precedence grammar as in Theorem 7.2. Prove that $\mathcal{A}_c$ is equivalent to $\mathcal{A}$ if and only if the following conditions are satisfied:

(1) (a) If $X \lessdot_c Y$, then $X \lessdot Y$.
    (b) If $X \doteq_c Y$, then $X \doteq Y$.
    (c) If $X \gtrdot_c a$, then $X \gtrdot a$.
(2) If $b \mathrel{?}_c a$, then $b \lessdot a$ is false.
(3) If $A \mathrel{?}_c a$ and $A \lessdot a$ or $A \doteq a$, then there is no derivation $A \underset{\text{rm}}{\Rightarrow} \alpha_1 X_1 \underset{\text{rm}}{\Rightarrow} \cdots \underset{\text{rm}}{\Rightarrow} \alpha_m X_m$, $m \geq 1$, such that for $1 \leq i < m$, $X_i \mathrel{?}_c a$ and $X_i \gtrdot a$, and $X_m \gtrdot_c a$, or X_m is a terminal and $X_m \gtrdot a$.
(4) If $A_1 \lessdot a$ or $A_1 \doteq a$ for some a, then there does not exist a derivation $A_1 \Rightarrow A_2 \Rightarrow \cdots \Rightarrow A_m \Rightarrow B\alpha$, $m \geq 1$, a symbol X, and a production $B \longrightarrow Y\beta$ such that
    (a) $X \mathrel{?}_c A_i$ but $X \lessdot A_i$, for $2 \leq i \leq m$;
    (b) $X \mathrel{?}_c B$ but $X \lessdot B$; and
    (c) $X \lessdot Y$.

7.1.14. Show that the parser using the precedence functions of Example 7.8 is equivalent to the canonical precedence parser for G_0.

7.1.15. Let M be a matrix of precedence relations constructed from M_c, the matrix of canonical Wirth–Weber precedence relations, by replacing some blank entries by $\gtrdot$. Show that the parsers constructed from M and M_c by Algorithm 5.12 (or 5.14) are equivalent.

*7.1.16. Consider a shift–reduce parsing algorithm for a simple precedence grammar in which after each reduction a check is made to determine whether the $\lessdot$ or $\doteq$ relation holds between the symbol that was immediately to the left of the handle and the nonterminal to which the handle is reduced. Under what conditions will an arbitrary matrix of precedence relations yield a parser that is exactly equivalent (or equivalent) to the parser of this form constructed from the canonical Wirth–Weber precedence relations?

**7.1.17. Show that every CFL has a precedence grammar (not necessarily uniquely invertible) for which linear precedence functions can be found.

Research Problems

7.1.18. Give an efficient algorithm to find linear precedence functions for a weak precedence grammar G that yields a parser which is equivalent to the canonical precedence parser for G.

7.1.19. Devise good error recovery routines to be used in conjunction with precedence functions.

Programming Exercises

7.1.20. Construct a program that implements Algorithm 7.1.

7.1.21. Write a program that implements a shift–reduce parsing algorithm using linear precedence functions to implement the f and g functions.

7.1.22. Write a program that determines whether a CFG is a precedence grammar that has linear precedence functions.

7.1.23. Write a program that takes as input a simple precedence grammar G that has linear precedence functions and constructs for G a shift–reduce parser utilizing the precedence functions.

BIBLIOGRAPHIC NOTES

Floyd [1963] used linear precedence functions to represent the matrix of operator precedence relations. Wirth and Weber [1966] suggested their use for representing Wirth–Weber precedence relations. Algorithms to compute linear precedence functions have been given by Floyd [1963], Wirth [1965], Bell [1969], Martin [1972], and Aho and Ullman [1972a].

Theorem 7.2 is from Aho and Ullman [1972b], which also contains answers to Exercises 7.1.13 and 7.1.15. Exercise 7.1.17 is from Martin [1972].

7.2. OPTIMIZATION OF FLOYD–EVANS PARSERS

A shift–reduce parsing algorithm provides a conceptually simple method of parsing. However, when we attempt to implement the two functions of the parser, we are confronted with problems of efficiency. In this section we shall discuss how a shift–reduce parsing algorithm for a uniquely invertible weak precedence grammar can be implemented using the Floyd–Evans production language. The emphasis in the discussion will be on methods by which we can reduce the size of the resulting Floyd–Evans production language program without changing the behavior of the parser. Although we only consider precedence grammars here, the techniques of this section are also applicable to the implementation of parsers for each of the other classes of grammars discussed in Chapter 5 (Volume I).

7.2.1. Mechanical Generation of Floyd–Evans Parsers for Weak Precedence Grammars

We begin by showing how a Floyd–Evans production language parser can be mechanically constructed for a uniquely invertible weak precedence grammar. The Floyd–Evans production language is described in Section 5.4.4 of Chapter 5. We shall illustrate the algorithm by means of an example.

As expected, we shall use for our example the weak precedence grammar G_0 with productions

$$(1)\ E \rightarrow E + T$$
$$(2)\ E \rightarrow T$$
$$(3)\ T \rightarrow T * F$$
$$(4)\ T \rightarrow F$$
$$(5)\ F \rightarrow (E)$$
$$(6)\ F \rightarrow a$$

The Wirth–Weber precedence relations for G_0 were shown in Fig. 7.9. (p. 553). From each row of this precedence matrix we shall generate statements of the Floyd–Evans parser. We use four types of statements: shift statements, reduce statements, checking statements, and computed goto statements.† We shall give statements symbolic labels that denote both the type of statement and the top symbol of the pushdown list. In these labels we shall use S for shift, R for reduce, C for checking, and G for goto, followed by the symbol assumed to be on top of the pushdown list.

We shall generate the shift statements first and then the reduce statements.

---

†The computed goto statement involves an extension of the production language of Section 5.4.4 in that the next label can be an expression involving the symbol #, which, as in Section 5.4.4, represents an unknown symbol matching the symbol at a designated position on the stack or in the lookahead. While we do not wish to discuss details of implementation, the reader should observe that such computed gotos as are used here can be easily implemented on his favorite computer.

For weak precedence grammars the precedence relations $\lessdot$ and $\doteq$ indicate shift and $\gtrdot$ indicates a reduction.

The E-row of Fig. 7.9 generates the statements

(7.2.1) SE: $E|) \longrightarrow E)|$ $* \, S)$

                    $E|+ \longrightarrow E+|$ $* \, S+$

                    $\$E|\$$ $|$ **accept**

                     $E|$ $|$ **error**

The first statement states that if E is on top of the pushdown list and the current input symbol is), then we shift) onto the pushdown list, read the next input symbol, and go to the statement labeled $S)$. If this statement does not apply, we see whether the current input symbol is $+$. If the second statement does not apply, we next see if the current input symbol is $\$$. The relevant action here would be to go into the halting state **accept** if the pushdown list contained $\$E$. Otherwise, we report error. Note that no reductions are possible if E is the top stack symbol.

Since the first component of the label indicates the symbol on top of the pushdown list, we can in many cases avoid unnecessary checking of the top symbol of the pushdown list if we know what it is. Knowing that E is on top of the pushdown list, we could replace the statements (7.2.1) by

       SE: $|) \longrightarrow)|$ $* \, S)$

                  $|+ \longrightarrow +|$ $* \, S+$

           $\$\#|\$$ $|$ **accept**

                 $|$ $|$ **error**

Notice that it is important that the error statement appear last. When E is on top of the pushdown list, the current input symbol must be), $+$, or $\$$. Otherwise we have an error. By ordering the statements accordingly, we can first check for), then for $+$, and then for $\$$, and if none of these is the current input symbol, we report error.

The row for T in Fig. 7.9 generates the statements

       ST: $|* \longrightarrow *|$ $* \, S*$

       RT: $E+T| \longrightarrow E|$ CT

               $T| \longrightarrow E|$ CT

(7.2.2) CT: $|)$ $|$ SE

                 $|+$ $|$ SE

                 $|\$$ $|$ SE

                 $|$ $|$ **error**

Here the precedence relation $T \doteq *$ generates the first statement. The precedence relations $T \gtrdot)$, $T \gtrdot +$, and $T \gtrdot \$$ indicate that with T on top of the pushdown list we are to reduce. Since we are dealing with a weak precedence grammar, we always reduce using the longest applicable production, by Lemma 5.4. Thus, we first look to see if $E + T$ appears on top of the pushdown list. If so, we replace $E + T$ by E. Otherwise, we reduce T to E. When the two RT statements are applicable, we know that T is on top of the pushdown list. Thus we could use

$$
\begin{array}{llll}
RT: & E + \# | & \longrightarrow E | & \quad CT \\
    & \# | & \longrightarrow E | & \quad CT
\end{array}
$$

and again avoid the unnecessary checking of the top symbol on the pushdown list.

After we perform the reduction, we check to see whether it was legal. That is, we check to see whether the current input symbol is either $)$, $+$, or $\$$. The group of checking statements labeled CT is used for this purpose. We report error if the current input symbol is not $)$, $+$, or $\$$. Reducing first and then checking to see if we should have made a reduction may not always be desirable, but by performing these actions in this order we shall be able to merge common checking operations.

To implement this checking, we shall introduce a computed goto statement of the form

$$
G: \quad \# | \qquad | \qquad S\#
$$

indicating that the top symbol of the pushdown list is to become the last symbol of the label.

Now we can replace the checking statements in (7.2.2) by the following sequence of statements:

$$
\begin{array}{llll}
CT: & |) & | & \quad G \\
    & | + & | & \quad G \\
    & | \$ & | & \quad G \\
    & | & | & \quad \textbf{error} \\
G: & \# | & | & \quad S\#
\end{array}
$$

We shall then be able to use these checking statements in other sequences. For example, if a reduction in G_0 is accomplished with T on top of the stack, the new top of the stack must be E. Thus, the statements in the CT group could all transfer to SE. However, in general, reductions to several different nonterminals could be made, and the computed goto is quite useful in establishing the new top of the stack.

Finally, for convenience we shall allow statements to have more than one label. The use of this feature, which is not difficult to implement, will become apparent later. We shall now give an algorithm which makes use of the preceding ideas.

ALGORITHM 7.2

Floyd–Evans parser from a uniquely invertible weak precedence grammar.

Input. A uniquely invertible weak precedence grammar $G = (\mathrm{N}, \Sigma, P, S)$.

Output. A Floyd–Evans production language parser for G.

Method.

(1) Compute the Wirth–Weber precedence relations for G.

(2) Linearly order the elements in $\mathrm{N} \cup \Sigma \cup \{\$\}$ as $(X_1, X_2, \ldots, X_m)$.

(3) Generate statements for $X_1, X_2, \ldots, X_m$ as follows. Suppose that X_i is not the start symbol. Suppose further that either $X_i \lessdot a$ or $X_i \doteq a$ for all a in $\{a_1, a_2, \ldots, a_j\}$, and $X_i \gtrdot b$ for all b in $\{b_1, \ldots, b_l\}$. Also, suppose $A_1 \rightarrow \alpha_1 X_i, A_2 \rightarrow \alpha_2 X_i, \ldots, A_k \rightarrow \alpha_k X_i$ are the productions having X_i as the last symbol on the right-hand side, arranged in an order such that $\alpha_p X_i$ is not a suffix of $\alpha_q X_i$ for $p < q$. Moreover, let us assume that $A_h \rightarrow \alpha_h X_i$ has number p_h, $1 \leq h \leq k$. Then generate the statements

$$
\begin{array}{lllll}
SX_i: & |a_1 \longrightarrow a_1| & & *\!\cdot Sa_1 \\
      & |a_2 \longrightarrow a_2| & & *\, Sa_2 \\
      & \qquad \vdots & & \\
      & |a_j \longrightarrow a_j| & & *\, Sa_k \\
RX_i: & \alpha_1 \# | \quad \longrightarrow A_1| & \text{emit } p_1 & CX_i \\
      & \alpha_2 \# | \quad \longrightarrow A_2| & \text{emit } p_2 & CX_i \\
      & \qquad \vdots & & \\
      & \alpha_k \# | \quad \longrightarrow A_k| & \text{emit } p_k & CX_i \\
      & | \qquad\qquad | & \text{error} & \\
CX_i: & |b_1 \qquad | & & G \\
      & |b_2 \qquad | & & G \\
      & \qquad \vdots & & \\
      & |b_l \qquad | & & G \\
      & | \qquad\qquad | & \text{error} &
\end{array}
$$

If j is zero, then the first statement of the RX_i group also has label SX_i. If k is zero, the error statement in the RX_i group has label RX_i. If X_i is the start symbol, then we do as above and also add the statement

$$\$\# \mid \$ \qquad \mid \qquad \textbf{accept}$$

to the end of the SX_i group. $S\$$ is the initial statement of the parser.

(4) Append the computed goto statement:

$$G: \qquad \# \mid \qquad \mid \qquad\qquad S\# \qquad\qquad \square$$

Example 7.9

Consider the grammar G_0. From the F row of the precedence matrix we would get the following statements:

$$SF: \quad RF\dagger: \quad T * \# \mid \quad \longrightarrow T \mid \quad \textbf{emit 3} \quad CF$$
$$\# \mid \quad \longrightarrow T \mid \quad \textbf{emit 4} \quad CF$$
$$\mid \qquad\qquad \mid \quad \textbf{error}$$
$$CF: \qquad \mid) \qquad \mid \qquad\qquad G$$
$$\mid + \qquad \mid \qquad\qquad G$$
$$\mid * \qquad \mid \qquad\qquad G$$
$$\mid \$ \qquad \mid \qquad\qquad G$$
$$\mid \qquad\qquad \mid \quad \textbf{error}$$

Note that the third statement is useless, as the second statement will always produce a successful match. We could, of course, incorporate a test into Algorithm 7.2 which would cause useless statements not to be produced. From now on we shall assume useless statements are not generated.

From the a row we get the following statements:

$$Sa: \quad Ra: \quad \# \mid \quad \longrightarrow F \mid \quad \textbf{emit 6} \quad Ca$$
$$Ca: \qquad \mid) \qquad \mid \qquad\qquad G$$
$$\mid + \qquad \mid \qquad\qquad G$$
$$\mid * \qquad \mid \qquad\qquad G$$
$$\mid \$ \qquad \mid \qquad\qquad G$$
$$\mid \qquad\qquad \mid \quad \textbf{error}$$

Notice that the checking statements for a are identical to those for F.

---

†Note the use of multiple labels for a location. Here, the SF group is empty.

In the next section we shall outline an algorithm which will merge redundant statements. In fact, the checking statements labeled CT could also be merged with CF if we write

$$Ca: \quad CF: \qquad | * \qquad | \qquad G$$
$$\qquad CT: \qquad |) \qquad | \qquad G$$
$$\qquad\qquad |+ \qquad | \qquad G$$
$$\qquad\qquad | \$ \qquad | \qquad G$$
$$\qquad\qquad | \qquad | \qquad \textbf{error}$$

Our merging algorithm will also consider partial mergers of this nature. The row labeled (in the precedence matrix generates the statements

$$S(: \qquad |(\longrightarrow (| \qquad * S(($$
$$\qquad |a \longrightarrow a| \qquad * Sa$$
$$\qquad | \qquad\qquad | \qquad \textbf{error}$$

Similar statements are also generated by the rows labeled $+$, $*$, and $\$$. $\square$

We shall leave the verification of the fact that Algorithm 7.2 produces a valid right parser for G for the Exercises.

7.2.2. Improvement of Floyd–Evans Parsers

In this section we shall consider techniques which can be used to reduce the number of shift and checking statements in the Floyd–Evans parser that results from Algorithm 7.2. Our basic technique will be to merge common shift statements and common checking statements. The procedure may introduce additional statements having the effect of an unconditional transfer, but we shall assume that these branch statements have relatively small cost. We shall treat the merger of shift statements here; the same technique can be used to merge checking statements.

Let $G = (N, \Sigma, P, S)$ be a uniquely invertible weak precedence grammar. Let M be its matrix of Wirth–Weber precedence relations. The matrix M determines the shift and checking statements that arise in Algorithm 7.2.

From the precedence matrix M, we construct a *merged shift matrix* M_s as follows:

(1) Delete all $\gtrdot$ entries and replace the $\doteq$ entries by $\lessdot$. (Since we care only about shifts, the $\lessdot$ and $\doteq$ relations can be identified.)

(2) If two or more rows of the resulting matrix are identical, replace

them by one row in M_s, with the new row identified with the set of symbols in $N \cup \Sigma \cup \{\$\}$ with which the original rows were associated.

(3) Delete all rows with no $\lessdot$ entries and call the resulting matrix M_s.

Example 7.10

The merged shift matrix for G_0 from Fig. 7.9 is shown in Fig. 7.15. This merged shift matrix is a concise representation of the situations in which the parser is to make a shift move. ☐

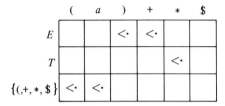

Fig. 7.15 Merged shift matrix.

From the merged shift matrix M_s, we construct an unordered labeled directed graph (A, R), called the *shift graph* associated with M_s, as follows:

(1) For each row of M_s labeled Y, there is a node in A labeled Y.

(2) There is one additional node labeled $\varnothing$ in A representing a fictitious empty row.

(3) If row Y of M_s *is covered by* row Z of M_s (that is, in whatever column Y has a $\lessdot$ entry, Z has a $\lessdot$ entry), then edge (Y, Z) is in R, and edge (Y, Z) is labeled with the number of columns in which Z, but not Y, has a $\lessdot$ entry. Note that Y may be the empty row. We let $l(Y, Z)$ denote the label of edge (Y, Z).

Example 7.11

Consider the shift matrix M_s given in Fig. 7.16. The shift graph associated with M is shown in Fig. 7.17. ☐

	a_1	a_2	a_3	a_4	a_5	a_6
Y_1	$\lessdot$		$\lessdot$	$\lessdot$	$\lessdot$	$\lessdot$
Y_2	$\lessdot$		$\lessdot$	$\lessdot$		$\lessdot$
Y_3	$\lessdot$			$\lessdot$		
Y_4	$\lessdot$					$\lessdot$
Y_5		$\lessdot$				

Fig. 7.16 Shift matrix M_s.

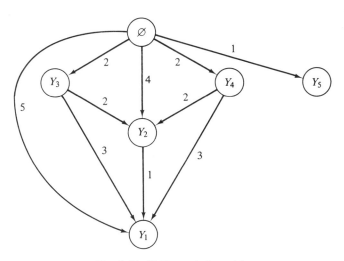

Fig. 7.17 Shift graph from M_s.

It should be clear that the shift graph is a directed acyclic graph with a single root, $\varnothing$. The number of shift statements generated by Algorithm 7.2 is equal to the number of shift ($\lessdot$ and $\doteq$) entries in the precedence matrix M. Using the shift matrix M_s and merging rows with similar shift entries, we can reduce the number of shift statements that are required. The technique is to construct a minimum cost *directed spanning tree* (subset of the edges which forms a tree, with all nodes included) for the shift graph, where the *cost* of a spanning tree is the sum of the labels of the edges in the tree.

A path from $\varnothing$ to Y to Z in the shift graph (A, R) has the following interpretation. The label $l(\varnothing, Y)$ gives the number of shift statements generated for row Y of M_s. Thus, the number of shift statements that would be generated for rows Y and Z is $l(\varnothing, Y) + l(\varnothing, Z)$. However, if there is a path from $\varnothing$ to Y to Z in the graph, we can first generate the shift statements for row Y. To generate the shift statements for row Z, we can use the shift statements for row Y and precede them by those shift statements for row Z which are not already present. Thus, we would generate the following sequence of shift statements for rows Y and Z:

> SZ: Shift statements for entries in Z but not in Y
>
> SY: Shift statements for entries in Y

The number of shift statements for Y and Z would thus be $l(\varnothing, Y) + l(Y, Z)$ $= l(\varnothing, Z)$, rather than $l(\varnothing, Y) + l(\varnothing, Z)$. We thus get the shift statements for row Y "for free."

We can generalize this technique in an algorithm which takes an arbitrary directed spanning tree for a shift graph and constructs a set of shift statements "corresponding" to that spanning tree. The number of shift statements is equal to the sum of the labels of the edges of the tree. The method is given in the following algorithm.

ALGORITHM 7.3

Set of shift statements from spanning tree.

Input. A shift matrix M_s and a spanning tree for its shift graph.

Output. A sequence of Floyd–Evans production language statements.

Method. For each node Y of the spanning tree except the root, construct the sequence of statements

$$
\begin{array}{lll}
L: & |a_1 \longrightarrow a_1| & * Sa_1 \\
   & |a_2 \longrightarrow a_2| & * Sa_2 \\
   & \qquad \cdot & \\
   & \qquad \cdot & \\
   & \qquad \cdot & \\
   & |a_n \longrightarrow a_n| & * Sa_n \\
   & | \qquad\quad | & L'
\end{array}
$$

where L is the label of row Y in M_s (i.e., the set of labels $SX_1, \ldots, SX_m$, where $X_1, \ldots, X_m$ are the symbols whose rows in the precedence matrix form row Y in M_s). L' is the label for the direct ancestor of node Y in the spanning tree; $a_1, \ldots, a_n$ are the columns covered by row Y of M_s but not by its direct ancestor.

For node $\varnothing$, we add a new computed goto statement:

$$
\varnothing: \quad \#| \qquad\qquad | \qquad R\#
$$

The statements for the nodes can be placed in any order. However, if the statement

$$
| \qquad\qquad | \qquad L'
$$

immediately precedes the statement labeled L', then the former statement may be deleted.   □

Example 7.12

The tree of Fig. 7.18 is a spanning tree for the shift graph of Fig. 7.17.

The following sequence of statements could be generated from the tree of Fig. 7.18 by Algorithm 7.3. Of course, the sequence of the statements is not completely fixed by Algorithm 7.3, and other sequences are possible. By SY_i is meant the set of labels corresponding to row Y_i in the shift graph.

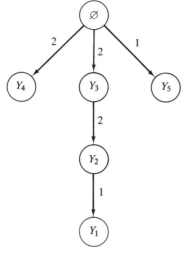

Fig. 7.18   Spanning tree.

$S Y_4:$ $|a_1 \longrightarrow a_1|$ $* S a_1$

$|a_6 \longrightarrow a_6|$ $* S a_6$

$|$ $|$ $\varnothing$

$S Y_1:$ $|a_5 \longrightarrow a_5|$ $* S a_5$

$S Y_2:$ $|a_3 \longrightarrow a_3|$ $* S a_3$

$|a_6 \longrightarrow a_6|$ $* S a_6$

$S Y_3:$ $|a_1 \longrightarrow a_1|$ $* S a_1$

$|a_4 \longrightarrow a_4|$ $* S a_4$

$|$ $|$ $\varnothing$

$S Y_5:$ $|a_2 \longrightarrow a_2|$ $* S a_2$

$\varnothing:$ $\#|$ $|$ $R\#$ $\square$

THEOREM 7.3

Algorithm 7.3 produces a sequence of production language statements which may replace the shift statements generated by Algorithm 7.2, with no change in the parsing action of the program.

Proof. We observe that when started at the sequence of statements generated by Algorithm 7.3 for node Y, the statements which may subsequently be executed are precisely those generated for the ancestors of node Y. It is straightforward to show that these statements test for the presence in the lookahead position of exactly those symbols whose columns are covered by row Y of the shift matrix.

The statement with label $\varnothing$ ensures that if no shift is made, we transfer to the proper R-group. $\square$

The spanning tree for a given shift graph which produces the fewest shift statements by Algorithm 7.3 is surprisingly easy to find. We observe that, neglecting the unconditional transfer statements, the number of statements generated by Algorithm 7.3 (all of which are of the form $|a \longrightarrow a| \quad * Sa$ for some a) is exactly the sum of the labels of the edges in the tree.

ALGORITHM 7.4

Minimum cost spanning tree from shift graph.

Input. Shift graph (A, R) for a precedence matrix M.

Output. Spanning tree (A, R') such that $\sum_{(X,Y)\in R'} l(X, Y)$ is minimal.

Method. For each node Y in A other than the root, choose a node X such that $l(X, Y)$ is smallest among all edges entering Y. Add (X, Y) to R'. □

Example 7.13

The spanning tree in Fig. 7.18 is obtained from the shift graph of Fig. 7.17 using Algorithm 7.4. □

THEOREM 7.4

The number of shift statements generated by Algorithm 7.3 from a spanning tree is minimized for a given shift graph when the tree produced by Algorithm 7.4 is chosen.

Proof. Since every node except the root of (A, R) has a unique direct ancestor, (A, R') must be a tree. Since in every spanning tree of (A, R) one edge enters each node other than the root, the minimality of (A, R') is immediate. □

We observe that we can define a *reduce matrix* M_r from a precedence matrix M by deleting all but the $\gtrdot$ entries and merging rows exactly as we did for the shift matrix. We can then define a *reduce graph* in exact analogy with the shift graph and minimize the number of checking statements by an obvious analog of Algorithm 7.4. We leave the details to the reader. We shall give an example of the minimization of the entire Floyd–Evans parser for G_0.

Example 7.14

The M_s matrix for G_0 is

	(	a	)	+	*
E			$\lessdot$	$\lessdot$	
T					$\lessdot$
Y	$\lessdot$	$\lessdot$			

where $Y = \{(, +, *, \$\}$. The M_r matrix (the matrix for reductions) is

	)	+	*	$
T	>	>		>
Z	>	>	>	>

where $Z = \{F, a,)\}$.

Employing Algorithm 7.4 for merging both shift statements and for merging checking statements, we generate the following Floyd–Evans parser for G_0. The initial statement is $S\$$.

```
 S(:  S+:  S*:  S$:      |(  ⟶ ( |                 * S(
                         |a  ⟶ a |                 * Sa
                         |       |                   ∅
            SE:          |)  ⟶ ) |                 * S)
                         |+  ⟶ + |                 * S+
                 $#† | $          |    accept
                         |       |                   ∅
            ST:          |*  ⟶ * |                 * S*
            ∅:          #|        |                 R#
            RT:  E + #|   ⟶ E |    emit 1         CT
                  #|   ⟶ E |    emit 2         CT
       SF:  RF:  T * #|   ⟶ T |    emit 3         CF
                  #|   ⟶ T |    emit 4         CF
       Sa:  Ra:   #|   ⟶ F |    emit 6         Ca
       S):  R):  (E#|   ⟶ F |    emit 5         C)
RE:  R(:  R+:  R*:  R$:   |        |    error
       CF:  Ca:  C):     |*       |                  G
            CT:        |)       |                  G
                       |+       |                  G
                       |$       |                  G
                       |        |    error
       G:        #|        |                 S#
```

†Here, this statement can be executed only with E on top of the stack. If it could be executed otherwise, we would have to replace $\#$ by E (or in general, by the start symbol).

The penultimate statement plays the role of $\varnothing$ for the checking statements.   □

There are other improvements that can be made to Floyd–Evans parsers. One is to combine two statements into a single statement. For example, the second statement of the parser for G_0 could have been combined with the statement labeled Sa into

$$|a \ \longrightarrow F| \qquad \textbf{emit } 6 \qquad Ca$$

If we are willing to change the behavior of the parser slightly, we can effect further changes. One change would be to delay error detection. For example, the parser in Section 5.4.3 for G_0 uses only 11 statements, but it delays error detection in some cases.

We should emphasize that all the parsing algorithms discussed in Chapter 5 can be implemented in the Floyd–Evans production language. To implement these parsing algorithms efficiently, we can use techniques similar to those presented in this section.

Finally, there is the question of implementing the Floyd–Evans production language parser itself. A production language statement may cause the following elementary operations to be performed: read an input symbol, compare symbols, place symbols on stack, pop symbols on the stack, generate output. These operations are quite straightforward to implement. Hence, we can construct a program that will map a Floyd–Evans parser into a sequence of these elementary operations. A small interpreter can then be provided to execute this sequence of elementary operations.

EXERCISES

7.2.1.   Use Algorithm 7.2 to generate Floyd–Evans parsers for the following weak precedence grammars:

  (a) $S \longrightarrow S + I | I$
  $I \longrightarrow (S) | a(S) | a$

  (b) $S \longrightarrow 0S1 | 01$

  (c) $E \longrightarrow E + T | T$
  $T \longrightarrow T * F | F$
  $F \longrightarrow F \uparrow P | P$
  $P \longrightarrow (E) | a$

7.2.2.   Use the techniques of this section to improve the parsers constructed in Exercise 7.2.1.

7.2.3.   For the weak precedence matrix of Fig. 7.19, find the shift and reduce matrices.

	X_1	X_2	X_3	X_4	X_5	X_6
X_1	<·	<·,≐	≐	·>		·>
X_2		<·	<·	≐	·>	·>
X_3	·>	≐	<·,≐	·>		·>
X_4	·>	≐	≐	≐	<·	
X_5		<·	·>	·>	·>	·>
X_6	<·	<·	·>	≐	≐	
X_7	≐	<·,≐	·>		·>	·>
X_8		<·	·>			<·

Fig. 7.19   Matrix of precedence relations.

7.2.4.   From the shift and reduce matrices constructed in Exercise 7.2.3, construct the shift and reduce graphs.

7.2.5.   Use Algorithm 7.3 to find shortest sequences of shift and checking statements for the graphs of Exercise 7.2.4.

*7.2.6.   Devise an algorithm to generate a deterministic left parser in production language for an LL(1) grammar.

7.2.7.   Using the algorithm developed in Exercise 7.2.6, construct a left parser in production language for the following LL(1) grammar:

$$E \longrightarrow TE'$$
$$E' \longrightarrow + TE' \,|\, e$$
$$T \longrightarrow FT'$$
$$T' \longrightarrow * FT' \,|\, e$$
$$F \longrightarrow (E) \,|\, a$$

*7.2.8.   Use the techniques of this section to improve the parser constructed in Exercise 7.2.7.

*7.2.9.   Devise an algorithm to generate a deterministic right parser in production language for an LR(1) grammar.

7.2.10.   Using the algorithm developed in Exercise 7.2.9, construct right parsers for G_0 and the grammar in Exercise 7.2.7.

*7.2.11.   Use the techniques of this section to improve the parsers constructed in Exercise 7.2.10. Compare the resulting parsers with those in Examples 5.47 and 7.14 and the one in Exercise 7.2.8.

*7.2.12.   Is it possible to test a production language parser to determine if it is a valid weak precedence parser for a given grammar?

*7.2.13. Construct an algorithm to generate a production language program that simulates a deterministic pushdown transducer. What improvements can be made to the resulting program?

Research Problems

It should be evident that this section does not go very deeply into its subject matter and that considerable further improvements can be made in parsers implemented in production language. We therefore suggest the following areas for further research.

7.2.14. Study the optimizations which are possible when various kinds of shift–reduce algorithms are to be implemented in production language. In particular, one might examine the algorithms used to parse LL(k), BRC, extended precedence, simple mixed strategy precedence, and LR(k) grammars.

7.2.15. Extend the parser optimizations given in this section by allowing post-ponement of error detection, statement merger and/or other reasonable alterations of the production language program.

7.2.16. Develop an alternative to production language for the implementation of parsing algorithms. Your language should have the property that each statement can be implemented by some constant number of machine statements per character in the statement of your language. A "reasonable" random access machine should serve as a benchmark here.

Programming Exercises

7.2.17. Design elementary operations that can be used to implement Floyd–Evans production language statements. Construct an interpreter that will execute these elementary operations.

7.2.18. Construct a compiler which will take a program in production language and generate for it a sequence of elementary operations which can be executed by the interpreter in Exercise 7.2.17.

7.2.19. Write a program that will construct production language parsers for a useful class of context-free grammars.

7.2.20. Construct a production language parser for one of the grammars in the Appendix of Volume I. Incorporate an error recovery routine which gets called whenever error is announced. The error recovery routine should adjust the stack and/or input so that normal parsing can resume.

BIBLIOGRAPHIC NOTES

Production language and variants thereof have been popular for implementing parsers. Techniques for the generation of production language parsers have been developed by a number of people, including Beals [1969], Beals et al. [1969], DeRemer [1968], Earley [1966], and Haynes and Schutte [1970]. The techniques presented in this section for generating production language parsers were originated by Cheatham [1967]. The use of computed goto's in production language and the optimization method in Section 7.2.2 is due to Ichbiah and Morse [1970]. Some error recovery techniques for production language parsers are described in LaFrance [1970].

7.3. TRANSFORMATIONS ON SETS OF LR(k) TABLES

We shall discuss the optimization of LR(k) parsers for the remainder of this chapter. The reason for devoting such a large amount of space to LR(k) parsers and their optimization is twofold. First, the LR(k) grammars are the largest natural class of unambiguous grammars for which we can construct deterministic parsers. Secondly, using optimizations it is possible to produce LR parsers that are quite competitive with other types of parsers.

In Chapter 5 the parsing algorithm for LR(k) grammars was given. The heart of this algorithm is a set of LR(k) tables which governs the behavior of the parser. In Section 5.2.5 an algorithm was presented which could be used to automatically construct the canonical set of LR(k) tables for an LR(k) grammar (Algorithm 5.7).

However, as we noted, this canonical set of LR(k) tables can be impractically large for a grammar of practical interest if $k \geq 1$. Nevertheless, the LR(k) parsing algorithm using the canonical set of LR(k) tables [the canonical LR(k) parser] has some desirable features:

(1) The parser is fast. An input string of length n can be parsed in cn moves, where c is a small constant.

(2) The parser has good error-detecting capability. For example, suppose that the string xa is a prefix of some sentence in the language at hand but that xab is not a prefix of any sentence. On an input string of the form $xaby$, the canonical LR(1) parser would parse x, shift a, and then announce error. Thus, it would announce error when the input symbol b becomes the lookahead string for the first time. In general, the canonical LR(k) parser will announce error at the earliest possible opportunity in a left-to-right scan of the input string.

Precedence parsers do not enjoy this early error-detecting capability. For example, in parsing the input string $xaby$ mentioned above, it is possible for a precedence parser to scan arbitrarily many symbols of y before announcing error. (See Exercise 7.3.5.)

LL(k) parsers share the fast speed and good error-detecting capability of LR(k) parsers. However, not every deterministic language has an LL grammar, and, in general, it is often possible to find a more "natural" LR grammar to describe a programming language and its translation. For this reason, for the remainder of this chapter we shall concentrate on techniques for constructing small LR(k) parsers. Many of these techniques can also be applied to LL(k) grammars.

In this section we shall discuss LR(k) parsers from a general point of view. We shall say that two LR(k) parsers are equivalent if given an input string w either they both accept w or they both announce error at the same symbol in w. This is exactly akin to the notion of "equivalence" we encountered in Example 7.8.

In this section we shall present several transformations which can be used to reduce the size of an LR(k) parser, while producing an equivalent LR(k) parser. In Section 7.4 we shall present techniques which can be used to produce directly, from certain types of LR(k) grammars, LR(k) parsers that are considerably smaller than, but equivalent to, the canonical LR(k) parser. In addition, the techniques discussed in this section can also be applied to these parsers. Finally, in Section 7.5 we shall consider a more detailed implementation of an LR parser in which common scanning actions can be merged.

7.3.1. The General Notion of an LR(k) Table

A set of LR(k) tables forms the basis of the LR(k) parsing algorithm (Algorithm 5.7). In general, there are many different sets of tables which can be used to construct equivalent parsers for the same LR(k) grammar. Consequently, we can search for a set of tables with certain desirable properties, e.g., smallness.

To understand what changes can be made to a set of LR(k) tables, let us examine the behavior of the LR(k) parsing algorithm in detail. This algorithm places LR(k) tables on the pushdown list. The LR(k) table on top of the pushdown list dictates the behavior of the parsing algorithm. Each table is a pair of functions $\langle f, g \rangle$. Recall that f, the parsing action function, given a lookahead string, tells us what parsing action to take. The action may be to (1) shift the next input symbol onto the pushdown list, (2) reduce the top of the pushdown list according to a named production, (3) announce completion of the parsing, or (4) declare that a syntactic error has been found in the input. The second function g, the goto function, is invoked after each shift action and each reduce action. Given a symbol of the grammar, the goto function returns either the name of another table or an error notation.

A sample LR(1) table is shown in Fig. 7.20. In the LR(k) parsing

$T_1:$	action			goto			
	a	b	e	S	A	a	b
	S	3	X	T_4	X	T_7	X

Fig. 7.20 LR(1) table.

algorithm, a table can influence the operation of the parser in two ways. First, suppose that table T_1 is at the top of the pushdown list. Then the parsing action function of T_1 influences events. For example, if b is the lookahead string, then the parser calls for a reduction using production 3. Or if a is the lookahead string, the parser shifts the current input symbol (here, a) onto the pushdown list, and since $g(a) = T_7$, the name of table T_7 follows a onto the top of the pushdown list.†

The second way in which a table can influence the action of the parser appears immediately after a reduction. Suppose that the pushdown list is $\alpha AT_1 bT_2 ST_3$ and that a reduction using the production $S \rightarrow bS$ is called for by T_3. The parser will then remove four symbols (two grammar symbols and two tables) from the stack, leaving αAT_1 there.‡ At this point table T_1 is exposed. The nonterminal S is then placed on top of the stack, and the goto function of T_1 is invoked to determine that table $T_4 = g(S)$ is to be placed on top of S.

We shall take the viewpoint that the important times in an LR parsing process occur when a new table has just been placed on top of the pushdown list. We call such a table a *governing table*. We shall examine the characteristics of an LR parser in terms of the sequence of governing tables. If a governing table T calls for a shift, then the next governing table is determined by the goto function of T in a straightforward manner. If T calls for a reduction, on the other hand, the next governing table is determined by the goto function of the ith table from the top of the pushdown list, where i is the length of the right-hand side of the reducing production. What table might be there may seem hard to decide, but we can give an algorithm to determine the set of possible tables.

With the viewpoint of governing tables in mind, we shall attempt to determine when two sets of LR(k) tables give rise to equivalent parsers. We shall set performance criteria that elaborate on what "equivalent" means. First, we shall give the definition of a set of LR(k) tables that extends the definition given in Section 5.2.5. Included as both a possible action and a possible goto entry will be a special symbol φ, which can be interpreted as "don't care." It turns out, as we shall see, that many of the error entries in a set of LR(k) tables are never exercised; that is, the LR(k) parsing algorithm will never consult certain error entries no matter what the input is. Thus, we can

---

†As we mentioned in Chapter 5, it is not necessary to write the grammar symbols on the pushdown list. However, since the action of an LR(k) parser is more evident with the grammar symbols present, in this section we shall assume that the grammar symbols also appear on the pushdown list.

‡Note that when the canonical LR(k) parser calls for a reduction according to production i, the right-hand side of production i will always be a suffix of the grammar symbols on the stack. Thus, in the parsing process it is not necessary to match the right-hand side of the production with the grammar symbols on the stack.

change these entries in any fashion whatsoever, and the parser will still operate in the same way.

DEFINITION

Let G be a CFG. A *set of LR(k) tables for* G is a pair $(\mathfrak{I}, T_0)$, where $\mathfrak{I}$ is a set of tables for G and T_0, called the *initial table*, is in $\mathfrak{I}$. A *table* for G is a pair of functions $\langle f, g \rangle$, where

(1) f is a mapping from Σ^{*k} to the set consisting of φ, **error**, **shift**, **accept**, and **reduce** i for all production indices i, and

(2) g maps $N \cup \Sigma$ to $\mathfrak{I} \cup \{\varphi, \text{error}\}$.

When T_0 is understood, we shall refer to $(\mathfrak{I}, T_0)$ simply as $\mathfrak{I}$. The canonical set of LR(k) tables constructed in Section 5.2.5 is a set of LR(k) tables in the formal sense used here. Note that φ never appears in a canonical set of LR(k) tables.

Example 7.15

Let G be defined by the productions

(1) $S \longrightarrow SA$
(2) $S \longrightarrow A$
(3) $A \longrightarrow aA$
(4) $A \longrightarrow b$

In Fig. 7.21 is a set of LR(1) tables for G.

	action			goto			
	a	b	e	S	A	a	b
T_1	S	S	X	X	T_3	T_1	T_2
T_2	4	4	4	φ	φ	φ	φ
T_3	2	φ	φ	T_1	X	T_2	φ

Fig. 7.21 Set of LR(1) tables.

We shall see that the tables of Fig. 7.21 do not in any sense parse according to the grammar G. They merely "fit" the grammar, in that the tables defined use only symbols in G, and the reductions called for use productions which actually exist in G. □

We can redefine the LR(k) parsing algorithm based on a set of LR(k) tables as defined above. This algorithm is essentially the same as Algorithm 5.7 when we consider a φ entry as an error entry. For completeness we shall restate the algorithm.

DEFINITION

Let $(\mathfrak{I}, T_0)$ be a set of LR(k) tables for a CFG $G = (N, \Sigma, P, S)$. A *configuration* of the LR(k) parser for $(\mathfrak{I}, T_0)$ is a triple $(T_0 X_1 T_1 \cdots X_m T_m, w, \pi)$, where

(1) T_i is in $\mathfrak{I}$, $0 \leq i \leq m$, and T_0 is the initial table;
(2) X_i is in $N \cup \Sigma$, $1 \leq i \leq m$;
(3) w is in Σ^*; and
(4) π is an output string of production numbers.

The first component of a configuration represents the contents of the pushdown list, the second the unused input, and the third the parse found so far.

An *initial configuration* of the parser is one of the form (T_0, w, e) for some w in Σ^*. As before, we shall express a move of the parsing algorithm by the relation $\vdash$ on configurations defined as follows.

Suppose that the parser is in configuration $(T_0 X_1 T_1 \cdots X_m T_m, w, \pi)$, where $T_m = \langle f, g \rangle$ is a table in $\mathfrak{I}$. Let w be in Σ^* and let $u = \text{FIRST}_k(w)$. That is, w is the string remaining on the input, and u is the lookahead string.

(1) If $f(u) = \textbf{shift}$ and $w = aw'$, where $a \in \Sigma$, then

$$(T_0 X_1 T_1 \cdots X_m T_m, aw', \pi) \vdash (T_0 X_1 T_1 \cdots X_m T_m aT, w', \pi)$$

where $T = g(a)$. Here, we make a shift move in which the next input symbol, a, is shifted onto the pushdown list and then the table $g(a)$ is placed on top of the pushdown list.

(2) Suppose that $f(u) = \textbf{reduce } i$ and that production i is $A \rightarrow \gamma$, where $|\gamma| = r$. Suppose further that $r \leq m$ and that $T_{m-r} = \langle f', g' \rangle$. T_{m-r} is the table that is exposed when the string $X_{m-r+1} T_{m-r+1} \cdots X_m T_m$ is removed from the pushdown list. Then we say that

$$(T_0 X_1 T_1 \cdots X_m T_m, w, \pi) \vdash (T_0 X_1 T_1 \cdots X_{m-r} T_{m-r} AT, w, \pi i)$$

where $T = g'(A)$. Here a reduction according to the production $A \rightarrow \gamma$ is made. The index of this production is appended to the output string, and a string of length $2|\gamma|$ is removed from the top of the pushdown list and replaced by AT, where $T = g'(A)$ and g' is the goto function of the table immediately below the last table removed. Note that in the reduction the symbols removed from the pushdown list are not examined. Thus, it may be possible to make a reduction such that the grammar symbols removed do not correspond to the right-hand side of the production governing the reduction.†

(3) If $f(u) = \varphi$, **error** or **accept**, there is no next configuration C such that $(T_0 X_1 T_1 \cdots X_m T_m, w, \pi) \vdash C$.

There is also no next configuration if in rule (1) $w = e$ (then there is no next input symbol) or $g(a)$ is not a table name, or in rule (2) $r > m$ (then

---

†This will never happen if the canonical set of tables is used. In general, this situation is undesirable and should only be permitted if we are sure an error will be declared shortly.

there are not enough symbols on the pushdown list) or $g'(a)$ is not a table name.

We call $(T_0X_1T_1 \cdots X_mT_m, w, \pi)$ an *error indication* if there is no next configuration. However, as an exception, we call (T_0ST_1, e, π) an *accepting configuration* if $T_1 = \langle f, g \rangle$ and $f(e) = $ **accept**.

We define $\vdash$, $\vdash^*$, and $\vdash^+$ in the usual manner. We say that configuration C is *accessible* if $C_0 \vdash^* C$ for some initial configuration C_0. We shall now summarize the parsing algorithm.

ALGORITHM 7.5

LR(k) parsing algorithm.

Input. A CFG $G = (N, \Sigma, P, S)$, a set $(\Im, T_0)$ of LR(k) tables for G, and an input string $w \in \Sigma^*$.

Output. A sequence of productions π or an error indication.

Method.

(1) Construct the initial configuration (T_0, w, e).

(2) Let C be the latest configuration constructed. Construct the next configuration C' such that $C \vdash C'$ and then repeat step (2). If there is no next configuration C', go to step (3).

(3) Let $C = (\alpha, x, \pi)$ be the last configuration constructed. If C is an accepting configuration, then emit π and halt. Otherwise, indicate error. $\square$

It should be evident that this algorithm can be implemented by a deterministic pushdown transducer with a right endmarker.

If Algorithm 7.5 reaches an accepting configuration, then the output string π is called a *parse* for the input string w. We say that π is *valid* if π is a right parse for w according to the grammar G. Likewise, we say that a set of LR(k) tables is *valid for a grammar* G if and only if Algorithm 7.5 produces a valid parse for each sentence in $L(G)$ and does not produce a parse for any w not in $L(G)$.

By Theorem 5.12 we know that the canonical set of LR(k) tables for an LR(k) grammar G is valid for G. However, an arbitrary set of LR(k) tables for a grammar G obviously need not be valid for G.

Example 7.16

Let us trace through the sequence of moves made by Algorithm 7.5 on input ab using the LR(1) tables of Fig. 7.21 (p. 582) with T_1 as the initial table.

The initial configuration is (T_1, ab, e). The action of T_1 on lookahead a is **shift** and the goto of T_1 on a is T_1, so

$$(T_1, ab, e) \vdash (T_1aT_1, b, e)$$

The action of T_1 on b is also **shift** but the goto is T_2, so

$$(T_1 a T_1, b, e) \vdash (T_1 a T_1 b T_2, e, e)$$

The action of T_2 on e is **reduce** 4; production 4 is $A \rightarrow b$. Thus, the topmost table and grammar symbol are removed from $T_1 a T_1 b T_2$, leaving $T_1 a T_1$. The goto of T_1 on A is T_3, so

$$(T_1 a T_1 b T_2, e, e) \vdash (T_1 a T_1 A T_3, e, 4)$$

The action of T_3 on lookahead e is φ. That is, no next configuration can be constructed. Since $(T_1 a T_1 A T_3, e, 4)$ is not an accepting configuration, we have an indication of error.

Since ab is in $L(G)$, this set of tables is obviously not valid for the grammar in Example 7.15. □

7.3.2. Equivalence of Table Sets

We can now describe what it means for two sets of LR(k) tables to be equivalent. The weakest equivalence we might be interested in would require that, using Algorithm 7.5, the two sets of tables produce the same parse for those sentences in the language $L(G)$ and that one would not parse a sentence not parsed by the other. The error condition might be detected at different times by the two sets of tables.

The strongest equivalence we might consider would be one which required that the two sets of tables produce identical sequences of parsing actions. That is, suppose that (T_0, w, e) and (T'_0, w, e) are initial configurations for two sets of tables $\Im$ and $\Im'$. Then for any $i \geq 0$

$$(T_0, w, e) \vdash^i (T_0 X_1 T_1 \cdots X_m T_m, x, \pi)$$

using tables in $\Im$ if and only if

$$(T'_0, w, e) \vdash^i (T'_0 X'_1 T'_1 \cdots X'_n T'_n, x', \pi')$$

using tables in $\Im'$, where $m = n$, $x = x'$, $\pi = \pi'$ and $X_i = X'_i$, for $1 \leq i \leq m$.

Each of these definitions allows us to develop techniques by which sets of tables can be modified while these equivalences are preserved. Here we shall consider an equivalence that is intermediate in stringency. We require, of course, that Algorithm 7.5 using one set of tables finds a parse for an input string w if and only if it finds the same parse for w using the other set of tables. Moreover, as in the strongest kind of equivalence, we further require that Algorithm 7.5 trace through the same sequence of parsing actions on each input string whenever both sets of tables specify parsing actions. However, we shall allow one set of tables to continue making reductions, even though the other set has stopped parsing. We have the following motivation for this definition.

When an error occurs, we wish to detect it using either set of tables, and we want the position of the error to be as apparent as possible. It will not do for one set of tables to detect an error while the other shifts a large number of input symbols before the error is detected. The reason for this requirement is that one would in practice like to discover an error as close to where it occurred as possible, for the purpose of producing intelligent and intelligible diagnostics.

In practice, on encountering an error, one would transfer to an error recovery routine which would modify the remaining input string and/or the contents of the pushdown list so that the parser could proceed to parse the rest of the input and detect as many errors as possible in one pass over the input. It would be unfortunate if large portions of the input had been processed in a meaningless way before the error was detected. We are thus motivated to make the following definition of equivalence on sets of LR tables. It is a special case of the informal notion of equivalence discussed in Section 7.1.

DEFINITION

Let $(\mathfrak{I}, T_0)$ and $(\mathfrak{I}', T_0')$ be two sets of LR(k) tables for a context-free grammar $G = (N, \Sigma, P, S)$.

Let w be an input string in Σ^*, $C_0 = (T_0, w, e)$, and $C_0' = (T_0', w, e)$. Let $C_0 \vdash C_1 \vdash C_2 \vdash \cdots$ and $C_0' \vdash C_1' \vdash C_2' \vdash \cdots$ be the respective sequences of configurations constructed by Algorithm 7.5. We say that $(\mathfrak{I}, T_0)$ and $(\mathfrak{I}', T_0')$ are *equivalent* if the following four conditions hold, for all $i \geq 0$ and for arbitrary w.

(1) If C_i and C_i' both exist, then we can express these configurations as $C_i = (T_0 X_1 T_1 \cdots X_m T_m, x, \pi)$ and $C_i' = (T_0' X_1 T_1' \cdots X_m T_m', x, \pi)$; that is, as long as both sequences of configurations exist, they are identical except for table names.

(2) C_i is an accepting configuration if and only if C_i' is an accepting configuration.

(3) If C_i is defined but C_i' is not, then the second components of C_{i-1} and C_i are the same.

(4) If C_i' is defined but C_i is not, then the second components of C_{i-1}' and C_i' are the same.

What conditions (3) and (4) are saying is that once one of the sets of tables has detected an error, the other must not consume any more input, that is, not call for any **shift** actions. However, conditions (3) and (4) allow one set of tables to call for one or more **reduce** actions while the other set has halted with a don't care or **error** action.

Notice that neither set of tables has to be valid for G. However, if two sets of tables are equivalent and one is valid for G, then the other must also be valid for G.

Example 7.17

Consider the LR(1) grammar G with the productions

$$(1)\ S \longrightarrow aSb$$
$$(2)\ S \longrightarrow ab$$

$(\mathfrak{I}, T_0)$, the canonical set of LR(1) tables for G, is shown in Fig. 7.22. Figure 7.23 shows another set of LR(1) tables, $(\mathfrak{U}, U_0)$, for G. Let us consider the

	action			goto		
	a	b	e	S	a	b
T_0	S	X	X	T_1	T_2	X
T_1	X	X	A	X	X	X
T_2	S	S	X	T_3	T_4	T_5
T_3	X	S	X	X	X	T_6
T_4	S	S	X	T_7	T_4	T_8
T_5	X	X	2	X	X	X
T_6	X	X	1	X	X	X
T_7	X	S	X	X	X	T_9
T_8	X	2	X	X	X	X
T_9	X	1	X	X	X	X

Fig. 7.22 $(\mathfrak{I}, T_0)$

behavior of the LR(1) parsing algorithm using $\mathfrak{I}$ and $\mathfrak{U}$ on the input string abb. Using $\mathfrak{I}$, the parsing algorithm would make the following sequence of moves:

$$(T_0,\ aab,\ e) \vdash (T_0 a T_2,\ bb,\ e)$$
$$\vdash (T_0 a T_2 b T_5,\ b,\ e)$$

The last configuration is an error indication. Using the set of tables $\mathfrak{U}$, the parsing algorithm would proceed as follows:

$$(U_0,\ abb,\ e) \vdash (U_0 a U_2,\ bb,\ e)$$
$$\vdash (U_0 a U_2 b U_4,\ b,\ e)$$
$$\vdash (U_0 S U_1,\ b,\ 2)$$

	action			goto		
	a	b	e	S	a	b
U_0	S	X	X	U_1	U_2	φ
U_1	φ	X	A	φ	φ	φ
U_2	S	S	X	U_3	U_2	U_4
U_3	φ	S	X	φ	φ	U_5
U_4	X	2	2	φ	φ	φ
U_5	X	1	1	φ	φ	φ

Fig. 7.23 $(\mathfrak{U}, U_0)$

The last configuration is an error configuration. Note that the canonical parser announces error as soon as it sees the second b in the input string for the first time. But the parser using the set of tables $\mathfrak{U}$ reduced ab to S before announcing error. However, the second b is not shifted onto the pushdown list, so the equivalence condition has not been violated.

It is not too difficult to show that $\mathfrak{I}$ and $\mathfrak{U}$ are indeed equivalent. There is an algorithm to determine whether an arbitrary set of LR(k) tables for an LR(k) grammar is equivalent to the canonical set of LR(k) tables for that grammar. We leave the algorithm as an exercise. $\square$

7.3.3. φ-Inaccessible Sets of Tables

Many of the **error** entries in a canonical set of LR(k) tables are never used by the LR(k) parsing algorithm. Such **error** entries can be replaced by φ's, which are truly don't cares in the sense that these entries never influence the computation of the next configuration for any accessible configuration. We show that all **error** symbols in the goto field of a canonical set of tables can be replaced by φ's and that if a given table can become the governing table only immediately after a reduction, then the same replacements can be made in the action field.

DEFINITION

Let $(\mathfrak{I}, T_0)$ be a set of LR(k) tables, $k \geq 1$, and let

$$C = (T_0 X_1 T_1 X_2 T_2 \cdots X_m T_m, w, \pi)$$

be any accessible configuration. Let $T = \langle f, g \rangle$ and $u = \text{FIRST}_k(w)$. We say that $\mathfrak{I}$ is *free of accessible φ entries*, or φ-*inaccessible* for short, if the following statements are true for arbitrary C:

(1) $f(u) \neq \varphi$.
(2) If $f(u) = $ **shift**, then $g(a) \neq \varphi$, where a is the first symbol of u.

(3) If $f(u) = $ **reduce** i, production i is $A \rightarrow Y_1 \cdots Y_r$, $r \geq 0$, and T_{m-r} is $\langle f', g' \rangle$, then $g'(A) \neq \varphi$.

Informally, a set of LR(k) tables is φ-inaccessible if whatever φ entries appear in the tables are never referred to by Algorithm 7.5 during the parsing of any input string. We shall now give an algorithm which replaces as many **error** entries as possible by φ in the canonical set of LR(k) tables while keeping the resulting set of tables φ-inaccessible.

Thus, we can identify the **error** entries in a canonical set of LR(k) tables which are never consulted by the LR(k) parsing algorithm by using this algorithm to change the unused error entries to φ's.

ALGORITHM 7.6

Construction of a φ-inaccessible set of LR(k) tables with as many φ's as possible.

Input. An LR(k) grammar $G = (N, \Sigma, P, S)$, with $k \geq 1$, and $(\mathfrak{I}, T_0)$, the canonical set of LR(k) tables for G.

Output. $(\mathfrak{I}', T_0')$, an equivalent set of LR(k) tables with all unused error entries replaced by φ.

Method.
(1) For each $T = \langle f, g \rangle$ in $\mathfrak{I}$, construct a new table $\langle f', g' \rangle$, where

$$g'(X) = \begin{cases} g(X) & \text{if } g(X) \neq \textbf{error} \\ \varphi & \text{otherwise} \end{cases}$$

Let $(\mathfrak{I}_1, T_0')$ be the set of tables so constructed.
(2) The set of tables $(\mathfrak{I}', T_0')$ is then constructed as follows:
  (a) T_0' is in $\mathfrak{I}'$.
  (b) For each table $T = \langle f, g \rangle$ in $\mathfrak{I}_1 - \{T_0'\}$ we add to $\mathfrak{I}'$ the table $T' = \langle f', g \rangle$, where f' is defined as follows:
     (i) $f'(u) = f(u)$ whenever $f(u) \neq \textbf{error}$.
     (ii) If $f(vb) = \textbf{error}$ for some v in Σ^{k-1} and b in Σ and for some $a \in \Sigma$ there is a table $\langle f_1, g_1 \rangle$ in $\mathfrak{I}_1$ such that $f_1(av) = \textbf{shift}$ and $g_1(a) = T$, then $f'(vb) = \textbf{error}$.
     (iii) If $f(u) = \textbf{error}$ for some u in $\Sigma^{*(k-1)}$ and for some $a \in \Sigma$ there is a table $\langle f_1, g_1 \rangle$ in $\mathfrak{I}_1$ such that $f_1(au) = \textbf{shift}$ and $g_1(a) = T$, then $f'(u) = \textbf{error}$.
     (iv) Otherwise $f'(u) = \varphi$. $\square$

In step (1) of Algorithm 7.6 all error entries in the goto functions are changed to φ entries, because when $k \geq 1$, a canonical LR(k) parser will always detect an error immediately after a shift move. Hence, an error entry in the goto field will never be exercised.

Step (2) of Algorithm 7.6 replaces **error** by φ in the action field of table

T if there is no table $\langle f_1, g_1 \rangle$ and lookahead string au such that $f_1(au) =$ **shift** and $g_1(a) = T$. Under these circumstances table T can appear on top of the stack only after a reduction. However, if an error has occurred, the canonical LR(1) parser would have announced error before making the reduction. Thus, all error entries in tables such as T will never be consulted and can therefore be treated as don't cares.

We should reiterate that Algorithm 7.6 as stated works only for sets of LR(k) tables where $k \geq 1$. For the LR(0) case, the lookahead string will always be the empty string. Therefore, all errors must be caught by the goto entries. Thus, in a set of LR(0) tables not all error entries in the goto field are don't cares. We leave it for the Exercises to deduce which of these entries are don't cares.

Example 7.18

Let G be the LR(1) grammar with productions

(1) $S \rightarrow SaSb$

(2) $S \rightarrow e$

The canonical set of LR(k) tables for G is shown in Fig. 7.24(a), and the tables after application of Algorithm 7.6 are shown in Fig. 7.24(b).

Note that in Fig. 7.24(b) all **error**'s in the right-hand portions of the tables (goto fields) have been replaced by φ's. In the action fields, T_0 has been left intact by rule (2a) of Algorithm 7.6. The only **shift** actions occur in tables T_3 and T_7; these result in T_4, T_5, or T_7 becoming the governing table. Thus, **error** entries in the action fields of these tables are left intact. We have changed **error** to φ elsewhere.   ☐

THEOREM 7.5

The set of tables $\mathfrak{I}'$ constructed by Algorithm 7.6 is φ-inaccessible and equivalent to the canonical set $\mathfrak{I}$.

Proof. The equivalence of $\mathfrak{I}$ and $\mathfrak{I}'$ is immediate, since in Algorithm 7.6, the only alterations of $\mathfrak{I}$ are to replace **error**'s by φ's, and the LR(k) parsing algorithm does not distinguish between error and φ in any way.† We shall now show that if a φ entry is encountered by Algo■ithm 7.5 using the set of tables $\mathfrak{I}'$, then $\mathfrak{I}'$ was not properly constructed from $\mathfrak{I}$.

Suppose that $\mathfrak{I}'$ is not φ-inaccessible. Then there must be some smallest i such that $C_0 \mathrel{\underset{\text{--}}{\mid}} C$, where C_0 is an initial configuration and in configuration C Algorithm 7.5 consults a φ-entry of $\mathfrak{I}'$. Since T_0 is not altered in step (2a), we must have $i > 0$. Let $C = (T_0 X_1 T_1 \cdots X_m T_m, w, \pi)$, where $T_m = \langle f, g \rangle$ and $\text{FIRST}_k(w) = u$. There are three ways in which a φ-entry might be encountered.

†The purpose of the φ's is only to mark entries which can be changed.

	action			goto		
	a	b	e	S	a	b
T_0	2	X	2	T_1	X	X
T_1	S	X	A	X	T_2	X
T_2	2	2	X	T_3	X	X
T_3	S	S	X	X	T_4	T_5
T_4	2	2	X	T_6	X	X
T_5	1	X	1	X	X	X
T_6	S	S	X	X	T_4	T_7
T_7	1	1	X	X	X	X

(a) Canonical Set of LR(1) Tables

	action			goto		
	a	b	e	S	a	b
T_0	2	X	2	T_1	φ	φ
T_1	S	φ	A	φ	T_2	φ
T_2	2	2	X	T_3	φ	φ
T_3	S	S	φ	φ	T_4	T_5
T_4	2	2	X	T_6	φ	φ
T_5	1	X	1	φ	φ	φ
T_6	S	S	φ	φ	T_4	T_7
T_7	1	1	X	φ	φ	φ

(b) ϕ-Free Set of Tables

Fig. 7.24 A set of LR(1) tables before and after application of Algorithm 7.6.

Case 1: Suppose that $f(u) = \varphi$. Then by step (2aii) and (2aiii) of Algorithm 7.6, the previous move of the parser could not have been shift and must have been reduce. Thus, $C_0 \models^{i-1} C' \models C$, where

$$C' = (T_0 X_1 T_1 \cdots X_{m-1} T_{m-1} Y_1 U_1 \cdots Y_r U_r, x, \pi'),$$

and the reduction was by production $X_m \rightarrow Y_1 \cdots Y_r$. ($\pi$ is π' followed by the number of this production.)

Let us consider the set of items from which the table U_r is constructed. (If $r = 0$, read T_{m-1} for U_r). This set of items must include the item

$[X_m \longrightarrow Y_1 \cdots Y_r \cdot, u]$. Recalling the definition of a valid item, there is some $y \in \Sigma^*$ such that the string $X_1 \cdots X_m uy$ is a right-sentential form. Suppose that the nonterminal X_m is introduced by production $A \longrightarrow \alpha X_m \beta$. That is, in the augmented grammar we have the derivation

$$S' \overset{*}{\underset{rm}{\Rightarrow}} \gamma A x \underset{rm}{\Rightarrow} \gamma \alpha X_m \beta x \overset{*}{\underset{rm}{\Rightarrow}} \gamma \alpha X_m uy$$

where $\gamma \alpha = X_1 \cdots X_{m-1}$. Since u is in FIRST(βx), item $[A \longrightarrow \alpha X_m \cdot \beta, v]$ must be valid for $X_1 \cdots X_m$ if $v = $ FIRST(x).

We may conclude that the parsing action of table T_m on u in the canonical set of tables was not error and thus could not have been changed to φ by Algorithm 7.6, contradicting what we had supposed.

Case 2: Suppose that $f(u) = $ **shift** and that a is the first symbol of u but that $g(a) = \varphi$. Since $f(u) = $ **shift**, in the set of items associated with table T_m there is an item of the form $[A \longrightarrow \alpha \cdot a \beta, v]$ such that u is in EFF($a\beta v$) and $[A \longrightarrow \alpha \cdot a \beta, v]$ is valid for the viable prefix $X_1 \cdots X_m$. (See Exercise 7.3.8.) But it then follows that $[A \longrightarrow \alpha a \cdot \beta, v]$ is valid for $X_1 \cdots X_m a$ and that $X_1 \cdots X_m a$ is also a viable prefix. Hence, the set of valid items for $X_1 \cdots X_m a$ is nonempty, and $g(a)$ should not be φ as supposed.

Case 3: Suppose that $f(u) = $ **reduce** p, where production p is $X_r \cdots X_m$, T_{r-1} is $\langle f', g' \rangle$, and $g'(A) = \varphi$. Then the item $[A \longrightarrow X_r \cdots X_m \cdot, u]$ is valid for $X_1 \cdots X_m$, and the item $[A \longrightarrow \cdot X_r \cdots X_m, u]$ is valid for $X_1 \cdots X_{r-1}$. In a manner similar to case 1 we claim that there is an item $[B \longrightarrow \alpha A \cdot \beta, v]$ which is valid for $X_1 \cdots X_{r-1} A$, and thus $g'(A)$ should not be φ. $\square$

We can also show that Algorithm 7.6 changes as many error entries in the canonical set of tables to φ as possible. Thus, if we change any **error** entry in $\Im'$ to φ, the resulting set of tables will no longer be φ-inaccessible.

7.3.4. Table Mergers by Compatible Partitions

In this section we shall present an important technique which can be used to reduce the size of a set of LR(k) tables. This technique is to merge two tables into one whenever this can be done without altering the behavior of the LR(k) parsing algorithm using this set of tables. Let us take a φ-inaccessible set of tables, and let T_1 and T_2 be two tables in this set. Suppose that whenever the action or goto entries of T_1 and T_2 disagree, one of them is φ. Then we say that T_1 and T_2 are *compatible*, and we can merge T_1 and T_2, treating them as one table.

In fact, we can do more. Suppose that T_1 and T_2 were almost compatible but disagreed in some goto entry by having T_3 and T_4 there. If T_3 and T_4 were themselves compatible, then we could simultaneously merge T_3 with

T_4 and T_1 with T_2. And if T_3 and T_4 missed being compatible only because they had T_1 and T_2 in corresponding goto entries, we could still do the merger.

We shall describe this merger algorithm by defining a compatible partition on a set of tables. We shall then show that all members of each block in the compatible partition may be simultaneously merged into a single table.

DEFINITION

Let $(\mathfrak{J}, T_0)$ be a set of φ-inaccessible LR(k) tables and let $\Pi = \{\mathcal{S}_1, \ldots, \mathcal{S}_p\}$ be a *partition* on $\mathfrak{J}$. That is, $\mathcal{S}_1 \cup \mathcal{S}_2 \cup \cdots \cup \mathcal{S}_p = \mathfrak{J}$, and for all $i \neq j$, $\mathcal{S}_i$ and $\mathcal{S}_j$ are disjoint. We say that Π is a *compatible partition of width p* if for all blocks $\mathcal{S}_i$, $1 \leq i \leq p$, whenever $\langle f_1, g_1 \rangle$ and $\langle f_2, g_2 \rangle$ are in $\mathcal{S}_i$, it follows that

(1) $f_1(u) \neq f_2(u)$ implies that at least one of $f_1(u)$ and $f_2(u)$ is φ and that
(2) $g_1(X) \neq g_2(X)$ implies that either
   (a) At least one of $g_1(X)$ and $g_2(X)$ is φ, or
   (b) $g_1(X)$ and $g_2(X)$ are in the same block of Π.

We can find compatible partitions of a set of LR(k) tables using techniques reminiscent of those used to find indistinguishable states of an incompletely specified finite automaton. Our goal is to find compatible partitions of least width. The following algorithm shows how we can use a compatible partition of width p on a set of LR(k) tables to find an equivalent set containing p tables.

ALGORITHM 7.7

Merger by compatible partitions.

Input. A φ-inaccessible set $(\mathfrak{J}, T_0)$ of LR(k) tables and a compatible partition $\Pi = \{\mathcal{S}_1, \ldots, \mathcal{S}_p\}$ on $\mathfrak{J}$.

Output. An equivalent φ-inaccessible set $(\mathfrak{J}', T_0')$ of LR(k) tables such that $\#\mathfrak{J}' = p$.

Method.

(1) For all i, $1 \leq i \leq p$, construct the table $U_i = \langle f, g \rangle$ from the block $\mathcal{S}_i$ of Π as follows:
   (a) Suppose that $\langle f', g' \rangle$ is in $\mathcal{S}_i$ and that for lookahead string u, $f'(u) \neq \varphi$. Then let $f(u) = f'(u)$. If there is no such table in $\mathcal{S}_i$, set $f(u) = \varphi$.
   (b) Suppose that $\langle f', g' \rangle$ is in $\mathcal{S}_i$ and that $g'(X)$ is in block $\mathcal{S}_j$. Then set $g(X) = U_j$. If there is no table in $\mathcal{S}_i$ with $g'(X)$ in $\mathcal{S}_j$, set $g(X) = \varphi$.
(2) T_0' is the table constructed from the block containing T_0.   □

The definition of compatible partition ensures us that the construction given in Algorithm 7.7 will be consistent.

Example 7.19

Consider G_0, our usual grammar for arithmetic expressions:

(1) $E \rightarrow E + T$
(2) $E \rightarrow T$
(3) $T \rightarrow T * F$
(4) $T \rightarrow F$
(5) $F \rightarrow (E)$
(6) $F \rightarrow a$

The φ-inaccessible set of LR(1) tables for G_0 is given in Fig. 7.25. We observe that T_3 and T_{10} are compatible and that T_{14} and T_{20} are compatible. Thus, we can construct a compatible partition with $\{T_3, T_{10}\}$ and $\{T_{14}, T_{20}\}$ as blocks and all other tables in blocks by themselves. If we replace $\{T_3, T_{10}\}$ by U_1 and $\{T_{14}, T_{20}\}$ by U_2, the resulting set of tables is as shown in Fig. 7.26. Note that goto entries T_3, T_{10}, T_{14}, and T_{20} have been changed to U_1 or U_2 as appropriate.

The compatible partition above is the best we can find. For example, T_{16} and T_{17} are almost compatible, and we would group them in one block of a partition if we could also group T_{10} and T_{20} in a block of the same partition. But T_{10} and T_{20} disagree irreconcilably in the actions for $+$, $*$, and $)$. $\square$

We shall now prove that Algorithm 7.7 produces as output an equivalent φ-inaccessible set of LR(k) tables.

THEOREM 7.6

Let $\mathfrak{I}'$ be the set of LR(k) tables constructed from $\mathfrak{I}$ using Algorithm 7.7. Then $\mathfrak{I}$ and $\mathfrak{I}'$ are equivalent and φ-inaccessible.

Proof. Let T' in $\mathfrak{I}'$ be the table constructed from the block of the compatible partition that contains the table T in $\mathfrak{I}$. Let $C_0 = (T_0, w, e)$ and $C'_0 = (T'_0, w, e)$ be initial configurations of the LR(k) parser using $\mathfrak{I}$ and $\mathfrak{I}'$, respectively. We shall show that

(7.3.1) $C_0 \mid\overset{i}{-} (T_0 X_1 T_1 \cdots X_m T_m, x, \pi)$ using $\mathfrak{I}$

if and only if $C'_0 \mid\overset{i}{-} (T'_0 X_1 T'_1 \cdots X_m T'_m, x, \pi)$ using $\mathfrak{I}'$

That is, the only difference between the LR(k) parser using $\mathfrak{I}$ and $\mathfrak{I}'$ is that in using $\mathfrak{I}'$ the parser replaces table T in $\mathfrak{I}$ by the representative of the block of T in the partition Π.

We shall prove statement (7.3.1) by induction on i. Let us consider the "only if" portion. The basis, $i = 0$, is trivial. For the inductive step, assume that statement (7.3.1) is true for i. Now consider the $i + 1$st move. Since $\mathfrak{I}$ is φ-inaccessible, the actions of T_m and T'_m on $\text{FIRST}_k(x)$ are the same.

	action						goto							
	a	$+$	$*$	$($	$)$	e	E	T	F	a	$+$	$*$	$($	$)$
T_0	S	X	X	S	X	X	T_1	T_2	T_3	T_4	φ	φ	T_5	φ
T_1	φ	S	φ	φ	φ	A	φ	φ	φ	φ	T_6	φ	φ	φ
T_2	φ	2	S	φ	φ	2	φ	φ	φ	φ	φ	T_7	φ	φ
T_3	φ	4	4	φ	φ	4	φ	φ	φ	φ	φ	φ	φ	φ
T_4	X	6	6	X	X	6	φ	φ	φ	φ	φ	φ	φ	φ
T_5	S	X	X	S	X	X	T_8	T_9	T_{10}	T_{11}	φ	φ	T_{12}	φ
T_6	S	X	X	S	X	X	φ	T_{13}	T_3	T_4	φ	φ	T_5	φ
T_7	S	X	X	S	X	X	φ	φ	T_{14}	T_4	φ	φ	T_5	φ
T_8	φ	S	φ	φ	S	φ	φ	φ	φ	φ	T_{16}	φ	φ	T_{15}
T_9	φ	2	S	φ	2	φ	φ	φ	φ	φ	φ	T_{17}	φ	φ
T_{10}	φ	4	4	φ	4	φ	φ	φ	φ	φ	φ	φ	φ	φ
T_{11}	X	6	6	X	6	X	φ	φ	φ	φ	φ	φ	φ	φ
T_{12}	S	X	X	S	X	X	T_{18}	T_9	T_{10}	T_{11}	φ	φ	T_{12}	φ
T_{13}	φ	1	S	φ	φ	1	φ	φ	φ	φ	φ	T_7	φ	φ
T_{14}	φ	3	3	φ	φ	3	φ	φ	φ	φ	φ	φ	φ	φ
T_{15}	X	5	5	X	X	5	φ	φ	φ	φ	φ	φ	φ	φ
T_{16}	S	X	X	S	X	X	φ	T_{19}	T_{10}	T_{11}	φ	φ	T_{12}	φ
T_{17}	S	X	X	S	X	X	φ	φ	T_{20}	T_{11}	φ	φ	T_{12}	φ
T_{18}	φ	S	φ	φ	S	φ	φ	φ	φ	φ	T_{16}	φ	φ	T_{21}
T_{19}	φ	1	S	φ	1	φ	φ	φ	φ	φ	φ	T_{17}	φ	φ
T_{20}	φ	3	3	φ	3	φ	φ	φ	φ	φ	φ	φ	φ	φ
T_{21}	X	5	5	X	5	X	φ	φ	φ	φ	φ	φ	φ	φ

Fig. 7.25 φ-inaccessible tables for G_0.

Suppose that the action is **shift**, that a is the first symbol of x, and that the goto entry of T_m on a is T. By Algorithm 7.7 and the definition of compatible partition, the goto of T'_m on a is T' if and only if T' is the representative of the block of Π containing T.

	action						goto						
	a	$+$	$*$	$($	$)$	e	E	T	F	a	$+$	$*$	$($	$)$
T_0	S	X	X	S	X	X	T_1	T_2	U_1	T_4	φ	φ	T_5	φ
T_1	φ	S	φ	φ	φ	A	φ	φ	φ	φ	T_6	φ	φ	φ
T_2	φ	2	S	φ	φ	2	φ	φ	φ	φ	φ	T_7	φ	φ
T_4	X	6	6	X	X	6	φ	φ	φ	φ	φ	φ	φ	φ
T_5	S	X	X	S	X	X	T_8	T_9	U_1	T_{11}	φ	φ	T_{12}	φ
T_6	S	X	X	S	X	X	φ	T_{13}	U_1	T_4	φ	φ	T_5	φ
T_7	S	X	X	S	X	X	φ	φ	U_2	T_4	φ	φ	T_5	φ
T_8	φ	S	φ	φ	S	φ	φ	φ	φ	φ	T_{16}	φ	φ	T_{15}
T_9	φ	2	S	φ	2	φ	φ	φ	φ	φ	φ	T_{17}	φ	φ
T_{11}	X	6	6	X	6	X	φ	φ	φ	φ	φ	φ	φ	φ
T_{12}	S	X	X	S	X	X	T_{18}	T_9	U_1	T_{11}	φ	φ	T_{12}	φ
T_{13}	φ	1	S	φ	φ	1	φ	φ	φ	φ	φ	T_7	φ	φ
T_{15}	X	5	5	X	X	5	φ	φ	φ	φ	φ	φ	φ	φ
T_{16}	S	X	X	S	X	X	φ	T_{19}	U_1	T_{11}	φ	φ	T_{12}	φ
T_{17}	S	X	X	S	X	X	φ	φ	U_2	T_{11}	φ	φ	T_{12}	φ
T_{18}	φ	S	φ	φ	S	φ	φ	φ	φ	φ	T_{16}	φ	φ	T_{21}
T_{19}	φ	1	S	φ	1	φ	φ	φ	φ	φ	φ	T_{17}	φ	φ
T_{21}	X	5	5	X	5	X	φ	φ	φ	φ	φ	φ	φ	φ
U_1	φ	4	4	φ	4	4	φ	φ	φ	φ	φ	φ	φ	φ
U_2	φ	3	3	φ	3	3	φ	φ	φ	φ	φ	φ	φ	φ

Fig. 7.26 Merged tables.

If the action is **reduce** by some production with r symbols on the right, then comparison of T_{m-r} and T'_{m-r} yields the inductive hypothesis for $i + 1$.

For the "if" portion of (7.3.1), we have only to observe that if T'_m has a non-φ action on FIRST(x), then T'_m must agree with T_m, since $\mathfrak{I}$ is φ-inaccessible. $\square$

We observe that Algorithm 7.7 preserves equivalence in the strongest sense. The two sets of tables involved always compute next configurations for the same number of steps regardless of whether the input has a parse.

7.3.5. Postponement of Error Checking

Our basic technique in reducing the size of a set of LR(k) tables is to merge tables wherever possible. However, two tables can be merged into one only if they are compatible. In this section we shall discuss a technique which can be used to change essential **error** entries in certain tables to **reduce** entries with the hope of increasing the number of compatible pairs of tables in a set of LR(k) tables.

As an example let us consider tables T_4 and T_{11} in Fig. 7.25 (p. 595) whose action fields are shown below:

action

	a	$+$	$*$	$($	$)$	e
T_4:	X	6	6	X	X	6
T_{11}:	X	6	6	X	6	X

If we changed the action of T_4 on lookahead) from **error** to **reduce** 6 and the action of T_{11} on e from **error** to **reduce** 6, then T_4 and T_{11} would be compatible and could be merged into a single table. However, before we make these changes, we would like to be sure that the error detected by T_4 on) and the error detected by T_{11} on e will be detected on a subsequent move before a shift move is made. In this section we shall derive conditions under which we can postpone error detection in time without affecting the position in the input string at which an LR(k) parser announces error. In particular, it is easy to show that any such change is permissible in the canonical set of tables.

Suppose that an LR(k) parser is in configuration $(T_0 X_1 T_1 \cdots X_m T_m, w, \pi)$ and that table T_m has action **error** on lookahead string $u = \text{FIRST}_k(w)$. Now, suppose that we change this **error** entry in T_m to **reduce** p, where p is production $A \rightarrow Y_1 \cdots Y_r$. There are two ways in which this error could be subsequently detected.

In the reduction process $2r$ symbols are removed from the pushdown list and table T_{m-r} is exposed. If the goto of T_{m-r} on A is φ, then error would be announced. We could change this φ to **error**. However, the goto of T_{m-r} on A could be some table T. If the action of T on lookahead u is **error** or φ (which we can change to **error** to preserve φ-inaccessibility), then we would catch the error at this point. We would also maintain error detection if the action of T on u was **reduce** p' and the process above was repeated. In short, we do not want any of the tables that become governing tables after the reduction by production p to call for a shift on lookahead u (or for acceptance).

Note that in order to change **error** entries to **reduce** entries, the full generality of the definition of equivalence of sets of LR(k) tables is needed here. While parsing, the new set of tables may compute next configurations several steps farther than the old set, but no input symbols will be shifted.

To describe the conditions under which this alteration can take place, we need to know, for each table appearing on top of the pushdown list during the parse, what tables can appear as the $r + 1$st table from the top of the pushdown list. We begin by defining three functions on tables and strings of grammar symbols.

DEFINITION

Let $(\mathfrak{I}, T_0)$ be a set of LR(k) tables for grammar $G = (N, \Sigma, P, S)$. We extend the GOTO function of Section 5.2.3 to tables and strings of grammar symbols. GOTO maps $\mathfrak{I} \times (N \cup \Sigma)^*$ to $\mathfrak{I}$ as follows:

(1) GOTO(T, e) $= T$ for all T in $\mathfrak{I}$.
(2) If $T = \langle f, g \rangle$, GOTO(T, X) $= g(X)$ for all X in $N \cup \Sigma$ and T in $\mathfrak{I}$.
(3) GOTO($T, \alpha X$) $=$ GOTO(GOTO(T, α), X) for all α in $(N \cup \Sigma)^*$ and T in $\mathfrak{I}$.

We say table that T in $(\mathfrak{I}, T_0)$ has *height* r if GOTO(T_0, α) $= T$ implies that $|\alpha| \geq r$.

We shall also have occasion to use GOTO^{-1}, the "inverse" of the GOTO function. GOTO^{-1} maps $\mathfrak{I} \times (N \cup \Sigma)^*$ to the subsets of $\mathfrak{I}$. We define GOTO$^{-1}(T, \alpha) = \{T' \,|\, \text{GOTO}(T', \alpha) = T\}$.

Finally, we define a function NEXT(T, p), where T is in $\mathfrak{I}$ and p is production $A \longrightarrow X_1 \cdots X_r$ as follows:

(1) If T does not have height r, then NEXT(T, p) is undefined.
(2) If T has height r, then NEXT(T, p) $= \{T' \,|\, \text{there exists } T'' \in \mathfrak{I} \text{ and } \alpha \in (N \cup \Sigma)^r \text{ such that } T'' \in \text{GOTO}^{-1}(T, \alpha) \text{ and } T' = \text{GOTO}(T'', A)\}$.

Thus, NEXT(T, p) gives all tables which could be the next governing table after T if T is on top of the pushdown list and calls for a reduction by production p. Note that there is no requirement that $X_1 \cdots X_r$ be the top r grammar symbols on the pushdown list. The only requirement is that there be at least r grammar symbols on the list. If the tables are the canonical ones, we can show that only for $\alpha = X_1 \cdots X_r$ among strings of length r will GOTO^{-1} (T, α) be nonempty.

Certain algebraic properties of the GOTO and NEXT functions are left for the Exercises.

The GOTO function for a set of LR(k) tables can be conveniently portrayed in terms of a labeled graph. The nodes of the GOTO graph are labeled by table names, and an edge labeled X is drawn from node T_i to node T_j if GOTO(T_i, X) $= T_j$. Thus, if GOTO($T, X_1 X_2 \cdots X_r$) $= T'$, then there will be a path from node T to node T' whose edge labels spell out the string $X_1 X_2 \cdots X_r$. The height of a table T can then be interpreted as the length of the shortest path from T_0 to T in the GOTO graph.

The NEXT function can be easily computed from the GOTO graph. To determine NEXT(T, i), where production i is $A \rightarrow X_1 X_2 \cdots X_r$, we find all nodes T'' in the GOTO graph such that there is a path of length r from T'' to T. We then add GOTO(T'', A) to NEXT(T, i) for each such T''.

Example 7.20

The GOTO graph for the set of tables in Fig. 7.25 (p. 595) is shown in Fig. 7.27.

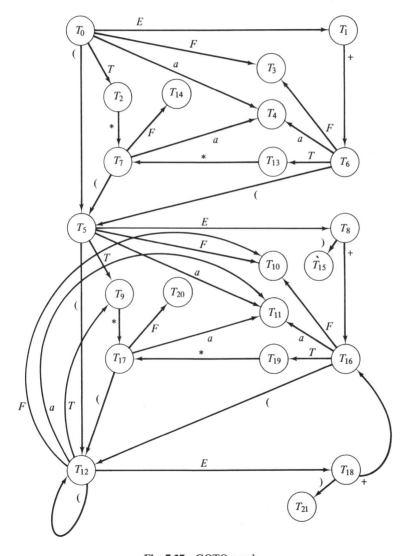

Fig. 7.27   GOTO graph.

From this graph we can deduce that $\text{GOTO}[T_6, (E)] = T_{15}$, since $\text{GOTO}[T_6, (] = T_5$, $\text{GOTO}[T_5, E] = T_8$, and $\text{GOTO}[T_8,)] = T_{15}$. Table T_6 has height 2, so $\text{NEXT}(T_6, 5)$, where production 5 is $F \rightarrow (E)$, is undefined.

Let us now compute $\text{NEXT}(T_{15}, 5)$. The only tables from which there is a path of length 3 to T_{15} are T_0, T_6, and T_7. Then $\text{GOTO}(T_0, F) = T_3$, $\text{GOTO}(T_6, F) = T_3$, and $\text{GOTO}(T_7, F) = T_{14}$, and so $\text{NEXT}(T_{15}, 5) = \{T_3, T_{14}\}$. □

We shall now give an algorithm whereby a set of φ-inaccessible tables can be modified to allow certain errors to be detected later in time, although not in terms of distance covered on the input. The algorithm we give here is not as general as possible, but it should give an indication of how the more general modifications can be performed.

We shall change certain **error** entries and φ-entries in the action field to **reduce** entries. For each entry to be changed, we specify the production to be used in the new reduce move. We collect permissible changes into what we call a postponement set. Each element of the postponement set is a triple (T, u, i), where T is a table name, u is a lookahead string, and i is a production number. The element (T, u, i) signifies that we are to change the action of table T on lookahead u to **reduce** i.

DEFINITION

Let $(\mathfrak{I}, T_0)$ be a set of $\text{LR}(k)$ tables for a grammar $G = (\text{N}, \Sigma, P, S)$. We call $\mathcal{P}$, a subset of $\mathfrak{I} \times \Sigma^{*k} \times P$, a *postponement set for* $(\mathfrak{I}, T_0)$ if the following conditions are satisfied.

If (T, u, i) is in $\mathcal{P}$ with $T = \langle f, g \rangle$, then

(1) $f(u) = $ **error** or φ;
(2) If production i is $A \rightarrow \alpha$ and $T = \text{GOTO}(T_0, \beta)$, then α is a suffix of β;
(3) There is no i' such that (T, u, i') is also in $\mathcal{P}$; and
(4) If T' is in $\text{NEXT}(T, i)$ and $T' = \langle f', g' \rangle$, then $f'(u) = $ **error** or φ.

Condition (1) states that only **error** entries and φ-entries are to be changed to **reduce** entries. Condition (2) ensures that a reduction by production i will occur only if α appears on top of the pushdown list. Condition (3) ensures uniqueness, and condition (4) implies that reductions caused by introducing extra **reduce** actions will eventually be caught without a **shift** occurring.

Referring to condition (4), note that (T', u, j) may also be in $\mathcal{P}$. In this case the value of $f'(u)$ will also be changed from **error** or φ to **reduce** j. Thus, several reductions may be made in sequence before error is announced.

Finding a postponement set for a set of $\text{LR}(k)$ tables which will maximize the total number of compatible tables in the set is a large combinatorial problem. In one of the examples to follow we shall hint at some heuristic techniques which can be used to find appropriate postponement sets. However, we shall first show how a postponement set is used to modify a given set of LR(k) tables.

ALGORITHM 7.8

Postponement of error checking.

Input. An LR(k) grammar $G = (N, \Sigma, P, S)$, a φ-inaccessible set $(\Im, T_0)$ of LR(k) tables for G, and a postponement set $\mathcal{P}$.

Output. A φ-inaccessible set $\Im'$ of LR(k) tables equivalent to $\Im$.

Method.

(1) For each (T, u, i) in $\mathcal{P}$, where $T = \langle f, g \rangle$, change $f(u)$ to **reduce** i.
(2) Suppose that (T, u, i) is in $\mathcal{P}$ and that production i is $A \longrightarrow \alpha$. For all $T' = \langle f', g' \rangle$ such that $\text{GOTO}(T', \alpha) = T$ and $g'(A) = \varphi$, change $g'(A)$ to **error**.
(3) Suppose that (T, u, i) is in $\mathcal{P}$ and that $T' = \langle f', g' \rangle$ is in $\text{NEXT}(T, i)$. If $f'(u) = \varphi$, change $f'(u)$ to **error**.
(4) Let $\Im'$ be the resulting set of tables with the original names retained.
□

Example 7.21

Consider the grammar G with productions

(1) $S \longrightarrow AS$
(2) $S \longrightarrow b$
(3) $A \longrightarrow aB$
(4) $B \longrightarrow aB$
(5) $B \longrightarrow b$

The φ-inaccessible set of LR(1) tables for G obtained by using Algorithm 7.6 on the canonical set of LR(1) tables for G is shown in Fig. 7.28.

We can choose to replace both **error** entries in the action field of T_4 with **reduce** 5 and the **error** entry in T_8 with **reduce** 2. That is, we pick a postponement set $\mathcal{P} = \{(T_4, a, 5), (T_4, b, 5), (T_8, e, 2)\}$. Production 5 is $B \longrightarrow b$, and $\text{GOTO}(T_0, b) = \text{GOTO}(T_2, b) = T_4$. Thus, the entries under B in T_0 and T_2 must be changed from φ to **error**. Similarly, the entries under S for T_3 and T_7 are changed to **error**. Since $\text{NEXT}(T_4, 5)$ and $\text{NEXT}(T_8, 2)$ are empty, no φ's in the action fields need be changed to **error**. The resulting set of tables is shown in Fig. 7.29.

If we wish, we can now apply Algorithm 7.7 with a compatible partition grouping T_4 with T_8, T_1 with T_2, and T_5 with T_6. (Other combinations of three pairs are also possible.) The resulting set of tables is given in Fig. 7.30.
□

THEOREM 7.7

Algorithm 7.8 produces a φ-inaccessible set of tables $\Im'$ which is equivalent to $\Im$.

	action			goto				
	a	b	e	S	A	B	a	b
T_0	S	S	X	T_1	T_2	φ	T_3	T_4
T_1	φ	φ	A	φ	φ	φ	φ	φ
T_2	S	S	φ	T_5	T_2	φ	T_3	T_4
T_3	S	S	X	φ	φ	T_6	T_7	T_8
T_4	X	X	2	φ	φ	φ	φ	φ
T_5	φ	φ	1	φ	φ	φ	φ	φ
T_6	3	3	φ	φ	φ	φ	φ	φ
T_7	S	S	X	φ	φ	T_9	T_7	T_8
T_8	5	5	X	φ	φ	φ	φ	φ
T_9	4	4	φ	φ	φ	φ	φ	φ

Fig. 7.28 φ-inaccessible tables for G.

	action			goto				
	a	b	e	S	A	B	a	b
T_0	S	S	X	T_1	T_2	X	T_3	T_4
T_1	φ	φ	A	φ	φ	φ	φ	φ
T_2	S	S	φ	T_5	T_2	X	T_3	T_4
T_3	S	S	X	X	φ	T_6	T_7	T_8
T_4	5	5	2	φ	φ	φ	φ	φ
T_5	φ	φ	1	φ	φ	φ	φ	φ
T_6	3	3	φ	φ	φ	φ	φ	φ
T_7	S	S	X	X	φ	T_9	T_7	T_8
T_8	5	5	2	φ	φ	φ	φ	φ
T_9	4	4	φ	φ	φ	φ	φ	φ

Fig. 7.29   Tables after postponement of error checking.

	action			goto				
	a	b	e	S	A	B	a	b
T_0	S	S	X	T_1	T_1	X	T_3	T_4
T_1	S	S	A	T_5	T_1	X	T_3	T_4
T_3	S	S	X	X	φ	T_5	T_7	T_4
T_4	5	5	2	φ	φ	φ	φ	φ
T_5	3	3	1	φ	φ	φ	φ	φ
T_7	S	S	X	X	φ	T_9	T_7	T_4
T_9	4	4	φ	φ	φ	φ	φ	φ

Fig. 7.30   Merged tables.

Proof. Let $C_0 = (T_0, w, e)$ be an initial configuration of the LR(k) parser (using either $\mathfrak{I}$ or $\mathfrak{I}'$ —the table names are the same). Let $C_0 \vdash C_1 \vdash \cdots \vdash C_n$ be the entire sequence of moves made by the parser using $\mathfrak{I}$ and let $C_0 \vdash C_1' \vdash \cdots \vdash C_m'$ be the corresponding sequence for $\mathfrak{I}'$. Since $\mathfrak{I}'$ is formed from $\mathfrak{I}$ by replacing only **error** entries and φ-entries, we must have $m \geq n$, and $C_i' = C_i$, for $1 \leq i \leq n$. (That is, the table names are the same, although different tables are represented.)

We shall now show that either $m = n$ or if $m > n$, then no shift or accept moves are made after configuration C_n' has been entered.

If $m = n$, the theorem is immediate, and if C_n is an accepting configuration, then $m = n$. Thus, assume that C_n declares an error and that $m > n$. By the definition of a postponement set, since the action in configuration C_n is **error** and the action in C_n' is not **error**, the action in configuration C_n' must be **reduce**. Thus, let s be the smallest integer greater than n such that the action in configuration C_s' is **shift** or **accept**. (If there is no such s, we have the theorem.)

Then there is some r, where $n < r \leq s$, such that the action entry consulted in configuration C_r' is one which was present in one of the tables of $\mathfrak{I}$. The case $r = s$ is not ruled out, as certainly the **shift** or **accept** entry of C_r' was present in $\mathfrak{I}$. The action entry consulted in configuration C_{r-1}' was of the form **reduce** i for some i. By our assumption on r, that entry must have been introduced by Algorithm 7.8.

Let T_1 and T_2 be the governing tables in configurations C_{r-1}' and C_r', respectively. Then T_2 is in NEXT(T_1, i), and condition (4) in the definition of a postponement set is violated. $\square$

We shall now give a rather extensive example in which we illustrate how postponement sets and compatible partitions might be found. There are a number of heuristics used in the example. Since these heuristics will not be delineated elsewhere, the reader is urged to examine this example with care.

Example 7.22

Consider the tables for G_0 shown in Fig. 7.25 (p. 595). Our general strategy will be to use Algorithm 7.8 to replace **error** actions by **reduce** actions in order to increase the number of tables with similar parsing action functions. In particular, we shall try to merge into one table all those tables which call for the same reductions.

Let us try to arrange to merge tables T_{15} and T_{21}, because they reduce according to production 5, and tables T_4 and T_{11}, which reduce according to production 6.

To merge T_{15} and T_{21}, we must make the action of T_{15} on) be **reduce** 5 and the action of T_{21} on e be **reduce** 5. Now we must check the actions of NEXT(T_{15}, 5) = $\{T_3, T_{14}\}$ and NEXT(T_{21}, 5) = $\{T_{10}, T_{20}\}$ on) and e. Since T_3 and T_{14} each have φ action on), we could change these φ's to **error**'s and be done with it. However, then T_3 and T_{10} would no longer be compatible— nor would T_{14} and T_{20}—so we would be wise to change the actions of T_3 and T_{14} on) instead to **reduce** 4 and **reduce** 3, respectively.

We must then check NEXT(T_3, 4) = NEXT(T_{14}, 3) = $\{T_2, T_{13}\}$. A similar argument tells us that we should not change the actions of T_2 and T_{13} on) to **error**, but rather to **reduce** 2 and **reduce** 1, respectively. Further, we see that NEXT(T_2, 2) = $\{T_1\}$ = NEXT(T_{13}, 1). There is nothing wrong with changing the action of T_1 on) to **error**, so at this point we have taken into account all modifications needed to change the action of T_{15} on) to **reduce** 5.

We must now consider what happens if we change the action of T_{21} on e to **reduce** 5. NEXT(T_{21}, 4) = $\{T_{10}, T_{20}\}$, but we do not want to change the actions of T_{10} and T_{20} on e to **error**, because then we could not possibly merge these tables with T_3 and T_{14}. We thus change the actions of T_{10} and T_{20} on e to **reduce** 4 and **reduce** 3, respectively. We find that

$$\text{NEXT}(T_{10}, 4) = \text{NEXT}(T_{20}, 3) = \{T_9, T_{19}\}.$$

We do not want to change the actions of T_9 and T_{19} on e to **error**, so let T_9 have action **reduce** 2 on e and T_{19} have action **reduce** 1 on e. We find NEXT(T_9, 2) = NEXT(T_{19}, 1) = $\{T_8, T_{18}\}$. These tables will have their actions on e changed to **error**.

We have now made T_{15} and T_{21} compatible without disturbing the possible compatibility of T_3 and T_{10}, of T_{14} and T_{20}, of T_2 and T_9, of T_{13} and T_{19}, or of T_{14} and T_{20}. Now let us consider making T_4 and T_{11} compatible by changing the action of T_4 on) to **reduce** 6 and the action of T_{11} on e to **reduce** 6. Since NEXT(T_4, 6) = $\{T_3, T_{14}\}$ and NEXT(T_{11}, 6) = $\{T_{10}, T_{20}\}$, the changes we have already made to T_3 and T_{14} and to T_{10} and T_{20} allow us to make these changes to T_4 and T_{11} without further ado. The complete postponement set consists of the following elements:

$$[T_2,), 2] \qquad [T_9, e, 2]$$
$$[T_3,), 4] \qquad [T_{10}, e, 4]$$
$$[T_4,), 6] \qquad [T_{11}, e, 6]$$
$$[T_{13},), 1] \qquad [T_{19}, e, 1]$$
$$[T_{14},), 3] \qquad [T_{20}, e, 3]$$
$$[T_{15},), 5] \qquad [T_{21}, e, 5]$$

The result of applying Algorithm 7.8 to the tables of Fig. 7.25 with this postponement set is shown in Fig. 7.31. Note that no **error** entries are introduced into the goto field.

Looking at Fig. 7.31, we see that the following pairs of tables are immediately compatible:

$$T_3\text{-}T_{10}$$
$$T_4\text{-}T_{11}$$
$$T_{14}\text{-}T_{20}$$
$$T_{15}\text{-}T_{21}$$

Moreover, if these pairs form blocks of a compatible partition, then the following pairs may also be grouped:

$$T_8\text{-}T_{18}$$
$$T_5\text{-}T_{12}$$
$$T_7\text{-}T_{17}$$
$$T_{13}\text{-}T_{19}$$
$$T_2\text{-}T_9$$
$$T_6\text{-}T_{16}$$

If we apply Algorithm 7.7 with the partition whose blocks are the above pairs and the singletons $\{T_0\}$ and $\{T_1\}$, we obtain the set of tables shown in Fig. 7.32. The smaller index of the paired tables is used as representative in each case. It is interesting to note that the "SLR" method of Section 7.4.1 can construct the particular set of tables shown in Fig. 7.32 directly from G_0.

To illustrate the effect of error postponement, let us parse the erroneous input string a). Using the tables in Fig. 7.25, the canonical parser would

	action						goto							
	a	$+$	$*$	$($	$)$	e	E	T	F	a	$+$	$*$	$($	$)$
T_0	S	X	X	S	X	X	T_1	T_2	T_3	T_4	φ	φ	T_5	φ
T_1	φ	S	φ	φ	X	A	φ	φ	φ	φ	T_6	φ	φ	φ
T_2	φ	2	S	φ	2	2	φ	φ	φ	φ	φ	T_7	φ	φ
T_3	φ	4	4	φ	4	4	φ	φ	φ	φ	φ	φ	φ	φ
T_4	X	6	6	X	6	6	φ	φ	φ	φ	φ	φ	φ	φ
T_5	S	X	X	S	X	X	T_8	T_9	T_{10}	T_{11}	φ	φ	T_{12}	φ
T_6	S	X	X	S	X	X	φ	T_{13}	T_3	T_4	φ	φ	T_5	φ
T_7	S	X	X	S	X	X	φ	φ	T_{14}	T_4	φ	φ	T_5	φ
T_8	φ	S	φ	φ	S	X	φ	φ	φ	φ	T_{16}	φ	φ	T_{15}
T_9	φ	2	S	φ	2	2	φ	φ	φ	φ	φ	T_{17}	φ	φ
T_{10}	φ	4	4	φ	4	4	φ	φ	φ	φ	φ	φ	φ	φ
T_{11}	X	6	6	X	6	6	φ	φ	φ	φ	φ	φ	φ	φ
T_{12}	S	X	X	S	X	X	T_{18}	T_9	T_{10}	T_{11}	φ	φ	T_{12}	φ
T_{13}	φ	1	S	φ	1	1	φ	φ	φ	φ	φ	T_7	φ	φ
T_{14}	φ	3	3	φ	3	3	φ	φ	φ	φ	φ	φ	φ	φ
T_{15}	X	5	5	X	5	5	φ	φ	φ	φ	φ	φ	φ	φ
T_{16}	S	X	X	S	X	X	φ	T_{19}	T_{10}	T_{11}	φ	φ	T_{12}	φ
T_{17}	S	X	X	S	X	X	φ	φ	T_{20}	T_{11}	φ	φ	T_{12}	φ
T_{18}	φ	S	φ	φ	S	X	φ	φ	φ	φ	T_{16}	φ	φ	T_{21}
T_{19}	φ	1	S	φ	1	1	φ	φ	φ	φ	φ	T_{17}	φ	φ
T_{20}	φ	3	3	φ	3	3	φ	φ	φ	φ	φ	φ	φ	φ
T_{21}	X	5	5	X	5	5	φ	φ	φ	φ	φ	φ	φ	φ

Fig. 7.31 Application of postponement algorithm.

make one move:

$$[T_0, a), e] \vdash [T_0 a T_4,), e]$$

The action of T_4 on $)$ is **error**.

	action						goto							
	a	+	*	(	)	e	E	T	F	a	+	*	(	)
T_0	S	X	X	S	X	X	T_1	T_2	T_3	T_4	φ	φ	T_5	φ
T_1	φ	S	φ	φ	X	A	φ	φ	φ	φ	T_6	φ	φ	φ
T_2	φ	2	S	φ	2	2	φ	φ	φ	φ	φ	T_7	φ	φ
T_3	φ	4	4	φ	4	4	φ	φ	φ	φ	φ	φ	φ	φ
T_4	X	6	6	X	6	6	φ	φ	φ	φ	φ	φ	φ	φ
T_5	S	X	X	S	X	X	T_8	T_2	T_3	T_4	φ	φ	T_5	φ
T_6	S	X	X	S	X	X	φ	T_{13}	T_3	T_4	φ	φ	T_5	φ
T_7	S	X	X	S	X	X	φ	φ	T_{14}	T_4	φ	φ	T_5	φ
T_8	φ	S	φ	φ	S	X	φ	φ	φ	φ	T_6	φ	φ	T_{15}
T_{13}	φ	1	S	φ	1	1	φ	φ	φ	φ	φ	T_7	φ	φ
T_{14}	φ	3	3	φ	3	3	φ	φ	φ	φ	φ	φ	φ	φ
T_{15}	X	5	5	X	5	5	φ	φ	φ	φ	φ	φ	φ	φ

Fig. 7.32   After application of merging algorithm.

However, using the tables in Fig. 7.32 to parse this same input string, the parser would now make the following sequence of moves:

$$[T_0, a), e] \vdash [T_0 a T_4,), e]$$
$$\vdash [T_0 F T_3,), 6]$$
$$\vdash [T_0 T T_2,), 64]$$
$$\vdash [T_0 E T_1,), 642]$$

Here three reductions are made before the announcement of error.   □

7.3.6. Elimination of Reductions by Single Productions

We shall now consider an important modification of LR(k) tables that does not preserve equivalence in the sense of the previous sections. This modification will never introduce additional shift actions, nor will it even cause a reduction when the unmodified tables detect error. However, this modification can cause certain reductions to be skipped altogether. As a result, a table appearing on the pushdown list may not be the one associated with the string of grammar symbols appearing below it (although it will be compatible with the table associated with that string). The modification of this section has to do with single productions, and we shall treat it rather more informally than we did previous modifications.

A production of the form $A \rightarrow B$, where A and B are nonterminals, is called a single production. Productions of this nature occur frequently in grammars describing programming languages. For instance, single productions often arise when a context-free grammar is used to describe the precedence levels of operators in programming languages. From example, if a string $a_1 + a_2 * a_3$ is to be interpreted as $a_1 + (a_2 * a_3)$, then we say the operator $*$ has *higher precedence* than the operator $+$.

Our grammar G_0 for arithmetic expressions makes $*$ of higher precedence than $+$. The productions in G_0 are

(1) $E \rightarrow E + T$
(2) $E \rightarrow T$
(3) $T \rightarrow T * F$
(4) $T \rightarrow F$
(5) $F \rightarrow (E)$
(6) $F \rightarrow a$

We can think of the nonterminals E, T, and F as generating expressions on different precedence levels reflecting the precedence levels of the operators. E generates the first level of expressions. These are strings of T's separated by $+$'s. The operator $+$ is on the first precedence level. T generates the second level of expressions consisting of F's separated by $*$'s. The third level of expressions are those generated by F, and we can consider these to be the primary expressions.

Thus, when we parse the string $a_1 + a_2 * a_3$ according to G_0, we must first parse $a_2 * a_3$ as a T before combining this T with a_1 into an expression E.

The only function served by the two single productions $E \rightarrow T$ and $T \rightarrow F$ is to permit an expression on a higher precedence level to be trivially reduced to an expression on a lower precedence level. In a compiler the translation rules usually associated with these single productions merely state that the translations for the nonterminal on the left are the same as those for the nonterminal on the right. Under this condition, we may, if we wish, eliminate reductions by the single production.

Some programming languages have operators on 12 or more different precedence levels. Thus, if we are parsing according to a grammar which reflects a hierarchy of precedence levels, the parser will often make many sequences of reductions by single productions. We can speed up the parsing process considerably if we can eliminate these sequences of reductions, and in most practical cases we can do so without affecting the translation that is being computed.

In this section we shall describe a transformation on a set of LR(k) tables which has the effect of eliminating reductions by single productions wherever desired.

Let $(\mathfrak{J}, T_0)$ be a φ-inaccessible set of LR(k) tables for an LR(k) grammar $G = (N, \Sigma, P, S)$, and assume that $\mathfrak{J}$ has as many φ-entries as possible. Suppose that $A \rightarrow B$ is a single production in P.

Now, suppose the LR(k) parsing algorithm using this set of tables has the property that whenever a handle $Y_1 Y_2 \cdots Y_r$ is reduced to B on lookahead string u, B is then immediately reduced to A. We can often modify this set of tables so that $Y_1 \cdots Y_r$ is reduced to A in one step. Let us examine the conditions under which this can be done.

Let the index of production $A \rightarrow B$ be p. Suppose that $T = \langle f, g \rangle$ is a table such that $f(u) = $ **reduce** p for some lookahead string u. Let $\mathfrak{J}' = $ GOTO$^{-1}(T, B)$ and let $\mathfrak{U} = \{U \mid U = $ GOTO(T', A) and $T' \in \mathfrak{J}'\}$. $\mathfrak{J}'$ consists of those tables which can appear immediately below B on the pushdown list when T is the table above B. If $(\mathfrak{J}, T_0)$ is the canonical set of LR(k) tables, then $\mathfrak{U}$ is NEXT(T, p) (Exercise 7.3.19).

To eliminate the reduction by production p, we would like to change the entry $g'(B)$ from T to $g'(A)$ for each $\langle f', g' \rangle$ in $\mathfrak{J}'$. Then instead of making the two moves

$$(\gamma T' Y_1 U_1 Y_2 U_2 \cdots Y_r U_r, w, \pi) \vdash (\gamma T' BT, w, \pi i)$$
$$\vdash (\gamma T' AU, w, \pi i p)$$

the parser would just make one move:

$$(\gamma T' Y_1 U_1 Y_2 U_2 \cdots Y_r U_r, w, \pi) \vdash (\gamma T' AU, w, \pi i)$$

We can make this change in $g'(B)$ provided that the entries in T and all tables in $\mathfrak{U}$ are in agreement except for those lookaheads which call for a reduction by production p. That is, let $T = \langle f, g \rangle$ and suppose $\mathfrak{U} = \{\langle f_1, g_1 \rangle, \langle f_2, g_2 \rangle, \ldots, \langle f_m, g_m \rangle\}$. Then we require that

(1) For all u in Σ^{*k} if $f(u)$ is not φ or reduce p, then $f_i(u)$ is either φ or the same as $f(u)$ for $1 \le i \le m$.

(2) For all X in $N \cup \Sigma$, if $g(X)$ is not φ, then $g_i(X)$ is either φ or the same as $g(X)$ for $1 \le i \le m$.

If both these conditions hold, then we modify the tables in $\mathfrak{J}'$ and $\mathfrak{U}$ as follows:

(3) We let $g'(B)$ be $g'(A)$ for all $\langle f', g' \rangle$ in $\mathfrak{J}'$.
(4) For $1 \le i \le m$
    (a) for each $u \in \Sigma^{*k}$ change $f_i(u)$ to $f(u)$ if $f_i(u) = \varphi$ and if $f(u)$ is not φ or **reduce** p, and
    (b) for each $X \in N \cup \Sigma$ change $g_i(X)$ to $g(X)$ if $g(X) \ne \varphi$.

The modification in rule (3) will make table T inaccessible if it is possible to reach T only via the entries $g'(B)$ in tables $\langle f', g' \rangle$ in $\mathfrak{J}'$.

Note that the modified parser can place symbols and tables on the pushdown list that were not placed there by the original parser. For example, suppose that the original parser makes a reduction to B and then calls for a shift, as follows:

$$(\gamma T' Y_1 U_1 Y_2 U_2 \cdots Y_r U_r, aw, \pi) \vdash (\gamma T' BT, aw, \pi i)$$
$$\vdash (\gamma T' BTaT'', w, \pi i)$$

The new parser would make the same sequence of moves, but different symbols would appear on the pushdown list. Here, we would have

$$(\gamma T' Y_1 U_1 Y_2 U_2 \cdots Y_r U_r, aw, \pi) \vdash (\gamma T' AU', aw, \pi i)$$
$$\vdash (\gamma T' AU'aT'', w, \pi i)$$

Suppose that $T = \langle f, g \rangle$, $T' = \langle f', g' \rangle$, and $U = \langle f_i, g_i \rangle$. Then, U is $g'(A)$. Table U' has been constructed from U according to rule (4) above. Thus, if $f(v) = $ **shift**, where $v = \text{FIRST}(aw)$, we know that $f_i'(v)$ is also **shift**. Moreover, we know that $g_i(a)$ will be the same as $g(a)$. Thus, the new parser makes a sequence of moves which is correct except that it ignores the question of whether the reduction by $A \rightarrow B$ was actually made or not.

In subsequent moves the grammar symbols on the pushdown list are never consulted. Since the goto entries of U' and T agree, we can be sure that the two parsers will continue to behave identically (except for reductions by single production $A \rightarrow B$).

We can repeat this modification on the new set of tables, attempting to eliminate as many reductions by semantically insignificant single productions as possible.

Example 7.23

Let us eliminate reductions by single productions wherever possible in the set of LR(1) tables for G_0 in Fig. 7.32 (p. 607). Table T_2 calls for reduction by production 2, which is $E \rightarrow T$. The set of tables which can appear immediately below T_2 on the stack is $\{T_0, T_5\}$, since $\text{GOTO}(T_0, E) = T_1$ and $\text{GOTO}(T_5, E) = T_8$.

We must check that except for the **reduce** 2 entries, tables T_2 and T_1 are compatible and T_2 and T_8 are compatible. The action of T_2 on $*$ is **shift**. The action of T_1 and T_8 on $*$ is φ. The goto of T_2 on $*$ is T_7. The goto of T_1 and T_8 on $*$ is φ. Therefore, T_2 and T_1 are compatible and T_2 and T_8 are compatible. Thus, we can change the goto of table T_0 on nonterminal T from T_2 to T_1 and the goto of T_5 on T from T_2 to T_8. We must also change the action of both T_1 and T_8 on $*$ from φ to **shift**, since the action of T_2 on $*$ is **shift**. Finally, we change the goto of both T_1 and T_8 on $*$ from φ to T_7 since the goto of T_2 on $*$ is T_7.

Table T_2 is now inaccessible from T_0 and thus can be removed.

Let us now consider the **reduce** 4 moves in table T_3. (Production 4 is $T \longrightarrow F$.) The set of tables which can appear directly below T_3 is $\{T_0, T_5, T_6\}$. Now $\text{GOTO}(T_0, T) = T_1$, $\text{GOTO}(T_5, T) = T_8$, and $\text{GOTO}(T_6, T) = T_{13}$. [Before the modification above, $\text{GOTO}(T_0, T)$ was T_2, and $\text{GOTO}(T_5, T)$ was T_2.] We must now check that T_3 is compatible with each of T_1, T_8, and T_{13}. This is clearly the case, since the actions of T_3 are either φ or **reduce** 4, and the gotos of T_3 are all φ.

Thus, we can change the goto of T_0, T_5, and T_6 on F to T_1, T_8, and T_{13}, respectively. This makes table T_3 inaccessible from T_0.

The resulting set of tables is shown in Fig. 7.33(a). Tables T_2 and T_3 have been removed.

There is one further observation we can make. The goto entries in the columns under E, T, and F all happen to be compatible. Thus, we can merge these three columns into a single column. Let us label this new column by E. The resulting set of tables is shown in Fig. 7.33(b).

The only additional change that we need to make in the parsing algorithm is to use E in place of T and F to compute the goto entries. In effect the set of tables in Fig. 7.33(b) is parsing according to the skeletal grammar

$$(1)\ E \longrightarrow E + E$$
$$(3)\ E \longrightarrow E * E$$
$$(5)\ E \longrightarrow (E)$$
$$(6)\ E \longrightarrow a$$

as defined in Section 5.4.3.

For example, let us parse the input string $(a + a) * a$ using the tables in Fig. 7.33(b). The LR(1) parser will make the following sequence of moves.

$$[T_0, (a + a) * a, e] \vdash [T_0(T_5, a + a) * a, e]$$
$$\vdash [T_0(T_5 a T_4, + a) * a, e]$$
$$\vdash [T_0(T_5 E T_8, + a) * a, 6]$$
$$\vdash [T_0(T_5 E T_8 + T_6, a) * a, 6]$$
$$\vdash [T_0(T_5 E T_8 + T_6 a T_4,) * a, 6]$$
$$\vdash [T_0(T_5 E T_8 + T_6 E T_{13},) * a, 66]$$
$$\vdash [T_0(T_5 E T_8,) * a, 661]$$
$$\vdash [T_0(T_5 E T_8) T_{15}, * a, 661]$$
$$\vdash [T_0 E T_1, * a, 6615]$$
$$\vdash [T_0 E T_1 * T_7, a, 6615]$$
$$\vdash [T_0 E T_1 * T_7 a T_4, e, 6615]$$
$$\vdash [T_0 E T_1 * T_7 E T_{14}, e, 66156]$$
$$\vdash [T_0 E T_1, e, 661563]$$

	action						goto							
	a	$+$	$*$	$($	$)$	e	E	T	F	a	$+$	$*$	$($	$)$
T_0	S	X	X	S	X	X	T_1	T_1	T_1	T_4	φ	φ	T_5	φ
T_1	φ	S	S	φ	X	A	φ	φ	φ	φ	T_6	T_7	φ	φ
T_4	X	6	6	X	6	6	φ	φ	φ	φ	φ	φ	φ	φ
T_5	S	X	X	S	X	X	T_8	T_8	T_8	T_4	φ	φ	T_5	φ
T_6	S	X	X	S	X	X	φ	T_{13}	T_{13}	T_4	φ	φ	T_5	φ
T_7	S	X	X	S	X	X	φ	φ	T_{14}	T_4	φ	φ	T_5	φ
T_8	φ	S	S	φ	S	X	φ	φ	φ	φ	T_6	T_7	φ	T_{15}
T_{13}	φ	1	S	φ	1	1	φ	φ	φ	φ	φ	T_7	φ	φ
T_{14}	φ	3	3	φ	3	3	φ	φ	φ	φ	φ	φ	φ	φ
i_{15}	X	5	5	X	5	5	φ	φ	φ	φ	φ	φ	φ	φ

(a) before column merger

	action						goto					
	a	$+$	$*$	$($	$)$	e	E	a	$+$	$*$	$($	$)$
T_0	S	X	X	S	X	X	T_1	T_4	φ	φ	T_5	φ
T_1	φ	S	S	φ	X	A	φ	φ	T_6	T_7	φ	φ
T_4	X	6	6	X	6	6	φ	φ	φ	φ	φ	φ
T_5	S	X	X	S	X	X	T_8	T_4	φ	φ	T_5	φ
T_6	S	X	X	S	X	X	T_{13}	T_4	φ	φ	T_5	φ
T_7	S	X	X	S	X	X	T_{14}	T_4	φ	φ	T_5	φ
T_8	φ	S	S	φ	S	X	φ	φ	T_6	T_7	φ	T_{15}
T_{13}	φ	1	S	φ	1	1	φ	φ	φ	T_7	φ	φ
T_{14}	φ	3	3	φ	3	3	φ	φ	φ	φ	φ	φ
T_{15}	X	5	5	X	5	5	φ	φ	φ	φ	φ	φ

(b) after column merger

Fig. 7.33   LR(1) tables after elimination of single productions.

The last configuration is an accepting configuration. In parsing this same input string the canonical LR(1) parser for G_0 would have made five additional moves corresponding to reductions by single productions. □

The technique for eliminating single productions is summarized in Algorithm 7.9. While we shall not prove it here in detail, this algorithm enables us to remove all reductions by single productions if the grammar has at most one single production for each nonterminal. Even if some nonterminal has more than one single production, this algorithm will still do reasonably well.

ALGORITHM 7.9

Elimination of reductions by single productions.

Input. An LR(k) grammar $G = (N, \Sigma, P, S)$ and a φ-inaccessible set of tables $(\mathfrak{I}, T_0)$ for G.

Output. A modified set of tables for G that will be "equivalent" to $(\mathfrak{I}, T_0)$ in the sense of detecting errors just as soon but which may fail to reduce by some single productions.

Method.

(1) Order the nonterminals so that $N = \{A_1, \ldots, A_n\}$, and if $A_i \rightarrow A_j$ is a single production, then $i < j$. The unambiguity of an LR grammar guarantees that this may be done.

(2) Do step (3) for $j = 1, 2, \ldots, n$, in turn.

(3) Let $A_i \rightarrow A_j$ be a single production, numbered p, and let T_1 be a table which calls for the **reduce** p action on one or more lookahead strings. Suppose that T_2 is in NEXT(T_1, p)† and that for all lookaheads either the actions of T_1 and T_2 are the same or one is φ or the action of T_1 is **reduce** p. Finally, suppose that the goto entries of T_1 and T_2 also either agree or one is φ. Then create a new table T_3 which agrees with T_1 and T_2 wherever they are not φ, except at those lookaheads for which the action of T_1 is **reduce** p. There, the action of T_3 is to agree with T_2. Then, modify every table $T = \langle f, g \rangle$ such that $g(A_i) = T_2$ and $g(A_j) = T_1$ by replacing T_1 and T_2 by T_3 in the range of g.

(4) After completing all modifications of step (3), remove all tables which are no longer accessible from the initial table. □

We shall state a series of results necessary to prove our contention that given an LR(1) grammar, Algorithm 7.9 completely eliminates reductions by single productions if no two having the same left or same right sides, provided that no nonterminal of the grammar derives the empty string only. (Such a

†NEXT must always be computed for the current set of tables, incorporating all previous modifications of step (3)

nonterminal can easily be removed without affecting the LR(1)-ness of the grammar.)

LEMMA 7.1

Let $G = (N, \Sigma, P, S)$ be an LR(1) grammar such that for each $C \in N$, there is some $w \neq e$ in Σ^* such that $C \overset{*}{\Rightarrow} w$. Suppose that $A \overset{+}{\Rightarrow} B$ by a sequence of single productions. Let α_1 and α_2 be the sets of LR(1) items that are valid for viable prefixes γA and γB, respectively. Then the following conditions hold:

(1) If $[C \rightarrow \alpha_1 \cdot X\beta_1, a]$ is in α_1 and $[D \rightarrow \alpha_2 \cdot Y\beta_2, b]$ is in α_2, then $X \neq Y$.

(2) If $[C \rightarrow \alpha_1 \cdot \beta_1, a]$ is in α_1 and b is in $\mathrm{EFF}(\beta_1 a)$,† then there is no item of the form $[D \rightarrow \alpha_2 \cdot \beta_2, c]$ in α_2 such that $b \in \mathrm{EFF}(\beta_2 c)$ except possibly for $[E \rightarrow B \cdot, b]$, where $A \overset{*}{\Rightarrow} E \Rightarrow B$ by a sequence of single productions.

Proof. A derivation of a contradiction of the LR(1) condition when condition (1) or (2) is violated is left for the Exercises. ☐

COROLLARY

The LR(1) tables constructed from α_1 and α_2 do not disagree in any action or goto entry unless one of them is φ or the table for α_2 calls for a reduction by a single production in that entry.

Proof. By Theorem 7.7, since the two tables are constructed from the sets of valid items for strings ending in a nonterminal, all **error** entries are don't cares. Lemma 7.1(1) assures that there are no conflicts in the goto entries; part (2) assures that there are no conflicts in the action entries, except for resolvable ones regarding single productions. ☐

LEMMA 7.2

During the application of Algorithm 7.9, if no two single productions have the same left or the same right sides, then each table is the result of merging a list (possibly of length 1) of LR(1) tables $T_1, \ldots, T_n$ which were constructed from the sets of valid items for some viable prefixes $\gamma A_1, \gamma A_2, \ldots,$ γA_n, where $A_i \rightarrow A_{i+1}$ is in P for $1 \leq i < n$.

Proof. Exercise. ☐

THEOREM 7.8

If Algorithm 7.9 is applied to an LR(1) grammar G and its canonical set of LR(1) tables $\mathfrak{I}$, if G has no more than one single production for any nonterminal, and if no nonterminal derives e alone, then the resulting set of tables has no reductions by single productions.

†Note that β_1 could be e here, in which case α_1 calls for a reduction on lookahead b. Otherwise, α_1 calls for a shift.

Proof. Intuitively, Lemmas 7.1 and 7.2 assure that all pairs T_1 and T_2 considered in step (3) do in fact meet the conditions of that step. A formal proof is left for the Exercises. $\square$

EXERCISES

7.3.1. Construct the canonical sets of LR(1) tables for the following grammars:

(a) $S \longrightarrow ABAC$
$A \longrightarrow aD$
$B \longrightarrow b \,|\, c$
$C \longrightarrow c \,|\, d$
$D \longrightarrow D0 \,|\, 0$

(b) $S \longrightarrow aSS \,|\, b$

(c) $S \longrightarrow SSa \,|\, b$

(d) $E \longrightarrow E + T \,|\, T$
$T \longrightarrow T * F \,|\, F$
$F \longrightarrow P \uparrow F \,|\, P$
$P \longrightarrow (E) \,|\, a \,|\, a(L)$
$L \longrightarrow L, E \,|\, E$

7.3.2. Use the canonical set of tables from Exercise 7.3.1(a) and Algorithm 7.5 to parse the input string $a0ba00c$.

7.3.3. Show how Algorithm 7.5 can be implemented by
(a) a deterministic pushdown transducer,
(b) a Floyd–Evans production language parser.

7.3.4. Construct a Floyd–Evans production language parser for G_0 from
(a) The LR(1) tables in Fig. 7.33(a).
(b) The LR(1) tables in Fig. 7.33(b).
Compare the resulting parsers with those in Exercise 7.2.11.

7.3.5. Consider the following grammar G which generates the language $L = \{a^n 0 a^i b^n \,|\, i, n \geq 0\} \cup \{0 a^n 1 a^i c^n \,|\, i, n \geq 0\}$:

$$S \longrightarrow A \,|\, 0B$$
$$A \longrightarrow aAb \,|\, 0 \,|\, 0C$$
$$B \longrightarrow aBc \,|\, 1 \,|\, 1C$$
$$C \longrightarrow aC \,|\, a$$

Construct a simple precedence parser and the canonical LR(1) parser for G. Show that the simple precedence parser will read all the a's following the 1 in the input string $a^n 1 a^i b$ before announcing error. Show that the canonical LR(1) parser will announce error as soon as it reads the 1.

7.3.6. Use Algorithm 7.6 to construct a φ-inaccessible set of LR(1) tables for each of the grammars in Exercise 7.3.1.

7.3.7. Use the techniques of this section to find a smaller equivalent set of LR(1) tables for each of the grammars of Exercise 7.3.1.

7.3.8. Let $\mathcal{S}$ be the canonical collection of sets of LR(k) items for an LR(k) grammar $G = (N, \Sigma, P, S)$. Let $\mathcal{C}$ be a set of items in $\mathcal{S}$. Show that

(a) If item $[A \longrightarrow \alpha \cdot \beta, u]$ is in $\mathcal{C}$, then $u \in \text{FOLLOW}_k(A)$.

(b) If $\mathcal{C}$ is not the initial set of items, then $\mathcal{C}$ contains at least one item of the form $[A \longrightarrow \alpha X \cdot \beta, u]$ for some X in $N \cup \Sigma$.

(c) If $[B \longrightarrow \cdot \beta, v]$ is in $\mathcal{C}$ and $B \neq S'$, then there is an item of the form $[A \longrightarrow \alpha \cdot B\gamma, u]$ in $\mathcal{C}$.

(d) If $[A \longrightarrow \alpha \cdot B\beta, u]$ is in $\mathcal{C}$ and $\text{EFF}_1(B\beta u)$ contains a, then there is an item of the form $[C \longrightarrow \cdot a\gamma, v]$ in $\mathcal{C}$ for some γ and v. (This result provides an easy method for computing the **shift** entries in an LR(1) parser.)

*7.3.9. Show that if an error entry is replaced by φ in $\mathcal{T}'$, the set of LR(k) tables constructed by Algorithm 7.6, the resulting set of tables will no longer be φ-inaccessible.

*7.3.10. Show that a canonical LR(k) parser will announce error either in the initial configuration or immediately after a shift move.

**7.3.11. Let G be an LR(k) grammar. Give upper and lower bounds on the number of tables in the canonical set of LR(k) tables for G. Can you give meaningful upper and lower bounds on the number of tables in an arbitrary valid set of LR(k) tables for G?

*7.3.12. Modify Algorithm 7.6 to construct a φ-inaccessible set of LR(0) tables for an LR(0) grammar.

*7.3.13. Devise an algorithm to find all φ-entries in an arbitrary set of LR(k) tables.

*7.3.14. Devise an algorithm to find all φ-entries in an arbitrary set of LL(k) tables.

**7.3.15. Devise an algorithm to find all φ-entries in an LC(k) parsing table.

*7.3.16. Devise a reasonable algorithm to find compatible partitions on a set of LR(k) tables.

7.3.17. Find compatible partitions for the sets of LR(1) tables in Exercise 7.3.1.

7.3.18. Show that the relation of compatibility of LR(k) tables is reflexive and symmetric but not transitive.

7.3.19. Let $(\mathcal{T}, T_0)$ be the canonical set of LR(k) tables for an LR(k) grammar G. Show that GOTO(T_0, α) is not empty if and only if α is a viable prefix of G. Is this true for an arbitrary valid set of LR(k) tables for G?

*7.3.20. Let $(\mathcal{T}, T_0)$ be the canonical set of LR(k) tables for G. Find an upper bound on the height of any table in $\mathcal{T}$ (as a function of G).

7.3.21. Let $\mathcal{T}$ be the canonical set of LR(k) tables for LR(k) grammar $G = (N, \Sigma, P, S)$. Show that for all $T \in \mathcal{T}$, NEXT(T, p) is the set $\{\text{GOTO}(T', A) \,|\, T' \in \text{GOTO}^{-1}(T, \alpha)\}$, where production p is $A \longrightarrow \alpha$.

7.3.22. Give an algorithm to compute NEXT(T, p) for an arbitrary set of LR(k) tables for a grammar G.

*7.3.23. Let $\mathfrak{I}$ be a canonical set of LR(k) tables. Suppose that for each $T \in \mathfrak{I}$ having one or more reduce actions, we select one production, p, by which T reduces and replace all **error** and φ actions by **reduce** p. Show that the resulting set of tables is equivalent to $\mathfrak{I}$.

*7.3.24. Show that reductions by single productions cannot always be eliminated from a set of LR(k) tables for an LR(k) grammar by Algorithm 7.9.

*7.3.25. Prove that Algorithm 7.9 results in a set of LR(k) tables which is equivalent to the original set of tables except for reductions by single productions.

7.3.26. A binary operator θ *associates from left to right* if $a\theta b\theta c$ is to be interpreted as $((a\theta b)\theta c)$. Construct an LR(1) grammar for expressions over the alphabet $\{a, (,)\}$ together with the operators $\{+, -, *, /, \uparrow\}$. All operators are binary except $+$ and $-$, which are both binary and (prefix) unary. All binary operators associate from left to right except $\uparrow$. The binary operators $+$ and $-$ have precedence level 1, $*$ and $/$ have precedence level 2, $\uparrow$ and the two unary operators have precedence level 3.

**7.3.27. Develop a technique for automatically constructing an LR(1) parser for expressions when the specification of the expressions is in terms of a set of operators together with their associativities and precedence levels, as in Exercise 7.3.26.

*7.3.28. Prove that $\mathfrak{I}$ and $\mathfrak{U}$ in Example 7.17 are equivalent sets of tables.

**7.3.29. Show that it is decidable whether two sets of LR(k) tables are equivalent.

DEFINITION

The following productions generate arithmetic expressions in which $\theta_1, \theta_2, \ldots, \theta_n$ represent binary operators on n different precedence levels. θ_1 has the lowest precedence, and θ_n the highest. The operators associate from left to right.

$$E_0 \longrightarrow E_0\theta_1 E_1 \mid E_1$$
$$E_1 \longrightarrow E_1\theta_2 E_2 \mid E_2$$
$$\vdots$$
$$E_{n-1} \longrightarrow E_{n-1}\theta_n E_n \mid E_n$$
$$E_n \longrightarrow (E_1) \mid a$$

We can also generate this same set of expressions by the following "tagged LR(1)" grammar:

$$
\begin{array}{lll}
(1) & E_i \longrightarrow E_i\theta_j E_j & 0 \le i < j \le n \\
(2) & E_i \longrightarrow (E_0) & 0 \le i \le n \\
(3) & E_i \longrightarrow a & 0 \le i \le n
\end{array}
$$

In these productions the subscripts are to be treated as tags on the nonterminal E and terminal θ. The conditions on the tags reflect the precedence levels of the operators. For example, the first production indicates that a level i expression can be a level i expression followed by an operator on the jth precedence level followed by a level j expression provided that $0 \leq i < j \leq n$. The start symbol has the tag 0.

The expression $a\theta_2(a\theta_1 a)$, which is analogous to $a * (a + a)$, has the parse tree shown in Fig. 7.34. In the tree we have shown the values of the tags associated with the nonterminals.

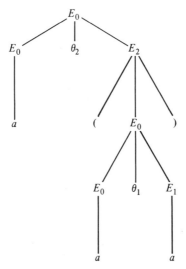

Fig. 7.34 Parse tree.

Although the tagged grammar is ambiguous without the tags, we can construct an LR(1)-like parser that uses tags with LR(1) tables wherever necessary to correctly parse input strings. Such an LR(1) parser is shown in Fig. 7.35.

To illustrate the behavior of the parser, let us parse the input string $a\theta_2(a\theta_1 a)$. The parser starts off in configuration $([T_0, 0], a\theta_2(a\theta_1 a), e)$ in which the tag 0 is associated with the initial table T_0. The parsing action of $[T_0, i]$ on input a is shift, and so the parser enters configuration

$$([T_0, 0]aT_2, \theta_2(a\theta_1 a), e)$$

The action of T_2 on θ_2 is reduce by production 3; that is, $E \longrightarrow a$. The goto of $[T_0, i]$ on E is $[T_1, i]$. The value of the tag is transmitted from T_0 to T_1. Therefore, the parser then enters configuration

$$([T_0, 0]E[T_1, 0], \theta_2(a\theta_1 a), 3)$$

	action					goto			
	a	θ_j	(	)	e	E	a	θ_j	(	)
$[T_0,i]$	S	X	S	X	X	$[T_1,i]$	T_2	X	$[T_3,0]$	X
$[T_1,i]$	X	S	X	X	A	X	X	$[T_4,j]$	X	X
T_2	X	3	X	3	3	X	X	X	X	X
$[T_3,0]$	S	X	S	X	X	$[T_5,i]$	T_2	X	$[T_3,0]$	X
$[T_4,j]$	S	X	S	X	X	$[T_6,i]$	T_2	X	$[T_3,0]$	X
$[T_5,i]$	X	S	X	S	X	X	X	$[T_4,j]$	X	T_7
$[T_6 i]$	X	$R1$	X	$R2$	$R2$	X	X	$[T_4,j]$	X	X
T_7	X	2	X	2	2	X	X	X	X	X

Fig. 7.35   LR(1) parser with tags.

The complete sequence of moves made by the parser would be as follows:

$([T_0, 0], a\theta_2(a\theta_1 a), e)$

$\vdash ([T_0, 0]aT_2, \theta_2(a\theta_1 a), e)$

$\vdash ([T_0, 0]E[T_1, 0], \theta_2(a\theta_1 a), 3)$

$\vdash ([T_0, 0]E[T_1, 0]\theta_2[T_4, 2], (a\theta_1 a), 3)$

$\vdash ([T_0, 0]E[T_1, 0]\theta_2[T_4, 2]([T_3, 0], a\theta_1 a), 3)$

$\vdash ([T_0, 0]E[T_1, 0]\theta_2[T_4, 2]([T_3, 0]aT_2, \theta_1 a), 3)$

$\vdash ([T_0, 0]E[T_1, 0]\theta_2[T_4, 2]([T_3, 0]E[T_5, 0], \theta_1 a), 33)$

$\vdash ([T_0, 0]E[T_1, 0]\theta_2[T_4, 2]([T_3, 0]E[T_5, 0]\theta_1[T_4, 1], a), 33)$

$\vdash ([T_0, 0]E[T_1, 0]\theta_2[T_4, 2]([T_3, 0]E[T_5, 0]\theta_1[T_4, 1]aT_2,), 33)$

$\vdash ([T_0, 0]E[T_1, 0]\theta_2[T_4, 2]([T_3, 0]E[T_5, 0]\theta_1[T_4, 1]E[T_6, 1],), 333)$

$\vdash ([T_0, 0]E[T_1, 0]\theta_2[T_4, 2]([T_3, 0]E[T_5, 0],), 3331_1)$

$\vdash ([T_0, 0]E[T_1, 0]\theta_2[T_4, 2]([T_3, 0]E[T_5, 0])T_7, e, 3331_1)$

$\vdash ([T_0, 0]E[T_1, 0]\theta_2[T_4, 2]E[T_6, 2], e, 3331_1 2)$

$\vdash ([T_0, 0]E[T_1, 0], e, 3331_1 21_2)$

**7.3.30. Show that the parser in Fig. 7.35 correctly parses all expressions generated by the tagged grammar.

7.3.31. Construct an LR(1) parser for the untagged grammar with operators on n different precedence levels. How big is this parser compared with the tagged parser in Fig. 7.35. Compare the operating speed of the two parsers.

*7.3.32. Construct a tagged LR(1)-like parser for expressions with binary operators of which some associate from left to right and others from right to left.

**7.3.33. The following tagged grammar will generate expressions with binary operators on n different precedence levels:

(1) $E_i \longrightarrow (E_0)R_{i.n}$ $\qquad$ $0 \leq i \leq n$
(2) $E_i \longrightarrow aR_{i,n}$ $\qquad\quad$ $0 \leq i \leq n$
(3) $R_{i,k} \longrightarrow \theta_j E_j R_{i,j-1}$ $\quad$ $0 \leq i < j \leq k \leq n$
(4) $R_{i,j} \longrightarrow e$ $\qquad\qquad$ $0 \leq i \leq j \leq n$

Construct a tagged LL(1)-like parser for this grammar. *Hint:* Although this grammar has two tags on R, only the first tag is needed by the parser.

7.3.34. Complete the proof of Lemma 7.1 and its corollary.

7.3.35. Prove Lemma 7.2.

7.3.36. Complete the proof of Theorem 7.8.

Open Problem

7.3.37. Under what conditions is it possible to merge all the goto columns for the nonterminals after eliminating reductions by single productions, as we did for G_0? The reader should consider the possibility of relating this question to operator precedence. Recall that G_0 is an operator precedence grammar.

Research Problems

7.3.38. Develop additional techniques for modifying sets of LR tables, while preserving "equivalence" in the sense we have been using the term.

7.3.39. Develop techniques for compactly representing LR tables, taking advantage of φ entries.

Programming Exercises

7.3.40. Design elementary operations that can be used to implement an LR(1) parser. Some of these operations might be: read an input symbol, push a symbol on the pushdown list, pop a certain number of symbols from the pushdown list, emit an output, and so forth. Construct an interpreter that will execute these elementary operations.

7.3.41. Construct a program that takes as input a set of LR(1) tables and produces as output a sequence of elementary instructions that implements the LR(1) parser using this set of tables.

7.3.42. Construct a program that takes as input a set of LL(1) tables and produces as output a sequence of elementary instructions that simulates the LL(1) parser using this set of tables.

7.3.43. Write a program to add don't care entries to the canonical set of LR tables.

*7.3.44. Write a program to apply some heuristics for error postponement and table merger, with the goal of producing small sets of tables.

7.3.45. Implement Algorithm 7.9 to eliminate reductions by single productions where possible.

BIBLIOGRAPHIC NOTES

The transformations considered in this section were developed by Aho and Ullman [1972c, 1972d]. Pager [1970] considers another approach to the simplification of LR(k) parsers in which a parser can be modified to such an extent that it may no longer detect errors at the same position on the input as the canonical LR(k) parser and may need to look at the stack to determine which reduction to make. The idea of using tags in LL grammars and parsers was suggested by P. M. Lewis, D. J. Rosenkrantz, and R. E. Stearns. Lewis and Rosenkrantz [1971] report that by using tags to handle expressions and conditional statements, the syntax analyzer in their ALGOL 60 compiler was reduced to a 29 by 37 LL(1) parsing table.

7.4. TECHNIQUES FOR CONSTRUCTING LR(k) PARSERS

The amount of work required to construct the sets of LR(k) items [and hence the canonical LR(k) parser] grows rapidly with the size of the grammar and with k, the length of the lookahead string. For large grammars the amount of computation needed to construct the canonical set of LR(k) tables is so large as to be impractical, even if $k = 1$. In this section we shall consider some more practical techniques which can be used to construct valid sets of LR(1) tables from certain LR(1) grammars.

The first technique that we shall consider is the construction of the canonical collection of sets of LR(0) items for a grammar G. If each set of LR(0) items is consistent,† then we can construct a valid set of LR(0) tables for G. If a set of LR(0) items is not consistent, then it is reasonable to attempt to use lookahead strings in this set of items to resolve parsing action conflicts.

---

†A set of LR(k) items, α, is consistent if we can construct an LR(k) table from α in which the parsing actions are unique.

The saving in this approach is due to the fact that we would use lookahead only where lookahead is needed. For many grammars this approach will produce a set of tables which is considerably smaller than the canonical set of LR(k) tables for G. However, for some LR(k) grammars this method does not work at all.

We shall also consider another approach to the design of LR(k) parsers. In this approach, we split a large grammar into smaller pieces, constructing sets of LR(k) items for the pieces and then combining the sets of items to form larger sets of items. However, not every splitting of an LR(k) grammar G is guaranteed to produce pieces from which we can construct a valid set of tables for G.

7.4.1. Simple LR Grammars

In this section we shall attempt to construct a parser for an LR(k) grammar G by first constructing the collection of sets of LR(0) items for G. The method that we shall consider works for a subclass of the LR grammars called the simple LR grammars.

DEFINITION

Let $G = (N, \Sigma, P, S)$ be a CFG [not necessarily LR(0)]. Let $\mathcal{S}_0$ be the canonical collection of sets of LR(0) items for G. Let $\mathcal{C}$ be any set of items in $\mathcal{S}_0$. Suppose that whenever $[A \longrightarrow \alpha \cdot \beta, e]$ and $[B \longrightarrow \gamma \cdot \delta, e]$ are two distinct items in $\mathcal{C}$, one of the following conditions is satisfied:

(1) Neither of β and δ are e.
(2) $\beta \neq e$, $\delta = e$, and $\text{FOLLOW}_k(B) \cap \text{EFF}_k(\beta\ \text{FOLLOW}_k(A))$† $= \varnothing$.
(3) $\beta = e$, $\delta \neq e$, and $\text{FOLLOW}_k(A) \cap \text{EFF}_k(\delta\ \text{FOLLOW}_k(B)) = \varnothing$.
(4) $\beta = \delta = e$ and $\text{FOLLOW}_k(A) \cap \text{FOLLOW}_k(B) = \varnothing$.

Then G is said to be a *simple* LR(k) grammar [SLR(k) grammar, for short].

Example 7.24

Let G_0 be our usual grammar

$$E \longrightarrow E + T \,|\, T$$
$$T \longrightarrow T * F \,|\, F$$
$$F \longrightarrow (E) \,|\, a$$

The canonical collection of sets of LR(0) items for G is listed in Fig. 7.36, with the second components, which are all e, omitted.

---

†We could use $\text{FOLLOW}_{k-1}(A)$ here, since β must generate at least one symbol of any string in $\text{EFF}_k(\beta\ \text{FOLLOW}_k(A))$.

$$\alpha_0 : \quad E' \longrightarrow \cdot E$$
$$E \longrightarrow \cdot E + T$$
$$E \longrightarrow \cdot T$$
$$T \longrightarrow \cdot T * F$$
$$T \longrightarrow \cdot F$$
$$F \longrightarrow \cdot (E)$$
$$F \longrightarrow \cdot a$$

$$\alpha_1 : \quad E' \longrightarrow E \cdot$$
$$E \longrightarrow E \cdot + T$$

$$\alpha_2 : \quad E \longrightarrow T \cdot$$
$$T \longrightarrow T \cdot * F$$

$$\alpha_3 : \quad T \longrightarrow F \cdot$$

$$\alpha_4 : \quad F \longrightarrow a \cdot$$

$$\alpha_5 : \quad F \longrightarrow (\cdot E)$$
$$E \longrightarrow \cdot E + T$$
$$E \longrightarrow \cdot T$$
$$T \longrightarrow \cdot T * F$$
$$T \longrightarrow \cdot F$$
$$F \longrightarrow \cdot (E)$$
$$F \longrightarrow \cdot a$$

$$\alpha_6 : \quad E \longrightarrow E + \cdot T$$
$$T \longrightarrow \cdot T * F$$
$$T \longrightarrow \cdot F$$
$$F \longrightarrow \cdot (E)$$
$$F \longrightarrow \cdot a$$

$$\alpha_7 : \quad T \longrightarrow T * \cdot F$$
$$F \longrightarrow \cdot (E)$$
$$F \longrightarrow \cdot a$$

$$\alpha_8 : \quad F \longrightarrow (E \cdot)$$
$$E \longrightarrow E \cdot + T$$

$$\alpha_9 : \quad E \longrightarrow E + T \cdot$$
$$T \longrightarrow T \cdot * F$$

$$\alpha_{10} : \quad T \longrightarrow T * F \cdot$$

$$\alpha_{11} : \quad F \longrightarrow (E) \cdot$$

Fig. 7.36 LR(0) items for G_0.

G_0 is not SLR(0) because, for example, α_1 contains the two items $[E' \longrightarrow E \cdot]$ and $[E \longrightarrow E \cdot + T]$ and

$$\text{FOLLOW}_0(E') = \{e\} = \text{EFF}_0[+ \ T \ \text{FOLLOW}_0(E)].\dagger$$

However, G_0 is SLR(1). To check the SLR(1) condition, it suffices to consider sets of items which

(1) Have at least two items, and
(2) Have an item with the dot at the right-hand end.

Thus, we need concern ourselves only with α_1, α_2, and α_9. For α_1, we observe that $\text{FOLLOW}_1(E') = \{e\}$ and $\text{EFF}_1[+ \ T \ \text{FOLLOW}_1(E)] = \{+\}$. Since $\{e\} \cap \{+\} = \varnothing$, α_1 satisfies condition (3) of the SLR(1) definition. α_2 and α_9 satisfy condition (3) similarly, and so we can conclude that G_0 is SLR(1). □

Now let us attempt to construct a set of LR(1) tables for an SLR(1) grammar G starting from $\mathcal{S}_0$, the canonical collection of sets of LR(0) items for G. Suppose that some set of items α in $\mathcal{S}_0$ has only the items $[A \longrightarrow \alpha \cdot, e]$ and $[B \longrightarrow \beta \cdot \gamma, e]$. We can construct an LR(1) table from this set of

†Note that for all α, $\text{FIRST}_0(\alpha) = \text{EFF}_0(\alpha) = \text{FOLLOW}_0(\alpha) = \{e\}$.

items as follows. The goto entries are constructed in the obvious way, as though the tables were LR(0) tables. But for lookahead a, what should the action be? Should we shift, or should we reduce by production $A \rightarrow \alpha$. The answer lies in whether or not $a \in \text{FOLLOW}_1(A)$. If $a \in \text{FOLLOW}_1(A)$, then it is impossible that a is in $\text{EFF}_1(\gamma)$, by the definition of an SLR(1) grammar. Thus, **reduce** is the appropriate parsing action. Conversely, if a is not in $\text{FOLLOW}_1(A)$, then it is impossible that **reduce** is correct. If a is in $\text{EFF}(\gamma)$, then **shift** is the action; otherwise, **error** is correct. This algorithm is summarized below.

ALGORITHM 7.10

Construction of a set of LR(k) tables for an SLR(k) grammar.

Input. An SLR(k) grammar $G = (\text{N}, \Sigma, P, S)$ and $\mathcal{S}_0$, the canonical collection of sets of LR(0) items for G.

Output. $(\mathcal{I}, T_0)$, a set of *LR(k)* tables for G, which we shall call the *SLR(k) set of tables* for G.

Method. Let $\mathcal{C}$ be a set of LR(0) items in $\mathcal{S}_0$. The LR(k) table T associated with $\mathcal{C}$ is the pair $\langle f, g \rangle$, constructed as follows:

(1) For all u in Σ^{*k},
    (a) $f(u) = \textbf{shift}$ if $[A \rightarrow \alpha \cdot \beta, e]$ is in $\mathcal{C}$, $\beta \neq e$, and u is in the set $\text{EFF}_k(\beta \text{ FOLLOW}_k(A))$.
    (b) $f(u) = \textbf{reduce } i$ if $[A \rightarrow \alpha \cdot, e]$ is in $\mathcal{C}$, $A \rightarrow \alpha$ is production i in P, and u is in $\text{FOLLOW}_k(A)$.
    (c) $f(e) = \textbf{accept}$ if $[S' \rightarrow S \cdot, e]$ is in $\mathcal{C}$.†
    (d) $f(u) = \textbf{error}$ otherwise.
(2) For all X in $\text{N} \cup \Sigma$, $g(X)$ is the table constructed from $\text{GOTO}(\mathcal{C}, X)$. T_0, the initial table, is the one associated with the set of items containing $[S' \rightarrow \cdot S, e]$. $\square$

We can relate Algorithm 7.10 to our original method of constructing a set of tables from a collection of sets of items given in Section 5.2.5. Let $\mathcal{C}'$ be the set of items $[A \rightarrow \alpha \cdot \beta, u]$ such that $[A \rightarrow \alpha \cdot \beta, e]$ is in $\mathcal{C}$ and u is in $\text{FOLLOW}_k(A)$. Let $\mathcal{S}_0'$ be $\{\mathcal{C}' | \mathcal{C} \in \mathcal{S}_0\}$. Then, Algorithm 7.10 yields the same set of tables that would be obtained by applying the construction given in Section 5.2.5 to $\mathcal{S}_0'$.

It should be clear from the definition that each set of items in $\mathcal{S}_0'$ is consistent if and only if G is an SLR(k) grammar.

Example 7.25

Let us construct the SLR(1) set of tables from the sets of items of Fig. 7.36 (p. 623). We use the name T_i for the table constructed from $\mathcal{C}_i$. We shall consider the construction of table T_2 only.

†The canonical collection of sets of items is constructed from the augmented grammar.

$\mathcal{a}_2$ is $\{[E \to T \cdot\,], [T \to T \cdot * F]\}$. Let $T_2 = \langle f, g \rangle$. Since FOLLOW($E$) is $\{+,), e\}$, we have $f(+) = f(]) = f(e) = \mathbf{reduce}\ 2$. (The usual production numbering is being used.) Since EFF($* F$ FOLLOW(T)) $= \{*\}$, $f(*) = \mathbf{shift}$. For the other lookaheads, we have $f(a) = f([) = \mathbf{error}$.

The only symbol X for which $g(X)$ is defined is $X = *$. It is easy to see by inspection of Fig. 7.36 that $g(*) = T_7$. The entire set of tables is given in Fig. 7.37.

	action						goto							
	a	$+$	$*$	$($	$)$	e	E	T	F	a	$+$	$*$	$($	$)$
T_0	S	X	X	S	X	X	T_1	T_2	T_3	T_4	X	X	T_5	X
T_1	X	S	X	X	X	A	X	X	X	X	T_6	X	X	X
T_2	X	2	S	X	2	2	X	X	X	X	X	T_7	X	X
T_3	X	4	4	X	4	4	X	X	X	X	X	X	X	X
T_4	X	6	6	X	6	6	X	X	X	X	X	X	X	X
T_5	S	X	X	S	X	X	T_8	T_2	T_3	T_4	X	X	T_5	X
T_6	S	X	X	S	X	X	X	T_9	T_3	T_4	X	X	T_5	X
T_7	S	X	X	S	X	X	X	X	T_{10}	T_4	X	X	T_5	X
T_8	X	S	X	X	S	X	X	X	X	X	T_6	X	X	T_{11}
T_9	X	1	S	X	1	1	X	X	X	X	X	T_7	X	X
T_{10}	X	3	3	X	3	3	X	X	X	X	X	X	X	X
T_{11}	X	5	5	X	5	5	X	X	X	X	X	X	X	X

Fig. 7.37   SLR(1) tables for G_0.

Except for names and φ entries, this set of tables is exactly the same as that in Fig. 7.32 (p. 607).   □

We shall now prove that Algorithm 7.10 will always produce a valid set of LR(k) tables for an SLR(k) grammar G. In fact, the set of tables produced is equivalent to the canonical set of LR(k) tables for G.

THEOREM 7.9

If G is an SLR(k) grammar, $(\mathfrak{I}, T_0)$, the SLR(k) set of tables constructed by Algorithm 7.10 for G is equivalent to $(\mathfrak{I}_c, T_c)$, the canonical set of LR(k) tables for G.

Proof. Let $\mathcal{S}_k$ be the canonical collection of sets of LR(k) items for G and let $\mathcal{S}_0$ be the collection of sets of LR(0) items for G. Let us define the *core* of a set of items $\mathcal{Q}$ as the set of bracketed first components of the items in that set. For example, the core of $[A \longrightarrow \alpha \cdot \beta, u]$ is $[A \longrightarrow \alpha \cdot \beta]$.† We shall denote the core of a set of items $\mathcal{Q}$ by CORE($\mathcal{Q}$).

Each set of items in $\mathcal{S}_0$ is distinct, but there may be several sets of items in $\mathcal{S}_k$ with the same core. However, it can easily be shown that $\mathcal{S}_0 = \{\text{CORE}(\mathcal{Q}) \,|\, \mathcal{Q} \in \mathcal{S}_k\}$.

Let us define the function h on tables which corresponds to the function CORE on sets of items. We let $h(T) = T'$ if T is the canonical LR(k) table associated with $\mathcal{Q}$ and T' is the SLR(k) table constructed by Algorithm 7.10 from CORE($\mathcal{Q}$). It is easy to verify that h commutes with the GOTO function. That is, GOTO($h(T), X$) = $h(\text{GOTO}(T, X))$.

As before, let

$$\mathcal{Q}' = \{[A \longrightarrow \alpha \cdot \beta, u] \,\big|\, [A \longrightarrow \alpha \cdot \beta, e] \in \mathcal{Q} \quad \text{and} \quad u \in \text{FOLLOW}_k(A)\}.$$

Let $\mathcal{S}_0' = \{\mathcal{Q}' \,|\, \mathcal{Q} \in \mathcal{S}_0\}$. We know that $(\mathfrak{I}, T_0)$ is the same set of LR(k) tables as that constructed from $\mathcal{S}_0'$ using the method of Section 5.2.5. We shall show that $(\mathfrak{I}, T_0)$ can also be obtained by applying a sequence of transformations to $(\mathfrak{I}_c, T_c)$, the canonical set of LR(k) tables for G. The necessary steps are the following.

(1) Let $\mathcal{P}$ be the postponement set consisting of those triples (T, u, i) such that the action of T on u is **error** and the action of $h(T)$ on u is **reduce** i. Use Algorithm 7.8 on $\mathcal{P}$ and $(\mathfrak{I}_c, T_c)$ to obtain another set of tables $(\mathfrak{I}_c', T_c')$.

(2) Apply Algorithm 7.7 to merge all pairs of tables T_1 and T_2 such that $h(T_1) = h(T_2)$. The resulting set of tables is $(\mathfrak{I}, T_0)$.

Let (T, u, i) be an element of $\mathcal{P}$. To show that $\mathcal{P}$ satisfies the requirements of being a postponement set for $\mathfrak{I}_c$, we must show that if $T'' = \langle f'', g'' \rangle$ is in NEXT(T, i), then $f''(u) = $ **error**. To this end, suppose that production i is $A \longrightarrow \alpha$ and $T'' = \text{GOTO}(T_0, \beta A)$ for some viable prefix βA. Then $T = \text{GOTO}(T_0, \beta \alpha)$.

In contradiction let us suppose that $f''(u) \neq$ **error**. Then there is some item $[B \longrightarrow \gamma \cdot \delta, v]$ valid for βA, where u is in EFF(δv).‡ Every set of items, except the initial set of items, contains an item in which there is at least one symbol to the left of the dot. (See Exercise 7.3.8.) The initial set of items is valid only for e. Thus, we may assume without loss of generality that $\gamma = \gamma' A$ for some γ'. Then $[B \longrightarrow \gamma' \cdot A\delta, v]$ is valid for β, and so is $[A \longrightarrow \cdot \alpha, u]$. Thus, $[A \longrightarrow \alpha \cdot, u]$ is valid for $\beta\alpha$, and $f(u)$ should not be **error** as assumed. We conclude that $\mathcal{P}$ is indeed a legitimate postponement set for $\mathfrak{I}_c$.

Let $\mathfrak{I}_1$ be the result of applying Algorithm 7.8 to $\mathfrak{I}_c$ using the postpone-

---

†We shall not bother to distinguish between $[A \longrightarrow \alpha \cdot \beta]$ and $[A \longrightarrow \alpha \cdot \beta, e]$.

‡Note that this statement is true independent of whether $\delta = e$ or not.

ment set $\mathcal{P}$. Now suppose that T is a table in $\mathfrak{I}_c$ associated with the set of items α and that T' is the corresponding modified table in $\mathfrak{I}_1$. Then the only difference between T and T' is that T' may call for a reduction when T announces an error. This will occur whenever u is in FOLLOW(A) and the only items in α of the form $[A \rightarrow \alpha \cdot, v]$ have $v \neq u$. This follows from the fact that because of rule (1b) in Algorithm 7.10, T' will call for a reduction on all u such that u is FOLLOW(A) and $[A \rightarrow \alpha \cdot]$ is an item in CORE(α).

We can now define a partition $\Pi = \{\mathfrak{B}_1, \mathfrak{B}_2, \ldots, \mathfrak{B}_r\}$ on $\mathfrak{I}_1$ which groups tables T_1 and T_2 in the same block if and only if $h(T_1) = h(T_2)$. The fact that h commutes with GOTO ensures that Π will be a compatible partition. Merging all tables in each block of this compatible partition using Algorithm 7.7 then produces $\mathfrak{I}$.

Since Algorithms 7.7 and 7.8 each preserve the equivalence of a set of tables, we have shown that $\mathfrak{I}$, the set of LR(k) tables for G, is equivalent to $\mathfrak{I}_c$, the canonical set of LR(k) tables for G. □

Before concluding our discussion of SLR parsing we should point out that the optimization techniques discussed in Section 7.3 also apply to SLR tables. Exercise 7.4.16 states which error entries in an SLR(1) set of tables are don't cares.

7.4.2. Extending the SLR Concept to non-SLR Grammars

There are two big advantages in attempting to construct a parser for a grammar from $\mathcal{S}_0$, the canonical collection of sets of LR(0) items. First, the amount of computation needed to produce $\mathcal{S}_0$ for a given grammar is much smaller in general than that required to generate $\mathcal{S}_1$, the sets of LR(1) items. Second, the number of sets of LR(0) items is generally considerably smaller than the number of sets of LR(1) items.

However, the following question arises: What should we do if we have a grammar in which the FOLLOW sets are not sufficient to resolve parsing action conflicts resulting from inconsistent sets of LR(0) items? There are several techniques we should consider before abandoning the LR(0) approach to parser design. One approach would be to try to use local context to resolve ambiguities. If this approach is unsuccessful, we might attempt to split one set of items into several. In each of the pieces the local context might result in unique parsing decisions. The following two examples illustrate each of these approaches.

Example 7.26

Consider the LR(1) grammar G with productions

(1) $S \rightarrow Aa$
(2) $S \rightarrow dAb$

(3) $S \longrightarrow cb$
(4) $S \longrightarrow dca$
(5) $A \longrightarrow c$

Even though $L(G)$ consists only of four sentences, G is not an SLR(k) grammar for any $k \geq 0$. The canonical collection of sets of LR(0) items for G is given in Fig. 7.38. The second components of the items have been omitted

α_0: $S' \longrightarrow \cdot S$
       $S \longrightarrow \cdot Aa \,|\, \cdot dAb \,|\, \cdot cb \,|\, \cdot dca$
       $A \longrightarrow \cdot c$

α_1: $S' \longrightarrow S \cdot$

α_2: $S \longrightarrow A \cdot a$

α_3: $S \longrightarrow d \cdot Ab \,|\, d \cdot ca$
       $A \longrightarrow \cdot c$

α_4: $S \longrightarrow c \cdot b$
       $A \longrightarrow c \cdot$

α_5: $S \longrightarrow Aa \cdot$

α_6: $S \longrightarrow dA \cdot b$

α_7: $S \longrightarrow dc \cdot a$
       $A \longrightarrow c \cdot$

α_8: $S \longrightarrow cb \cdot$

α_9: $S \longrightarrow dAb \cdot$

α_{10}: $S \longrightarrow dca \cdot$

Fig. 7.38 Sets of LR(0) items.

and we have used the notation $A \longrightarrow \alpha_1 \cdot \beta_1 \,|\, \alpha_2 \cdot \beta_2 \,|\, \cdots \,|\, \alpha_n \cdot \beta_n$ as shorthand for the n items $[A \longrightarrow \alpha_1 \cdot \beta_1], [A \longrightarrow \alpha_2 \cdot \beta_2], \ldots, [A \longrightarrow \alpha_n \cdot \beta_n]$. There are two sets of items that are inconsistent, α_4 and α_7. Moreover, since FOLLOW(A) = $\{a, b\}$, Algorithm 7.10 will not produce unique parsing actions from α_4 and α_7 on the lookaheads b and a, respectively.

However, let us examine the GOTO function on the sets of items as graphically shown in Fig. 7.39.† We see that the only way to get to α_4 from α_0 is to have c on the pushdown list. If we reduce c to A, from the productions of the grammar, we see that a is the only symbol that can then follow A. Thus, T_4, the table constructed from α_4, would have the following unique parsing actions:

	a	b	c	d
T_4:	reduce 5	shift	error	error

†Note that this graph is acyclic but that, in general, a goto graph has cycles.

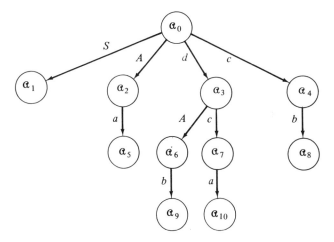

Fig. 7.39 GOTO graph.

Similarly, from the GOTO graph we see that the only way to get to α_7 from α_0 is to have dc on the pushdown list. In this context if c is reduced to A, the only symbol that can then legitimately follow A is b. Thus, the parsing actions for T_7, the table constructed from α_7, would be

	a	b	c	d
T_7:	shift	reduce 5	error	error

The remaining LR(1) tables for G can be constructed using Algorithm 7.10 directly. ☐

The grammar in Example 7.26 is not an SLR grammar. However, we were able to use lookahead to resolve all ambiguities in parsing action decisions in the sets of LR(0) items. The class of LR(k) grammars for which we can always construct LR parsers in this fashion is called the class of *lookahead LR(k) grammars*, *LALR(k)* for short (see Exercise 7.4.11 for a more precise definition). The LALR(k) grammars are the largest natural subclass of the LR(k) grammars for which k symbol lookahead will resolve all parsing action conflicts arising in δ_0, the canonical collection of sets of LR(0) items. The lookaheads can be computed directly from the GOTO graph for δ_0 or by merging the sets of LR(k) items with identical cores. LALR grammars include all SLR grammars, but not all LR grammars are LALR grammars.

We shall now give an example in which a set of items can be "split" to obtain unique parsing decisions.

Example 7.27

Consider the LR(1) grammar G with productions

$$
\begin{array}{ll}
(1) & S \longrightarrow Aa \\
(2) & S \longrightarrow dAb \\
(3) & S \longrightarrow Bb \\
(4) & S \longrightarrow dBa \\
(5) & A \longrightarrow c \\
(6) & B \longrightarrow c
\end{array}
$$

This grammar is quite similar to the one in Example 7.26, but it is not an LALR grammar. The canonical collection of sets of LR(0) items for the augmented grammar is shown in Fig. 7.40. The set of items $\mathcal{C}_5$ is inconsistent because we do not know whether we should reduce by production $A \longrightarrow c$ or $B \longrightarrow c$. Since FOLLOW(A) = FOLLOW(B) = $\{a, b\}$, using these sets as lookaheads will not resolve this ambiguity. Thus G is not SLR(1).

$$
\begin{array}{ll}
\mathcal{C}_0: & S' \longrightarrow \cdot S \\
               & S \longrightarrow \cdot Aa \\
               & S \longrightarrow \cdot dAb \\
               & S \longrightarrow \cdot Bb \\
               & S \longrightarrow \cdot dBa \\
               & A \longrightarrow \cdot c \\
               & B \longrightarrow \cdot c \\
\mathcal{C}_1: & S' \longrightarrow S\cdot \\
\mathcal{C}_2: & S \longrightarrow A\cdot a \\
\mathcal{C}_3: & S \longrightarrow B\cdot b \\
\mathcal{C}_4: & S \longrightarrow d\cdot Ab \\
               & S \longrightarrow d\cdot Ba \\
               & A \longrightarrow \cdot c \\
               & B \longrightarrow \cdot c
\end{array}
\qquad
\begin{array}{ll}
\mathcal{C}_5: & A \longrightarrow c\cdot \\
               & B \longrightarrow c\cdot \\
\mathcal{C}_6: & S \longrightarrow Aa\cdot \\
\mathcal{C}_7: & S \longrightarrow Bb\cdot \\
\mathcal{C}_8: & S \longrightarrow dA\cdot b \\
\mathcal{C}_9: & S \longrightarrow dB\cdot a \\
\mathcal{C}_{10}: & S \longrightarrow dAb\cdot \\
\mathcal{C}_{11}: & S \longrightarrow dBa\cdot
\end{array}
$$

Fig. 7.40   LR(0) items.

Examining the productions of the grammar, we know that if we have only c on the pushdown list and if the next input symbol is a, then we should use production $A \longrightarrow c$ to reduce c. If the next input symbol is b, we should use production $B \longrightarrow c$. However, if dc appears on the pushdown list and the next input symbol is a, we should use production $B \longrightarrow c$ to reduce c. If the next input symbol is b, we should use $A \longrightarrow c$.

The GOTO function for the set of items is shown in Fig. 7.41. Unfortunately, $\mathcal{C}_5$ is accessible from $\mathcal{C}_0$ under both c and dc. Thus, $\mathcal{C}_5$ does not tell us whether we have c or dc on the pushdown list, and hence G is not LALR(1).

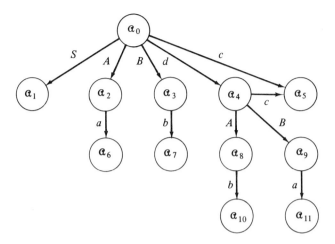

Fig. 7.41   GOTO graph.

However, we can construct an LR(1) parser for G by replacing $\mathcal{C}_5$ by two identical sets of items $\mathcal{C}_5'$ and $\mathcal{C}_5''$ such that $\mathcal{C}_5'$ is accessible only from $\mathcal{C}_4$ and $\mathcal{C}_5''$ is accessible from only $\mathcal{C}_0$. These new sets of items provide the additional needed information about what has appeared on the pushdown list.

From $\mathcal{C}_5'$ and $\mathcal{C}_5''$ we can construct the tables with unique parsing actions as follows:

	a	b	c	d
T_5':	reduce 6	reduce 5	error	error
T_5'':	reduce 5	reduce 6	error	error

The value of the goto functions of T_5' and T_5'' is always **error**.   □

7.4.3. Grammar Splitting

In this section we shall discuss another technique for constructing LR parsers. It is not as easy to apply as the SLR approach, but it does work in situations where the SLR approach does not. Here, we partition a grammar $G = (N, \Sigma, P, S)$ into several component grammars by treating certain nonterminal symbols as terminal symbols. Let $N' \subseteq N$ be such a set of "splitting" nonterminals. For each A in N' we can find G_A, the *component grammar with start symbol A*, using the following algorithm.

ALGORITHM 7.11

Grammar splitting.

Input. A CFG $G = (N, \Sigma, P, S)$ and N', a subset of N.

Output. A set of component grammars G_A for each $A \in N'$.

Method. For each $A \in N'$, construct G_A as follows:

(1) On the right-hand side of each production in P, replace every non-terminal $B \in N'$ by $\hat{B}$. Let $\hat{N}$ be $\{\hat{B} | B \in N'\}$ and let the resulting set of productions be $\hat{P}$.

(2) Define $G'_A = (N - N' \cup \{A\}, \Sigma \cup \hat{N}, \hat{P}, A)$.

(3) Apply Algorithm 2.9 to eliminate useless nonterminals and productions from G'_A. Call the resulting reduced grammar G_A. $\square$

Here we consider the building of LR(1) parsers for each component grammar and the merger of these parsers. Alternatives involve the design of different kinds of parsers for the various components. For example, we could use an LL(1) parser for everything but expressions, for which we would use an operator precedence parser. Research extending the techniques of this section to several types of parsers is clearly needed.

Example 7.28

Let G_0 be the usual grammar and let $N' = \{E, T\}$ be the splitting nonterminals. Then $\hat{P}$ consists of

$$E \longrightarrow \hat{E} + \hat{T} | \hat{T}$$

$$T \longrightarrow \hat{T} * F | F$$

$$F \longrightarrow (\hat{E}) | a$$

Thus, $G_E = (\{E\}, \{\hat{E}, \hat{T}, +\}, \{E \rightarrow \hat{E} + \hat{T} | \hat{T}\}, E)$, and G_T is given by $(\{T, F\}, \{\hat{T}, \hat{E}, (,), a, *\}, \{T \rightarrow \hat{T} * F | F, F \rightarrow (\hat{E}) | a\}, T)$. $\square$

We shall now describe a method of constructing LR(1) parsers for certain large grammars. The procedure is to initially partition a given grammar into a number of smaller grammars. If a collection of consistent sets of LR(1) items can be found for each component grammar and if certain conditions relating these sets of items are satisfied, then a set of LR(1) items can be constructed for the original grammar by combining the sets of items for the component grammars. The underlying philosophy of this procedure is that much less work is usually involved in building the collections of sets of LR(1) items for smaller grammars and merging them together than in constructing the canonical collection of sets of LR(1) items for one large grammar. Moreover, the resulting LR(1) parser will most likely turn out to be considerably smaller than the canonical parser.

In the grammar-splitting algorithm we treat A as the start symbol of its own grammar and use FOLLOW(A) as the set of possible lookahead strings for the initial set of items for the subgrammar G_A. The net effect will be to merge certain sets of items having common cores. The similarity to the SLR algorithm should be apparent. In fact, we shall see that the SLR algorithm is really a grammar-splitting algorithm with $N' = N$.

The complete technique can be summarized as follows.

(1) Given a grammar $G = (N, \Sigma, P, S)$, we ascertain a suitable splitting set of nonterminals $N' \subseteq N$. We include S in N'. This set should be large enough so that the component grammars are small, and we can readily construct sets of LR(1) tables for each component. At the same time, the number of components should not be so large that the method will fail to produce a set of tables. (This comment applies only to non-SLR grammars. If the grammar is SLR, any choice for N' will work, and choosing $N = N'$ yields the smallest set of tables.)

(2) Having chosen N', we compute the component grammars using Algorithm 7.11.

(3) Using Algorithm 7.12, below, we compute the sets of LR(1) items for each component grammar.

(4) Then, using Algorithm 7.13, we combine the component sets of items into $\mathcal{S}$, a collection of sets of items for the original grammar. This process may not always yield a collection of consistent sets of items for the original grammar. However, if $\mathcal{S}$ is consistent, we then construct a set of LR(1) tables from $\mathcal{S}$ in the usual manner.

ALGORITHM 7.12

Construction of sets of LR(1) items for the component grammars of a given grammar.

Input. A grammar $G = (N, \Sigma, P, S)$, a subset N' of N, with $S \in N'$, and the component grammars G_A for each $A \in N'$.

Output. Sets of LR(1) items for each component grammar.

Method. For notational convenience let $N' = \{S_1, S_2, \ldots, S_m\}$. We shall denote G_{S_i} as G_i.

If $\mathcal{Q}$ is a set of LR(1) items, we compute $\mathcal{Q}'$, the *closure of $\mathcal{Q}$ with respect to G_A*, in a manner similar, but not identical, to Algorithm 5.8. $\mathcal{Q}'$ is defined as follows:

(1) $\mathcal{Q} \subseteq \mathcal{Q}'$. (That is, all items in $\mathcal{Q}$ are in $\mathcal{Q}'$.)

(2) If $[B \longrightarrow \alpha \cdot C\beta, u]$ is in $\mathcal{Q}'$ and $C \longrightarrow \gamma$ is a production in G_A, then $[C \longrightarrow \cdot \gamma, v]$ is in $\mathcal{Q}'$ for all v in $\mathrm{FIRST}_1^G(\beta'u)$, where β' is β with each symbol in $\hat{N}$ replaced by the original symbol in N.

Thus all lookahead strings are in Σ^*, while the first components of the items reflect productions in G_A.

For each G_i, we construct $\mathcal{S}_i$, the collection of sets of LR(1) items for G_i, as follows:

(1) Let $\mathfrak{a}_0^i$ be the closure (with respect to G_i) of

$$\{[S_i \longrightarrow \cdot \, \alpha, a] \, | \, S_i \longrightarrow \alpha \text{ is a production in } G_i \text{ and } a \text{ is in } \text{FOLLOW}_1^G(S_i)\}.$$

Let $\mathcal{S}_i = \{\mathfrak{a}_0^i\}$.

(2) Then repeat step (3) until no new sets of items can be added to $\mathcal{S}_i$.

(3) If $\mathfrak{a}$ is in $\mathcal{S}_i$, let $\mathfrak{a}'$ be $\{[A \longrightarrow \alpha X \cdot \beta, u] \, | \, [A \longrightarrow \alpha \cdot X\beta, u] \text{ is in } \mathfrak{a}\}$. Here X is in $N \cup \Sigma \cup \hat{N}$. Add $\mathfrak{a}''$, the closure (with respect to G_i) of $\mathfrak{a}'$, to $\mathcal{S}_i$. Thus, $\mathfrak{a}'' = \text{GOTO}(\mathfrak{a}, X)$. $\quad\square$

Note that we have chosen to add FOLLOW(A) to the lookahead set of each initial set of items rather than augmenting each component grammar with a zeroth production. The effect will be the same.

Example 7.29

Let us apply Algorithm 7.12 to G_0, with $N' = \{E, T\}$. We find that FOLLOW(E) $= \{+,), e\}$ and FOLLOW(T) $= \{+, *,), e\}$. Thus, by step (1), $\mathfrak{a}_0^E$ consists of

$$[E \longrightarrow \cdot \, \hat{E} + \hat{T}, + \, / \,) \, / \, e]$$
$$[E \longrightarrow \cdot \, \hat{T}, + \, / \,) \, / \, e]$$

Likewise, $\mathfrak{a}_0^T$ consists of

$$[T \longrightarrow \cdot \, \hat{T} * F, + \, / * \, / \,) \, / \, e]$$
$$[T \longrightarrow \cdot \, F, + \, / * \, / \,) \, / \, e]$$
$$[F \longrightarrow \cdot \, (\hat{E}), + \, / * \, / \,) \, / \, e]$$
$$[F \longrightarrow \cdot \, a, + \, / * \, / \,) \, / \, e]$$

The complete sets of items generated for G_E are shown in Fig. 7.42, and those for G_T are shown in Fig. 7.43.

Note that when $\mathfrak{a}_3^E$ is constructed from $\mathfrak{a}_1^E$, for example, the symbol $\hat{T}$ is a terminal, and the closure operation yields no new items. $\quad\square$

We now give an algorithm that takes the sets of items generated by Algorithm 7.12 for the component grammars and combines them to form

$$\mathfrak{a}_0^E: \quad \begin{cases} [E \longrightarrow \cdot \hat{E} + \hat{T}, + \,) \, / \, e] \\ [E \longrightarrow \cdot \hat{T}, \qquad + \,) \, / \, e] \end{cases}$$

$$\mathfrak{a}_1^E: \quad [E \longrightarrow \hat{E} \cdot + \hat{T}, \; + \,) \, / \, e]$$

$$\mathfrak{a}_2^E: \quad [E \longrightarrow \hat{T} \cdot, \qquad + \,) \, / \, e]$$

$$\mathfrak{a}_3^E: \quad [E \longrightarrow \hat{E} + \cdot \hat{T}, \; + \,) \, / \, e]$$

$$\mathfrak{a}_4^E: \quad [E \longrightarrow \hat{E} + \hat{T} \cdot, + \,) \, / \, e]$$

Fig. 7.42 Sets of items for G_E.

$$\mathcal{C}_0^T: \begin{cases} [T \longrightarrow \cdot \hat{T} * F, \; + \,/\, * \,/\,) \,/\, e] \\ [T \longrightarrow \cdot F, \quad\quad + \,/\, * \,/\,) \,/\, e] \\ [F \longrightarrow \cdot (\hat{E}), \quad + \,/\, * \,/\,) \,/\, e] \\ [F \longrightarrow \cdot a, \quad\quad + \,/\, * \,/\,) \,/\, e] \end{cases}$$

$$\mathcal{C}_1^T: \quad [T \longrightarrow \hat{T} \cdot * F, \; + \,/\, * \,/\,) \,/\, e]$$

$$\mathcal{C}_2^T: \quad [T \longrightarrow F \cdot, \quad + \,/\, * \,/\,) \,/\, e]$$

$$\mathcal{C}_3^T: \quad [F \longrightarrow (\cdot \hat{E}), \quad + \,/\, * \,/\,) \,/\, e]$$

$$\mathcal{C}_4^T: \quad [F \longrightarrow a \cdot, \quad + \,/\, * \,/\,) \,/\, e]$$

$$\mathcal{C}_5^T: \begin{cases} [T \longrightarrow \hat{T} * \cdot F, \; + \,/\, * \,/\,) \,/\, e] \\ [F \longrightarrow \cdot (\hat{E}), \quad + \,/\, * \,/\,) \,/\, e] \\ [F \longrightarrow \cdot a, \quad\quad + \,/\, * \,/\,) \,/\, e] \end{cases}$$

$$\mathcal{C}_6^T: \quad [F \longrightarrow (\hat{E} \cdot), \quad + \,/\, * \,/\,) \,/\, e]$$

$$\mathcal{C}_7^T: \quad [T \longrightarrow \hat{T} * F \cdot, \; + \,/\, * \,/\,) \,/\, e]$$

$$\mathcal{C}_8^T: \quad [F \longrightarrow (\hat{E}) \cdot, \quad + \,/\, * \,/\,) \,/\, e]$$

Fig. 7.43 Sets of items for G_T.

a set of LR(1) tables for the original grammar, provided that certain conditions hold.

ALGORITHM 7.13

Construction of a set of LR(1) tables from the sets of LR(1) items of component grammars.

Input. A CFG $G = (\mathrm{N}, \Sigma, P, S_1)$, a splitting set $\mathrm{N}' = \{S_1, S_2, \ldots, S_m\}$, and a collection $\{\mathcal{C}_0^i, \mathcal{C}_1^i, \ldots, \mathcal{C}_{n_i}^i\}$ of sets of LR(1) items for each component grammar G_i.

Output. A valid set of LR(1) tables for G or an indication that the sets of items will not yield a valid set of tables.

Method.

(1) In the first component of each item, replace each symbol of the form $\hat{S}_i$ by S_i. Each such S_i is in N'. Retain the original name for each set of items so altered.

(2) Let $\mathcal{I}_0 = \{[S_1' \longrightarrow \cdot \, S_1, e]\}$. Apply the following augmenting operation to $\mathcal{I}_0$, and call the resulting set of items $\mathcal{I}_0$. $\mathcal{I}_0$ will then be the "initial" set of items in the merged collection of sets of items.

Augmenting Operation. If a set of items $\mathcal{C}$ contains an item with a first component of the form $A \longrightarrow \alpha \cdot B\beta$ and $B \underset{G}{\overset{*}{\Longrightarrow}} S_j \gamma$ for some S_j in N', γ in $(\mathrm{N} \cup \Sigma)^*$, then add $\mathcal{C}_0^j$ to $\mathcal{C}$. Repeat this process until no new sets of items can be added to $\mathcal{C}$.

(3) We shall now construct $\mathcal{S}$, the collection of sets of items accessible from $\mathcal{I}_0$. Initially, let $\mathcal{S} = \{\mathcal{I}_0\}$. We then perform step (4) until no new sets of items can be added to $\mathcal{S}$.

(4) Let $\mathcal{I}$ be in $\mathcal{S}$. $\mathcal{I}$ can be written as $\mathcal{Q} \cup \mathcal{Q}_{i_1}^{j_1} \cup \mathcal{Q}_{i_2}^{j_2} \cup \cdots \cup \mathcal{Q}_{i_r}^{j_r}$, where $\mathcal{Q}$ is either the empty set or $\{[S_1' \rightarrow \cdot S_1, e]\}$ or $\{[S_1' \rightarrow S_1 \cdot, e]\}$. For each X in $N \cup \Sigma$, let $\mathcal{Q}' = \text{GOTO}(\mathcal{Q}, X)$ and $\mathcal{Q}_{h_n}^{j_n} = \text{GOTO}(\mathcal{Q}_{i_n}^{j_n}, X)$.† Let $\mathcal{I}'$ be the union of $\mathcal{Q}'$ and these $\mathcal{Q}_{h_n}^{j_n}$'s. Then apply the augmenting operation to $\mathcal{I}'$ and call the resulting set of items $\mathcal{I}'$. Let KGOTO‡ be the function such that $\text{KGOTO}(\mathcal{I}, X) = \mathcal{I}'$ if $\mathcal{I}$, X, and $\mathcal{I}'$ are related as above. Add $\mathcal{I}'$ to $\mathcal{S}$ if it is not already there. Repeat this process until for all $\mathcal{I}$ in $\mathcal{S}$ and X in $N \cup \Sigma$, $\text{KGOTO}(\mathcal{I}, X)$ is in $\mathcal{S}$.

(5) When no new set of items can be added to $\mathcal{S}$, construct a set of LR(1) tables from $\mathcal{S}$ using the methods of Section 5.2.5. If table $T = \langle f, g \rangle$ is being constructed from the set of items $\mathcal{I}$, then $g(X)$ is $\text{KGOTO}(\mathcal{I}, X)$. If any set of items produces parsing action conflicts, report failure.   ☐

Example 7.30

Let us apply Algorithm 7.13 to the sets of items in Figs. 7.42 and 7.43. The effect of step (1) should be obvious. Step (2) first creates the set of items $\mathcal{I}_0 = \{[E' \rightarrow \cdot E, e]\}$, and after applying the augmenting operation, $\mathcal{I}_0 = \{[E' \rightarrow \cdot E, e]\} \cup \mathcal{Q}_0^E \cup \mathcal{Q}_0^T$.

At the beginning of step (3), $\mathcal{S} = \{\mathcal{I}_0\}$. Applying step (4), we first compute

$$\mathcal{I}_1 = \text{GOTO}(\mathcal{I}_0, E) = \{[E' \rightarrow E \cdot, e]\} \cup \mathcal{Q}_1^E.$$

That is, $\text{GOTO}(\{[E' \rightarrow \cdot E, e]\}, E) = \{[E' \rightarrow E \cdot, e]\}$ and $\text{GOTO}(\mathcal{Q}_0^E, E) = \mathcal{Q}_1^E$. $\text{GOTO}(\mathcal{Q}_0^T, E)$ is empty. The augmenting operation does not enlarge $\mathcal{I}_1$. We then compute $\mathcal{I}_2 = \text{GOTO}(\mathcal{I}_0, T) = \mathcal{Q}_2^E \cup \mathcal{Q}_1^T$. The augmenting operation does not enlarge $\mathcal{I}_2$. Continuing in this fashion, we obtain the following collection of sets of items for $\mathcal{S}$:

$$\mathcal{I}_0 = \{[E' \longrightarrow \cdot E, e]\} \cup \mathcal{Q}_0^E \cup \mathcal{Q}_0^T$$
$$\mathcal{I}_1 = \{[E' \longrightarrow E \cdot, e]\} \cup \mathcal{Q}_1^E$$
$$\mathcal{I}_2 = \mathcal{Q}_2^E \cup \mathcal{Q}_1^T$$
$$\mathcal{I}_3 = \mathcal{Q}_2^T$$
$$\mathcal{I}_4 = \mathcal{Q}_4^T$$
$$\mathcal{I}_5 = \mathcal{Q}_0^E \cup \mathcal{Q}_0^T \cup \mathcal{Q}_3^T$$
$$\mathcal{I}_6 = \mathcal{Q}_3^E \cup \mathcal{Q}_0^T$$
$$\mathcal{I}_7 = \mathcal{Q}_5^T$$
$$\mathcal{I}_8 = \mathcal{Q}_1^E \cup \mathcal{Q}_6^T$$

†The GOTO function for G_{j_n} is meant here. However if X is splitting nonterminal then use $\hat{X}$ in place of X.

‡The K honors A. J. Korenjak, inventor of the method being described.

$$\mathcal{I}_9 = \mathcal{C}_4^E \cup \mathcal{C}_1^T$$

$$\mathcal{I}_{10} = \mathcal{C}_7^T$$

$$\mathcal{I}_{11} = \mathcal{C}_8^T$$

All sets of items in $\mathcal{S}$ are consistent, and so from $\mathcal{S}$ we can construct the set of LR(1) tables shown in Fig. 7.44. Table T_i is constructed from $\mathcal{I}_i$. This set of tables is identical to that in Fig. 7.37 (p. 625). We shall see that this is not a coincidence. □

	action						goto							
	a	+	*	(	)	e	E	T	F	a	+	*	(	)
T_0	S	X	X	S	X	X	T_1	T_2	T_3	T_4	X	X	T_5	X
T_1	X	S	X	X	X	A	X	X	X	X	T_6	X	X	X
T_2	X	2	S	X	2	2	X	X	X	X	X	T_7	X	X
T_3	X	4	4	X	4	4	X	X	X	X	X	X	X	X
T_4	X	6	6	X	6	6	X	X	X	X	X	X	X	X
T_5	S	X	X	S	X	X	T_8	T_2	T_3	T_4	X	X	T_5	X
T_6	S	X	X	S	X	X	X	T_9	T_3	T_4	X	X	T_5	X
T_7	S	X	X	S	X	X	X	X	T_{10}	T_4	X	X	T_5	X
T_8	X	S	X	X	S	X	X	X	X	X	T_6	X	X	T_{11}
T_9	X	1	S	X	1	1	X	X	X	X	X	T_7	X	X
T_{10}	X	3	3	X	3	3	X	X	X	X	X	X	X	X
T_{11}	X	5	5	X	5	5	X	X	X	X	X	X	X	X

Fig. 7.44   Tables for G_0 from Algorithm 7.13.

We shall now show that this approach yields a set of LR(1) tables that is equivalent to the canonical set of LR(1) tables. We begin by characterizing the merged collection of sets of items generated in step (4) of Algorithm 7.13.

DEFINITION

Let KGOTO be the function in step (4) of Algorithm 7.13. We extend KGOTO to strings in the obvious way; i.e.,

(1) KGOTO($\mathcal{I}, e$) = $\mathcal{I}$, and
(2) KGOTO($\mathcal{I}, \alpha X$) = KGOTO(KGOTO($\mathcal{I}, \alpha$), X).

Let $G = (N, \Sigma, P, S)$ be a CFG and N' a splitting set. We say that item $[A \rightarrow \alpha \cdot \beta, a]$ is *quasi-valid* for string γ if it is valid (as defined in Section 5.2.3) or if there is a derivation $S' \xrightarrow[rm]{*} \delta_1 Bx \xrightarrow[rm]{*} \delta_1 \delta_2 Ax \underset{rm}{\Rightarrow} \delta_1 \delta_2 \alpha \beta x$ in the augmented grammar such that

(1) $\delta_1 \delta_2 \alpha = \gamma$,
(2) B is in N', and
(3) a is in FOLLOW(B).

Note that if $[A \rightarrow \alpha \cdot \beta, a]$ is quasi-valid for γ, then there exists a lookahead b such that $[A \rightarrow \alpha \cdot \beta, b]$ is valid for γ. (b might be a.)

LEMMA 7.3

–Let $G = (N, \Sigma, P, S)$ be a CFG as above and let KGOTO($\mathcal{I}_0, \gamma$) = $\mathcal{I}$ for some γ in $(N \cup \Sigma)^*$. Then $\mathcal{I}$ is the set of quasi-valid items for γ.

Proof. We prove the result by induction on $|\gamma|$. The basis, $\gamma = e$, is omitted, as it follows from observations made during the inductive step.

Assume that $\gamma = \gamma'X$ and $\mathcal{K}$, the set of quasi-valid items for γ', is KGOTO($\mathcal{I}_0, \gamma'$). Let $\mathcal{K} = \mathcal{I}_{i_1}^{j_1} \cup \cdots \cup \mathcal{I}_{i_k}^{j_k}$. The case where $[S' \rightarrow \cdot S, e]$ or $[S' \rightarrow S \cdot, e]$ is in $\mathcal{K}$ can be handled easily, and we shall omit these details here. Suppose that $[A \rightarrow \alpha \cdot \beta, a]$ is in $\mathcal{I} =$ KGOTO($\mathcal{I}_0, \gamma'X$). There are three ways in which $[A \rightarrow \alpha \cdot \beta, a]$ can be added to $\mathcal{I}$.

Case 1: Suppose that $[A \rightarrow \alpha \cdot \beta, a]$ is in GOTO($\mathcal{I}_{i_p}^{j_p}, X$) for some p, $\alpha = \alpha'X$ and that $[A \rightarrow \alpha' \cdot X\beta, a]$ is in $\mathcal{I}_{i_p}^{j_p}$. Then $[A \rightarrow \alpha' \cdot X\beta, a]$ is quasi-valid for γ', and it follows that $[A \rightarrow \alpha \cdot \beta, a]$ is quasi-valid for γ.

Case 2: Suppose that $[A \rightarrow \alpha \cdot \beta, a]$ is in GOTO($\mathcal{I}_{i_p}^{j_p}, X$) and that $\alpha = e$. Then there is an item $[B \rightarrow \delta_1 X \cdot C\delta_2, b]$ in GOTO($\mathcal{I}_{i_p}^{j_p}, X$), and $C \xrightarrow[rm]{*} Aw$, where $a \in$ FIRST($w\delta_2 b$). Then $[B \rightarrow \delta_1 \cdot XC\delta_2, b]$ is quasi-valid for γ', and $[B \rightarrow \delta_1 X \cdot C\delta_2, b]$ is quasi-valid for γ. If a is the first symbol of w or $w = e$ and a comes from δ_2, then $[A \rightarrow \alpha \cdot \beta, a]$ is valid for γ. Likewise, if $[B \rightarrow \delta_1 X \cdot C\delta_2, b]$ is valid for γ, so is $[A \rightarrow \alpha \cdot \beta, a]$.

Thus, suppose that $w = e$, $\delta_2 \xRightarrow{*} e$, $a = b$, and $[B \rightarrow \delta_1 X \cdot C\delta_2, b]$ is quasi-valid, but not valid for γ. Then there is a derivation

$$S' \xrightarrow[rm]{*} \delta_3 Dx \xrightarrow[rm]{*} \delta_3 \delta_4 Bx \underset{rm}{\Rightarrow} \delta_3 \delta_4 \delta_1 XC\delta_2 x \xrightarrow[rm]{*} \delta_3 \delta_4 \delta_1 XAx,$$

where $\delta_3 \delta_4 \delta_1 X = \gamma$, D is in N', and b is in FOLLOW(D). Thus, item $[A \rightarrow \alpha \cdot \beta, a]$ is quasi-valid for γ, since $a = b$.

Case 3: Suppose that $[A \rightarrow \alpha \cdot \beta, a]$ is added to $\mathcal{I}$ during the augmenting operation in step (4). Then $\alpha = e$, and there must be some $[B \rightarrow \delta_1 X \cdot C\delta_2, b]$ in GOTO($\mathcal{I}_{i_p}^{j_p}, X$) such that $C \xrightarrow[rm]{*} Dw_1 \xrightarrow[rm]{*} Aw_2 w_1$, D is in N', and a is in FIRST($w_2 c$) for some c in FOLLOW(D). That is, D is S_r, where $[A \rightarrow \alpha \cdot \beta, a]$ is added to $\mathcal{K}$ when $\mathcal{I}_0^r$ is adjoined. The argument now proceeds as in case 2.

We must now show the converse of the above, that if $[A \rightarrow \alpha \cdot \beta, a]$ is quasi-valid for γ, then it is in $\mathfrak{s}$. We omit the easier case, where the item is actually valid for γ. Let us assume that $[A \rightarrow \alpha \cdot \beta, a]$ is quasi-valid, but not valid. Then there is a derivation

$$S' \overset{*}{\underset{rm}{\Rightarrow}} \delta_1 Bx \overset{*}{\underset{rm}{\Rightarrow}} \delta_1 \delta_2 Ax \underset{rm}{\Rightarrow} \delta_1 \delta_2 \alpha \beta x$$

where $\gamma = \delta_1 \delta_2 \alpha$, B is in N', and a is in FOLLOW(B). If $\alpha \neq e$, then we may write $\alpha = \alpha' X$. Then $[A \rightarrow \alpha' \cdot X\beta, a]$ is quasi-valid for γ' and is therefore in $\mathfrak{K}$. It is immediate that $[A \rightarrow \alpha \cdot \beta, a]$ is in $\mathfrak{s}$.

Thus, suppose that $\alpha = e$. We consider two cases, depending on whether $\delta_2 \neq e$ or $\delta_2 = e$.

Case 1: $\delta_2 \neq e$. Then there is a derivation $B \overset{*}{\underset{rm}{\Rightarrow}} \delta_3 C \underset{rm}{\Rightarrow} \delta_3 \delta_4 X \delta_5$ and $\delta_5 \overset{*}{\underset{rm}{\Rightarrow}} A$. Then $[C \rightarrow \delta_4 \cdot X\delta_5, a]$ is quasi-valid for γ' and hence is in $\mathfrak{K}$. It follows that $[C \rightarrow \delta_4 X \cdot \delta_5, a]$ is in $\mathfrak{s}$. Since $\delta_5 \overset{*}{\underset{rm}{\Rightarrow}} A$, it is not hard to show that either in the closure operation or in the augmenting operation $[A \rightarrow \alpha \cdot \beta, a]$ is placed in $\mathfrak{s}$.

Case 2: $\delta_2 = e$. Then there is a derivation $S' \overset{*}{\underset{rm}{\Rightarrow}} \delta_3 Cy \underset{rm}{\Rightarrow} \delta_3 \delta_4 X \delta_5 y$, where $\delta_5 y \overset{*}{\underset{rm}{\Rightarrow}} Bx$. Then $[C \rightarrow \delta_4 \cdot X\delta_5, c]$ is valid for γ', where c is FIRST(y). Hence, $[C \rightarrow \delta_4 X \cdot \delta_5, c]$ is in $\mathfrak{s}$. Then, since $\delta_5 y \overset{*}{\underset{rm}{\Rightarrow}} Bx$, in the augmenting operation, all items of the form $[B \rightarrow \cdot \epsilon, b]$ are added to $\mathfrak{s}$, where $B \rightarrow \epsilon$ is a production and b is in FOLLOW(B). Then, since $B \overset{*}{\underset{rm}{\Rightarrow}} A$, the item $[A \rightarrow \alpha \cdot \beta, a]$ is added to $\mathfrak{s}$, either in the modified closure of the set containing $[B \rightarrow \cdot \epsilon, b]$ or in a subsequent augmenting operation. $\square$

THEOREM 7.10

Let (N, Σ, P, S) be a CFG. Let ($\mathfrak{I}$, T_0) be the set of LR(1) tables for G generated by Algorithm 7.13. Let ($\mathfrak{I}_c$, T_c) be the canonical set. Then the two sets of tables are equivalent.

Proof. We observe by Lemma 7.3 that the table of $\mathfrak{I}$ associated with string γ agrees in action with the table of $\mathfrak{I}_c$ associated with γ wherever the latter is not **error**. Thus, if the two sets are inequivalent, we can find an input w such that $(T_c, w) \overset{*}{\vdash} (T_c X_1 T_1 \cdots X_m T_m, x)$† using $\mathfrak{I}_c$, and an error is then declared, while

$$(T_0, w) \overset{*}{\vdash} (T_0 X_1 T'_1 \cdots X_m T'_m, x)$$
$$\overset{*}{\vdash} (T_0 Y_1 U_1 \cdots Y_n U_n, x)$$
$$\vdash (T_0 Y_1 U_1 \cdots Y_n U_n a U, x')$$

using $\mathfrak{I}$.

†We have omitted the output field in these configurations for simplicity.

Suppose that table U_n is constructed from the set of items $\mathcal{I}$. Then $\mathcal{I}$ has some member $[A \longrightarrow \alpha \cdot \beta, b]$ such that $\beta \neq e$ and a is in $\text{EFF}(\beta)$. Since $[A \longrightarrow \alpha \cdot \beta, b]$ is quasi-valid for $Y_1 \cdots Y_n$, by Lemma 7.3, there is a derivation $S' \underset{\text{rm}}{\overset{*}{\Rightarrow}} \gamma A y \underset{\text{rm}}{\Rightarrow} \gamma \alpha \beta y$ for some y, where $\gamma \alpha = Y_1 \cdots Y_n$. Since we have derivation $Y_1 \cdots Y_n \overset{*}{\underset{\text{rm}}{\Rightarrow}} X_1 \cdots X_m$, it follows that there is an item $[B \longrightarrow \delta \cdot \epsilon, c]$ valid for $X_1 \cdots X_m$, where a is in $\text{EFF}(\epsilon c)$. (The case $\epsilon = e$, where $a = c$, is not ruled out. In fact, it will occur whenever the sequence of steps

$$(T_0 X_1 T'_1 \cdots X_m T'_m, x) \mid \overset{*}{-} (T_0 Y_1 U_1 \cdots Y_n U_n, x)$$

is not null. If that sequence is null, then $[A \longrightarrow \alpha \cdot \beta, b]$ suffices for $[B \longrightarrow \delta \cdot \epsilon, c]$.)

Since $a = \text{FIRST}(x)$, the hypothesis that $\mathfrak{I}'$ declares an error in configuration $(T_0 X_1 T'_1 \cdots X_m T'_m, x)$ is false, and we may conclude the theorem.   □

Let us compare the grammar-splitting algorithm with the SLR approach. The grammar-splitting algorithm is a generalization of the SLR method in the following sense.

THEOREM 7.11

Let $G = (N, \Sigma, P, S)$ be a CFG. Then G is SLR(1) if and only if Algorithm 7.13 succeeds, with splitting set N. If so, then the sets of tables produced by the two methods are the same.

Proof. If $N' = N$, then $[A \longrightarrow \alpha \cdot \beta, a]$ is quasi-valid for γ if and only if $[A \longrightarrow \alpha \cdot \beta, b]$ is valid for some b and a is in $\text{FOLLOW}(A)$. This is a consequence of the fact that if $B \overset{*}{\underset{\text{rm}}{\Rightarrow}} \delta C$, then $\text{FOLLOW}(B) \subseteq \text{FOLLOW}(C)$. It follows from Lemma 7.3 that the SLR sets of items are the same as those generated by Algorithm 7.13.   □

Theorem 7.9 is thus a corollary of Theorems 7.10 and 7.11.

Algorithm 7.13 brings the full power of the canonical LR(1) parser construction procedure to bear on each component grammar. Thus, from an intuitive point of view, if a grammar is not SLR, we would like to isolate in a single component each aspect of the given grammar that results in its being non-SLR. The following example illustrates this concept.

Example 7.31

Consider the following LR(1) grammar:

(1) $S \longrightarrow Aa$
(2) $S \longrightarrow dAb$
(3) $S \longrightarrow cb$

(4) $S \rightarrow BB$
(5) $A \rightarrow c$
(6) $B \rightarrow Bc$
(7) $B \rightarrow b$

This grammar is not SLR because of productions (1), (2), (3), and (5). Using the splitting set $\{S, B\}$, these four productions will be together in one component grammar to which the full LR(1) technique will then be applied. With this splitting set Algorithm 7.13 would produce the set of LR(1) tables in Fig. 7.45. □

| | action | | | | | goto | | | | | | |
	a	b	c	d	e	S	A	B	a	b	c	d
T_0	X	S	S	S	X	T_1	T_2	T_3	X	T_4	T_5	T_6
T_1	X	X	X	X	A	X	X	X	X	X	X	X
T_2	S	X	X	X	X	X	X	X	T_7	X	X	X
T_3	X	S	S	X	X	X	X	T_8	X	T_4	T_9	X
T_4	X	7	7	X	7	X	X	X	X	X	X	X
T_5	5	S	X	X	X	X	X	X	X	T_{10}	X	X
T_6	X	X	S	X	X	X	T_{11}	X	X	X	T_{12}	X
T_7	X	X	X	X	1	X	X	X	X	X	X	X
T_8	X	X	S	X	4	X	X	X	X	X	T_9	X
T_9	X	6	6	X	6	X	X	X	X	X	X	X
T_{10}	X	X	X	X	3	X	X	X	X	X	X	X
T_{11}	X	S	X	X	X	X	X	X	X	T_{13}	X	X
T_{12}	X	5	X	X	X	X	X	X	X	X	X	X
T_{13}	X	X	X	X	2	X	X	X	X	X	X	X

Fig. 7.45   LR(1) tables.

Finally, we observe that neither Algorithm 7.10 nor Algorithm 7.13 make maximal use of the principles of error postponement and table merger. For example, the SLR(1) grammar in Exercise 7.3.1(a) has a canonical set of 18 LR(1) tables. Algorithm 7.13 will yield a set of LR(1) tables containing at least 14 tables and Algorithm 7.10 will produce a set of 14 SLR(1) tables.

But a judicious application of error postponement and table merger can result in an equivalent set of 7 LR(1) tables.

EXERCISES

*7.4.1. Consider the class $\{G_1, G_2, \ldots\}$ of LR(0) grammars, where G_n has the following productions:

$$S \longrightarrow A_i \qquad 1 \leq i \leq n$$
$$A_i \longrightarrow a_j A_i \qquad 1 \leq i \neq j \leq n$$
$$A_i \longrightarrow a_i B_i \,|\, b_i \qquad 1 \leq i \leq n$$
$$B_i \longrightarrow a_j B_i \,|\, b_i \qquad 1 \leq i, j \leq n$$

Show that the number of tables in the canonical set of LR(0) tables for G_n is exponential in n.

7.4.2. Show that each grammar in Exercise 7.3.1 is SLR(1).

7.4.3. Show that every LR(0) grammar is an SLR(0) grammar.

*7.4.4. Show that every SMSP grammar is an SLR(1) grammar.

7.4.5. Show that the grammar in Example 7.26 is not SLR(k) for any $k \geq 0$.

*7.4.6. Show that every LL(1) grammar is an SLR(1) grammar. Is every LL(2) grammar an SLR(2) grammar?

7.4.7. Using Algorithm 7.10, construct a parser for each grammar in Exercise 7.3.1.

7.4.8. Let $\mathcal{S}_c$ be the canonical collection of sets of LR(k) items for G. Let $\mathcal{S}_0$ be the sets of LR(0) items for G. Show that $\mathcal{S}_c$ and $\mathcal{S}_0$ have the same sets of cores. *Hint:* Let $\mathcal{C} = \text{GOTO}(\mathcal{C}_0, \alpha)$, where $\mathcal{C}_0$ is the initial set of $\mathcal{S}_c$, and proceed by induction on $|\alpha|$.

7.4.9. Show that $\text{CORE}(\text{GOTO}(\mathcal{C}, \alpha)) = \text{GOTO}(\text{CORE}(\mathcal{C}), \alpha)$, where $\mathcal{C} \in \mathcal{S}_c$ as above.

DEFINITION

A grammar $G = (N, \Sigma, P, S)$ is said to be *lookahead* LR(k) [LALR(k)] if the following algorithm succeeds in producing LR(k) tables:

(1) Construct $\mathcal{S}_c$, the canonical collection of sets of LR(k) items for G.

(2) For each $\mathcal{C} \in \mathcal{S}_c$, let $\mathcal{C}'$ be the union of those $\mathcal{B} \in \mathcal{S}_c$ such that $\text{CORE}(\mathcal{B}) = \text{CORE}(\mathcal{C})$.

(3) Let $\mathcal{S}$ be the set of those $\mathcal{C}'$ constructed in step (2). Construct a set of LR(k) tables from $\mathcal{S}$ in the usual manner.

7.4.10. Show that if G is SLR(k), then it is LALR(k).

7.4.11. Show that the LALR table-constructing algorithm above yields a set of tables equivalent to the canonical set.

7.4.12. (a) Show that the grammar in Example 7.26 is LALR(1).

(b) Show that the grammar in Example 7.27 is not LALR(k) for any k.

7.4.13. Let G be defined by

$$S \longrightarrow L = R \mid R$$
$$L \longrightarrow * R \mid a$$
$$R \longrightarrow L$$

Show that G is LALR(1) but not SLR(1).

7.4.14. Show that there are LALR grammars that are not LL, and conversely.

*7.4.15. Let G be an LALR(1) grammar. Let $\mathcal{S}_0$ be the canonical collection of sets of LR(0) items for G. We say that $\mathcal{S}_0$ has a *shift–reduce conflict* if some $\mathcal{Q} \in \mathcal{S}_0$ contains items $[A \to \alpha \cdot]$ and $[B \to \beta \cdot a\gamma]$ where $a \in$ FOLLOW(A). Show that the LALR parser resolves each shift–reduce conflict in the LR(0) items in favor of shifting.

*7.4.16. Let $(\mathfrak{I}, T_0)$ be the set of SLR(1) tables for an SLR(1) grammar $G = (N, \Sigma, P, S)$. Show that:

(1) All error entries in the goto field of each table are don't cares.

(2) An error entry on input symbol a in the action field of table T is essential (not a don't care) if and only if one of the following conditions holds.

(a) T is T_0, the initial table.

(b) There is a table $T' = (f, g)$ in $\mathfrak{I}$ such that $T = g(b)$ for some b in Σ.

(c) There is some table $T' = (f, g)$ such that $T \in$ NEXT (T', i) and $f(a) = $ **reduce** i.

*7.4.17. Let $G = (N, \Sigma, P, S)$ be a CFG. Show that G is LR(k) if and only if, for each splitting set $N' \subseteq N$, all component grammars G_A are LR(k), $A \in N'$. [*Note:* G may not be LR(k) but yet have some splitting set N' such that each G_A is LR(k) for $A \in N'$.]

7.4.18. Repeat Exercise 7.4.17 for LL(k) grammars.

7.4.19. Use Algorithms 7.12 and 7.13 to construct a set of LR(1) tables for G_0 using the splitting set $\{E, T, F\}$. Compare the set of tables obtained with that in Fig. 7.44 (p. 637).

**7.4.20. Under what conditions will all splitting sets on the nonterminals of a grammar G cause Algorithms 7.12 and 7.13 to produce the same set of LR(1) tables for G?

*7.4.21. Suppose that the LALR(1) algorithm fails to produce a set of LR(1) tables for a grammar $G = (N, \Sigma, P, S)$ because a set of items containing $[A \longrightarrow \alpha \cdot, a]$ and $[B \longrightarrow \beta \cdot \gamma, b]$ is generated such that $\gamma \neq e$ and

$a \in \text{EFF}(\gamma b)$. Show that if $\text{N}' \subseteq \text{N}$ is a splitting set and $A \in \text{N}'$, then Algorithm 7.13 will also not produce a set of LR(1) tables with unique parsing actions.

7.4.22. Use Algorithms 7.12 and 7.13 to try to construct a set of LR(1) tables for the grammar in Example 7.27 using the splitting set $\{S, A\}$.

7.4.23. Use Algorithms 7.12 and 7.13 to construct a set of LR(1) tables for the grammar in Exercise 7.3.1(a) using the splitting set $\{S, A\}$.

*7.4.24. Use error postponement and table merger to find an equivalent set of LR(1) tables for the grammar in Exercise 7.3.1(a) that has seven tables.

*7.4.25. Give an example of a (1, 1)-BRC grammar which is not SLR(1).

*7.4.26. Show that if Algorithm 7.9 is applied to a set of SLR(1) tables for a grammar having at most one single production for any nonterminal, then all reductions by single productions are eliminated.

Research Problems

7.4.27. Find additional ways of constructing small sets of LR(k) tables for LR(k) grammars without resorting to the detailed transformations of Section 7.3. Your methods need not work for all LR(k) grammars but should be applicable to at least some of the practically important grammars, such as those listed in the Appendix of Volume 1.

7.4.28. When an LR(k) parser enters an error configuration, in practice we would call an error recovery routine that modifies the input and the pushdown list so that normal parsing can resume. One method of modifying the error configuration of an LR(1) parser is to search forward on the input tape until we find one of certain input symbols. Once such an input symbol a has been found, we look down into the pushdown list for a table $T = \langle f, g \rangle$ such that T was constructed from a set of items $\mathfrak{A}$ containing an item of the form $[A \longrightarrow \cdot \alpha, a]$, $A \neq S$. The error recovery procedure is to delete all input symbols up to a and to remove all symbols and tables above T on the pushdown list. The nonterminal A is then placed on top of the pushdown list and table $g(A)$ is placed on top of A. Because of Exercise 7.3.8(c), $g(A) \neq$ **error**. The effect of this error recovery action is to assume that the grammar symbols above T on the pushdown list together with the input symbols up to a form an instance of A. Evaluate the effectiveness of this error recovery procedure, either empirically or theoretically. A reasonable criterion of effectiveness is the likelihood of properly correcting the errors chosen from a set of "likely" programmer errors.

7.4.29. When a grammar is split, the component grammars can be parsed in different ways. Investigate ways to combine various types of parsers for the components. In particular, is it possible to parse one component bottom up and another top down?

Programming Exercises

7.4.30. Write a program that constructs the SLR(1) set of tables from an SLR(1) grammar.

7.4.31. Write a program that finds all inaccessible error entries in a set of LR(1) tables.

7.4.32. Write a program to construct an LALR(1) parser from an LALR(1) grammar.

7.4.33. Construct an SLR(1) parser with error recovery for one of the grammars in the Appendix of Volume I.

BIBLIOGRAPHIC NOTES

Simple LR(k) grammars and LALR(k) grammars were first studied by DeRemer [1969, 1971]. The technique of constructing the canonical set of LR(0) items for a grammar and then using lookahead to resolve parsing decision ambiguities was also advocated by DeRemer. The grammar-splitting approach to LR parser design was put forward by Korenjak [1969].

Exercise 7.4.1 is from Earley [1968]. The error recovery procedure in Exercise 7.4.28 was suggested by Leinius [1970]. Exercise 7.4.26 is from Aho and Ullman [1972d].

7.5. PARSING AUTOMATA

Instead of looking at an LR parser as a routine which treats the LR tables as data, in this section we shall take the point of view that the LR tables control the parser. Adopting this point of view, we can develop another approach to the simplification of LR parsers.

The central idea of this section is that if the LR tables are in control of the parser, then each table can be considered as the state of an automaton which implements the LR parsing algorithm. The automaton can be considered as a finite automaton with "side effects" that manipulate a pushdown list. Minimization of the states of the automaton can then take place in a manner similar to Algorithm 2.2.

7.5.1. Canonical Parsing Automata

An LR parsing algorithm makes its decision to shift or reduce by looking at the next k input symbols and consulting the governing table, the table on top of the pushdown list. If a reduction is made, the new governing table is determined by examining the table on the pushdown list which is exposed during the reduction.

It is entirely possible to imagine that the tables themselves are parts of a program, and that program control lies with the governing table itself. Typically, the program will be written in some easily interpreted language, so the distinction between a set of tables driving a parsing routine and an interpreted program is not significant.

Let G be an LR(0) grammar and $(\mathfrak{I}, T_0)$ the set of LR(0) tables for G. From the tables we shall construct a parsing automaton for G that mimics the behavior of the LR(0) parsing algorithm for G using the set of tables $\mathfrak{I}$.

We notice that if $T = \langle f, g \rangle$ is an LR(0) table in $\mathfrak{I}$, then $f(e)$ is either **shift**, **reduce**, or **accept**. Thus, we can refer to tables as "shift" tables or "reduce" tables as determined by the parsing action function. We shall initially have one program for each table. We can interpret these programs as *states* of the parsing automaton for G.

A *shift state* $T = \langle f, g \rangle$ does the following:

(1) T, the name of the state, is placed on top of the pushdown list.

(2) The next input symbol, say a, is removed from the input and control passes to the state $g(a)$.

In the previous versions of LR parsing we also placed the input symbol a on the pushdown list on top of the table T. But, as we have pointed out, storing the grammar symbols on the pushdown list is not necessary, and for the remainder of this section we shall not place any grammar symbols on the pushdown list.

A *reduce state* does the following:

(1) Let $A \longrightarrow \alpha$ be production i according to which the reduction is to be made. The top $|\alpha| - 1$ symbols are removed (popped) from the pushdown list.† (If $\alpha = e$, then the controlling state is placed on top of the pushdown list.)

(2) The state name now on top of the pushdown list is determined. Suppose that that state is $T = \langle f, g \rangle$. Control passes to the state $g(A)$ and the production number i is emitted.

A special case occurs when the "reduce" action really means **accept**. In that case, the entire process terminates and the automaton enters an (accepting) final state.

It is straightforward to show that the collection of states defined above will do to the pushdown list exactly what the LR(k) parser does (except here we have not written any grammar symbols on the pushdown list) if we identify the state names and the tables from which the states are derived. The only exception is that the LR(k) parsing algorithm places the name of the governing table on top of the pushdown list, while here the name of

---

†We remove $|\alpha| - 1$ symbols, rather than $|\alpha|$ symbols because the table corresponding to the rightmost symbol of α is in control and does not appear on the list.

that table does not appear but is indicated by the fact that program control lies with that table.

We shall now define the parsing automaton which executes these parsing actions directly. There is a state of the automaton for each state (i.e., table) in the above sense. The input symbols for the automaton are the terminals of the grammar and the state names themselves. A shift state makes transitions only on terminals, and a reduce state makes transitions only on state names. In fact, a state T calling for a reduction according to production $A \longrightarrow \alpha$ need have a transition specified for state T' only when T is in GOTO(T', α).

We should remember that this automaton is more than a finite automaton, in that the states have side effects on a pushdown list. That is, each time a state transition occurs, something happens to the pushdown list which is not reflected in the finite automaton model of the system. Nevertheless, we can reduce the number of states of the parsing automaton in a manner similar to Algorithm 2.2. The difference in this case is that we must be sure that all subsequent side effects are the same if two states are to be placed in the same equivalence class. We now give a formal definition of a parsing automaton.

DEFINITION

Let $G = (N, \Sigma, P, S)$ be an LR(0) grammar and $(\mathfrak{I}, T_0)$ its set of LR(0) tables. We define an incompletely specified automaton M, called the *canonical parsing automaton* for G. M is a 5-tuple $(\mathfrak{I}, \Sigma \cup \mathfrak{I} \cup \{\$\}, \delta, T_0, \{T_1\})$, where

(1) $\mathfrak{I}$ is the set of states.

(2) $\Sigma \cup \mathfrak{I}$ is the set of possible input symbols. The symbols in Σ are on the input tape, and those in $\mathfrak{I}$ are on the pushdown list. Thus, $\mathfrak{I}$ is both the set of states and a subset of the inputs to the parsing automaton.

(3) δ is a mapping from $\mathfrak{I} \times (\Sigma \cup \mathfrak{I})$ to $\mathfrak{I}$. δ is defined as follows:

    (a) If $T \in \mathfrak{I}$ is a shift state, $\delta(T, a) = \text{GOTO}(T, a)$ for all $a \in \Sigma$.

    (b) If $T \in \mathfrak{I}$ is a reduce state calling for a reduction by production $A \longrightarrow \alpha$ and if T' is in GOTO$^{-1}(T, \alpha)$ [i.e., $T = \text{GOTO}(T', \alpha)$], then $\delta(T, T') = \text{GOTO}(T', A)$.

    (c) $\delta(T, X)$ is undefined otherwise.

The canonical parsing automaton is a finite transducer with side effects on a pushdown list. Its behavior can be described in terms of configurations consisting of 4-tuples of the form (α, T, w, π), where

(1) α represents the contents of the pushdown list (with the topmost symbol on the right).

(2) T is the governing state.

(3) w is the unexpended input.

(4) π is the output string to this point.

Moves can be reflected by a relation $\vdash$ on configurations. If T is a shift state and $\delta(T, a) = T'$, we write $(\alpha, T, aw, \pi) \vdash (\alpha T, T', w, \pi)$. If T calls for a reduction according to the ith production $A \longrightarrow \gamma$ and $\delta(T, T') = T''$, we write $(\alpha T' \beta, T, w, \pi) \vdash (\alpha T', T'', w, \pi i)$ for all β of length $|\gamma| - 1$. If $|\gamma| = 0$, then $(\alpha, T, w, \pi) \vdash (\alpha T, T'', w, \pi i)$. In this case, T and T' are the same. Note that if we had included the controlling state symbol as the top symbol of the pushdown list, we would have the configurations of the usual LR parsing algorithm.

We define $\vdash^i$, $\vdash^*$, and $\vdash^+$ in the usual fashion. An *initial* configuration is one of the form (e, T_0, w, e), and an *accepting* configuration is one of the form (T_0, T_1, e, π). If $(e, T_0, w, e) \vdash^* (T_0, T_1, e, \pi)$, then we say that π is *the parse produced by M for w.*

Example 7.32

Let us consider the LR(0) grammar G

$$
\begin{align}
&(1) \ S \longrightarrow aA \\
&(2) \ S \longrightarrow aB \\
&(3) \ A \longrightarrow bA \\
&(4) \ A \longrightarrow c \\
&(5) \ B \longrightarrow bB \\
&(6) \ B \longrightarrow d
\end{align}
$$

generating the regular set $ab^*(c + d)$. The ten LR(0) tables for G are listed in Fig. 7.46.

	action			goto				
	e	S	A	B	a	b	c	d
T_0	S	T_1	X	X	T_2	X	X	X
T_1	A	X	X	X	X	X	X	X
T_2	S	X	T_3	T_4	X	T_5	T_6	T_7
T_3	1	X	X	X	X	X	X	X
T_4	2	X	X	X	X	X	X	X
T_5	S	X	T_8	T_9	X	T_5	T_6	T_7
T_6	4	X	X	X	X	X	X	X
T_7	6	X	X	X	X	X	X	X
T_8	3	X	X	X	X	X	X	X
T_9	5	X	X	X	X	X	X	X

Fig. 7.46 LR(0) tables.

T_0, T_2, and T_5 are shift states. Thus, we have a parsing automaton with the following shift rules:

$$\delta(T_0, a) = T_2$$
$$\delta(T_2, b) = T_5$$
$$\delta(T_2, c) = T_6$$
$$\delta(T_2, d) = T_7$$
$$\delta(T_5, b) = T_5$$
$$\delta(T_5, c) = T_6$$
$$\delta(T_5, d) = T_7$$

We compute the transition rules for the reduce states T_3, T_4, T_6, T_7, T_8 and T_9. Table T_3 reduces using production $S \rightarrow aA$. Since $\text{GOTO}^{-1}(T_3, aA) = \{T_0\}$ and $\text{GOTO}(T_0, S) = T_1$, $\delta(T_3, T_0) = T_1$ is the only rule for T_3. Table T_7 reduces by $B \rightarrow d$. Since $\text{GOTO}^{-1}(T_7, d) = \{T_2, T_5\}$, $\text{GOTO}(T_2, B) = T_4$, and $\text{GOTO}(T_5, B) = T_9$, the rules for T_7 are $\delta(T_7, T_2) = T_4$ and $\delta(T_7, T_5) = T_9$. The reduce rules are summarized below:

$$\delta(T_3, T_0) = T_1$$
$$\delta(T_4, T_0) = T_1$$
$$\delta(T_6, T_2) = T_3 \qquad \delta(T_6, T_5) = T_8$$
$$\delta(T_7, T_2) = T_4 \qquad \delta(T_7, T_5) = T_9$$
$$\delta(T_8, T_2) = T_3 \qquad \delta(T_8, T_5) = T_8$$
$$\delta(T_9, T_2) = T_4 \qquad \delta(T_9, T_5) = T_9$$

The transition graph of the parsing automaton is shown in Fig. 7.47. With input abc, this canonical automaton would enter the following sequence of configurations:

$$(e, T_0, abc, e) \vdash (T_0, T_2, bc, e)$$
$$\vdash (T_0 T_2, T_5, c, e)$$
$$\vdash (T_0 T_2 T_5, T_6, e, e)$$
$$\vdash (T_0 T_2 T_5, T_8, e, 4)$$
$$\vdash (T_0 T_2, T_3, e, 43)$$
$$\vdash (T_0, T_1, e, 431)$$

Thus, the parsing automaton produces the parse 431 for the input abc.

$\square$

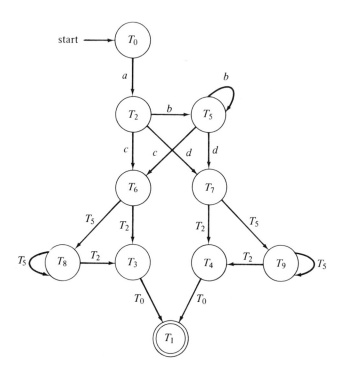

Fig. 7.47   Transition graph of canonical automaton.

7.5.2. Splitting the Functions of States

One good feature of the parsing automaton approach to parser design is that we can often split the functions of certain states and attribute them to two separate states, connected in series. If state A is split into two states A_1 and A_2 while B is split into B_1 and B_2, it may be possible to merge, say A_2 and B_2, while it was not possible to merge A and B. Since the amount of work done by A_1 and A_2 (or B_1 and B_2) exactly equals the amount done by A (or B), no increase in cost occurs if the split is made. However, if state mergers can be made, then improvement is possible. In this section we shall explore ways in which the functions of certain states can be split with the hope of merging common actions.

We shall split every reduce state into a *pop state* followed by an *interrogation state*. Suppose that T is a reduce state calling for a reduction by production $A \longrightarrow \alpha$ whose number is i. When we split T, we create a pop state whose sole function is to remove $|\alpha| - 1$ symbols from the top of the pushdown list. If $\alpha = e$, the pop state will actually add the name T to the top of the pushdown list. In addition, the pop state will emit the production number i.

Control is then transferred to the interrogation state which examines the state name now on top of the pushdown list, say U, and then transfers control to GOTO(U, A).

In the transition graph we can replace a reduce state T by a pop state, which we shall also call T, and an interrogation state, which we shall call T'. All edges entering the old T still enter the new T, but all edges leaving the old T now leave T'. One unlabeled edge goes from the new T to T'. This transformation is sketched in Fig. 7.48, where production i is $A \rightarrow \alpha$. Shift states and the accept state will not be split here.

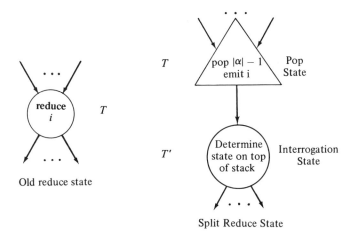

Fig. 7.48 Splitting reduce states.

The automaton constructed from a canonical parsing automaton in the above manner is called a *split canonical parsing automaton*.

Example 7.33

The split parsing automaton from Fig. 7.47 is shown in Fig. 7.49. We show shift states by □, pop states by △, and interrogation and accept states by ○.

To compare the behavior of this split automaton with the automaton in Example 7.32, consider the sequence of moves the split automaton makes on input abc:

$$(e, T_0, abc, e) \vdash (T_0, T_2, bc, e)$$
$$\vdash (T_0 T_2, T_5, c, e)$$
$$\vdash (T_0 T_2 T_5, T_6, e, e)$$
$$\vdash (T_0 T_2 T_5, T'_6, e, 4)$$

$$\vdash (T_0 T_2 T_5, T_8, e, 4)$$
$$\vdash (T_0 T_2, T_8', e, 43)$$
$$\vdash (T_0 T_2, T_3, e, 43)$$
$$\vdash (T_0, T_3', e, 431)$$
$$\vdash (T_0, T_1, e, 431)$$

☐

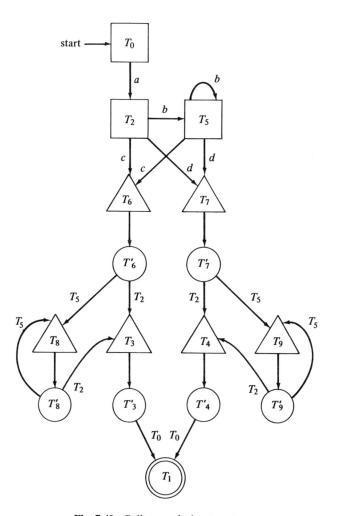

Fig. 7.49 Split canonical automaton.

If M_1 and M_2 are two parsing automata for a grammar G, then we say that M_1 and M_2 are *equivalent* if, for each input string w, they both produce the same parse or they both produce an error indication after having read the same number of input symbols. Thus, we are using the same definition of equivalence as for two sets of LR(k) tables.

If the canonical and split canonical automata are run side by side, then it is easy to see that the resulting pushdown lists are the same each time the split automaton enters a shift or interrogation state. Thus, it should be evident that these two automata are equivalent.

There are two kinds of simplifications that can be made to split parsing automata. The first is to eliminate certain states completely if their actions are not needed. The second is to merge states which are indistinguishable. The first kind of simplification eliminates certain interrogation states.

If an interrogation state has out-degree 1, it may be removed. The pop state connected to it will be connected directly, by an unlabeled edge, to the state to which the interrogation state was connected.

We call the automaton constructed from a split canonical automaton by applying this simplification a *semireduced automaton*.

Example 7.34

Let us consider the split parsing automaton of Fig. 7.49. T'_3 and T'_4 have only one transition, on T_0. Applying our transformation, these states and the T_0 transitions are eliminated. The resulting semireduced automaton is shown in Fig. 7.50. $\quad\square$

THEOREM 7.12

A split canonical parsing automaton M_1 and its semireduced automaton M_2 are equivalent.

Proof. An interrogation state does not change the symbols appearing on the pushdown list. Moreover, if an interrogation state T has only one transition, then the state labeling that transition must appear at the top of the pushdown list whenever M_1 enters state T. This follows from the definition of the GOTO function and of the canonical automaton. Thus, the first transformation does not affect any sequence of stack, input or output moves made by the automaton. $\quad\square$

We now turn to the problem of minimizing the states of a semireduced automaton by merging states whose side effects (other than placing their own name on the pushdown list) are the same and which transfer on corresponding edges to states that are themselves indistinguishable. The minimization algorithm is similar in spirit to Algorithm 2.2, although modifications are necessary because we must account for the operations on the pushdown list.

DEFINITION

Let $M = (Q, \Sigma, \delta, q_0, \{q_1\})$ be a semireduced parsing automaton, where q_0 is the initial state and q_1 the accept state. Note that $Q \subseteq \Sigma$. Also, we shall

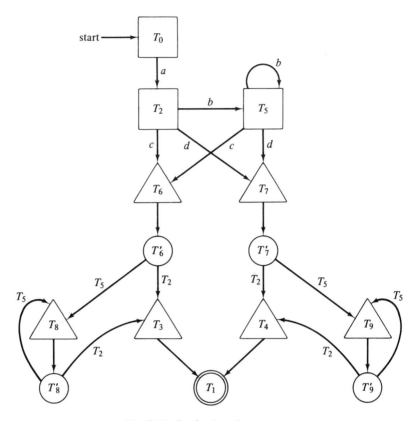

Fig. 7.50   Semi-reduced automaton.

use e to "label" transitions hitherto unlabeled. We say that p and q in Q are *0-indistinguishable*, written $p \overset{0}{=} q$, if one of the following conditions is satisfied by the transition diagram for M (the case $p = q$ is not excluded):

   (1) p and q are both shift states.
   (2) p and q are both interrogation states.
   (3) p and q are both pop states, and they pop the same number of symbols from the pushdown list and cause the same production number to be emitted. (That is, p and q reduce according to the same production.)
   (4) $p = q = q_1$ (the final state).

   Otherwise, p and q are 0-distinguishable. In particular, states of different types are always 0-distinguishable.
   We say that p and q are *k-indistinguishable*, written $p \overset{k}{=} q$, if they are $(k - 1)$-indistinguishable and one of the following holds:

(1) p and q are shift states and

    (a) For every $a \in \Sigma \cup \{e\}$, an edge labeled a leaves either both or neither of p and q. If an edge labeled a leaves each of p and q and enters p' and q', respectively, then p' and q' are $(k - 1)$-indistinguishable states.

    (b) There is no interrogation state with transitions on p and q to $(k - 1)$-distinguishable states.

(2) p and q are pop states and the edges leaving them go to $(k - 1)$-indistinguishable states.

(3) p and q are interrogation states, and for all states s either both or neither of p and q have transitions on s. If both do, then the transitions lead to $(k - 1)$-indistinguishable states.

Otherwise, p and q are k-*distinguishable*. We say that p and q are *indistinguishable*, written $p \equiv q$, if they are k-indistinguishable for all $k \geq 0$. Otherwise, p and q are *distinguishable*.

LEMMA 7.4

Let $M = (Q, \Sigma, \delta, q_0, \{q_1\})$ be a semireduced automaton. Then

(1) For all k, $\overset{k}{\equiv}$ is an equivalence relation on Q, and

(2) If $\overset{k}{\equiv} = \overset{k+1}{\equiv}$, then $\overset{k+1}{\equiv} = \overset{k+2}{\equiv} = \cdots$.

Proof. Exercise similar to Lemma 2.11. $\square$

Example 7.35

Consider the semireduced automaton of Fig. 7.50. Recalling the LR(0) tables from which that automaton was constructed (Fig. 7.46 on p. 648), we see that all six pop states reduce according to different productions and hence are 0-distinguishable. The other kinds of states are, by definition, 0-indistinguishable from those of the same kind, and so $\overset{0}{\equiv}$ has equivalence classes $\{T_0, T_2, T_5\}$, $\{T_1\}$, $\{T_3\}$, $\{T_4\}$, $\{T_6\}$, $\{T_7\}$, $\{T_8\}$, $\{T_9\}$, $\{T'_6, T'_7, T'_8, T'_9\}$.

To compute $\overset{1}{\equiv}$, we observe that T_2 and T_5 are 1-distinguishable, because T'_6 branches to 0-distinguishable states T_3 and T_8 on T_2 and T_5, respectively. Also, T_0 is 1-distinguishable from T_2 and T_5, because the former has a transition on a, while the latter do not. T'_6 and T'_7 are 1-distinguishable because they branch on T_2 to 0-distinguishable states. Likewise, the pairs T'_6–T'_7, T'_7–T'_8 and T'_8–T'_9 are 1-distinguishable. The other pairs which are 0-indistinguishable are also 1-indistinguishable. Thus, the equivalence classes of $\overset{1}{\equiv}$ which have more than one member are $\{T'_6, T'_8\}$ and $\{T'_7, T'_9\}$. We find that $\overset{2}{\equiv} = \overset{1}{\equiv}$. $\square$

DEFINITION

Let $M_1 = (Q, \Sigma, \delta, q_0, \{q_1\})$ be a semireduced automaton. Let Q' be the set of equivalence classes of $\equiv$ and let $[q]$ stand for the equivalence class containing q. The *reduced automaton* for M_1 is $M_2 = (Q', \Sigma', \delta', [q_0], \{[q_1]\})$, where

(1) $\Sigma' = (\Sigma - Q) \cup Q'$;
(2) For all $q \in Q$ and $a \in \Sigma \cup \{e\} - Q$, $\delta'([q], a) = [\delta(q, a)]$; and
(3) For all q and $p \in Q$, $\delta'([q], [p]) = [\delta(q, p)]$.

Example 7.36

In Example 7.35 we found that $T'_6 \equiv T'_8$ and $T'_7 \equiv T'_9$. The transition graph of the reduced automaton for Fig. 7.50 is shown in Fig. 7.51. T'_6 and T'_7 have been chosen as representatives for the two equivalence classes with more than one member.   □

From the definition of $\equiv$, it follows that the definition of the reduced automaton is consistent; that is, rules (2) and (3) of the definition do not depend on which representative of an equivalence class is chosen.

We can also show in a straightforward way that the reduced and semi-

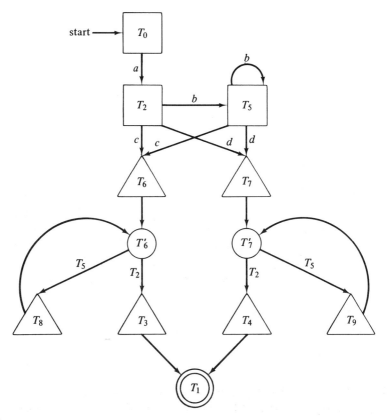

Fig. 7.51 Reduced automaton.

reduced automata are equivalent. Essentially, the two automata will always make similar sequences of moves. The reduced automaton enters a state representing the equivalence class of each state entered by the semireduced automaton. We state the correspondence formally as follows.

THEOREM 7.13

Let M_1 be a semireduced automaton and M_2 the corresponding reduced automaton. Then for all $i \geq 0$, there exist $T_1, \ldots, T_m, T$ such that

$$(e, T_0, w, e) \mathrel{|\frac{i}{M_1}} (T_0 T_1 \cdots T_m, T, x, \pi)$$

if and only if

$$(e, [T_0], w, e) \mathrel{|\frac{i}{M_2}} ([T_0][T_1] \cdots [T_m], [T], x, \pi),$$

where T_0 is the initial state of M_1 and $[u]$ denotes the equivalence class of state u.

Proof. Elementary induction on i. $\square$

COROLLARY

M_1 and M_2 are equivalent. $\square$

7.5.3. Generalizations to LR(k) Parsers

We can also construct a canonical parsing automaton from a set of LR(k) tables for an LR(k) grammar with $k > 0$. Here we consider the case in which $k = 1$. The parsing automaton behaves in much the same fashion as the canonical parsing automaton for an LR(0) grammar, except that we now cannot classify each table solely as a shift, reduce, or accept table.

As before, there will be a state of the automaton corresponding to each table. If the automaton is in configuration $(T_0 T_1 \cdots T_m, T, w, \pi)$, the automaton behaves as follows:

(1) The lookahead string $a = \text{FIRST}(w)$ is determined.
(2) A decision is made whether to shift or reduce. That is, if $T = \langle f, g \rangle$, then $f(a)$ is determined.
  (a) If $f(a) = \textbf{shift}$, then the automaton moves into the configuration $(T_0 T_1 \cdots T_m T, T', w', \pi)$, where $T' = g(a)$ and $aw' = w$.
  (b) If $f(a) = \textbf{reduce}\ i$ and production i is $A \rightarrow \alpha$, where $|\alpha| = r > 0$, the automaton enters configuration $(T_0 T_1 \cdots T_{m-r+1}, T', w, \pi i)$, where $T' = g'(A)$ if $T_{m-r+1} = \langle f', g' \rangle$. [If the production is $A \rightarrow e$, then the resulting configuration will be $(T_0 T_1 \cdots T_m T, T', w, \pi i)$, where $T' = g(A)$, assuming that $T = \langle f, g \rangle$.]
  (c) If $f(a) = \textbf{accept}$ or $\textbf{error}$, then the automaton halts and reports acceptance or rejection of the input.

It is possible to split states in various ways, so that particular pushdown list operations can be isolated with the hope of merging common operations. Here, we shall consider the following state-splitting scheme.

Let T be a state corresponding to table $T = \langle f, g \rangle$. We split this state into read, push, pop, and interrogation states as follows:

(1) We create a *read* state labeled T which reads the next input symbol. Read states are indicated by $\bigcirc$.

(2) If $f(a) =$ **shift**, we then create a *push* state labeled T^a and draw an edge with label a from the read state T to this push state. If $g(a) = T'$, we then draw an unlabeled edge from T^a to the read state labeled T'. The push state T^a has two side effects. The input symbol a is removed from the input, and the table name T is pushed on top of the pushdown list. We indicate push states by $\square$.

(3) If $f(a) =$ **reduce** i, then we create a pop state T_1 and an interrogation state T_2. An edge labeled a is drawn from T to T_1. If production i is $A \rightarrow \alpha$, then the action of state T_1 is to remove $|\alpha| - 1$ symbols from the top of the pushdown list and to emit the production number i. If $\alpha = e$, then T_1 places the original table name T on the pushdown list. Pop states are indicated by $\triangle$. An unlabeled edge is then drawn from T_1 to T_2. The action of T_2 is to examine the symbol now on top of the pushdown list. If $\text{GOTO}^{-1}(T, \alpha)$ contains T' and $\text{GOTO}(T', A) = T''$, then an edge labeled T' is drawn from T_2 to the read state of T''. Interrogation states are also indicated by $\bigcirc$. The labels on the edges leaving distinguish these circles from read states.

Thus, state T would be represented as in Fig. 7.52 if $f(a) =$ **shift** and $f(b) =$ **reduce** i.

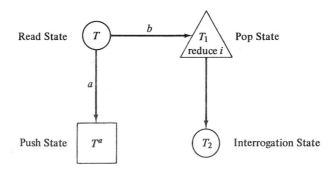

Fig. 7.52   Possible representation for state T.

(4) The accepting state is not split.

Example 7.37

Let us consider the LR(1) grammar G

$$(1) \ S \longrightarrow AB$$
$$(2) \ A \longrightarrow aAb$$
$$(3) \ A \longrightarrow e$$
$$(4) \ B \longrightarrow bB$$
$$(5) \ B \longrightarrow b$$

A set of LR(1) tables for G is shown in Fig. 7.53.

	action			goto				
	a	b	e	S	A	B	a	b
T_0	S	3	X	T_1	T_2	X	T_3	X
T_1	X	X	A	X	X	X	X	X
T_2	X	S	X	X	X	T_4	X	T_5
T_3	S	3	X	X	T_6	X	T_3	X
T_4	X	X	1	X	X	X	X	X
T_5	X	S	5	X	X	T_7	X	T_5
T_6	X	S	X	X	X	X	X	T_8
T_7	X	X	4	X	X	X	X	X
T_8	X	2	X	X	X	X	X	X

Fig. 7.53   LR(1) tables.

The parsing automaton which results from splitting states as described above is shown in Fig. 7.54.   ☐

There are several ways in which the number of states in a split automaton for an LR(1) grammar can be reduced:

(1) If an interrogation state has only one edge leaving, the interrogation state can be eliminated. This simplification is exactly like the corresponding LR(0) simplification.

(2) Let T be a read state such that in every path into T the last edge entering a pop state is always labeled by the same input symbol or always by e. Then the read state may be eliminated. (One can show that in this case the read state has only one edge leaving and that the edge is labeled by that symbol.)

Example 7.38

Let us consider the automaton of Fig. 7.54. There are three interrogation states with out-degree 1, namely T'_0, T'_3, and T'_4. These states and the edges leaving can all be eliminated.

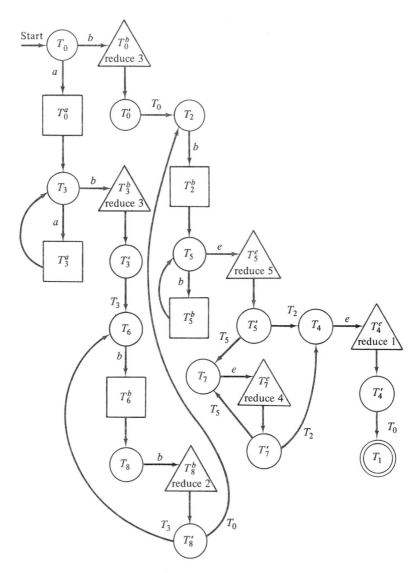

Fig. 7.54   Split automaton for LR(1) grammar.

Next, let us consider read state T_6. The only way T_6 can be reached is via the paths from T_3 and T'_3 or T_8 and T'_8. The previous input symbol label is b in either case, meaning that if T_3 or T_8 see b on the input, they transfer to T^b_3 or T^b_8 for a reduction. The b remains on the input until T_6 examines it and decides to transfer to T^b_6 for a shift. Since we know that the b is there, T_6 is superfluous; T^b_6 can push the state name T_6 on the pushdown list without looking at the next input symbol, since that input symbol must be b if the automaton has reached state T_6.

Similarly, T_2 can be eliminated. The resulting automaton is shown in Fig. 7.55. ☐

As with the LR(0) semireduced automaton, we can also merge compatible states without affecting the action of the automaton. We leave these matters to the reader. In Fig. 7.55, the only pair of states which can be merged is T'_5 and T'_7.

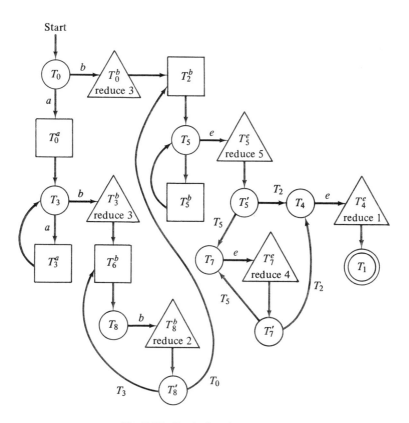

Fig. 7.55 Semireduced automaton.

7.5.4. Chapter Summary

In this chapter we have seen a large number of techniques that can be used to reduce the size and increase the speed of parsers. In view of all these possibilities, how should one go about constructing a parser for a given grammar?

First a decision whether to use a top-down or bottom-up parser must be made. This decision is affected by the types of translations which need to be computed. The matter will be discussed in Chapter 9.

If a top-down parser is desired, an LL(1) parser is recommended. To construct such a parser, we need to perform the following steps:

(1) The grammar must be first transformed into an LL(1) grammar. Very rarely will the initial grammar be LL(1). Left factoring and elimination of left recursion are the primary tools in attempting to make a grammar LL(1), but there is no guarantee that these transformations will always succeed. (See Examples 5.10 and 5.11 on p. 345 of Volume I.)

(2) However, if we can obtain an equivalent LL(1) grammar G, then using the techniques of Section 5.1 (Algorithm 5.1 in particular), we can readily produce an LL(1) parsing table for G. The entries in this parsing table will in practice be calls to routines that manipulate the pushdown list, produce output, or generate error messages.

(3) There are two techniques that can be used to reduce the size of the parsing table:

(a) If a production begins with a terminal symbol, then it is not necessary to stack the terminal symbol if we advance the input pointer. (That is, if production $A \rightarrow a\alpha$ is to be used and a is the current input symbol, then we put α on the stack and move the input head one symbol to the right.) This technique can reduce the number of different symbols that can appear on the pushdown list and hence the number of rows in the LL(1) parsing table.

(b) Several nonterminals with similar parsing actions can be combined into a single nonterminal with a "tag" which describes what nonterminal it represents. Nonterminals representing expressions are amenable to this combination. (See Exercises 7.3.28 and 7.3.31.)

If a bottom-up parser is desired, then we recommend a deterministic shift–reduce parsing algorithm such as an SLR(1) parser or LALR(1) parser, if necessary. It is easy to describe the syntax of most programming languages by an SLR(1) grammar, so little preliminary modification of the given grammar should be necessary. The size of an SLR(1) or LALR(1) parser can be reduced significantly by a few optimizations. It is usually worthwhile to eliminate reductions by single productions.

Further space optimization is possible if we implement an LALR(1) parser in the style of the production language parsers of Section 7.2. The parsing action entries of each LR(1) table could be implemented as a sequence of shift statements, followed by a sequence of reduce statements, followed by one unconditional error statement. If all reduce statements involve the same production, then all these reduce statements and the following error statement could be replaced by one statement which reduces by that production regardless of the input. The error-detecting capability of the parser would not be affected by this optimization. See Exercises 7.3.23 and 7.5.13. The non-φ goto entries for each LR(1) table could be stored as a list of pairs (A, T) meaning on nonterminal A place T on top of the stack. The gotos on terminals could be encoded in the shift statements themselves. Note that no φ-entries would have to be stored. The optimizations of Section 7.2 merging common sequences of statements would then be applicable.

These approaches to parser design have several practical advantages. First, we can mechanically debug the resulting parser by generating input strings that will check the behavior of the parser. For example, we can easily construct input strings that cause each useful entry in an LL(1) or LR(1) table to be exercised. Another advantage of LL(1) and LR(1) parsers, especially the former, is that minor changes to the syntax or semantics can be made by simply changing the appropriate entries in a parsing table.

Finally, the reader should be aware that certain ambiguous grammars have "LL" or "LR" parsers that are formed by resolving parsing action conflicts in an apparently arbitrary manner (see Exercise 7.5.14). Design of parsers of this type warrants further research.

EXERCISES

7.5.1. Construct a parsing automaton M for G_0. Construct from M an equivalent split, a semireduced, and a reduced automaton.

7.5.2. Construct parsing automata for each grammar in Exercise 7.3.1.

7.5.3. Split states to construct reduced parsing automata from the parsing automata in Exercise 7.5.2.

7.5.4. Prove Lemma 7.4.

7.5.5. Prove that the definition of the reduced automaton in Section 7.5.2 is consistent; that is, if $p \equiv q$, then $\delta(p, a) \equiv \delta(q, a)$ for all a in $\Sigma' \cup \{e\}$.

7.5.6. Prove Theorem 7.13.

DEFINITION

Let $G = (N, \Sigma, P, S')$ be an augmented CFG with productions numbered $0, 1, \ldots$ such that the zeroth production is $S' \rightarrow S$. Let $\Sigma' = \{\#_0, \#_1, \ldots, \#_p\}$ be a set of special symbols not in $N \cup \Sigma$. Let the ith production be $A \rightarrow \beta$ and suppose that $S' \stackrel{*}{\Rightarrow} \alpha A w \underset{rm}{\Rightarrow} \alpha \beta w$. Then $\alpha \beta \#_i$ is called a *characteristic* string of the right-sentential form $\alpha \beta w$.

*7.5.7. Show that the set of characteristic strings for a CFG is a regular set.

7.5.8. Show that a CFG G is unambiguous if and only if each right-sentential form of G, except S', has a unique characteristic string.

7.5.9. Show that a CFG is LR(k) if and only if each right-sentential form $\alpha\beta w$ such that $S' \overset{*}{\underset{rm}{\Rightarrow}} \alpha Aw \underset{rm}{\Rightarrow} \alpha\beta w$ has a characteristic string which may be determined from only $\alpha\beta$ and $\mathrm{FIRST}_k(w)$.

7.5.10. Let $G = (\mathrm{N}, \Sigma, P, S)$ be an LR(0) grammar and $(\mathfrak{I}, T_0)$ its canonical set of LR(0) tables. Let $M = (\mathfrak{I}, \Sigma \cup \mathfrak{I}, \delta, T_0, \{T_1\})$ be the canonical parsing automaton for G. Let $M' = (\mathfrak{I} \cup \{q_f\}, \Sigma \cup \Sigma', \delta', T_0, \{q_f\})$ be the deterministic finite automaton constructed from M by letting

(1) $\delta'(T, a) = \delta(T, a)$ for all T in $\mathfrak{I}$ and a in Σ.

(2) $\delta'(T, \#_i) = q_f$ if $\delta(T, T')$ is defined and T' is a reduce state calling for a reduction using production i.

Show that $L(M')$ is the set of characteristic strings for G.

7.5.11. Give an algorithm for merging "equivalent" states of the semireduced automaton constructed for an LR(1) grammar, where equivalence is taken to mean that the two states have transitions on the same set of symbols and transitions on each symbol are to equivalent states.†

*7.5.12. Suppose that we modify the definition of "equivalence" in Exercise 7.5.11 to admit the equivalence of states that transfer to equivalent states on symbol a whenever both states have a transition on a. Is the resulting automaton equivalent (in the formal sense, meaning one may not shift if the other declares error) to the semireduced automation?

7.5.13. Suppose a read state T of an LR(1) parsing automaton has all its transitions to pop states which reduce by the same production. Show that if we delete T and merge all those pop states to one, the new automaton will make the reduction independent of the lookahead, but will be equivalent to the original automaton,

*7.5.14. Let G be the ambiguous grammar with productions

$$S \to \text{if } b \text{ then } SE \mid a$$
$$E \to \text{else } S \mid e$$

(a) Show that $L(G)$ is not an LL language.

(b) Construct a 1-predictive parser for G assuming that whenever E is on top of the stack and **else** is the next input symbol, production $E \to \text{else } S$ is to be applied.

(c) Construct an LR(1) parser for G by making an analogous assumption.

Research Problems

7.5.15. Apply the technique used here—breaking a parser into a large number of active components and merging or eliminating some of them—to parsers other than LR ones. For example, the technique in Section 7.2

---

†This definition can be made precise by defining relations $\overset{0}{\equiv}, \overset{1}{\equiv}, \ldots$ as in Lemma 7.2.

effectively treated the rows of a precedence matrix as active elements. Develop techniques applicable to LL parsers and various kinds of precedence parsers.

7.5.16. Certain states of a canonical parsing automaton may recognize only regular sets. Consider splitting the shift states of a parsing automaton into scan states and push states. The scan state might remove input symbols and emit output but would not affect the pushdown list. Then a scan state might transfer control to another scan state or a push state. Thus, a set of scan states can behave as a finite transducer. A push state would place the name of the current state on the pushdown list. Develop transformations that can be used to optimize parsing automata with scan and push states as well as split reduce states.

7.5.17. Express the optimizations of Section 7.3 and 7.5 in each other's terms.

Programming Exercises

7.5.18. Design elementary operations that can be used to implement split canonical parsing automata. Construct an interpreter for these elementary operations.

7.5.19. Write a program that will take a split canonical parsing automaton and construct from it a sequence of elementary operations that simulates the behavior of the parsing automaton.

7.5.20. Construct two LR(1) parsers for one of the grammars in the Appendix of Volume 1. One LR(1) parser should be the interpretive LR(1) parser working from a set of LR(1) tables. The other should be a sequence of elementary operations simulating the parsing automaton. Compare the size and speed of the parsers.

BIBLIOGRAPHIC NOTES

The parsing automaton approach was suggested by DeRemer [1969]. The definition of characteristic string preceding Exercise 7.5.7 is from the same source. Classes of ambiguous grammars that can be parsed by LL or LR means are discussed by Aho, Johnson, and Ullman [1972].

8 THEORY OF DETERMINISTIC PARSING

In Chapter 5 we were introduced to various classes of grammars for which we can construct efficient deterministic parsers. In that chapter some inclusion relations among these classes of grammars were demonstrated. For example, it was shown that every (m, k)-BRC grammar is an $LR(k)$ grammar. In this chapter we shall complete the hierarchy of relationships among these classes of grammars.

One can also ask what class of languages is generated by the grammars in a given class. In this chapter we shall see that most of the classes of grammars in Chapter 5 generate exactly the deterministic context-free languages. Specifically, we shall show that each of the following classes of grammars generates exactly the deterministic context-free languages:

(1) $LR(1)$,
(2) $(1, 1)$-BRC,
(3) Uniquely invertible $(2, 1)$-precedence, and
(4) Simple mixed strategy precedence.

In deriving these results we provide algorithms to convert grammars of one kind into another. Thus, for each deterministic context-free language we can find a grammar that can be parsed by a UI $(2, 1)$-precedence or simple mixed strategy precedence algorithm. However, if these conversion algorithms are used indiscriminately, the resulting grammars will often be too large for practical use.

There are three interesting proper subclasses of the deterministic context-free languages:

(1) The simple precedence languages,
(2) The operator precedence languages, and
(3) The LL languages.

The operator precedence languages are a proper subset of the simple precedence languages and incommensurate with the LL languages. In Chapter 5 we saw that the class of UI weak precedence languages is the same as the simple precedence languages. Thus, we have the hierarchy of languages shown in Fig. 8.1.

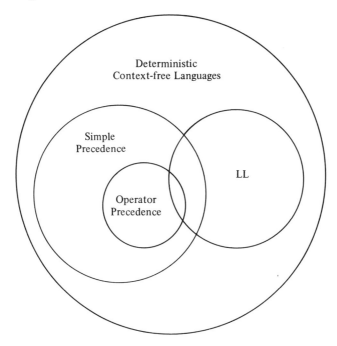

Fig. 8.1   Hierarchy of deterministic context-free languages.

In this chapter we shall derive this hierarchy and mention the most striking features of each class of languages. This chapter is organized into three sections. In the first, we shall discuss LL languages and their properties. In the second, we shall investigate the class of deterministic languages, and in the third section we shall discuss the simple precedence and operator precedence languages.

This chapter is the caviar of the book. However, it is not essential to a strict diet of "theory of compiling," and it can be skipped on a first reading.†

8.1. THEORY OF LL LANGUAGES

We begin by deriving the principal results about LL languages and grammars. In this section we shall bring out the following six results:

†Readers who dislike caviar can skip it on subsequent readings as well.

(1) Every LL(k) grammar is an LR(k) grammar (Theorem 8.1).

(2) For every LL(k) language there is a Greibach normal form LL($k + 1$) grammar (Theorem 8.5).

(3) It is decidable whether two LL grammars are equivalent (Theorem 8.6).

(4) An e-free language is LL(k) if and only if it has an e-free LL($k + 1$) grammar (Theorem 8.7).

(5) For $k \geq 0$, the LL(k) languages are a proper subset of the LL($k + 1$) languages (Theorem 8.8).

(6) There exist LR languages which are not LL languages (Exercise 8.1.11).

8.1.1. LL and LR Grammars

Our first task is to prove that every LL(k) grammar is an LR(k) grammar. This result can be intuited by the following argument. Consider the derivation tree sketched in Fig. 8.2.

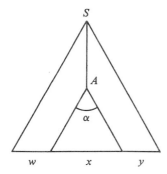

Fig. 8.2 Sketch of derivation tree.

In scanning the input string wxy, the LR(k) condition requires us to recognize the production $A \rightarrow \alpha$ knowing wx and $\text{FIRST}_k(y)$. On the other hand, the LL(k) condition requires us to recognize the production $A \rightarrow \alpha$ knowing only w and $\text{FIRST}_k(xy)$. Thus, it would appear that the LL(k) condition is more stringent than the LR(k) condition, so that every LL(k) grammar is LR(k). We shall now formalize this argument.

Suppose that we have an LL(k) grammar G and two parse trees in G. Moreover, suppose that the frontiers of the two trees agree for the first m symbols. Then to every node of one tree such that no more than $m - k$ leaves labeled with terminals appear to its left, there corresponds an "essentially identical" node in the other tree. This relationship is represented pictorially in Fig. 8.3, where the shaded region represents the "same" nodes. We assume that $|w| = m - k$ and that $\text{FIRST}_k(x_1) = \text{FIRST}_k(x_2)$. We can state this observation more precisely as the following lemma.

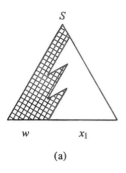 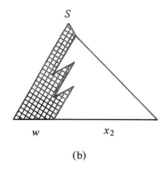

$$\begin{array}{cc} \text{(a)} & \text{(b)} \end{array}$$

Fig. 8.3 Two parse trees for an LL(k) grammar.

LEMMA 8.1

Let G be an LL(k) grammar and let

$$S \underset{\text{lm}}{\overset{m_1}{\Rightarrow}} w_1 A\alpha \underset{\text{lm}}{\overset{*}{\Rightarrow}} w_1 x_1 \text{ and } S \underset{\text{lm}}{\overset{m_2}{\Rightarrow}} w_2 B\beta \underset{\text{lm}}{\overset{*}{\Rightarrow}} w_2 x_2$$

be two leftmost derivations such that $\text{FIRST}_l(w_1 x_1) = \text{FIRST}_l(w_2 x_2)$ for $l = k + \max(|w_1|, |w_2|)$. (That is, $w_1 x_1$ and $w_2 x_2$ agree at least k symbols beyond w_1 and w_2.)

(1) If $m_1 = m_2$, then $w_1 = w_2$, $A = B$, and $\alpha = \beta$.

(2) If $m_1 < m_2$, then $S \underset{\text{lm}}{\overset{m_1}{\Rightarrow}} w_1 A\alpha \underset{\text{lm}}{\overset{m_2-m_1}{\Longrightarrow}} w_2 B\beta \overset{*}{\Rightarrow} w_2 x_2$.

Proof. Examining the LL(k) definition, we find that if $m_1 \leq m_2$, each of the first m_1 steps of the derivation $S \underset{\text{lm}}{\overset{m_2}{\Rightarrow}} w_2 B\beta$ are the same as those of $S \underset{\text{lm}}{\overset{m_1}{\Rightarrow}} w_1 A\alpha$, since the lookahead strings are the same at each step. (1) and (2) follow immediately. □

THEOREM 8.1

Every LL(k) grammar† is LR(k).

Proof. Let $G = (\text{N}, \Sigma, P, S)$ be an LL(k) grammar and suppose that it is not LR(k). Then there exist two rightmost derivations in the augmented grammar

(8.1.1) $S' \underset{\text{rm}}{\overset{i}{\Longrightarrow}} \alpha A x_1 \underset{\text{rm}}{\Longrightarrow} \alpha\beta x_1$

(8.1.2) $S' \underset{\text{rm}}{\overset{j}{\Longrightarrow}} \gamma B y \underset{\text{rm}}{\Longrightarrow} \gamma\delta y$

such that $\gamma\delta y = \alpha\beta x_2$ for some x_2 for which $\text{FIRST}_k(x_2) = \text{FIRST}_k(x_1)$. Since G is assumed not to be LR(1), we can assume that $\alpha A x_2 \neq \gamma B y$.

---

†Throughout this book we are assuming that a grammar has no useless productions.

In these derivations, we can assume that i and j are both greater than zero. Otherwise, we would have, for example,

$$S' \overset{0}{\Longrightarrow} S' \Longrightarrow S$$

$$S' \overset{+}{\Longrightarrow} By \Longrightarrow S\beta y$$

which would imply that G was left-recursive and hence that G was not LL. Thus, for the remainder of this proof we can assume that we can replace S' by S in derivations (8.1.1) and (8.1.2).

Let x_α, x_β, x_γ, and x_δ be terminal strings derived from α, β, γ, and δ, respectively, such that $x_\alpha x_\beta x_2 = x_\gamma x_\delta y$. Consider the leftmost derivations which correspond to the derivations

(8.1.3) $\qquad S \overset{*}{\underset{rm}{\Longrightarrow}} \alpha A x_1 \underset{rm}{\Longrightarrow} \alpha \beta x_1 \overset{*}{\underset{rm}{\Longrightarrow}} x_\alpha x_\beta x_1$

and

(8.1.4) $\qquad S \overset{*}{\underset{rm}{\Longrightarrow}} \gamma B y \underset{rm}{\Longrightarrow} \gamma \delta y \overset{*}{\underset{rm}{\Longrightarrow}} x_\gamma x_\delta y$

Specifically, let

(8.1.5) $\qquad S \overset{*}{\underset{lm}{\Longrightarrow}} x_\alpha A \eta \underset{lm}{\Longrightarrow} x_\alpha \beta \eta \overset{*}{\underset{lm}{\Longrightarrow}} x_\alpha x_\beta \eta \overset{*}{\underset{lm}{\Longrightarrow}} x_\alpha x_\beta x_1$

and

(8.1.6) $\qquad S \overset{*}{\underset{lm}{\Longrightarrow}} x_\gamma B \theta \underset{lm}{\Longrightarrow} x_\gamma \delta \theta \overset{*}{\underset{lm}{\Longrightarrow}} x_\gamma x_\delta \theta \overset{*}{\underset{lm}{\Longrightarrow}} x_\gamma x_\delta y$

where η and θ are the appropriate strings in $(N \cup \Sigma)^*$.

By Lemma 8.1, the sequence of steps in the derivation $S \overset{*}{\underset{lm}{\Longrightarrow}} x_\alpha A \eta$ is the initial sequence of steps in the derivation $S \overset{*}{\underset{lm}{\Longrightarrow}} x_\gamma B \theta$ or conversely. We assume the former case; the converse can be handled in a symmetric manner. Thus, derivation (8.1.6) can be written as

(8.1.7) $\quad S \overset{*}{\underset{lm}{\Longrightarrow}} x_\alpha A \eta \underset{lm}{\Longrightarrow} x_\alpha \beta \eta \overset{*}{\underset{lm}{\Longrightarrow}} x_\gamma B \theta \underset{lm}{\Longrightarrow} x_\gamma \delta \theta \overset{*}{\underset{lm}{\Longrightarrow}} x_\gamma x_\delta \theta \overset{*}{\underset{lm}{\Longrightarrow}} x_\gamma x_\delta y$

Let us fix our attention on the parse tree T of derivation (8.1.7). Let n_A be the node corresponding to A in $x_\alpha A \eta$ and n_B the node corresponding to B in $x_\gamma B \theta$. These nodes are shown in Fig. 8.4. Note that n_B may be a descendant of n_A. There cannot really be overlap between x_β and x_δ. Either they are disjoint or x_δ is a subword of x_β. We depict them this way merely to imply either case.

Let us now consider two rightmost derivations associated with parse tree T. In the first, T is expanded rightmost up to (and including) node n_A; in the second the parse tree is expanded up to node n_B. The latter derivation can be written as

$$S \overset{*}{\underset{rm}{\Longrightarrow}} \gamma B y \underset{rm}{\Longrightarrow} \gamma \delta y$$

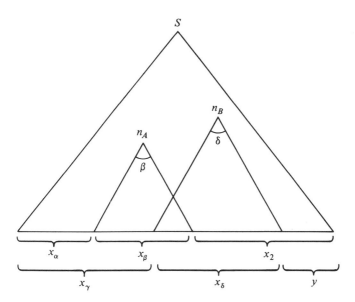

Fig. 8.4   Parse tree T.

This derivation is in fact derivation (8.1.2). The rightmost derivation up to node n_A is

$$(8.1.8) \qquad S \underset{\text{rm}}{\overset{*}{\Longrightarrow}} \alpha' A x_2 \underset{\text{rm}}{\Longrightarrow} \alpha' \beta x_2$$

for some α'. We shall subsequently prove that $\alpha' = \alpha$.

Let us temporarily assume that $\alpha' = \alpha$. We shall then derive a contradiction of the LL(k)-ness of G and thus be able to conclude the theorem. If $\alpha' = \alpha$, then $\gamma \delta y = \alpha' \beta x_2 = \alpha \beta x_2$. Thus, the same rightmost derivations can be used to extend derivations (8.1.2) and (8.1.8) to the string of terminals $x_\gamma x_\delta y$. But since we assume that nodes n_A and n_B are distinct, derivations (8.1.2) and (8.1.8) are different, and thus the completed derivations are different. We may conclude that $x_\gamma x_\delta y$ has two different rightmost derivations and that G is ambiguous. By Exercise 5.1.3, no LL grammar is ambiguous. Hence, G cannot be LL, a contradiction of what was assumed.

Now we must show that $\alpha' = \alpha$. We note that α' is the string formed by concatenating the labels from the left of those nodes of T whose direct ancestor is an ancestor of n_A. (The reader should verify this property of rightmost derivations.) Now let us again consider the leftmost derivation (8.1.5), which has the same parse tree as the rightmost derivation (8.1.3). Let T' be the parse tree associated with derivation (8.1.3). The steps of derivation (8.1.5) up to $x_\alpha A \eta$ are the same as those of derivation (8.1.7) up to $x_\alpha A \eta$. Let n'_A be the node of T' corresponding to the nonterminal replaced in derivation (8.1.7) at the step $x_\alpha A\eta \underset{\text{lm}}{\Longrightarrow} x_\alpha \beta\eta$. Let Π be the preordering† of the interior nodes of parse tree T up to node n_A and Π' the preordering of the interior nodes of T' up to node n'_A. The ith node in Π matches the ith node in Π' in that both these nodes have the same label and that corresponding descendants either are matched or are to the right of n_A and n'_A, respectively.

The nodes in T' whose direct ancestor is an ancestor of n'_A have labels which, concatenated from the left, form α. But these nodes are matched with those in T which form α', so that $\alpha' = \alpha$. The proof is thus complete. $\square$

The grammar

$$S \longrightarrow A \mid B$$
$$A \longrightarrow aAb \mid 0$$
$$B \longrightarrow aBbb \mid 1$$

is an LR(0) grammar but not an LL grammar (Example 5.4), so the containment of LL grammars in LR grammars is proper. In fact, if we consider the LL and LR grammars along with the classes of grammars that are left- or right-parsable (by a DPDT with an endmarker), we have, by Theorems 5.5, 5.12, and 8.1, the containment relations shown in Fig. 8.5.

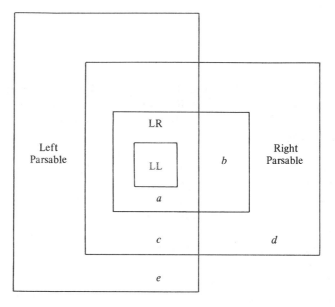

Fig. 8.5   Relations between classes of grammars.

†Π is the sequence of interior nodes of T in the order in which the nodes are expanded in a leftmost derivation.

We claim that each of the six classes of grammars depicted in Fig. 8.5 is nonempty. We know that there exists an LL grammar, so we must show the following.

THEOREM 8.2

There exist grammars which are

(1) LR and left-parsable but not LL.
(2) LR but not left-parsable.
(3) Left- and right-parsable but not LR.
(4) Right-parsable but not LR or left-parsable.
(5) Left-parsable but not right-parsable.

Proof. Each of the following grammars inhabits the appropriate region.

(1) The grammar G_a with productions

$$S \longrightarrow A \,|\, B$$
$$A \longrightarrow aaA \,|\, aa$$
$$B \longrightarrow aaB \,|\, a$$

is LR(1) and left-parsable but not LL.

(2) The grammar G_b with productions

$$S \longrightarrow Ab \,|\, Ac$$
$$A \longrightarrow AB \,|\, a$$
$$B \longrightarrow a$$

is LR(1) but not left-parsable. See Example 3.27 (p. 272 of Volume I).

(3) The grammar G_c with productions

$$S \longrightarrow Ab \,|\, Bc$$
$$A \longrightarrow Aa \,|\, a$$
$$B \longrightarrow Ba \,|\, a$$

is both left- and right-parsable but is not LR.

(4) The grammar G_d with productions

$$S \longrightarrow Ab \,|\, Bc$$
$$A \longrightarrow AC \,|\, a$$
$$B \longrightarrow BC \,|\, a$$
$$C \longrightarrow a$$

is right-parsable but neither LR nor left-parsable.

(5) The grammar G_e with productions

$$S \longrightarrow BAb \mid CAc$$
$$A \longrightarrow BA \mid a$$
$$B \longrightarrow a$$
$$C \longrightarrow a$$

is left-parsable but not right-parsable. See Example 3.26 (p. 271, Volume I).
□

8.1.2. LL Grammars in Greibach Normal Form

In this section we shall consider transformations which can be applied to LL grammars while preserving the LL property. Our first results involve e-productions. We shall give two algorithms which together convert an LL(k) grammar into an equivalent LL($k + 1$) grammar without e-productions. The first algorithm modifies a grammar so that each right-hand side is either e or begins with a symbol (possibly a terminal) which does not derive the empty string. The second algorithm converts a grammar satisfying that condition to one without e-productions. Both algorithms preserve the LL-ness of grammars.

DEFINITION

Let $G = (N, \Sigma, P, S)$ be a CFG. We say that nonterminal A is *nullable* if A can derive the empty string. Otherwise, a symbol in $N \cup \Sigma$ is said to be *nonnullable*. Every terminal is thus nonnullable. We say that G is *nonnullable* if each production in P is of the form $A \rightarrow e$ or $A \rightarrow X_1 \cdots X_k$, where X_1 is a nonnullable symbol.

ALGORITHM 8.1

Conversion to a nonnullable grammar.

Input. CFG $G = (N, \Sigma, P, S)$.

Output. A nonnullable context-free grammar $G_1 = (N_1, \Sigma, P_1, S_1)$ such that $L(G_1) = L(G) - \{e\}$.

Method.

(1) Let $N' = N \cup \{\bar{A} \mid A \text{ is a nullable nonterminal in } N\}$. The barred nonterminal $\bar{A}$ will generate the same strings as A except e. Hence $\bar{A}$ is nonnullable.

(2) If e is in $L(G)$, let $S_1 = \bar{S}$. Otherwise $S_1 = S$.

(3) Each non-e-production in P can be uniquely written in the form $A \rightarrow B_1 \cdots B_m X_1 \cdots X_n$ (with $m \geq 0$, $n \geq 0$, and $m + n > 0$), where each B_i is a nullable symbol, and if $n > 0$, X_1 is a nonnullable symbol. The

remaining X_j, $1 < j \leq n$, can be either nullable or nonnullable. Thus, X_1 is the leftmost nonnullable symbol on the right-hand side of the production. For each non-e-production $A \rightarrow B_1 \cdots B_m X_1 \cdots X_n$, we construct P' as follows:

(a) If $m \geq 1$, add to P' the m productions

$$A \longrightarrow \bar{B}_1 B_2 \cdots B_m X_1 \cdots X_n$$
$$A \longrightarrow \bar{B}_2 B_3 \cdots B_m X_1 \cdots X_n$$
$$\vdots$$
$$A \longrightarrow \bar{B}_m X_1 \cdots X_n$$

(b) If $n \geq 1$ and $m \geq 0$, add to P' the production

$$A \longrightarrow X_1 \cdots X_n$$

(c) In addition, if A is itself nullable, we also add to P' all the productions in (a) and (b) above with $\bar{A}$ instead of A on the left.

(4) If $A \rightarrow e$ is in P, we add $A \rightarrow e$ to P'.

(5) Let $G_1 = (N_1, \Sigma, P_1, S_1)$ be $G' = (N', \Sigma, P', S_1)$ with all useless symbols and productions removed. □

Example 8.1

Let G be the LL(1) grammar with productions

$$S \longrightarrow AB$$
$$A \longrightarrow aA \,|\, e$$
$$B \longrightarrow bA \,|\, e$$

Each of the nonterminals is nullable, so we introduce new nonterminals $\bar{S}$, $\bar{A}$, and $\bar{B}$; the first of these is the new start symbol. Productions $A \rightarrow aA$ and $B \rightarrow bA$ each begin with a nonnullable symbol, and so their right-hand sides are of the form $X_1 X_2$ for the purpose of step (3) of Algorithm 8.1. Thus, we retain these productions and also add $\bar{A} \rightarrow aA$ and $\bar{B} \rightarrow bA$ to the set of productions.

In the production $S \rightarrow AB$, each symbol on the right is nullable, and so we can write the right-hand side as $B_1 B_2$. This production is replaced by the following four productions:

$$S \longrightarrow \bar{A}B \,|\, \bar{B}$$
$$\bar{S} \longrightarrow \bar{A}B \,|\, \bar{B}$$

Since $\bar{S}$ is the new start symbol, we find that S is now inaccessible. The final set of productions constructed by Algorithm 8.1 is

$$\bar{S} \longrightarrow \bar{A}B \mid \bar{B}$$
$$\bar{A} \longrightarrow aA$$
$$A \longrightarrow aA \mid e$$
$$\bar{B} \longrightarrow bA$$
$$B \longrightarrow bA \mid e \quad \square$$

The following theorem shows that Algorithm 8.1 preserves the LL(k)-ness of a grammar.

THEOREM 8.3

If G_1 is constructed from G by Algorithm 8.1, then

(1) $L(G_1) = L(G) - \{e\}$, and
(2) If G is LL(k), then so is G_1.

Proof.

(1) Straightforward induction on the length of strings shows that for all A in N,

(a) $A \xoverset{*}{\underset{G_1}{\Longrightarrow}} w$ if and only if $A \xoverset{*}{\underset{G}{\Longrightarrow}} w$ and

(b) $\bar{A} \xoverset{*}{\underset{G_1}{\Longrightarrow}} w$ if and only if $w \neq e$ and $A \xoverset{*}{\underset{G}{\Longrightarrow}} w$.

The details are left for the Exercises.

For part (2), assume the contrary. Then we can find derivations in G_1

$$S_1 \xoverset{*}{\underset{G_1 \, lm}{\Longrightarrow}} w\hat{A}\alpha \underset{G_1 \, lm}{\Longrightarrow} w\beta\alpha \xoverset{*}{\underset{G_1 \, lm}{\Longrightarrow}} wx$$
$$S_1 \xoverset{*}{\underset{G_1 \, lm}{\Longrightarrow}} w\hat{A}\alpha \underset{G_1 \, lm}{\Longrightarrow} wy\alpha \xoverset{*}{\underset{G_1 \, lm}{\Longrightarrow}} wy$$

where $\text{FIRST}_k(x) = \text{FIRST}_k(y)$, $\beta \neq \gamma$, and $\hat{A}$ is either A or $\bar{A}$.

We can construct from these two derivations corresponding derivations in G of wx and wy as follows. First define $h(A) = h(\bar{A}) = A$ for $A \in$ N and $h(a) = a$ for $a \in \Sigma$.

For each production $\hat{B} \longrightarrow \delta$ in P_1 we can find a production $B \longrightarrow \delta'h(\delta)$ in P from which it was constructed in step (3) of Algorithm 8.1. That is, $B = h(\hat{B})$, and δ' is some (possibly empty) string of nullable symbols. Each time production $\hat{B} \longrightarrow \delta$ is used in one of the derivations in G_1, in the corresponding derivation in G we replace it by $B \longrightarrow \delta'h(\delta)$, followed by a leftmost derivation of e from δ' if $\delta' \neq e$. In this manner, we construct the derivations in G:

$$S \underset{G \text{ lm}}{\overset{*}{\Longrightarrow}} wAh(\alpha) \underset{G \text{ lm}}{\Longrightarrow} w\beta'h(\beta)h(\alpha) \underset{G \text{ lm}}{\overset{*}{\Longrightarrow}} wh(\beta)h(\alpha) \underset{G \text{ lm}}{\overset{*}{\Longrightarrow}} wx$$

$$S \underset{G \text{ lm}}{\overset{*}{\Longrightarrow}} wAh(\alpha) \underset{G \text{ lm}}{\Longrightarrow} w\gamma'h(\gamma)h(\alpha) \underset{G \text{ lm}}{\overset{*}{\Longrightarrow}} wh(\gamma)h(\alpha) \underset{G \text{ lm}}{\overset{*}{\Longrightarrow}} wy$$

We can write the steps between $w\beta'h(\beta)h(\alpha)$ and $wh(\beta)h(\alpha)$ as

$$w\beta'h(\beta)h(\alpha) = w\delta_1 \underset{\text{lm}}{\Longrightarrow} w\delta_2 \underset{\text{lm}}{\Longrightarrow} \cdots \underset{\text{lm}}{\Longrightarrow} w\delta_n = wh(\beta)h(\alpha)$$

and those between $w\gamma'h(\gamma)h(\alpha)$ and $wh(\gamma)h(\alpha)$ as

$$w\gamma'h(\gamma)h(\alpha) = w\epsilon_1 \underset{\text{lm}}{\Longrightarrow} w\epsilon_2 \underset{\text{lm}}{\Longrightarrow} \cdots \underset{\text{lm}}{\Longrightarrow} w\epsilon_m = wh(\gamma)h(\alpha).$$

If $z = \text{FIRST}(x) = \text{FIRST}(y)$, then we claim that z is in $\text{FIRST}(\delta_i)$ and $\text{FIRST}(\epsilon_i)$ for all i, since β' and γ' consist only of nullable symbols (if β' and γ' are not e). Since G is LL(k), it follows that $\delta_i = \epsilon_i$ for all i. In particular, $\beta'h(\beta) = \gamma'h(\gamma)$. Thus, β and γ are formed from the same production by Algorithm 8.1. If $\beta' \neq \gamma'$, then in one of the above derivations, a nonterminal derives e, while in the other it does not. We may contradict the LL(k)-ness of G in this way and so conclude that $\beta' = \gamma'$. Since β and γ are assumed to be different, they cannot both be e, and so they each start with the same, nonnullable symbol. It is then possible to conclude that $m = n$ and arrive at the contradiction $\beta = \gamma$. $\square$

Our next transformation will eliminate e-productions entirely from an LL grammar G. We shall assume that $e \notin L(G)$. Our strategy will be to first apply Algorithm 8.1 to an LL(k) grammar, and then to combine nonnullable symbols in derivations with all following nullable symbols, replacing such a string by a single symbol. If the grammar is LL(k), then there is a limit to the number of consecutive nullable symbols which can follow a nonnullable symbol.

DEFINITION

Let $G = (N, \Sigma, P, S)$ be a CFG. Let V_G be the set of symbols of the form $[XB_1 \cdots B_n]$ such that

(1) X is a nonnullable symbol of G (possibly a terminal).
(2) $B_1, \ldots, B_n$ are nullable symbols (hence nonterminals).
(3) If $i \neq j$, then $B_i \neq B_j$. (That is, the list $B_1, \ldots, B_n$ contains no repeats.)

Define the homomorphism g from V_G to $(N \cup \Sigma)^*$ by $g([\alpha]) = \alpha$.

LEMMA 8.2

Let $G = (N, \Sigma, P, S)$ be a nonnullable $LL(k)$ grammar such that every nonterminal derives at least one nonempty terminal string. Let V_G and g be as defined above. Then for each left-sentential form α of G such that $\alpha \neq e$ there is a unique β in V_G^* such that $h(\beta) = \alpha$.

Proof. We can write α uniquely as $\alpha_1\alpha_2 \cdots \alpha_m$, $m \geq 1$, where each α_i is a nonnullable symbol X followed by some string of nullable symbols (because every non-e-sentential form of G begins with a nonnullable symbol). It suffices to show that $[\alpha_i]$ is in V_G for each i. If not, then we can write α_i as $X\beta B\gamma B\delta$, where B is some nullable symbol and β, γ, and δ consist only of nullable symbols, i.e., α_i does not satisfy condition (3) of the definition of V_G. Let w be a nonempty string such that $B \underset{G}{\overset{*}{\Rightarrow}} w$. Then there are two distinct leftmost derivations:

$$\beta B\gamma B\delta \underset{1m}{\overset{*}{\Longrightarrow}} B\gamma B\delta \underset{1m}{\overset{*}{\Longrightarrow}} w\gamma B\delta \underset{1m}{\overset{*}{\Longrightarrow}} w$$

and

$$\beta B\gamma B\delta \underset{1m}{\overset{*}{\Longrightarrow}} B\delta \underset{1m}{\overset{*}{\Longrightarrow}} w\delta \underset{1m}{\overset{*}{\Longrightarrow}} w$$

From these, it is straightforward to show that G is ambiguous and hence not LL. $\square$

The following algorithm can be used to prove that every $LL(k)$ language without e has an $LL(k + 1)$ grammar with no e-productions.

ALGORITHM 8.2

Elimination of e-productions from an $LL(k)$ grammar.

Input. An $LL(k)$ grammar $G_1 = (N_1, \Sigma, P_1, S_1)$.

Output. An $LL(k + 1)$ grammar $G = (N, \Sigma, P, S)$ such that $L(G) = L(G_1) - \{e\}$.

Method.

(1) First apply Algorithm 8.1 to obtain a nonnullable $LL(k)$ grammar $G_2 = (N_2, \Sigma, P_2, S_2)$.

(2) Eliminate from G_2 each nonterminal A that derives only the empty string by deleting A from the right-hand sides of productions in which it appears and then deleting all A-productions. Let the resulting grammar be $G_3 = (N_3, \Sigma, P_3, S_2)$.

(3) Construct grammar $G = (N, \Sigma, P, S)$ as follows:

    (a) Let N be the set of symbols $[X\alpha]$ such that

        (i) X is a nonnullable symbol of G_3,

        (ii) α is a string of nullable symbols,

   (iii) $X\alpha \notin \Sigma$ (i.e., we do not have $X \in \Sigma$ and $\alpha = e$ simultaneously),
   (iv) α has no repeating symbols, and
   (v) $X\alpha$ actually appears as a substring of some left-sentential form of G_3.
(b) $S = [S_2]$.
(c) Let g be the homomorphism $g([\alpha]) = \alpha$ for all $[\alpha]$ in N and let $g(a) = a$ for a in Σ. Since $g^{-1}(\beta)$ contains at most one member, we use $g^{-1}(\beta)$ to stand for γ if γ is the lone member of $g^{-1}(\beta)$. We construct P as follows:
   (i) Let $[A\alpha]$ be in N and let $A \rightarrow \beta$ be a production in P_3. Then $[A\alpha] \rightarrow g^{-1}(\beta\alpha)$ is a production in P.
   (ii) Let $[a\alpha A\beta]$ be in N, with $a \in \Sigma$ and $A \in N_3$. Let $A \rightarrow \gamma$ be in P_3, with $\gamma \neq e$. Then $[a\alpha A\beta] \rightarrow ag^{-1}(\gamma\beta)$ is in P.
   (iii) Let $[a\alpha A\beta]$ be in N with $a \in \Sigma$. Then $[a\alpha A\beta] \rightarrow a$ is also in P. □

Example 8.2

Let us consider the grammar of Example 8.1. Algorithm 8.1 has already been applied in that example. Step (2) of Algorithm 8.2 does not affect the grammar. We shall generate the productions of grammar G as needed to assure that each nonterminal involved appears in some left-sentential form. The start symbol is $[\bar{S}]$. There are two $\bar{S}$-productions, with right-hand sides $\bar{A}B$ and $\bar{B}$. Since $\bar{A}$ and $\bar{B}$ are nonnullable but B is nullable, $g^{-1}(\bar{A}B) = [\bar{A}B]$ and $g^{-1}(\bar{B}) = [\bar{B}]$. Thus, by rule (i) of step (3c), we have productions

$$[\bar{S}] \longrightarrow [\bar{A}B] \,|\, [\bar{B}]$$

Let us consider nonterminal $[\bar{A}B]$. $\bar{A}$ has one production, $\bar{A} \rightarrow aA$. Since $g^{-1}(aAB) = [aAB]$, we add production

$$[\bar{A}B] \longrightarrow [aAB]$$

Consideration of $[\bar{B}]$ causes us to add

$$[\bar{B}] \longrightarrow [bA]$$

We now apply rules (ii) and (iii) to the nonterminal $[aAB]$. There is one non-e-production for A and one for B. Since $g^{-1}(aAB) = [aAB]$, we add

$$[aAB] \longrightarrow a[aAB]$$

corresponding to the A-production. Since $g^{-1}(bA) = [bA]$, we add

$$[aAB] \longrightarrow a[bA]$$

corresponding to the B-production. By step (iii), we add

$$[aAB] \longrightarrow a$$

Similarly, from nonterminal $[bA]$ we get

$$[bA] \longrightarrow b[aA] \,|\, b$$

Then, considering the newly introduced nonterminal $[aA]$, we add productions

$$[aA] \longrightarrow a[aA] \,|\, a$$

Thus, we have constructed the productions for all nonterminals introduced and so completed the construction of G. $\quad\square$

THEOREM 8.4

The grammar G constructed from G_1 in Algorithm 8.2 is such that

(1) $L(G) = L(G_1) - \{e\}$, and
(2) If G_1 is LL(k), then G is LL($k + 1$).

Proof. Let g be the homomorphism in step (3c) of Algorithm 8.2.

(1) A straightforward inductive argument shows that $A \overset{*}{\underset{G_3}{\Rightarrow}} \beta$, where $A \in N$ and $\beta \in (N \cup \Sigma)^*$, if and only if $g(A) \overset{*}{\underset{G}{\Rightarrow}} g(\beta)$ and $\beta \neq e$. Thus, $[S_2] \overset{*}{\underset{G_3}{\Rightarrow}} w$, for w in Σ^*, if and only if $S_2 \overset{*}{\underset{G}{\Rightarrow}} w$ and $w \neq e$. Hence, $L(G) = L(G_3)$. That $L(G_2) = L(G_1) - \{e\}$ is part (1) of Theorem 8.3, and it is easy to see that step (2) of Algorithm 8.2, converting G_2 to G_3, does not change the language generated.

(2) Here, the argument is similar to that of the second part of Theorem 8.2. Given a leftmost derivation in G, we find a corresponding one in G_3 and show that an LL($k + 1$) conflict in the former implies an LL(k) conflict in the latter. The intuitive reason for the parameter $k + 1$, instead of k, is that if a production of G constructed in step (3cii) or (iii) is used, the terminal a is still part of the lookahead when we must determine which production to apply for $\alpha A\beta$. Let us suppose that G is not LL($k + 1$). Then there exist derivations

$$S \overset{*}{\underset{G\ \mathrm{lm}}{\Longrightarrow}} wA\alpha \underset{G\ \mathrm{lm}}{\Longrightarrow} w\beta\alpha \overset{*}{\underset{G\ \mathrm{lm}}{\Longrightarrow}} wx$$

and

$$S \overset{*}{\underset{G\ \mathrm{lm}}{\Longrightarrow}} wA\alpha \underset{G\ \mathrm{lm}}{\Longrightarrow} w\gamma\alpha \overset{*}{\underset{G\ \mathrm{lm}}{\Longrightarrow}} wy$$

where $\beta \neq \gamma$, but $\mathrm{FIRST}_{k+1}(x) = \mathrm{FIRST}_{k+1}(y)$. We construct corresponding derivations in G_3 as follows:

(a) Each time production $[A\alpha] \to g^{-1}(\beta\alpha)$, which is in P because of rule (3ci), is used, we use production $A \to \beta$ of G_3.

(b) Each time production $[a\alpha A\beta] \to ag^{-1}(\gamma\beta)$, which is in P by rule (3cii), is used, we do a leftmost derivation of e from α, followed by an application of production $A \to \gamma$.

(c) Each time production $[a\alpha A\beta] \to a$ is used, we do a leftmost derivation of e from $\alpha A\beta$. Note that this derivation will involve one or more steps, since $\alpha A\beta \neq e$.

Thus, corresponding to the derivation $S \underset{G\,\text{lm}}{\overset{*}{\Longrightarrow}} wA\alpha$ is a unique derivation $g(S) \underset{G_3\,\text{lm}}{\overset{*}{\Longrightarrow}} wg(A)g(\alpha)$. In the case that A is a bracketed string of symbols beginning with a terminal, say a, the border† of $wg(A)g(\alpha)$ is one symbol to the right of w. Otherwise it is immediately to the right of w. In either case, since x and y agree for $k + 1$ symbols and G_3 is LL(k), the steps in G_3 corresponding to the application of productions $A \to \beta$ and $A \to \gamma$ in G must be the same.

Straightforward examination of the three different origins of productions of G and their relation to their corresponding derivations in G_3 suffices to show that we must have $\beta = \gamma$, contrary to hypothesis. That is, let $A = [\delta]$. If δ begins with a nonterminal, say $\delta = C\delta'$, case (2a) above must apply in both derivations. There is one production of G_3, say $C \to \delta''$, such that $\beta = \gamma = g^{-1}(\delta''\delta')$.

If δ begins with a terminal, say $\delta = a\delta'$, case (2b) or (2c) must apply. The two derivations in G_3 replace a certain prefix of δ by e, followed by the application of a non-e-production in case (2b). It is easy to argue that $\beta = \gamma$ in either case. $\square$

We shall now prove that every LL(k) language has an LL($k + 1$) grammar in Greibach normal form (GNF). This theorem has several important applications and will be used as a tool to derive other results. Two preliminary lemmas are needed.

LEMMA 8.3

No LL(k) grammar is left-recursive.

Proof. Suppose that $G = (N, \Sigma, P, S)$ has a left-recursive nonterminal A. Then there is a derivation $A \overset{+}{\Rightarrow} A\alpha$. If $\alpha \overset{*}{\Rightarrow} e$, then it is easy to show that G is ambiguous and hence cannot be LL. Thus, assume that $\alpha \overset{*}{\Rightarrow} v$ for some $v \in \Sigma^+$. We can further assume that $A \overset{*}{\Rightarrow} u$ for some $u \in \Sigma^*$ and that there exists a derivation

$$S \underset{\text{lm}}{\overset{*}{\Longrightarrow}} wA\delta \underset{\text{lm}}{\overset{*}{\Longrightarrow}} wA\alpha^k\delta \underset{\text{lm}}{\overset{*}{\Longrightarrow}} wuv^k x$$

†Border as in Section 5.1.1.

Hence, there is another derivation:

$$S \xrightarrow[lm]{*} wA\delta \xrightarrow[lm]{*} wA\alpha^k\delta \xrightarrow[lm]{*} wA\alpha^{k+1}\delta \xrightarrow[lm]{*} wuv^{k+1}x$$

Since $\text{FIRST}_k(uv^kx) = \text{FIRST}_k(uv^{k+1}x)$, we can readily obtain a contradiction of the LL(k) definition from these two derivations, for arbitrary k.   □

LEMMA 8.4

Let $G = (N, \Sigma, P, S)$ be a CFG with $A \rightarrow B\alpha$ in P, where $B \in N$. Let $B \rightarrow \beta_1 | \beta_2 | \cdots | \beta_m$ be all the B-productions of G and let $G_1 = (N, \Sigma, P_1, S)$ be formed by deleting $A \rightarrow B\alpha$ from P and substituting the productions $A \rightarrow \beta_1\alpha | \beta_2\alpha | \cdots | \beta_m\alpha$. Then $L(G_1) = L(G)$, and if G is LL(k), then so is G_1.

Proof. By Lemma 2.14, $L(G_1) = L(G)$. To show that G_1 is LL(k) when G is, we observe that leftmost derivations in G_1 are essentially the same as those of G, except that the successive application of the productions $A \rightarrow B\alpha$ and $B \rightarrow \beta_i$ in G is done in one step in G_1. Informally, since $B\alpha$ begins with a nonterminal, the two steps in G are dictated by the same k symbol lookahead string. Thus, when parsing according to G_1, that lookahead dictates the use of the production $A \rightarrow \beta_i\alpha$. A more detailed proof is left for the Exercises.   □

ALGORITHM 8.3

Conversion of an LL(k) grammar to an LL($k + 1$) grammar in GNF.

Input. LL(k) grammar $G_1 = (N_1, \Sigma, P_1, S_1)$.

Output. LL($k + 1$) grammar $G = (N, \Sigma, P, S)$ in Greibach normal form, such that $L(G) = L(G_1) - \{e\}$.

Method.

(1) Using Algorithm 8.2, construct from G_1 an LL($k + 1$) grammar $G_2 = (N_2, \Sigma, P_2, S)$ with no e-productions.

(2) Number the nonterminals of N_2, say $N_2 = \{A_1, \ldots, A_m\}$, such that if $A_i \rightarrow A_j\alpha$ is in P_2, then $j > i$. Since, by Lemma 8.3, G is not left-recursive, we can do this ordering by Lemma 2.16.

(3) Successively, for $i = m - 1, m - 2, \ldots, 1$, replace all productions $A_i \rightarrow A_j\alpha$ by those $A_i \rightarrow \beta\alpha$ such that $A_j \rightarrow \beta$ is currently a production. We shall show that this operation causes all productions to have right-hand sides that begin with terminals. Call the new grammar $G_3 = (N_3, \Sigma, P_3, S)$.

(4) For each a in Σ, let X_a be a new nonterminal symbol. Let

$$N = N_3 \cup \{X_a | a \in \Sigma\}.$$

Let P be formed from P_3 by replacing each instance of terminal a, which is not the leftmost symbol of its string, by X_a and by adding productions $X_a \rightarrow a$ for each a. Let $G = (N, \Sigma, P, S)$. G is in GNF. $\square$

THEOREM 8.5

Every LL(k) language has an LL($k + 1$) grammar in GNF.

Proof. It suffices to show that G constructed in Algorithm 8.3 is LL($k + 1$) if G_1 is LL(k). By Lemma 8.4, G_3 is LL($k + 1$). We claim that the right-hand side of every production of G_3 begins with a terminal. Since G_1 is not left-recursive, the argument is the same as for Algorithm 2.14.

It is easy to show that the construction of step (4) preserves the LL($k + 1$) property and the language generated. It is also clear that G is in GNF. The proofs are left for the Exercises. $\square$

8.1.3. The Equivalence Problem for LL Grammars

We are almost prepared to give an algorithm to test if two LL(k) grammars are equivalent. However, one additional concept is necessary.

DEFINITION

Let $G = (N, \Sigma, P, S)$ be a CFG. For α in $(N \cup \Sigma)^*$, we define the *thickness* of α in G, denoted $\mathrm{TH}^G(\alpha)$, to be the length of the shortest string w in Σ^* such that $\alpha \overset{*}{\underset{G}{\Rightarrow}} w$. We leave for the Exercises the observations that $\mathrm{TH}^G(\alpha\beta) = \mathrm{TH}^G(\alpha) + \mathrm{TH}^G(\beta)$ and that if $\alpha \overset{*}{\Rightarrow} \beta$, then $\mathrm{TH}^G(\alpha) \leq \mathrm{TH}^G(\beta)$.

We further define $\mathrm{TH}_k^G(\alpha, w)$, where α is in $(N \cup \Sigma)^*$ and w is in Σ^{*k}, to be the length of the shortest string x in Σ^* such that $\alpha \overset{*}{\underset{G}{\Rightarrow}} x$ and $w = \mathrm{FIRST}_k(x)$. If no such x exists, $\mathrm{TH}_k^G(\alpha, w)$ is undefined. We omit k and G from TH_k^G or TH^G where obvious.

The algorithm to test the equivalence of two LL(k) grammars is based on the following lemma.

LEMMA 8.5

Let $G_1 = (N_1, \Sigma, P_1, S_1)$ and $G_2 = (N_2, \Sigma, P_2, S_2)$ be LL(k) grammars in GNF such that $L(G_1) = L(G_2)$. Then there is a constant p, depending on G_1 and G_2, with the following property. Suppose that $S_1 \underset{G_1 \,\mathrm{lm}}{\overset{*}{\Longrightarrow}} w\alpha \underset{G_1 \,\mathrm{lm}}{\overset{*}{\Longrightarrow}} wx$ and that $S_2 \underset{G_2 \,\mathrm{lm}}{\overset{*}{\Longrightarrow}} w\beta \underset{G_2 \,\mathrm{lm}}{\overset{*}{\Longrightarrow}} wy$, where α and β are the open portions of $w\alpha$ and $w\beta$, and $\mathrm{FIRST}_k(x) = \mathrm{FIRST}_k(y)$. Then $|\,\mathrm{TH}^{G_1}(\alpha) - \mathrm{TH}^{G_2}(\beta)\,| \leq p$.†

Proof. Let t be the maximum of $\mathrm{TH}^{G_1}(\gamma)$ or $\mathrm{TH}^{G_2}(\gamma)$ such that γ is a right-hand side of a production in P_1 or P_2, respectively. Let $p = t(k + 1)$, and suppose in contradiction that

(8.1.9) $\mathrm{TH}^{G_1}(\alpha) - \mathrm{TH}^{G_2}(\beta) > p$

---

†Absolute value, not length, is meant here by $|\quad|$.

We shall show that as a consequence of this assumption, $L(G_1) \neq L(G_2)$. Let $z = \text{FIRST}(x) = \text{FIRST}(y)$. We claim that $\text{TH}^{G_2}(\beta, z) \leq \text{TH}^{G_2}(\beta) + p$, for there is a derivation $\beta \underset{G_2 \, \text{lm}}{\overset{*}{\Longrightarrow}} y$, and hence, since G_2 is in GNF, there is a derivation, $\beta \underset{G_2 \, \text{lm}}{\overset{*}{\Longrightarrow}} z\delta$ for some δ, requiring no more than k steps. It is easy to show that

$$\text{TH}^{G_2}(\delta) \leq \text{TH}^{G_2}(\beta) + kt$$

since "at worst" δ is β with most of the right-hand sides of k productions appended. We conclude that

$$(8.1.10) \qquad \text{TH}^{G_2}(\beta, z) \leq k + \text{TH}^{G_2}(\delta) \leq \text{TH}^{G_2}(\beta) + p$$

It is trivial to show that $\text{TH}^{G_1}(\alpha, z) \geq \text{TH}^{G_1}(\alpha)$, and so from (8.1.9) and (8.1.10) we have

$$(8.1.11) \qquad \text{TH}^{G_1}(\alpha, z) > \text{TH}^{G_2}(\beta, z)$$

If we let u be a shortest string derivable from δ, then $\text{TH}^{G_1}(\beta, z) \leq |zu|$. The string wzu is in $L(G_2)$, since $S \underset{G_2}{\overset{*}{\Rightarrow}} w\beta \underset{G_2}{\overset{*}{\Rightarrow}} wz\delta \underset{G_2}{\overset{*}{\Rightarrow}} wzu$. But it is impossible that $\alpha \underset{G_2}{\overset{*}{\Rightarrow}} zu$, because by (8.1.11) $\text{TH}^{G_1}(\alpha, z) > |zu|$. Since G_1 is LL(k), if there is any leftmost derivation of wzu in G_1, it begins with the derivation $S_1 \underset{G_1 \, \text{lm}}{\overset{*}{\Longrightarrow}} w\alpha$. Thus, wzu is not in $L(G_1)$, contradicting the assumption that $L(G_1) = L(G_2)$. We conclude that $\text{TH}^{G_1}(\alpha) - \text{TH}^{G_2}(\beta) \leq p = t(k + 1)$. The case $\text{TH}^{G_2}(\beta) - \text{TH}^{G_1}(\alpha) > p$ is handled symmetrically. □

LEMMA 8.6

It is decidable, for DPDA P, whether P accepts all strings over its input alphabet.

Proof. By Theorem 2.23, $\overline{L(P)}$, the complement of $L(P)$, is a deterministic language and hence a CFL. Moreover, we can effectively construct a CFG G such that $L(G) = \overline{L(P)}$. Algorithm 2.7 can be used to test if $L(G) = \varnothing$. Thus, we can determine whether P accepts all strings over its input alphabet. □

We are now ready to describe the algorithm to test the equivalence of two LL(k) grammars.

THEOREM 8.6

It is decidable, for two LL(k) grammars $G_1 = (N_1, \Sigma_1, P_1, S_1)$ and $G_2 = (N_2, \Sigma_2, P_2, S_2)$, whether $L(G_1) = L(G_2)$.

Proof. We first construct, by Algorithm 8.3, GNF grammars G_1' and G_2' equivalent to G_1 and G_2, respectively (except possibly for the empty string, which can be handled in an obvious way). We then construct a DPDA P which accepts an input string w in $(\Sigma_1 \cup \Sigma_2)^*$ if and only if

(1) w is in both $L(G_1)$ and $L(G_2)$ or
(2) w is in neither $L(G_1)$ nor $L(G_2)$.

Thus, $L(G_1) = L(G_2)$ if and only if $L(P) = (\Sigma_1 \cup \Sigma_2)^*$. We can use Lemma 8.6 for this test.

Thus, to complete the proof, all we need to do is show how we construct the DPDA P. P has a pushdown list consisting of two parallel tracks. P processes an input string by simultaneously parsing its input top-down according to G_1' and G_2'.

Suppose that P's input is of the form wx. After simulating $|w|$ steps of the leftmost derivations in G_1' and G_2', P will have on its pushdown list the contents of each stack of the k-predictive parser for G_1' and G_2', as shown in Fig. 8.6. We note from Algorithm 5.3 that the stack contents are in each

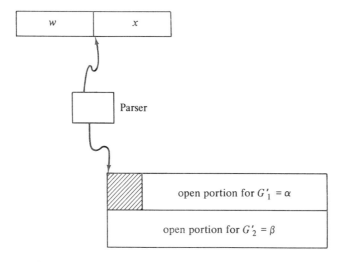

Fig. 8.6   Representation of left sentential forms $w\alpha$ and $w\beta$.

case the open portions of the two current left-sentential forms, together with some extra information appended to the nonterminals to guide the parsing. We can thus think of the stack contents as consisting of symbols of G_1' and G_2'. The extra information is carried along automatically.

Note that the two open portions may not take the same amount of space. However, since we can bound from above the difference in their thicknesses, then, whenever $L(G_1) = L(G_2)$, we know that P can simulate both derivations by reading and writing a fixed distance down its pushdown list. Since G_1' and G_2' are in GNF, P alternately simulates one step of the derivation in G_1', one in G_2', and then moves its input head one position. If one parse reaches an error condition, the simulation of the parse in the remaining grammar continues until it reaches an error or accepting configuration.

It is necessary only to explain how the two open portions can be placed so that they have approximately the same length, on the assumption that $L(G_1) = L(G_2)$. By Lemma 8.5, there is a constant p such that the thicknesses of the two open portions, resulting from processing the prefix of any input string, do not differ by more than p.

For each grammar symbol of thickness t, P will reserve t cells of the appropriate track of its pushdown list, placing the symbol on one of them. Since G_1' and G_2' are in GNF, there are no nullable symbols in either grammar, and so $t \geq 1$ in each case. Since the two strings α and β of Fig. 8.6 differ in thickness by at most p, their representations on P's pushdown list differ in length by at most p cells.

To complete the proof, we design P to reject its input if the two open portions on its pushdown list ever have thicknesses differing by more than p symbols. By Lemma 8.5, $L(G_1) \neq L(G_2)$ in this case. Also, should the thicknesses never differ by more than p, P accepts its input if and only if it finds a parse of that input in both G_1' and G_2' or in neither of G_1' and G_2'. Thus, P accepts all strings over its input alphabet if and only if $L(G_1) = L(G_2)$. $\square$

8.1.4. The Hierarchy of LL Languages

We shall show that for all $k \geq 0$ the LL(k) languages are a proper subset of the LL($k + 1$) languages. As we shall see, this situation is in direct contrast to the situation for LR languages, where for each LR language we can find an LR(1) grammar.

Consider the sequence of languages $L_1, L_2, \ldots, L_k, \ldots$, where

$$L_k = \{a^n w \mid n \geq 1 \text{ and } w \text{ is in } \{b, c, b^k d\}^n\}.$$

In this section, we shall show that L_k is an LL(k) language but not an LL($k - 1$) language, thereby demonstrating that there is an infinite proper hierarchy of LL(k) languages. The following LL(k) grammar generates L_k:

$$S \longrightarrow aT$$
$$T \longrightarrow SA \mid A$$
$$A \longrightarrow bB \mid c$$
$$B \longrightarrow b^{k-1}d \mid e$$

We now show that every LL(k) grammar for L_k must contain at least one e-production.

LEMMA 8.7

L_k is not generated by any LL(k) grammar without e-productions.

Proof. Assume the contrary. Then we may, by steps (2)–(4) of Algorithm 8.3, find an LL(k) grammar, $G = (N, \{a, b, c, d\}, P, S)$, in GNF such that $L(G) = L_k$. We shall now proceed to show that any such grammar must generate sentences not in L_k.

Consider the sequence of strings α_i, $i = 1, 2, \ldots$, such that

$$S \underset{\text{lm}}{\overset{i}{\Rightarrow}} a^i\alpha_i \underset{\text{lm}}{\overset{k-1}{\Rightarrow}} a^{i+k-1}\delta$$

for some δ. Since G is LL(k) and in GNF, α_i is unique for each i. For if not, let $\alpha_i = \alpha_j$. Then it is easy to show that $a^{i+k}b^{j+k}$ is in $L(G)$, which is contrary to assumptions if $i \neq j$. Thus, we can find i such that $|\alpha_i| \geq 2k - 1$.

Pick a value of i such that $\alpha_i = \beta B \gamma$ for some β and γ in N* and $B \in$ N such that $|\beta|$ and $|\gamma|$ are at least $k - 1$. Since G is LL(k), the derivation of the sentence $a^{i+k-1}b^{i+k-1}$ is of the form

$$S \underset{\text{lm}}{\overset{*}{\Rightarrow}} a^i\beta B\gamma \underset{\text{lm}}{\overset{*}{\Rightarrow}} a^{i+k-1}b^{i+k-1}.$$

Since G is in GNF and $|\beta| \geq k - 1$, we must have $\beta \overset{*}{\Rightarrow} a^{k-1}b^j$, $B \overset{*}{\Rightarrow} b^l$, and $\gamma \overset{*}{\Rightarrow} b^m$ for some $j \geq 0$, $l \geq 1$, and $m \geq k - 1$, where

$$i + k - 1 = j + l + m.$$

If we consider the derivation of the sentence $a^{i+k-1}c^{i+k-1}$, we can also conclude that $B \overset{*}{\Rightarrow} c^n$ for some $n \geq 1$.

Finally, if we consider the derivation of the sentence $a^{i+k-1}b^{j+l+k-1}db^m$, we find that

$$S \underset{\text{lm}}{\overset{*}{\Rightarrow}} a^i\beta B\gamma \underset{\text{lm}}{\overset{*}{\Rightarrow}} a^{i+k-1}b^j B\gamma \underset{\text{lm}}{\overset{*}{\Rightarrow}} a^{i+k-1}b^{j+l}\gamma \underset{\text{lm}}{\overset{*}{\Rightarrow}} a^{i+k-1}b^{j+l+k-1}db^m.$$

The existence of the latter derivation follows from the fact that the sentence $a^{i+k-1}b^{j+l+k-1}db^m$ agrees with $a^{i+k-1}b^{i+k-1}$ for $(i + k - 1) + (j + l + k - 1)$ symbols. Thus, $\gamma \overset{*}{\Rightarrow} b^{k-1}db^m$.

Putting these partial derivations together, we can obtain the derivation

$$S \underset{\text{lm}}{\overset{*}{\Rightarrow}} a^i\beta B\gamma \underset{\text{lm}}{\overset{*}{\Rightarrow}} a^{i+k-1}b^j B\gamma \underset{\text{lm}}{\overset{*}{\Rightarrow}} a^{i+k-1}b^j c^n\gamma \underset{\text{lm}}{\overset{*}{\Rightarrow}} a^{i+k-1}b^j c^n b^{k-1}db^m$$

But the result of this derivation is not in L_k, because it contains a substring of the form $cb^{k-1}d$. (Every d must have k b's before it.) We conclude that L_k has no LL(k) grammar without e-productions. □

We now show that if a language L is generated by an LL(k) grammar with no e-productions, then L is an LL($k - 1$) language.

THEOREM 8.7

If a language L has an LL(k) grammar without e-productions, $k \geq 2$, then L has an LL($k - 1$) grammar.

Proof. By the third step of Algorithm 8.3 we can find an LL(k) grammar in GNF for L. Let $G = (N, \Sigma, P, S)$ be such a grammar. From G, we can construct LL($k - 1$) grammar $G_1 = (N_1, \Sigma, P_1, S)$, where

(1) $N_1 = N \cup \{[A, a] \,|\, A \in N, \ a \in \Sigma, \text{ and } A \rightarrow a\alpha \text{ is in } P \text{ for some } \alpha\}$ and

(2) $P_1 = \{A \rightarrow a[A, a] \,|\, A \rightarrow a\alpha \text{ is in } P\} \cup \{[A, a] \rightarrow \alpha \,|\, A \rightarrow a\alpha \text{ is in } P\}$. It is left for the Exercises to prove that G_1 is LL($k - 1$). Note that the construction here is an example of left factoring. ☐

Example 8.3

Let us consider G_k, the natural LL($k + 1$) grammar for the language L_k of Lemma 8.7, defined by

$$S \longrightarrow aSA \,|\, aA$$
$$A \longrightarrow b^k d \,|\, b \,|\, c$$

We construct an LL(k) grammar for L_k by adding the new symbols $[S, a]$, $[A, b]$, and $[A, c]$. This new grammar G'_k is defined by productions

$$S \longrightarrow a[S, a]$$
$$A \longrightarrow b[A, b] \,|\, c[A, c]$$
$$[S, a] \longrightarrow SA \,|\, A$$
$$[A, b] \longrightarrow b^{k-1} d \,|\, e$$
$$[A, c] \longrightarrow e$$

It is left for the Exercises to prove that G_k and G'_k are, respectively, LL($k + 1$) and LL(k). ☐

THEOREM 8.8

For all $k \geq 1$, the class of LL($k - 1$) languages is properly included within the LL(k) languages.

Proof. Clearly, the LL(0) languages are a proper subset of the LL(1) languages. For $k > 1$, using Lemma 8.7, the language L_k has no LL(k) grammar without e-productions. Hence, by Theorem 8.4 it has no LL($k - 1$) grammar. It does, as we have seen, have an LL(k) grammar. ☐

EXERCISES

8.1.1. Give additional examples of grammars which are
(a) LR and (deterministically) left-parsable but not LL.
(b) Right- and left-parsable but not LR.
(c) LR but not left-parsable.

8.1.2. Convert the following LL(1) grammar to an LL(2) grammar with no e-productions:

$$E \longrightarrow TE'$$
$$E' \longrightarrow + TE' \mid e$$
$$T \longrightarrow FT'$$
$$T' \longrightarrow * FT' \mid e$$
$$F \longrightarrow a \mid (E)$$

8.1.3. Convert the grammar of Exercise 8.1.2 to an LL(2) grammar in GNF.

8.1.4. Prove part (1) of Theorem 8.3.

8.1.5. Complete the proof of Lemma 8.4.

8.1.6. Complete the proof of Theorem 8.5.

8.1.7. Show that G_1, constructed in the proof of Theorem 8.7, is LL($k - 1$).

8.1.8. Show that a language is LL(0) if and only if it is $\varnothing$ or a singleton.

8.1.9. Show that G_k and G'_k in Example 8.3 are, respectively, LL($k + 1$) and LL(k).

*8.1.10. Prove that each of the grammars in Theorem 8.2 has the properties attributed to it there.

*8.1.11. Show that the language $L = \{a^n b^n \mid n \geq 1\} \cup \{a^n c^n \mid n \geq 1\}$ is a deterministic language which is not an LL language. *Hint:* Assume that L has an LL(k) grammar G in GNF. Show that $L(G)$ must contain strings not in L by considering left-sentential forms of the appearance $a^i \alpha$ for $i \geq 1$.

8.1.12. Show that $L = \{a^n b^m \mid 1 \leq m \leq n\}$ is a deterministic language which is not LL. Note that L is the concatenation of the two LL(1) languages a^* and $\{a^n b^n \mid n \geq 1\}$.

*8.1.13. Show that every LL(k) language has an LL($k + 1$) grammar in CNF.

**8.1.14. Let $L = L_1 \cup L_2 \cup \cdots \cup L_m$, where each L_i is an LL language, $1 \leq i \leq m$. Show that if L is regular, then L_i is regular for all i.

**8.1.15. Show that if L is an LL language but not regular, then $\bar{L}$ is not LL.

*8.1.16. Show that the LL languages are not closed under union, intersection, complementation, concatenation, reversal, or e-free homomorphism. *Hint:* See Exercises 8.1.11, 8.1.12, and 8.1.15.

8.1.17. Prove that $TH^G(\alpha\beta) = TH^G(\alpha) + TH^G(\beta)$ and that if $\alpha \overset{*}{\Rightarrow} \beta$, then $TH^G(\alpha) \leq TH^G(\beta)$.

8.1.18. Give algorithms to compute $TH^G(\alpha)$ and $TH^G(\alpha, z)$.

8.1.19. Show that G_1 of Algorithm 8.1 left-covers G of that algorithm.

8.1.20. Show that every $LL(k)$ grammar G is left-covered by an $LL(k + 1)$ grammar in GNF.

8.1.21. For $k \geq 2$, show that every $LL(k)$ grammar without e-productions is left-covered by an $LL(k - 1)$ grammar.

**8.1.22. Show that it is decidable, given an $LR(k)$ grammar G, whether there exists a k' such that G is $LL(k')$.

BIBLIOGRAPHIC NOTES

Theorem 8.1 was first suggested by Knuth [1967]. The results in Sections 8.1.2 and 8.1.3 first appeared in Rosenkrantz and Stearns [1970]. Solutions to Exercises 8.1.14–8.1.16 and 8.1.22 can be found in there also. The hierarchy of $LL(k)$ languages was first noted by Kurki-Suonio [1969].

Several earlier papers gave decidability results related to Theorem 8.6. Korenjak and Hopcroft [1966] showed that it was decidable whether two simple $LL(1)$ grammars were equivalent. McNaughton [1967] showed that equivalence was decidable for *parenthesis grammars*, which are grammars in which the right-hand side of each production is surrounded by a pair of parentheses, which do not appear elsewhere within any production. Independently, Paull and Unger [1968a] showed that it was decidable whether two grammars were *structurally equivalent*, meaning that they generate the same strings, and that their parse trees are the same except for labels. (Two grammars are structurally equivalent if and only if the parenthesis grammars constructed from them are equivalent.)

8.2. CLASSES OF GRAMMARS GENERATING THE DETERMINISTIC LANGUAGES

In this section we shall see that various classes of grammars generate exactly the deterministic languages. Among these are the $LR(1)$, $(1, 1)$-BRC, simple MSP, and UI $(2, 1)$-precedence grammars. In addition, if a deterministic language has the prefix property, then it has $LR(0)$ and $(1, 0)$-BRC grammars. Note that any language can be given the prefix property by appending a right endmarker to each sentence in the language.

8.2.1. Normal Form DPDA's and Canonical Grammars

The general strategy of Section 8.2 is to construct grammars from DPDA's having certain special properties. These grammars, or simple modifications of them, will be in the classes mentioned above. We shall first define the special properties desired in a DPDA.

DEFINITION

A DPDA $P = (Q, \Sigma, \Gamma, \delta, q_0, Z_0, F)$ is in *normal form* if it has all the following properties:

(1) P is loop-free. Thus, on each input, P can make only a bounded number of moves.

(2) F has a single member, q_f, and if $(q_0, w, Z_0) \mathrel{\vdash^*} (q_f, e, \gamma)$, then $\gamma = Z_0$. That is, if P accepts an input string, then P is in the final state q_f and the pushdown list consists of the start symbol alone.

(3) Q can be written as $Q = Q_s \cup Q_w \cup Q_e \cup \{q_f\}$, where Q_s, Q_w, and Q_e are disjoint sets, called the *scan*, *write*, and *erase* states, respectively; q_f is in none of these three sets. The states have the following properties:

    (a) If q is in Q_s, then for each $a \in \Sigma$, there is some state p_a such that $\delta(q, a, Z) = (p_a, Z)$ for all Z. Thus, if P is in a scan state, the next move is to scan the input symbol. In addition, this move is always independent of the symbol on top of the pushdown list.

    (b) If q is in Q_w, then $\delta(q, e, Z) = (p, YZ)$ for some p and Y and for all Z. A write state always prints a new symbol on top of the pushdown list, and the move is independent of the current input symbol and the symbol on top of the pushdown list.

    (c) If q is in Q_e, then for each $Z \in \Gamma$, there is some state p_Z such that $\delta(q, e, Z) = (p_Z, e)$. An erase state always removes the topmost symbol from the pushdown list without scanning a new input symbol.

    (d) $\delta(q_f, a, Z) = \varnothing$ for all a in $\Sigma \cup \{e\}$ and $Z \in \Gamma$. No moves are possible in the final state.

(4) If $(q, w, Z) \mathrel{\vdash^+} (p, e, Z)$, then $w \neq e$. That is, a sequence of moves which (possibly) enlarges the stack and returns to the same level cannot occur on e input. A sequence of moves $(q, w, Z) \mathrel{\vdash^+} (p, e, Z)$ will be called a *traverse*. Note that the possibility or impossibility of a traverse for given q, p, and w is independent of Z, the symbol on top of the pushdown list.

In short, a scan state reads the next input symbol, a write state prints a new symbol on the stack, and an erase state examines the top stack symbol, erasing it. Only scan states may shift the input head.

THEOREM 8.9

If $L \subseteq \Sigma^*$ is a deterministic language, and $\cent$ is not in Σ, then $L\cent$ is $L(P)$ for some DPDA P in normal form.

Proof. We shall construct a sequence of six DPDA's P_1–P_6, constructing P_{i+1} from P_i such that P_{i+1} has more of the properties of a normal form DPDA than P_i does. P_6 will be our desired DPDA in normal form.

For P_1 we use Lemma 2.28 to find a continuing, and hence loop-free, DPDA such that $L = L(P_1)$. We then transform P_1 into P_2 using the construction of Lemma 2.21, treating P_1 as an extended DPDA. The resulting DPDA P_2 will be continuing, and each state will act either as an erase or write state or will leave the stack fixed, although any state of P_2 may advance the input.

Then we use the construction of Theorem 2.23 to construct P_3 from P_2. P_3 will have all the properties of P_2 and, in addition, will make no e-move in a final state.

Next, we construct P_4 from P_3, so that P_4 has all the properties of P_3 mentioned but accepts $L\phi$, where ϕ is not in the alphabet of L. P_4 will have a unique final state, q_f, and will only accept if the stack consists of its start symbol only. P_4 has two bottom markers, Z_0 and Z_1. Z_0 is the start symbol, and the first two moves of P_4 print Z_1 above Z_0 and P_3's start symbol above Z_1. P_4 then simulates P_3. If P_3 accepts, then on input ϕ, P_4 enters a new state q_e and erases its stack down to Z_1. Then, P_4 erases Z_1, enters state q_f, and makes no further moves.

To put P_4 in normal form, it remains to

(1) Separate the (input) scan operation from the stack manipulations and
(2) Eliminate traverses on input e.

For (1), we modify P_4 to create P_5. For each state q of P_4 on which an e-move is not possible, except $q = q_f$, we create new states q_a for each a in Σ. We have q transfer to q_a on input a and then have P_5 make the move from state q_a on input e that P_4 made from state q on input a.

Finally, we observe that it is decidable whether $(q, e, Z) \vdash^+_{P_5} (p, e, Z)$ for each q and p. This question is independent of Z because of the construction of P_2. An algorithm to decide this question is left for the Exercises. We observe that all DPDA's constructed, including P_5, are loop-free. Hence, for each state q there is a unique state q' (possibly $q' = q$) such that

$$(q, e, Z) \vdash^* (q', e, Z),$$

but for no q'' does $(q', e, Z) \vdash^+ (q'', e, Z)$. We construct the final DPDA P_6 in our sequence from P_5 by giving q the moves of q' in each situation above. P_6 is then the desired DPDA P.

The detailed construction corresponding to these intuitive ideas is left for the Exercises. □

We next give a method of constructing what we call the canonical grammar from a normal form DPDA. This method is somewhat different from that of Lemma 2.26 in that here we make use of the special properties of a normal form DPDA.

DEFINITION

Let $M = (Q, \Sigma, \Gamma, \delta, q_0, Z_0, \{q_f\})$ be a normal form DPDA with pushdown top at the left. *The canonical grammar* for P is $G = (N, \Sigma, P, [q_0 q_f])$, where

(1) N' is the set of pairs $[qp]$ in $Q \times Q$ such that q is a scan or write state and p is arbitrary. The nonterminal $[qp]$ will generate exactly those terminal strings w such that M can make a traverse from state q to state p under input w. That is, $[qp] \overset{*}{\Rightarrow} w$ if and only if $(q, w, Z) \vdash^{+} (p, e, Z)$ for all Z in Γ.

(2) The set of productions P' is constructed as follows:

(a) If $\delta(q, a, Z) = (q', Z)$, then we add

$$[qq'] \rightarrow a$$

to P. Also, for all $r \in Q_s \cup Q_w$ we add

$$[rq'] \rightarrow [rq]a$$

to P'. Note that here q is a scan state.

(b) If $\delta(q, e, Z) = (s, YZ)$ and $\delta(p, e, Y) = (q', e)$, then we add

$$[qq'] \rightarrow [sp]$$

to P', and for all $r \in Q_s \cup Q_w$,

$$[rq'] \rightarrow [rq][sp]$$

is added to P'. Here, q is a write state and p an erase state.

(3) N and P are constructed by eliminating useless nonterminals and productions from N' and P'. The productions in P will be of the forms

(1) $[qq'] \rightarrow a$,
(2) $[qq'] \rightarrow [pp']a$,
(3) $[qq'] \rightarrow [pp']$, and
(4) $[qq'] \rightarrow [pp'][rr']$.

We say that a production of the ith form is of *type i* for $1 \leq i \leq 4$.

We make the following observations about canonical grammars.

(1) If $[qq'] \rightarrow a$ is in P, then q is a scan state.
(2) If $[qq'] \rightarrow [pp']a$ is in P, then p' is a scan state.
(3) If $[qq'] \rightarrow [pp']$ is in P, then q is a write state and p' is an erase state.
(4) If $[qq'] \rightarrow [pp'][rr']$ is in P, then p' is a write state and r' an erase state.

The next observation is also useful. Let q be any write state of M. From state q, M can write only a fixed number of symbols on its pushdown list before scanning another input symbol. That is, there exists a finite sequence of states $q_1, \ldots, q_k$ such that $q_1 = q$, $\delta(q_i, e, Z) = (q_{i+1}, Y_i Z)$ for $1 \leq i < k$ and all Z, and q_k is a scan state. The sequence has no repeats, and $k = 1$ is possible. The justification is that should there be a repeat, then M is not loop-free; if the sequence is longer than $\#Q$, then there must be a repeat. We call this sequence of states the *write sequence for state q*.

THEOREM 8.10

If $G = (N, \Sigma, P, S)$ is the canonical grammar constructed from a normal form DPDA $M = (Q, \Sigma, \Gamma, \delta, q_0, Z_0, \{q_f\})$, then $L(G) = L(M) - \{e\}$.

Proof. Here we shall prove that $[qq']$ generates exactly the input strings for which a traverse from q to q' is possible. To do so, we shall prove the following statement inductively:

(8.2.1) $[qq'] \overset{n}{\Rightarrow} w$ for some n and $w \neq e$ if and only if

$$(q, w, Z) \overset{m}{\vdash} (q', e, Z) \quad \text{for some } m > 0 \text{ and arbitrary } Z$$

If: The basis, $m = 1$, is trivial. In this case, w must be a symbol in Σ, and $[qq'] \rightarrow w$ must be a production in P. For the inductive step, assume that (8.2.1) is true for values smaller than m and that $(q, w, Z) \overset{m}{\vdash} (q', e, Z)$. Then the configuration immediately before (q', e, Z) must be either of the form (p, a, Z) or (p, e, YZ).

In the first case, p is a scan state, and $(q, w, Z) \overset{m-1}{\vdash} (p, a, Z)$. Hence, $(q, w', Z) \overset{m-1}{\vdash} (p, e, Z)$ if $w'a = w$. By the inductive hypothesis, $[qp] \overset{*}{\Rightarrow} w'$. By definition of G, $[qq'] \rightarrow [qp]a$ is in P, so $[qq'] \overset{*}{\Rightarrow} w$.

In the second case, we must be able to find states r and s and express w as $w_1 w_2$, so that

$$(q, w_1 w_2, Z) \overset{m_1}{\vdash} (r, w_2, Z)$$
$$\vdash (s, w_2, YZ)$$
$$\overset{m_2}{\vdash} (p, e, YZ)$$
$$\vdash (q', e, Z)$$

where $m_1 < m$, $m_2 < m$, and the sequence $(s, w_2, YZ) \overset{m_2}{\vdash} (p, e, YZ)$ never erases the explicitly shown Y. If $m_1 = 0$, then $r = q$ and $w_2 = w$. It follows that $[qq'] \rightarrow [sp]$ is in P. It also follows from the form of the moves that $(s, w_2, Y) \overset{m_2}{\vdash} (p, e, Y)$, and hence, $[sp] \overset{*}{\Rightarrow} w_2$. Thus, $[qq'] \overset{*}{\Rightarrow} w$.

If $m_1 > 0$, then $(q, w_1, Z) \overset{m_1}{\vdash} (r, e, Z)$, and so by hypothesis, $[qr] \overset{*}{\Rightarrow} w_1$. As above, we also have $[sp] \overset{*}{\Rightarrow} w_2$. The construction of G assures that

$[qq'] \rightarrow [qr][sp]$ is in P, and so $[qq'] \overset{*}{\Rightarrow} w$.

Only if: This portion is another straightforward induction and is left for the Exercises. The special case of (8.2.1) where $q = q_0$ and $q' = q_f$ yields the theorem.

$\square$

COROLLARY 1

If L is a deterministic language with the prefix property and e is not in L,† then L is generated by a canonical grammar.

Proof. The construction of a normal form DPDA for such a language is similar to the construction in Theorem 8.9. $\square$

COROLLARY 2

If $L \subseteq \Sigma^*$ is a deterministic language and $\not\in$ is not in Σ, then $L\not\in$ has a canonical grammar. $\square$

8.2.2. Simple MSP Grammars and Deterministic Languages

We shall now proceed to prove that every canonical grammar is a simple MSP grammar. Recall that a simple MSP grammar is a (not necessarily UI) weak precedence grammar $G = (N, \Sigma, P, S)$ such that if $A \rightarrow \alpha$ and $B \rightarrow \alpha$ are in P, then $l(A) \cap l(B) = \varnothing$, where $l(C)$ is the set of nonterminal or terminal symbols which may appear immediately to the left of C in a right-sentential form; i.e., $l(C) = \{X \mid X \lessdot C \text{ or } X \doteq C\}$.

We begin by showing that a canonical grammar is a $(1, 1)$-precedence grammar (nòt necessarily UI).

LEMMA 8.8

A canonical grammar is proper (i.e., has no useless symbols, e-productions, or cycles).

Proof. The construction of a canonical grammar eliminates useless symbols and e-productions. It suffices to show that there are no cycles. A cycle can occur only if there is a sequence of productions of type 3, say $[q_i q_i'] \rightarrow [q_{i+1} q_{i+1}']$, $1 \leq i < j$, where $[q_1 q_1'] = [q_j q_j']$. But then the rules for the construction of a canonical grammar imply that the write sequence for q_1 begins with $q_1, q_2, \ldots, q_j$ and thus has a repeat. This would imply that the underlying normal form DPDA has a loop, and we may therefore conclude that no cycles occur. $\square$

---

†Note that if L has the prefix property and e is in L, then $L = \{e\}$.

LEMMA 8.9

A canonical grammar is a (not necessarily UI) (1, 1)-precedence grammar.†

Proof. Let $G = (N, \Sigma, P, S)$ be a canonical grammar. We consider the three possible precedence conflicts and show that none can occur.

Case 1: Suppose that $X \lessdot Y$ and $X \doteq Y$. Since $X \doteq Y$, there must be a production $A \rightarrow XY$ of type 2 or 4. Thus, $X = [qq']$, and either $Y \in \Sigma$ and q' is a scan state or $Y = [pp']$ and p' is an erase state.

Since $X \lessdot Y$, there must also be a production $B \rightarrow XC$ of type 4, where $C \overset{+}{\Rightarrow} Y\alpha$ for some α. Let $X = [qq']$ as above. Then q' must be a write state, because $B \rightarrow XC$ is a type 4 production. Moreover, Y must be of the form $[pp']$, where p' is an erase state, and hence $A \rightarrow XY$ is of type 4. We may conclude from the form of type 4 productions that p is the second state in the write sequence of q'. Because $B \rightarrow XC$ is a type 4 production, we may also conclude that $C = [pp'']$ for some p''.

Now, let us consider the derivation $C \overset{+}{\underset{\text{lm}}{\Rightarrow}} Y\alpha$, which we may write as

$$[s_1 s_1'] \underset{\text{lm}}{\Rightarrow} [s_2 s_2']\alpha_2 \underset{\text{lm}}{\Rightarrow} \cdots \underset{\text{lm}}{\Rightarrow} [s_n s_n']\alpha_n,$$

where $[s_1 s_1'] = [pp'']$ and $[s_n s_n'] = [pp']$. We observe from the form of productions that for each i either $s_{i+1} = s_i$ (if $[s_i s_i']$ is replaced by a production of type 2 or 4) or s_{i+1} is the state following s_i in the write sequence of q' (if $[s_i s_i']$ is replaced by a production of type 3). Only in the latter case will s_{i+1}' be an erase state, and thus we may conclude that since $s_n' (= p')$ is an erase state, $s_n (= p)$ follows s_{n-1} on the write sequence of q'. Since s_{n-1} is either p or follows p on that sequence, we may conclude that p appears twice in the write sequence of q'. Since this would imply a loop, we conclude that there are no conflicts between $\lessdot$ and $\doteq$ in a canonical grammar.

Case 2: $X \lessdot Y$ and $X \gtrdot Y$. Since $X \lessdot Y$, we may conclude as in case 1 that $X = [qq']$, where q' is a write state. But if $X \gtrdot Y$, then there is a production $A \rightarrow BZ$, where $B \overset{+}{\Rightarrow} \alpha X$ and $Z \overset{*}{\Rightarrow} Y\beta$. The form of the productions assures us that if $B \overset{+}{\Rightarrow} \alpha[qq']$, then q' is an erase state. But we already found q' to be a write state. We may conclude that no conflicts between $\lessdot$ and $\gtrdot$ exist.

Case 3: $X \doteq Y$ and $X \gtrdot Y$. Since $X \doteq Y$, we may conclude as in case 1 that $X = [qq']$, where q' is a write or scan state. But, since $X \gtrdot Y$, we may conclude as in case 2 that q' is an erase state.

Thus, a canonical grammar is a precedence grammar.   ☐

---

†To prove that a canonical grammar is simple MSP, we need only prove it to be weak precedence, rather than (1, 1)–precedence. However, the additional portion of this lemma is interesting and easy to prove.

THEOREM 8.11

A canonical grammar is a simple mixed strategy precedence grammar.

Proof. By Theorem 8.10 and Lemmas 8.8 and 8.9, it suffices to show that for every canonical grammar $G = (N, \Sigma, P, S)$

(1) If $A \rightarrow \alpha X Y \beta$ and $B \rightarrow Y \beta$ are in P, then X is not in $l(B)$; and
(2) If $A \rightarrow \alpha$ and $B \rightarrow \alpha$ are in P, $A \neq B$, then $l(A) \cap l(B) = \varnothing$.

We have (1) immediately, since if $X \lessdot B$ or $X \doteq B$, then $X \lessdot Y$. But if $A \rightarrow \alpha X Y \beta$ is a production, then $X \doteq Y$, and so we have a precedence conflict, in violation of Lemma 8.9.

Now let us consider (2). $A \rightarrow \alpha$ and $B \rightarrow \alpha$ cannot be distinct type 2 productions, for if $A = [qq']$, $B = [pp']$, and $\alpha = [rr']a$, and if G comes from a DPDA $M = (Q, \Sigma, \Gamma, \delta, q_0, Z_0, \{q_f\})$, we have

$$\delta(r', a, Z) = (q', Z) = (p', Z).$$

Thus $q' = p'$. But the form of type 2 productions assures us that $q = p = r$, so $A = B$, which we assumed not to be the case. A similar argument, left for the Exercises, shows that $A \rightarrow \alpha$ and $B \rightarrow \alpha$ cannot be distinct type 4 productions.

Let us now consider the case $\alpha = a$, i.e., where $A \rightarrow \alpha$ and $B \rightarrow \alpha$ are productions of type 1. In general, if $X \lessdot Y$ or $X \doteq Y$, we have seen that X must be a nonterminal (proof of Lemma 8.9, case 1). Thus, suppose that C is in both $l(A)$ and $l(B)$. Then there exist productions $D_1 \rightarrow CD_2$ and $E_1 \rightarrow CE_2$, where $D_2 \overset{*}{\Rightarrow} A\beta$ and $E_2 \overset{*}{\Rightarrow} B\gamma$. The cases $A = D_2$ or $B = E_2$ are not ruled out. Let $C = [qq']$, $A = [pp']$, and $B = [rr']$. Then p and r are scan states, since $[pp'] \rightarrow a$ and $[rr'] \rightarrow a$ are type 1 productions. By a previous argument, p and r must each appear in the write sequence of q', and thus each must end that sequence. Hence, $p = r$. Since

$$\delta(p, a, Z) = (p', Z) = (r', Z)$$

we have $p' = r'$ and $A = B$, in contradiction. Thus, $A \rightarrow \alpha$ and $B \rightarrow \alpha$ may not be of type 1.

Last, suppose that $A \rightarrow \alpha$ and $B \rightarrow \alpha$ are of type 3. As in the previous paragraph, let C be in $l(A) \cap l(B)$, with $C = [qq']$, $A = [pp']$, and $B = [rr']$. Then p and r are each in the write sequence of q'. If $p = r$, let $\delta(p, e, Z)$ be (s, Y). Then $\alpha = [ss']$ for some s', and $\delta(s', e, Y) = (p', e) = (r', e)$. Thus, $r' = p'$, and again $A = B$, which we know not to be the case.

We conclude that $p \neq r$. However, if $\alpha = [ss']$, then s follows both p and r in the write sequence of q' and thus appears twice. We conclude that $A \rightarrow \alpha$ and $B \rightarrow \alpha$ are not of type 3 and that condition (2) does not occur. Thus, G is simple MSP. □

As a consequence of Theorem 8.11, $L\cent$ has a simple MSP grammar for every deterministic language L, where $\cent$ is an endmarker. In fact, we can prove more, by showing that $\cent$ can be removed from the end of each string generated by a canonical grammar; the modified grammar will also be simple MSP. As the construction which eliminates endmarkers will be used several times, we shall give it the status of an algorithm.

ALGORITHM 8.4

Elimination of the right endmarker from the sentences generated by a proper grammar.

Input. A proper grammar $G = (N, \Sigma \cup \{\cent\}, P, S)$, where $\cent$ is not in Σ and $L(G)$ is of the form $L\cent$ for some $L \subseteq \Sigma^+$.

Output. A grammar $G_1 = (N_1, \Sigma, P_1, S)$ such that $L(G_1) = L$.

Method.

(1) Remove all productions of the form $A \rightarrow \cent$ from P.

(2) Replace all productions in P of the form $A \rightarrow \alpha\cent$, where $\alpha \neq e$, by $A \rightarrow \alpha$.

(3) If $A \rightarrow \alpha B$ is in P, $\alpha \neq e$, and $B \overset{*}{\underset{G}{\Rightarrow}} \cent$, then add $A \rightarrow \alpha$ to P.

(4) Remove useless nonterminals and productions from N and the resultant set of productions. Let N_1 and P_1 be the nonterminals and productions remaining. $\square$

THEOREM 8.12

If G_1 is the grammar constructed in Algorithm 8.4, then $L(G_1) = L$.

Proof. Since every sentence w in $L(G)$ is of the form $x\cent$ for $x \in \Sigma^+$, it follows that for every $A \in N$, either $A \overset{*}{\underset{G}{\Rightarrow}} u$ implies $u \in \Sigma^+$, or $A \overset{*}{\underset{G}{\Rightarrow}} u$ implies $u = v\cent$, where $v \in \Sigma^*$. Let us call nonterminals of the first kind *intermediate* and nonterminals of the latter type *completing*. A straightforward induction on the length of derivations shows that if A is an intermediate nonterminal, then $A \overset{*}{\underset{G}{\Rightarrow}} u$ if and only if $A \overset{*}{\underset{G_1}{\Rightarrow}} u$, $u \in \Sigma^*$. Likewise, if A is a completing nonterminal, then $A \overset{*}{\underset{G}{\Rightarrow}} v\cent$ if and only if $A \overset{*}{\underset{G_1}{\Rightarrow}} v$. The proof is left for the Exercises.

We now have $S \overset{*}{\underset{G}{\Rightarrow}} w\cent$ if and only if $S \overset{*}{\underset{G_1}{\Rightarrow}} w$. Thus, $L(G_1) = L$. $\square$

THEOREM 8.13

If L is a deterministic language and e is not in L, then L is generated by a simple MSP grammar.

Proof. Let $L \subseteq \Sigma^+$ and $\cent$ not be in Σ. Then by Corollary 2 to Theorem 8.10, $L\cent$ is generated by a canonical grammar $G = (N, \Sigma, P, S)$, which by Theorem 8.11 is a simple MSP grammar. Let $G_1 = (N_1, \Sigma, P_1, S)$ be the grammar constructed from G by Algorithm 8.4. Then $L(G_1) = L$, and we shall show that G_1 is also simple MSP.

It is easy to show that G_1 will have no e-productions or useless symbols. If G_1 had a cycle, it would have to involve a production $A \rightarrow B$ which is in P_1 but not in P. Suppose that $A \rightarrow BX$ is in P for some X such that $X \underset{G}{\overset{*}{\Rightarrow}} \notin$. Suppose further that $A \underset{G_1}{\Rightarrow} B \underset{G_1}{\overset{*}{\Rightarrow}} A$. It follows that $A \underset{G}{\overset{+}{\Rightarrow}} Aw\notin$ for some w in $(\Sigma \cup \{\notin\})^*$, and hence G generates words with more than one $\notin$. Since we know this not to be the case, we conclude that G_1 is proper.

Next, we must show that G_1 is a precedence grammar. Since $\notin$ appears only at the right-hand end of strings generated by S in G, it is easy to show that the only new relations for G_1 that do not hold for G involve \$ (the end-marker in the precedence formalism) on the right. But $X > \$$ is the only relation that can hold with \$ on the right, and so G_1 must be a precedence grammar.

Third, we must show that no new conflicts $A \rightarrow \alpha XY\beta$ and $B \rightarrow Y\beta$, with X in $l(B)$, occur in G_1. As in Theorem 8.10, the simple precedence property rules out such problems.

Last, we must show that there is no pair of productions $A \rightarrow \alpha$ and $B \rightarrow \alpha$ in P_1, where $A \neq B$. Three cases need to be considered.

Case 1: Suppose that $\alpha = C$ and that $A \rightarrow CX$ and $B \rightarrow CY$ are in P, where $X \underset{G}{\overset{*}{\Rightarrow}} \notin$ and $Y \underset{G}{\overset{*}{\Rightarrow}} \notin$. Let $C = [qq']$. If q' is a scan state, then $X = Y = \notin$. As we saw in the proof of Theorem 8.11, the left-hand side of a type 2 production is uniquely determined by its right-hand side, and so $A = B$, contrary to hypothesis. If q' is a write state, let p be the unique scan state in the write sequence of q' and let $\delta(p, \notin, Z) = (p', Z)$, where δ is the move function of the DPDA from which G was constructed. After entering state p', the DPDA can do nothing but erase its stack, because if it scans or writes, either it accepts a string with $\notin$ in the middle or X or Y are useless symbols. There is then a unique state p'' in which the DPDA finds itself after erasing the symbols pushed on the pushdown list during the write sequence of q'. Thus, $X = Y$ again, and we conclude that $A = B$.

Case 2: Suppose that $\alpha = C$ and that $A \rightarrow C$ and $B \rightarrow CX$ are in P, where $X \overset{*}{\Rightarrow} \notin$. If $C = [qq']$, then q' is an erase state, as $A \rightarrow C$ is a type 3 production. But since $B \rightarrow CX$ is a type 2 or 4 production, q' must be a write or scan state. We thus have a contradiction.

Case 3: If $\alpha = C$ and $A \rightarrow CX$ and $B \rightarrow C$ are in P, then we have a situation symmetric to case 2.

We conclude that G_1 is simple MSP. $\square$

8.2.3. BRC Grammars, LR Grammars, and Deterministic Languages

We shall show that a canonical grammar is also a $(1, 0)$-BRC grammar and hence, by Theorem 5.21, an LR(0) grammar. Intuitively, the reason that no lookahead is needed for the shift–reduce parsing of a canonical grammar is that every terminal and every nonterminal $[qq']$, where q' is an erase state, indicates the right-hand end of a handle. We shall give a formal proof incorporating this idea.

THEOREM 8.14

A canonical grammar is a $(1, 0)$-BRC grammar.

Proof. Let $G = (N, \Sigma, P, S)$ be a canonical grammar. Suppose that G were not $(1, 0)$-BRC. Then we can find derivations in the augmented grammar $G' = (N \cup \{S'\}, \Sigma, P \cup \{S' \to S\}, S')$ namely $\$S' \overset{*}{\underset{\text{rm}}{\Rightarrow}} \alpha XAw \underset{\text{rm}}{\Rightarrow} \alpha X\beta w$ and $\$S' \overset{*}{\underset{\text{rm}}{\Rightarrow}} \gamma Bx \underset{\text{rm}}{\Rightarrow} \gamma \delta x$, where $\gamma \delta x$ can be written as $\alpha' X\beta y$ with $|x| \leq |y|$ but $\alpha' XAy \neq \gamma Bx$. We observe that every right-sentential form of G has an open portion consisting of nonterminals only, and so $X \in N$ and α, α' and γ are in N^*. We shall consider four cases, depending on the type of the production $A \to \beta$.

Case 1: Suppose that $\beta = a$, where $a \in \Sigma$. Since $|x| \leq |y|$, we must have $x = y$ and either $\delta = a$ or $\delta = Xa$. In the first case, X is in $l(A) \cap l(B)$, which can only occur if $A = B$, since we know G to simple MSP. In the second case, we have productions $A \to a$ and $B \to Xa$, with $X \in l(A)$, again violating the simple MSP condition.

Case 2: Suppose that $\beta = Ca$ for some $C \in N$. Then since $|x| \leq |y|$, we must have $x = y$ and $\delta = a$ or $\delta = Ca$. If $\delta = Ca$, then $A = B$, since productions of type 2 are uniquely invertible, as we saw in Theorem 8.11. It then follows that $\alpha' XAy = \gamma Bx$, contrary to hypothesis. If $\delta = a$, we have $C \doteq a$ from $A \to Ca$. Since C must be the last symbol of γ, we have $C \lessdot B$ or $C \doteq B$, and hence, $C \lessdot a$, in violation of the fact that G is a precedence grammar.

Case 3: Suppose $\beta = C$ for some $C \in N$. Either $\delta = C$, $\delta = a$ or $\delta = Ca$ for some $a \in \Sigma$, or $\delta = XC$. If $\delta = C$, then X is in $l(A) \cap l(B)$, which violates the simple MSP condition. Let $C = [qq']$. Then q' is an erase state. If $\delta = a$ then C is the last symbol of γ. Since B appears to the right of C in a right sentential form, q' must be a write state. We thus have a contradiction. If $\delta = Ca$, then q' would be a scan state, and so we eliminate this possibility. If $\delta = XC$, then since X is in $l(A)$, we have a violation of the simple MSP condition, with productions $A \to C$ and $B \to XC$.

Case 4: Suppose that $\beta = CD$ for C and D in N. Then δ is one of D, a or Da for some $a \in \Sigma$, or CD. Since type 4 productions are uniquely invertible (proof of Theorem 8.11), if $\delta = CD$, then $A = B$ and $\alpha' XAy = \gamma Bx$. Let $D = [qq']$. Because of production $A \to CD$, q' is an erase state. If $\delta = Da$, then q' would be a scan state, and so we eliminate this possibility. If $\delta = a$, then as in Case 3, we can show that q' is a write state. If $\delta = D$, then the last symbol of γ is C, and so C is in $l(B)$. With productions $A \rightarrow CD$ and $B \rightarrow D$, we have a violation of the simple MSP condition. $\square$

COROLLARY 1

Every deterministic language L with the prefix property has a $(1, 0)$-BRC grammar.

Proof. If e is not in L, the result is immediate. If $e \in L$, then $L = \{e\}$. It is easy to find a $(1, 0)$-BRC grammar for this language. $\square$

COROLLARY 2

If $L \subseteq \Sigma^*$ is a deterministic language and $\not{c}$ is not in Σ, then $L\not{c}$ has a $(1, 0)$-BRC grammar. $\square$

We can now prove a theorem about arbitrary deterministic languages which is almost a restatement of Corollary 2 above.

THEOREM 8.15

Every deterministic language is generated by a $(1, 1)$-BRC grammar.

Proof. Let G be a canonical grammar and construct G_1 from G by Algorithm 8.4. It is necessary to show that G_1 is $(1, 1)$-BRC. Intuitively, the problem is to recognize when a production $A \rightarrow B$ of G_1, which is not a production of G, is to be used for a reduction. However, the one-symbol lookahead allows us to make such a reduction only when \$, the BRC end-marker, is the lookahead. A formal proof is left for the Exercises. $\square$

THEOREM 8.16

(1) Every deterministic language with the prefix property has an LR(0) grammar.

(2) Every deterministic language has an LR(1) grammar.

Proof. From Theorem 5.21, every (m, k)-BRC grammar is an LR(k) grammar. The result is thus immediate from Theorem 8.15 and Corollary 1 to Theorem 8.14. $\square$

8.2.4. Extended Precedence Grammars and Deterministic Languages

Up to this point we have seen that if L is a deterministic context-free language, then

(1) There is a normal form DPDA P such that $L(P) = L\not{c}$,

(2) There is a simple mixed strategy precedence grammar G such that $L(G) = L - \{e\}$, and

(3) There is a $(1, 1)$-BRC grammar G such that $L(G) = L$.

We shall now show that there is also a UI $(2, 1)$-precedence grammar G such that $L(G) = L - \{e\}$. We already know that a canonical grammar is a $(1, 1)$-precedence grammar, although it is not necessarily UI. To obtain our result, we shall perform several transformations on a canonical grammar that will convert it to a UI $(2, 1)$-precedence grammar. These transformations are summarized as follows:

(1) Each nonterminal is augmented to record the symbol to its left in a rightmost derivation.

(2) Single productions are eliminated by replacing the productions $A \longrightarrow B$ and $B \longrightarrow \alpha_1 \mid \cdots \mid \alpha_m$ by the productions $A \longrightarrow \alpha_1 \mid \cdots \mid \alpha_m$.

(3) Nonterminals are "split" so that each nonterminal either has one production of the form $A \longrightarrow a$ or has no production of that form.

(4) Finally, nonterminals are "strung out" to restore unique invertibility to nonterminals whose production is $A \longrightarrow a$. That is, a set of productions $A_1 \longrightarrow a, \ldots, A_k \longrightarrow a$ will be replaced by $A_1 \longrightarrow A_2, \ldots, A_{k-1} \longrightarrow A_k$ and $A_k \longrightarrow a$.

The first three operations each preserve the $(1, 1)$-precedence nature of the grammar. The fourth step may make the grammar $(2, 1)$-precedence at worst, but the fourth step is needed to ensure unique invertibility. We now give the complete algorithm.

ALGORITHM 8.5

Conversion of a canonical grammar to a UI $(2, 1)$-precedence grammar.

Input. A canonical grammar $G = (N, \Sigma, P, S)$.

Output. An equivalent uniquely invertible $(2, 1)$-precedence grammar $G_4 = (N_4, \Sigma, P_4, S_4)$.

Method.

(1) Construct $G_1 = (N_1, \Sigma, P_1, S_1)$ from G as follows:
   (a) Let N_1 be the set of symbols A_X, where $A \in N$ and $X \in N \cup \{\$\}$.
   (b) Let $S_1 = S_\$$.
   (c) P_1' consists of productions $A_X \longrightarrow B_X$, $A_X \longrightarrow B_X C_B$, $A_X \longrightarrow B_X a$, and $A_X \longrightarrow a$, for all $X \in N \cup \{\$\}$, whenever $A \longrightarrow B$, $A \longrightarrow BC$, $A \longrightarrow Ba$, and $A \longrightarrow a$ are in P, respectively.
   (d) N_1 and P_1 are formed from N_1' and P_1', respectively, by deleting useless symbols and productions.

(2) Construct $G_2 = (N_2, \Sigma, P_2, S_1)$ from G_1 as follows:
   (a) Remove all single productions from P_1 by performing the following operation until no further change is possible. If $A \longrightarrow B$ is currently a production of P_1, add $A \longrightarrow \alpha$ for each production $B \longrightarrow \alpha$ in P_1 and delete $A \longrightarrow B$.
   (b) Let N_2 and P_2 be the resulting set of useful nonterminals and productions.

(3) Construct $G_3 = (N_3, \Sigma, P_3, S_1)$ from G_2 as follows:
   (a) Let N'_3 consist of N_2 and all symbols A^a such that $A \rightarrow a$ is in P_2.
   (b) Add to P'_3 the production $A^a \rightarrow a$ for all A^a in N'_3.
   (c) If A is in N_2, $A \rightarrow \alpha$ is in P_2, and α is not a single terminal, add $A \rightarrow \alpha'$ to P'_3 for each α' in $h^{-1}(\alpha)$, where h is the homomorphism:

$$h(a) = a \quad \text{for all } a \ \in \Sigma$$
$$h(B^a) = B \quad \text{for all } B^a \in N'_3$$
$$h(B) = B \quad \text{for all } B \ \in N_2$$

   (d) Let N_3 and P_3 be the useful portions of N'_3 and P'_3.
(4) Construct $G_4 = (N_4, \Sigma, P_4, S_4)$ from G_3 as follows:
   (a) $N_4 = N_3$ and $S_4 = S_1$.
   (b) P_4 is P_3 with the following change. If $A_1 \rightarrow a, A_2 \rightarrow a, \ldots,$ $A_k \rightarrow a$ are all the productions with a on the right in P_3 in some order and $k > 1$, then these productions are replaced in P_4 by $A_1 \rightarrow A_2, A_2 \rightarrow A_3, \ldots, A_{k-1} \rightarrow A_k$ and $A_k \rightarrow a$. □

Example 8.4

Let G be defined by the following productions:

$$S \longrightarrow AB$$
$$A \longrightarrow a \,|\, b$$
$$B \longrightarrow AC$$
$$C \longrightarrow D$$
$$D \longrightarrow a$$

Then G_1 is defined by

$$S_\$ \longrightarrow A_\$ B_A$$
$$A_\$ \longrightarrow a \,|\, b$$
$$B_A \longrightarrow A_A C_A$$
$$A_A \longrightarrow a \,|\, b$$
$$C_A \longrightarrow D_A$$
$$D_A \longrightarrow a$$

In step (2) of Algorithm 8.5, $C_A \rightarrow D_A$ is replaced by $C_A \rightarrow a$. D_A is then useless.

In step (3), we add nonterminals $A^a_\$, A^b_\$, A^a_A, A^b_A$, and C^a_A. Then $A_\$, A_A$, and C_A become useless, so the resulting productions of G_3 are

$$S_\$ \longrightarrow A^a_\$ B_A \,|\, A^b_\$ B_A$$
$$A^a_\$ \longrightarrow a$$
$$A^b_\$ \longrightarrow b$$

$$B_A \longrightarrow A_A^a C_A^a \mid A_A^b C_A^a$$
$$A_A^a \longrightarrow a$$
$$A_A^b \longrightarrow b$$
$$C_A^a \longrightarrow a$$

In step (4), we string out $A_\$^a$, A_A^a, and C_A^a, and we string out $A_\$^b$ and A_A^b. The resulting productions of G_4 are

$$S_\$ \longrightarrow A_\$^a B_A \mid A_\$^b B_A$$
$$B_A \longrightarrow A_A^a C_A^a \mid A_A^b C_A^a$$
$$A_\$^a \longrightarrow A_A^a$$
$$A_A^a \longrightarrow C_A^a$$
$$C_A^a \longrightarrow a$$
$$A_\$^b \longrightarrow A_A^b$$
$$A_A^b \longrightarrow b \quad \square$$

We shall now prove by a series of lemmas that G_4 is a UI (2, 1)-precedence grammar.

LEMMA 8.10

In Algorithm 8.5,

(1) $L(G_1) = L(G)$,
(2) G_1 is a (1, 1)-precedence grammar, and
(3) If $A \rightarrow \alpha$ and $B \rightarrow \alpha$ are in P_1 and α is not a single terminal, then $A = B$.

Proof. Assertion (1) is a straightforward induction on lengths of derivations. For (2), we observe that if X and Y are related by $\lessdot$, $\doteq$, or $\gtrdot$ in G_1, then X' and Y', which are X and Y with subscripts (if any) deleted, are similarly related in G. Thus G_1 is a (1, 1)-precedence grammar, since G is.

For (3), we have noted that productions of types 2 and 4 are uniquely invertible in G. That is, if $A \rightarrow CX$ and $B \rightarrow CX$ are in P, then $A = B$. It thus follows that if $A_Y \rightarrow C_Y X_C$ and $B_Y \rightarrow C_Y X_C$ are in P_1, then $A_Y = B_Y$. Similarly, if X is a terminal, and $A_Y \rightarrow C_Y X$ and $B_Y \rightarrow C_Y X$ are in P_1, then $A_Y = B_Y$.

We must consider productions in P_1 derived from type 3 productions; that is, suppose that we have $A_X \rightarrow C_X$ and $B_X \rightarrow C_X$. Since we have eliminated useless productions in G_1, there must be right-hand sides XD and XE of productions of G such that $D \overset{*}{\underset{G}{\Rightarrow}} A\alpha$ and $E \overset{*}{\underset{G}{\Rightarrow}} B\beta$ for some α and β. Let $X = [qq']$, $A = [pp']$, $B = [rr']$, and $C = [ss']$. Then p and r are in the write sequence of q', and s follows both of them. We may conclude that $p = r$. Since $A \rightarrow C$ and $B \rightarrow C$ are both type 3 productions, we have

$p' = r'$. That is, let δ be the transition function of the DPDA underlying G. Then $\delta(p, e, Z) = (s, YZ)$ for some Y, and $\delta(s', e, Y) = (p', e) = (r', e)$. Thus, $A = B$, and $A_X = B_X$.

The case $X = \$$ is handled similarly, with q_0, the start state of the underlying DPDA, playing the role of q' in the above. $\quad\square$

LEMMA 8.11

The three properties of G_1 stated in Lemma 8.10 apply equally to G_2 of Algorithm 8.5.

Proof. Again (1) is a simple induction. To prove (2), we observe that step (2) of Algorithm 8.5 introduces no new right-hand sides and hence no new $\doteq$ relationships. Also, every right-sentential form of G_2 is a right-sentential form of G_1, and so it is easy to show that no $<$ or $>$ relationships are introduced.

For (3), it suffices to show that if $A_X \longrightarrow B_X$ is a production in P_1, then B_X appears on the right of no other production and hence is useless and eliminated in step (2b). We already know that there is no production $C_X \longrightarrow B_X$ in P_1 if $C \neq A$. The only possibilities are productions $C_X \longrightarrow B_X a$, $C_X \longrightarrow B_X D_B$, or $C_Y \longrightarrow X_Y B_X$. Now $A \longrightarrow B$ is a type 3 production, and so if $B = [qq']$, then q' is an erase state. Thus, $C_X \longrightarrow B_X a$ and $C_X \longrightarrow B_X D_B$ are impossible, because $C \longrightarrow Ba$ and $C \longrightarrow BD$ are of types 2 and 4, respectively.

Let us consider a production $C_Y \longrightarrow X_Y B_X$. Let $X = [pp']$ and $A = [rr']$. Then q is the second state in the write sequence of p', because $C \longrightarrow XB$ is a type (4) production. Also, since $A \longrightarrow B$ is a type 3 production, q follows r in any write sequence in which r appears. But since X can appear immediately to the left of A in a right-sentential form of G, r appears in the write sequence of p', and $r \neq p'$. Thus, q appears twice in the write sequence of p', which is impossible. $\quad\square$

LEMMA 8.12

The three properties of G_1 stated in Lemma 8.10 apply equally to G_3 of Algorithm 8.5.

Proof. Again, (1) is straightforward. To prove (2), we note that if X and Y are related in G_3 by $<$, $\doteq$, or $>$, then X' and Y' are so related in G_2, where X' and Y' are X and Y with superscripts (if any) removed. Thus, G_3 is (1, 1)-precedence, and (2) holds. Part (3) is straightforward. $\quad\square$

THEOREM 8.17

G_4 of Algorithm 8.5 is a UI (2, 1)-precedence grammar.

Proof. Since for each a in Σ, P_4 has at most one production $A \longrightarrow a$, it should be clear that G_4 is UI. It is easy to show that the only new

(1, 1)-precedence conflicts which might be introduced involve new relations (1) $A_X^a \gtrdot b$ and (2) $C \lessdot A_X^a$.

Conflicts of form (1) occur because some $B_Y^a \gtrdot b$ or $B_Y^a \doteq b$ holds in G_3, and $B_Y^a \underset{G_4}{\overset{+}{\Rightarrow}} A_X^a$. We might also have $A_X^a \doteq b$ or $A_X^a \lessdot b$ in G_3 and hence in G_4. Conflicts of form (2) occur by essentially the same mechanism. We could have $C \doteq B_C^a$ or $C \lessdot B_{C'}^a$ in G_3, and $B_{C'}^a \underset{G_4}{\overset{+}{\Rightarrow}} A_X^a$. We could also have $C \doteq A_X^a$ in G_3 and hence in G_4. (C' is C with subscripts and superscripts deleted.)

We shall show that potential conflicts of form (1) are resolved by considering (2, 1)-precedence relations. Those of form (2) cannot occur.

Case 1: Suppose for some $C \in N_4$ that $CA_X^a \gtrdot b$ in G_4 and that either $CA_X^a \doteq b$ or $CA_X^a \lessdot b$ in both G_3 and G_4. Then $C = X_Z^d$ for some Z and d; the latter symbol may not actually appear. We observed that since $A_X^a \gtrdot b$ is a relation in G_4 but not in G_3, there must exist a derivation $B_Y^a \underset{G_4}{\overset{+}{\Rightarrow}} A_X^a$ such that C can appear to the left of B_Y^a in a rightmost derivation of G_3. Thus, $Y = X$.

We must show that there cannot be two distinct nonterminals B_X^a and A_X^a in N_3. That is, there cannot exist B_X and A_X in N_2, with $A \neq B$, $A \underset{G}{\overset{*}{\Rightarrow}} a$, and $B \underset{G}{\overset{*}{\Rightarrow}} a$. Let $A = [qq']$, $B = [pp']$, and $X = [rr']$. We observe that q and p are both in the write sequence of r'. Also, if $[ss'] \underset{G}{\overset{*}{\Rightarrow}} a$ and $[ss''] \underset{G}{\overset{*}{\Rightarrow}} a$, then referring to the DPDA underlying G, we may conclude that $s' = s''$. Thus, q' is uniquely determined by q, and p' by p, given that $[qq'] \underset{G}{\overset{*}{\Rightarrow}} a$ and $[pp'] \underset{G}{\overset{*}{\Rightarrow}} a$.

It follows that since q and p are in the write sequence of r' and $q \neq p$, then either B appears as a sentential form in the derivation $A \underset{G}{\overset{*}{\Rightarrow}} a$ or A appears in $B \underset{G}{\overset{*}{\Rightarrow}} a$.

Assume the former without loss of generality. Then there is a nontrivial derivation of B from A in G, and this derivation must use only type (3) productions. Then $A_X \underset{G_1}{\overset{+}{\Rightarrow}} B_X$, and B_X should have been removed in step (2) of Algorithm 8.5. In contradiction, we conclude that B_Y^a does not exist in G_4.

The case where \$ replaces C in the above is handled similarly. Here, q_0, the start state of the underlying DPDA, plays the role of r'.

Case 2: Suppose that for some C, we have $C \lessdot A_X^a$ in G_4 and $C \doteq A_X^a$ in both G_3 and G_4. Then there is some B_X^a such that $C \lessdot B_X^a$ or $C \doteq B_X^a$ in G_3 and $B_X^a \underset{G_4}{\overset{+}{\Rightarrow}} A_X^a$. By the same argument as in case 1, we conclude that $C = X_Z^d$ and that $A_X \underset{G_1}{\overset{+}{\Rightarrow}} B_X$, or vice versa. Thus, A_X or B_X should have been removed in step (2) of Algorithm 8.5. Note that there cannot be a (1, 1)-precedence conflict here, let alone a (2, 1)-precedence conflict.

We conclude that G_4 is a UI (2, 1)-precedence grammar. $\square$

COROLLARY 1

Every deterministic language L with the prefix property but without e has a UI (2, 1)-precedence grammar. $\square$

COROLLARY 2

If $L \subseteq \Sigma^*$ is a deterministic language and $\mathcal{c}$ is not in Σ, then $L\mathcal{c}$ has a UI (2, 1)-precedence grammar. $\square$

We can strengthen Theorem 8.17 by deleting the endmarker in Corollary 2.

THEOREM 8.18

Every deterministic language without e has a UI (2, 1)-precedence grammar.

Proof. Let $L\mathcal{c}$ have canonical grammar G. Apply Algorithm 8.5 to G and Algorithm 8.4 to the resulting G_4. We claim that the grammar constructed by Algorithm 8.4 is also a UI (2, 1)-precedence grammar. The proof is left for the Exercises. $\square$

EXERCISES

8.2.1. Find a normal form DPDA accepting
(a) $\{wcw^R \mid w \in (a + b)^*\}$.
(b) $\{a^m b^n a^n b^m \mid m, n \geq 1\}$.
(c) $L(G_0)$.

8.2.2. Find the canonical grammar for the normal form DPDA

$$P = (\{q_0, q_1, q_2, q_3, q_f\}, \{0, 1\}, \{Z_0, Z_1, X\}, \delta, q_0, Z_0, \{q_f\})$$

where δ is given, for all Y, by

$$\delta(q_0, e, Y) = (q_1, Z_1 Y)$$
$$\delta(q_1, 0, Y) = (q_2, Y)$$
$$\delta(q_1, 1, Y) = (q_3, Y)$$
$$\delta(q_2, e, Y) = (q_1, XY)$$
$$\delta(q_3. e, X) = (q_1, e)$$
$$\delta(q_3, e, Z_1) = (q_f, e)$$
$$\delta(q_3, e, Z_0) = (q_f, e)\dagger$$

8.2.3. Identify the write, scan, and erase states in Exercise 8.2.2.

8.2.4. Give formal constructions for Theorem 8.9.

The following three exercises refer to a canonical grammar $G = (N, \Sigma, P, S)$.

8.2.5. Show that
(a) If $[qq'] \longrightarrow a$ is in P, then q is a scan state.
(b) If $[qq'] \longrightarrow [pp']a$ is in P, then p' is a scan state.

†This rule is never used but appears for the sake of the normal form.

(c) If $[qq'] \rightarrow [pp']$ is in P, then q is a write state and p' an erase state.

(d) If $[qq'] \rightarrow [pp'][rr']$ is in P, then p' is a write state and r' is an erase state.

8.2.6. Show that if $[qq'][pp']$ appears as a substring in a right-sentential form of G, then

(a) q' is a write state.

(b) $q' \neq p$.

(c) p is in the write sequence of q'.

8.2.7. Show that if $[qq'] \overset{+}{\Rightarrow} \alpha[pp']$, then p' is an erase state.

8.2.8. Prove the "only if" portion of Theorem 8.10.

8.2.9. Give a formal proof of Theorem 8.15.

8.2.10. Use Algorithm 8.5 to find UI (2, 1)-precedence grammars for the following deterministic languages:

(a) $\{a0^n c0^n \mid n \geq 0\} \cup \{b0^n c0^{2n} \mid n \geq 0\}$.

(b) $\{0^n a1^n 0^m \mid n \geq 0, m \geq 0\} \cup \{0^m b1^n 0^n \mid n \geq 0, m \geq 0\}$.

8.2.11. Complete the case $X = \$$ in Lemma 8.10.

8.2.12. Complete the proof of Theorem 8.17.

8.2.13. Prove Theorem 8.18.

*8.2.14. Show that a CFL has an LR(0) grammar if and only if it is deterministic and has the prefix property.

8.2.15. Show that a CFL has a (1, 0)-BRC grammar if and only if it is deterministic and has the prefix property.

**8.2.16. Show that every deterministic language has an LR(1) grammar in

(a) CNF.

(b) GNF.

8.2.17. Show that if $A \rightarrow \alpha$ and $B \rightarrow \alpha$ are type 4 productions of a canonical grammar, then $A = B$.

*8.2.18. If G of Algorithm 8.4 is a canonical grammar, does G_1 constructed in that algorithm right-cover G? What if G is an arbitrary grammar?

8.2.19. Complete the proof of Theorem 8.12.

*8.2.20. Show that every LR(k) grammar is right-covered by a (1, k)-BRC grammar. *Hint:* Modify the LR(k) grammar by replacing each terminal a on the right of productions by a new nonterminal X_a and adding production $X_a \rightarrow a$. Then modify nonterminals of the grammar to record the set of valid items for the viable prefix to their right.

**8.2.21. Show that every LR(k) grammar is right-covered by an LR(k) grammar which is also a (not necessarily UI) (1, 1)-precedence grammar.

*8.2.22. Show that G_4 of Algorithm 8.5 right-covers G of that algorithm.

Open Problems

8.2.23. Is every LR(k) grammar covered by an LR(1) grammar?

8.2.24. Is every LR(k) grammar covered by a UI (2, 1)-precedence grammar? A positive answer here would yield a positive answer to Exercise 8.2.23.

8.2.25. We stated this one in Chapter 2, but no one has solved it yet, so we shall state it again. Is the equivalence problem for DPDA's decidable? Since all the constructions of this section can be effectively carried out, we have many equivalent forms for this problem. For example, one might show that the equivalence problem for simple MSP grammars or for UI (2, 1)-precedence grammars is decidable.

BIBLIOGRAPHIC NOTES

Theorem 8.11 was first derived by Aho, Denning, and Ullman [1972]. Theorems 8.15 and 8.16 initially appeared in Knuth [1965]. Theorem 8.18 is from Graham [1970]. Exercise 8.2.21 is from Gray and Harrison [1969].

8.3. THEORY OF SIMPLE PRECEDENCE LANGUAGES

We have seen that many classes of grammars generate exactly the deterministic languages. However, there are also several important classes of grammars which do not generate all the deterministic languages. The LL grammars are such a class. In this section we shall study another such class, the simple precedence grammars. We shall show that the simple precedence languages are a proper subset of the deterministic languages and are incommensurate with the LL languages. We shall also show that the operator precedence languages are a proper subset of the simple precedence languages.

8.3.1. The Class of Simple Precedence Languages

As we remarked in Chapter 5, every CFL has a UI grammar and a precedence grammar. When these properties occur simultaneously in a grammar, we have a simple precedence grammar and language. It is interesting to examine the power of simple precedence grammars. They can generate only deterministic languages, since each simple precedence grammar has a deterministic parser. We shall now prove the two main results regarding the class of simple precedence languages. First, we show that

$$L_1 = \{a0^n1^n \,|\, n \geq 1\} \cup \{b0^n1^{2n} \,|\, n \geq 1\}$$

is not a simple precedence language.

THEOREM 8.19

The simple precedence languages form a proper subset of the deterministic languages.

Proof. Clearly, every simple precedence grammar is an LR(1) grammar. To prove proper inclusion, we shall show that there is no simple precedence grammar that generates the deterministic language L_1. Intuitively, the reason for this is that any simple precedence parser for L_1 cannot keep count of the number of 0's in an input string and at the same time know whether an a or a b was seen at the beginning of the input. If the parser stores the first input symbol on the pushdown list followed by the succeeding string of 0's, then, when the 1's are encountered on the input, the parser will not know whether to match one or two 1's with each 0 on the pushdown list without first erasing all the 0's stored on the stack. On the other hand, if the parser tries to maintain on top of the pushdown list an indication of whether an a or b was initially seen, then it must make a sequence of reductions while reading the 0's, which destroys the count of the number of 0's seen on the input.

We shall now construct a formal proof motivated by this intuitive reasoning. Suppose that $G = (N, \Sigma, P, S)$ is a simple precedence grammar such that $L(G) = L_1$. We shall show as a contradiction that any such grammar must also derive sentences not in L_1.

Suppose that an input string $a0^n w$, $w \in 1^*$, is to be parsed by the simple precedence parser constructed for G according to Algorithm 5.12. As $a0^n$ is the prefix of some sentence in L_1 for all n, each 0 must eventually be shifted onto the stack. Let α_i be the stack contents after the ith 0 is shifted. If $\alpha_i = \alpha_j$ for some $i < j$, then $a0^j 1^i$ and $a0^j 1^j$ would either both be accepted or both be rejected by the parser, and so $\alpha_i \neq \alpha_j$ if $i \neq j$.

Thus, for any constant c we can find an α_i such that $|\alpha_i| > c$ and α_i is a prefix of every α_j, $j > i$ (for if not, then we could construct an arbitrarily long sequence $\alpha_{s_1}, \alpha_{s_2}, \ldots$ such that $|\alpha_{s_t}| = |\alpha_{s_{t-1}}|$ for $t \geq 2$ and thus find two identical α's). Choose i as small as possible. Then there must be some shortest string $\beta \neq e$ such that for each k, $\alpha_i \beta^k$ is α_{i+mk} for some $m > 0$. The reason is that since α_i is never erased as long as 0's appear on the input, the symbols written on the stack by the parser do not depend on α_i. The behavior of the parser on input $a0^n$ must be cyclic, and it must enlarge the stack or repeat the same stack contents (and we have just argued that it may not do the latter).

Now, let us consider the behavior of the parser on an input string of the form $b0^n x$. Let γ_k be the stack after reading $b0^k$. We may argue as above, that for some γ_j, j as small as possible, there is a shortest string $\delta \neq e$ such that for each k, $\gamma_j \delta^k = \gamma_{j+qk}$ for some $q > 0$. In fact, since γ_j is never erased, we must have $\delta = \beta$ and $q = m$. That is, a simple induction on $r \geq 0$ shows that if after reading $a0^{i+r}$ the stack holds $\alpha_i \epsilon_r$, then after reading $b0^{j+r}$, the stack will hold $\gamma_j \epsilon_r$.

Consider the moves made by the parser acting on the input string $a0^{i+mk}1^{i+mk}$. After reading $a0^{i+mk}$, the stack will contain $\alpha_i \beta^k$. Then let s be the largest number such that after reading 1^{i+mk-s} the parser will have $\alpha_i \zeta$ left on its stack for some ζ in $(N \cup \Sigma)^*$ (i.e., on the next 1 input, one of the symbols of α_i is involved in a reduction). It is easy to show that s is unique; otherwise, the parser would accept a string not in L_1.

Similarly, let r be the largest number such that beginning with $\gamma_j \beta^k$ on its stack the parser with input $1^{2(j+mk)-r}$ makes a sequence of moves ending up with some $\gamma_j \zeta$ on its stack. Again, r must be unique.

Then for all k, the input $b0^{j+mk}1^{i+mk-s+r}$ must be accepted, since $b0^{j+mk}$ causes the stack to become $\alpha_j \beta^k$, and 1^{i+mk-s} causes the stack to become $\alpha_j \zeta$. The erasure of the β's occurs independently of whether α_i or α_j is below, and 1^r causes acceptance. But since $m \neq 0$, it is impossible that we have $i + mk - s + r = 2(j + mk)$ for all k.

We conclude that L_1 is not a simple precedence language.   □

THEOREM 8.20

The classes of LL and simple precedence languages are incommensurate.

Proof. L_1 of Theorem 8.19 is an LL(1) language which is not a simple precedence language. The natural grammar for L_1

$$S \longrightarrow aA \mid bB$$
$$A \longrightarrow 0A1 \mid 01$$
$$B \longrightarrow 0B11 \mid 011$$

is easily shown to be an LL(2) grammar. Left factoring converts it to an LL(1) grammar.

We claim that the language $L_2 = \{0^n a1^n \mid n \geq 1\} \cup \{0^n b2^n \mid n \geq 1\}$ is not an LL language. (See Exercise 8.3.2.) L_2 is a simple precedence language; it has the following simple precedence grammar:

$$S \longrightarrow A \mid B$$
$$A \longrightarrow 0A1 \mid a$$
$$B \longrightarrow 0B2 \mid b$$ □

8.3.2. Operator Precedence Languages

Let us now turn our attention to the class of languages generated by the operator precedence grammars. Although there are ambiguous operator precedence grammars (the grammar $S \longrightarrow A \,|\, B$, $A \longrightarrow a$, $B \longrightarrow a$ is a simple example), we shall discover that operator precedence languages are a proper subset of the simple precedence languages. We begin by showing that every operator precedence language has an operator grammar which has no single productions and which is uniquely invertible.

LEMMA 8.13

Every (not necessarily UI) operator precedence grammar is equivalent to one with no single productions.

Proof. Algorithm 2.11, which removes single productions, is easily seen to preserve the operator precedence relations between terminals.   ☐

We shall now provide an algorithm to make any context-free grammar with no single productions uniquely invertible.

ALGORITHM 8.6

Conversion of a CFG with no single productions to an equivalent UI CFG.

Input. A CFG $G = (N, \Sigma, P, S)$ with no single productions.

Output. An equivalent UI CFG $G_1 = (N_1, \Sigma, P_1, S_1)$.

Method.

(1) The nonterminals of the new grammar will be nonempty subsets of N. Formally, let $N'_1 = \{M \,|\, M \subseteq N$ and $M \neq \varnothing\} \cup \{S_1\}$.

(2) For each $w_0, w_1, \ldots, w_k$ in Σ^* and $M_1, \ldots, M_k$ in N'_1, place in P'_1 the production $M \longrightarrow w_0 M_1 w_1 \cdots M_k w_k$, where

$$M = \{A \,|\, \text{there is a production of the form } A \longrightarrow w_0 B_1 w_1 \cdots B_k w_k,$$
$$\text{where } B_i \in M_i, \text{ for } 1 \leq i \leq k\}$$

provided that $M \neq \varnothing$. Note that only a finite number of productions are so generated.

(3) For all $M \subseteq N$ such that $S \in M$, add the production $S_1 \longrightarrow M$ to P'_1.

(4) Remove all useless nonterminals and productions, and let N_1 and P_1 be the useful portions of N'_1 and P'_1, respectively.   ☐

Example 8.5

Consider the grammar

$$S \longrightarrow a \,|\, aAbS$$
$$A \longrightarrow a \,|\, aSbA$$

From step (2) we obtain the productions

$$\{S\} \longrightarrow a\{A\}b\{S\} \mid a\{S, A\}b\{S\} \mid a\{A\}b\{S, A\}$$
$$\{A\} \longrightarrow a\{S\}b\{A\} \mid a\{S, A\}b\{A\} \mid a\{S\}b\{S, A\}$$
$$\{S, A\} \longrightarrow a \mid a\{S, A\}b\{S, A\}$$

From step (3) we obtain the productions

$$S_1 \longrightarrow \{S\} \mid \{S, A\}$$

From step (4) we discover that all $\{S\}$- and $\{A\}$-productions are useless, and so the resulting grammar is

$$S_1 \longrightarrow \{S, A\}$$
$$\{S, A\} \longrightarrow a \mid a\{S, A\}b\{S, A\} \qquad \square$$

LEMMA 8.14

The grammar G_1 constructed from G in Algorithm 8.6 is UI if G has no single productions and is an operator precedence grammar if G is operator precedence. Moreover, $L(G_1) = L(G)$.

Proof. Step (2) certainly enforces unique invertibility, and since G has no single productions, step (3) cannot introduce a nonuniquely invertible right side. A proof that Algorithm 8.6 preserves the operator precedence relations among terminals is straightforward and left for the Exercises. Finally, it is easy to verify by induction on the length of a derivation that if $A \in M$, then $A \overset{*}{\underset{G}{\Rightarrow}} w$ if and only if $M \overset{*}{\underset{G_1}{\Rightarrow}} w$. $\square$

We thus have the following normal form for operator precedence grammars.

THEOREM 8.21

If L is an operator precedence language, then $L = L(G)$ for some operator precedence grammar $G = (N, \Sigma, P, S)$ such that

(1) G is UI,
(2) S appears on the right of no production, and
(3) The only single productions in P have S on the left.

Proof. Apply Algorithms 2.11 and 8.6 to an arbitrary operator precedence grammar. $\square$

We shall now take an operator precedence grammar G in the normal form given in Theorem 8.21 and change G into a UI weak precedence grammar G_1 such that $L(G_1) = \phi L(G)$, where ϕ is a left endmarker. We can then construct a UI weak precedence grammar G_2 such that $L(G_2) = L(G)$. In this way we shall show that the operator precedence languages are a subset of the simple precedence languages.

ALGORITHM 8.7

Conversion of an operator precedence grammar to a weak precedence grammar.

Input. A UI operator precedence grammar $G = (N, \Sigma, P, S)$ satisfying the conditions of Theorem 8.21.

Output. A UI weak precedence grammar $G_1 = (N_1, \Sigma \cup \{\phi\}, P_1, S_1)$ such that $L(G_1) = \phi L(G)$, where ϕ is not in Σ.

Method.

(1) Let N'_1 consist of all symbols $[XA]$ such that $X \in \Sigma \cup \{\phi\}$ and $A \in N$.
(2) Let $S_1 = [\phi S]$.
(3) Let h be the homomorphism from $N'_1 \cup \Sigma \cup \{\phi\}$ to $N \cup \Sigma$ such that
   (a) $h(a) = a$, for $a \in \Sigma \cup \{\phi\}$, and
   (b) $h([aA]) = aA$.

Then $h^{-1}(\alpha)$ is defined only for strings α in $(N \cup \Sigma)^*$ which begin with a symbol in $\Sigma \cup \{\phi\}$ and do not have adjacent nonterminals. Moreover, $h^{-1}(\alpha)$ is unique if it is defined. That is, h^{-1} combines a nonterminal with the terminal appearing to its left. Let P'_1 consist of all productions $[aA] \rightarrow h^{-1}(a\alpha)$ such that $A \rightarrow \alpha$ is in P and a is in $\Sigma \cup \{\phi\}$.

(4) Let N_1 and P_1 be the useful portions of N'_1 and P'_1, respectively.   □

Example 8.6

Let G be defined by

$$S \longrightarrow A$$
$$A \longrightarrow aAbAc \,|\, aAd \,|\, a$$

We shall generate only the useful portion of N'_1 and P'_1 in Algorithm 8.7. We begin with nonterminal $[\phi S]$. Its production is $[\phi S] \rightarrow [\phi A]$. The productions for $[\phi A]$ are $[\phi A] \rightarrow \phi[aA][bA]c$, $[\phi A] \rightarrow \phi[aA]d$, and $[\phi A] \rightarrow \phi a$. The productions for $[aA]$ and $[bA]$ are constructed similarly. Thus, G_1 is

$$[\phi S] \longrightarrow [\phi A]$$
$$[\phi A] \longrightarrow \phi[aA][bA]c \,|\, \phi[aA]d \,|\, \phi a$$
$$[aA] \longrightarrow a[aA][bA]c \,|\, a[aA]d \,|\, aa$$
$$[bA] \longrightarrow b[aA][bA]c \,|\, b[aA]d \,|\, ba$$ □

LEMMA 8.15

In Algorithm 8.7 the grammar G_1 is a UI weak precedence grammar such that $L(G_1) = \not\!\! c L(G)$.

Proof. Unique invertibility is easy to show, and we omit the proof. To show that G_1 is a weak precedence grammar, we must show that $\lessdot$ and $\doteq$ are disjoint from $\gtrdot$ in G_1†. Let us define the homomorphism g by

(1) $g(a) = a$ for $a \in \Sigma$,
(2) $g(\not\!\! c) = \$$, and
(3) $g([aA]) = a$.

It suffices to show that

(1) If $X \lessdot Y$ in G_1, then $g(X) \lessdot g(Y)$ or $g(X) \doteq g(Y)$ in G.
(2) If $X \doteq Y$ in G_1, then $g(X) \lessdot g(Y)$ or $g(X) \doteq g(Y)$ in G.
(3) If $X \gtrdot Y$ in G_1, then $g(X) \gtrdot g(Y)$ in G.

Case 1: Suppose that $X \lessdot Y$ in G_1, where $X \neq \not\!\! c$ and $X \neq \$$. Then there is a right-hand side in P_1, say $\alpha X[aA]\beta$, such that $[aA] \underset{G_1}{\overset{+}{\Rightarrow}} Y\gamma$ for some γ. If α is not e, then it is easy to show that there is a right-hand side in P with substring $h(X[aA])$‡ and thus $g(X) \doteq a$ in G. But the form of the productions in P_1 implies that $g(Y)$ must be a. Thus, $g(X) \doteq g(Y)$.

If α is e and $X \in \Sigma$, then the left-hand side associated with right-hand side $\alpha X[aA]\beta$ is of the form $[XB]$ for some $B \in N$. Then there must be a production in P whose right-hand side has substring XB. Moreover, $B \rightarrow aAh(\beta)$ is a production in P. Hence, $X \lessdot a$ in G. Since $g(X) = X$ in this case, the conclusion $g(X) \lessdot g(Y)$ follows. If α is e and $X = [bB]$ for some $b \in \Sigma$ and $B \in N$, let the left-hand side associated with right-hand side $\alpha X[aA]\beta$ be $[bC]$. Then there is a right-hand side in P with substring bC, and $C \rightarrow BaAh(\beta)$ is in P. Thus, $b \lessdot a$ in G, and $g(X) \lessdot g(Y)$ follows. The case in which $\alpha = e$ and $X = [\not\!\! c B]$ for some $B \in N$ is easily handled, as is the case where X itself is $\not\!\! c$ or $\$$.

Case 2: The case $X \doteq Y$ is handled similarly to case 1.

Case 3: $X \gtrdot Y$. Assume that $Y \neq \$$. Then there is some right-hand side in P_1, say $\alpha[aA]Z\beta$, such that $[aA] \underset{G_1}{\overset{+}{\Rightarrow}} \gamma X$ and $Z \underset{G_1}{\overset{*}{\Rightarrow}} Y\delta$ for some γ and δ. The form of productions in P_1 again implies that either $Z = Y$ and both are in $\Sigma \cup \{\$\}$ or $Z = [aB]$ and $Y = [aC]$ or $Y = a$, for some B and C in N. In any case, $g(Z) = g(Y)$.

There must be a right-hand side in P with substring $Ag(Z)$ because

---

†Here and subsequently, the symbols $\lessdot$, $\doteq$, and $\gtrdot$ refer to operator precedence relations in G and Wirth–Weber precedence relations in G_1.

‡h is the homomorphism in Algorithm 8.7.

$\alpha[aA]Z\beta$ is a right-hand side of P_1. Since G has no single productions except for starting productions, γ is not e, and so $g(X)$ is derived from A rather than a in the derivation $[aA] \underset{G_1}{\overset{+}{\Rightarrow}} \gamma X$. Thus, $g(X) > g(Z)$, and $g(X) > g(Y)$ in G.

The case $Y = \$$ is handled easily.

To complete the proof that G_1 is a weak precedence grammar, we must show that if $A \rightarrow \alpha X\beta$ and $B \rightarrow \beta$ are in P_1, then neither $X \lessdot B$ nor $X \doteq B$ holds. Let $B = [aC]$, and suppose for the moment that $C \neq S$. Then, since G has no single productions without S on the left, we know that $\beta = Y\beta'$ for some $\beta' \neq e$, where $h(Y) = a$. Since $\beta' \neq e$, $h(\beta')$ has at least one terminal; let b be the leftmost one. Then, since a can appear to the left of C in a right-sentential form of G, we know that $a \lessdot b$ in G. But since $\alpha X\beta$ is a right-hand side in P_1, $h(\beta)$ is a subword of some right-hand side in P, and so $a \doteq b$ in G. We thus rule out the possibility that $C \neq S$.

If $C = S$, then by Theorem 8.21(2), we must have $a = \phi$. But then, since $\alpha X\beta$ is a right-hand side in P_1, ϕ must appear in a right-hand side in P, which we assumed not to be the case.

We conclude that G_1 is a weak precedence grammar. The proof that $L(G_1) = \phi L(G)$ is straightforward and will be omitted. $\square$

THEOREM 8.22

If L is an operator precedence language, then L is a simple precedence language.

Proof. By Theorem 8.21 and Lemma 8.15, if $L \subseteq \Sigma^+$ is an operator precedence language, then ϕL is a UI weak precedence language, where ϕ is not in Σ. A straightforward generalization of Algorithm 8.4 allows us to remove the left endmarker from the grammar for ϕL constructed by Algorithm 8.7. (The form of productions in Algorithm 8.7 assures that the resulting grammar will be UI and proper.) The actual proof is left for the Exercises. By Theorem 5.16, L is a simple precedence language. $\square$

8.3.3. Chapter Summary

We have, in Chapter 8, shown the inclusion relations for classes of languages indicated in Fig. 8.7. All inclusions are proper.

Examples of languages which are contained in the regions shown in Fig. 8.7 are

(1) $\{0^n 1^n \,|\, n \geq 1\}$ is LL(1) and operator precedence.

(2) $\{0^n 1^n \,|\, n \geq 1\} \cup \{0^n 2^n \,|\, n \geq 1\}$ is operator precedence but not LL.

(3) $\{a0^n 1^n 0^m \,|\, m, n \geq 1\} \cup \{b0^m 1^n 0^n \,|\, m, n \geq 1\} \cup \{a0^n 2^n 0^m \,|\, m, n \geq 1\}$ is simple precedence but neither operator precedence nor LL.

(4) $\{a0^n 1^n 0^m \,|\, m, n \geq 1\} \cup \{b0^m 1^n 0^n \,|\, m, n \geq 1\}$ is LL(1) and simple precedence but not operator precedence.

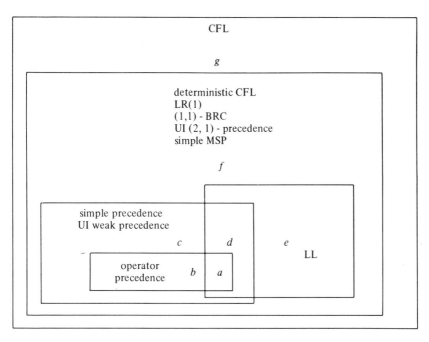

Fig. 8.7   Subclasses of deterministic languages.

(5) $\{a0^n1^n \mid n \geq 1\} \cup \{b0^n1^{2n} \mid n \geq 1\}$ is LL(1) but not simple precedence.

(6) $\{a0^n1^n \mid n \geq 1\} \cup \{a0^n2^{2n} \mid n \geq 1\} \cup \{b0^n1^{2n} \mid n \geq 1\}$ is deterministic but not LL or simple precedence.

(7) $\{0^n1^n \mid n \geq 1\} \cup \{0^n1^{2n} \mid n \geq 1\}$ is context-free but not deterministic.

Proofs that these languages have the ascribed properties are requested in the Exercises.

EXERCISES

8.3.1.   Show that the grammar for L_1 given in Theorem 8.20 is LL(2). Find an LL(1) grammar for L_1.

*8.3.2.   Prove that the language $L_2 = \{0^n a1^n \mid n \geq 1\} \cup \{0^n b2^n \mid n \geq 1\}$ is not an LL language. *Hint:* Assume that L_2 has an LL(k) grammar in GNF.

*8.3.3.   Show that L_2 of Exercise 8.3.2 is an operator precedence language.

8.3.4.   Prove that Algorithm 2.11 (elimination of single productions) preserves the properties of
(a) Operator precedence.
(b) (m, n)-precedence.
(c) (m, n)-BRC.

8.3.5.   Prove Lemma 8.14.

*8.3.6. Why does Algorithm 8.6 not necessarily convert an arbitrary precedence grammar into a simple precedence grammar?

8.3.7. Convert the following operator precedence grammar to an equivalent simple precedence grammar:

$$S \longrightarrow \text{if } b \text{ then } S_1 \text{ else } S \,|\, \text{if } b \text{ then } S \,|\, a$$
$$S_1 \longrightarrow \text{if } b \text{ then } S_1 \text{ else } S_1 \,|\, a$$

8.3.8. Prove case 2 of Lemma 8.15.

8.3.9. Give an algorithm to remove the left endmarker from the language generated by a grammar. Show that your algorithm preserves the UI weak precedence property when applied to a grammar constructed by Algorithm 8.7.

8.3.10. Show that the simple precedence language

$$L = \{a0^n 1^n 0^m \,|\, n \geq 1, m \geq 1\} \cup \{b0^m 1^n 0^n \,|\, n \geq 1, m \geq 1\}$$

is not an operator precedence language.
Hint: Show that any grammar for L must have $1 \lessdot 1$ and $1 \gtrdot 1$ as part of the operator precedence relations.

*8.3.11. Show that L of Exercise 8.3.10 is a simple precedence language.

*8.3.12. Prove that the languages given in Section 8.3.3 have the properties ascribed to them.

8.3.13. Give additional examples of languages which belong to the various regions in Fig. 8.7.

8.3.14. Generalize Theorem 8.18 to show that L_1 of that theorem is not UI $(1, k)$-precedence for any k.

8.3.15. Show that G_1 of Algorithm 8.7 right-covers G of that algorithm.

8.3.16. Does G_1 constructed in Algorithm 8.6 right-cover G of that algorithm if G is proper?

**8.3.17. Let L be the simple precedence language

$$\{a^n 0 a^i b^n \,|\, i, n \geq 0\} \cup \{0a^n 1a^i c^n \,|\, i, n \geq 0\}.$$

Show that there is no simple precedence parser for L that will announce error immediately after reading the 1 in an input string of the form $a^n 1 a^i b$. (See Exercise 7.3.5.)

Open Question

8.3.18. What is the relationship of the class of UI $(1, k)$-precedence languages, $k > 1$, to the classes shown in Fig. 8.7? The reader should be aware of Exercise 8.3.14.

BIBLIOGRAPHIC NOTES

The proper inclusion of the simple precedence languages in the deterministic context-free languages and the proper containment of the operator precedence languages in the simple precedence languages were first proved by Fischer [1969].

9   TRANSLATION AND CODE GENERATION

A compiler designer is usually presented with an incomplete specification of the language for which he is to design a compiler. Much of the syntax of the language can be precisely defined in terms of a context-free grammar. However, the object code that is to be generated for each source program is more difficult to specify. Broadly applicable formal methods for specifying the semantics of a programming language are still a subject of current research.

In this chapter we shall present and give examples of declarative formalisms that can be used to specify some of the translations performed within a compiler. Then we shall investigate techniques for mechanically implementing the translations defined by these formalisms.

9.1. THE ROLE OF TRANSLATION IN COMPILING

We recall from Chapter 1 that a compiler is a translator that maps strings into strings. The input to the compiler is a string of symbols that constitutes the *source program*. The output of the compiler, called the *object* (or *target*) *program*, is also a string of symbols. The object program can be

(1) A sequence of absolute machine instructions,
(2) A sequence of relocatable machine instructions,
(3) An assembly language program, or
(4) A program in some other language.

Let us briefly discuss the characteristics of each of these forms of the object program.

(1) Mapping a source program into an absolute machine language pro-

gram that can immediately be executed is one way of achieving very fast compilation. WATFOR is an example of such a compiler. This type of compilation is best suited for small programs that do not use separately compiled subroutines.

(2) A relocatable machine instruction is an instruction that references memory locations relative to some movable origin. An object program in the form of a sequence of relocatable machine instructions is usually called a relocatable *object deck*. This object deck can be linked together with other object decks such as separately compiled user subprograms, input–output routines, and library functions to produce a single relocatable object deck, often called a *load module*. The program that produces the load module from a set of binary decks is called a *link editor*. The load module is then put into memory by a program called a *loader* that converts the relocatable addresses into absolute addresses. The object program is then ready for execution.

Although linking and loading consume time, most commercial compilers produce relocatable binary decks because of the flexibility in being able to use extensive library subroutines and separately compiled subprograms.

(3) Translating a source program into an assembly language program that is then run through an assembler simplifies the design of the compiler. However, the total time now required to produce an executable machine language program is rather high because assembling the output of this type of compiler may take as much time as the compilation itself.

(4) Certain compilers (e.g., SNOBOL) map a source program into another program in a special internal language. This internal program is then executed by simulating the sequence of instructions in the internal program. Such compilers are usually called *interpreters*. However, we can view the mapping of the source program into the internal language as an instance of compilation in itself.

In this book we shall not assume any fixed format for the output of a compiler, although in many examples we use assembly language as the object code. In this section we shall review compiling and the main processes that map a source program into object code.

9.1.1. Phases of Compilation

In Chapter 1 we saw that a compiler can be partitioned into several subtranslators, each of which participated in translating some representation of the source program toward the object program. We can model each subtranslator by a mapping that defines a *phase* of the compilation such that the composition of all the phases models the entire compilation.

What we choose to call a phase is somewhat arbitrary. However, it is convenient to think of lexical analysis, syntactic analysis, and code generation as the main phases of compilation. However, in many sophisticated compilers these phases are often subdivided into several subphases, and other phases (e.g., code optimization) may also be present.

The input to a compiler is a string of symbols. The lexical analyzer is the first phase of compilation. It maps the input into a string consisting of tokens and symbol table entries. During lexical analysis the original source program is compressed in size somewhat because identifiers are replaced by tokens and unnecessary blanks and comments are removed. After lexical analysis, the original source program is still essentially a string, but certain portions of this string are pointers to information in a symbol table.

A finite transducer is a good model for a lexical analyzer. We discussed finite transducers and their application to lexical analysis in Section 3.3. In Chapter 10 we shall discuss techniques that can be used to insert and retrieve information from symbol tables.

The syntax analyzer takes the output of the lexical analyzer and parses it according to some underlying grammar. This grammar is similar to the one used in the specification of the source language. However, the grammar for the source language usually does not specify what constructs are to be treated as lexical items. Keywords and identifiers such as labels, variable names, and constants are some of the constructs that are usually recognized during lexical analysis. But these constructs could also be recognized by the syntax analyzer, and in practice there is no hard and fast rule as to what constructs are to be recognized lexically and what should be left for the syntactic analyzer.

After syntactic analysis, we can visualize that the source program has been transformed into a tree, called the *syntax tree*. The syntax tree is closely related to the derivation tree for the source program, often being the derivation tree with chains of single productions deleted. In the syntax tree interior nodes generally correspond to operators, and the leaves represent operands consisting of pointers into the symbol table. The structure of the syntax tree reflects the syntactic rules of the programming language in which the source program was written. There are several ways of physically representing the syntax tree, which we shall discuss in the next section. We shall call a representation of the syntax tree an *intermediate program*.

The actual output of the syntactic analyzer can be a sequence of commands to construct the intermediate program, to consult and modify the symbol table, and to produce diagnostic messages where necessary. The model that we have used for a syntactic analyzer in Chapters 4–7 produced a left or right parse for the input. However, it is the nature of syntax trees used in practice that one may easily replace the production numbers in a left or right parse by commands that construct the syntax tree and perform symbol table operations. Thus, it is an appealing simplification to regard the left or right parses produced by the parsers of Chapters 4–7 as the intermediate program itself, and to avoid making a major distinction between a syntax tree and a parse tree.

A compiler must also check that certain semantic conventions of the source language have been obeyed. Some common examples of conventions of this nature are

(1) Each statement label referenced must actually appear as the label of an appropriate statement in the source program.

(2) No identifier can be declared more than once.

(3) All variables must be defined before use.

(4) The arguments of a function call must be compatible both in number and in attributes with the definition of the function.

The checking of these conventions by a compiler is called *semantic analysis*. Semantic analysis often occurs immediately after syntactic analysis, but it can also be done in some later phases of compilation. For example, checking that variables are defined before use can be done during code optimization if there is a code optimization phase. Checking of operands for correct attributes can be deferred to the code generation phase.

In Chapter 10, we shall discuss property grammars, a formalism that can be used to model aspects of syntactic and semantic analysis.

After syntactic analysis, the intermediate program is mapped by the code generator into the object program. However, to generate correct object code, the code generator must also have access to the information in the symbol table. For example, the attributes of the operands of a given operator determine the code that is to be generated for the operator. For instance, when A and B are floating-point variables, different object code will be generated for $A + B$ than will be generated when A and B are integer variables.

Storage allocation also occurs during code generation (or in some subphase of code generation). Thus, the code generator must know whether a variable represents a scalar, an array, or a structure. This information is contained in the symbol table.

Some compilers have an optimizing phase before code generation. In this optimizing phase the intermediate program is subjected to transformations that attempt to put the intermediate program into a form from which a more efficient object language program can be produced. It is often difficult to distinguish some optimizing transformations from good code generation techniques. In Chapter 11 we shall discuss some of the optimizations that can be performed on intermediate programs or while generating intermediate programs.

An actual compiler may implement a phase of the compilation process in one or more passes, where a *pass* consists of reading input from secondary memory and then writing intermediate results into secondary memory. What is implemented in a pass is a function of the size of the machine on which the compiler is to run, the language for which the compiler is being developed, the number of people engaged in implementing the compiler, and so forth. It is even possible to implement all phases in one pass. What the optimal number of passes to implement a given compiler should be is a topic that is beyond the scope of this book.

9.1.2. Representations of the Intermediate Program

In this section we shall discuss some possible representations for the intermediate program that is produced by the syntactic analyzer. The intermediate program should reflect the syntactic structure of the source program. However, it should also be relatively easy to translate each statement of the intermediate program into machine code.

Compilers performing extensive amounts of code optimization create a detailed representation of the intermediate program, explicitly showing the flow of control inherent in the source program. In other compilers the representation of the intermediate program is a simple representation of the syntax tree, such as Polish notation. Other compilers, doing little code optimization, will generate object code as the parse proceeds. In this case, the "intermediate" program appears only figuratively, as a sequence of steps taken by the parser.

Some of the more common representations for the intermediate program are

(1) Postfix Polish notation,
(2) Prefix Polish notation,
(3) Linked list structures representing trees,
(4) Multiple address code with named results, and
(5) Multiple address code with implicitly named results.

Let us examine some examples of these representations.

We defined Polish notation for arithmetic expressions in Section 3.1.1. For example, the assignment statement

$$(9.1.1) \qquad\qquad A = B + C * - D$$

with the normal order of precedence for the operators and assignment symbol $(=)$ has the postfix Polish representation†

$$ABCD - * + =$$

and the prefix Polish representation

$$= A + B * C - D$$

†In this representation, $-$ is a unary operator and $*$, $+$, and $=$ are all binary operators.

In postfix Polish notation, the operands appear from left to right in the order in which they are used. The operators appear right after the operands and in the order in which they are used. Postfix Polish notation is often used as an intermediate language by interpreters. The execution phase of the interpreter can evaluate the postfix expression using a pushdown list for an accumulator. (See Example 9.4.)

Both types of Polish expressions are linear representations of the syntax tree for expression (9.1.1), shown in Fig. 9.1. This tree reflects the syntactic structure of expression (9.1.1). We can also use this tree itself as the intermediate program, encoding it as a linked list structure.

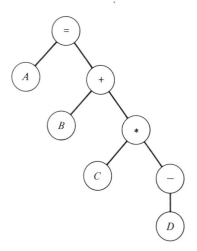

Fig. 9.1   Syntax tree.

Another method of encoding of the syntax tree is to use multiple address code. For example, using multiple address code with named results, expression (9.1.1) could be represented by the following sequence of assignment statements:

$$T_1 \longleftarrow -D$$
$$T_2 \longleftarrow *CT_1$$
$$T_3 \longleftarrow +BT_2$$
$$A \longleftarrow T_3†$$

A statement of the form $A \longleftarrow \theta B_1 \cdots B_r$ means that r-ary operator θ is to be applied to the current values of variables $B_1, \cdots, B_r$ and that the resulting

---

†Note that the assignment operator must be treated differently from other operators. A simple "optimization" is to replace T_3 by A in the third line and to delete the fourth line.

value is to be assigned to variable A. We shall formally define this particular intermediate language in Section 11.1.

Multiple address code with named results requires a temporary variable name in each assignment instruction to hold the value of the expression computed by the right-hand side of each statement. We can avoid the use of the temporary variables by using multiple address code with implicitly named results. In this notation we label each assignment statement by a number. We then delete the left-hand side of the statement and reference temporary results by the number assigned to the statement generating the temporary result. For example, expression (9.1.1) would be represented by the sequence

$$1: \quad -D$$
$$2: \quad *C\,(1)$$
$$3: \quad +B\,(2)$$
$$4: \quad =A\,(3)$$

Here a parenthesized number refers to the expression labeled by that number.

Multiple address code representations are computationally convenient if a code optimization phase occurs after the syntactic analysis phase. During the code optimization phase the representation of the program may change considerably. It is much more difficult to make global changes on a Polish representation than a linked list representation of the intermediate program.

As a second example let us consider representations for the statement

$$(9.1.2) \qquad\qquad \textbf{if } I = J \textbf{ then } S_1 \textbf{ else } S_2$$

where S_1 and S_2 represent arbitrary statements.

A possible postfix Polish representation for this statement might be

$$I\ J\ \text{EQUAL?}\ L_2\ \text{JFALSE}\ S_1'\ L\ \text{JUMP}\ S_2'$$

Here, S_1' and S_2' are the postfix representations of S_1 and S_2, respectively; EQUAL? is a Boolean-valued binary operator that has the value **true** if its two arguments are equal and **false** otherwise. L_2 is a constant which names the beginning of S_2'. JFALSE is a binary operator which causes a jump to the location given by its second argument if the value of the first argument is **false** and has no effect if the first argument is **true**. L is a constant which is the first instruction following S_2'. JUMP is a unary operator that causes a jump to the location given by its argument.

A derivation tree for statement (9.1.2) is shown in Fig. 9.2. The important syntactic information in this derivation tree can be represented by the syntax tree shown in Fig. 9.3, where S_1' and S_2' represent syntax trees for S_1 and S_2.

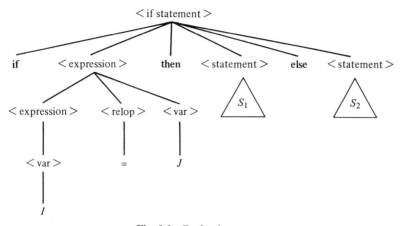

Fig. 9.2   Derivation tree.

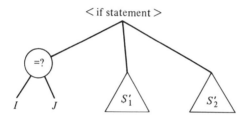

Fig. 9.3   Syntax tree.

A syntactic analyzer generating an intermediate program would parse expression (9.1.2) tracing out the tree in Fig. 9.2, but its output would be a sequence of commands that would construct the syntax tree in Fig. 9.3.

In general, in the syntax tree an interior node represents an operator whose operands are given by its direct descendants. The leaves of the syntax tree correspond to identifiers. The leaves will actually be pointers into the symbol table where the names and attributes of these identifiers are kept.

Part of the output of the syntax analyzer will be commands to enter information into the symbol table. For example, a source language statement of the form

INTEGER *I*

will be translated into a command that enters the attribute "integer" in the symbol table location reserved for identifier *I*. There will be no explicit representation for this statement in the intermediate program.

9.1.3. Models for Code Generation

Code generation is a mapping from the intermediate program to a string. We shall consider this mapping to be a function defined on the syntax tree and information in the symbol table. The nature of this mapping depends on the source language, the target machine, and the quality of the object code desired.

One of the simplest code generation schemes would map each multiple address statement into a sequence of object language instructions independent of the context of the multiple address instructions. For example, an assignment instruction of the form

$$A \longleftarrow +BC$$

might be mapped into the three machine instructions

$$
\begin{array}{ll}
\text{LOAD} & B \\
\text{ADD} & C \\
\text{STORE} & A
\end{array}
$$

Here we are assuming a one accumulator machine, where the instruction LOAD B places the value of memory location B in the accumulator, ADD C adds† the value of memory location C to the accumulator, and STORE A places the value in the accumulator into memory location A. The STORE instruction leaves the contents of the accumulator unchanged.

However, if the accumulator initially contained the value of memory location B (because, for example, the previous assignment instruction was $B \longleftarrow + DE$), then the LOAD B instruction would be unnecessary. Also, if the next assignment instruction is $F \longleftarrow +AG$ and no other reference is made to A, then the STORE A instruction is not needed.

In Sections 11.1 and 11.2 of Chapter 11 we shall consider some techniques for generating code from multiple address statements.

EXERCISES

9.1.1. Draw syntax trees for the following source language statements:
(a) $A = (B - C)/(B + C)$ (as in FORTRAN).
(b) $I = \text{LENGTH}(C1 \,||\, C2)$ (as in PL/I).
(c) **if** $B > C$ **then**
       if $D > E$ **then** $A := B + C$ **else** $A := B - C$
     else $A := B * C$ (as in ALGOL).

---

†Let us assume for simplicity that there is only one type of arithmetic. If more than one, e.g., fixed and floating, is available, then the translation of $+$ will depend on symbol table information about the attributes of B and C.

9.1.2. Define postfix Polish representations for the programs in Exercise 9.1.1.

9.1.3. Generate multiple address code with named results for the statements in Exercise 9.1.1.

9.1.4. Construct a deterministic pushdown transducer that maps prefix Polish notation into postfix Polish notation.

9.1.5. Show that there is no deterministic pushdown transducer that maps postfix Polish notation into prefix Polish notation. Is there a nondeterministic pushdown transducer that performs this mapping? Hint: see Theorem 3.15.

9.1.6. Devise an algorithm using a pushdown list that will evaluate a postfix Polish expression.

9.1.7. Design a pushdown transducer that takes as input an expression w in $L(G_0)$ and produces as output a sequence of commands that will build a syntax tree (or multiple address code) for w.

9.1.8. Generate assembly code for your favorite computer for the programs in Exercise 9.1.1.

*9.1.9. Devise algorithms to generate assembly code for your favorite computer for intermediate programs representing arithmetic assignments when the intermediate program is in
(a) Postfix Polish notation.
(b) Multiple address code with named results.
(c) Multiple address code with implicitly named results.
(d) The form of a syntax tree.

*9.1.10. Design an intermediate language that is suitable for the representation of some subset of FORTRAN (or PL/I or ALGOL) programs. The subset should include assignment statements and some control statements. Subscripted variables should also be allowed.

**9.1.11. Design a code generator that will map an intermediate program of Exercise 9.1.10 into machine code for your favorite computer.

BIBLIOGRAPHIC NOTES

Unfortunately, it is impossible to specify the best object code even for common source language constructs. However, there are several papers and books that discuss the translation of various programming languages. Backus et al. [1957] give the details of an early FORTRAN compiler. Randell and Russell [1964] and Grau et al. [1967] discuss the implementation of ALGOL 60. Some details of PL/I implementation are given in IBM [1969].

There are many publications describing techniques that are useful in code generation. Knuth [1968a] discusses and analyzes various storage allocation techniques. Elson and Rake [1970] consider the generation of code from a tree-structured intermediate language. Wilcox [1971] presents some general models for code generation.

9.2. SYNTAX-DIRECTED TRANSLATIONS

In this section we shall consider a compiler model in which syntax analysis and code generation are combined into a single phase. We can view such a model as one in which code generation operations are interspersed with parsing operations. The term *syntax-directed compiling* is often used to describe this type of compilation.

The techniques discussed here can also be used to generate intermediate code instead of object or assembly code, and we give one example of translation to intermediate code. The remainder of our examples are to assembly code.

Our starting point is the syntax-directed translation scheme of Chapter 3. We show how a syntax-directed translation can be implemented on a deterministic pushdown transducer that does top-down or bottom-up parsing. Throughout this section we shall assume that a DPDT uses a special symbol $ to delimit the right-hand end of the input string. Then we add various features to make the SDTS more versatile. First, we allow semantic rules that permit more than one translation to be defined at various nodes of the parse tree. We also allow repetition and conditionals in the formulas for these translations. We then consider translations which are not strings; integers and Boolean variables are useful additional types of translations. Finally, we allow translations to be defined in terms of other translations found not only at the direct descendants of the node in question but at its direct ancestor.

First, we shall show that every simple SDTS on an LL grammar can be implemented by a deterministic pushdown transducer. We shall then investigate what simple SDTS's on an LR grammar can be so implemented. We shall discuss an extension of the DPDA, called a pushdown processor, to implement the full class of SDT's whose underlying grammar is LL or LR. Then, the implementation of syntax-directed translations in connection with backtrack parsing algorithms is studied briefly.

9.2.1. Simple Syntax-Directed Translations

In Chapter 3 we saw that a simple syntax-directed translation scheme can be implemented by a nondeterministic pushdown transducer. In this section we shall discuss deterministic implementations of certain simple syntax-directed translation schemes.

The grammar G underlying an SDTS can determine the translations definable on $L(G)$ and the efficiency with which these translations can be directly implemented.

Example 9.1

Suppose that we wish to map expressions generated by the grammar G, below, into prefix Polish expressions, on the assumption that *'s are to take precedence over $+$'s, e.g., $a * a + a$ has prefix expression $+ * aaa$, not $* a + aa$. G is given by $E \longrightarrow a + E \,|\, a * E \,|\, a$. However, there is no syntax-directed translation scheme which uses G as an underlying grammar and which can define this translation. The reason for this is that the output grammar of such an SDTS must be a linear CFG, and it is not difficult to show that the set of prefix Polish expressions over $\{+, *, a\}$ corresponding to the infix expressions in $L(G)$ is not a linear context free language. However, this particular translation can be defined using a simple SDTS with G_0 [except for production $F \longrightarrow$ (E)] as the underlying grammar. $\square$

In Theorem 3.14 we showed that if (x, y) is an element of a simple syntax-directed translation, then the output y can be generated from the left parse of x using a deterministic pushdown transducer. As a consequence, if a grammar G can be deterministically parsed top-down in the natural manner using a DPDT M, then M can be readily modified to implement any simple SDTS whose underlying grammar is G. If G is an LL(k) grammar, then any simple SDT defined on G can be implemented by a DPDT in the following manner.

THEOREM 9.1

Let $T = (N, \Sigma, \Delta, R, S)$ be a semantically unambiguous simple SDTS with an underlying LL(k) grammar. Then $\{(x\$, y) \,|\, (x, y) \in \tau(T)\}$ can be defined by a deterministic pushdown transducer.

Proof. The proof follows from the methods of Theorems 3.14 and 5.4. If G is the underlying grammar of T, then we can construct a k-predictive parsing algorithm for G using Algorithm 5.3. We can construct a DPDT M with an endmarker to simulate this k-predictive parser and perform the translation as follows.

Let $\Delta' = \{a' \,|\, a \in \Delta\}$, assume $\Delta' \cap \Sigma = \varnothing$, and let $h(a) = a'$ for all $a \in \Delta$. The parser of Algorithm 5.3 repeatedly replaces nonterminals by right-hand sides of productions, carrying along LL(k) tables with the nonterminals. M will do essentially the same thing. Suppose that the left parser replaces A by $w_0 B_1 w_1 \cdots B_m w_m$ [with some LL(k) tables, not shown, appended to the nonterminals]. Let

$$A \longrightarrow w_0 B_1 w_1 \cdots B_m w_m, \; x_0 B_1 x_1 \cdots B_m x_m$$

be a rule of R. Then M will replace A by $w_0 h(x_0) B_1 w_1 h(x_1) \cdots B_m w_m h(x_m)$.

As in Algorithm 5.3, whenever a symbol of Σ appears on top of the pushdown list, it is compared with the current input symbol, and if a match occurs, the symbol is deleted from the pushdown list, and the input head moves right one cell. When a symbol a' in Δ' is found on top of the pushdown list, M emits a and removes a' from the top of the pushdown list without moving the input head. M does not emit production indices.

A more formal construction of M is left to the reader. $\square$

Example 9.2

Let T be the simple SDTS with the rules

$$S \longrightarrow aSbSc, 1S2S3$$
$$S \longrightarrow d, 4$$

The underlying grammar is a simple LL(1) grammar. Therefore, no LL tables need be kept on the stack. Let M be the deterministic pushdown transducer $(Q, \Sigma, \Delta, \Gamma, \delta, q, S, \{\text{accept}\})$, where

$$Q = \{q, \text{accept}, \text{error}\}$$
$$\Sigma = \{a, b, c, d, \$\}$$
$$\Gamma = \{S, \$\} \cup \Sigma \cup \Delta$$
$$\Delta = \{1, 2, 3, 4\}$$

Since $\Sigma \cap \Delta = \varnothing$, we shall let $\Delta' = \Delta$. δ could be defined as follows:

$$\delta(q, a, S) = (q, Sb2Sc3, 1)\dagger$$
$$\delta(q, d, S) = (q, e, 4)$$
$$\delta(q, b, b) = (q, e, e)$$
$$\delta(q, c, c) = (q, e, e)$$
$$\delta(q, e, 2) = (q, e, 2)$$
$$\delta(q, e, 3) = (q, e, 3)$$
$$\delta(q, \$, \$) = (\text{accept}, e, e)$$

Otherwise,

$$\delta(q, X, Y) = (\text{error}, e, e)$$

It is easy to verify that $\tau(M) = \{(x\$, y) \,|\, (x, y) \in \tau(T)\}$.   □

Let us now consider a simple SDTS in which the underlying grammar is LR(k). Since the class of LR(k) grammars is larger than the class of LL(k) grammars, it is interesting to investigate what class of simple SDTS's with underlying LR(k) grammars can be implemented by DPDT's. It turns out that there are semantically unambiguous simple SDT's which have an underlying LR(k) grammar but which cannot be performed by any DPDT. Intui-

---

†In these rules we have taken the liberty of producing an output symbol and shifting the input as soon as a production has been recognized, rather than doing these actions in separate steps as indicated in the proof of Theorem 9.1.

tively, the reason for this is that a translation element may require the generation of output long before it can be ascertained that the production to which this translation element is attached is actually used.

Example 9.3

Consider the simple SDTS T with the rules

$$S \longrightarrow Sa, aSa$$
$$S \longrightarrow Sb, bSb$$
$$S \longrightarrow e, e$$

The underlying grammar is LR(1), but by Lemma 3.15 there is no DPDT defining $\{(x\$, y) | (x, y) \in \tau(T)\}$. The intuitive reason for this is that the first rule of this SDTS requires that an a be emitted before the use of production $S \longrightarrow Sa$ can be recognized.   □

However, if a simple SDTS with an underlying LR(k) grammar does not require the generation of any output until after a production is recognized, then the translation can be implemented on a DPDT.

DEFINITION

An SDTS $T = (N, \Sigma, \Delta, R, S)$ will be called a *postfix* SDTS if each rule in R is of the form $A \longrightarrow \alpha, \beta$, where β is in $N^*\Delta^*$. That is, each translation element is a string of nonterminals followed by a string of output symbols.

THEOREM 9.2

Let $T = (N, \Sigma, \Delta, R, S)$ be a semantically unambiguous simple postfix SDTS with an underlying LR(k) grammar. Then $\{(x\$, y) | (x, y) \in \tau(T)\}$ can be defined by a deterministic pushdown transducer.

Proof. Using Algorithm 5.11, we can construct a deterministic right parser M with an endmarker for the underlying LR(k) grammar. However, rather than emitting the production number, M can emit the string of output symbols of the translation element associated with that production. That is, if $A \longrightarrow \alpha, \beta x$ is a rule in R where $\beta \in N^*$ and $x \in \Delta^*$, then when the production number of $A \longrightarrow \alpha$ is to be emitted by the parser, the string x is emitted by M. In this fashion M defines $\{(x\$, y) | (x, y) \in \tau(T)\}$.   □

We leave the converse of Theorem 9.2, that every deterministic pushdown transduction can be expressed as a postfix simple SDTS on an LR(1) grammar, for the Exercises.

Example 9.4

Postfix translations are more useful than it might appear at first. Here, let us consider an extended DPDT that maps the arithmetic expressions of

$L(G_0)$ into machine code for a very convenient machine. The computer for this example has a pushdown stack for an accumulator. The instruction

$$\text{LOAD } X$$

puts the value held in location X on top of the stack; all other entries on the stack are pushed down. The instructions ADD and MPY, respectively, add and multiply the top two levels of the stack, removing the two levels but then pushing the result on top of the stack. We shall use semicolons to separate these instructions.

The SDTS we have in mind is

$$E \longrightarrow E + T, \; ET \quad \text{'ADD;'}$$
$$E \longrightarrow T, \quad\quad T$$
$$T \longrightarrow T * F, \; TF \quad \text{'MPY;'}$$
$$T \longrightarrow F, \quad\quad F$$
$$F \longrightarrow (E), \quad E$$
$$F \longrightarrow a, \quad\quad \text{'LOAD } a\text{;'}$$

In this example and the ones to follow we shall use the SNOBOL convention of surrounding literal strings in translation rules by quote marks. Quote marks are not part of the output string.

With input $a + (a * a)\$$, the DPDT enters the following sequence of configurations; we have deleted the LR(k) tables from the pushdown list. We have also deleted certain obvious configurations from the sequence as well as the states and bottom of stack marker.

$$[e, \quad\quad a + (a * a)\$, \; e]$$
$$\vdash [a, \quad\quad + (a * a)\$, \; e]$$
$$\vdash [F, \quad\quad + (a * a)\$, \; \text{LOAD } a;]$$
$$\vdash^2 [E, \quad\quad + (a * a)\$, \; \text{LOAD } a;]$$
$$\vdash^3 [E + (a, \quad * a)\$, \quad\quad \text{LOAD } a;]$$
$$\vdash [E + (F, \quad * a)\$, \quad\quad \text{LOAD } a; \text{LOAD } a;]$$
$$\vdash [E + (T, \quad * a)\$, \quad\quad \text{LOAD } a; \text{LOAD } a;]$$
$$\vdash^2 [E + (T * a, \;)\$, \quad\quad \text{LOAD } a; \text{LOAD } a;]$$
$$\vdash [E + (T * F, \;)\$, \quad\quad \text{LOAD } a; \text{LOAD } a; \text{LOAD } a;]$$
$$\vdash [E + (T, \quad)\$, \quad\quad \text{LOAD } a; \text{LOAD } a; \text{LOAD } a; \text{MPY;}]$$
$$\vdash [E + (E, \quad)\$, \quad\quad \text{LOAD } a; \text{LOAD } a; \text{LOAD } a; \text{MPY;}]$$

$\vdash [E + (E),$ $\$,$ LOAD a; LOAD a; LOAD a; MPY;]

$\vdash^{2} [E + T,$ $\$,$ LOAD a; LOAD a; LOAD a; MPY;]

$\vdash [E,$ $\$,$ LOAD a; LOAD a; LOAD a; MPY; ADD;]

Note that if the different a's representing identifiers are indexed, so that the input expression becomes, say, $a_1 + (a_2 * a_3)$, then the output code would be

$$\text{LOAD } a_1$$
$$\text{LOAD } a_2$$
$$\text{LOAD } a_3$$
$$\text{MPY}$$
$$\text{ADD}$$

which computes the expression correctly on this machine. ☐

While the computer model used in Example 9.4 was designed for the purpose of demonstrating a syntax-directed translation of expressions with few of the complexities of generating code for more common machine models, the postfix scheme is capable of defining useful classes of translations. In the remainder of this chapter, we shall show how object code can be generated for other machine models using a pushdown transducer operating on what is in essence a simple postfix SDTS with an underlying LR grammar.

Suppose that we have a simple SDTS which has an underlying LR(k) grammar, but which is not postfix. How can such a translation be performed? One possible technique is to use the following multipass translation scheme. This technique illustrates a cascade connection of DPDT's. However, in practice this translation would be implemented in one pass using the techniques of the next section for arbitrary SDTS's.

Let $T = (N, \Sigma, \Delta, R, S)$ be a semantically unambiguous simple SDTS with an underlying LR(k) grammar G. We can design a four-stage translation scheme to implement $\tau(T)$. The first stage consists of a DPDT. The input to the first stage is the input string $w\$$. The output of the first stage is π, the right parse for w according to the underlying input grammar G. The second stage reverses π to create π^R, the right parse in reverse.†

The input to the third stage will be π^R. The output of the third stage will be the translation defined by the simple SDTS $T' = (N, \Sigma', \Delta, R', S)$, where

---

†Recall that π, the right parse, is the reverse of the sequence of productions used in a rightmost derivation. Thus, π^R begins with the first production used and ends with the last production used in a rightmost derivation. To obtain π^R we can merely read the buffer in which π is stored backward.

R' contains the rule

$$A \longrightarrow i B_m B_{m-1} \cdots B_1, y_m B_m \cdots y_1 B_1 y_0$$

if and only if $A \to x_0 B_1 x_1 \cdots B_m x_m, y_0 B_1 y_1 \cdots B_m y_m$ is a rule in R and $A \to x_0 B_1 x_1 \cdots B_m x_m$ is the ith production in the underlying LR(k) grammar. It is easy to prove that (π^R, y^R) is in $\tau(T')$ if and only if $(S, S) \underset{T}{\Rightarrow} \pi^R (w, y)$.

T' is a simple SDTS based on an LL(1) grammar and can thus be implemented on a DPDT. The fourth stage merely reverses the output of the third stage. If the output of the third stage is put on a pushdown list, then the fourth stage merely pops off the symbols from the pushdown list, emitting each symbol as it is popped off.

Figure 9.4 summarizes this procedure.

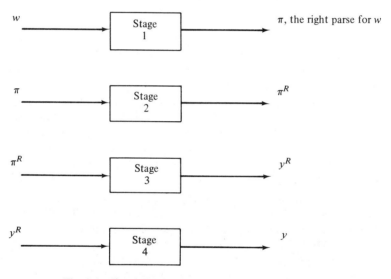

Fig. 9.4 Simple SDT on an LR(k) grammar.

Each of these three stages requires a number of basic operations that is linearly proportional to the length of w. Thus, we can state the following result.

THEOREM 9.3

Any simple SDTS with an underlying LR(k) grammar can be implemented in time proportional to its input length.

Proof. A formalization of the discussion above.   □

9.2.2. A Generalized Transducer

While the pushdown transducer is adequate for defining all simple SDTS's on an LL grammar and for some simple SDTS's on an LR grammar, we need a more versatile model of a translator when doing

(1) Nonsimple SDTS's,
(2) Nonpostfix simple SDTS's on an LR grammar,
(3) Simple SDTS's on a non-LR grammar, and
(4) Syntax-directed translation when the parsing is not deterministic one pass, such as the algorithms of Chapters 4 and 6.

We shall now define a new device called a *pushdown processor* (PP) for defining syntax-directed translations that map strings into graphs. A pushdown processor is a PDT whose output is a labeled directed graph, generally a tree or part of a tree which the processor is constructing. The major feature of the PP is that its pushdown list, in addition to pushdown symbols, can hold pointers to nodes in the output graph.

Like the extended PDA, the pushdown processor can examine the top k cells of its pushdown list for any finite k and can manipulate the contents of these cells arbitrarily. Unlike the PDA, if these k cells include some pointers to the output graph, the PP can modify the output graph by adding or deleting directed edges connected to the nodes pointed to. The PP can also create new nodes, label them, create pointers to them, and create edges between these nodes and the nodes pointed to by those pointers on the top k cells of the pushdown list.

As it is difficult to develop a concise lucid notation for such manipulations, we shall use written descriptions of the moves of the PP. Since each move of the PP can involve only a finite number of pointers, nodes, and edges, such descriptions are, in principle, possible, but we feel that a formal notation would serve to obscure the essential simplicity of the translation algorithms involved. We proceed directly to an example.

Example 9.5

Let us design a pushdown processor P to map the arithmetic expressions of $L(G_0)$ into syntax trees. In this case, a syntax tree will be a tree in which each interior node is labeled by $+$ or $*$ and leaves are labeled by a. The following table gives the parsing and output actions that the pushdown processor is to take under various combinations of current input symbol and symbol on top of the pushdown list. P has been designed from the SLR(1) parser for G_0 given in Fig. 7.37 (p. 625).

However, here we have eliminated table T_4 from Fig. 7.37, treating $F \longrightarrow a$ as a single production, and have renamed the tables as follows:

Old name	T_0	T_1	T_5	T_6	T_7	T_8	T_9	T_{10}	T_{11}
New name	T_0	T_1	(	+	*	T_2	T_3	T_4	)

In addition $ is used as a right endmarker on the input. The parsing and output actions of P are given in Figs. 9.5 and 9.6. P uses the LR(1) tables to determine its actions. In addition P will attach a pointer to tables T_1, T_2, T_3, and T_4 when these tables are placed on the pushdown list.† These pointers are to the output graph being generated. However, the pointers do not affect the parsing actions. In parsing we shall not place the grammar symbols on the pushdown list. However, the table names indicate what that grammar symbol would be.

The last column of Fig. 9.5 gives the new LR(1) table to be placed on top of the pushdown list after a reduce move. Blank entries denote error situations. A new input symbol is read only after a shift move. The numbers in the table refer to the actions described in Fig. 9.6.

Let us trace the behavior of P on input $a_1 * (a_2 + a_3)$\$. We have subscripted the a's for clarity. The sequence of moves made by P is as follows:

	Pushdown List	Input
(1)	T_0	$a_1 * (a_2 + a_3)$\$
(2)	$T_0[T_1, p_1]$	$* (a_2 + a_3)$\$
(3)	$T_0[T_1, p_1] *$	$(a_2 + a_3)$\$
(4)	$T_0[T_1, p_1] * ($	$a_2 + a_3)$\$
(5)	$T_0[T_1, p_1] * ([T_2, p_2]$	$+ a_3)$\$
(6)	$T_0[T_1, p_1] * ([T_2, p_2] +$	$a_3)$\$
(7)	$T_0[T_1, p_1] * ([T_2, p_2] + [T_3, p_3]$	$)$\$
(8)	$T_0[T_1, p_1] * ([T_2, p_4]$	$)$\$
(9)	$T_0[T_1, p_1] * ([T_2, p_4])$	\$
(10)	$T_0[T_1, p_1] * [T_4, p_4]$	\$
(11)	$T_0[T_1, p_5]$	\$

Let us examine the interesting moves in this sequence. In going from configuration (1) to configuration (2), P creates a node n_1 labeled a and sets a pointer p_1 to this node. The pointer p_1 is stored with the LR(1) table T_1 on the pushdown list. Similarly, going from configuration (4) to configuration (5), P creates a new node n_2 labeled a_2 and places a pointer p_2 to this node on the pushdown list with LR(1) table T_2. In configuration (7) another node n_3 labeled a_3 is created and p_3 is established as a pointer to n_3.

---

†In practice, these pointers can be stored immediately below the tables on the pushdown list.

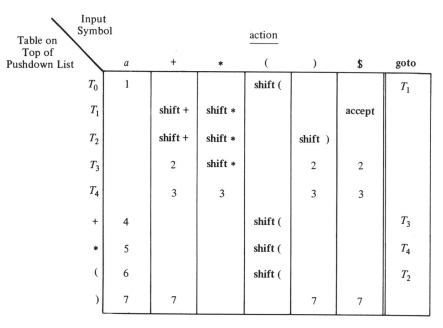

Table on Top of Pushdown List	Input Symbol	action						goto
	a	$+$	$*$	$($	$)$	$\$$		
T_0	1			shift $($				T_1
T_1		shift $+$	shift $*$			accept		
T_2		shift $+$	shift $*$		shift $)$			
T_3		2	shift $*$		2	2		
T_4		3	3		3	3		
$+$	4			shift $($				T_3
$*$	5			shift $($				T_4
$($	6			shift $($				T_2
$)$	7	7			7	7		

Fig. 9.5 Pushdown processor P.

(1) Create a new node n labeled a. Push the symbol $[T_1, p]$ on top of the pushdown list, where p is a pointer to n. Read a new input symbol.

(2) At this point, the top of the pushdown list contains a string of four symbols of the form $X[T_i, p_1] + [T_j, p_2]$, where p_1 and p_2 are pointers to nodes n_1 and n_2, respectively. Create a new node n labeled $+$. Make n_1 and n_2 the left and right direct descendants of n. Replace $[T_i, p_1] + [T_j, p_2]$ by $[T, p]$, where $T = \mathbf{goto}(X)$ and p is a pointer to node n.

(3) Same as (2) above with $*$ in place of $+$.

(4) Same as (1) with T_3 in place of T_1.

(5) Same as (1) with T_4 in place of T_1.

(6) Same as (1) with T_2 in place of T_1.

(7) The pushdown list now contains $X([T, p])$, where p is a pointer to some node n. Replace $([T, p])$ by $[T', p]$, where $T' = \mathbf{goto}(X)$.

Fig. 9.6 Processor output actions.

In going to configuration (8), P creates the output graph shown in Fig. 9.7. Here, p_4 is a pointer to node n_4. After entering configuration (11), the output graph is as shown in Fig. 9.8. Here p_5 is a pointer to node n_5. In configuration (11), the action of T_1 on input $\$$ is **accept**, and so the tree in Fig. 9.8 is the final output. This tree is the syntax tree for the expression $a_1 * (a_2 + a_3)$. □

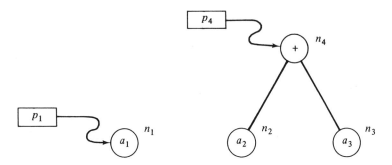

Fig. 9.7   Output after configuration (8).

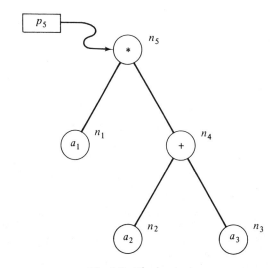

Fig. 9.8   Final output.

9.2.3.   Deterministic One-Pass Bottom-Up Translation

This is the first of three sections showing how various parsing algorithms can be extended to implement an SDTS by the use of a deterministic pushdown processor instead of a pushdown transducer. We begin by giving an algorithm to implement an arbitrary SDTS with an underlying LR grammar.

ALGORITHM 9.1

SDTS on an LR grammar.

Input. A semantically unambiguous SDTS $T = (N, \Sigma, \Delta, R, S)$ with underlying LR(k) grammar $G = (N, \Sigma, P, S)$ and an input w in Σ^*.

Output. An output tree whose frontier is the output for w.

Method. The tree is constructed by a pushdown processor M, which simulates $\mathcal{C}$, an LR(k) parser for G. M will hold on its pushdown list (top at the right) the symbols in $N \cup \Sigma$ and the LR(k) tables exactly as $\mathcal{C}$ does. In addition, immediately below each nonterminal, M will have a pointer to the output graph being generated. The **shift, reduce,** and **accept** actions of M are as follows:

(1) When $\mathcal{C}$ shifts symbol a onto its stack, M does the same.
(2) If $\mathcal{C}$ reduces $X_1 \cdots X_m$ to nonterminal A, M does the following:
   (a) Let $A \longrightarrow X_1 \cdots X_m, w_0 B_1 w_1 \cdots B_r w_r$ be a rule of the SDTS, where the B's are in one-to-one correspondence with those of the X's which are nonterminals.
   (b) M removes $X_1 \cdots X_m$ from the top of its stack, along with intervening pointers, LR(k) tables, and, if X_1 is in N, the pointer immediately below X_1.
   (c) M creates a new node n, labels it A, and places a pointer to n below the symbol A on top of its stack.
   (d) The direct descendants of n have labels reading, from the left, $w_0 B_1 w_1 \cdots B_r w_r$. Nodes are created for each of the symbols of the w's. The node for B_i, $1 \leq i \leq r$, is the node pointed to by the pointer which was immediately below X_j on the stack of M, where X_j is the nonterminal corresponding to B_i in this particular rule of the SDTS.

(3) If $\mathcal{C}$'s input becomes empty (we have reached the right endmarker) and only pS and two LR(k) tables appear on M's pushdown list, then M accepts if $\mathcal{C}$ accepts; p points to the root of the output tree of M. $\square$

Example 9.6

Let Algorithm 9.1 be applied to the SDTS

$$S \longrightarrow aSA, 0AS$$
$$S \longrightarrow b, 1$$
$$A \longrightarrow bAS, 1SA$$
$$A \longrightarrow a, 0$$

with input *abbab*. The underlying grammar is SLR(1), and we shall omit discussion of the LR(1) tables, assuming that they are there and guide the parse properly. We shall list the successive stack contents entered by the pushdown processor and then show the tree structure pointed to by each of the pointers. The LR(1) tables on the stack have been omitted.

$$(e, abbab\$) \vdash^2 (ab, bab\$)$$
$$\vdash (ap_1S, bab\$)$$
$$\vdash^2 (ap_1Sba, b\$)$$
$$\vdash (ap_1Sbp_2A, b\$)$$
$$\vdash (ap_1Sbp_2Ab, \$)$$
$$\vdash (ap_1Sbp_2Ap_3S, \$)$$
$$\vdash (ap_1Sp_4A, \$)$$
$$\vdash (p_5S, \$)$$

The trees constructed after the third, fifth, seventh, eighth, and ninth indicated configurations are shown in Fig. 9.9(a)–(e).

Note that when bp_2Ap_3S is reduced to A, the subtree formerly pointed to by p_3 appears to the left of that pointed to by p_2, because the translation element associated with $A \longrightarrow bSA$ permutes the S and A on the right. A similar permutation occurs at the final reduction. Observe that the yield of Fig. 9.9(e) is 01101. ☐

THEOREM 9.4

Algorithm 9.1 correctly produces the translation of the input word according to the given SDTS.

Proof. Elementary induction on the order in which the pointers are created by Algorithm 9.1. ☐

We comment that if we "implement" a pushdown processor on a reasonable random access computer, a single move of the PP can be done in a finite number of steps of the random access machine. Thus, Algorithm 9.1 takes time which is a linear function of the input length.

9.2.4. Deterministic One-Pass Top-Down Translation

Suppose that we have a predictive (top-down) parser. Converting such a parser to a translator requires a somewhat different approach from the way in which a bottom-up parser was converted into a translator. Let us suppose that we have an SDTS with an underlying LL grammar. The parsing process builds a tree top-down, and at any stage in the process, we can imagine that a partial tree has been constructed. Those leaves in this partial tree labeled by nonterminals correspond to the nonterminals contained on the pushdown list of the predictive parser generated by Algorithm 5.3. The expansion of a nonterminal is tantamount to the creation of descendants for the corresponding leaf of the tree.

The translation strategy is to maintain a pointer to each leaf of the "cur-

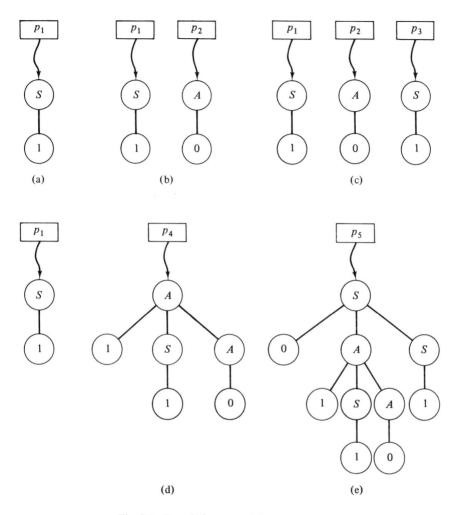

Fig. 9.9 Translation by pushdown processor.

rent" tree having a nonterminal label. While doing ordinary LL parsing, that pointer will be kept on the pushdown list immediately below the nonterminal corresponding to the node pointed to. When a nonterminal is expanded according to some production, new leaves are created for the corresponding translation element, and nodes with nonterminal labels are pointed to by newly created pointers on the pushdown list. The pointer below the expanded nonterminal disappears. It is therefore necessary to keep, outside the pushdown processor, a pointer to the root of the tree being created. For example, if the pushdown list contains Ap, and the production $A \rightarrow aBbCc$, with translation element $0C1B2$, is used to expand A, then the pushdown processor will replace Ap by aBp_1bCp_2c. If p pointed to the leaf labeled A before the expansion, then after the expansion A is the root of the following subtree:

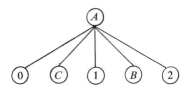

where p_1 points to node B and p_2 points to node C.

ALGORITHM 9.2

Top-down implementation of an SDTS on an LL grammar.

Input. A semantically unambiguous SDTS $T = (N, \Sigma, \Delta, R, S)$ with an underlying LL(k) grammar $G = (N, \Sigma, P, S)$.

Output. A pushdown processor which produces a tree whose frontier is the output for w for each w in $L(G)$.

Method. We shall construct a pushdown processor M which simulates the LL(k) parser α for G. The simulation of α by M proceeds as follows. As in Algorithm 9.1, we ignore the handling of tables. It is the same for M as for α.

(1) Initially, M will have Sp_r on its pushdown stack (the top is at the left), where p_r is a pointer to the root node n_r.

(2) If α has a terminal on top of its pushdown list and compares it with the current input symbol, deleting both, M does the same.

(3) Suppose that α expands a nonterminal A [possibly with an associated LL(k) table] by production $A \rightarrow X_1 \cdots X_m$, having translation element $y_0B_1y_1 \cdots B_ry_r$, and that the pointer immediately below A (it is easy to show that there will always be one) points to node n. Then M does the following:

    (a) M creates direct descendant nodes for n labeled, from the left, with the symbols of $y_0B_1y_1 \cdots B_ry_r$.

    (b) On the stack M replaces A and the pointer below by $X_1 \cdots X_m$, with pointers immediately below those of $X_1 \cdots X_m$ which are nonterminals. The pointer below X_j points to the node created for B_i if X_j and B_i correspond in the rule

$$A \rightarrow X_1 \cdots X_m, y_0B_1y_1 \cdots B_ry_r$$

(4) If M's pushdown list becomes empty when it has reached the end of the input sentence, it accepts; the output is the tree which has been constructed with root n_r. □

Example 9.7

We shall consider an example drawn from the area of natural language translation. It is a little known fact that an SDTS forms a precise model for the translation of English to another commonly spoken natural language, pig Latin. The following rules informally define the translation of a word in English to the corresponding word in pig Latin:

(1) If a word begins with a vowel, add the suffix YAY.

(2) If a word begins with a nonempty string of consonants, move all consonants before the first vowel to the back of the word and append suffix AY.

(3) One-letter words are not changed.

(4) U following a Q is a consonant.

(5) Y beginning a word is a vowel if it is not followed by a vowel.

We shall give an SDTS that incorporates only rules (1) and (2). It is left for the Exercises to incorporate the remaining rules.

The rules of the SDTS are as follows:

$\langle$word$\rangle \longrightarrow \langle$consonants$\rangle\langle$vowel$\rangle\langle$letters$\rangle$,
$\qquad\qquad\qquad \langle$vowel$\rangle\langle$letters$\rangle\langle$consonants$\rangle$ 'AY'

$\langle$word$\rangle \longrightarrow \langle$vowel$\rangle\langle$letters$\rangle$, $\langle$vowel$\rangle\langle$letters$\rangle$ 'YAY'

$\langle$consonants$\rangle \longrightarrow \langle$consonant$\rangle\langle$consonants$\rangle$, $\langle$consonant$\rangle\langle$consonants$\rangle$

$\langle$consonants$\rangle \longrightarrow \langle$consonant$\rangle$, $\langle$consonant$\rangle$

$\langle$letters$\rangle \longrightarrow \langle$letter$\rangle\langle$letters$\rangle$, $\langle$letter$\rangle\langle$letters$\rangle$

$\langle$letters$\rangle \longrightarrow e, e$

$\langle$vowel$\rangle \longrightarrow$ 'A', 'A'

$\langle$vowel$\rangle \longrightarrow$ 'E', 'E'

    .
    .
    .

$\langle$vowel$\rangle \longrightarrow$ 'U', 'U'

$\langle$consonant$\rangle \longrightarrow$ 'B', 'B'

$\langle$consonant$\rangle \longrightarrow$ 'C', 'C'

    .
    .
    .

$\langle$consonant$\rangle \longrightarrow$ 'Z', 'Z'

$\langle$letter$\rangle \longrightarrow \langle$vowel$\rangle$, $\langle$vowel$\rangle$

$\langle$letter$\rangle \longrightarrow \langle$consonant$\rangle$, $\langle$consonant$\rangle$

The underlying grammar is easily seen to be LL(2). Let us compute the output translation corresponding to the input word "THE". As in the previous two examples, we shall first list the configurations entered by the processor and then show the tree at various stages in its construction. The pushdown top is at the left this time.

	Input	Stack
(1)	THE\$	$\langle$word$\rangle p_1$
(2)	THE\$	$\langle$consonants$\rangle p_2 \langle$vowel$\rangle p_3 \langle$letters$\rangle p_4$
(3)	THE\$	$\langle$consonant$\rangle p_5 \langle$consonants$\rangle p_6 \langle$vowel$\rangle p_3 \langle$letters$\rangle p_4$
(4)	THE\$	T$\langle$consonants$\rangle p_6 \langle$vowel$\rangle p_3 \langle$letters$\rangle p_4$
(5)	HE\$	$\langle$consonants$\rangle p_6 \langle$vowel$\rangle p_3 \langle$letters$\rangle p_4$
(6)	HE\$	$\langle$consonant$\rangle p_7 \langle$vowel$\rangle p_3 \langle$letters$\rangle p_4$
(7)	HE\$	H$\langle$vowel$\rangle p_3 \langle$letters$\rangle p_4$
(8)	E\$	$\langle$vowel$\rangle p_3 \langle$letters$\rangle p_4$
(9)	E\$	E$\langle$letters$\rangle p_4$
(10)	\$	$\langle$letters$\rangle p_4$
(11)	\$	e

The tree structure after steps 1, 2, 6, and 11 are shown in Fig. 9.10(a)–(d), respectively. □

As in the previous section, there is an easy proof that the current algorithm performs the correct translation and that on a suitable random access machine the algorithm can be implemented to run in time which is linear in the input length. For the record, we state the following theorem.

THEOREM 9.5

Algorithm 9.2 constructs a pushdown processor which produces as output a tree whose frontier is the translation of the input string.

Proof. We can prove by induction that an input string w has the net effect of erasing nonterminal A and pointer p from the pushdown list if and only if $(A, A) \underset{T}{\overset{*}{\Rightarrow}} (w, x)$, where x is the frontier of the subtree whose root is the node pointed to by p (after erasure of A and p and the symbols to which A is expanded). Details are left for the Exercises. □

9.2.5. Translation in a Backtrack Environment

The ideas central to the pushdown processor can be applied to backtrack parsing algorithms as well. To be specific, we shall discuss how the parsing machine of Section 6.1 can be extended to incorporate tree construction. The chief new idea is that the processor must be able to "destroy," if need be, subtrees which it has constructed. That is, certain subtrees can become inaccessible, and while we shall not discuss it here, the memory cells used to

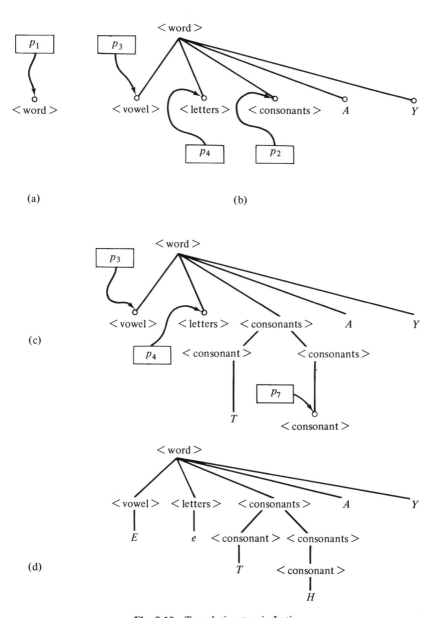

(a)

(b)

(c)

(d)

Fig. 9.10 Translation to pig Latin.

represent the subtree are in practice returned to the available memory. We shall modify the parsing machine of Section 6.1 to give it the capability of placing pointers to nodes of a graph on its pushdown list. (Recall that the parsing machine already has pointers to its input; these pointers are kept on one cell along with an information symbol.) The rules for manipulating these pointers are the same as for the pushdown processor, and we shall not discuss the matter in any more detail.

Before giving the translation algorithm associated with the parsing machine, let us discuss how the notion of a syntax-directed translation carries over to the GTDPL programs of Section 6.1. It is reasonable to suppose that we shall associate a translation with a "call" of a nonterminal if and only if that call succeeds.

Let $P = (N, \Sigma, R, S)$ be a GTDPL program. Let us interpret a GTDPL statement $A \to a$, where a is in $\Sigma \cup \{e\}$, as though it were an attempt to apply production $A \to a$ in a CFG. Then, in analogy with the SDTS, we would expect to find associated with that rule a string of output symbols. That is, the complete rule would be $A \to a$, w, where w is in Δ^*, Δ being the "output alphabet."

The only other GTDPL statement which might yield a translation is $A \to B[C, D]$, where A, B, C, and D are in N. We can suppose that two CFG productions are implied here, namely $A \to BC$ and $A \to D$. If B and C succeed, we want the translation of A to involve the translations of B and C. Therefore, it appears natural to associate with rule $A \to B[C, D]$ a translation element of the form $wBxCy$ or $wCxBy$, where w, x, and y are in Δ^*. (If $B = C$, then there must be a correspondence specified between the nonterminals of the rule and those of the translation element.)

If B fails, however, we want the translation of A to involve the translation of D. Thus, a second translation element, of the form uDv, must be associated with the rule $A \to B[C, D]$. We shall give a formal definition of such a translation-defining method and then discuss how the parsing machine can be generalized to perform such translations.

DEFINITION

A *GTDPL program with output* is a system $P = (N, \Sigma, \Delta, R, S)$, where N, Σ, and S are as for any GTDPL program, Δ is a finite set of *output symbols*, and R is a set of *rules* of the following forms:

(1) $A \to f, e$
(2) $A \to a, y$ where $a \in \Sigma \cup \{e\}$ and $y \in \Delta^*$
(3) (a) $A \to B[C, D], y_1 B y_2 C y_3, y_4 D y_5$
    (b) $A \to B[C, D], y_1 C y_2 B y_3, y_4 D y_5$
    where y_i is in Δ^*

There is at most one rule for each nonterminal.

We define relations $\xrightarrow{n}$ between nonterminals and triples of the form $(u \restriction v, y, r)$, where u and v are in Σ^*, $y \in \Delta^*$, and r is s or f. Here, the first component is the input string, with input head position indicated; the second component is an output string, and the third is the outcome, either success or failure.

(1) If A has rule $A \rightarrow a, y$, then for all u in Σ^*, $A \overset{1}{\Rightarrow} (a \upharpoonright u, y, s)$. If v is in Σ^* but does not begin with a, then $A \overset{1}{\Rightarrow} (\upharpoonright v, e, f)$.

(2) If A has rule $A \rightarrow B[C, D], y_1 E y_2 F y_3, y_4 D y_5$, where $E = B$ and $F = C$ or vice versa, then the following hold:

(a) If $B \overset{n_1}{\Rightarrow} (u_1 \upharpoonright u_2 u_3, x_1, s)$ and $C \overset{n_2}{\Rightarrow} (u_2 \upharpoonright u_3, x_2, s)$, then

$$A \overset{n_1+n_2+1}{\Longrightarrow} (u_1 u_2 \upharpoonright u_3, y_1 x_1 y_2 x_2 y_3, s)$$

if $E = B$ and $F = C$, and

$$A \overset{n_1+n_2+1}{\Longrightarrow} (u_1 u_2 \upharpoonright u_3, y_1 x_2 y_2 x_1 y_3, s)$$

if $E = C$ and $F = B$. In case $B = C$, we presume that the correspondence between E and F on the one hand and the positions held by B and C on the other is indicated by superscripts, e.g., $A \rightarrow B^{(1)}[B^{(2)}, D], y_1 B^{(2)} y_2 B^{(1)} y_3, y_4 D y_5$.

(b) If $B \overset{n_1}{\Rightarrow} (u_1 \upharpoonright u_2, x, s)$ and $C \overset{n_2}{\Rightarrow} (\upharpoonright u_2, e, f)$, then

$$A \overset{n_1+n_2+1}{\Longrightarrow} (\upharpoonright u_1 u_2, e, f)$$

(c) If $B \overset{n_1}{\Rightarrow} (\upharpoonright u_1 u_2, e, f)$ and $D \overset{n_2}{\Rightarrow} (u_1 \upharpoonright u_2, x, s)$, then

$$A \overset{n_1+n_2+1}{\Longrightarrow} (u_1 \upharpoonright u_2, y_4 x y_5, s)$$

(d) If $B \overset{n_1}{\Rightarrow} (\upharpoonright u, e, f)$ and $D \overset{n_2}{\Rightarrow} (\upharpoonright u, e, f)$, then $A \overset{n_1+n_2+1}{\Longrightarrow} (\upharpoonright u, e, f)$.

Note that if $A \overset{n}{\Rightarrow} (u \upharpoonright v, y, f)$, then $u = e$ and $y = e$. That is, on failure the input pointer is not moved and no translation is produced. It also should be observed that in case (2b) the translation of B is "canceled" when C fails.

We let $\overset{+}{\Rightarrow}$ be the union of $\overset{n}{\Rightarrow}$ for $n \geq 1$. The *translation defined by P*, denoted $\tau(P)$, is $\{(w, x) \mid S \overset{+}{\Rightarrow} (w \upharpoonright, x, s)\}$.

Example 9.8

Let us define a GTDPL program with output that performs the pig Latin translation of Example 9.7. Here we shall use lowercase output and the following nonterminals, whose correspondence with the previous example is listed below. Note that X and C_3 represent strings of nonterminals.

Here	Example 9.7
W	$\langle\text{word}\rangle$
C_1	$\langle\text{consonant}\rangle$
C_2	$\langle\text{consonants}\rangle$
C_3	$\langle\text{consonant}\rangle$*
L_1	$\langle\text{letter}\rangle$
L_2	$\langle\text{letters}\rangle$
V	$\langle\text{vowel}\rangle$
X	$\langle\text{vowel}\rangle\langle\text{letters}\rangle$

In addition, we shall use nonterminals S and F with rules $S \rightarrow e$ and $F \rightarrow f$. Finally, the rules for C_1, V, and L must be such that they match any consonant, vowel, or letter, respectively, giving a translation which is the letter matched. These rules involve additional nonterminals and will be omitted. The important rules are

$$W \longrightarrow C_2[X, X], \quad XC_2 \text{ 'ay'}, \quad X \text{ 'yay'}$$

$$C_2 \longrightarrow C_1[C_3, F], \quad C_1C_3, \quad F$$

$$C_3 \longrightarrow C_1[C_3, S], \quad C_1C_3, \quad S$$

$$L_2 \longrightarrow L_1[L_2, S], \quad L_1L_2, \quad S$$

$$X \longrightarrow V[L_2, F], \quad VL_2, \quad F$$

For example, if we consider the input string 'and', we observe that $V \overset{+}{\Rightarrow} (a \upharpoonright \text{nd}, a, s)$ and that $L_2 \overset{+}{\Rightarrow} (\text{nd} \upharpoonright, \text{nd}, s)$. Thus, $X \overset{+}{\Rightarrow} (\text{and} \upharpoonright, \text{and}, s)$. Since $C_1 \overset{+}{\Rightarrow} (\upharpoonright \text{and}, e, f)$, it follows that $C_2 \overset{+}{\Rightarrow} (\upharpoonright \text{and}, e, f)$. Thus, we have $W \overset{+}{\Rightarrow} (\text{and} \upharpoonright, \text{andyay}, s)$. $\square$

Such a translation can be implemented by a modification of the parsing machine of Section 6.1. The action of this modified machine is based on the following observation. If procedure A with rule $A \rightarrow B[C, D]$ is called, then A will produce a translation only if B and C succeed or if B fails and D succeeds. The following algorithm describes the behavior of the modified parsing machine.

ALGORITHM 9.3

Implementation of GTDPL programs with output.

Input. $P = (\text{N}, \Sigma, \Delta, R, S)$, a GTDPL program with output.

Output. A modified parsing machine M such that for each input w, M produces a tree with frontier x if and only if (w, x) is in $\tau(P)$.

Method. If we ignore the translation elements of the rules of P, we have a GTDPL program P' in the sense of Section 6.1. Then we can use Lemma 6.6 to construct M', a parsing machine that recognizes $L(P')$.

We shall now informally describe the modifications of M' we need to make to obtain the modified parsing machine M. The modified machine M simulates M' and also creates nodes in an output tree, placing pointers to these nodes on its pushdown list.

With an input string w, M has initial configuration $(\textbf{begin}, \upharpoonright w, (S, 0)p_r)$. Here p_r is a pointer to a root node n_r.

(1) (a) Suppose that $A \rightarrow B[C, D]$, $y_1 E y_2 F y_3$, $y_4 D y_5$ is the rule for A. Suppose that M makes the following sequence of moves implementing a call of procedure A under the rule $A \rightarrow B[C, D]$:

$$(\textbf{begin}, u_1 \upharpoonright u_2 u_3, (A, i)\gamma) \vdash (\textbf{begin}, u_1 \upharpoonright u_2 u_3, (B, j)(A, i)\gamma)$$
$$\vdash^* (\textbf{success}, u_1 u_2 \upharpoonright u_3, (A, i)\gamma)$$
$$\vdash (\textbf{begin}, u_1 u_2 \upharpoonright u_3, (C, i)\gamma)$$

Then M would make the following sequence of moves corresponding to the moves above made by M':

(9.2.1) $(\textbf{begin}, u_1 \upharpoonright u_2 u_3, (A, i)p_A\gamma')$

(9.2.2) $\vdash (\textbf{begin}, u_1 \upharpoonright u_2 u_3, (B, j)p_B(A, i)p_B p_A\gamma')$

(9.2.3) $\vdash^* (\textbf{success}, u_1 u_2 \upharpoonright u_3, (A, i)p_B p_A\gamma')$

(9.2.4) $\vdash (\textbf{begin}, u_1 u_2 \upharpoonright u_3, (C, i)p_C\gamma')$

In configuration (9.2.1) M has a pointer p_A, to a leaf n_A, directly below A. (We shall ignore the pointers to the input in this discussion.) In going to configuration (9.2.2), M creates a new node n_B, makes it a direct descendant of n_A, and places a pointer p_B to n_B immediately below and above A. Then M places B on top of the pushdown list. In (9.2.3) M returns to A in state **success**. In going to configuration (9.2.4), M creates a direct descendant of n_A for each symbol of $y_1 E y_2 F y_3$ and orders them from the left. Node n_B, which has already been created, becomes the node for E or F, whichever is B. Let the node for the other of E and F be n_C. Then in configuration (9.2.4), M has replaced $Ap_B p_A$ by Cp_C, where p_C is a pointer to n_C. Thus if $E = C$ and $F = B$, then at configuration (9.2.4), node n_A is root of the following subtree:

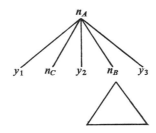

(b) If, on the other hand, B returns **failure** in rule $A \rightarrow B[C, D]$, M will make the following sequence of moves:

(9.2.1) $(\textbf{begin}, u_1 \upharpoonright u_2 u_3, (A, i)p_A \gamma')$

(9.2.2) $\vdash (\textbf{begin}, u_1 \upharpoonright u_2 u_3, (B, j)p_B (A, i)p_B p_A \gamma')$

(9.2.5) $\vdash^{*} (\textbf{failure}, u_1 \upharpoonright u_2 u_3, (A, i)p_B p_A \gamma')$

(9.2.6) $\vdash (\textbf{begin}, u_1 \upharpoonright u_2 u_3, (D, i)p_D \gamma')$

In going from configuration (9.2.5) to (9.2.6), M first deletes n_B and all its descendants from the output tree, using the pointer p_B below A to locate n_B. Then M creates a direct descendant of n_A for each symbol of $y_4 D y_5$ in order from the left and replaces $A p_B p_A$ on top of its pushdown list by $D p_D$, where p_D is the pointer to the node created for D.

(2) If $A \rightarrow a$, y is a rule a in $\Sigma \cup \{e\}$, then M would make one of the following moves:

(a) $(\textbf{begin}, u \upharpoonright av, (A, i)p_A y) \vdash (\textbf{success}, ua \upharpoonright v, \gamma)$. In this move a direct descendant of n_A (the node pointed to by p_A) would be created for each symbol of y. If $y = e$, then one node, labeled e, would be created as a direct descendant.

(b) $(\textbf{begin}, u \upharpoonright v, (A, i)p_A y) \vdash (\textbf{failure}, u' \upharpoonright v', \gamma)$, where $|u'| = i$ and v does not begin with an a.

(3) If $A \rightarrow f$, e is a rule, then M would make the move in (2b).

(4) If M' reads its entire input w and erases all symbols on its pushdown list, then the tree constructed with root n_r will be the translation of w. □

THEOREM 9.6

Algorithm 9.3 defines a modified parsing machine which for an input w produces a tree whose frontier is the translation of w.

Proof. This is another straightforward inductive argument on the number of moves made by M. The inductive hypothesis is that if M, started in state **begin** with A and a pointer p to node n on top of its pushdown list and uv to the right of its input head, uses input u with the net effect of deleting A and p from the stack and ending in state **success**, then the node pointed to by p will be the root of a subtree with frontier y such that $A \overset{*}{\Rightarrow} (u \upharpoonright v, y, s)$. □

Example 9.9

Let us show how a parsing machine would implement the translation of Example 9.8. The usual format will be followed. Configurations will be indicated, followed by the constructed tree. Moves representing recognition by C_1, V, and L_1 of consonants, vowels, and letters will not be shown.

State	Input	Pushdown List
begin	⊢ and	Wp_1
begin	⊢ and	$C_2p_2Wp_2p_1$
begin	⊢ and	$C_1p_3C_2p_3p_2Wp_2p_1$
	⋮	
failure	⊢ and	$C_2p_3p_2Wp_2p_1$
begin	⊢ and	$Fp_4Wp_2p_1$
failure	⊢ and	Wp_2p_1
begin	⊢ and	Xp_5
begin	⊢ and	$Vp_6Xp_6p_5$
	⋮	
success	a ⊢ nd	Xp_6p_5
begin	a ⊢ nd	L_2p_7
begin	a ⊢ nd	$L_1p_8L_2p_8p_7$
	⋮	
success	an ⊢ d	$L_2p_8p_7$
begin	an ⊢ d	L_2p_9
begin	an ⊢ d	$L_1p_{10}L_2p_{10}p_9$
	⋮	
success	and ⊢	$L_2p_{10}p_9$
begin	and ⊢	L_2p_{11}
begin	and ⊢	$L_1p_{12}L_2p_{12}p_{11}$
	⋮	
failure	and ⊢	$L_2p_{12}p_{11}$
begin	and ⊢	Sp_{13}
success	and ⊢	e

We show the tree after every fourth-listed configuration in Fig. 9.11(a)–(e).   □

Although we shall not discuss it, the techniques suggested in Algorithm 9.3 are applicable to the other top-down parsing algorithms, such as Algorithm 4.1 and translation built on a TDPL program.

EXERCISES

9.2.1. Construct a pushdown transducer to implement the following simple SDTS:

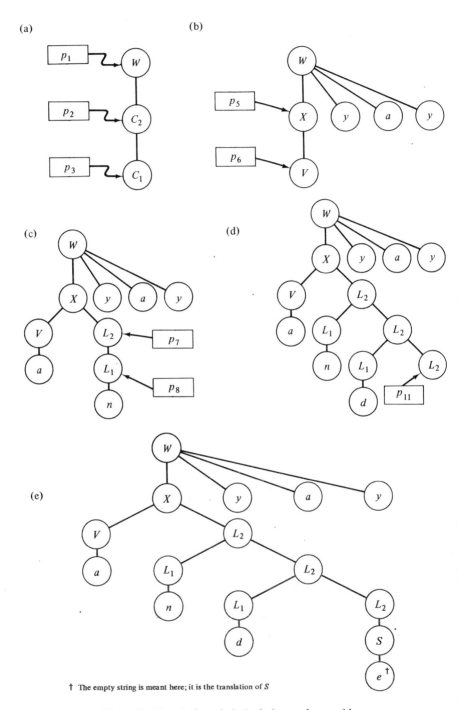

(a)

(b)

(c)

(d)

(e)

† The empty string is meant here; it is the translation of S

Fig. 9.11 Translation of pig Latin by parsing machine.

$$E \longrightarrow E + T, \ ET \text{ 'ADD;'}$$
$$E \longrightarrow T, \qquad T$$
$$T \longrightarrow T * F, \ TF \text{ 'MPY;'}$$
$$T \longrightarrow F, \qquad F$$
$$F \longrightarrow F \uparrow P, \ FP \text{ 'EXP;'}$$
$$F \longrightarrow P, \qquad P$$
$$P \longrightarrow (E), \qquad E$$
$$P \longrightarrow a, \qquad \text{'}LOAD \ a\text{;'}$$

The transducer should be based on an SLR(1) parsing algorithm. Give the sequence of output strings during the processing of
(a) $a \uparrow a * (a + a)$.
(b) $a + a * a \uparrow a$.

9.2.2. Repeat Exercise 9.2.1 for a pushdown processor parsing in an LL(1) manner. Modify the underlying grammar when necessary.

9.2.3. Show how a pushdown transducer working as an LL(1) parser would translate the following strings according to the simple SDTS

$$E \longrightarrow TE', \quad TE'$$
$$E' \longrightarrow + TE', \ T \text{ 'ADD;'} E'$$
$$E' \longrightarrow e, \qquad e$$
$$T \longrightarrow FT', \qquad FT'$$
$$T' \longrightarrow * FT', \ F \text{ 'MPY;'} T'$$
$$T' \longrightarrow e, \qquad e$$
$$F \longrightarrow (E), \qquad E$$
$$F \longrightarrow a, \qquad \text{'LOAD } a\text{;'}$$

(a) $a * (a + a)$.
(b) $((a + a) * a) + a$.

9.2.4. Show how a pushdown processor would translate the word *abbaaaa* according to the SDTS

$$S \longrightarrow aA^{(1)}A^{(2)}, \ 0A^{(2)}A^{(1)}1$$
$$S \longrightarrow b, \qquad 2$$
$$A \longrightarrow bS^{(1)}S^{(2)}, \ 1S^{(1)}S^{(2)}0$$
$$A \longrightarrow a, \qquad e$$

(a) Parsing in an LL(1) mode.
(b) Parsing in an LR(1) mode.

9.2.5. Show that there is no SDTS which performs the translation of Example 9.1 on the given grammar $E \longrightarrow a + E \mid a * E \mid a$.

9.2.6. Give a formal construction for the PDT M of Theorem 9.1.

*9.2.7. Prove that every DPDT defines a postfix simple syntax-directed translation on an LR(1) grammar. *Hint:* Show that every DPDT can be put in a normal form analogous to that of Section 8.2.1.

*9.2.8. Show that there exist translations $T = \{(x\$, y)\}$ such that T is definable by a DPDT but $\{(x, y) \mid (x\$, y) \in T\}$ is not definable any DPDT. Contrast this result with Exercise 2.6.20(b).

9.2.9. Give a formal proof of Theorem 9.3.

9.2.10. Prove Theorem 9.4.

9.2.11. Extend the SDTS of Example 9.7 to incorporate rules (3), (4), and (5) for pig Latin.

9.2.12. Can the SDTS of Example 9.7 be replaced by a simple SDTS if we assume that no English word begins with more than four consonants? What happens to the number of rules of the SDTS?

9.2.13. Show how a parsing machine with pointers would translate the word *abb* according to the following GTDPL program with output:

$$S \longrightarrow A[B, C], 0BA, 11C$$
$$A \longrightarrow a, \qquad 0$$
$$B \longrightarrow S[C, A], 0CS, 1A$$
$$C \longrightarrow b, \qquad 1$$

**9.2.14. Construct P, a GTDPL program with output, such that $\tau(P) = \{(x, y) \mid x$ is a string with n a's and n b's, $n \geq 0$, and $y = a^n b^n\}$. Construct M, a modified parsing machine, from P so that $\tau(M) = \tau(P)$. Is there (a) a TDPL program with output or (b) an SDTS that defines the same translation?

9.2.15. Prove Theorem 9.5.

9.2.16. Prove Theorem 9.6.

*9.2.17. Extend the notion of a processor with pointers to a graph and give translation algorithms for SDTS's based on the following algorithms:
(a) Algorithm 4.1.
(b) Algorithm 4.2.
(c) The Cocke–Younger–Kasami algorithm.
(d) Earley's algorithm.
(e) A two-stack parser (see Section 6.2).
(f) A Floyd–Evans parser.

Research Problem

9.2.18. In implementing a translation, we are often concerned with the efficiency with which the translation is performed. Develop optimization techniques similar to those in Chapter 7 to find efficient translators for useful classes of syntax-directed translations.

Programming Exercises

9.2.19. Construct a program that takes as input a simple SDTS on an LL(1) grammar and produces as output a translator which implements the given SDTS.

9.2.20. Construct a program that produces a translator which implements a postfix simple SDTS on an LALR(1) grammar.

9.2.21. Construct a program that produces a translator which implements an arbitrary SDTS on an LALR(1) grammar.

BIBLIOGRAPHIC NOTES

Lewis and Stearns [1968] were the first to prove that a simple SDTS with an underlying LL(k) grammar can be implemented by a deterministic pushdown transducer. They also showed that a simple postfix SDTS on an LR(k) grammar can be performed on a DPDT and that every DPDT translation can be effectively described by a simple postfix SDTS on an LR(k) grammar (Exercise 9.2.7). The pushdown processor was introduced by Aho and Ullman [1969a].

In many compiler-compilers and compiler writing systems, the formalism used to describe the object compiler is similar to a syntax-directed translation scheme. The syntax of the language for which a compiler is being constructed is specified in terms of a context-free grammar. Semantic routines are also specified and associated with each production. The object compiler that is produced can be modeled by a pushdown processor; as the object compiler parses its input, the semantic routines are invoked to compute the output. TDPL with output is a simplified model of the TMG compiler writing system [McClure, 1965]. McIlroy [1972] has implemented an extension of TMG to allow GTDPL-type parsing rules and simulation of bottom-up parsers. GTDPL with output is a simplified model for the META family of compiler-compilers [Schorre, 1964].

Two classes of simple SDTS's which each include the simple SDTS's on an LL grammar and the postfix simple SDTS's on an LR grammar are mentioned by Lewis and Stearns [1968] and Aho and Ullman [1972g]. Each of these classes is implementable on a DPDT.

9.3. GENERALIZED TRANSLATION SCHEMES

In this section we shall consider how the idealized translations discussed previously can be extended in a natural way to enable us to perform a wider

and more useful class of translations. Here we shall adopt the point of view
that the most general translation element that can be associated with a production can be any type of function. The main extensions are to allow several
translations at each node of the parse tree, to allow use of other than string-
valued variables, and to allow a translation at one node to depend on translations at its direct ancestor, as well as its direct descendants.

We shall also discuss the important matter of the timing of the evaluation
of translations at various nodes.

9.3.1. Multiple Translation Schemes

Our first extension of the SDTS will allow each node in the parse tree to
possess several string-valued translations. As in the SDTS, each translation
depends on the translations of the various direct descendants of the node in
question. However, the translation elements can be arbitrary strings of output
symbols and symbols representing the translations at the descendants. Thus,
translation symbols can be repeated.

DEFINITION

A *generalized syntax-directed translation scheme* (GSDTS) is a system
$T = (N, \Sigma, \Delta, \Gamma, R, S)$, where N, Σ, and Δ are finite sets of *nonterminals, input symbols*, and *output symbols*, respectively. Γ is a finite set of *translation
symbols* of the form A_i, where $A \in N$ and i is an integer. We assume that
$S_1 \in \Gamma$. S is the *start symbol*, a member of N. Finally, R is a set of *rules* of
the form

$$A \longrightarrow \alpha, A_1 = \beta_1, A_2 = \beta_2, \ldots, A_m = \beta_m$$

subject to the following constraints:

(1) $A_j \in \Gamma$ for $1 \leq j \leq m$.
(2) Each symbol of $\beta_1, \ldots, \beta_m$ is either in Δ or a symbol B_k in Γ such
that B is a nonterminal which appears in α.
(3) If α has more than one symbol B, then each B_k in the β's is associated
by a superscript to one of these instances of B.

We call $A \longrightarrow \alpha$ the *underlying production* of the rule. We call A_i a *translation* of A and $A_i = \beta_i$ a *translation element* associated with this rule. If P
denotes the set of *underlying productions* of all rules, then $G = (N, \Sigma, P, S)$
is the *underlying grammar* of T. If no two rules have the same underlying
production, then T is said to be *semantically unambiguous*.

We define the output of a GSDTS in a bottom-up fashion. With each
interior node n of a parse tree (in the underlying grammar) labeled A, we
associate one string for each A_i in Γ. This string is called the *value* (or
translation) of A_i at node n. Each value is computed by substituting the values

defined at the direct descendants of n for the translation symbols of the translation element for A_i. The proper translation element for A_i is the one associated with the production used at n. For example, suppose that

$$A \rightarrow BaC, \quad A_1 = bB_1C_2B_1, \quad A_2 = C_1cB_2$$

is a rule in a GSDTS and that the underlying production $A \rightarrow BaC$ is used to expand a node labeled A in the derivation tree, as shown in Fig. 9.12. Then if

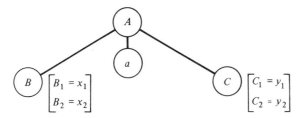

Fig. 9.12   Portion of a parse tree.

the values of B_1 and B_2 at node B and of C_1 and C_2 at node C are as in Fig. 9.12, the value of A_1 defined at the node labeled A is $bx_1y_2x_1$ and the value of A_2 at that node is y_1cx_2.

The *translation defined by* T, denoted $\tau(T)$, is the set of pairs

$$\{(x, y) \mid x \text{ has a parse tree in the underlying grammar of } T,$$
$$\text{and } y \text{ is the value of } S_1 \text{ at the root of that tree}\}.$$

Example 9.10

Let $T = (\{S\}, \{a\}, \{a\}, \{S_1, S_2\}, R, S)$ be a· GSDTS, where R consists of the following rules:

$$S \longrightarrow aS, \quad S_1 = S_1S_2S_2a, \quad S_2 = S_2a$$
$$S \longrightarrow a, \quad S_1 = a, \quad\quad\quad S_2 = a$$

Then $\tau(T) = \{(a^n, a^{n^2}) \mid n \geq 1\}$. For example, a^4 has the parse tree of Fig. 9.13(a). The values of the two translations at each interior node are shown in Fig. 9.13(b).

For example, to calculate the value of S_1 at the root, we substitute into the expression $S_1S_2S_2a$ the values for S_1 and S_2 at the node below the root. These values are a^9 and a^3, respectively. A proof that $\tau(T)$ maps a^n to a^{n^2} reduces to observing that $(n + 1)^2 = n^2 + 2n + 1$. $\square$

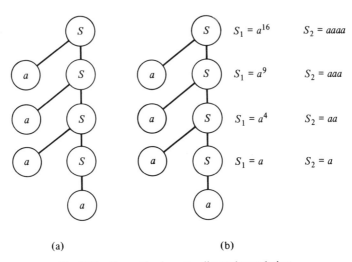

Fig. 9.13   Generalized syntax directed translation.

Example 9.11

We shall give an example of formal differentiation of expressions involving the constants 0 and 1, the variable x, and the functions sine, cosine, $+$, and $*$. The following grammar generates the expressions:

$$E \longrightarrow E + T \,|\, T$$
$$T \longrightarrow T * F \,|\, F$$
$$F \longrightarrow (E) \,|\, \sin(E) \,|\, \cos(E) \,|\, x \,|\, 0 \,|\, 1$$

We associate with each of E, T, and F two translations indicated by subscripts 1 and 2. Subscript 1 indicates an undifferentiated expression; 2 indicates a differentiated expression. E_2 is the distinguished translation. The appropriate laws for the derivatives are

$$d(f(x) + g(x)) = df(x) + dg(x)$$
$$df(x)g(x) = f(x)dg(x) + g(x)df(x)$$
$$d\sin(f(x)) = \cos(f(x))df(x)$$
$$d\cos(f(x)) = -\sin(f(x))df(x)$$
$$dx = 1$$
$$d0 = 0$$
$$d1 = 0$$

The following GSDTS, T, reflects these laws:

$$E \longrightarrow E + T \qquad E_1 = E_1 + T_1$$
$$E_2 = E_2 + T_2$$
$$E \longrightarrow T \qquad E_1 = T_1$$
$$E_2 = T_2$$
$$T \longrightarrow T * F \qquad T_1 = T_1 * F_1$$
$$T_2 = T_1 * F_2 + (T_2) * F_1$$
$$T \longrightarrow F \qquad T_1 = F_1$$
$$T_2 = F_2$$
$$F \longrightarrow (E) \qquad F_1 = (E_1)$$
$$F_2 = (E_2)$$
$$F \longrightarrow \sin(E) \qquad F_1 = \sin(E_1)$$
$$F_2 = \cos(E_1) * (E_2)$$
$$F \longrightarrow \cos(E) \qquad F_1 = \cos(E_1)$$
$$F_2 = -\sin(E_1) * (E_2)$$
$$F \longrightarrow x \qquad F_1 = x$$
$$F_2 = 1$$
$$F \longrightarrow 0 \qquad F_1 = 0$$
$$F_2 = 0$$
$$F \longrightarrow 1 \qquad F_1 = 1$$
$$F_2 = 0$$

We leave for the Exercises a proof that if (α, β) is in $\tau(T)$, then β is the derivative of α. β may contain some redundant parentheses.

The derivation tree for $\sin(\cos(x)) + x$ is given in Fig. 9.14.

The values of the translation symbols at each of the interior nodes are listed below:

Nodes	E_1, T_1, or F_1	E_2, T_2 or F_2
n_3, n_2	x	1
n_{12}, n_{11}, n_{10}	x	1
n_9, n_8, n_7	$\cos(x)$	$-\sin(x) * (1)$
n_6, n_5, n_4	$\sin(\cos(x))$	$\cos(\cos(x)) * (-\sin(x) * (1))$
n_1	$\sin(\cos(x)) + x$	$\cos(\cos(x)) * (-\sin(x) * (1)) + 1$

$\square$

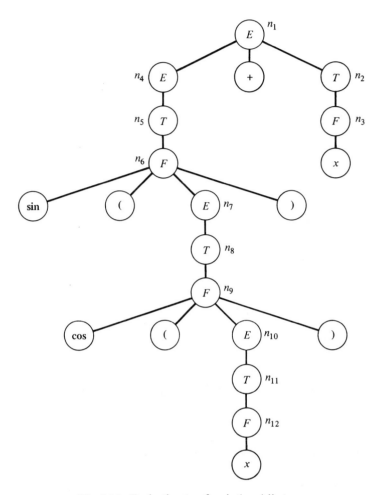

Fig. 9.14   Derivation tree for sin (cos (x)) $+ x$.

The implementation of a GSDTS is not much different from that of an SDTS using Algorithms 9.1 and 9.2. We shall generalize Algorithm 9.1 to produce as output a directed acyclic graph (dag) rather than a tree. It is then possible to "walk" over the dag in such a way that the desired translation can be obtained.

ALGORITHM 9.4

Bottom-up execution of a GSDTS.

Input. A semantically unambiguous GSDTS $T = (N, \Sigma, \Delta, \Gamma, R, S)$, whose underlying grammar G is LR(k), and an input string $x \in \Sigma^*$.

Output. A dag from which we can recover the output y such that (x, y) is in T.

Method. Let α be an LR(k) parser for G. We shall construct a pushdown processor M with an endmarker, which will simulate α and construct a dag. If α has nonterminal A on its pushdown list, M will place below A one pointer for each translation symbol $A_i \in \Gamma$. Thus, corresponding to a node labeled A on the parse tree will be as many nodes of the dag as there are translations of A, i.e., symbols A_i in Γ. The action of M is as follows:

(1) If α shifts, M does the same.

(2) Suppose that α is about to reduce according to production $A \rightarrow \alpha$, with translation elements $A_1 = \beta_1, \ldots, A_m = \beta_m$. At this point M will have α on top of its pushdown list, and immediately below each nonterminal in α there will be pointers to each of the translations of that nonterminal. When M makes the reduction, M first creates m nodes, one for each translation symbol A_i. The direct descendants of these nodes are determined by the symbols in $\beta_1, \ldots, \beta_m$. New nodes for output symbols are created. The node for translation symbol $B_k \in \Gamma$ is the node indicated by that pointer below the nonterminal B in α which represents the kth translation of B. (As usual, if there is more than one B in α, the particular instance of B referred to will be indicated in the translation element by a superscript.) In making the reduction, M replaces α and its pointers by A and the m pointers to the translations for A. For example, suppose that α reduces according to the underlying production of the rule

$$A \longrightarrow BaC, \quad A_1 = bB_1C_2B_1, \quad A_2 = C_1cB_2$$

Then M would have the string $p_{B_2}p_{B_1}Bap_{C_2}p_{C_1}C$ on top of its pushdown list (C is on top), where the p's are pointers to nodes representing translations. In making the reduction, M would replace this string by $p_{A_2}p_{A_1}A$, where p_{A_1} and p_{A_2} are pointers to the first and second translations of A. After the reduction the output dag is as shown in Fig. 9.15. We assume that p_{X_i} points to the node for X_i.

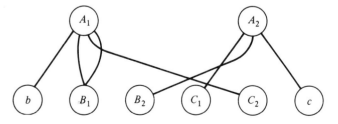

Fig. 9.15 Portion of output dag.

(3) If M has reached the end of the input string and its pushdown list contains S and some pointers, then the pointer to the node for S_1 is the root of the desired output dag.   ☐

We shall delay a complete example until we have discussed the interpretation of the dag. Apparently, each node of the dag "represents" the value of a translation symbol at some node of the parse tree. But how can that value be produced from the dag? It should be evident from the definition of the translation associated with a dag that the value represented by a node n should be the concatenation, in order from the left, of the values represented by the direct descendants of node n. Note that two or more direct descendants may in fact be the same node. In that case, the value of that node is to be repeated.

With the above in mind, it should be clear that the following method of walking through a dag will produce the desired output.

ALGORITHM 9.5

Translation from dag.

Input. A dag with leaves labeled and a single root.

Output. A sequence of the symbols used to label the leaves.

Method. We shall use a recursive procedure $R(n)$, where n is a node of the dag. Initially, $R(n_0)$ is called, where n_0 is the root.

Procedure $R(n)$.

(1) Let $a_1, a_2, \ldots, a_m$ be the edges leaving n in this order. Do step (2) for $a_1, a_2, \ldots, a_m$ in order.
(2) Let a_i be the current edge.
    (a) If a_i enters a leaf, emit the label of that leaf.
    (b) If a_i enters an interior node n', perform $R(n')$.   ☐

THEOREM 9.7

If Algorithm 9.5 is applied to the dag produced by Algorithm 9.4, then the output of Algorithm 9.5 is the translation of the input x to Algorithm 9.4.

Proof. Each node n produced by Algorithm 9.4 corresponds in an obvious way to the value of a translation symbol at a particular node of the parse tree for x. A straightforward induction on the height of a node shows that $R(n)$ does produce the value of that translation symbol.   ☐

Example 9.12

Let us apply Algorithms 9.4 and 9.5 to the GSDTS of Example 9.10 (p. 759), with input *aaaa*.

The sequence of configurations of the processor is [with LR(1) tables omitted, as usual]

Pushdown List	Input
(1) e	$aaaa\$$
(2) a	$aaa\$$
(3) aa	$aa\$$
(4) aaa	$a\$$
(5) $aaaa$	$\$$
(6) $aaap_1p_2S$	$\$$
(7) aap_3p_4S	$\$$
(8) ap_5p_6S	$\$$
(9) p_7p_8S	$\$$

The trees constructed after steps 6, 7, and 9 are shown in Fig. 9.16(a)–(c). Nodes on the left correspond to values of S_1 and those on the right to values of S_2.

The application of Algorithm 9.5 to the dag of Fig. 9.16(c) requires many invocations of the procedure $R(n)$. We begin with node n_1, since that corresponds to S_1. The sequence of calls of $R(n)$ and the generations of output a will be listed. A call of $R(n_i)$ is indicated simply as n_i. The sequence is

$n_1n_3n_5n_7an_8an_8aan_6n_8aan_6n_8aaan_4n_6n_8aaan_4n_6n_8aaaa$.　□

9.3.2.　Varieties of Translations

Heretofore, we have considered only string-valued translation variables in a translation scheme. The same principles that enabled us to define SDTS's and GSDTS's will allow us to define and implement translation schemes containing arithmetic and Boolean variables, for example, in addition to string variables.

The strings produced in the course of code generation can fall into several different classes:

(1) Machine or assembly code which is to be output of the compiler.

(2) Diagnostic messages; also output of the compiler but not in the same stream as (1).

(3) Instructions indicating that certain operations should be performed on data managed by the compiler itself.

Under (3), we would include instructions which do bookkeeping operations, arithmetic operations on certain variables used by the compiler other than in the parsing mechanism, and operations that allocate storage and generate new labels for output statements. We defer discussion of when these instructions are executed to the next section.

A few examples of types of translations which we might find useful during code generation are

(1) Elements of a finite set of modes (real, integer, and so forth) to indicate the mode of an arithmetic expression,

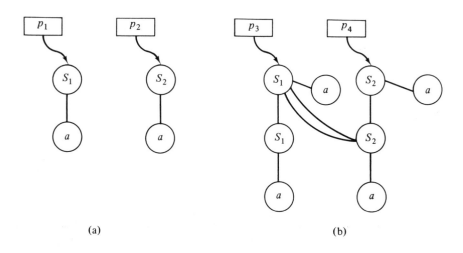

(a)   (b)

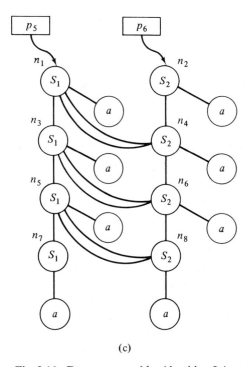

(c)

Fig. 9.16   Dag constructed by Algorithm 9.4.

(2) Strings representing the labels of certain statements when compiling flow of control structures (**if–then–else**, for example), and

(3) Integers indicating the height of a node in the parse tree.

We shall generalize the types of formulas that can be used in a syntax-directed translation scheme to compute translations. Of course, when dealing with numbers or Boolean variables, we shall use Boolean and arithmetic operators to express translations. However, we find it convenient to also use conditional statements of the form **if** B **then** E_1 **else** E_2, where B is a Boolean expression and E_1 and E_2 are arbitrary expressions, including conditionals.

For example, we might have a production $A \to BC$, where B has a Boolean translation B_1 and C has two string-valued translations C_1 and C_2. The formula for the translation of A_1 might be **if** B_1 **then** C_1 **else** C_2. That is, if the left direct descendant of the node whose translation A_1 is being computed has translation B_1 = **true**, then take C_1, the first translation of the right direct descendant, as A_1; otherwise, take C_2. Alternatively, B might have an integer-valued translation B_2, and the formula for A_2 might be **if** B_2 = 1 **then** C_1 **else** C_2. This statement would cause A_2 to be the same as C_2 unless B_2 had the value 1.

We observe that it is not hard to generalize Algorithm 9.4, a bottom-up algorithm, to incorporate the possibility that certain translations are numbers, Boolean values, or elements of some finite set. In a bottom-up scheme the formulas for these variables (and the string-valued variables) are evaluated only when all arguments are known.

In fact, it will often be the case that all but one of the translations associated with a node are Boolean, integer or elements of a finite set. If the remaining (string-valued) translation can be produced by rules that are essentially postfix simple SDTS rules (with conditionals, perhaps), then we can implement the entire translation on a DPDT which keeps the non-string translations on its pushdown list. These translations can be easily "attached" to the pushdown cells holding the nonterminals, there being an obvious connection between nonterminals on the pushdown list and interior nodes of the parse tree. If some translation is integer-valued, we have gone outside the DPDT formalism, but the extension should pose no problem to the person implementing the translator on a computer.

However, generalizing Algorithms 9.2 and 9.3, which are top-down, is not as easy. When only strings are to be constructed, we have allowed the formulas to be expanded implicitly, i.e., with pointers to nodes which will eventually represent the desired string. However, it may not be possible to treat arithmetic or conditional formulas in the same way.

Referring to Algorithm 9.2, we can make the following modification. If a nonterminal A on top of the pushdown list is expanded, we leave the pointer immediately below A on the pushdown list. This pointer indicates the node n which this instance of A represents. When the expansion of A is complete, the pointer will again be at the top of the pushdown list, and the translations for all descendants of n will have been computed. (We can show this inductively.) It is then possible to compute the translation of n exactly as if the parse were bottom-up. We leave the details of such a generalization for the Exercises.

We conclude this section with several examples of more general translation schemes.

Example 9.13

We shall elaborate on Section 1.2.5, wherein we spoke of the generation of code for arithmetic expressions for a single accumulator random access machine. Specifically, we assume that the assembly language instructions

$$\begin{array}{ll} \text{ADD} & \alpha \\ \text{MPY} & \alpha \\ \text{LOAD} & \alpha \\ \text{STORE} & \alpha \end{array}$$

are available and have the obvious meanings.

We shall base our translation on the grammar G_0. Nonterminals E, T, and F will each have two translation elements. The first will produce a string of output characters that will cause the value of the corresponding input expression to be brought to the accumulator. The second translation will be an integer, representing the height of the node in a parse tree. We shall not, however, count the productions $E \rightarrow T$, $T \rightarrow F$, or $F \rightarrow (E)$ when determining height. Since the only need for this height measure is to determine a safe temporary location name, it is permissible to disregard these productions. Put another way, we shall really measure height in the syntax tree.

The six productions and their translation elements are listed below:

(1) $E \longrightarrow E + T$ $E_1 = T_1$ ';STORE \$' E_2 ';' E_1 ';ADD \$' E_2

$E_2 = \mathbf{max}(E_2, T_2) + 1$

(2) $E \longrightarrow T$ $E_1 = T_1 \dagger$

$E_2 = T_2$

(3) $T \longrightarrow T * F$ $T_1 = F_1$ ';STORE \$' T_2 ';' T_1 ';MPY \$' T_2

$T_2 = \mathbf{max}(T_2, F_2) + 1$

---

† If we were working from the syntax tree, rather than the parse tree, reductions by $E \rightarrow T$, $T \rightarrow F$ and $F \rightarrow (E)$ would not appear. We would then have no need to implement the trivial translation rules associated with these productions.

(4) $\quad T \longrightarrow F \qquad T_1 = F_1$

$\qquad\qquad\qquad\qquad\quad T_2 = F_2$

(5) $\quad F \longrightarrow (E) \qquad F_1 = E_1$

$\qquad\qquad\qquad\qquad\quad F_2 = E_2$

(6) $\quad F \longrightarrow a \qquad\; F_1 = $ 'LOAD' NAME(a)

$\qquad\qquad\qquad\qquad\quad F_2 = 1$

Again we use the SNOBOL convention in the translation elements for the definition of strings. Quotes surround strings that denote themselves. Unquoted symbols denote their current value, which is to be substituted for that symbol. Thus, in rule (1), the translation element for E_1 states that the value of E_1 is to be the concatenation of

(1) The value of T_1 followed by a semicolon;

(2) The instruction STORE with an address $\$n$, where n is the height of the node for E (on the right-hand side of the production), followed by a semicolon;

(3) The value of E_1 (the left argument of $+$) followed by a semicolon; and

(4) The instruction ADD $\$n$, where n is the same as in (2).

Here $\$n$ is intended to be a temporary location, and the translation for E_1 (on the right-hand side of the translation element) will not use that location because of the way E_2, T_2, and F_2 are handled.

The rule for production (6) uses the function NAME(a), where NAME is a bookkeeping function that retrieves the internal (to the compiler) name of the identifier represented by the token a. Recall that the terminal symbols of all our grammars are intended to be tokens. If a token represents an identifier, the token will contain a pointer to the place in the symbol table where information about the particular identifier is stored. This information tells which identifier the token really represents, as well as giving attributes of that identifier.

The parse tree of $(a + a) * (a + a)$, with values of some of the translation symbols, is shown in Fig. 9.17. We assume that the function NAME(a) yields a_1, a_2, a_3, and a_4, respectively, for the four identifiers represented by a. $\quad \square$

Example 9.14

The code produced by Example 9.13 is by no means optimal. A considerable improvement can be made by observing that if the right operand is a single identifier, we need not load it and store it in a temporary. We shall therefore add a third translation for E, T, and F, which is a Boolean variable

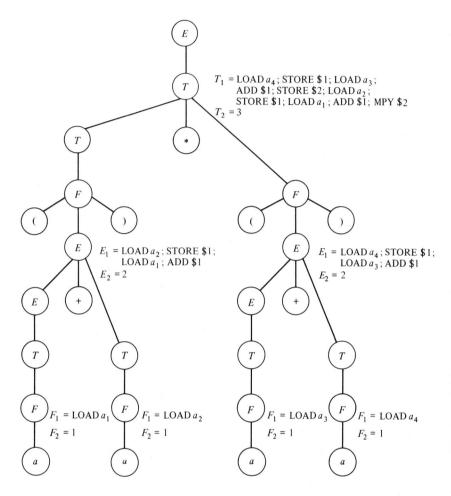

Fig. 9.17   Parse tree and translations.

with value **true** if and only if the expression dominated by the node is a single identifier.

The first translation of E, T, and F is again code to compute the expression. However, if the expression is a single identifier, then this translation is only the "NAME" of that identifier. Thus, the translation scheme does not "work" for single identifiers. This should cause little trouble, since the expression grammar is presumably part of a grammar for assignment and the translation for assignments such as $A \longleftarrow B$ can be handled at a higher level.

The new rules are the following:

(1) $E \longrightarrow E + T$ $\quad E_1 =$ **if** T_3 **then**

$\qquad$ **if** E_3 **then** 'LOAD' E_1 ';ADD' T_1

$\qquad$ **else** E_1 ';ADD' T_1

$\qquad$ **else if** E_3 **then** T_1 ';STORE $1;LOAD' E_1

$\qquad$ ';ADD $1'

$\qquad$ **else** T_1 ';STORE $' E_2 ';' E_1 ';ADD $' E_2

$\quad E_2 = $ **max**$(E_2, T_2) + 1$

$\quad E_3 = $ **false**

(2) $E \longrightarrow T$ $\quad E_1 = T_1$

$\quad E_2 = T_2$

$\quad E_3 = T_3$

(3) $T \longrightarrow T * F$ $\quad T_1 = $ **if** F_3 **then**

$\qquad$ **if** T_3 **then** 'LOAD' T_1 ';MPY' F_1

$\qquad$ **else** T_1 ';MPY' F_1

$\qquad$ **else if** T_3 **then** F_1 ';STORE $1;LOAD' T_1

$\qquad$ ';MPY $1'

$\qquad$ **else** F_1 ';STORE $' T_2 ';' T_1 ';MPY $' T_2

$\quad T_2 = $ **max**$(T_2, F_2) + 1$

$\quad T_3 = $ **false**

(4) $T \longrightarrow F$ $\quad T_1 = F_1$

$\quad T_2 = F_2$

$\quad T_3 = F_3$

(5) $F \longrightarrow (E)$ $\quad F_1 = E_1$

$\quad F_2 = E_2$

$\quad F_3 = E_3$

(6) $F \longrightarrow a$ $\quad F_1 = $ NAME(a)

$\quad F_2 = 1$

$\quad F_3 = $ **true**

In rule (1), the formula for E_1 checks whether either or both arguments are single identifiers. If the right-hand argument is a single identifier, then the code generated causes the left-hand argument to be computed and the right-hand argument to be added to the accumulator. If the left-hand argument is a single identifier, then the code generated for this argument is the identifier name. Thus, 'LOAD' must be prefixed to it. Note that $E_2 = 1$ in this case, and so \$1 can be used as the temporary store rather than '\$' E_2 (which would be \$1 in this case anyway).

The code produced for $(a + a) * (a + a)$ is

$$\text{LOAD } a_3; \text{ ADD } a_4; \text{ STORE \$2}; \text{ LOAD } a_1; \text{ ADD } a_2; \text{ MPY \$2}$$

Note that these rules do not assume that $+$ and $*$ are commutative. □

Our next example again deals with arithmetic expressions. It shows how if three address code is chosen as the intermediate language, we can write what is essentially a simple SDTS, implementable by a deterministic pushdown transducer that holds some extra information at the cells of its pushdown list.

Example 9.15

Let us translate $L(G_0)$ to a sequence of three address statements of the form $A \leftarrow + BC$ and $A \leftarrow * BC$, meaning that A is to be assigned the sum or product, respectively, of B and C. In this example A will be a string of the form \$$i$, where i is an integer. The principal translations, E_1, T_1, and F_1, will be a sequence of three address statements which evaluate the expression dominated by the node in question; E_2, T_2, and F_2 are integers indicating levels, as in the previous examples. E_3, T_3, and F_3 will be the name of a variable which has been assigned the value of the expression by the aforementioned code. This name is a program variable in the case that the expression is a single identifier and a temporary name otherwise. The following is the translation scheme:

$$E \longrightarrow E + T \qquad E_1 = E_1 T_1 \text{ '\$' } \mathbf{max}(E_2, T_2) \text{ '}\leftarrow +\text{' } E_3 T_3 \text{ ';'}$$
$$E_2 = \mathbf{max}(E_2, T_2) + 1$$
$$E_3 = \text{ '\$' } \mathbf{max}(E_2, T_2)$$

$$E \longrightarrow T \qquad E_1 = T_1$$
$$E_2 = T_2$$
$$E_3 = T_3$$

$$T \longrightarrow T * F \qquad T_1 = T_1 F_1 \text{ '\$' } \mathbf{max}(T_2, F_2) \text{ '}\leftarrow *\text{' } T_3 F_3 \text{ ';'}$$
$$T_2 = \mathbf{max}(T_2, F_2) + 1$$
$$T_3 = \text{ '\$' } \mathbf{max}(T_2, F_2)$$

$$T \longrightarrow F \qquad T_1 = F_1$$
$$T_2 = F_2$$
$$T_3 = F_3$$

$$F \longrightarrow (E) \qquad F_1 = E_1$$
$$F_2 = E_2$$
$$F_3 = E_3$$
$$F \longrightarrow a \qquad F_1 = e$$
$$F_2 = 1$$
$$F_3 = \text{NAME}(a)$$

As an example, the output for the input $a_1 * (a_2 + a_3)$ is

$$\$1 \longleftarrow + a_2 a_3;$$
$$\$2 \longleftarrow * a_1 \$1;$$

We leave it to the reader to observe that the rules for E_1, T_1, and F_1 form a postfix simple SDTS if we assume that the values of second and third translations of E, T, and F are output symbols. A practical method of implementation is to parse G_0 in an LR(1) manner by a DPDT which keeps the values of the second and third translations on its stack. That is, each pushdown cell holding E will also hold the values of E_2 and E_3 for the associated node of the parse tree (and similarly for cells holding T and F).

The translation is implemented by emitting

$$\text{`\$' } \max(E_2, T_2) \text{ `}\longleftarrow +\text{' } E_3 T_3 \text{ `;'}$$

every time a reduction of $E + T$ to E is called for, where E_2, E_3, T_2, and T_3 are the values attached to the pushdown cells involved in the reduction. Reductions by $T \longrightarrow T * F$ are treated analogously, and nothing is emitted when other reductions are made.

We should observe that since the second and third translations of E, T, and F can assume an infinity of values, the device doing the translation is not, strictly speaking, a DPDT. However, the extension is easy to implement in practice on a random access computer.   □

Example 9.16

We shall generate assembly code for control statements of the **if–then–else** form. We presume that the nonterminal S stands for a statement and that one of its productions is $S \longrightarrow$ **if** B **then** S **else** S. We suppose that S has a translation S_1 which is code to execute that statement. Thus, if a production for S other than the one shown is used, we can presume that S_1 is correctly computed.

Let us assume that B stands for a Boolean expression and that it has two translations, B_1 and B_2, which are computed by other rules of the translation system. Specifically, B_1 is code that causes a jump to location B_2 if the Boolean expression has value **false**.

To generate the expected code, S will need another translation S_2, which is the location to be transferred to after execution of S is finished. We assume that our computer has an instruction JUMP α which transfers control to the location named α.

To generate names for these locations, we shall assume the existence of a function NEWLABEL, which when invoked generates a name for a label that has never been used before. For example, the compiler might keep a global integer i available. Each time NEWLABEL is invoked, it might increment i by 1 and return the name $\$\$i$. The function NEWLABEL is not actually invoked for this S-production but will be invoked for some other S-productions and for B-productions.

We also make use of a convenient assembler pseudo-operation, the likes of which is found in most assembly languages. This assembly instruction is of the form

$$\text{EQUAL} \quad \alpha, \beta$$

It generates no code but causes the assembler to treat the locations named α and β as the same location.

The EQUAL instruction is needed because the two instances of S on the right-hand side of the production $S \longrightarrow$ **if** B **then** S **else** S each have a name for the instruction they expect to execute next. We must make sure that a location allotted for one serves for the other as well.

The translation elements for the production mentioned are

$$S \longrightarrow \textbf{if } B \textbf{ then } S^{(1)} \textbf{ else } S^{(2)} \qquad S_1 = \text{'EQUAL' } S_2^{(1)} \text{ ',' } S_2^{(2)} \text{ ';'}$$
$$B_1 \text{ ';' } S_1^{(1)} \text{ ';JUMP'}$$
$$S_2^{(1)} \text{ ';' } B_2 \text{ ':' } S_1^{(2)}$$
$$S_2 = S_2^{(1)}$$

That is, the translation for S consists of the concatenation of

(1) An instruction to cause $S_2^{(1)}$ and $S_2^{(2)}$ to represent the same location;

(2) Object code for the Boolean expression (B_1), which causes a jump to location B_2 if false;

(3) Object code for the first statement $(S_1^{(1)})$ followed by a jump to the location labeled $S_2^{(1)}$ (the location with that label exists outside the statement being compiled); and

(4) Object code for the second statement $(S_1^{(2)})$. The first location for that code is given label B_2.

The translation for S_2 is the same as translation S_2 of the first substatement. Thus, whether B is true or false, the location $S_2^{(1)}$ (which now equals $S_2^{(2)}$) will be reached.

Let us consider the nested statement

$$\text{if } B^{(1)} \text{ then if } B^{(2)} \text{ then } S^{(1)} \text{ else } S^{(2)} \text{ else } S^{(3)}$$

generated by two applications of the production in question. (The superscripts are just for reference and strictly speaking should not appear.) The object code generated for this nested statement would be (with semicolons replaced by new lines)

$$\text{EQUAL } S_2^{(1)}, \ S_2^{(3)}$$
$$\text{code for } B^{(1)}$$
$$\text{EQUAL } S_2^{(1)}, \ S_2^{(2)}$$
$$\text{code for } B^{(2)}$$
$$\text{code for } S^{(1)}$$
$$\text{JUMP } S_2^{(1)}$$

$B_2^{(2)}:$ code for $S^{(2)}$

  JUMP $S_2^{(1)}$

$B_2^{(1)}:$ code for $S^{(3)}$ □

Example 9.17

As the last example in this section, we consider generating object code for a call of the form

$$\text{call } X(E^{(1)}, \ldots, E^{(n)})$$

We suppose that there is an assembly instruction CALL X which transfers to location X and places the current location in a register reserved for returning from a function call. We translate **call** $X(E^{(1)}, \ldots, E^{(n)})$ into code which computes the values denoted by each of the expressions $E^{(1)}, \ldots, E^{(n)}$ and stores their values in temporary locations $t_1, \ldots, t_n$. These computations are followed by the assembly instruction CALL X and n "argument-holding" instructions ARG $t_1, \ldots,$ ARG t_n, which are used as pointers to the arguments of this call of X.

We should comment that an alternative method of implementing a call is to place the values of $E^{(1)}, \ldots, E^{(n)}$ directly in the locations following the instruction CALL X. A translation scheme generating this type of call is left for the Exercises.

The important productions describing the call statement are

$$S \longrightarrow \text{call } a \ A$$

$$A \longrightarrow e \,|\, (L)$$
$$L \longrightarrow E, L \,|\, E$$

That is, a statement can be the keyword **call** followed by an identifier and an argument list (A). The argument list can be the empty string or a parenthesized list (L) of expressions. We assume that each expression E has two translations E_1 and E_2, where the translation of E_1 is object code that leaves the value of E in the accumulator and the translation of E_2 is the name of a temporary location for storing the value of E. The names for the temporaries are created by the function NEWLABEL. The following rules perform the desired translation:

$$S \longrightarrow \textbf{call } a \, A \qquad S_1 = A_1 \; \text{`;CALL' NAME}(a) \, A_2$$
$$A \longrightarrow (L) \qquad A_1 = L_1$$
$$\qquad\qquad A_2 = \text{`;'} \, L_2$$
$$A \longrightarrow e \qquad A_1 = e$$
$$\qquad\qquad A_2 = e$$
$$L \longrightarrow E, L \qquad L_1 = E_1 \; \text{`;STORE'} \, E_2 \; \text{`;'} \, L_1$$
$$\qquad\qquad L_2 = \text{`ARG'} \, E_2 \; \text{`;'} \, L_2$$
$$L \longrightarrow E \qquad L_1 = E_1 \; \text{`;STORE'} \, E_2$$
$$\qquad\qquad L_2 = \text{`ARG'} \, E_2$$

For example, the statement **call** $AB(E^{(1)}, E^{(2)})$ would, if the temporaries for $E^{(1)}$ and $E^{(2)}$ were \$\$1 and \$\$2, respectively, be compiled into

> code for $E^{(1)}$
> STORE \$\$1
> code for $E^{(2)}$
> STORE \$\$2
> CALL AB
> ARG \$\$1
> ARG \$\$2

9.3.3. Inherited and Synthesized Translations

There is another generalization of the syntax-directed translation that may be useful in certain applications. We have considered translations of nonterminals which are functions only of translations at the direct descendant nodes. It is also possible that the value of a translation could be a function of the values of the translations at its direct ancestor as well as its direct descendants. We make the following definition.

DEFINITION

A translation of a nonterminal in a translation scheme is said to be a *synthesized translation* if it is a function only of translations at itself and the direct descendants of the nodes at which it is computed. The translation is an *inherited translation* if it is a function only of translations at itself and the direct ancestor of nodes at which it is computed. All translations considered so far have been synthesized and, in fact, have not had formulas involving translations at the same node.

We shall define translation elements associated with a production in the usual way if the translation defined is synthesized. However, the rules for inherited translations associated with a production may use as arguments the translations associated with the left-hand side of the production and compute a translation associated with some particular symbol on the right. It is thus necessary that we distinguish the nonterminal on the left from any instances of that symbol on the right. As usual, superscripts will be used for this task.

Example 9.18

Let us consider the translation rule

$$A^{(1)} \longrightarrow A^{(2)}A^{(3)} \qquad A_1^{(1)} = aA_2^{(2)}A_2^{(3)}b$$
$$A_2^{(2)} = A_1^{(1)}$$
$$A_2^{(3)} = aA_1^{(1)}$$

Here A has two translations A_1, which is synthesized, and A_2, which is inherited. The rule for A_1 is of the type with which we are familiar. The rules for $A_2^{(2)}$ and $A_2^{(3)}$ are examples of rules for inherited attributes. Let us refer to the portion of a tree in Fig. 9.18. The rule for $A_2^{(2)}$ says that translation A_2 at node n_2 is to be made equal to the translation A_1 at n_1. Since A_1 at n_1 is defined in terms of A_2 at n_2, here we have a simple example of circular definition, and this rule is not acceptable as it stands.   ☐

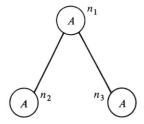

Fig. 9.18   Portion of a tree.

Implementation of a translation scheme with both inherited and synthesized attributes is not easy. In the most general case, one must first construct
the entire parse tree and then compute at each node whatever translations
can be computed in terms of the already computed translations at the descendant and ancestor nodes. Presumably, one begins with the synthesized
attributes at nodes of height 1. When a translation is recomputed, all translations depending on it, whether inherited or synthesized, must be recomputed. It is thus possible that there is no end to the sequence of translations
which must be recomputed. Such a translation scheme is said to be *circular*.
It is decidable whether a translation scheme is circular, although the decision
algorithm is complicated, and we shall leave it for the Exercises. We shall
give one example in which for any parse tree there is a natural order in which
to compute the various translations.

Example 9.19

Let us compile code for arithmetic expressions to be executed on a
machine with two fast registers, denoted the A and B registers. The relevant
instructions are

$$\begin{array}{ll} \text{LOADA} & \alpha \\ \text{LOADB} & \alpha \\ \text{STOREA} & \alpha \\ \text{STOREB} & \alpha \\ \text{ADDA} & \alpha \\ \text{ADDB} & \alpha \\ \text{MPY} & \alpha \\ \text{ATOB} & \end{array}$$

The meaning of the first six instructions should be obvious. We can load,
store, or perform addition in either register. We presume that the MPY
instruction takes its left argument in the B register and leaves the result in
the A register, as is the case for floating-point arithmetic on some computers.
The last instruction, ATOB, with no argument, transfers the contents of
the A register to the B register.

We shall build our translation on G_0, exactly as we did in Example 9.13.
The translations E_1, T_1, and F_1 will represent code to compute the value of
the associated input expression, sometimes leaving the result in the A register
and sometimes in B. However, the code for E_1 at the root of the parse tree
for the input expression will always leave the value of the expression in the A
register. E_2, T_2, and F_2 are integers which measure the height of the node,
as in Example 9.13. There will be translations E_3, T_3, and F_3 which are
Boolean and have the value **true** if and only if the value of the expression is

to be left in the A register. These last three translations are all inherited, while the first six are synthesized. We dispense with the code-improving feature of Example 9.14. The rules of the translation scheme are

$E^{(1)} \longrightarrow E^{(2)} + T$ $E_1^{(1)} = $ **if** $E_3^{(1)}$ **then**

$$T_1 \text{ ';STOREA \$' } E_2^{(2)} \text{ ';' } E_1^{(2)}$$

$$\text{';ADDA \$' } E_2^{(2)}$$

$$\textbf{else } T_1 \text{ ';STOREA \$' } E_2^{(2)} \text{ ';' } E_1^{(2)}$$

$$\text{';ADDB \$' } E_2^{(2)}$$

$$E_2^{(1)} = \max(E_2^{(2)}, T_2) + 1$$

$$E_3^{(2)} = E_3^{(1)}\dagger$$

$$T_3 = \textbf{true}$$

$E \longrightarrow T$ $E_1 = T_1$

$$E_2 = T_2$$

$$T_3 = E_3$$

$T^{(1)} \longrightarrow T^{(2)} * F$ $T_1^{(1)} = $ **if** $T_3^{(1)}$ **then**

$$F_1 \text{ ';STOREA \$' } T_2^{(2)} \text{ ';' } T_1^{(2)}$$

$$\text{';MPY \$' } T_2^{(2)}$$

$$\textbf{else } F_1 \text{ ';STOREA \$' } T_2^{(2)} \text{ ';' } T_1^{(2)}$$

$$\text{';MPY \$' } T_2^{(2)} \text{ ';ATOB'}$$

$$T_2^{(1)} = \max(T_2^{(2)}, F_2) + 1$$

$$T_3^{(2)} = \textbf{false}$$

$$F_3 = \textbf{true}$$

$T \longrightarrow F$ $T_1 = F_1$

$$T_2 = F_2$$

$$F_3 = T_3$$

$F \longrightarrow (E)$ $F_1 = E_1$

$$F_2 = E_2$$

$$E_3 = F_3$$

$F \longrightarrow a$ $F_1 = $ **if** F_3 **then** 'LOADA' NAME(a)

$$\textbf{else 'LOADB' NAME}(a)$$

$$F_2 = 1$$

†We assume that all Boolean translations initially have the value **true**. Thus, if $E_3^{(1)}$ refers to the root, it is already defined.

The strategy is to compute all right-hand operands in register A. The left-hand operand of $*$ is always computed in B, and the left-hand operand of $+$ is computed in either A or B, depending on where the value of the complete expression is desired. Thus, the translation element for $E_1^{(1)}$ associated with production $E \rightarrow E + T$ gives a translation which computes T in register A, stores it in a safe temporary, then computes E in either A or B, whichever is desired, and performs the addition. The rule for $T_1^{(1)}$ associated with production $T \rightarrow T * F$ computes F in register A, stores it, computes T in register B, multiplies, and, if desired, transfers the result in register B.

The parse tree of $(a + a) * a$ is shown in Fig. 9.19, with some interior

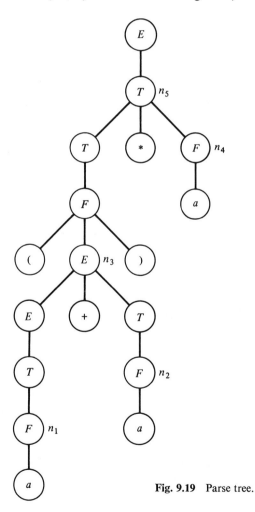

Fig. 9.19 Parse tree.

nodes named. Inherited and synthesized attributes propagate unchanged up and down chains $E \rightarrow T \rightarrow F$. Here, we describe one sequence of computation of the translations, omitting the propagation of translations from E to T to F and conversely:

Translation	At Node	Value
T_3	n_5	**true**
E_3	n_3	**false**
F_3	n_1	**false**
F_3	n_2	**true**
F_1	n_2	LOADA a_2
F_2	n_2	1
F_1	n_1	LOADB a_1
F_2	n_1	1
E_1	n_3	LOADA a_2; STOREA \$1; LOADB a_1; ADDB \$1
E_2	n_3	2
F_3	n_4	**true**
F_1	n_4	LOADA a_3
F_2	n_4	1
T_1	n_5	LOADA a_3; STOREA \$2; LOADA a_2; STOREA \$1; LOADB a_1; ADDB \$1; MPY \$2
T_2	n_5	3

□

9.3.4. A Word About Timing

We have pictured a compiler as though the three steps of lexical analysis, syntactic analysis, and code generation were done one at a time, in that order. However, this time division is only for representational purposes and may not occur in practice.

First, the lexical analysis phase normally produces tokens only as they are needed by the parser. The input string of tokens, which we have shown when demonstrating the action of parsers, does not necessarily exist in reality. The tokens are found only when the parser is about to look at them. Of course, this difference does not affect the action of the parser in any way.

As we have already indicated, the parsing and code generation phases may occur simultaneously. Thus, the three phases can operate in lock-step. When the parser cannot parse further, it gets another token from the lexical analyzer. After each reduction (if bottom-up) or nonterminal expansion (if top-down) by the parser, the code generation phase operates on the node or nodes of the parse tree that have just been produced.

If the translation being produced were one string, there would be little concern about when different pieces of the translation were produced. However, we recall that the various pieces of translation being produced may be of several types: for example, object code, diagnostics, and instructions to be executed by the compiler itself, such as instructions to enter information into the bookkeeping mechanism.

Should the method of translation be a pushdown transducer, or a similar device, where a single stream of output emerges from the device, we again have little problem with the timing of translations. Symbols are deemed output as they emerge from the device. If we assume that different kinds of output are differentiated by metasymbols, then the output stream can be divided as it emerges. For example, intermediate code is passed to the optimization phase, diagnostics are placed on their own list to await printing, and bookkeeping instructions are executed immediately.

Let us suppose that one of the more general versions of Algorithms 9.1–9.4 is being used to perform some generalized syntax-directed translation. We could wait until the entire tree or dag is constructed and then construct a single output stream. The division of the stream into object code and instructions would occur exactly as for a pushdown transducer. This means that bookkeeping instructions would not be executed until the entire output was constructed and that the instructions are reached as the output is processed. This arrangement requires an extra pass over the output and a large random access memory but may be the most practical arrangement if the power of the more general syntax-directed translation schemes is needed.

Alternatively, one could adopt the convention that bookkeeping and other compiler instructions are associated with particular nodes of the parse tree and are executed just as soon as that node is constructed. However, if the parsing algorithm involves backtrack, one must be careful not to execute an instruction associated with a node which is subsequently found not to be part of the parse. In such a situation, a mechanism to negate the effect of such an instruction is needed.

EXERCISES

9.3.1. Find GSDTS's for the following translations:
(a) $\{(a^n, a^{n^3}) \mid n \geq 1\}$.
(b) $\{(a^n, a^{2^n}) \mid n \geq 1\}$.
(c) $\{(w, ww) \mid w \in (0 + 1)^*\}$.

9.3.2. Show that there exist GSDTS definable translations that are not SDT's.

**9.3.3. Let T be a semantically unambiguous GSDTS with infinite domain whose underlying CFG is proper. Show that one of the following three conditions must hold:

(1) There exist constants c_1 and c_2 greater than 1 such that if $(x, y) \in \tau(T)$, then $|y| \leq c_2^{|x|}$, and for an infinity of x, there exists $(x, y) \in \tau(T)$ with $|y| \geq c_1^{|x|}$.

(2) There exist constants c_1 and c_2 greater than 0 and an integer $i \geq 1$ such that if $(x, y) \in \tau(T)$ and $x \neq e$, then $|y| \leq c_2 |x|^i$, and for an infinity of x, there exists $(x, y) \in \tau(T)$ with $|y| \geq c_1 |x|^i$.

(3) The range of T is finite.

9.3.4. Show that the translation $\{(a^n, a^m) \mid m$ is the integer part of $\sqrt{n}\}$ cannot be defined by any GSDTS.

9.3.5. For Exercise 9.3.1(a)–(c), give the dags produced by Algorithm 9.4 with inputs a^3, a^4, and 011, respectively.

9.3.6. Give the sequence of nodes visited by Algorithm 9.5 when applied to the three dags of Exercise 9.3.5.

*9.3.7. Embellish Example 9.16 to include the production $S \longrightarrow$ **while** B **do** S, with the intended meaning that alternately expression B is to be tested, and then the statement S done, until such time as the value of B becomes **false**.

9.3.8. The following grammar generates PL/I-like declarations:

$$D \longrightarrow (L)M$$
$$L \longrightarrow a, L \mid D, L \mid a \mid D$$
$$M \longrightarrow m_1 \mid m_2 \mid \cdots \mid m_k$$

The terminal a stands for any identifier; $m_1, \ldots, m_k$ are the k possible attributes of identifiers in the language. Comma and parentheses are also terminal symbols. L stands for a list of identifiers and declarations; D is a declaration, which consists of a parenthesized list of identifiers and declarations. The intention is that the attribute derived from M is to apply to all those identifiers generated by L in the production $D \longrightarrow (L)M$ even if the identifier is within a nested declaration. For example, the declaration $(a_1, (a_2, a_3)m_1)m_2$ assigns attribute m_1 to a_2 and a_3 and attribute m_2 to a_1, a_2, and a_3. Build a translation scheme, involving any type of translation, that will translate strings generated by D into k lists; list i is to hold exactly those identifiers which are given attribute m_i.

9.3.9. Modify Example 9.17 to place values of the expressions, rather than pointers to those values, in the ARG instructions.

9.3.10. Consider the following translation scheme:

$$
\begin{aligned}
N &\longrightarrow L^{(1)} \cdot L^{(2)} & N_1 &= L_1^{(1)} + L_1^{(2)} / 2^{L_2^{(2)}} \\
N &\longrightarrow L & N_1 &= L_1 \\
L &\longrightarrow LB & L_1 &= 2L_1 + B_1 \\
& & L_2 &= L_2 + 1 \\
L &\longrightarrow B & L_1 &= B_1 \\
& & L_2 &= 1 \\
B &\longrightarrow 0 & B_1 &= 0 \\
B &\longrightarrow 1 & B_1 &= 1
\end{aligned}
$$

In the underlying grammar, N is the start symbol and derives binary numbers (possibly with a binary point). L stands for a list of bits and B for bit. The translation elements are arithmetic formulas. The translation element N_1 represents a rational number, the value of the binary number derived by the nonterminal N. The translation elements L_1, L_2, and B_1 take integer values. For example, 11.01 has the translation $3\frac{1}{4}$. Show that $\tau(T) = \{(b, d) \mid b$ is a binary number and d is the value of $b\}$.

*9.3.11. Consider the following translation scheme with the same underlying grammar as in Exercise 9.3.10 but involving both synthesized and inherited attributes:

$$N \longrightarrow L^{(1)} \cdot L^{(2)} \qquad N_1 = L_1^{(1)} + L_1^{(2)}$$
$$L_2^{(1)} = 0$$
$$L_2^{(2)} = -L_3^{(2)}$$
$$N \longrightarrow L \qquad N_1 = L_1$$
$$L_2 = 0$$
$$L^{(1)} \longrightarrow L^{(2)}B \qquad L_1^{(1)} = L_1^{(2)} + B_1$$
$$B_2 = L_2^{(1)}$$
$$L_2^{(2)} = L_2^{(1)} + 1$$
$$L_3^{(1)} = L_3^{(2)} + 1$$
$$L \longrightarrow B \qquad L_1 = B_1$$
$$B_2 = L_2$$
$$L_3 = 1$$
$$B \longrightarrow 0 \qquad B_1 = 0$$
$$B \longrightarrow 1 \qquad B_1 = 2^{B_2}$$

The parse tree for 11.01 together with the values of the translation elements associated with each node is shown in Fig. 9.20. Note that to compute the translation element N_1 we must first compute the L_3's to the right of the radix point bottom-up, then the L_2's top-down, and finally the L_1's bottom-up. Show that this translation scheme defines the same translation as the scheme in Exercise 9.3.10.

*9.3.12. Show that any translation that can be performed using inherited and synthesized translations can be performed using synthesized translations only. *Hint:* There is no restriction on the structure of a translation. Thus, one translation defined at a node can be the entire subtree that it dominates.

9.3.13. Can every translation using synthesized translations be performed using inherited translations only?

**9.3.14. Give an algorithm to test whether a given translation scheme involving inherited and synthesized attributes is circular.

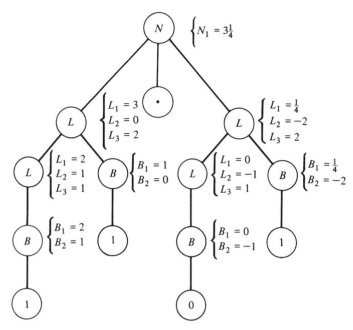

Fig. 9.20   Parse tree with translations.

9.3.15. Modify Example 9.18 to incorporate the code-improving feature of Example 9.14.

*9.3.16. The differentiation algorithm of Example 9.11 allowed the generation of expressions such as $1 * \cos(x)$ or $0 * x + (1) * 1$ (the formal derivative of $1 * x$). We can detect and eliminate expressions which are *explicitly* 0 or 1, where the definition of *explicit* is as follows:

   (1) 0 is explicitly 0; 1 is explicitly 1.
   (2) If E_1 is explicitly 0 and E_2 is any expression, then $E_1 * E_2$ and $E_2 * E_1$ are explicitly 0.
   (3) If E_1 and E_2 are explicitly 1, then $E_1 * E_2$ is explicitly 1.
   (4) If E_1 is explicitly 0 and E_2 is explicitly 1, then $E_1 + E_2$ and $E_2 + E_1$ are explicitly 1.
   (5) If E_1 and E_2 are explicitly 0, then $E_1 + E_2$ is explicitly 0.

Modify the GSDTS, including the underlying grammar, if necessary, so that no subexpressions which are explicitly 0 appear in the translation, and no explicit 1 appears as a multiplicative factor.

9.3.17. Consider the following grammar for assignment statements involving subscripted variables:

$$A \longrightarrow I := E$$
$$E \longrightarrow E\langle\text{adop}\rangle T \mid T$$

$$T \longrightarrow T\langle \text{mulop}\rangle F \,|\, F$$
$$F \longrightarrow (E) \,|\, I$$
$$I \longrightarrow a \,|\, a(L)$$
$$L \longrightarrow E, L \,|\, E$$
$$\langle \text{adop}\rangle \longrightarrow + \,|\, -$$
$$\langle \text{mulop}\rangle \longrightarrow * \,|\, /$$

An example of a statement generated by this grammar would be

$$a(a, a) := a(a + a, a * (a + a)) + a$$

Here, a is a token representing an identifier. Construct a translation scheme based on this grammar that will generate suitable assembly or multiple address code for assignment statements.

9.3.18. Show that the GSDTS of Example 9.11 correctly produces an expression for the derivative of its input expression.

**9.3.19. Show that

$$\{(a_1 \ldots a_n b_1 \ldots b_n, a_1 b_1 \ldots a_n b_n) \,|\, n \geq 1,$$
$$a_i \in \{0, 1\} \text{ and } b_i \in \{2, 3\} \text{ for } 1 \leq i \leq n\}$$

is not definable by a GSDTS.

Research Problem

9.3.20. Translation of arithmetic expressions can become quite complicated if operands can be of many different data types. For example, we could be dealing with identifiers that could be Boolean, string, integer, real, or complex—the last three in single, double, or perhaps higher precisions. Moreover, some identifiers could be in dynamically allocated storage, while others are statically allocated. The number of combinations can easily be large enough to make the translation elements associated with a production such as $E \longrightarrow E + T$ quite cumbersome. Given a translation which spells out the desired code for each case, can you develop an automatic way of simplifying the notation? For instance, in Example 9.19, the **then** and **else** portions of the translation of $E_1^{(1)}$ differ only in the single character A or B at the end of ADD. Thus, almost a factor of 2 in space could be saved if a more versatile defining mechanism were used.

Programming Exercise

*9.3.21. Construct a translation scheme that maps a subset of FORTRAN into intermediate language as in Exercise 9.1.10. Write a program to implement this translation scheme. Implement the code generator designed in Exercise 9.1.11. Combine these programs with a lexical analyzer to produce a compiler for the subset of FORTRAN. Design test strings that will check the correct operation of each program.

BIBLIOGRAPHIC NOTES

Generalized syntax-directed translation schemes are discussed by Aho and Ullman [1971], and a solution to Exercise 9.3.3 can be found there. Knuth [1968b] defined translation schemes with inherited and synthesized attributes. The GSDT's in Exercises 9.3.10 and 9.3.11 are discussed there.

The solution to Exercise 9.3.14 is found in Bruno and Burkhard [1970] and Knuth [1968b]. Exercise 9.3.12 is from Knuth [1968b].

10 BOOKKEEPING

This chapter discusses methods by which information can be quickly stored in tables and accessed from these tables. The primary application of these techniques is the storage of information about tokens during lexical analysis and the retrieval of this information during code generation. We shall discuss two ideas—simple information retrieval techniques and the formalism of property grammars. The latter is a method of associating attributes and identifiers while ensuring that the proper information about each identifier is available at each node of the parse tree for translation purposes.

10.1. SYMBOL TABLES

The term *symbol table* is given to a table which stores names and information associated with these names. Symbol tables are an integral feature of virtually all compilers. A symbol table is pictured in Fig. 10.1. The entries in the name field are usually identifiers. If names can be of different lengths, then it is more convenient for the entry in the name field to be a pointer to a storage area in which the names are actually stored.

The entries in the data field, sometimes called *descriptors*, provide information that has been collected about each name. In some situations a dozen or more pieces of information are associated with a given name. For example, we might need to know the data type (real, integer, string, and so forth) of an identifier; whether it was perhaps a label, a procedure name, or a formal parameter of a procedure; whether it was to be given statically or dynamically allocated storage; or whether it was an identifier with structure (e.g., an array), and if so, what the structure was (e.g., the dimensions of an array). If the number of pieces of information associated with a given name is vari-

NAME	DATA
I	INTEGER
LOOP	LABEL
X	REAL ARRAY

Fig. 10.1   Symbol table.

able, then it is again convenient to store a pointer in the data field to this information.

10.1.1. Storage of Information About Tokens

A compiler uses a symbol table to store information about tokens, particularly identifiers. This information is then used for two purposes. First, it is used to check for the semantic correctness of a source program. For example, if a statement of the form

$$\text{GOTO} \quad \text{LOOP}$$

is found in the source program, then the compiler must check that the identifier LOOP appears as the label of an appropriate statement in the program. This information will be found in the symbol table (although not necessarily at the time at which the goto statement is processed). The second use of the information in the symbol table is in generating code. For example, if we have a FORTRAN statement of the form

$$A = B + C$$

in the source program, then the code that is generated for the operator $+$ depends on the attributes of identifiers B and C (e.g., are they fixed- or floating-point, in or out of "common," and so forth).

The lexical analyzer enters names and information into the symbol table. For example, whenever the lexical analyzer discovers an identifier, it consults the symbol table to see whether this token has previously been used. If not, the lexical analyzer inserts the name of this identifier into the symbol table along with any associated information. If the identifier is already present in the symbol table at some location l, then the lexical analyzer produces the token ($\langle$identifier$\rangle$, l) as output.

Thus, every time the lexical analyzer finds a token, it consults the symbol table. Therefore, to design an efficient compiler, we must, given an instance of an identifier, be able to rapidly determine whether or not a location in the symbol table has been reserved for that identifier. If no such entry exists, we must then be able to insert the identifier quickly into the table.

Example 10.1

Let us suppose that we are compiling a FORTRAN-like language and wish to use a single token type ⟨identifier⟩ for all variable names. When the (direct) lexical analyzer first encounters an identifier, it could enter into a symbol table information as to whether this identifier was fixed- or floating-point. The lexical analyzer obtains the information by observing the first letter of the identifier. Of course, a previous declaration of the identifier to be a function or subroutine or not to obey the usual fixed–floating convention would already appear in the symbol table and would already overrule the attempt by the lexical analyzer to store its information.   □

Example 10.2

Let us suppose that we are compiling a language in which array declarations are defined by the following productions:

⟨array statement⟩ ⟶ **array** ⟨array list⟩

⟨array list⟩ ⟶ ⟨array definition⟩, ⟨array list⟩|⟨array definition⟩

⟨array definition⟩ ⟶ ⟨identifier⟩ (⟨integer⟩)

An example of an array declaration in this language is

(10.1.1)   **array** $AB(10)$, $CD(20)$

For simplicity, we are assuming that arrays are one-dimensional here. The parse tree for statement (10.1.1) is shown in Fig. 10.2, treating AB and CD identifiers and 10 and 20 as integers.

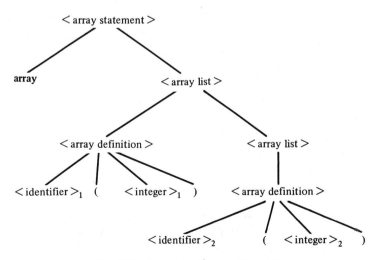

Fig. 10.2   Parse tree of array statement.

In this parse tree the tokens $\langle\text{identifier}\rangle_1$, $\langle\text{identifier}\rangle_2$, $\langle\text{integer}\rangle_1$, and $\langle\text{integer}\rangle_2$ represent AB, CD, 10, and 20, respectively.

The array statement is, naturally, nonexecutable; it is not compiled into machine code. However, it makes sense to think of its translation as a sequence of bookkeeping steps to be executed immediately by the compiler. That is, if the translation of an identifier is a pointer to the place in the symbol table reserved for it and the translation of an integer is itself, then the syntax-directed translation of a node labeled $\langle\text{array definition}\rangle$ can be instructions for the bookkeeping mechanism to record that the identifier is an array and that its size is measured by the integer. ☐

The ways in which the information stored in the symbol table is used are numerous. As a simple example, every subexpression in an arithmetic expression may need mode information, so that the arithmetic operators can be interpreted as fixed, floating, complex, and so forth. This information is collected from the symbol table for those leaves which have identifier or constant labels and are passed up the tree by rules such as fixed + floating = floating, and floating + complex = complex. Alternatively, the language, and hence the compiler, may prohibit mixed mode expressions altogether (e.g., as in some versions of FORTRAN).

10.1.2. Storage Mechanisms

We conclude that there is a need in a compiler for a bookkeeping method which rapidly stores and retrieves information about a large number of different items (e.g., identifiers). Moreover, while the number of items that actually occur is large, say on the order of 100 to 1000 for a typical program, the number of possible items is orders of magnitude larger; most of the possible identifiers do not appear in a given program.

Let us briefly consider possible ways of storing information in tables in order to better motivate the use of the hash or scatter storage tables, to be discussed in the next section.

Our basic problem can be formulated as follows. We have a large collection of possible items that may occur. Here, an item can be considered to be a name consisting of a string of symbols. We encounter items in an unpredictable fashion, and the exact number of items to be encountered is unknown in advance. As each item is encountered, we wish to check a table to determine whether that item has been previously encountered and if it has not, to enter the name of the item into the table. In addition, there will be other information about items which we wish to store in the table.

We might initially consider using a direct access table to store information about items. In such a table a distinct location is reserved for each possible item. Information concerning the item would be stored at that location, and the name of the item need not be entered in the table. If the number of possible items is small and a unique location can readily be assigned to each item, then the direct access table provides a very fast mechanism for storing and retrieving information about items. However, we would quickly discard the idea of using a direct access table for most symbol table applications, since the size of the table would be prohibitive and most of it would never be used. For example, the number of FORTRAN identifiers (a letter followed by up to five letters or digits) is about 1.33×10^9.

Another possible method of storage is to use a pushdown list. If a new item is encountered, its name and a pointer to information concerning that item is pushed onto the pushdown list. Here, the size of the table is proportional to the number of items actually encountered, and new items can be inserted very quickly. However, the retrieval of information about an item requires that we search the list until the item is found. Thus, retrieval on the average requires time proportional to the number of items on the list. This technique is often adequate for small lists. In addition, it has advantages when a block-structured language is being compiled, as a new declaration of a variable can be pushed on top of an old one. When the block ends, all its declarations are popped off the list and the old declarations of the variables are still there.

A third method, which is faster than the pushdown list, is to use a *binary search tree*. In a binary search tree each node can have a *left direct descendant* and a *right direct descendant*. We assume that data items can be linearly ordered by some relation $<$, e.g., the relation "precedes in alphabetical order." Items are stored as the labels of the nodes of the tree. When the first item, say α_1, is encountered, a root is created and labeled α_1. If α_2 is the next item and $\alpha_2 < \alpha_1$, then a leaf labeled α_2 is added to the tree and this leaf is made the left direct descendant of the root. (If $\alpha_1 < \alpha_2$, then this leaf would have been made the right direct descendant.) Each new item causes a new leaf to be added to the tree in such a position that at all times the tree will have the following property. Suppose that N is any node in the tree and that N is labeled β. If node N has a left subtree containing a node labeled α, then $\alpha < \beta$. If node N has a right subtree with a node labeled γ, then $\beta < \gamma$.

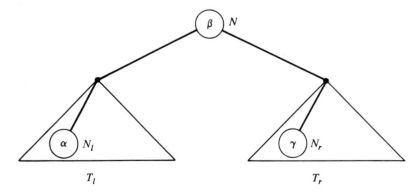

The following algorithm can be used to insert items into a binary search tree.

ALGORITHM 10.1

Insertion of items into a binary search tree.

Input. A sequence $\alpha_1, \ldots, \alpha_n$ of items from a set of items A with a linear order $<$ on A.

Output. A binary tree whose nodes are each labeled by one of $\alpha_1, \ldots, \alpha_n$, with the property that if node N is labeled α and some descendant N' of N is labeled β, then $\beta < \alpha$ if and only if N' is in the left subtree of N.

Method.

(1) Create a single node (the root) and label it α_1.

(2) Suppose that $\alpha_1, \ldots, \alpha_{i-1}$ have been placed in the tree, $i > 0$. If $i = n + 1$, halt. Otherwise, insert α_i in the tree by executing step (3) beginning at the root.

(3) Let this step be executed at node N with label β.

    (a) If $\alpha_i < \beta$ and N has a left direct descendant, N_l, execute step (3) at N_l. If N has no left direct descendant, create such a node and label it α_i. Return to step (2).

    (b) If $\beta < \alpha_i$ and N has a right direct descendant, N_r, execute step (3) at N_r. If N has no right direct descendant, create such a node and label it α_i. Return to step (2). ☐

The method of retrieval of items is essentially the same as the method for insertion, except that one must check at each node encountered in step (3) whether the label of that node is the desired item.

Example 10.3

Let the sequence of items input to Algorithm 10.1 be XY, M, QB, ACE, and OP. We assume that the ordering is alphabetic. The tree constructed is shown in Fig. 10.3. ☐

It can be shown that, after n items have been placed in a binary search tree, the expected number of nodes which must be searched to retrieve one of them is proportional to log n. This cost is acceptable, although hash tables, which we shall discuss next, give a faster expected retrieval time.

10.1.3. Hash Tables

The most efficient and commonly used method for the bookkeeping necessary in a compiler is the *hash table*. A hash storage symbol table is shown schematically in Fig. 10.4.

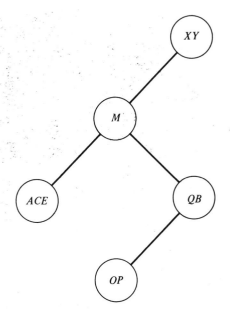

Fig. 10.3   Binary search tree.

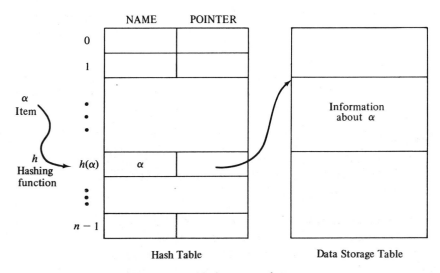

Fig. 10.4   Hash storage scheme.

The hash storage mechanism uses a *hashing function*, *h*, a *hash table*, and a *data storage table*. The hash table has *n* entries, where *n* is fixed before-hand. Each entry in the hash table consists of two fields—a name field and

a pointer field. Initially, each entry in the hash table is assumed to be empty.†
If an item α has been encountered, then some location in the hash table,
usually $h(\alpha)$, contains an entry whose name field contains α (or possibly
a pointer to a location in a name table in which α is stored) and whose pointer
field holds a pointer to a block in the data storage table containing the information associated with α.

The data storage table need not be physically distinct from the hash
table. For example, if k words of information are needed for each item,
then it is possible to use a hash table of size kn. Each item stored in the hash
table would occupy a block of k consecutive words of storage. The appropriate location in the hash table for an item α can then readily be found by
multiplying $h(\alpha)$, the hash address for α, by k and using the resulting address
as the location of the first word in the block of words for α.

The hashing function h is actually a list of functions $h_0, h_1, \ldots, h_m$, each
from the set of items to the set of integers $\{0, 1, \ldots, n - 1\}$. We shall call
h_0 the *primary hashing function*. When a new item α is encountered, we can
use the following algorithm to compute $h(\alpha)$, the hash address of α. If α has
been previously encountered, $h(\alpha)$ is the location in the hash table at which
α is stored. If α has not been encountered, then $h(\alpha)$ is an empty location
into which α can be stored.

ALGORITHM 10.2

Computation of a hash table address.

Input. An item α, a hashing function h consisting of a sequence of functions
$h_0, h_1, \ldots, h_m$ each from the set of items to the set of integers $\{0, 1, \ldots, n - 1\}$
and a (not necessarily empty) hash table with n locations.

Output. The hash address $h(\alpha)$ and an indication of whether α has been
previously encountered. If α has already been entered into the hash table,
$h(\alpha)$ is the location assigned to α. If α has not been encountered, $h(\alpha)$ is
an empty location into which α is to be stored.

Method.

(1) We compute $h_0(\alpha), h_1(\alpha), \ldots, h_m(\alpha)$ in order using step (2) until no
"collision" occurs. If $h_m(\alpha)$ produces a collision, we terminate this algorithm
with a failure indication.

(2) Compute $h_i(\alpha)$ and do the following:

(a) If location $h_i(\alpha)$ in the hash table is empty, let $h(\alpha) = h_i(\alpha)$,
report that α has not been encountered, and halt.

(b) If location $h_i(\alpha)$ is not empty, check the name entry of this loca-

---

†Sometimes it is convenient to put the reserved words and standard functions in the
symbol table at the start.

tion.† If the name is α, let $h(\alpha) = h_i(\alpha)$, report that α has already been entered, and halt. If the name is not α, a *collision* occurs and we repeat step (2) to compute the next alternate address.

☐

Each time a location $h_i(\alpha)$ is examined, we say that a *probe* of the table is made.

When the hash table is sparsely filled, collisions are rare, and for a new item α, $h(\alpha)$ can be computed very quickly, usually just by evaluating the primary hashing function, $h_0(\alpha)$. However, as the table fills, it becomes increasingly likely that for each new item α, $h_0(\alpha)$ will already contain another item. Thus, collisions become more frequent as more items are inserted into the table, and thus the number of probes required to determine $h(\alpha)$ increases. However, it is possible to design hash tables whose overall performance is much superior to binary search trees.

Ideally, for each distinct item encountered we would like the primary hashing function h_0 to yield a distinct location in the hash table. This, of course, is not generally feasible because the total number of possible items is usually much larger than n, the number of locations in the table. In practice, n will be somewhat larger than the number of distinct items expected. However, some course of action must be planned in case the table overflows.

To store information about an item α, we first compute $h(\alpha)$. If α has not been previously encountered, we store the name α in the name field of location $h(\alpha)$. [If we are using a separate name table, we store α in the next empty location in the name table and put a pointer to this location in the name field of location $h(\alpha)$.] Then we seize the next available block of storage in the data storage table and put a pointer to this block in the pointer field of location $h(\alpha)$. We can then insert the information in this block of data storage table.

Likewise, to fetch information about an item α, we can compute $h(\alpha)$, if it exists, by Algorithm 10.2. We can then use the pointer in the pointer field to locate the information in the data storage table associated with item α.

Example 10.4

Let us choose $n = 10$ and let an item consist of any string of capital Roman letters. We define CODE(α), where α is a string of letters to be the sum of the "numerical value" of each letter in α, where A has numerical value of 1, B has value 2, and so forth. Let us define $h_j(\alpha)$, for $0 \leq j \leq 9$,

---

†If the name entry contains a pointer to a name table, we need to consult the name table to determine the actual name.

to be $(CODE(\alpha) + j)$mod 10.† Let us insert the items A, W, and EF into the hash table.

We find that $h_0(A) = (1 \bmod 10) = 1$, so A is assigned to location 1. Next, W is assigned to location $h_0(W) = (23 \bmod 10) = 3$. Then, EF is encountered. We find $h_0(EF) = (5 + 6)$mod $10 = 1$. Since location 1 is already occupied, we try $h_1(EF) = (5 + 6 + 1)$mod $10 = 2$. Thus, EF is given location 2. The hash storage contents are now as depicted in Fig. 10.5.

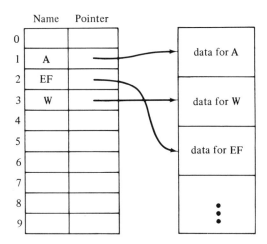

Fig. 10.5   Hash table contents.

Now, suppose that we wish to determine whether item HX is in the table. We find $h_0(HX) = 2$. By Algorithm 10.2, we examine location 2 and find that a collision occurs, since location 2 is filled but not with HX. We then examine location $h_1(HX) = 3$ and have another collision. Finally, we compute $h_2(HX) = 4$ and find that location 4 is empty. Thus, we can conclude that the item HX is not in the table.   □

10.1.4. Hashing Functions

It is desirable to use a primary hashing function h_0 that scatters items uniformly throughout the hash table. Functions which do not map onto the entire range of locations or tend to favor certain locations, as well as those which are expensive to compute, should be avoided.

Some commonly used primary hashing functions are the following.

---

†a mod b is the remainder when a is divided by b.

(1) If an item α is spread across several computer words, we can numerically sum these words (or exclusive-or these words) to obtain a *single word representation* of α. We can then treat this word as a number, square it, and use the middle $\log_2 n$ bits of the result as $h_0(\alpha)$. Since the middle bits of the square depend on all symbols in the item, distinct items are likely to yield different addresses regardless of whether the items share common prefixes or suffixes.

(2) We can partition the single word representation of α into sections of some fixed length ($\log_2 n$ bits is common). These sections can then be summed, and the $\log_2 n$ low-order bits of the sum determine $h_0(\alpha)$.

(3) We can divide the single word representation of α by the table size n and use the remainder as $h_0(\alpha)$. (n should be a prime here.)

Let us now consider methods of resolving collisions, that is, the design of the alternate functions $h_1, h_2, \ldots, h_m$. First we note that $h_i(\alpha)$ should be different from $h_j(\alpha)$ for all $i \neq j$. If $h_i(\alpha)$ produces a collision, it would be senseless to then probe $h_{i+r}(\alpha)$ if $h_{i+r}(\alpha) = h_i(\alpha)$. Also, in most cases we want $m = n - 1$, because we always want to find an empty slot in the table if one exists. In general the method used to resolve collisions can have a significant effect on the overall efficiency of a scatter store system.

The simplest, but as we shall see one of the worst, choices for the functions $h_1, h_2, \ldots, h_{n-1}$ is to use

$$h_i(\alpha) = [h_0(\alpha) + i] \bmod n \text{ for } 1 \leq i \leq n - 1.$$

Here we search forward from the primary location $h_0(\alpha)$ until no collision occurs. If we reach location $n - 1$, we proceed to location 0. This method is simple to implement, but clusters tend to occur once several collisions are encountered. For example, given that $h_0(\alpha)$ produces a collision, the probability that $h_1(\alpha)$ will also produce a collision is greater than average.

A more efficient method of generating alternate addresses is to use

$$h_i(\alpha) = (h_0(\alpha) + r_i) \bmod n \text{ for } 1 \leq i \leq n - 1$$

where r_i is a pseudorandom number. The most rudimentary random number generator that generates every integer between 1 and $n - 1$ exactly once will often suffice. (See Exercise 10.1.8.) Each time the alternate functions are used, the random number generator is initialized to the same point. Thus, the same sequence $r_1, r_2, \ldots$ is generated each time h is invoked, and the "random" number generator is quite predictable.

Other possibilities for the alternate functions are

$$h_i(\alpha) = [i(h_0(\alpha) + 1)] \bmod n$$

and

$$h_i(\alpha) = [h_0(\alpha) + ai^2 + bi]\bmod n,$$

where a and b are suitably chosen constants.

A somewhat different method of resolving collisions, called chaining, is discussed in the Exercises.

10.1.5. Hash Table Efficiency

We shall now address ourselves to the question, "How long, on the average, does it take to insert or retrieve data from a hash table?" A companion question is, "Given a set of probabilities for the various items, how should the functions $h_0, \ldots, h_{n-1}$ be selected to optimize the performance of the hash table?" Interestingly, there are a number of open questions in this area.

As we have noted, it is foolish to have duplications in the sequence of locations $h_0(\alpha), \ldots, h_{n-1}(\alpha)$ for any α. We shall thus assume that the best system of hashing functions avoids duplication. For example, the sequence $h_0, \ldots, h_9$ of Example 10.4 never causes the same location to be examined twice for the same item.

If n is the size of the hash table with locations numbered from 0 to $n - 1$ and $h_0, \ldots, h_{n-1}$ are the hashing functions, we can associate with each item α a permutation Π_α of $\{0, \ldots, n - 1\}$, namely $\Pi_\alpha = [h_0(\alpha), \ldots, h_{n-1}(\alpha)]$. Thus, the first component of Π_α gives the primary location to be assigned to α, the second component gives the next alternate location, and so forth. If we know p_α, the probability of item α occurring, for all items α, we can define the *probability of permutation* Π to be $\sum p_\alpha$, where the sum is taken over all items α such that $\Pi_\alpha = \Pi$. Hereafter we shall assume that we have been given the probabilities of the permutations.

It should be clear that we can calculate the expected number of locations which must be examined to insert an item into a hash table or find an item knowing only the probabilities of the permutations. It is not necessary to know the actual functions $h_0, \ldots, h_{n-1}$ to evaluate the efficiency of a particular hashing function. In this section we shall study properties of hashing functions as measured by the probabilities of the permutations.

We are thus motivated to make the following definition, which abstracts the problem of hash table design to a question of what is a desirable set of probabilities for permutations.

DEFINITION

A *hashing system* is a number n, the *table size*, and a probability function p on permutations of the integers 0 through $n - 1$. We say that a hashing system is *random* if $p(\Pi) = 1/n!$ for all permutations Π.

The important functions associated with a hashing system are

(1) $p(i_1 i_2 \cdots i_k)$, the probability that some item will have i_1 as its primary location, i_2 the first alternate, i_3 the next alternate, and so forth (each i_j here is an integer between 0 and $n - 1$), and

(2) $p(\{i_1, i_2, \ldots, i_k\})$, the probability that a sequence of k items will fill exactly the set of locations $\{i_1, \ldots, i_k\}$.

The following formulas are easy to derive:

(10.1.2) $\qquad p(i_1 \cdots i_k) = \sum_{i \text{ not among } i_1, \cdots, i_k} p(i_1 \cdots i_k i) \qquad$ if $k < n$

(10.1.3) $\qquad\qquad\qquad p(i_1 \cdots i_n) = p(\Pi)$

where Π is the permutation $[i_1, \ldots, i_n]$.

(10.1.4) $\qquad\qquad p(S) = \sum_{i \in S} p(S - \{i\}) \sum_{w} p(wi)$

where S is any subset of $\{0, \ldots, n - 1\}$ of size k and the rightmost sum is taken over all w such that w is any string of $k - 1$ or fewer distinct locations in $S - \{i\}$. We take $p(\varnothing) = 1$.

Formula (10.1.2) allows us to compute the probability of any sequence of locations occurring as alternates, starting with the probabilities of the permutations. Formula (10.1.4) allows us to compute the probability that the locations assigned to k items will be exactly those in set S. This probability is the sum of the probability that the first $k - 1$ items will fill all locations in S except location i and that the last item will fill i, taken over all i in S.

Example 10.5

Let $n = 3$ and let the probabilities of the six permutations be

Permutation	Probability
[0, 1, 2]	.1
[0, 2, 1]	.2
[1, 0, 2]	.1
[1, 2, 0]	.3
[2, 0, 1]	.2
[2, 1, 0]	.1

By (10.1.3) the probability that the string of locations 012 is generated by applying the hashing function to some item is just the probability of the permutation $[0, 1, 2]$. Thus, $p(012) = .1$. By (10.1.2) the probability that 01 is generated is $p(012)$. Likewise, $p(02)$ is the probability of permutation $[0, 2, 1]$, which is .2. Using formula (10.1.2), $p(0) = p(01) + p(02) = .3$.

The probability of each string of length 2 or 3 is the probability of the unique permutation of which it is a prefix. The probabilities of strings 1 and 2 are, respectively, $p(10) + p(12) = .4$ and $p(20) + p(21) = .3$.

Let us now compute the probabilities that various sets of locations are filled. For sets S of one element, (10.1.4) reduces to $p(\{i\}) = p(i)$. Let us compute $p(\{0, 1\})$ by (10.1.4). Direct substitution gives

$$p(\{0, 1\}) = p(\{0\})[p(1) + p(01)] + p(\{1\})[p(0) + p(10)]$$
$$= .3[.4 + .1] + .4[.3 + .1] = .31$$

Similarly, we obtain

$$p(\{0, 2\}) = .30 \quad \text{and} \quad p(\{1, 2\}) = .39$$

To compute $p(\{0, 1, 2\})$ by (10.1.4), we must evaluate

$$p(\{0, 1\})[p(2) + p(02) + p(12) + p(012) + p(102)]$$
$$+ p(\{0, 2\})[p(1) + p(01) + p(21) + p(021) + p(201)]$$
$$+ p(\{1, 2\})[p(0) + p(10) + p(20) + p(120) + p(210)]$$

which sums to 1, of course.   □

The figure of merit which we shall use to evaluate a hashing system is the expected number of probes necessary to insert an item α into a table in which k out of n locations are filled. We shall succeed on the first probe if $h_0(\alpha) = i$ and location i is one of the $n - k$ empty locations. Thus, the probability that we succeed on the first probe is given by

$$\sum_{i=0}^{n-1} p(i) \sum_{S} p(S)$$

where the rightmost sum is taken over all sets S of k locations which do not contain i.

If $h_0(\alpha)$ is in S but $h_1(\alpha) \notin S$, then we shall succeed on the second try. Therefore, the probability that we fail on the first try but succeed on the second is given by

$$\sum_{i=0}^{n-1} \sum_{j=0}^{n-1} p(ij) \sum_{S} p(S)$$

where the rightmost sum is taken over all sets S such that $\#S = k$, $i \in S$, and $j \notin S$. Note that $p(ij) = 0$ if $i = j$.

Proceeding in this manner, we arrive at the following formula for $E(k, n)$, *the expected number of probes required to insert an item into a table in which* *k out of n locations are filled, k < n:*

$$(10.1.5) \qquad E(k, n) = \sum_{m=1}^{k+1} m \sum_{w} p(w) \sum_{S} p(S)$$

where

(1) The middle summation is taken over all w which are strings of distinct locations of length m and
(2) The rightmost sum is taken over all sets S of k locations such that all but the last symbol of w is in S. (The last symbol of w is not in S.)

The first summation assumes that m steps are required to compute the primary location and its first $m - 1$ alternates. Note that if $k < n$, an empty location will always be found after at most $k + 1$ tries.

Example 10.6

Let us use the statistics of Example 10.5 to compute $E(2, 3)$. Equation (10.1.5) gives

$$E(2, 3) = \sum_{m=1}^{3} m \sum_{|w|=m} p(w) \sum_{\substack{S \text{ such that } \#S=2 \text{ and all but} \\ \text{the last symbol of } w \text{ is in } S}} p(S)$$

$$= p(0)p(\{1, 2\}) + p(1)p(\{0, 2\}) + p(2)p(\{0, 1\})$$
$$+ 2[p(01)p(\{0, 2\}) + p(10)p(\{1, 2\}) + p(02)p(\{0, 1\})$$
$$+ p(20)p(\{1, 2\}) + p(12)p(\{0, 1\}) + p(21)p(\{0, 2\})]$$
$$+ 3[p(012)p(\{0, 1\}) + p(021)p(\{0, 2\}) + p(102)p(\{0, 1\})$$
$$+ p(120)p(\{1, 2\}) + p(201)p(\{0, 2\}) + p(210)p(\{1, 2\})]$$
$$= 2.008$$

$\square$

Another figure of merit used to evaluate hashing systems is $R(k, n)$, *the expected number of probes required to retrieve an item from a table in which k out of n locations are filled.* However, this figure of merit can be readily computed from $E(k, n)$. We can assume that each of the k items in the table is equally likely to be retrieved. Thus, the expected retrieval time is equal to the average number of probes that were required to originally insert these k items into the table. That is,

$$R(k, n) = \frac{1}{k} \sum_{i=0}^{k-1} E(i, n)$$

For this reason, we shall consider $E(k, n)$ as the exclusive figure of merit.

A natural conjecture is that performance is best when a hashing system is random, on the grounds that any nonrandomness can only make certain locations more likely to be filled than others and that these are exactly the locations more likely to be examined when we attempt to insert new items. While this will be seen not to be precisely true, the exact optimum is not known. Random hashing is conjectured to be optimum in the sense of minimum retrieval time, and other common hashing systems do not compare favorably with a random hashing system. We shall therefore calculate $E(k, n)$ for a random hashing system.

LEMMA 10.1

If a hashing system is random, then

(1) For all sequences w of locations such that $1 \leq |w| \leq n$,

$$p(w) = (n - |w|)!/n!$$

(2) For all subsets S of $\{0, 1, \ldots, n - 1\}$,

$$p(S) = \frac{1}{\binom{n}{\#S}}$$

Proof.

(1) Using (10.1.2), this is an elementary induction on $(n - |w|)$, starting at $|w| = n$ and ending at $|w| = 1$.

(2) A simple argument of symmetry assures us that $p(S)$ is the same for all S of size k. Since the number of sets of size k is $\binom{n}{k}$, part (2) is immediate. $\square$

LEMMA 10.2

If $n \geq k$, then $\sum_{j=0}^{k} \binom{n-j}{k-j} = \binom{n+1}{k}$.

Proof. Exercise. $\square$

THEOREM 10.1

If a hashing system is random, then $E(k, n) = (n + 1)/(n + 1 - k)$.

Proof. Let us suppose that we have a hash table with k out of n locations filled. We wish to insert the $k + 1$st item α. It follows from Lemma 10.1(2) that every set of k locations has the same probability of being filled. Thus $E(k, n)$ is independent of which k locations are actually filled. We can therefore assume without loss of generality that locations $0, 1, 2, \ldots, k - 1$ are filled.

To determine the expected number of probes required to insert α, we examine the sequence of addresses obtained by applying h to α. Let this sequence be $h_0(\alpha), h_1(\alpha), \ldots, h_{n-1}(\alpha)$. By definition, all such sequences of n locations are equally probable.

Let q_j be the probability that the first $j - 1$ locations in this sequence are in $\{0, 1, \ldots, k - 1\}$ but that the jth is not. Clearly, $E(k, n)$, the expected number of probes to insert α, is $\sum_{j=1}^{k+1} jq_j$. We observe that

$$(10.1.6) \qquad \sum_{j=1}^{k+1} jq_j = \sum_{m=1}^{k+1} \sum_{j=1}^{m} q_m = \sum_{j=1}^{k+1} \sum_{m=j}^{k+1} q_m$$

But $\sum_{m=j}^{k+1} q_m$ is just the probability that the first $j - 1$ locations in the sequence $h_0(\alpha), h_1(\alpha), \ldots, h_{n-1}(\alpha)$ are between 0 and $k - 1$, i.e., that at least j probes are required to insert the $k + 1$st item. By Lemma 10.1(1), this quantity is

$$\left(\frac{k}{n}\right)\left(\frac{k - 1}{n - 1}\right) \cdots \left(\frac{k - j + 2}{n - j + 2}\right) = \frac{k!}{(k - j + 1)!} \frac{(n - j + 1)!}{n!} = \frac{\binom{n - j + 1}{k - j + 1}}{\binom{n}{k}}$$

Then,

$$E(k, n) = \sum_{j=1}^{k+1} \frac{\binom{n - j + 1}{k - j + 1}}{\binom{n}{k}} = \frac{\binom{n + 1}{k}}{\binom{n}{k}} = \frac{n + 1}{n - k + 1}$$

using Lemma 10.2.   □

We observe from Theorem 10.1 that for large n and k, the expected time to insert an item depends only on the ratio of k and n and is approximately $1/(1 - \rho)$, where $\rho = k/n$. This function is plotted in Fig. 10.6.

The ratio k/n is termed the *load factor*. When the load factor is small, the insertion time increases with k, the number of filled locations, at a slower rate than $\log k$, and hashing is thus superior to a binary search. Of course, if k approaches n, that is, as the table gets filled, insertion becomes very expensive, and at $k = n$, further insertion is impossible unless some mechanism is provided to handle overflows. One method of dealing with overflows is suggested in Exercises 10.1.11 and 10.1.12.

The expected number of trials to insert an item is not the only criterion of goodness of a hashing scheme. One also desires that the computation of the hashing functions be simple. The hashing schemes we have considered compute the alternate functions $h_1(\alpha), \ldots, h_{n-1}(\alpha)$ not from α itself but from $h_0(\alpha)$, and this is characteristic of most hashing schemes. This arrangement is efficient because $h_0(\alpha)$ is an integer of known length, while α may be arbitrarily long. We shall call such a method *hashing on locations*. A more restricted case, and one that is even easier to implement, is *linear hashing*, where $h_i(\alpha)$ is given by $(h_0(\alpha) + i) \bmod n$. That is, successive locations in the table are tried until an empty one is found; if the bottom of the table is reached, we proceed to the top. Example 10.4 (p. 796) is an example of linear hashing.

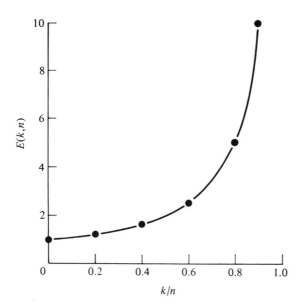

Fig. 10.6   Expected insertion time as a function of load factor for random hashing.

We shall give an example to show that linear hashing can be inferior to random hashing in the expected number of trials for insertion. We shall then discuss hashing on locations and show that at least in one case it, too, is inferior to random hashing.

Example 10.7

Let us consider a linear hashing system with $n = 4$ and probability $1/4$ for each of the four permutations [0123], [1230], [2301], and [3012]. The reader can show that performance is made worse only if these probabilities are made unequal. For random hashing, Theorem 10.1 gives $E(2, 4) = 5/3$.

By (10.1.4), we can calculate the probabilities that a set of two locations is filled. These probabilities are

$$p(\{0, 1\}) = p(\{1, 2\}) = p(\{2, 3\}) = p(\{3, 0\}) = 3/16$$

and

$$p(\{0, 2\}) = p(\{1, 3\}) = 1/8$$

Then, by (10.1.5), we compute $E(2, 4)$ for linear hashing to be $27/16$, which is greater than $5/3$, the cost for random hashing.   ☐

We shall next compare hashing on locations with random hashing in the special case that the third item is entered into the table. We note that when we hash on locations there is, for each location i, exactly one permutation, Π_i, that begins with i and has nonzero probability. We can denote the probability of Π_i by p_i. We shall denote the second entry in Π_i, the first alternate of i, by a_i. If $p_i = 1/n$ for each i, we call the system *random hashing on locations*.

THEOREM 10.2

$E(2, n)$ is smaller for random hashing than for random hashing on locations for all $n > 3$.

Proof. We know by Theorem 10.1 that $E(2, n)$ for random hashing is $(n + 1)/(n - 1)$. We shall derive a lower bound on $E(2, n)$ for hashing on locations. Let us suppose that the first three items to be entered into the table have permutations Π_i, Π_j, and Π_k, respectively. We shall consider two cases, depending on whether $i = j$ or not.

Case 1: $i \neq j$. This occurs with probability $(n - 1)/n$. The expected number of trials to insert the third item is seen to be

$$1 + (2/n) + (2/n)[1/(n - 1)] = (n + 1)/(n - 1).$$

Case 2: $i = j$. This occurs with probability $1/n$. Then with probability $(n - 2)/n$, the third item is inserted in one try, that is, $k \neq i$ and $k \neq a_i$, the second location filled. With probability $1/n$, $k = a_i$, and at least two tries are made. Also with probability $1/n$, $k = i$, and three tries must be made. (This follows because we know that the second try is for a_i, which was filled by j.) The expected number of tries in this case is thus at least $[(n - 2)/n] + (2/n) + (3/n) = (n + 3)/n$.

Weighting the two cases according to their likelihoods, we get, for random hashing on location,

$$E(2, n) \geq \left(\frac{n + 1}{n - 1}\right)\left(\frac{n - 1}{n}\right) + \left(\frac{n + 3}{n}\right)\left(\frac{1}{n}\right) = \frac{n^2 + 2n + 3}{n^2}$$

The latter expression exceeds $(n + 1)/(n - 1)$ for $n > 3$. $\square$

The point of the previous example and theorem is that many simple hashing schemes do not meet the performance of random hashing. Intuitively, the cause is that when nonrandom schemes are used, there is a tendency for the same location to be tried over and over again. Even if the load factor is small, with high probability there will still be some locations that have been tried many times. If a scheme such as hashing on locations is used, each time a primary location $h_0(\alpha)$ is filled, all the alternates of $h_0(\alpha)$ which were tried before will be tried again, resulting in poor performance.

The foregoing does not imply that one should not use a scheme such as hashing on locations if there is a compensating saving in time per insertion try.

In fact, it is at least possible that random hashing is not the best we can do. The following example shows that $E(k, n)$ does not always attain a minimum when random hashing is used. We conjecture, however, that random hashing does minimize $R(k, n)$, the expected retrieval time.

Example 10.8

Let the permutations [0123] and [1032] have probability .2 and let [2013], [2103], [3012], and [3102] have probability .15, all others having zero probability. We can calculate $E(2, 4)$ directly by (10.1.5), obtaining the value 1.665. This value is smaller than the figure 5/3 for random hashing. $\square$

EXERCISES

10.1.1. Use Algorithm 10.1 to insert the following sequence of items into a binary search tree: T, D, H, F, A, P, O, Q, W, TO, TH. Assume that the items have alphabetic order.

10.1.2. Design an algorithm which will take a binary search tree as input and list all elements stored in the tree in order. Apply your algorithm to the tree constructed in Exercise 10.1.1.

*10.1.3. Show that the expected time to insert (or retrieve) one item in a binary search tree is $0(\log n)$, where n is the number of nodes in the tree. What is the maximum amount of time required to insert any one item?

*10.1.4. What information about FORTRAN variables and constants is needed in the symbol table for code generation?

10.1.5. Describe a symbol table storage mechanism for a block-structured language such as ALGOL in which the scope of a variable X is limited to a given block and all blocks contained in that block in which X is not redeclared.

10.1.6. Choose a table size and a primary hashing function h_0. Compute $h_0(\alpha)$, where α is drawn from the set of (a) FORTRAN keywords, (b) ALGOL keywords, and (c) PL/I keywords. What is the maximum number of items with the same primary hash address? You may wish to do this calculation by computer. Sammet [1969] will provide the needed sets of keywords.

*10.1.7. Show that $R(k, n)$ for random hashing approximates $(-1/\rho) \log (1-\rho)$, where $\rho = k/n$. Plot this function.
Hint: Approximate $(n/k) \sum_{i=0}^{k-1} (n + 1)/(n - i + 1)$ by an integral.

*10.1.8. Consider the following pseudorandom number generator. This generator creates a sequence $r_1, r_2, \ldots, r_{n-1}$ of numbers which can be used to compute $h_i(\alpha) = [h_0(\alpha) + r_i] \bmod n$ for $1 \leq i \leq n - 1$. Each time that a sequence of numbers is to be generated, the integer R is initially set to 1. We assume that $n = 2^p$. Each time another number is required, the following steps are executed:

(1) $R = 5 * R$.
(2) $R = R \bmod 4n$.
(3) Return $r = [R/4]$.

Show that for each i, the differences $r_{i+k} - r_i$ are all distinct for $k \geq 1$ and $i + k \leq n - 1$.

10.1.9. Show that if $h_i = [h_0 + ai^2 + bi] \bmod n$ for $1 \leq i \leq n - 1$, then at most half the locations in the sequence $h_0, h_1, h_2, \ldots, h_{n-1}$ are distinct. Under what conditions will exactly half the locations in this sequence be distinct?

10.1.10. How many distinct locations are there in the sequence $h_0, h_1, \ldots, h_{p-1}$ if for $1 \leq i < p/2$

$$h_{2i-1} = [h_0 + i^2] \bmod p$$

$$h_{2i} = h_0 - \left[\left(\frac{p-1}{2}\right) + i\right]^2 \bmod p$$

and p is a prime number?

DEFINITION

Another technique for resolving collisions that is more efficient in terms of insertion and retrieval time is *chaining*. In this method one field is set aside in each entry of the hash table to hold a pointer to additional entries with the same primary hash address. All entries with the same primary address are chained on a linked list starting at that primary location.

There are several methods of implementing chaining. One method, called *direct chaining*, uses the hash table itself to store all items. To insert an item α, we consult location $h_0(\alpha)$.

(1) If that location is empty, α is installed there. If $h_0(\alpha)$ is filled and is the head of a chain, we find an empty entry in the hash table by any convenient mechanism and place this entry on the chain headed by $h_0(\alpha)$.

(2) If $h_0(\alpha)$ is filled but not by the head of a chain, we move the current entry β in $h_0(\alpha)$ to an empty location in the hash table and insert α in $h_0(\alpha)$. [We must recompute $h(\beta)$ to keep β in the proper chain.]

This movement of entries is the primary disadvantage of direct chaining. However, the method is fast. Another advantage of the technique is that when the table becomes full, additional items can be placed in an overflow table with the same insertion and retrieval strategy.

10.1.11. Show that if alternate locations are chosen randomly, then $R(k, n)$, the expected retrieval time for direct chaining, is $1 + p/2$, where $p = k/n$. Compare this function with $R(k, n)$ in Exercise 10.1.7.

Another chaining technique which does not require items to be moved uses an index table in front of the hash table. The primary hashing function h_0 computes addresses in the index table. The entries in the index table are pointers to the hash table, whose entries are filled in sequence.

To insert an item α in this new scheme, we compute $h_0(\alpha)$, which is an address in the index table. If $h_0(\alpha)$ is empty, we seize the next available location in the hash table and insert α into that location. We then place a pointer to this location in $h_0(\alpha)$.

If $h_0(\alpha)$ already contains a pointer to a location in the hash table, we go to that location. We then search down the chain headed by that location. Once we reach the end of the chain, we take the next available location in the hash table, insert α into that location, and then attach this location to the end of the chain.

If we fill the hash table in order beginning from the top, we can find the next available location very quickly. In this scheme no items ever need to be moved because each entry in the index table always points to the head of a chain.

Moreover, overflows can be simply accommodated in this scheme by adding additional space to the end of the hash table.

*10.1.12. What is the expected retrieval time for a chaining scheme with an index table? Assume that the primary locations are uniformly distributed.

10.1.13. Consider a random hashing system with n locations as in Section 10.1.5. Show that if S is a set of k locations and $i \notin S$, then $\sum_w p(wi) = 1/(n - k)$, where the sum is taken over all w such that w is a string of k or fewer distinct locations in S.

*10.1.14. Prove the following identities:

(a) $\displaystyle\sum_{i=0}^{k} \binom{n + i}{i} = \binom{n + k + 1}{k}.$

(b) $\displaystyle\sum_{i=0}^{k} \binom{n - i}{k - i} = \binom{n + 1}{k}.$

(c) $\displaystyle\sum_{i=0}^{k} i\binom{n + i}{i} = k\binom{n + k + 1}{k} - \binom{n + k + 1}{k - 1}.$

*10.1.15. Suppose that items are strings of from one to six capital Roman letters. Let $\text{CODE}(\alpha)$ be the function defined in Example 10.4. Suppose that item α has probability $(1/6)26^{-|\alpha|}$. Compute the probabilities of the permutations on $\{0, 1, \ldots, n - 1\}$ if

(a) $h_i(\alpha) = (\text{CODE}(\alpha) + i) \bmod n,\ 0 \leq i \leq n - 1.$

(b) $h_i(\alpha) = (i(h_0(\alpha) + 1))\bmod n, 1 \le i \le n-1$ where

$$h_0(\alpha) = \mathrm{CODE}(\alpha) \bmod n$$

10.1.16. Show that for linear hashing with the primary location $h_0(\alpha)$ randomly distributed, the limit of $E(k, n)$ as k and n approach ∞ with $k/n = p$ is given by $1 + [p(1 - p/2)/(1 - p)^2]$. How does this compare with the corresponding function of p for random hashing?

DEFINITION

A hashing system is said to be *k-uniform* if for each set $S \subseteq \{0, 1, 2, \ldots, n - 1\}$ such that $\#S = k$ the probability that a sequence of k distinct locations consists of exactly the locations of S is $1/\binom{n}{k}$. (Most important, the probability is independent of S.)

*10.1.17. Show that if a hashing system is k-uniform, then

$$E(k, n) = (n + 1)/(n + 1 - k),$$

as for random hashing.

*10.1.18. Show that for each hashing system such that there exists k for which $E(k, n) < (n + 1)/(n + 1 - k)$, there exists $k' < k$ such that

$$E(k', n) > (n + 1)/(n + 1 - k')$$

Thus, if a given hashing system is better than random for some k, there is a smaller k' for which performance is worse than random. *Hint:* Show that if a hashing system is $(k - 1)$-uniform but not k-uniform, then $E(k, n) > (n + 1)/(n - k + 1)$.

*10.1.19. Give an example of a hashing system which is k-uniform for all k but is not random.

*10.1.20. Generalize Example 10.7 to the case of unequal probabilities for the cyclic permutations.

*10.1.21. Strengthen Theorem 10.2 to include systems which hash on locations but do not have equal p_i's.

Open Problems

10.1.22. Is random hashing optimal in the sense of expected retrieval time? That is, is it true that $R(k, n)$ is always bounded below by

$$(1/k) \sum_{i=0}^{k-1} (n + 1)/(n + 1 - i)?$$

We conjecture that random hashing is optimal.

10.1.23. Find the greatest lower bound on $E(k, n)$ for systems which hash on locations. Any lower bound that exceeds $(n + 1)/(n + 1 - k)$ would be of interest.

10.1.24. Find the greatest lower bound on $E(k, n)$ for arbitrary hashing systems. We saw in Example 10.8 that $(n + 1)/(n + 1 - k)$ is not such a bound.

Research Problem

10.1.25. In certain uses of a hash table, the items entered are known in advance. Examples are tables of library routines or tables of assembly language operation codes. If we know what the residents of the hash table are, we have the opportunity to select our hashing system to minimize the expected lookup time. Can you provide an algorithm which takes the list of items to be stored and yields a hashing system which is efficient to implement, yet has a low lookup time for this particular loading of the hash table?

Programming Exercises

10.1.26. Implement a hashing system that does hashing on locations. Test the behavior of the system on FORTRAN keywords and common function names.

10.1.27. Implement a hashing system that uses chaining to resolve collisions. Compare the behavior of this system with that in Exercise 10.1.26.

BIBLIOGRAPHIC NOTES

Hash tables are also known as scatter storage tables, key transformation tables, randomized tables, and computed entry tables. Hash tables have been used by programmers since the early 1950's. The earliest paper on hash addressing is by Peterson [1957]. Morris [1968] provides a good survey of hashing techniques. The answer to Exercise 10.1.7 can be found there.

Methods of computing the alternate functions to reduce the expected number of collisions are discussed by Maurer [1968], Radke [1970], and Bell [1970]. An answer to Exercise 10.1.10 can be found in Radke [1970]. Ullman [1972] discusses k-uniform hashing systems.

Knuth [1973] is a good reference on binary search trees and hash tables.

10.2. PROPERTY GRAMMARS

An interesting and highly structured method of assigning properties to the identifiers of a programming language is through the formalism of "property grammars." These are context-free grammars with an additional mechanism to record information about identifiers and to handle some of the non-context-free aspects of the syntax of programming languages (such as requiring identifiers to be declared before their use). In this section we provide an introduction to the theory of property grammars and show how a property grammar can be implemented to model a syntactic analyzer that combines parsing with certain aspects of semantic analysis.

10.2.1. Motivation

Let us try first to understand why it is not always sufficient to establish the properties of each identifier as it is declared and to place these properties in some location in a symbol table reserved for that identifier. If we consider a block-structured language such as ALGOL or PL/I, we realize that the properties of an identifier may change many times, as it may be defined in an outer block and redefined in an inner block. When the inner block terminates, the properties return to what they were in the outer block.

For example, consider the diagram in Fig. 10.7 indicating the block structure of a program. The letters indicate regions in the program. This block structure can be presented by the tree in Fig. 10.8.

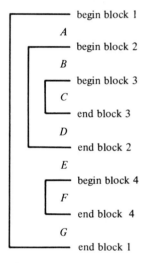

begin block 1

A

begin block 2

B

begin block 3

C

end block 3

D

end block 2

E

begin block 4

F

end block 4

G

end block 1   **Fig. 10.7**   Block structure of a program.

Suppose that an identifier *I* is defined in block 1 of this program and is recorded in a symbol table as soon as it is encountered. Suppose that *I* is then redefined in block 2. In regions *B*, *C*, and *D* of this program, *I* has the new definition. Thus, on encountering the definition of *I* in block 2, we must enter the new definition of *I* in the symbol table. However, we cannot merely replace the definition that *I* had in block 1 by the new definition in block 2, because once region *E* is encountered we must revert to the original definition of *I*.

One way to handle this problem is to associate two numbers—a *level* number and an *index*—with each definition of an identifier. The level number is the nesting depth, and each block with the same level number is given a distinct index. For example, identifiers in areas *B* and *D* of block 2 would

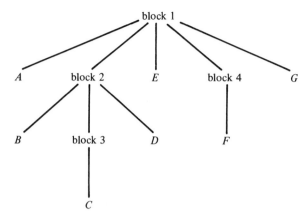

Fig. 10.8   Tree representation of block structure.

have level number 2 and index 1. Identifiers in area F of block 4 would have level number 2 and index 2.

If an identifier in the block with level i and index j is referenced, we look in the symbol table for a definition of that identifier with the same level number and index. However, if that identifier is nowhere defined in the block with level number i, we would then look for a definition of that identifier in the block of level number $i - 1$ which contained the block of level number i and index j, and so forth. If we encounter a definition at the desired level but with too small an index, we may delete the definition, as it will never again apply. Thus, a pushdown list is useful for the storing of definitions of each identifier as encountered. The search described is also facilitated if the index of the currently active block at each level is available.

For example, if an identifier K is encountered in region C and no definition of K appeared in region C, we would accept a definition of K appearing in region B (or D, if declarations after use are permitted). However, if no definition of K appeared in regions B or D, we would then accept a definition of K in regions A, E, or G. But we would not look in region F for a definition of K.

The level–index method of recording definitions can be used for languages with the conventional nesting of definitions, e.g., ALGOL and PL/I. However, in this section we shall discuss a more general formalism, called property grammars, which permits arbitrary conventions regarding scope of definition. Property grammars have an inherent generality and elegance which stem from the uniformity of the treatment of identifiers and their properties. Moreover, they can be implemented in an amount of time which is essentially linear in the length of the compiler input. While the constant of proportionality may be high, we present the concept in the hope that future research may make it a practical compiler technique.

10.2.2. Definition of Property Grammar

Informally, a property grammar consists of an underlying CFG to whose nonterminal and terminal symbols we have attached "property tables." We can picture a property table as an abstraction of a symbol table. When we parse bottom-up according to the underlying grammar, the property tables attached to the nonterminals together represent the information available in the symbol table at that point of the parse.

A property table T is a mapping from an index set I to a property set V. Here we shall use the set of nonnegative integers as the index set. We can interpret each integer in the index set as a pointer into a symbol table. Thus, if the entry pointed to in the symbol table represents an identifier, we can treat the integer as the name of that identifier.

The set V is a set of "properties" or "values" and we shall use a finite set of integers for V. One integer (usually 0) is distinguished as the "neutral" property. Other integers can be associated with various properties which are of interest. For example, the integer 1 might be associated with the property "this identifier has been referenced," 2 with "declared real," and so forth.

In tables associated with terminals all but one index is mapped to the neutral property. The remaining index can be mapped to any property (including the neutral one). However, if the terminal is the token ⟨identifier⟩, the index which represents the name of the particular token (that is, the data component of the token) would be mapped onto a property such as "this is the identifier mentioned here."

For example, if we encounter the declaration **real** B in a program, this string might be parsed as

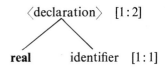

where the data component of the token ⟨identifier⟩ refers to the string B. With the terminal ⟨identifier⟩ is associated the table [1: 1], which associates the property 1 (perhaps "mentioned") with the index 1 (which now corresponds to B) and the neutral property with all other indices. The terminal token **real** is associated with a table which maps all indices to the neutral property. Such a table will normally not be explicitly present.

With the nonterminal ⟨declaration⟩ in the parse tree we associate a table which would be constructed by merging the tables of its direct descendants according to some rule. Here, the table that is constructed is [1: 2], which associates property 2 with index 1 and the neutral property with all other indices. This table can then be interpreted as meaning that the identifier associated with index 1 (namely B) has the property "declared real." In general if we have the structure

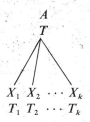

$$A$$
$$T$$

$$X_1 \ X_2 \ \cdots \ X_k$$
$$T_1 \ T_2 \ \cdots \ T_k$$

in a parse tree, then the property of index i in table T is a function only of the property of index i in tables $T_1, T_2, \ldots, T_k$. That is, each index is treated independently of all others.

We shall now define a property grammar precisely.

DEFINITION

A *property grammar* is an 8-tuple $G = (N, \Sigma, P, S, V, v_0, F, \mu)$, where

(1) (N, Σ, P, S) is a CFG, called the *underlying* CFG;
(2) V is a finite set of *properties*;
(3) v_0 in V is the *neutral property*;
(4) $F \subseteq V$ is the set of *acceptable properties*; v_0 is always in F; and
(5) μ is a mapping from $P \times V^*$ to V, such that
   (a) If $\mu(p, s)$ is defined, then production p has a right-hand side exactly as long as s, where s is a string of properties;
   (b) $\mu(p, v_0 v_0 \cdots v_0)$ is v_0 if the string of v_0's is as long as the right-hand side of production p, and is undefined otherwise.

The function μ tells how to assign properties in the tables associated with interior nodes of parse trees. Depending on the production used at that node, the property associated with each integer is computed independently of the property of any other integer. Condition (5b) establishes that the table of some interior node can have a nonneutral property for some integer only if one of its direct descendants has a nonneutral property for that integer.

A *sentential form* of G is a string $X_1 T_1 X_2 T_2 \cdots X_n T_n$, where the X's are symbols in $N \cup \Sigma$ and the T's are property tables. Each table is assumed to be attached to the symbol immediately to its left and represents a mapping from indices to V such that all but a finite number of indices are mapped to v_0.

We define the relation $\Rightarrow$, or $\underset{G}{\Rightarrow}$ if G is understood, on sentential forms as follows. Let $\alpha A T \beta$ be a sentential form of G and $A \rightarrow X_1 \cdots X_k$ be production p in P. Then $\alpha A T \beta \Rightarrow \alpha X_1 T_1 \cdots X_k T_k \beta$ if for all indices i,

$$\mu(p, T_1(i)T_2(i) \cdots T_k(i)) = T(i).$$

Let $\overset{*}{\underset{G}{\Rightarrow}}$, or $\overset{*}{\Rightarrow}$ if G is understood, be the reflexive, transitive closure of $\underset{G}{\Rightarrow}$. The language defined by G, denoted $L(G)$, is the set of all $a_1T_1a_2T_2 \cdots a_nT_n$ such that for some table T

(1) $ST \overset{*}{\Rightarrow} a_1T_1a_2T_2 \cdots a_nT_n$;
(2) Each a_j is in Σ;
(3) For all indices i, $T(i)$ is in F; and
(4) For each j, T_j maps all indices, or all but one index, to v_0.

We should observe that although the definition of a derivation is top-down, the definition of a property grammar lends itself well to bottom-up parsing. If we can determine the tables associated with the terminals, we can construct the tables associated with each node of the parse tree deterministically, since μ is a function of the tables associated with the direct descendants of a node.

It should be clear that if G is a property grammar, then the set

$$\{a_1a_2 \cdots a_n \,|\, a_1T_1a_2T_2 \cdots a_nT_n \text{ is in } L(G)$$
$$\text{for some sequence of tables } T_1, T_2, \ldots, T_n\}$$

is a context-free language, because any string generated by the underlying CFG can be given all-neutral tables and generated in the property grammar.

CONVENTION

We continue to use the convention regarding context-free grammars, $a, b, c, \ldots$ are in Σ and so forth, except v now represents a property and s a string of properties. If T maps all integers to the neutral property, we write X instead of XT.

Example 10.9

We shall give a rather lengthy example using property grammars to handle declarations in a block-structured language. We shall also show how, if the underlying CFG is deterministically parsable in a bottom-up way, the tables can be deterministically constructed as the parse proceeds.[†]

Let $G = (N, \Sigma, P, S, V, 0, \{0\}, \mu)$ be a property grammar with

(i) N = {⟨block⟩, ⟨statement⟩, ⟨declaration list⟩, ⟨statement list⟩, ⟨variable list⟩}. The nonterminal ⟨variable list⟩ generates a list of variables used in a statement. We are going to represent a statement by the actual variables used in the statement rather than giving its entire structure. This

---

[†]Our example grammar happens to be ambiguous but will illustrate the points to be made.

abstraction brings out the salient features of property grammars without involving us in too much detail.

(ii) $\Sigma = \{$**begin, end, declare, label, goto,** $a\}$. The terminal **declare** stands for the declaration of one identifier. We do not show the identifier declared, as this information will be in the property table attached to **declare**. Likewise, **label** stands for the use of an identifier as a statement label. The identifier itself is not explicitly shown. The terminal **goto** stands for **goto**$\langle$label$\rangle$, but again we do not show the label explicitly, since it will be in the property table attached to **goto**. The terminal a represents a variable.

(iii) P consists of the following productions.

(1) $\langle$block$\rangle \longrightarrow$ **begin** $\langle$declaration list$\rangle \langle$statement list$\rangle$ **end**

(2) $\langle$statement list$\rangle \longrightarrow \langle$statement list$\rangle \langle$statement$\rangle$

(3) $\langle$statement list$\rangle \longrightarrow \langle$statement$\rangle$

(4) $\langle$statement$\rangle \longrightarrow \langle$block$\rangle$

(5) $\langle$statement$\rangle \longrightarrow$ **label** $\langle$variable list$\rangle$

(6) $\langle$statement$\rangle \longrightarrow \langle$variable list$\rangle$

(7) $\langle$statement$\rangle \longrightarrow$ **goto**

(8) $\langle$variable list$\rangle \longrightarrow \langle$variable list$\rangle$ a

(9) $\langle$variable list$\rangle \longrightarrow e$

(10) $\langle$declaration list$\rangle \longrightarrow$ **declare** $\langle$declaration list$\rangle$

(11) $\langle$declaration list$\rangle \longrightarrow e$

Informally, production (1) says that a block is a declaration list and a list of statements surrounded by **begin** and **end**. Production (4) says that a statement can be a block; productions (5) and (6) say that a statement is a list of the variables used therein, possibly prefixed with a label. Production (7) says that a statement can be a goto statement. Productions (8) and (9) say that a variable list is a string of 0 or more a's, and productions (10) and (11) say that a declaration list is a string of 0 or more **declare**'s.

(iv) $V = \{0, 1, 2, 3, 4\}$ is a set of properties with the following meanings:

0   Identifier does not appear in the string derived from this node (neutral property).

1   Identifier is declared to be a variable.

2   Identifier is a label of a statement.

3   Identifier is used as a variable but is not (insofar as the descendants of the node in question are concerned) yet declared.

4   Identifier is used as a goto target but has not yet appeared as a label.

(v) We define the function μ on properties with the following ideas in mind:

(a) If an invalid use of a variable or label is found, there will be no way to construct further tables, and so the process of table computation will "jam." (We could also have defined an "error" property.)

(b) An identifier used in a **goto** must be the label of some statement of the block in which it is used.†

(c) An identifier used as a variable must be declared within its block or a block in which its block is nested.

We shall give $\mu(p, w)$ for each production in turn, with comments as to the motivation.

(1) $\langle$block$\rangle \longrightarrow$ **begin** $\langle$declaration list$\rangle \langle$statement list$\rangle$ **end**

s	$\mu(1, s)$
0 0 0 0	0
0 1 0 0	0
0 1 3 0	0
0 0 3 0	3
0 0 2 0	0

The only possible property for all integers associated with **begin** and **end** is 0 and hence the two columns of 0's. In the declaration list each identifier will have property 0 ($=$ not declared) or 1 ($=$ declared). If an identifier is declared, then within the body of the block, i.e., the statement list, it can be used only as a variable (3) or not used (0). In either case, the identifier is not declared insofar as the program outside the block is concerned, and so we give the identifier the 0 property. Thus, the second and third lines appear as they do.

If an identifier is not declared in this block, it may still be used, either as a label or variable. If used as a variable (property 3), this fact must be transmitted outside the block, so we can check that it is declared at some appropriate place, as in line 4. If an identifier is defined as a label within the block, this fact is not transmitted outside the block (line 5), because a label within the block may not be transferred to from outside the block.

Since μ is not defined for other values of s, the property grammar catches uses of labels not found within the block as well as uses of declared variables as labels within the block. A label used as a variable will be caught at another point.

---

†This differs from the convention of ALGOL, e.g., in that ALGOL allows transfers to a block which surrounds the current one. We use this convention to make the handling of labels differ from that of identifiers.

(2) $\langle$statement list$\rangle \longrightarrow \langle$statement list$\rangle\langle$statement$\rangle$

s		$\mu(2, s)$
0	0	0
3	3	3
0	3	3
3	0	3
4	4	4
0	4	4
4	0	4
4	2	2
2	4	2
0	2	2
2	0	2

Lines 2–4 say that an identifier used as a variable in $\langle$statement list$\rangle$ or $\langle$statement$\rangle$ on the right-hand side of the production is used as a variable insofar as the $\langle$statement list$\rangle$ on the left is concerned. Lines 5–7 say the same thing about labels. Lines 8–11 say that a label defined in either $\langle$statement list$\rangle$ or $\langle$statement$\rangle$ on the right is defined for $\langle$statement list$\rangle$ on the left, whether or not that label has been used.

At this point, we catch uses of an identifier as both a variable and label within one block.

(3) $\langle$statement list$\rangle \longrightarrow \langle$statement$\rangle$

s	$\mu(3, s)$
0	0
2	2
3	3
4	4

Properties are transmitted naturally. Property 1 is impossible for a statement.

(4) $\langle$statement$\rangle \longrightarrow \langle$block$\rangle$

s	$\mu(4, s)$
0	0
3	3

The philosophy for production (3) also applies for production (4).

(5) $\langle$statement$\rangle \longrightarrow$ **label** $\langle$variable list$\rangle$

s	$\mu(5, s)$
0 0	0
0 3	3
2 0	2

The use of an identifier as a label in **label** or variable in $\langle$variable list$\rangle$ is transmitted to the $\langle$statement$\rangle$ on the right.

(6) $\langle$statement$\rangle \longrightarrow \langle$variable list$\rangle$

s	$\mu(6, s)$
0	0
3	3

Here, the use of a variable in $\langle$variable list$\rangle$ is transmitted to $\langle$statement$\rangle$.

(7) $\langle$statement$\rangle \longrightarrow$ **goto**

s	$\mu(7, s)$
0	0
4	4

The use of a label in **goto** is transmitted to $\langle$statement$\rangle$.

(8) $\langle$variable list$\rangle \longrightarrow \langle$variable list$\rangle a$

s	$\mu(8, s)$
0 0	0
3 0	3
0 3	3
3 3	3

Any use of a variable is transmitted to $\langle$variable list$\rangle$.

(9) $\langle$variable list$\rangle \longrightarrow e$

s	$\mu(9, s)$
e	0

The one value for which μ is defined is $s = e$. The property must be 0 by definition of the neutral property.

(10)   ⟨declaration list⟩ ⟶ **declare** ⟨declaration list⟩

s	$\mu(10, s)$
0 0	0
0 1	1
1 0	1
1 1	1

Declared identifiers are transmitted to ⟨declaration list⟩.

(11)   ⟨declaration list⟩ ⟶ e

s	$\mu(11, s)$
e	0

The situation with regard to production (9) also applies here.

We shall now give an example of how tables are constructed bottom-up on a parse tree. We shall use the notation $[i_1 : v_1, i_2 : v_2, \ldots, i_n : v_n]$ for the table which assigns to index i_j the property v_j for $1 \leq j \leq n$ and assigns the neutral property to all other indices.

Let us consider the input string

> **begin**
>> **declare** $[1 : 1]$
>> **declare** $[2 : 1]$
>>> **begin**
>>>> **label** $[1 : 2]\ a\ [2 : 3]$
>>>> **goto** $[1 : 4]$
>>> **end**
>> $a\ [1 : 3]$
> **end**

That is, in the outer block, identifiers 1 and 2 are declared as variables by symbols **declare**$[1 : 1]$ and **declare**$[2 : 1]$. Then, in the inner block, identifier 1 is declared and used as a label (which is legitimate) by symbols **label**$[1 : 2]$ and **goto**$[1 : 4]$, respectively, and identifier 2 is used as a variable by symbol $a[2 : 3]$. Returning to the outer block, 1 is used as a variable by symbol $a[1 : 3]$.

A parse tree with tables associated with each node is given in Fig. 10.9.

□

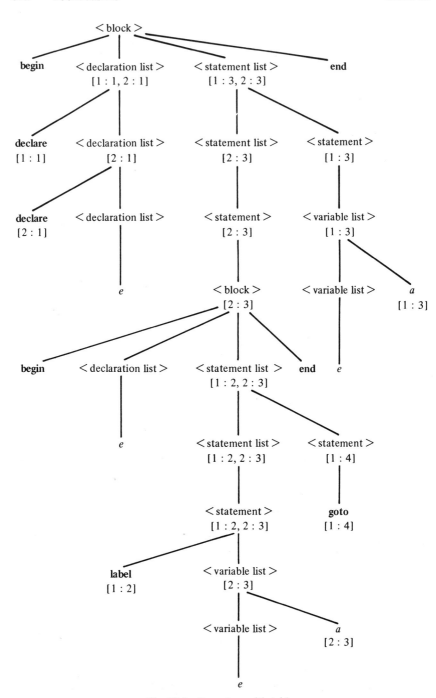

Fig. 10.9   Parse tree with tables.

The notion of a property grammar can be generalized. For example,

(1) The mapping μ can be made nondeterministic; that is, let $\mu(p, w)$ be a subset of V.

(2) The existence of a neutral property need not be assumed.

(3) Constraints may be placed on the class of tables which may be associated with symbols, e.g., the all-neutral table may not appear.

Certain theorems about property grammars in this more general formulation are reserved for the Exercises.

10.2.3. Implementation of Property Grammars

We shall discuss the implementation of a property grammar when the underlying CFG can be parsed bottom-up deterministically by a shift–reduce algorithm. When parsing top-down, or using any of the other parsing algorithms discussed in this book, one encounters the same timing problems in the construction of tables as one has timing the construction of translation strings in syntax-directed translation. Since the solutions are essentially those presented in Chapter 9, we shall discuss only the bottom-up case.

In our model of a compiler the input to the lexical analyzer does not have tables associated with its terminals. Let us assume that the lexical analyzer will signal whether a token involved is an identifier or not. Thus, each token, when it becomes input to the parser, will have one of two tables, an all-neutral table or a table in which one index has the nonneutral property. We shall thus assume that unused input to the parser will have no tables at all; these are constructed when the symbol is shifted onto the pushdown list.

We also assume that the tables do not influence the parse, except to interrupt it when there is an error. Thus, our parsing mechanism will be the normal shift-reduce mechanism, with a pointer to a representation of the property table for each symbol on the pushdown list.

Suppose that we have $[B, T_1][C, T_2]$ on top of the pushdown list and that a reduction according to the production $A \rightarrow BC$ is called for. Our problem is to construct the table associated with A from T_1 and T_2 quickly and conveniently. Since most indices in a table are mapped to the neutral property, it is desirable to have entries only for those indices which do not have the neutral property.

We shall implement the table-handling scheme in such a way that all table-handling operations and inquiries about the property of a given index can be accomplished in time that is virtually linear in the number of operations and inquiries. We make the natural assumption that the number of table inquiries is proportional to the length of the input. The assumption is correct if we are parsing deterministically, as the number of reductions made (and hence the number of table mergers) is proportional to the length of the input. Also, a reasonable translation algorithm would not inquire of properties more than a constant number of times per reduction.

In what follows, we shall assume that we have a property grammar whose underlying CFG is in Chomsky normal form. Generalizations of the algorithms are left for the Exercises. We shall also assume that each index (identifier) with a nonneutral property in any property table has a location in a hash table and that we may construct data structures out of elementary building blocks called *cells*. Each cell is of the form

DATUM1	$\cdots$	DATUMm	POINTER1	$\cdots$	POINTERn

consisting of one or more fields, each of which can contain some data or a pointer to another cell. The cells will be used to construct linked lists.

Suppose that there are k properties in V. The property table associated with a grammar symbol on the pushdown list is represented by a data structure consisting of up to k *property lists* and an *intersection list*. Each property list is headed by a *property list header cell*. The intersection list is headed by an *intersection list leader cell*. These header cells are linked as shown in Fig. 10.10.

The property header cell has three fields:

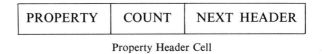

Property Header Cell

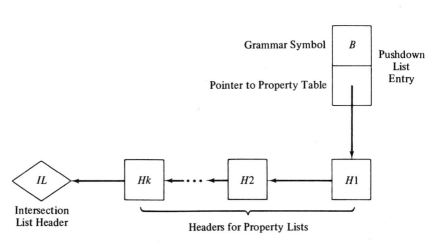

Fig. 10.10 A pushdown list entry with structure representing property table.

The intersection list header cell contains only a pointer to the first cell on the intersection list. All cells on the property lists and the intersection lists are *index cells.* An index cell consists of four pointer fields:

TOWARD PROPERTY	INTERSECTION LIST	TOWARD HASH TABLE	AWAY FROM HASH TABLE

Index Cell

Suppose that T is a property table associated with a symbol on the pushdown list. Then T will be represented by p property lists, where p is the number of distinct properties in T, and one intersection list. For each index in T having a nonneutral property j, there is one index cell on the property list headed by the property list header cell for property j.

All index cells having the same property are linked into a tree whose root is the header for that property. The first pointer in an index cell is to its direct ancestor in that tree.

If an index cell is on the intersection list, then the second pointer in that cell is to the next cell on the intersection list. The pointer is absent if an index cell is not on the intersection list.

The last two pointers link index cells which represent the same index but in different property tables. Suppose that $\delta T_3 \gamma T_2 \beta T_1 \alpha$ represents a string of tables on the pushdown list such that T_1, T_2, and T_3 each contain index i with a nonneutral property and that all tables in α, β, γ, or δ give index i the neutral property.

If table T_1 is closest to the top of the pushdown list, then C_1, the index cell representing i in T_1, will have in its third field a pointer to the symbol table location for i. The fourth field in C_1 has a pointer to C_2, the cell in T_2 that represents i. In C_2, the third field has a pointer to cell C_1 and the fourth field has a pointer to the cell representing i in T_3.

Thus, an additional structure is placed on the index cells: All index cells representing the same index in all tables on the pushdown list are in a doubly linked list, with the hash table entry for the index at the head.

A cell is on the intersection list of a table if and only if some table above it on the pushdown list has an index cell representing the same index. In the example above, the cell C_2 above will be on the intersection list for T_2.

Example 10.10

Suppose that we have a pushdown list containing grammar symbols B and C with C on top. Let the tables associated with these entries be, respectively,

$$T_1 = [1 : v_1, 2 : v_2, 5 : v_2, 6 : v_1, 8 : v_2]$$

and

$$T_2 = [2 : v_1, 3 : v_1, 4 : v_1, 5 : v_1, 7 : v_2, 8 : v_3]$$

Then a possible implementation for these tables is shown in Fig. 10.11. Circles

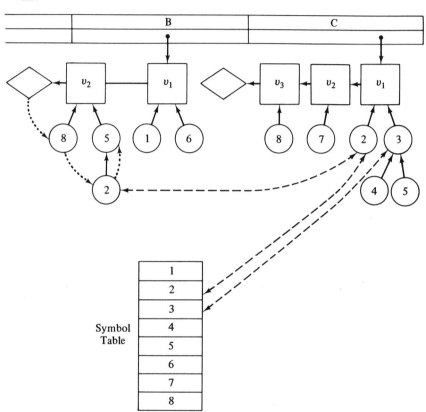

Fig. 10.11   Implementation of property tables.

indicate index cells. The number inside the circle is the index represented by that cell. Dotted lines indicate the links of the intersection list. Note that the intersection list of the topmost table is empty, by definition, and that the intersection list of table T_1 consists of index cells for indices 2, 5, and 8. Dashed lines indicate links to the hash table and to cells representing the same index on other tables. We show these only for indices 2 and 3 to avoid clutter. ☐

Suppose that we are parsing and that the parser calls for BC on its stack to be reduced to A. We must compute table T for A from tables T_1 and T_2 for B and C, respectively. Since C is the top symbol, the intersection list of T_1 contains exactly those indices having a nonneutral property on both T_1 and T_2 (hence the name "intersection list"). These indices will be set aside for later consideration.

Those indices which are not on the intersection list of T_1 have the neutral property on at least one of T_1 or T_2. Thus, their property on T is a function only of their one nonneutral property. Neglecting those indices on the intersection list, the data structure representing table T can be constructed by combining various trees of T_1 and T_2. After doing so, each entry on the intersection list of T_1 is treated separately and made to point to the appropriate cell of T.

Before formalizing these ideas, we should point out that in practice we would expect that the properties can be partitioned into disjoint subsets such that we can express V as $V_1 \times V_2 \times \cdots \times V_m$ for some relatively large m. The various components, $V_1, V_2, \ldots$ would in general be small. For example, V_1 might contain two elements designating "real" and "integer". V_2 might have two elements "single precision" and "double precision"; V_3 might consist of "dynamically allocated" and "statically allocated," and so on. One element of each of $V_1, V_2, \ldots$ can be considered the default condition and the product of the default elements is the neutral property. Finally, we may expect that the various components of an identifier's property can be determined independently of the others.

If this situation pertains, it is possible to create one property header for each nondefault element of V_1, one for each nondefault element of V_2, and so on. Each index cell is linked to several property headers, but at most one from any V_i. If the links to the headers for V_i are made distinct from those to the headers of V_j for $i \neq j$, then the ideas of this section apply equally well to this situation, and the total number of property headers will approximate the sum of the sizes of the V_i's rather than their product.

We shall now give a formal algorithm for implementing a property grammar. For simplicity in exposition, we restrict our consideration to property grammars whose underlying CFG is in Chomsky normal form.

ALGORITHM 10.3

Table handling for property grammar implementation.

Input. A property grammar $G = (N, \Sigma, P, S, V, v_0, F, \mu)$ whose underlying CFG is in Chomsky normal form. We shall assume that a nonneutral property is never mapped into the neutral property; that is, if $\mu(p, v_1v_2) = v_0$, then $v_1 = v_2 = v_0$. [This condition may be easily assumed, because if we find $\mu(i, v_1v_2) = v_0$ but v_1 or v_2 is not v_0, we could on the right-hand side replace v_0 by v_0', a new, nonneutral property, and introduce rules that would make v_0' "look like" v_0.] Also, part of the input to this algorithm is a shift–reduce parsing algorithm for the underlying CFG.

Output. A modified shift–reduce parsing algorithm for the underlying CFG, which while parsing computes the tables associated with those nodes of the parse tree corresponding to the symbols or the pushdown list.

Method. Let us suppose that each table has the format of Fig. 10.10, that is, an intersection list and a list of headers, at most one for each property, with a tree of indices with that property attached to each header. The operation of the table mechanism will be described in two parts, depending on whether a terminal or two nonterminals are reduced. (Recall that the underlying grammar is in Chomsky normal form.)

Part 1: Suppose that a terminal symbol a is shifted onto the pushdown list and reduced to a nonterminal A. Let the required table for A be $[i : v]$. To implement this operation, we shall shift A onto the pushdown list directly and create the table $[i : v]$ for A as follows.

(1) In the entry for A at the top of the pushdown list, place a pointer to a single property header cell having property v and count 1. This property header points to an intersection list header with an empty intersection list.

(2) Create C, an index cell for i.

(3) Place a pointer in the first field of C to the property header cell.

(4) Make the second field of C blank.

(5) Place a pointer in the third field of C to the hash table entry for i and also make that hash table entry point to C.

(6) If there was previously another cell C' which was linked to the hash table entry for i, place C' on the intersection list of its table. (Specifically, make the intersection list header point to C' and make the third field in C' point to the previous first cell of the intersection list if there was one.)

(7) Place a pointer in the fourth field of C to C'.

(8) Make the pointer in the third field of C' point to C.

Part 2: Now, suppose that two nonterminals are reduced to one, say by production $A \rightarrow BD$. Let T_1 and T_2 be the tables associated with B and D, respectively. Then do the following to compute T, the table for A.

(1) Consider each index cell on the intersection list of T_1. (Recall that T_2 has no intersection list.) Each such cell represents an entry for some index i on both T_1 and T_2. Find the properties of this index on these tables by Algorithm 10.4.† Let these properties be v_1 and v_2. Compute $v = \mu(p, v_1 v_2)$,

---

†Obviously, one can find the property of the index by going from its cells on the two tables to the roots of the trees on which the cells are found. However, in order that the table handling as a whole be virtually linear in time, it is necessary that following the path to the root be done in a special way. This method will be described subsequently in Algorithm 10.4.

where p is production $A \to BD$. Make a list of all index cells on the intersection list along with their new properties and the old contents of the cells on T_1 and T_2.

(2) Consider the property header cells of T_1. Change the property of the header cell with property v to the property $\mu(p, vv_0)$. That is, assume that all indices with property v on T_1 have the neutral property on T_2.

(3) Consider the property header cells of T_2. Change the property of the header cell with property v to $\mu(p, v_0v)$. That is, assume that all indices with property v on T_2 have the neutral property on T_1.

(4) Now, several of the property header cells formerly belonging to T_1 and T_2 may have the same property. These are merged by the following steps, which combine two trees into one:

(a) Change the property header cell with the smaller count (break ties arbitrarily) into a dummy index cell not corresponding to any index.

(b) Make the new index cell point to the property header cell with the larger count.

(c) Adjust the count of the remaining property header cell to be the sum of the counts of the two headers plus 1, so that it reflects the number of index cells in the tree, including dummy cells.

(5) Now, consider the list of indices created in step (1). For each such index,

(a) Create a new index cell C.

(b) Place a pointer in the first field of C to the property header cell with the correct property and adjust the count in that header cell.

(c) Place pointers in the third field of C to the hash table location for that index and from this hash table entry to C.

(d) Place a pointer in the fourth field of C to the first index cell below (on the pushdown list) having the same index.

(e) Now, consider C_1 and C_2, the two original cells representing this index on T_1 and T_2. Make C_1 and C_2 into "dummy" cells by preserving the pointers in the first field of C_1 and C_2 (their links to their ancestors in their trees) but by removing the pointers in the third and fourth fields (their links to the hash table and to cells on other tables having the same index). Thus, the newly created index cell C plays the role of the two cells C_1 and C_2 that have been made dummy cells.

(6) Dummy cells that are leaves can be returned to available storage. ☐

Example 10.11

Let us consider the two property tables of Example 10.10 (Fig. 10.11 on p. 826). Suppose that $\mu(p, st)$ is given by the following table:

s	t	$\mu(p, st)$
v_0	v_1	v_1
v_0	v_2	v_2
v_0	v_3	v_3
v_1	v_0	v_1
v_2	v_0	v_2
v_2	v_1	v_3
v_2	v_3	v_2

In part 2 of Algorithm 10.3 we must first consider the intersection list of T_1, which consists of index cells 2, 5, and 8. (See Fig. 10.11.) Inspection of the above table shows that these indices will have properties v_3, v_3, and v_2, respectively, on the new property table T.

Then, we consider the property header cells of T_1 and T_2. $\mu(p, v_0 v_i) = v_i$ and $\mu(p, v_i v_0) = v_i$, so the properties in the header cells all remain the same. Now, we merge the tree for v_1 on T_1 into the tree for v_1 on T_2, since the latter is the larger. The resulting tree is shown in Fig. 10.12(a). Then, we merge the tree for v_2 on T_2 into the tree for v_2 on T_1. The resulting tree is shown in Fig. 10.12(b). It should be observed that in Fig. 10.12(a) node 5

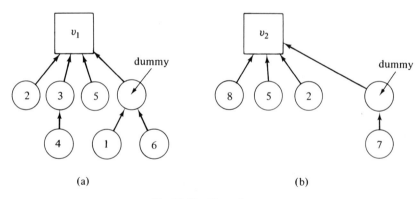

(a)   (b)

Fig. 10.12   Merged trees.

has been made a direct descendant of the header, while in Fig. 10.11 it was a direct descendant of the node numbered 3. This is an effect of Algorithm 10.4 and occurred when the intersection list of T_1 was examined. Node 2 in Fig. 10.12(b) has been moved for the same reason.

In the last step, we consider the indices on the intersection list of T_1. New index cells are created for these indices; the new cells point directly to the appropriate header. All other cells for that index in table T are made dummy cells. Dummy cells with no descendants are then removed. The resulting table T is shown in Fig. 10.13. The symbol table is not shown. Note that the intersection list of T is empty.

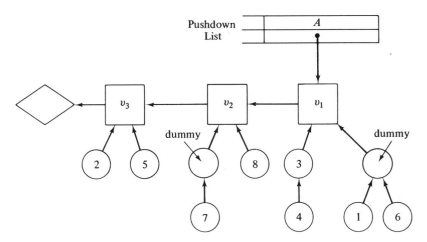

Fig. 10.13   New table T.

Now suppose that an input symbol is shifted onto the pushdown list and reduced to $D[2 : v_1]$. Then the index cell for 2, which points to v_3 in Fig. 10.13, is linked to the intersection list of its table. The changes are shown in Fig. 10.14.   □

We shall now give the algorithm whereby we inquire about the property of index i on table T. This algorithm is used in Algorithm 10.3 to find the property of indices on the intersection list.

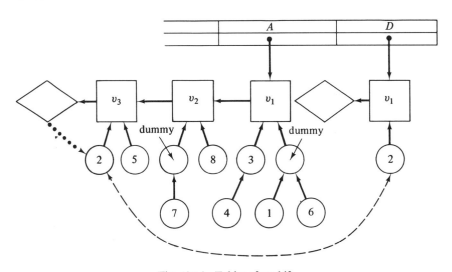

Fig. 10.14   Tables after shift.

ALGORITHM 10.4

Finding the property of an index.

Input. An index cell on some table T. We assume that tables are structured as in Algorithm 10.3.

Output. The property of that index in table T.

Method.

(1) Follow pointers from the index cell to the root of the tree on which it appears. Make a list of all cells encountered on this path.

(2) Make each cell on the path, except the root itself, point to the root directly. (Of course, the cell on the path immediately before the root already does so.)   □

Note that it is step (2) of Algorithm 10.4, which is essentially a "side effect" of the algorithm, that is of significance. It is step (2) which guarantees that the aggregate time spent on the table handling will be virtually proportional to input length.

10.2.4.   Analysis of the Table Handling Algorithm

The remainder of this chapter is devoted to the analysis of the time complexity of Algorithms 10.3 and 10.4. To begin, we define two functions F and G which will be used throughout this section.

DEFINITION

We define $F(n)$ by the recurrence:

$$F(1) = 1$$
$$F(n) = 2^{F(n-1)}$$

The following table shows some values of $F(n)$.

n	$F(n)$
1	1
2	2
3	4
4	16
5	65536

Now let us define $G(n)$ to be the least integer i such that $F(i) \geq n$. $G(n)$ grows so slowly that it is reasonable to say that $G(n) \leq 6$ for all n which are representable in a single computer word, even in floating-point notation. Alternatively, we could define $G(n)$ to be the number of times we have to apply $\log_2$ to n in order to produce a number equal to or less than 0.

The remainder of this section is devoted to proving that Algorithm 10.3 requires $0(nG(n))$ steps of a random access computer when the input string is of length n. We begin by showing that exclusive of the time spent in Algorithm 10.4, the time complexity of Algorithm 10.3 is $0(n)$.

LEMMA 10.3

Algorithm 10.3, exclusive of calls to Algorithm 10.4, can be implemented to run in time $0(n)$ on a random access computer, where n is the length of the input string being parsed.

Proof. Each execution of part 1 requires a fixed amount of time, and there are exactly n such executions.

In part 2, we note that steps (1) and (5) take time proportional to the length of the intersection list. (Again recall that we are not counting the time spent in calls of Algorithm 10.4.) But the only way for an index cell to find its way onto an intersection list is in part 1. Each execution of part 1 places at most one index cell on an intersection list. Thus, at most n indices are placed on all the intersection lists of all tables. After execution of part 2, all index cells are removed from the intersection list, and so the aggregate amount of time spent in steps (1) and (5) of part 2 is $0(n)$.

The other steps of part 2 are easily seen to require a constant amount of time per execution of part 2. Since part 2 is executed exactly $n - 1$ times, we conclude that all time spent in Algorithm 10.3, exclusive of calls to Algorithm 10.4, is $0(n)$. ☐

We shall now define an abstract problem and provide a solution, mirroring the ideas of Algorithms 10.3 and 10.4 in terms that are somewhat more abstract but easier to analyze.

DEFINITION

For the remainder of this section let us define a *set merging problem* as

(1) A collection of *objects* $a_1, \ldots, a_n$;
(2) A collection of set *names*, including $A_1, A_2, \ldots, A_n$; and
(3) A sequence of instructions $I_1, I_2, \ldots, I_m$, where each I_i is of the form
   (a) **merge**(A, B, C) or
   (b) **find**(a),
   where A, B, and C are set names and a is an object.

(Think of the set names as pairs consisting of a table and a property. Think of the objects as index cells.)

The instruction **merge**(A, B, C) creates the union of the sets named A and B and calls the resulting set C. No output is generated.

The instruction **find**(a) prints the name of the set of which a is currently a member.

Initially, we assume that each object a_i is in the set A_i; that is, $A_i = \{a_i\}$.

The *response to a sequence of instructions* $I_1, I_2, \ldots, I_m$ is the sequence of outputs generated when each instruction is executed in turn.

Example 10.12

Suppose that we have objects $a_1, a_2, \ldots, a_6$ and the sequence of instructions

$$\mathbf{merge}(A_1, A_2, A_2)$$
$$\mathbf{merge}(A_3, A_4, A_4)$$
$$\mathbf{merge}(A_5, A_6, A_6)$$
$$\mathbf{merge}(A_2, A_4, A_4)$$
$$\mathbf{merge}(A_4, A_6, A_6)$$
$$\mathbf{find}(a_3)$$

After executing the first instruction, A_2 is $\{a_1, a_2\}$. After the second instruction, A_4 is $\{a_3, a_4\}$. After the third instruction, A_6 is $\{a_5, a_6\}$. Then after the instruction $\mathbf{merge}(A_2, A_4, A_4)$, A_4 becomes $\{a_1, a_2, a_3, a_4\}$. After the last merge instruction, $A_6 = \{a_1, a_2, \ldots, a_6\}$. Then, the instruction $\mathbf{find}(a_3)$ prints the name A_6, which is the response to this sequence of instructions. ☐

We shall now give an algorithm to execute any instruction sequence of length $0(n)$ on n objects in $0(nG(n))$ time. We shall make certain assumptions about the way in which objects and sets can be accessed. While it may not initially appear that the property grammar implementation of Algorithms 10.3 and 10.4 meets these conditions, a little reflection will suffice to see that in fact objects (index cells) are easily accessible at times when we wish to determine their property and that sets (property headers) are accessible when we want to merge them.

ALGORITHM 10.5

Computation of the response to a sequence of instructions.

Input. A collection of objects $\{a_1, \ldots, a_n\}$ and a sequence of instructions $I_1, \ldots, I_m$ of the type described above.

Output. The response to the sequence $I_1, \ldots, I_m$.

Method. A set will be stored as a tree in which each node represents one element of the set. The root of the tree has a label which gives

(1) The name of the set represented by the tree and
(2) The number of nodes in that tree (*count*).

We assume that it is possible to find the node representing an object or the root of the tree representing a set in a fixed number of steps. One way of accomplishing this is to use two vectors OBJECT and SET such that OBJECT(a) is a pointer to the node representing a and SET(A) is a pointer to the root of the tree representing set A.

Initially, we construct n nodes, one for each object a_i. The node for a_i is the root of a one-node tree. Initially, this root is labeled A_i and has a count of 1.

(1) To execute the instruction **merge**(A, B, C), locate the roots of the trees for A and B [via SET(A) and SET(B)]. Compare the counts of the trees named A and B. The root of the smaller tree is made a direct descendant of the larger. (Break ties arbitrarily.) The larger root is given the name C, and its count becomes the sum of the counts of A and B.† Place a pointer in location SET(C) to the root of C.

(2) To execute the instruction **find**(a), determine the node representing a via OBJECT(a). Then follow the path from that node to the root r of its tree. Print the name found at r. Make all nodes on this path, except r, direct descendants of r.‡ ☐

Example 10.13

Let us consider the sequence of instructions in Example 10.12. After executing the first three merge instructions, we would have three trees, as shown in Fig. 10.15. The roots are labeled with a set name and a count.

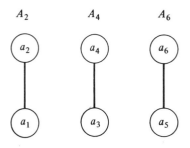

Fig. 10.15 Trees after three merge instructions.

(The count is not shown.) Then executing the instruction **merge**(A_2, A_4, A_4), we obtain the structure of Fig. 10.16. After the final merge instruction **merge**(A_4, A_6, A_6), we obtain Fig. 10.17. Then, executing the instruction **find**(a_3), we print the name A_6 and make nodes a_3 and a_4 direct descendants of the root. (a_4 is already a direct descendant.) The final structure is shown in Fig. 10.18. ☐

---

†The analogy between this step and the merge procedure of Algorithm 10.3 should be obvious. The discrepancy in the way counts are handled has to do simply with the question of whether the root is counted or not. Here it is; in Algorithm 10.3 it was not.

‡The analogy to Algorithm 10.4 should be obvious.

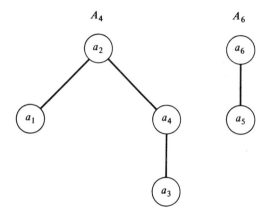

Fig. 10.16 Trees after next merge instruction.

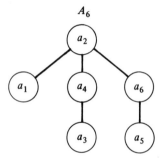

Fig. 10.17 Tree after last merge instruction.

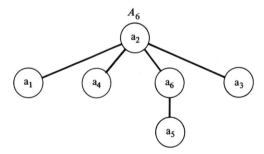

Fig. 10.18 Tree after find instruction.

We shall now show that Algorithm 10.5 can be executed in $0(nG(n))$ time on the reasonable assumption that execution of a **merge** instruction requires one unit of time and an instruction of the form **find**(a) requires time proportional to the length of the path from the node representing a to the root. All subsequent results are predicated on this assumption. From this point on we shall assume that n, the number of objects, has been fixed, and that the sequence of instructions is of length $0(n)$.

DEFINITION

We define the *rank* of a node on one of the structures created by Algorithm 10.5 as follows.

(1) A leaf is of rank 0.

(2) If a node N ever has a direct descendant of rank i, then N is of rank at least $i + 1$.

(3) The rank of a node is the least integer consistent with (2).

It may not be immediately apparent that this definition is consistent. However, if node M is made a direct descendant of node N in Algorithm 10.5, then M will never subsequently be given any more direct descendants. Thus the rank of M may be fixed at that time. For example, in Fig. 10.17 the rank of node a_6 can be fixed at 1 since a_6 has one direct descendant of rank 0 and a_6 subsequently acquires no new descendants.

The next three lemmas state some properties of the rank of a node.

LEMMA 10.4

Let N be a root of rank i created by Algorithm 10.5. Then N has at least 2^i descendants.

Proof. The basis, $i = 0$, is clear, since a node is trivially its own descendant. For the inductive step, suppose node N is a root of rank i. Then, N must have at some time been given a direct descendant M of rank $i - 1$. Moreover, M must have been made a direct descendant of N in step (1) of Algorithm 10.5, or else the rank of N would be at least $i + 1$. This implies that M was then a root so that, by the inductive hypothesis, M has at least 2^{i-1} descendants at that time, and in step (1) of Algorithm 10.5, N has at least 2^{i-1} descendants at that time. Thus, N has at least 2^i descendants after merger. As long as N remains a root, it cannot lose descendants. $\square$

LEMMA 10.5

At all times during the execution of Algorithm 10.5, if N has a direct descendant M, then the rank of N is greater than the rank of M.

Proof. Straightforward induction on the number of instructions executed. $\square$

The following lemma gives a bound on the number of nodes of rank i.

LEMMA 10.6

There are at most $n2^{-i}$ nodes of rank i.

Proof. The structure created by Algorithm 10.5 is a collection of trees.

Thus, no node is a descendant of two different nodes of rank i. Since there are n nodes in the structure, the result follows immediately from Lemma 10.4. ☐

COROLLARY

No node has rank greater than $\log_2 n$. ☐

DEFINITION

With the number of objects n fixed, define *groups* of ranks as follows. We say *integer i is in group j* if and only if

$$\log_2^{(j)}(n) \geq i > \log_2^{(j+1)}(n),$$

where $\log_2^{(1)}(n) = \log_2 n$ and $\log_2^{(k+1)}(n) = \log_2^{(k)}(\log_2(n))$. That is, $\log_2^{(k)}$ is the function which applies the $\log_2$ function k times. For example,

$$\log_2^{(3)}(65536) = \log_2^{(2)}(16) = \log_2(4) = 2.$$

A node of rank r is said to be in *rank group j* if r is in group j. Since $\log_2^{(k)}(F(k)) = 1$ and no node has rank greater than $\log_2 n$, we note that no node is in a rank group higher than $G(n)$. For example, if $n = 65536$, we have the following rank groups.

Rank of Node	Rank Group
0	5
1	4
2	3
3, 4	2
5, 6, ..., 16	1

We are now ready to prove that Algorithm 10.5 is of time complexity $O(nG(n))$.

THEOREM 10.3

The cost of executing any sequence σ of $O(n)$ instructions on n objects is $O(nG(n))$.

Proof. Clearly the total cost of the **merge** instructions in σ is $O(n)$ units of time. We shall account for the lengths of the paths traversed by the **find** instructions in σ in two ways. In executing a **find** instruction suppose we move from node M to node N going up a path. If M and N are in different rank groups, then we charge one unit of time to the **find** instruction itself. We also charge 1 if N is the root. Since there are at most $G(n)$ different rank groups along any path, no **find** instruction is charged more than $G(n)$ units.

If, on the other hand, M and N are in the same rank group, and N is not a root, we charge 1 time unit to node M itself. Note that M must be moved in this case. By Lemma 10.5, the new direct ancestor of M is of higher rank than its previous direct ancestor. Thus, if M is in rank group j, M may be charged at most $\log_2^{(j)}(n)$ time units before its direct ancestor becomes one of a lower rank group. From that time on, M will never be charged; the cost of moving M will be borne by the **find** instruction executed, as described in the paragraph above.

Clearly the charge to all the **find** instructions is $O(nG(n))$. To find an upper bound on the total charge to all the objects we sum over all rank groups the maximum charge to each node in the group times the maximum number of nodes in the group. Let g_j be the number of nodes in rank group j and c_j the charge to all nodes in group j. Then:

$$(10.2.1) \qquad g_j \leq \sum_{k=\log_2^{(j+1)}(n)}^{\log_2^{(j)}(n)} n2^{-k}$$

by Lemma 10.6.

The terms of (10.2.1) form a geometric series with ratio $1/2$, so their sum is no greater than twice the first term. Thus $g_j \leq 2n\,2^{-\log_2^{(j+1)}(n)}$, which is $2n/\log_2^{(j)}(n)$. Now c_j is bounded above by $g_j \log_2^{(j)}(n)$, so $c_j \leq 2n$. Since j may vary only from 1 to $G(n)$, we see that $O(nG(n))$ units of time are charged to nodes. It follows that the total cost of executing Algorithm 10.5 is $O(nG(n))$. $\square$

Now we apply our abstract result to property grammars.

THEOREM 10.4

Suppose that the parsing and table-handling mechanism constructed in Algorithms 10.3 and 10.4 is applied to an input of length n. Also, assume that the number of inquiries regarding properties of an index in tables is $O(n)$ and that these inquiries are restricted to the top table on the pushdown list for which the index has a nonneutral property.[†] Then the total time spent in table handling on a random access computer is $O(nG(n))$.

Proof. First, we must observe that the assumptions of our model apply, namely that the time needed in Algorithm 10.3 to reach any node which we want to manipulate is fixed, independent of n. The property headers (roots of trees) can be reached in fixed time since there are a finite number of them per table and they are linked. The index cells (nodes for objects) are directly accessible either from the hash table when we wish to inquire of their properties (this is why we assume that we inquire only of indices on the top table) or in turn as we proceed down an intersection list.

[†]If we think of the typical use of these properties, e.g., when a is reduced to F in G_0 and properties of the particular identifier a are desired, we see that the assumption is quite plausible.

It thus suffices to show that each index and header cell we create can be modeled as an object node, that there are $0(n)$ of them, and that all manipulations can be expressed exactly as some sequence of **merge** and **find** instructions. The following is a complete list of all the cells ever created.

(1) $2n$ "objects" correspond to the n header cells and n index cells created during the shift operation (part 1 of Algorithm 10.3). We can cause the index cell to point to the header cell by a **merge** operation.

(2) At most n objects correspond to the new index cells created in step (5) of part 2 of Algorithm 10.3. These cells can be made to point to the correct root by an appropriate **merge** operation.

Thus, there are at most $3n$ objects (and n in Algorithm 10.5 means $3n$ here). Moreover, the number of instructions needed to manipulate the sets and objects when "simulating" Algorithms 10.3 and 10.4 by Algorithm 10.5 is $0(n)$. We have commented that at most $3n$ **merge** instructions suffice to initialize tables after a shift [(1) above] and to attach new index cells to headers [(2) above]. In addition, $0(n)$ **merge** instructions suffice in step (4) of part 2 of Algorithm 10.3 when two sets of indices having the same property are merged. This follows from the fact that the number of distinct properties is fixed and that only $n - 1$ reductions can be made.

Lemma 10.3 implies that $0(n)$ **find** instructions suffice to account for the examination of properties of indices on an intersection list [step (1) of part 2 of Algorithm 10.3]. Finally, we assume in the hypothesis of the theorem that $0(n)$ additional **find** instructions are needed to determine properties of indices (presumably for use in translation). If we put all these instructions in the order dictated by the parser and Algorithm 10.3, we have a sequence of $0(n)$ instructions. Thus, the present theorem follows from Lemma 10.3 and Theorem 10.3. $\square$

EXERCISES

10.2.1. Let G be the CFG with productions

$$E \longrightarrow E + T \mid E \oplus T \mid T$$
$$T \longrightarrow (E) \mid a$$

where a represents an identifier, $+$ represents fixed-point addition, and $\oplus$ represents floating-point addition. Create from G a property grammar that will do the following:

(1) Assume that each a has a table with one nonneutral entry.

(2) If node n in a parse tree uses production $E \longrightarrow E + T$, then all the a's whose nodes are dominated by n are said to be "used in a fixed-point addition."

(3) If, as in (2), production $E \longrightarrow E \oplus T$ is used, all a's dominated by n are "used in a floating-point addition."

(4) The property grammar must parse according to G, but check that an identifier which is used in a floating-point addition is not subsequently (higher up the parse tree) used in a fixed-point addition.

10.2.2. Use the property grammar of Example 10.9 and give a parse tree, if one exists, for each of the following input strings:

(a) **begin**
    declare[1 : 1]
    declare[1 : 1]
    begin
        a[1 : 3]
    end
    label[2 : 2]a[1 : 3]
    begin
        declare[3 : 1]
        a[3 : 3]
    end
    goto[2 : 4]
  end

(b) **begin**
    declare[1 : 1]
    a[1 : 3]
    begin
        declare[2 : 1]
        goto[1 : 4]
    end
  end

DEFINITION

A *nondeterministic property grammar* is defined exactly as a property grammar, except that

(1) The range of μ is, the subsets of V, and

(2) There is no requirement as to the existence of a neutral property.

Using the conventions of this section, we say that $\alpha A T \beta \Longrightarrow \alpha X_1 T_1 \cdots X_n T_n \beta$ if $A \longrightarrow X_1 \cdots X_n$ is some production, say p, and for each i, $T(i)$ is a member of $\mu(p, T_1(i) \cdots T_n(i))$. The $\overset{*}{\Longrightarrow}$ relation and the language generated are defined exactly as for the deterministic case.

*10.2.3. Prove that for every nondeterministic property grammar G there is a property grammar G' (possibly without a neutral property) generating the same language, in which μ is a function.

10.2.4. Show that if the grammar G of Exercise 10.2.3 has a neutral property (i.e., all but a finite number of integers must have that property in each table of each derivation), then grammar G' is a property grammar with the neutral property.

10.2.5. Generalize Algorithm 10.3 to grammars which are not in CNF. Your generalized algorithm should have the same time complexity as the original.

*10.2.6. Let us modify our property grammar definition by requiring that no terminal symbol have the all-neutral table. If G is such a property grammar, let $L'(G)$ be $\{a_1 \cdots a_n \mid a_1 T_1 \cdots a_n T_n$ is in $L(G)$ for some (not all-neutral) tables $T_1, \ldots, T_n\}$. Show that $L'(G)$ need not be a CFG. *Hint:* Show that $\{a^i b^j c^k \mid i \leq j \leq k\}$ can be so generated.

**10.2.7. Show that for "property grammar" G, as modified in Exercise 10.2.6, it is undecidable whether $L'(G) = \varnothing$, even if the underlying CFG of G is right-linear.

10.2.8. Let G be the underlying CFG of Example 10.9. Suppose the terminal **declare** associates one of two properties with an index—either "declared real" or "declared integer." Define a property grammar on G such that if the implementation of Algorithm 10.3 is used, the highest table on the pushdown list having a particular index i with nonneutral property (i.e., the one with the cell for i pointed to by the hash table entry for i) will have the currently valid declaration for identifier i as the property for i. Thus, the decision whether an identifier is real or integer can be made as soon as its use is detected on the input stream.

10.2.9. Find the output of Algorithm 10.5 and the final tree structure when given a set of objects $\{a_1, \ldots, a_{12}\}$ and the following sequence of instructions. Assume that in case of tie counts, the root of A_i becomes a descendant of the root of A_j if $i < j$.

$$\text{merge}(A_1, A_2, A_1)$$

$$\text{merge}(A_3, A_1, A_1)$$

$$\text{merge}(A_4, A_5, A_4)$$

$$\text{merge}(A_6, A_4, A_4)$$

$$\text{merge}(A_7, A_8, A_7)$$

$$\text{merge}(A_9, A_7, A_7)$$

$$\text{merge}(A_{10}, A_{11}, A_{10})$$

$$\text{merge}(A_{12}, A_{10}, A_{10})$$

$$\text{find}(a_1)$$

$$\text{merge}(A_1, A_4, A_1)$$

$$\text{merge}(A_7, A_{10}, A_2)$$

$$\text{find}(a_7)$$

$$\text{merge}(A_1, A_2, A_1)$$

$$\text{find}(a_3)$$

$$\text{find}(a_4)$$

**10.2.10.   Suppose that Algorithm 10.5 were modified to allow either root to be made a descendant of the other when mergers were made. Show that the revised algorithm is of time complexity at best $O(n \log n)$.

Open Problems

10.2.11.   Is Algorithm 10.5 as stated in this book really $O(nG(n))$ in complexity, or is it $O(n)$, or perhaps something in between?

10.2.12.   Is the revised algorithm of Exercise 10.2.10 of time complexity $O(n \log n)$?

Research Problem

10.2.13.   Investigate or characterize the kinds of properties of identifiers which can be handled correctly by property grammars.

BIBLIOGRAPHIC NOTES

Property grammars were first defined by Stearns and Lewis [1969]. Answers to Exercises 10.2.6 and 10.2.7 can be found there. An $n \log \log n$ method of implementing property grammars is discussed by Stearns and Rosenkrantz [1969].

To our knowledge, Algorithm 10.5 originated with R. Morris and M. D. McIlroy, but was not published. The analysis of the algorithm is due to Hopcroft and Ullman [1972a]. Exercise 10.2.10 is from Fischer [1972].

11 CODE OPTIMIZATION

One of the most difficult and least understood problems in the design of compilers is the generation of "good" object code. The two most common criteria by which the goodness of a program is judged are its running time and size. Unfortunately, for a given program it is generally impossible to ascertain the running time of the fastest equivalent program or the length of the shortest equivalent program. As mentioned in Chapter 1, we must be content with code improvement, rather than true optimization when programs have loops.

Most code improvement algorithms can be viewed as the application of various transformations on some intermediate representation of the source program in an attempt to manipulate the intermediate program into a form from which more efficient object code can be produced. These code improvement transformations can be applied at any point in the compilation process. One common technique is to apply the transformations to the intermediate language program that occurs after syntactic analysis but before code generation.

Code improvement transformations can be classified as being either machine-independent or machine-dependent. An example of machine-independent optimization would be the removal of useless statements from a program, those which do not in any way affect its output.† Such machine-independent transformations would be beneficial in all compilers.

Machine-dependent transformations would attempt to transform a program into a form whereby advantage could be taken of special-purpose

†Since such statements should not normally appear in a program, it is likely that an error is present, and thus the compiler ought to inform the user of the uselessness of the statement.

· machine instructions. As a consequence, machine-dependent transformations are hard to characterize in general, and for this reason they will not be discussed further here.

In this chapter we shall study various machine-independent transformations that can be applied to the intermediate programs occurring within a compiler after syntactic analysis but before code generation. We shall begin by showing how optimal code can be generated for a certain simple but important class of straight-line programs. We shall then extend this class of programs to include loops and examine some of the code improvement techniques that can be applied to these programs.

11.1. OPTIMIZATION OF STRAIGHT-LINE CODE

We shall first consider a program schema that models a block of code consisting of a sequence of assignment statements, each of which has the form $A \leftarrow f(B_1, \ldots, B_r)$, where A and $B_1, \ldots, B_r$ are scalar variables and f is a function of r variables for some r. For this restricted class of programs, we develop a set of transformations and show how these transformations can be used to find an optimal program under a rather general cost function. Since the actual cost of a program depends on the nature of the machine code that will eventually be produced, we shall consider what portions of the optimization procedure are machine-independent and how the rest depends on the actual machine model chosen.

11.1.1. A Model of Straight-Line Code

We shall begin by defining a *block*. A block models a portion of an intermediate language program that contains only multiple-address assignment statements.

DEFINITION

Let Σ be a countable set of *variable names* and Θ a finite set of *operators*. We assume that each operator θ in Θ takes a known fixed number of operands. We also assume that Θ and Σ are disjoint.

A *statement* is a string of the form

$$A \longleftarrow \theta B_1 \cdots B_r$$

where $A, B_1, \ldots, B_r$ are variables in Σ and θ is an r-ary operator in Θ. We say that this statement *assigns* (or *sets*) A and *references* $B_1, \ldots, B_r$.

A *block* $\mathcal{B}$ is a triple (P, I, U), where

(1) P is a list of statements $S_1; S_2; \ldots; S_n$, where $n \geq 0$;

(2) I is a set of *input* variables; and

(3) U is a set of *output* variables.

We shall assume that if statement S_j references A, then A is either an input variable or assigned by some statement before S_j (i.e., by some S_i such that $i < j$). Thus, in a block all variables referenced are previously defined, either internally, as assigned variables, or externally, as input variables. Similarly, we assume each output variable either is an input variable or is set by some statement.

A typical statement is $A \leftarrow + BC$, which is just the prefix form of the more common assignment "$A \leftarrow B + C$." If a statement sets variable A, we can associate a "value" with that assignment of A. This value is the formula for A in terms of the (unknown) initial values of the input variables. This formula can be written as a prefix expression involving the input variables and the operators.

For the time being we are assuming that the input variables have unknown values and should be treated as algebraic unknowns. Moreover, the meaning of the operators and the set of quantities on which they are defined is not specified, and so a formula, rather than a quantity, is all that we can expect as a value.

DEFINITION

To be more precise, let (P, I, U) be a block with $P = S_1; \ldots; S_n$. We define $v_t(A)$, the *value* of variable A immediately after time t, $0 \le t \le n$, to be the following prefix expression:

(1) If A is in I, then $v_0(A) = A$.
(2) If statement S_t is $A \leftarrow \theta B_1 \cdots B_r$, then
   (a) $v_t(A) = \theta v_{t-1}(B_1) \cdots v_{t-1}(B_r)$.
   (b) $v_t(C) = v_{t-1}(C)$ for all $C \ne A$, provided that $v_{t-1}(C)$ is defined.
(3) For all A in Σ, $v_t(A)$ is undefined unless defined by (1) or (2) above.

We observe that since each operator takes a known number of operands, every value expression is either a single symbol of Σ or can be uniquely written as $\theta E_1 \cdots E_r$, where θ is an r-ary operator and $E_1, \ldots, E_r$ are value expressions. (See Exercise 3.1.17.)

The *value* of block $\mathfrak{B} = (P, I, U)$, denoted $v(\mathfrak{B})$, is the set

$$\{v_n(A) \,|\, A \in U, \text{ and } n \text{ is the number of statements of } P\}$$

Two blocks are (*topologically*) *equivalent* ($\equiv$) if they have the same value. Note that the strings forming prefix expressions are equal if and only if they are identical. That is, we assume no algebraic identities for the time being. In Section 11.1.6 we shall study equivalence of blocks under certain algebraic laws.

Example 11.1

Let $I = \{A, B\}$, let $U = \{F, G\}$, and let P consist of the statements†

$$T \longleftarrow A + B$$
$$S \longleftarrow A - B$$
$$T \longleftarrow T * T$$
$$S \longleftarrow S * S$$
$$F \longleftarrow T + S$$
$$G \longleftarrow T - S$$

Initially, $v_0(A) = A$ and $v_0(B) = B$. After the first statement, $v_1(T) = A + B$ [in prefix notation $v_1(T) = +AB$], $v_1(A) = A$, and $v_1(B) = B$. After the second statement, $v_2(S) = A - B$, and other variables retain their previous values. After the third statement, $v_3(T) = (A + B) * (A + B)$. The last three statements cause the following values to be computed (other values carry over from the previous step):

$$v_4(S) = (A - B) * (A - B)$$
$$v_5(F) = (A + B) * (A + B) + (A - B) * (A - B)$$
$$v_6(G) = (A + B) * (A + B) - (A - B) * (A - B)$$

Since $v_6(F) = v_5(F)$, the value of the block is

$$\{(A + B) * (A + B) + (A - B) * (A - B),$$
$$(A + B) * (A + B) - (A - B) * (A - B)\}.‡$$

Note that we are assuming that no algebraic laws pertain. If the usual laws of algebra applied, then we could write $F = 2(A^2 + B^2)$ and $G = 4AB$. $\quad\square$

To avoid undue complexity, we shall not consider statements involving structured variables (arrays and so forth) at this time. One way to handle arrays is the following. If A is an array, treat an assignment such as $A(I) = J$ as if A were a scalar variable assigned some function of I, J and its former value. That is, we write $A \longleftarrow \theta AIJ$, where θ is an operator symbolizing assignment in an array. Similarly, an assignment such as $J = A(I)$ could be expressed as $J \longleftarrow \psi AI$.

---

†In displaying a list of statements we often use a new line in place of a semicolon to separate statements. In examples we shall use infix notation for binary operators.

‡In prefix notation the value of the block is

$$\{+*+AB+AB*-AB-AB, \quad -*+AB+AB*-AB-AB\}.$$

In addition, we make several other assumptions which make this theory less than generally applicable. For example, we ignore test statements, constants, and assignments of the form $A \leftarrow B$. However, changing the assumptions will lead to a similar theory, and we make our assumptions primarily for convenience, in order to give an example of this family of theories.

Our principal assumptions are:

(1) The important thing about a block is the set of functions of the input variables (variables defined outside the block) computed within the block. The number of times a particular function is computed is not important. This philosophy stems from the view that the blocks of a program pass values from one to another. We assume that it is never necessary for a block to pass two copies of a value to another block.

(2) The variable names given to the functions computed are not important. This assumption is not a good one if the block is part of a loop and the function computed is fed back. That is, if $I \leftarrow I + 1$ is computed, it would not do to change this computation to $J \leftarrow I + 1$ and then repeat the block, expecting the computation to be the same. Nevertheless, we make this assumption because it lends a certain symmetry to the solution and is often valid. In the Exercises, the reader is asked to make the modifications necessary to allow certain output values to be given fixed names.

(3) We do not include statements of the form $X \leftarrow Y$. If such a statement occurred, we could substitute Y for X and delete it anyway, provided that assumption (2) holds. Again, this assumption lends symmetry to the model, and the reader is asked to modify the theory to include such statements.

11.1.2. Transformations on Blocks

We observe that given two blocks $\mathcal{B}_1$ and $\mathcal{B}_2$, we can test whether $\mathcal{B}_1$ and $\mathcal{B}_2$ are equivalent by computing their values $v(\mathcal{B}_1)$ and $v(\mathcal{B}_2)$ and determining whether $v(\mathcal{B}_1) = v(\mathcal{B}_2)$. However, there are an infinity of blocks equivalent to any given block.

For example, if $\mathcal{B} = (P, I, U)$ is a block, X is a variable not mentioned in $\mathcal{B}$, A is an input variable, and θ is any operator, then we can append the statement $X \leftarrow \theta A \cdots A$ to P as many times as we choose without changing the value of $\mathcal{B}$.

Under a reasonable cost function, all equivalent blocks are not equally efficient. Given a block $\mathcal{B}$, there are various transformations that we can apply to map $\mathcal{B}$ into an equivalent, and possibly more desirable block $\mathcal{B}'$. Let $\mathcal{I}$ be the set of all transformations which preserve the equivalence of blocks. We shall show that each transformation in $\mathcal{I}$ can be implemented by a finite sequence of four primitive transformations on blocks. We shall then characterize those sequences of transformations which lead to a block that is optimal under a reasonable cost criterion.

DEFINITION

Let $\mathfrak{B} = (P, I, U)$ be a block with $P = S_1; S_2; \ldots; S_n$. For notational uniformity we shall adopt the convention that all members of the input set I are assigned at a zeroth statement, S_0, and all members of the output set U are referenced at an $n + 1$st statement, S_{n+1}.

Variable A is *active* immediately after time t, if

(1) A is assigned by some statement S_i;
(2) A is not assigned by statements $S_{i+1}, S_{i+2}, \ldots, S_j$;
(3) A is referenced by statement S_{j+1}; and
(4) $0 \leq i \leq t \leq j \leq n$.

If j above is as large as possible, then the sequence of statements S_{i+1}, $S_{i+2}, \ldots, S_{j+1}$ is said to be the *scope* of statement S_i and the scope of this assignment of variable A. If A is an output variable and not assigned after S_i, then $j = n + 1$, and U is also said to be in the scope of S_i. (This follows from the above convention; we state it only for emphasis.)

If a block contains a statement S such that the variable assigned in S is not active immediately after this statement, then the scope of S is null, and S is said to be a *useless* statement. Put another way, S is useless if S sets a variable that is neither an output variable nor subsequently referenced.

Example 11.2

Consider the following block, where α, β, and γ are lists of zero or more statements:

$$\alpha$$
$$A \longleftarrow B + C$$
$$\beta$$
$$D \longleftarrow A * E$$
$$\gamma$$

If A is not assigned in the sequence of statements β or referenced in γ, then the scope of $A \longleftarrow B + C$ includes all of β and the statement $D \longleftarrow A * E$. If no statement in γ references D, and D is not an output variable, then the statement $D \longleftarrow A * E$ is useless. $\square$

We shall now define four primitive equivalence-preserving transformations on blocks. We assume that $\mathfrak{B} = (P, I, U)$ is a block and that P is $S_1; S_2; \ldots; S_n$. As before, we assume that S_0 assigns all input variables and that S_{n+1} references all output variables. We shall define our transformations in terms of their effect on this block $\mathfrak{B}$. Our first transformation is intuitively appealing. We remove from a block any input variable or statement that does not affect an output variable.

T_1: *Elimination of Useless Assignments*

If statement S_i, $0 \le i \le n$, assigns A, and A is not active after time i, then

(1) If $i > 0$, S_i can be deleted from P, or
(2) If $i = 0$, A can be deleted from I.

Example 11.3

Let $\mathcal{B} = (P, I, U)$, where $I = \{A, B, C\}$, $U = \{F, G\}$, and P consists of

$$F \longleftarrow A + A$$
$$G \longleftarrow F * C$$
$$F \longleftarrow A + B$$
$$G \longleftarrow A * B$$

The second statement is useless, since its scope is null. Thus one application of T_1 maps $\mathcal{B}$ into $\mathcal{B}_1 = (P_1, I, U)$, where P_1 is

$$F \longleftarrow A + A$$
$$F \longleftarrow A + B$$
$$G \longleftarrow A * B$$

In $\mathcal{B}_1$, the input variable C is now useless, and the first statement in P_1 is also useless. Thus, we can apply transformation T_1 twice in succession to obtain $\mathcal{B}_2 = (P_2, \{A, B\}, U)$, where P_2 consists of

$$F \longleftarrow A + B$$
$$G \longleftarrow A * B$$

Note that $\mathcal{B}_2$ is obtained whether we first remove input variable C or whether we first remove the first statement in P_1. $\quad \square$

A systematic method of eliminating all useless statements from a block $\mathcal{B} = (P, I, U)$ is to determine the set of useful variables (those that are used directly or indirectly in computing an output) after each statement of the block, beginning with the last statement in P and working up. Certainly, $U_n = U$ is the set of variables that are useful after the last statement S_n.

Suppose that statement S_i is $A \leftarrow \theta B_1 \cdots B_r$ and that U_i is the set of variables useful after S_i.

(1) If $A \in U_i$, S_i is a useful statement, since the variable A is used to compute an output variable. Then U_{i-1}, the set of useful variables after statement S_{i-1}, is found by replacing A in U_i by the variables $B_1, \ldots, B_r$ [i.e., $U_{i-1} = (U_i - \{A\}) \cup \{B_1, \ldots, B_r\}$].

(2) If $A \notin U_i$, then statement S_i is useless and can be deleted. In this case $U_{i-1} = U_i$.

(3) Once we have computed U_0, we can remove all input variables in I which do not appear in U_0.

Our second transformation on blocks merges common expressions as follows.

T_2: *Elimination of Redundant Computations*

Now let us suppose that $\mathfrak{B} = (P, I, U)$ is a block in which P is of the form

$$\alpha$$
$$A \longleftarrow \theta\, C_1 \cdots C_r$$
$$\beta$$
$$B \longleftarrow \theta\, C_1 \cdots C_r$$
$$\gamma$$

where none of $C_1, \ldots, C_r$ is A or is assigned in a statement of β. Transformation T_2 maps $\mathfrak{B}$ into $\mathfrak{B}' = (P', I, U')$, where P' is

$$\alpha$$
$$D \longleftarrow \theta\, C_1 \cdots C_r$$
$$\beta'$$
$$\gamma'$$

and

(1) β' is β with all references to A changed to D in the scope of the explicitly shown A, and

(2) γ' is γ with all references to A and B changed to D in the scopes of the explicitly shown A and B.

If the scope of A or B extends to S_{n+1}, then U' is U with A or B changed to D. Otherwise $U' = U$.

D can be any symbol which does not change the value of the block. Any symbol not mentioned in P is suitable, and some symbols of P might also be usable.

Example 11.4

Suppose that $\mathfrak{B} = (P, \{A, B\}, \{F, G\})$, where P consists of

$$S \longleftarrow A + B$$
$$F \longleftarrow A * S$$

$$R \leftarrow B + B$$
$$T \leftarrow A * S$$
$$G \leftarrow T * R$$

The second and fourth statements perform redundant computations, so transformation T_2 can be applied to $\mathcal{B}$ to produce $\mathcal{B}' = (P', \{A, B\}, \{D, G\})$, where P' consists of

$$S \leftarrow A + B$$
$$D \leftarrow A * S$$
$$R \leftarrow B + B$$
$$G \leftarrow D * R$$

The output set becomes $\{D, G\}$. D may be any new symbol or one of the variables F, A, S, or T. It is easy to check that letting D be B, R, or G changes the value of the program. ☐

T_3: *Renaming*

Clearly, the name of an assigned variable is irrelevant insofar as the value of a block $\mathcal{B} = (P, I, U)$ is concerned. Suppose that statement S_i in P is $A \leftarrow \theta B_1 \cdots B_r$ and that C is a variable that is not active in the scope of S_i. Then we can let $\mathcal{B}' = (P', I, U')$, where P' is P with S_i replaced by $C \leftarrow \theta B_1 \cdots B_r$ and with all references to A replaced by references to C in the scope of S_i. If U is in the scope of S_i, then U' is U with A changed to C. Otherwise $U' = U$. Transformation T_3 maps $\mathcal{B}$ into $\mathcal{B}'$.

Example 11.5

Let $\mathcal{B} = (P, \{A, B\}, \{F\})$, where P is

$$T \leftarrow A * B$$
$$T \leftarrow T + A$$
$$F \leftarrow T * T$$

One application of T_3 enables us to change the name of the first assigned variable from T to S. Thus T_3 maps $\mathcal{B}$ into $\mathcal{B}' = (P', \{A, B\}, \{F\})$, where P' is

$$S \leftarrow A * B$$
$$T \leftarrow S + A$$
$$F \leftarrow T * T$$

Note that only the first assignment of T has been replaced by S. ☐

T_4: Flipping

Let $\mathcal{B} = (P, I, U)$ be a block in which statement S_i is $A \leftarrow \theta\, B_1 \cdots B_r$, statement S_{i+1} is $C \leftarrow \psi D_1 \cdots D_s$, A is not one of $C, D_1, \ldots, D_s$, and C is not one of $A, B_1, \ldots, B_r$. Then transformation T_4 maps the block $\mathcal{B}$ into $\mathcal{B}' = (P', I, U)$, where P' is P with S_i and S_{i+1} interchanged.

Example 11.6

Let $\mathcal{B} = (P, \{A, B\}, \{F, G\})$ in which P is

$$F \longleftarrow A + B$$
$$G \longleftarrow A * B$$

T_4 can be applied to transform $\mathcal{B}$ into $(P', \{A, B\}, \{F, G\})$, where P' is

$$G \longleftarrow A * B$$
$$F \longleftarrow A + B$$

However, T_4 can not map the block $\mathcal{B}_1 = (P_1, \{A, B\}, \{F, G\})$, where P_1 is

$$F \longleftarrow A + B$$
$$G \longleftarrow F * A$$

into the block $\mathcal{B}_2 = (P_2, \{A, B\}, \{F, G\})$, where P_2 is

$$G \longleftarrow F * A$$
$$F \longleftarrow A + B$$

In fact, $\mathcal{B}_2$ is not even a block, because variable F is used without a previous definition. $\square$

We shall now define certain equivalence relations that reflect the action of the four transformations defined.

DEFINITION

Let S be a subset of $\{1, 2, 3, 4\}$. We say that $\mathcal{B}_1 \underset{S}{\Rightarrow} \mathcal{B}_2$ if one application of transformation T_i changes $\mathcal{B}_1$ into $\mathcal{B}_2$, where i is in S. We say $\mathcal{B}_1 \underset{S}{\overset{*}{\leftrightarrow}} \mathcal{B}_2$ if there is a sequence $\mathcal{C}_0, \ldots, \mathcal{C}_n$ of blocks such that

(1) $\mathcal{C}_0 = \mathcal{B}_1$.
(2) $\mathcal{C}_n = \mathcal{B}_2$.
(3) For each i, $0 \le i < n$, either $\mathcal{C}_i \underset{S}{\Rightarrow} \mathcal{C}_{i+1}$ or $\mathcal{C}_{i+1} \underset{S}{\Rightarrow} \mathcal{C}_i$.

Thus, $\underset{S}{\overset{*}{\leftrightarrow}}$ is the least equivalence relation containing $\underset{S}{\Rightarrow}$ and reflects the idea that the transformations can be applied in either direction.

CONVENTION

We shall represent subsets of $\{1, 2, 3, 4\}$ without braces, so, for example, $\underset{\{1,2\}}{\Longrightarrow}$ would be written $\underset{1,2}{\Longrightarrow}$.

We would now like to show that $\mathcal{B}_1$ and $\mathcal{B}_2$ are equivalent blocks if and only if there is a sequence of transformations involving only T_1 through T_4 which transforms $\mathcal{B}_1$ into $\mathcal{B}_2$. That is, $\mathcal{B}_1 \equiv \mathcal{B}_2$ if and only if $\mathcal{B}_1 \underset{1,2,3,4}{\overset{*}{\longleftrightarrow}} \mathcal{B}_2$. The "if" portion of this statement is easy to verify. All that is needed is to show that each transformation individually preserves the value of a block.

THEOREM 11.1

If $\mathcal{B}_1 \underset{1,2,3,4}{\Longrightarrow} \mathcal{B}_2$, then $\mathcal{B}_1 \equiv \mathcal{B}_2$.

Proof. Exercise. The reader should also show that any new name may be chosen for D in T_2, as stated in the description of that transformation. $\square$

COROLLARY

If $\mathcal{B}_1 \underset{1,2,3,4}{\overset{*}{\longleftrightarrow}} \mathcal{B}_2$, then $\mathcal{B}_1 \equiv \mathcal{B}_2$. $\square$

We shall prove the converse of the corollary to Theorem 11.1 in Section 11.1.4.

11.1.3. A Graphical Representation of Blocks

In this section we shall show that for each block $\mathcal{B} = (P, I, U)$ we can find a directed acyclic graph (dag) D that represents $\mathcal{B}$ in a natural way. Each leaf of D corresponds to one input variable in I and each interior node of D corresponds to a statement of P. The transformations on blocks considered in the previous section can then be applied to dags with equal ease.

DEFINITION

Let $\mathcal{B} = (P, I, U)$ be a block. We construct a labeled ordered dag, denoted $D(\mathcal{B})$, from $\mathcal{B}$ as follows:

(1) Let $P = S_1; \ldots ; S_n$.
(2) For each A in I, create a node with label A. At this point in the algorithm, the node for A is said to be *the last definition* of A.
(3) For $i = 1, 2, \ldots, n$, do the following. Let S_i be $A \leftarrow \theta B_1 \cdots B_r$. Create a new node labeled θ, with r directed edges leaving. Order the edges from the left, and let the jth edge from the left point to the last definition of B_j, $1 \leq j \leq r$. The new node labeled θ becomes the last definition of A. This node *corresponds* to statement S_i in P.
(4) After step (3), those nodes which are the last definition of an output variable are further labeled "distinguished." We shall circle distinguished nodes.

Example 11.7

Let $\mathfrak{B} = (P, \{A, B\}, \{F, G\})$ be a block, where P consists of the statements

$$T \longleftarrow A + B$$
$$F \longleftarrow A * T$$
$$T \longleftarrow B + F$$
$$G \longleftarrow B * T$$

The dag $D(\mathfrak{B})$ is given in Fig. 11.1.

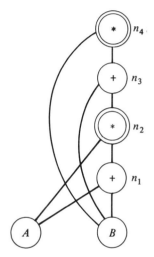

Fig. 11.1   Example of a dag.

Note in Fig. 11.1 that the four statements of $\mathfrak{B}$ correspond in order to nodes n_1, n_2, n_3, n_4. Also note that the right descendant of n_4 is n_3 rather than n_1, because when n_4 is created, n_3 is the last definition of T. $\quad \square$

Each dag represents an equivalence class of $\xleftrightarrow[3,4]{*}$ in a natural way. That is, if a block $\mathfrak{B}_1$ can be transformed into $\mathfrak{B}_2$ by some sequence of transformations T_3 and T_4, then blocks $\mathfrak{B}_1$ and $\mathfrak{B}_2$ have the same dag, and conversely. Half of this assertion is the following lemma, which is left to the reader to check using the definitions.

Lemma 11.1

If $\mathfrak{B}_1 \underset{3,4}{\Rightarrow} \mathfrak{B}_2$, then $D(\mathfrak{B}_1) = D(\mathfrak{B}_2)$.

Proof. Exercise. $\quad \square$

Corollary

If $\mathfrak{B}_1 \xleftrightarrow[3,4]{*} \mathfrak{B}_2$, then $D(\mathfrak{B}_1) = D(\mathfrak{B}_2)$. $\quad \square$

The more difficult portion of our assertion is the other direction. For its proof we need the following definition and lemma.

DEFINITION

A block $\mathfrak{B} = (P, I, U)$ is said to be *open* if

(1) No statement in P is of the form $A \leftarrow \alpha$, where A is in I, and
(2) No two statements in P assign the same variable.

In an open block $\mathfrak{B} = (P, I, U)$, a distinct variable X_i not in I is assigned by each statement S_i in P. The following lemma states that an open block can always be created by renaming variables using only transformation T_3.

LEMMA 11.2

Let $\mathfrak{B} = (P, I, U)$ be a block. Then there is an equivalent open block $\mathfrak{B}' = (P', I, U')$ such that $\mathfrak{B} \overset{*}{\underset{3}{\longleftrightarrow}} \mathfrak{B}'$.

Proof. Exercise. $\square$

The following theorem shows that two blocks have the same dag if and only if one block can be transformed into the other by renaming and flipping.

THEOREM 11.2

$D(\mathfrak{B}_1) = D(\mathfrak{B}_2)$ if and only if $\mathfrak{B}_1 \overset{*}{\underset{3,4}{\longleftrightarrow}} \mathfrak{B}_2$.

Proof. The "if" portion is the corollary to Lemma 11.1. Thus, it suffices to consider two blocks $\mathfrak{B}_1 = (P_1, I_1, U_1)$ and $\mathfrak{B}_2 = (P_2, I_2, U_2)$ such that $D(\mathfrak{B}_1) = D(\mathfrak{B}_2) = D$. Since the dags are identical, the input sets must be the same, and so we may let $I_1 = I_2 = I$. Also, the number of statements in P_1 and P_2 must be the same, and so we may suppose $P_1 = S_1; \ldots; S_n$ and $P_2 = R_1; \ldots; R_n$.

Using T_3, the renaming transformation, we can construct two open blocks $\mathfrak{B}'_1 = (P'_1, I'_1, U'_1)$ and $\mathfrak{B}'_2 = (P'_2, I'_2, U'_2)$ having the same set of assigned variables, such that

(1) $\mathfrak{B}'_1 \overset{*}{\underset{3}{\longleftrightarrow}} \mathfrak{B}_1$;

(2) $\mathfrak{B}'_2 \overset{*}{\underset{3}{\longleftrightarrow}} \mathfrak{B}_2$;

(3) Let $P'_1 = S'_1; \ldots; S'_n$ and $P'_2 = R'_1; \ldots; R'_n$. Then S'_i and R'_j assign the same variable if and only if they correspond to the same node of D. [Observe by the corollary to Lemma 11.1 that $D(\mathfrak{B}'_1) = D(\mathfrak{B}'_2) = D$.]

In creating the open blocks, we first rename all the variables of $\mathfrak{B}_1$ and $\mathfrak{B}_2$ with entirely new names. Then, we can rename again to satisfy condition (3).

Now we shall construct a sequence of blocks $\mathfrak{C}_0, \ldots, \mathfrak{C}_n$ such that

(4) $\mathfrak{C}_0 = \mathfrak{B}'_1$;

(5) $\mathfrak{C}_n = \mathfrak{B}'_2$;

(6) $\mathfrak{C}_i \overset{*}{\underset{4}{\longleftrightarrow}} \mathfrak{C}_{i+1}$ for $0 \le i < n$;

(7) The statements of $\mathcal{C}_i$ are $R'_1 ; \ldots ; R'_i$ followed by those statements among $S'_1 ; \ldots ; S'_n$ which do not set variables also assigned by any of $R'_1, \ldots, R'_i$. Clearly $D(\mathcal{C}_i) = D$, and statements defining the same variable in $\mathcal{C}_i$ and $\mathcal{B}'_2$ create the same node in D.

We begin with $\mathcal{C}_0 = \mathcal{B}'_1$. Condition (7) is satisfied trivially. Suppose that we have constructed $\mathcal{C}_i$, $i \geq 0$. We can write the list of statements in $\mathcal{C}_i$ as $R'_1 ; \ldots ; R'_i ; S'_{j_1} ; \ldots ; S'_{j_{n-i}}$, in which the statements $S'_{j_1}, \ldots, S'_{j_{n-i}}$ satisfy condition (7). By definition of P'_1 and P'_2, we can find S'_{j_k}, which assigns the same variable as R'_{i+1}. Since S'_{j_k} and R'_{i+1} correspond to the same node of D, it follows that S'_{j_k} references only variables which are in I or assigned by $R'_1 ; \cdots ; R'_i$, and, in fact, $R_{i+1} = S'_{j_k}$. Thus, by repeated application of T_4, we may move S'_{j_k} in front of all of $S'_{j_1} ; \cdots ; S'_{j_{n-i}}$. The resulting block is $\mathcal{C}_{i+1}$, and conditions (6) and (7) are easily checked.

When i in condition (7) is equal to n, we obtain condition (5). Thus

$$\mathcal{B}_1 \xleftrightarrow[3]{*} \mathcal{B}'_1 \xleftrightarrow[4]{*} \mathcal{B}'_2 \xleftrightarrow[3]{*} \mathcal{B}_2,$$

from which $\mathcal{B}_1 \xleftrightarrow[3,4]{*} \mathcal{B}_2$ is immediate. $\quad\square$

COROLLARY

If $D(\mathcal{B}_1) = D(\mathcal{B}_2)$, then $\mathcal{B}_1 \equiv \mathcal{B}_2$.

Proof. Immediate from Theorems 11.1 and 11.2. $\quad\square$

By the above corollary, we can naturally give a value to a dag, namely the value of any block having that dag.

Example 11.8

Consider the two blocks $\mathcal{B}_1 = (P_1, \{A, B\}, \{F\})$ and $\mathcal{B}_2 = (P_2, \{A, B\}, \{F\})$, with P_1 and P_2 as follows:

P_1	P_2
$C \leftarrow A * A$	$C \leftarrow B * B$
$D \leftarrow B * B$	$D \leftarrow A * A$
$E \leftarrow C - D$	$E \leftarrow D + C$
$F \leftarrow C + D$	$C \leftarrow D - C$
$F \leftarrow E/F$	$F \leftarrow C/E$

Blocks $\mathcal{B}_1$ and $\mathcal{B}_2$ have the same dag, which is shown in Fig. 11.2. Using T_3, we can map $\mathcal{B}_1$ and $\mathcal{B}_2$ into open blocks $\mathcal{B}'_1 = (P'_1, \{A, B\}, \{X_5\})$ and $\mathcal{B}'_2 = (P'_2, \{A, B\}, \{X_5\})$ so that condition (3) in the proof of Theorem 11.2 is satisfied. P'_1 and P'_2 are shown on the following page.

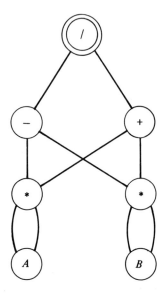

Fig. 11.2   Dag for $\mathcal{B}_1$ and $\mathcal{B}_2$.

P_1'	P_2'
$X_1 \leftarrow A * A$	$X_2 \leftarrow B * B$
$X_2 \leftarrow B * B$	$X_1 \leftarrow A * A$
$X_3 \leftarrow X_1 - X_2$	$X_4 \leftarrow X_1 + X_2$
$X_4 \leftarrow X_1 + X_2$	$X_3 \leftarrow X_1 - X_2$
$X_5 \leftarrow X_3/X_4$	$X_5 \leftarrow X_3/X_4$

Then, beginning with block $\mathcal{C}_0$ having the list of statements P_1', we can readily construct the blocks $\mathcal{C}_1$, $\mathcal{C}_2$, $\mathcal{C}_3$, $\mathcal{C}_4$, and $\mathcal{C}_5$ in the proof of Theorem 11.2. Block $\mathcal{C}_1$ is obtained by using T_4 to move the second statement in front of the first, as shown below:

$\mathcal{C}_1$	$\mathcal{C}_3$
$X_2 \leftarrow B * B$	$X_2 \leftarrow B * B$
$X_1 \leftarrow A * A$	$X_1 \leftarrow A * A$
$X_3 \leftarrow X_1 - X_2$	$X_4 \leftarrow X_1 + X_2$
$X_4 \leftarrow X_1 + X_2$	$X_3 \leftarrow X_1 - X_2$
$X_5 \leftarrow X_3/X_4$	$X_5 \leftarrow X_3/X_4$

Then $\mathcal{C}_2 = \mathcal{C}_1$. Block $\mathcal{C}_3$ is constructed from $\mathcal{C}_2$, using T_4 to move the fourth statement in front of the third as shown above, and $\mathcal{C}_4$ and $\mathcal{C}_5$ are both the same as $\mathcal{C}_3$. $\square$

11.1.4. Characterization of Equivalences Between Blocks

We shall now show that $\mathcal{B}_1 \equiv \mathcal{B}_2$ if and only if $\mathcal{B}_1 \underset{1,2,3,4}{\overset{*}{\longleftrightarrow}} \mathcal{B}_2$. In fact there is a stronger result, namely that $\mathcal{B}_1 \equiv \mathcal{B}_2$ if and only if $\mathcal{B}_1 \underset{1,2}{\overset{*}{\longleftrightarrow}} \mathcal{B}_2$. That is, transformations T_1 and T_2 are sufficient to map any block into any other equivalent block. We shall leave the proof of this stronger result for the Exercises. (See Exercises 11.1.9 and 11.1.10.)

DEFINITION

A block $\mathcal{B}$ is *reduced* if there is no block $\mathcal{B}'$ such that $\mathcal{B} \underset{1,2}{\Longrightarrow} \mathcal{B}'$.

A reduced block contains no useless statements or redundant computations. Given any block $\mathcal{B}$, we can find a reduced block equivalent to it by repeatedly applying T_1 and T_2 in their forward directions. Since each application of T_1 or T_2 reduces the length of the block, we must eventually come upon a reduced block. Our goal is to show that for reduced blocks $\mathcal{B}_1$ and $\mathcal{B}_2$, we have $\mathcal{B}_1 \equiv \mathcal{B}_2$ if and only if $D(\mathcal{B}_1) = D(\mathcal{B}_2)$. Thus, given a block $\mathcal{B}$, we can find one dag corresponding to all reduced blocks obtainable from $\mathcal{B}$ by any sequence of transformations T_1 and T_2 whatsoever. Finding this dag is an important step in the "optimization" of the block, whatever machine model we are using.

DEFINITION

Let $P = S_1; \ldots ; S_n$ be the list of statements in a block. Let $E(P)$ be the set of expressions computed by P. Formally,

$$E(P) = \{v_t(A) \,|\, S_t \text{ assigns } A, 1 \leq t \leq n\}.$$

Expression η is computed k times by P if there are exactly k distinct values of t such that $v_t(A) = \eta$ and S_t sets A.

LEMMA 11.3

If $\mathcal{B} = (P, I, U)$ is a reduced block, then P does not compute any expression more than once.

Proof. If two statements compute the same expression, find the "first" instance of an expression computed twice. That is, if S_i and S_j, $i < j$, compute the same expression η, we say that (i, j) is the *first* instance if for all pairs S_k and S_l, $k < l$, which compute the same expression, either $i < k$ or both $i = k$ and $j < l$. It is left for the Exercises to show that an application of T_2 in the forward direction would be applicable to S_i and S_j contradicting the assumption that P is reduced. □

LEMMA 11.4

If $\mathfrak{B}_1 = (P_1, I_1, U_1)$ and $\mathfrak{B}_2 = (P_2, I_2, U_2)$ are equivalent reduced blocks, then $E(P_1) = E(P_2)$.

Proof. If $E(P_1) \neq E(P_2)$, we may, without loss of generality, let η be the last computed expression in $E(P_1) - E(P_2)$. Since $v(\mathfrak{B}_1) = v(\mathfrak{B}_2)$ and each expression may be uniquely split into subexpressions, it follows that η is not a subexpression of any expression in $v(\mathfrak{B}_1)$. Thus, the statement computing η in P_1 is useless and can be eliminated using transformation T_1, contradicting the assumption that $\mathfrak{B}_1$ was reduced. Details are left for the Exercises. $\square$

THEOREM 11.3

Let $\mathfrak{B}_1$ and $\mathfrak{B}_2$ be two reduced blocks. Then $\mathfrak{B}_1 \equiv \mathfrak{B}_2$ if and only if $D(\mathfrak{B}_1) = D(\mathfrak{B}_2)$.

Proof. The "if" portion is a special case of the corollary to Theorem 11.2. Thus, let $\mathfrak{B}_1 \equiv \mathfrak{B}_2$. By the previous two lemmas, there is a one-to-one correspondence between those statements of $\mathfrak{B}_1$ and $\mathfrak{B}_2$ which compute the same expression.

Suppose that $D(\mathfrak{B}_1) \neq D(\mathfrak{B}_2)$. We shall attempt to "match" the nodes of $D(\mathfrak{B}_1)$ and $D(\mathfrak{B}_2)$ as far "up" the dag as possible. Clearly, the leaves of the two dags must match, for if not, the input sets of $\mathfrak{B}_1$ and $\mathfrak{B}_2$ would be different. We could then find an input variable of one which was not referenced and apply T_1 to eliminate that input variable. Since $\mathfrak{B}_1$ and $\mathfrak{B}_2$ are reduced, we would have a contradiction.

We proceed to match nodes; if a node of $D(\mathfrak{B}_1)$ and a node of $D(\mathfrak{B}_2)$ have the same (operator) label, if their edges leaving are equal in number, and if corresponding edges (from the left) point to matching nodes, then the two nodes in question are matched. If in so doing we match all nodes of $D(\mathfrak{B}_1)$ and $D(\mathfrak{B}_2)$, then these dags are the same.

Otherwise, we shall come to some node of $D(\mathfrak{B}_1)$ or $D(\mathfrak{B}_2)$ which does not match a node in the other dag. Without loss of generality, we can assume that such a node occurs in $D(\mathfrak{B}_1)$ and that we pick the "lowest" such node, one such that each edge leaving it points to a node which is matched. Let this node be n_1. We observe that matched nodes of $D(\mathfrak{B}_1)$ and $D(\mathfrak{B}_2)$ are created by statements of $\mathfrak{B}_1$ and $\mathfrak{B}_2$ which compute the same expression. An easy induction on the order of matching shows this.

However, by Lemma 11.3, no node can possibly be matched with two nodes of the other dag. By Lemma 11.4, there is a node n_2 of $D(\mathfrak{B}_2)$ which is created by a statement of $\mathfrak{B}_2$ which computes the same expression as the statement of $\mathfrak{B}_1$ which creates n_1. Since expressions "parse" uniquely, the direct descendants of n_1 and n_2 are matched. This follows from our assumption that n_1 was as "low" on $D(\mathfrak{B}_1)$ as possible. Thus, n_1 and n_2

could have been matched, contrary to hypothesis. Hence, $D(\mathcal{B}_1) = D(\mathcal{B}_2)$.

☐

COROLLARY

All reduced blocks equivalent to a given block have the same dag.   ☐

We can now put the various pieces together to obtain the result that the four transformations are sufficient to transform a block into any of its equivalents.

THEOREM 11.4

$\mathcal{B}_1 \equiv \mathcal{B}_2$ if and only if $\mathcal{B}_1 \overset{*}{\underset{1,2,3,4}{\longleftrightarrow}} \mathcal{B}_2$.

Proof. The "if" portion is the corollary to Theorem 11.1. Conversely, assume that $\mathcal{B}_1 \equiv \mathcal{B}_2$. Then there exist reduced blocks $\mathcal{B}'_1$ and $\mathcal{B}'_2$ such that $\mathcal{B}_1 \overset{*}{\underset{1,2}{\longleftrightarrow}} \mathcal{B}'_1$ and $\mathcal{B}_2 \overset{*}{\underset{1,2}{\longleftrightarrow}} \mathcal{B}'_2$. By the corollary to Theorem 11.1, $\mathcal{B}_1 \equiv \mathcal{B}'_1$ and $\mathcal{B}_2 \equiv \mathcal{B}'_2$. Thus, $\mathcal{B}'_1 \equiv \mathcal{B}'_2$. By Theorem 11.3 $D(\mathcal{B}'_1) = D(\mathcal{B}'_2)$. By Theorem 11.2, $\mathcal{B}'_1 \overset{*}{\underset{3,4}{\longleftrightarrow}} \mathcal{B}'_2$. Hence, $\mathcal{B}_1 \overset{*}{\underset{1,2,3,4}{\longleftrightarrow}} \mathcal{B}_2$.   ☐

11.1.5. Optimization of Blocks

Let us now consider the question of transforming a block $\mathcal{B}$ into a block $\mathcal{B}'$ which is optimal with respect to some cost criterion on blocks. In practice, we have the situation portrayed in Fig. 11.3. Given a block $\mathcal{B}$, we want

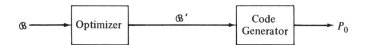

Fig. 11.3   Optimization scheme.

to ultimately produce an object language program that is optimal with respect to some cost function on object programs such as program size or execution speed. Our optimizer applies a sequence of transformations to $\mathcal{B}$ in order to produce $\mathcal{B}'$, a block equivalent to $\mathcal{B}$, from which an optimal object language program can be generated. Thus, one problem is to find some cost criterion on blocks that mirrors the cost of the object program which will ultimately be produced.

There are certain cost criteria on blocks for which the idea of optimization does not even make sense. For example, if we said that the longer a block is, the better it is, then there would be no optimal block equivalent to a given block. Here we shall restrict our thinking to cost functions on blocks that reflect most of the common criteria applied to object language programs, such as speed of execution or amount of storage used.

DEFINITION

A *cost criterion* on blocks is a function from blocks to real numbers. A block $\mathcal{B}$ is *optimal* under cost criterion C if $C(\mathcal{B}) \leq C(\mathcal{B}')$ for all $\mathcal{B}'$ equivalent to $\mathcal{B}$. A cost criterion C is *reasonable* if $\mathcal{B}_1 \underset{1,2}{\Rightarrow} \mathcal{B}_2$ implies that $C(\mathcal{B}_2) \leq C(\mathcal{B}_1)$, and every block has an optimal equivalent under C. That is, a cost criterion is reasonable if transformations T_1 and T_2 applied in the forward direction do not increase the cost of a block.

LEMMA 11.5

If C is a reasonable cost criterion, then every block has a reduced equivalent which is optimal under C.

Proof. Immediate from definitions. □

Lemma 11.5 states that given a block $\mathcal{B}$ we can confine our search for an equivalent optimal block to the set of reduced blocks equivalent to $\mathcal{B}$. The following lemma states that only reduced blocks equivalent to a given reduced block $\mathcal{B}$ will be found by applying a sequence of transformations T_3 and T_4 to $\mathcal{B}$.

LEMMA 11.6

If $\mathcal{B}_1$ is a reduced block and $\mathcal{B}_1 \underset{3,4}{\overset{*}{\longleftrightarrow}} \mathcal{B}_2$, then $\mathcal{B}_2$ is reduced.

Proof. Exercise. □

Our next result shows that if we have an open block initially, then a sequence of renamings followed by a flip can be replaced by the flip followed by the renamings.

LEMMA 11.7

Let $\mathcal{B}_1$ be an open block and $\mathcal{B}_1 \underset{3}{\overset{*}{\longleftrightarrow}} \mathcal{B}_2 \underset{4}{\Rightarrow} \mathcal{B}_3$. Then there exists a block $\mathcal{B}_2'$ such that $\mathcal{B}_1 \underset{4}{\Rightarrow} \mathcal{B}_2' \underset{3}{\overset{*}{\longleftrightarrow}} \mathcal{B}_3$.

Proof. Exercise. □

We are now prepared to give a general framework for optimizing blocks according to any reasonable cost criterion. The following theorem provides the basis for this optimization.

THEOREM 11.5

Let $\mathcal{B}$ be any block. There exists a block $\mathcal{B}'$ equivalent to $\mathcal{B}$ such that if C is any reasonable cost criterion, then there also exist blocks $\mathcal{B}_1$ and $\mathcal{B}_2$ such that

(1) $\mathcal{B}' \underset{4}{\overset{*}{\longleftrightarrow}} \mathcal{B}_1$,

(2) $\mathcal{B}_1 \underset{3}{\overset{*}{\longleftrightarrow}} \mathcal{B}_2$, and

(3) $\mathcal{B}_2$ is optimal under C.

Proof. Let $\mathcal{B}''$ be any reduced block equivalent to $\mathcal{B}$. We can transform $\mathcal{B}''$ into $\mathcal{B}'$, an open block equivalent to $\mathcal{B}''$ using only T_3. By Lemma 11.6, $\mathcal{B}'$ is reduced as well as open.

Let $\mathcal{B}_2$ be an optimal reduced block equivalent to $\mathcal{B}$. By Lemma 11.5, $\mathcal{B}_2$ exists. Thus, $D(\mathcal{B}_2) = D(\mathcal{B}')$ by the corollary to Theorem 11.3. By Theorem 11.2, $\mathcal{B}' \underset{3,4}{\overset{*}{\longleftrightarrow}} \mathcal{B}_2$. We observe that T_3 and T_4 are their own "inverses," that is, $\mathcal{C} \underset{3,4}{\Longrightarrow} \mathcal{C}'$ if and only if $\mathcal{C}' \Longrightarrow \mathcal{C}$. Hence, we can find a sequence of blocks $\mathcal{C}_1, \ldots, \mathcal{C}_n$ such that $\mathcal{B}' = \mathcal{C}_1$, $\mathcal{B}_2 = \mathcal{C}_n$, and $\mathcal{C}_i \underset{3,4}{\Longrightarrow} \mathcal{C}_{i+1}$ for $1 \leq i < n$. Using Lemma 11.7 iteratively, we can move all uses of T_4 ahead of those of T_3. Thus, we can find $\mathcal{B}_1$ such that $\mathcal{B}' \underset{4}{\overset{*}{\longleftrightarrow}} \mathcal{B}_1 \underset{3}{\overset{*}{\longleftrightarrow}} \mathcal{B}_2$. $\quad\square$

If we examine Theorem 11.5, we see that it divides the optimization process into three stages. Suppose that we wish to optimize a given block $\mathcal{B}$:

(1) From $\mathcal{B}$ we can first eliminate redundant and useless computations and rename variables to obtain a reduced open block $\mathcal{B}'$.

(2) In $\mathcal{B}'$ we can then reorder statements by flipping, until a block $\mathcal{B}_1$ is obtained in which the statements are in the best order.

(3) Finally we can rename variables in $\mathcal{B}_1$ until an optimal block $\mathcal{B}_2$ is found.

We note that step (1) can be performed efficiently (as a function of block length). It is left to the reader to give an algorithm for step (1) which takes time $0(n \log n)$ on a block having n statements.

Often, one of steps (2) and (3) is trivial. Our next example shows how statements in our intermediate language can be converted to assembly language in such a way that the number of assembly language instructions executed is minimized. This optimization algorithm will be seen not to need step (3). Renaming of variables will not subsequently affect the cost.

Example 11.9

We shall now take an example that has some interesting ideas not found elsewhere in the book. The reader is urged to examine it closely. Let us consider generating machine code for blocks. We postulate a computer with a single accumulator and the following assembly language instructions with meanings as shown.

(1) LOAD M. Here the contents of memory location M are loaded into the accumulator.

(2) STORE M. Here the contents of the accumulator are stored into memory location M.

(3) $\theta\, M_2 M_3, \cdots, M_r$. Here θ is the name of an r-ary operator. The first argument of θ is in the accumulator, the second in memory location M_2, the third in memory location M_3, and so forth. The result obtained by applying θ to its arguments is placed in the accumulator.

A code generator would translate a statement of the form $A \leftarrow \theta B_1 \cdots B_r$ into the following sequence of machine instructions:

$$\text{LOAD} \quad B_1$$
$$\theta \qquad B_2, \ldots, B_r$$
$$\text{STORE} \quad A$$

However, if the value of B_1 is already in the accumulator (i.e., the previous statement assigned B_1), then the first LOAD instruction need not be generated. Likewise, if the value of A is not required, except as the first argument of the next statement, then the final STORE instruction is not necessary.

The cost of the statement $A \leftarrow \theta B_1 \cdots B_n$ can thus be 1, 2, or 3. It is 3 if B_1 is not found in the accumulator and there is a subsequent reference to this assignment of A that is not the first argument of the next statement (i.e., A has to be stored). It is 1 if B_1 is already in the accumulator and there is no reference to this computation of A other than as the first argument of the next statement. Otherwise, the cost is 2.

We should point out that this cost assumption glosses over a number of considerations. To show that it correctly reflects the number of instructions needed to execute the block on our machine, we should first rigorously define the effect of a sequence of assembly instructions. If this is done in the expected way, then every assembly language program can be related to a block in our intermediate language by identifying assembly instructions of type (3), the operations, with statements of the block. All these details are left for the Exercises. In this example we shall take the cost function on blocks to be as we have stated it.

Let us consider the block $\mathfrak{B}_1 = (P_1, \{A, B, C\}, \{F, G\})$, which might be obtained from the FORTRAN statements

$$F = (A + B) * (A - B)$$
$$G = (A - B) * (A - C) * (B - C)$$

The list of statements in P_1 is

$$T \longleftarrow A + B$$
$$S \longleftarrow A - B$$
$$F \longleftarrow T * S$$
$$T \longleftarrow A - B$$
$$S \longleftarrow A - C$$
$$R \longleftarrow B - C$$

$$T \longleftarrow T * S$$
$$G \longleftarrow T * R$$

There are no useless statements. However, we note one instance of redundancy, between the second and fourth statements. We can eliminate this redundancy and then give each statement a new variable name to assign, obtaining the reduced open block $\mathfrak{B}_2 = (P_2, \{A, B, C\}, \{X_3, X_7\})$. $\mathfrak{B}_2$ plays the role of $\mathfrak{B}'$ in Theorem 11.5. The statements of P_2 are

$$X_1 \longleftarrow A + B$$
$$X_2 \longleftarrow A - B$$
$$X_3 \longleftarrow X_1 * X_2$$
$$X_4 \longleftarrow A - C$$
$$X_5 \longleftarrow B - C$$
$$X_6 \longleftarrow X_2 * X_4$$
$$X_7 \longleftarrow X_6 * X_5$$

The dag for $\mathfrak{B}_2$ is shown in Fig. 11.4. Node n_i is created from the statement of P_2 which sets X_i.

We observe that there are a large number of programs into which $\mathfrak{B}_2$ can be transformed using only T_4. We leave it for the Exercises to show that this number is the same as the number of linear orders of which the partial order represented by Fig. 11.4 is a subset.

An upper bound on that number would be 7!, the number of permutations of the seven statements. However, the actual number will be less in this case, as not all statements of P_2 can ever pass over each other by using T_4. For example, the third statement of P_2 must always follow the second, because the third references X_2 and the second defines it. Note that an application of T_3 may change the name of X_2 but that the same relation will hold with a new name.

Another interpretation of the limits on T_4's ability to reorder the block is to observe that in any such reordering, each node of $D(\mathfrak{B}_2)$ will correspond to some statement. The statement corresponding to an interior node n cannot precede any statement corresponding to an interior node which is a descendant of node n.

While the problem of this example is simple enough to enumerate all linear orderings of P_2, we cannot afford the time to do this for an arbitrary block. Some heuristic that will produce good, although not necessarily optimal, orderings quickly is needed. We propose one here. The following algorithm produces a linear ordering of the nodes of a dag. The desired block has statements corresponding to these nodes in reverse order. We express the algorithm as follows:

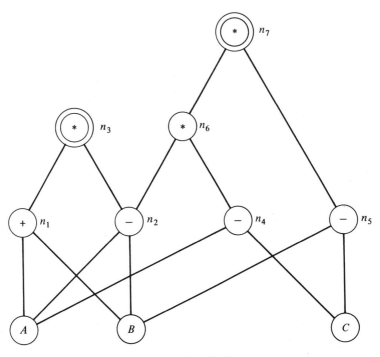

Fig. 11.4   Dag for $\mathcal{B}_2$.

(1) We construct a list L. Initially, L is empty.

(2) Choose a node n of the dag such that n is not on L, and if there are any edges entering n, they come from nodes already on L. Add n to L. If no such n exists, end.

(3) If n_1 is the last node added to L, the leftmost edge leaving n_1 points to an interior node n not in L, and all of n's direct ancestors are already in L, add n to L and repeat step (3). Otherwise go to step (2).

For example, using the dag of Fig. 11.4, we might begin with $L = n_3$. By step (3), we would add n_1 to L. Then we would choose n_7, add it to L, and follow it by n_6 and n_2. Two more uses of rule (2) would add n_4 and n_5, so a candidate for L is $n_3, n_1, n_7, n_6, n_2, n_4, n_5$. Recalling that the statement assigning X_i creates node n_i and that the list L corresponds to the statements in reverse, we obtain the block $\mathcal{B}_3 = (P_3, \{A, B, C\}, \{X_3, X_7\})$. It is easy to check that $\mathcal{B}_2 \overset{*}{\underset{4}{\longleftrightarrow}} \mathcal{B}_3$. The list of statements in P_3 is

$$X_5 \longleftarrow B - C$$
$$X_4 \longleftarrow A - C$$
$$X_2 \longleftarrow A - B$$

$$X_6 \longleftarrow X_2 * X_4$$
$$X_7 \longleftarrow X_6 * X_5$$
$$X_1 \longleftarrow A + B$$
$$X_3 \longleftarrow X_1 * X_2$$

The assembly language programs obtained from $\mathfrak{B}_2$ and $\mathfrak{B}_3$ are shown in Fig. 11.5. □

LOAD	A	LOAD	B
ADD	B	SUBTR	C
STORE	X_1	STORE	X_5
LOAD	A	LOAD	A
SUBTR	B	SUBTR	C
STORE	X_2	STORE	X_4
LOAD	X_1	LOAD	A
MULT	X_2	SUBTR	B
STORE	X_3	STORE	X_2
LOAD	A	MULT	X_4
SUBTR	C	MULT	X_5
STORE	X_4	STORE	X_7
LOAD	B	LOAD	A
SUBTR	C	ADD	B
STORE	X_5	MULT	X_2
LOAD	X_2	STORE	X_3
MULT	X_4		
MULT	X_5		
STORE	X_7		
(a) From $\mathfrak{B}_2$		(b) From $\mathfrak{B}_3$	

Fig. 11.5   Assembly language programs.

11.1.6. Algebraic Transformations

In many programming languages certain algebraic laws are known to hold among some operators and operands. These algebraic laws can often be used to reduce the cost of a program in a manner which would not be possible using only the four topological transformations hitherto considered. Some useful, common algebraic laws are the following:

(1) A binary operator θ is *commutative* if $\alpha\,\theta\,\beta = \beta\,\theta\,\alpha$ for all expressions α and β. Integer addition and multiplication are examples of commutative operators.†

---

†However, care must be exercised if the operands of a commutative operator are functions with side effects. For example, $f(x) + g(y)$ may not be equal to $g(y) + f(x)$ if the function f alters the value of y.

(2) A binary operator θ is *associative* if $\alpha \theta (\beta \theta \gamma) = (\alpha \theta \beta) \theta \gamma$ for all α, β, and γ. For example, addition is associative because

$$\alpha + (\beta + \gamma) = (\alpha + \beta) + \gamma.\dagger$$

(3) A binary operator θ_1 *distributes* over a binary operator θ_2 if $\alpha \theta_1 (\beta \theta_2 \gamma) = (\alpha \theta_1 \beta) \theta_2 (\alpha \theta_1 \gamma)$. For example, multiplication distributes over addition because $\alpha * (\beta + \gamma) = \alpha * \beta + \alpha * \gamma$. The same caveats as for (1) and (2) also apply here.

(4) A unary operator θ is a *self-inverse* if $\theta\theta\alpha = \alpha$ for all α. For example, Boolean **not** and unary minus are self-inverses.

(5) An expression ϵ is said to be an *identity* under a (binary) operator θ if $\epsilon \theta \alpha = \alpha \theta \epsilon = \alpha$ for all α. Some common examples of identity expressions are

    (a) The constant 0 is an identity under addition. So is any expression which has the value 0, such as $\alpha - \alpha$, $\alpha * 0$, $(-\alpha) + \alpha$, and so forth.

    (b) The constant 1 is a multiplicative identity.

    (c) The Boolean constant **true** is a conjunctive identity. (That is, α **and true** $= \alpha$ for all α).

    (d) The Boolean constant **false** is a disjunctive identity. (That is, α **or false** $= \alpha$ for all α).

If $\mathcal{Q}$ is a set of algebraic laws, we say that *expression α is equivalent to expression β under $\mathcal{Q}$*, written $\alpha \equiv_\mathcal{Q} \beta$, if α can be transformed into β using the algebraic laws in $\mathcal{Q}$.

Example 11.10

Suppose that we have the expression

$$A * (B * C) + (B * A) * D + A * E$$

Using the associative law of $*$ we can write $A * (B * C)$ as $(A * B) * C$. Using the commutative law for $*$, we can write $B * A$ as $A * B$. Then using the distributive law, we can write the entire expression as

$$(A * B) * (C + D) + A * E$$

Finally, applying the associative law to the first term and then the distributive law, we can write the expression as

$$A * (B * (C + D) + E)$$

---

†One must also use this transformation with care. For example, suppose x is very much larger than y, $z = -x$, and floating-point calculation is done. Then $(y + x) + z$ may give 0 as a result, while $y + (x + z)$ gives y as an answer.

Thus, this expression is equivalent to the original under the associative, commutative, and distributive laws for + and *. However, this final expression can be evaluated using two multiplications and two additions, while the original expression required five multiplications and two additions. ☐

We can extend the definition of equivalence under a set of algebraic laws $\mathfrak{A}$ to blocks. We say that *blocks $\mathfrak{B}_1$ and $\mathfrak{B}_2$ are equivalent under $\mathfrak{A}$*, written $\mathfrak{B}_1 \equiv_\mathfrak{a} \mathfrak{B}_2$, if for each expression α in $v(\mathfrak{B}_1)$ there is an expression β in $v(\mathfrak{B}_2)$ such that $\alpha \equiv_\mathfrak{a} \beta$, and conversely.

Each algebraic law induces a corresponding transformation on blocks (and dags).

Example 11.11

If + is commutative, then the transformation on blocks corresponding to this algebraic law would allow us to replace a statement of the form $X \leftarrow A + B$ in a block by the statement $X \leftarrow B + A$.

The associated transformation on dags would allow us to replace the structure

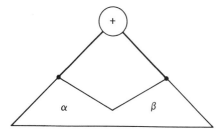

by the structure

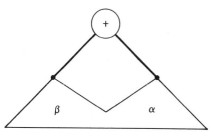

anywhere within a dag. ☐

Example 11.12

Let us consider the transformation on blocks corresponding to the associative law for +. Here we can replace a sequence of two statements of the form

$$X \longleftarrow B + C$$
$$Y \longleftarrow A + X$$

by the three statements

$$X \longleftarrow B + C$$
$$X' \longleftarrow A + B$$
$$Y \longleftarrow X' + C$$

where X' is a new variable. This transformation would have the following analog on dags:

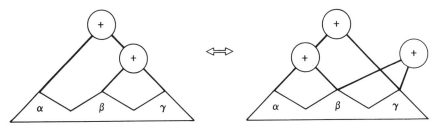

Note that we preserve the statement $X \longleftarrow B + C$, because the variable X may be referenced by some later statement. However, if the statement $X \longleftarrow B + C$ is useless after the transformation, then we may remove this statement using transformation T_1. If, in addition, the statement $X' \longleftarrow A + B$ can be removed by T_2, we have used the associative law to advantage. (See Exercise 11.1.17.)   □

Given a finite set of algebraic laws and the corresponding transformations on blocks, we would like to use these in conjunction with the four topological transformations of Section 11.1.2 on a given block to find an optimal equivalent block. Unfortunately, for a particular set of algebraic laws, there may be no effective way of applying these transformations to find an optimal block.

The approach usually taken is to apply algebraic transformations in limited ways, in the hopes of doing most of the possible "simplification" of expressions and of producing as many common subexpressions as possible. A typical scheme would uniformly replace $\beta \theta \alpha$ by $\alpha \theta \beta$ if θ were a commutative binary operator and α preceded β under some lexicographic ordering of variable names. If θ were an associative and commutative binary operator, then $\alpha_1 \theta \alpha_2 \theta \cdots \theta \alpha_n$ would be transformed by ordering the names $\alpha_1, \ldots, \alpha_n$ lexicographically and grouping from the left.

We conclude this section with an example that illustrates the possible effect of algebraic transformations on blocks.

Example 11.13

Consider the block $\mathcal{B} = (P, I, \{Y\})$, where $I = \{A, B, C, D, E, F\}$ and P is the following sequence of statements:

$$X_1 \leftarrow B - C$$
$$X_2 \leftarrow A * X_1$$
$$X_3 \leftarrow E * F$$
$$X_4 \leftarrow D * X_3$$
$$Y \leftarrow X_2 * X_4$$

$\mathcal{B}$ computes the expression

$$Y = (A * (B - C)) * (D * (E * F))$$

The dag for $\mathcal{B}$ is shown in Fig. 11.6.

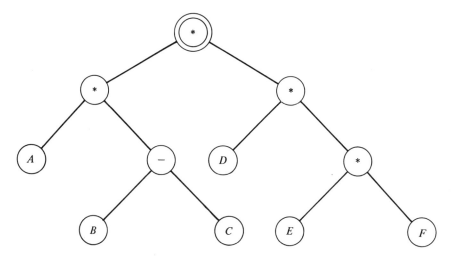

Fig. 11.6   Dag for $\mathcal{B}$.

Suppose that we wish to generate an assembly code program for $\mathcal{B}$ where we are using the assembly code and cost function of Example 11.9 (p. 863). If we generate assembly code directly from $\mathcal{B}$, the resulting assembly language program would have a cost of 15.

Now let us suppose that $*$ is a commutative and associative operator and that we wish to find an optimal block for $\mathcal{B}$ that is equivalent to $\mathcal{B}$ under the associative and commutative law for $*$. We shall apply to $\mathcal{B}$ the algebraic transformations corresponding to the two algebraic laws for $*$. Our goal in applying these transformations will be to try to obtain a sequence of statements in which intermediate results can be immediately used by the following instruction without being stored.

Assuming that $*$ is associative, in ⑥ we can replace the two statements

$$X_3 \longleftarrow E * F$$
$$X_4 \longleftarrow D * X_3$$

by the three statements

$$X_3 \longleftarrow E * F$$
$$X_3' \longleftarrow D * E$$
$$X_4 \longleftarrow X_3' * F$$

Now the statement $X_3 \longleftarrow E * F$ is useless and can be deleted by transformation T_1. Then using the associative transformation, we can replace the statements

$$X_4 \longleftarrow X_3' * F$$
$$Y \longleftarrow X_2 * X_4$$

by the statements

$$X_4 \longleftarrow X_3' * F$$
$$X_4' \longleftarrow X_2 * X_3'$$
$$Y \longleftarrow X_4' * F$$

The statement $X_4 \longleftarrow X_3' * F$ is now useless and can be deleted. At this point we have the statements

$$X_1 \longleftarrow B - C$$
$$X_2 \longleftarrow A * X_1$$
$$X_3' \longleftarrow D * E$$
$$X_4' \longleftarrow X_2 * X_3'$$
$$Y \longleftarrow X_4' * F$$

Now if we apply the associative transformation once more to the third and fourth statements, we obtain (after deleting the resulting useless statement) the block

$$X_1 \longleftarrow B - C$$
$$X_2 \longleftarrow A * X_1$$
$$X_3'' \longleftarrow X_2 * D$$

$$X'_4 \longleftarrow X''_3 * E$$
$$Y \longleftarrow X'_4 * F$$

Finally, if we assume that $*$ is commutative, we can permute the operands of the second statement to obtain the following block $\mathcal{B}'$:

$$X_1 \longleftarrow B - C$$
$$X_2 \longleftarrow X_1 * A$$
$$X''_3 \longleftarrow X_2 * D$$
$$X'_4 \longleftarrow X''_3 * E$$
$$Y \longleftarrow X'_4 * F$$

The dag for $\mathcal{B}'$ is shown in Fig. 11.7. $\mathcal{B}'$ has a cost of 7, the lowest possible cost for a block equivalent to $\mathcal{B}'$. In the next section we shall give a systematic method for optimizing arithmetic expressions using the associative and commutative algebraic laws. □

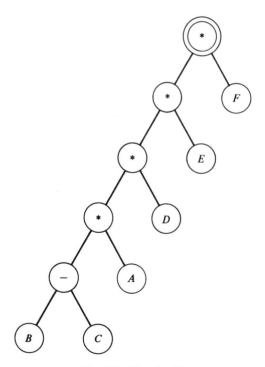

Fig. 11.7   Dag for $\mathcal{B}'$.

EXERCISES

11.1.1. Let $\mathcal{B} = (P, \{A, B, C\}, \{F, G\})$ be a block in which P is

$$T \longleftarrow A + B$$
$$R \longleftarrow A * T$$
$$S \longleftarrow B + C$$
$$F \longleftarrow R * S$$
$$T \longleftarrow A * A$$
$$R \longleftarrow A + B$$
$$S \longleftarrow A * R$$
$$G \longleftarrow S + T$$

(a) What is $v(\mathcal{B})$?

(b) Indicate the scope of each statement in P.

(c) Does P have any useless statements?

(d) Transformation T_2 is applicable to the first and sixth statements What values may D (as defined on p. 851) take in this application. of T_2?

(e) Draw a dag for $\mathcal{B}$.

(f) Find an equivalent reduced block for $\mathcal{B}$.

(g) How many different reduced blocks are equivalent to $\mathcal{B}$ except for renaming? (More technically, let $\mathcal{B}'$ be an open reduced block equivalent to $\mathcal{B}$. What is the cardinality of $\{\mathcal{B}'' \mid \mathcal{B}'' \overset{*}{\underset{4}{\Longleftrightarrow}} \mathcal{B}'\}$?)

(h) Find a block equivalent to $\mathcal{B}$ that is optimal according to the cost criterion of Example 11.9 (p. 863).

11.1.2. Prove that transformations T_1, T_3, and T_4 preserve block equivalence (that is, if $\mathcal{B} \underset{i}{\Longrightarrow} \mathcal{B}'$, then $v(\mathcal{B}) = v(\mathcal{B}')$ for $i = 1, 3$, and 4).

11.1.3. Show that in transformation T_2, as presented on p. 851, if D is any symbol not mentioned in P, then $v(\mathcal{B}) = v(\mathcal{B}')$.

*11.1.4. Give an algorithm to determine the set of permissible names for D in transformation T_2.

11.1.5. Prove that the algorithm following Example 11.3 removes all useless statements and input variables from a block. Show that the number of steps required to implement this algorithm is linearly proportional to the number of statements in a block.

*11.1.6. Devise an algorithm to remove all redundant computations (transformation T_2) from a block in time $0(n \log n)$, where n is the number of statements in the block.† (Note the similarity to minimizing finite state machines by Algorithm 2.6.)

---

†Do not forget that the set of possible names of variables is infinite. Thus, some bookkeeping techniques such as those mentioned in Section 10.1 must be used.

11.1.7. Devise an algorithm to compute the scope of a statement in a block.

11.1.8. Define the transformations on dags that are analogous to the transformations T_1–T_4 on blocks.

Exercises 11.1.9 and 11.1.10 show that if $\mathcal{B}_1 \overset{*}{\underset{1,2\ 3,4}{\longleftrightarrow}} \mathcal{B}_2$, then $\mathcal{B}_1 \overset{*}{\underset{1,2}{\longleftrightarrow}} \mathcal{B}_2$.

*11.1.9. Show that if $\mathcal{B}_1 \underset{3}{\Longrightarrow} \mathcal{B}_2$, then there is a block $\mathcal{B}_3$ such that $\mathcal{B}_3 \underset{2}{\Longrightarrow} \mathcal{B}_2$ and $\mathcal{B}_3 \underset{1}{\Longrightarrow} \mathcal{B}_1$. Thus, transformation T_3 can be implemented using one application of T_1 in reverse followed by one application of T_2.

*11.1.10. Show that if $\mathcal{B}_1 \underset{4}{\Longrightarrow} \mathcal{B}_2$, then there is a block $\mathcal{B}_3$ such that $\mathcal{B}_3 \underset{2}{\Longrightarrow} \mathcal{B}_2$ and $\mathcal{B}_3 \underset{1}{\Longrightarrow} \mathcal{B}_1$.

DEFINITION

A set S of transformations on blocks is *complete* if $v(\mathcal{B}_1) = v(\mathcal{B}_2)$ implies that $\mathcal{B}_1 \overset{*}{\underset{S}{\longleftrightarrow}} \mathcal{B}_2$. S is *minimal complete* if no proper subset of S is complete.

Exercises 11.1.9 and 11.1.10 show that $\{T_1, T_2\}$ is complete. The following two exercises show that $\{T_1, T_2\}$ is minimal complete.

*11.1.11. Show that block $\mathcal{B} = (P, \{A, B\}, \{C, D\})$ cannot be transformed into $\mathcal{B}' = (P', \{A, B\}, \{C, D\})$, where P and P' are as shown, using only transformations T_1, T_3, and T_4.

P	P'
$E \leftarrow A + B$	$C \leftarrow A + B$
$D \leftarrow E * E$	$D \leftarrow C * C$
$C \leftarrow A + B$	

Hence, $\{T_1, T_3, T_4\}$ is not complete, and so $\{T_1\}$ cannot be complete.

*11.1.12. Show that block $\mathcal{B} = (P, \{A, B\}, \{C\})$ cannot be transformed into $\mathcal{B}' = (P', \{A, B\}, \{C\})$ using only transformations T_2, T_3, and T_4, where P and P' are

P	P'
$C \leftarrow A * B$	$C \leftarrow A + B$
$C \leftarrow A + B$	

11.1.13. Provide an algorithm to determine whether two blocks are equivalent.

11.1.14. Let $P = S_1; S_2; \ldots; S_n$ be a sequence of assignment statements. Let I be a set of input variables. Give an algorithm to locate all undefined (referenced before being assigned) variables in P.

*11.1.15. Consider blocks as defined but also include statements of the form $A \leftarrow B$ with the obvious meaning. Find a complete set of transformations for such blocks.

**11.1.16. Assume that addition is commutative. Let T_5 be the transformation which replaces a statement $A \leftarrow B + C$ by $A \leftarrow C + B$. Show that T_5 together with transformations T_1 and T_2 transform two blocks into one another if and only if they are equivalent under the commutative law of addition.

**11.1.17. Assume that addition is associative. Let T_6 be the transformation which replaces two statements $X \leftarrow A + B$; $Y \leftarrow X + C$ by the three statements $X \leftarrow A + B$; $X' \leftarrow B + C$; $Y \leftarrow A + X'$ or the statements $X \leftarrow B + C$; $Y \leftarrow A + X$ by $X \leftarrow B + C$; $X' \leftarrow A + B$; $Y \leftarrow X' + C$, where X' is a new variable. Show that T_6, T_1, and T_2 transform two blocks into one another if and only if they are equivalent under the associative law of addition.

11.1.18. What is the transformation on blocks that corresponds to the distributive law of $*$ over $+$? What is the corresponding transformation on dags?

**11.1.19. Show that there exist sets of algebraic laws for which it is recursively undecidable whether two expressions are equivalent.

DEFINITION

An algebraic law is *operand-preserving* if no operands are created or destroyed by one application of the algebraic law. For example, the commutative and associative laws are operand-preserving but the distributive law is not.

An algebraic law is *operator-preserving* if the number of operators is not affected by one application of the law. The algebraic law $\theta\, \theta\, \alpha = \alpha$ (self-inverse) is not operator-preserving, but the law $(\alpha - \beta) - \gamma = \alpha - (\beta + \gamma)$ is.

The number of interior nodes and the number of leaves in the dag associated with a block are preserved when the transformations corresponding to operator- and operand-preserving algebraic laws are applied to the block.

*11.1.20. Show that under a set of operator- and operand-preserving algebraic laws it is decidable whether two blocks are equivalent.

**11.1.21. Extend Theorem 11.5 to apply to optimization of blocks using both the topological transformations of Section 11.1.2 and an arbitrary collection of operator- and operand-preserving algebraic transformations.

*11.1.22. Consider blocks in which variables can represent one-dimensional arrays. Let us consider assignment statements of the form

(1) $A(X) \leftarrow B$ and
(2) $B \leftarrow A(X)$,

where A is a one-dimensional array and B and X are scalars. If we have block in which each statement is of form (1) or (2) or $B \leftarrow \theta C_1 \cdots C_r$, where $B, C_1, \ldots, C_r$ are scalars, find some transformations that can be applied to these blocks making use of the fact that A is an array.

11.1.23. Prove Lemma 11.1.

11.1.24. Prove Lemma 11.2.

11.1.25. Complete the proof of Lemma 11.3.

11.1.26. Complete the proof of Lemma 11.4.

*11.1.27. Give an example of a cost criterion C such that if $\mathfrak{B}_1 \underset{1,2}{\Longrightarrow} \mathfrak{B}_2$, then $C(\mathfrak{B}_2) \leq C(\mathfrak{B}_1)$, yet not every block has an optimal block under C.

11.1.28. Prove Lemma 11.6.

11.1.29. Show that if $\mathfrak{B}_1$ is open and $\mathfrak{B}_1 \underset{3}{\Longrightarrow} \mathfrak{B}_2 \underset{4}{\Longrightarrow} \mathfrak{B}_3$, then there is a block $\mathfrak{B}$ such that $\mathfrak{B}_1 \underset{4}{\Longrightarrow} \mathfrak{B} \underset{3}{\Longrightarrow} \mathfrak{B}_3$.

11.1.30. Prove Lemma 11.7. *Hint:* Use Exercise 11.1.29.

*11.1.31. Suppose that we have a machine with N registers such that operations can be done with any or all arguments in registers, the result appearing in any designated register. Show that the output values of a block can be computed on such a machine with no store instructions (the results appearing in registers) if and only if that block has an equivalent block in which no more than N variable names appear in the instructions.

*11.1.32. Show that if T_1 and T_2 are applied to a given block $\mathfrak{B}$ in any order until a reduced block is obtained, then a unique block (up to renaming) results.

Research Problems

11.1.33. Using the cost criterion of Example 11.9, or some other interesting cost criterion, find a fast algorithm to find an optimal block equivalent to a given one.

11.1.34. Find a collection of algebraic transformations that is useful in optimizing a large class of programs. Devise efficient techniques for applying these transformations.

Programming Exercises

11.1.35. Using a suitable representation for dags, implement transformations T_1 and T_2 of this section.

11.1.36. Implement the heuristic suggested in Example 11.9 to "optimize" code for a one-accumulator machine.

BIBLIOGRAPHIC NOTES

The presentation in this section follows Aho and Ullman [1972e]. Igarishi [1968] discusses transformations on similar blocks with $A \leftarrow B$ statements permitted and names of output variables considered important. DeBakker [1971] considers blocks in which all statements are of the form $A \leftarrow B$. Bracha [1972] treats straight line blocks with foward jumps.

Richardson [1968] proved that no algorithm to "simplify" expressions exists when the expressions are taken to be over quite simple operators. The answer to Exercise 11.1.19 can be found in his article. Caviness [1970] also treats classes of algebraic laws for which equivalence of blocks is undecidable.

Floyd [1961a] and Breuer [1969] have considered algorithms to find common subexpressions in straight-line blocks when certain algebraic laws pertain. Aho and Ullman [1972f] discuss the equivalence of blocks with structured variables as in Exercise 11.1.22. Some techniques useful for Exercise 11.1.32 can be found in Aho, Sethi, and Ullman [1972].

11.2. ARITHMETIC EXPRESSIONS

Let us now turn our attention to the design of a code generator which produces assembly language code for blocks. The input to the code generator is a block consisting of a sequence of assignment statements. The output is an equivalent assembly language program.

We would like the resulting assembly language program to be good under some cost function such as number of assembly language instructions or number of memory fetches. Unfortunately, as mentioned in the last section, there is no efficient algorithm known that will produce optimal assembly code, even for the simple "one-accumulator" machine of Example 11.9.

In this section we shall provide an efficient algorithm for generating assembly code for a restricted class of blocks—those that represent one expression with no identical operands. For this class of blocks our algorithm will generate assembly language code that is optimal under a variety of cost criteria, including program length and number of accumulators used.

While the assumption of no identical operands is certainly not realistic, it is often a good first-order approximation. Moreover, if we are to generate code using a syntax directed translation with synthesized attributes only, the assumption is quite convenient. Finally, experience has shown that the problem of generating optimal code for expressions with even one pair of identical operands is extremely difficult in comparison.

A block representing one expression has only one output variable. For example, the assignment statement $F = Z * (X + Y)$ can be represented by the block $\mathcal{B} = (P, \{X, Y, Z\}, \{F\})$, where P is

$$R \longleftarrow X + Y$$
$$F \longleftarrow Z * R$$

The restriction that the assignment involve an expression with no identical operands is equivalent to requiring that the dag for the expression be a tree.

For convenience we shall assume that all operators are binary. This restriction is not serious, since it is straightforward to generalize the results of this section to expressions involving arbitrary operators.

We shall generate assembly code for a machine having N accumulators, where $N \geq 1$. The cost criterion will be the length of the assembly language program (i.e., the number of instructions). The algorithm is then extended to take advantage of operators which we know are commutative or associative.

11.2.1. The Machine Model

We consider a computer with $N \geq 1$ general-purpose accumulators and four types of instructions.

DEFINITION

An *assembly language instruction* is a string of symbols of one of the following four types:

LOAD M, A

STORE A, M

OP θ A, M, B

OP θ A, B, C

In these instructions, M is a memory location and A, B, and C are accumulator names (possibly the same). OP θ is the operation code for the binary operator θ. We assume that each operator θ has a corresponding machine instruction of type (3) and (4).

These instructions perform the following actions:

(1) LOAD M, A places the contents of memory location M into accumulator A.

(2) STORE A, M places the contents of accumulator A into memory location M.

(3) OP θ A, M, B applies the binary operator θ to the contents of accumulator A and memory location M and places the result in accumulator B.

(4) OP θ A, B, C applies the binary operator θ to the contents of accumulators A and B and stores the result in accumulator C.

If there is but one accumulator, this set of instructions reduces to that in

Example 11.9, except for type (4) instructions, which become OP θ A, A, A. The algorithm we have in mind does not take advantage of such an instruction, and so for these purposes, our instruction set can be thought of as a generalization of one-address, single-accumulator instructions.

An *assembly language program* (program for short) is a sequence of assembly language instructions.

If $P = I_1; I_2; \ldots; I_n$ is a program, we can define the *value of register R after instruction t*, denoted $v_t(R)$, as follows. (A *register* is either an accumulator or a memory location.)

(1) $v_0(R) = R$ if R is a memory location and is undefined if R is an accumulator.

(2) Let I_t be LOAD M, A. Then $v_t(A) = v_{t-1}(M)$.

(3) Let I_t be STORE A, M. Then $v_t(M) = v_{t-1}(A)$.

(4) Let I_t be OP θ A, R, C. Then $v_t(C) = \theta\, v_{t-1}(A)\, v_{t-1}(R)$. Note that R may be an accumulator or a memory location.

(5) If $v_t(R)$ is not defined by (2)–(4) but $v_{t-1}(R)$ has been defined, then $v_t(R) = v_{t-1}(R)$. Otherwise, $v_t(R)$ is undefined.

Thus, values are computed exactly as one would expect. LOAD's and STORE's move values from one register to another, leaving them also in the original register. Operations place the computed value in the accumulator designated by the third argument, leaving other registers unchanged in value. We say that a program P *computes* expression α, leaving the result in accumulator A, if after the last statement of P, accumulator A has the value α.

Example 11.14

Consider the following assembly language program with two accumulators A and B. The values of the accumulators after each instruction are shown beside each instruction in infix notation, as usual.

	$v(A)$	$v(B)$
LOAD X, A	X	Undefined
ADD A, Y, A	$X + Y$	Undefined
LOAD Z, B	$X + Y$	Z
MULT B, A, A	$Z * (X + Y)$	Z

The value of accumulator A at the end of the program corresponds to the (infix) expression $Z * (X + Y)$. Thus, this program computes $Z * (X + Y)$, leaving the result in accumulator A. (Technically, the expression Z is also computed.)   □

In this section we shall formally define an (arithmetic) *syntax tree* as a labeled binary tree T having one or more nodes such that

(1) Each interior node is labeled by a binary operator θ in Θ, and
(2) Each leaf is labeled by a distinct variable name X in Σ.

For convenience we assume that Θ and Σ are disjoint. Figure 11.8 shows the tree for $Z * (X + Y)$.

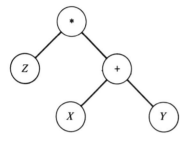

Fig. 11.8   Tree for $Z * (X + Y)$.

We can assign *values* to the nodes of a tree from the bottom as follows:

(1) If node n is a leaf labeled X, then n has value X.
(2) If n is an interior node labeled θ with direct descendants n_1 and n_2 whose values are v_1 and v_2, then n has value $\theta v_1 v_2$.

The *value of a tree* is the value of its root. For example, the value of the tree in Fig. 11.8 is $Z * (X + Y)$ in infix notation.

Let us briefly discuss the relation between the intermediate language blocks of Section 11.1 and the assembly language programs we have just defined. First, given a reduced block in which

(1) All operators are binary,
(2) Each input variable is referenced once, and
(3) There is exactly one output variable,

the dag associated with the block will be a tree. This tree is a syntax tree in our current terminology. The value of the expression is also the value of the block.

We can naturally convert the intermediate language block to an assembly language program, statement by statement. It turns out that if this conversion takes account of the possibility that desired values are already in accumulators, then we can produce an optimal assembly program from a given reduced open block using only transformation T_4, as suggested by Theorem 11.5, and then performing conversion to assembly language.

However, it may not be entirely obvious that the above is true; the reader should verify these facts for himself. What we achieve by essentially reworking many of the definitions of Section 11.1 for assembly language programs is to show that there is no strange optimal assembly language program which is not related by any natural statement-by-statement conversion to an intermediate language block obtainable from a reduced open block and transformation T_4.

11.2.2. The Labeling of Trees

Fundamental to our algorithm for generating code for expressions is a method of attaching additional labels to the nodes of a syntax tree. These labels are integers, and we shall subsequently refer to them as the labels of nodes, even though each node is also labeled by an operator or variable. The integer label determines the number of accumulators needed to evaluate an expression optimally.

ALGORITHM 11.1

Labeling of syntax trees.

Input. A syntax tree T.

Output. A labeled syntax tree.

Method. We assign integer labels to the nodes of T recursively from the bottom as follows:

(1) If a node is a leaf and either the left direct descendant of its direct ancestor, or a root (i.e., the tree consists of this one node), label this node 1; if it is a leaf and the right direct descendant, label it 0.

(2) Let node n have direct descendants n_1 and n_2 with labels l_1 and l_2. If $l_1 \neq l_2$, let the label of n be the larger of l_1 and l_2. If $l_1 = l_2$, let the label of n be one greater than l_1.   □

Example 11.15

The arithmetic expression $A * (B - C)/(D * (E - F))$ is expressed in tree form in Fig. 11.9. The integer labels are shown.   □

The following algorithm converts a labeled syntax tree into an assembly language program for a machine with N accumulators. We shall show that for each N the program produced is optimal under a variety of cost criteria, including program length.

ALGORITHM 11.2

Assembly code for expressions.

Input. A labeled syntax tree T and N accumulators $A_1, A_2, \ldots, A_N$ for some $N \geq 1$.

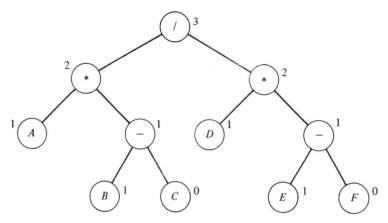

Fig. 11.9 Labeled syntax tree.

Output. An assembly language program P such that $v(A_1)$ after the last instruction of P is $v(T)$; i.e., P computes the expression represented by T, leaving the result in accumulator A_1.

Method. We assume that T has been labeled using Algorithm 11.1. We then execute the following procedure **code**(n, i) recursively. The input to **code** is a node n of T and an integer i between 1 and N. The integer i means that accumulators $A_i, A_{i+1}, \ldots, A_N$ are currently available to compute the expression for node n. The output of **code**(n, i) is a sequence of assembly language instructions which computes the value $v(n)$, leaving the result in accumulator A_i.

Initially we execute **code**$(n_0, 1)$, where n_0 is the root of T. The sequence of instructions generated by this call of the procedure **code** is the desired assembly language program.

Procedure **code**(n, i).

We assume that n is a node of T and that i is an integer between 1 and N.

(1) If node n is a leaf, do step (2). Otherwise, do step (3).

(2) If **code**(n, i) is called and n is a leaf, then n will always be a left direct descendant (or the root if n is the only node in the tree). If leaf n has variable name X associated with it, then

$$\text{code}(n, i) = \text{‘LOAD } X, A_i\text{’}$$

[meaning that the output of **code**(n, i) is the instruction LOAD X, A_i]. End.

(3) We reach this point only if n is an interior node. Let n have operator θ associated with it and direct descendants n_1 and n_2 with labels l_1 and l_2

as shown:

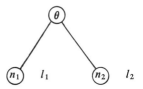

The next step is determined by the values of labels l_1 and l_2:
    (a) If $l_2 = 0$ (node n_2 is a right leaf), then do step (4).
    (b) If $1 \leq l_1 < l_2$ and $l_1 < N$, then do step (5).
    (c) If $1 \leq l_2 \leq l_1$ and $l_2 < N$, then do step (6).
    (d) If $N \leq l_1$ and $N \leq l_2$, then do step (7).

(4) $\mathbf{code}(n, i) = \mathbf{code}(n_1, i)$

                           'OP θ A_i, X, A_i'

Here X is the variable associated with leaf n_2, and OP θ is the operation code for operation θ. The output of $\mathbf{code}(n, i)$ is the output of $\mathbf{code}(n_1, i)$ followed by the instruction OP θ A_i, X, A_i.

(5) $\mathbf{code}(n, i) = \mathbf{code}(n_2, i)$
                          $\mathbf{code}(n_1, i + 1)$
                          'OP θ A_{i+1}, A_i, A_i'

(6) $\mathbf{code}(n, i) = \mathbf{code}(n_1, i)$
                          $\mathbf{code}(n_2, i + 1)$
                          'OP θ A_i, A_{i+1}, A_i'

(7) $\mathbf{code}(n, i) = \mathbf{code}(n_2, i)$
                          $T \longleftarrow \mathbf{newtemp}$
                          'STORE A_i, T'
                          $\mathbf{code}(n_1, i)$
                          'OP θ A_i, T, A_i'

Here $\mathbf{newtemp}$ is a function which whenever invoked produces a new temporary memory location for storing intermediate results.   ☐

    Later we shall show that the following relationships between l_1, l_2, and i hold when steps (5), (6), and (7) of Algorithm 11.2 are invoked:

Step	Relation
(5)	$i \leq N - l_1$
(6)	$i \leq N - l_2$
(7)	$i = 1$

Note also that Algorithm 11.2 requires instructions of type (4) of the form

$$\text{OP } \theta \quad A, B, A$$
$$\text{OP } \theta \quad A, B, B$$

By making the procedure **code** slightly more complicated in step (5), we can eliminate the need for instructions of the form

$$\text{OP } \theta \quad A, B, B$$

which is not part of the instruction repertoire of some multiregister machines. (See Exercise 11.2.11.)

We can view **code**(n, i) as a function which computes a translation at each node of an expression in terms of the translations and labels of the direct descendants of the node. To get acquainted with Algorithm 11.2, let us consider several examples.

Example 11.16

Let T be the syntax tree consisting of the single node X (labeled 1). From step (2) **code** is the single instruction LOAD X, A_1. □

Example 11.17

Let T be the labeled syntax tree in Fig. 11.10. The assembly language program for T using Algorithm 11.2 with $N = 2$ is produced as follows. The following sequence of calls of **code**(n, i) is generated. We also show the step of Algorithm 11.2 which is invoked during each call. Here, we indicate a node by the variable or operator associated with it.

Call	Step of Algorithm 11.2
code$(*, 1)$	(3c)
code$(Z, 1)$	(2)
code$(+, 2)$	(3a)
code$(X, 2)$	(2)

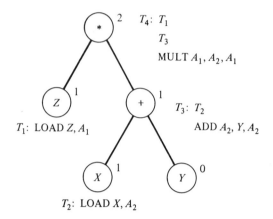

Fig. 11.10   Labeled syntax tree with translations.

The call **code**(X, 2) generates the instruction LOAD X, A_2, which is the translation associated with node X. The call **code**($+$, 2) generates the instruction sequence

$$\text{LOAD} \quad X, A_2$$
$$\text{ADD} \quad A_2, Y, A_2$$

which is the translation for node $+$.

The call **code**(Z, 1) generates the instruction LOAD Z, A_1, the translation for node Z. The call **code**($*$, 1) generates the final program which is the translation for the root:

$$\text{LOAD} \quad Z, A_1$$
$$\text{LOAD} \quad X, A_2$$
$$\text{ADD} \quad A_2, Y, A_2$$
$$\text{MULT} \quad A_1, A_2, A_1$$

This program is similar (but not identical) to that in Example 11.14. The value in accumulator A_1 at the end of this program is clearly $Z * (X + Y)$.   □

Example 11.18

Let us apply Algorithm 11.2 with $N = 2$ to the syntax tree in Fig. 11.9 (p. 883). The following sequence of calls of **code**(n, i) is generated. Here $*_L$ refers to the left descendant of $/$, $*_R$ to the right descendant of $/$, $-_L$ to the right descendant of $*_L$, and $-_R$ to the right descendant of $*_R$. The step of Algorithm 11.2 which is applicable during each call is also shown.

Call	Step
code(/, 1)	(3d)
code(∗$_R$, 1)	(3c)
code(D, 1)	(2)
code(−$_R$, 2)	(3a)
code(E, 2)	(2)
code(∗$_L$, 1)	(3c)
code(A, 1)	(2)
code(−$_L$, 2)	(3a)
code(B, 2)	(2)

The following program is generated by **code**(/, 1):

$$\text{LOAD} \quad D, A_1$$

$$\text{LOAD} \quad E, A_2$$

$$\text{SUBTR} \quad A_2, F, A_2$$

$$\text{MULT} \quad A_1, A_2, A_1$$

$$\text{STORE} \quad A_1, \text{TEMP1}$$

$$\text{LOAD} \quad A, A_1$$

$$\text{LOAD} \quad B, A_2$$

$$\text{SUBTR} \quad A_2, C, A_2$$

$$\text{MULT} \quad A_1, A_2, A_1$$

$$\text{DIV} \quad A_1, \text{TEMP1}, A_1$$

Here TEMP1 is a memory location generated by **newtemp**.   ☐

We shall prove that the label of the root of the labeled syntax tree produced by Algorithm 11.1 is the smallest number of accumulators needed to compute that expression without using any STORE instructions.

We begin by making several observations about Algorithm 11.2.

LEMMA 11.8

The program produced by procedure **code**(n, i) in Algorithm 11.2 correctly computes the value of node n, leaving that value in the ith accumulator.

Proof. An elementary induction on the height of a node.   ☐

LEMMA 11.9

If Algorithm 11.2, with N accumulators available, is applied to the root of a syntax tree, then when procedure **code**(n, i) is called on node n with label l either

(1) $l \geq N$ and N accumulators are available for this call (i.e., $i = 1$), or
(2) $l < N$ and at least l accumulators are available for this call (i.e., $i \leq N - l + 1$).

Proof. Another elementary induction, this time on the number of calls of **code**(n, i) made prior to the call in question. □

THEOREM 11.6

Let T be a syntax tree and let N be the number of available accumulators. Let l be the label of the root of T. Then there exists a program to compute T which uses no STORE instructions if and only if $l \leq N$.

Proof.

If: If $l \leq N$, then step (7) of procedure **code**(n, i) is never executed. That is, a node whose two direct descendants have labels equal to or greater than N has a label at least $N + 1$ itself. Step (7) is the only step which generates a STORE instruction. Therefore, if $l \leq N$, the program constructed by Algorithm 11.2 has no STORE's.

Only if: Assume that $l > N$. Since $N \geq 1$, we must have $l \geq 2$. Suppose that the conclusion is false. Then we may assume without loss of generality that T has a program P which computes it using N accumulators, that P has no STORE statements, and that there is no syntax tree T' which has fewer nodes than T and also violates the conclusion. Since the label of the root of T exceeds 1, T cannot be a single leaf. Let n be the root and let n_1 and n_2 be its direct descendants, with labels l_1 and l_2, respectively.

Case 1: $l_1 = l$. The only way the value of n can be computed is for the value of n_1 to appear at some time in an accumulator, since n_1 cannot be a leaf. We form a new program P' from P by deleting those statements following the computation of the value of n_1. Then P' computes the subtree with root n_1 and has no STORE's. Thus, a violation with fewer nodes than T occurs, contrary to our assumption about T.

Case 2: $l_2 = l$. This case is similar to case 1.

Case 3: $l_1 = l_2 = l - 1$. We have assumed that no two leaves have the same associated variable name. We can assume without loss of generality that P is "as short as possible," in the sense that if any statement were deleted, the value of n would no longer appear in the same accumulator at the end of P. Thus, the first statement of P must be LOAD X, A, where X is the variable name associated with some leaf of T, for any other first statement could be deleted.

Let us assume that X is the value of a leaf which is a descendant of n_1 (possibly n_1 itself). The case in which X is a value of a descendant of n_2 is symmetric and will be omitted. Then until n_1 is computed, there is always at least one accumulator which holds a value involving X. This value could not be used in a correct computation of the value of n_2. We may conclude that from P we can find a program P' which computes the value of n_2, with label $l - 1$, which uses no STORE's and no more than $N - 1$ accumulators at any time. We leave it to the reader to show that from P' we can find an equivalent P'' which never mentions more than $N - 1$ different accumulators. (Note that P' may mention all N accumulators, even though it is not "using" more than $N - 1$ at any time.) Thus, the subtree of n_2 forms a smaller violation of our conditions, contradicting the minimality of T. We conclude that no violation can occur. $\quad\square$

11.2.3. Programs with STORE's

We shall now consider how many LOAD's and STORE's are needed to compute a syntax tree using N accumulators when the root has a label greater than N. The following definitions are useful.

DEFINITION

Let T be a syntax tree and let N be the number of available accumulators. A node of T is *major* if each of its direct descendants has a label equal to or greater than N. A node is *minor* if it is a leaf and the left direct descendant of its direct ancestor (i.e., a leaf with label 1).

Example 11.19

Consider the syntax tree of Fig. 11.9 (p. 883) again, with $N = 2$. The only major node is the root. There are four minor nodes, the leaves with values A, B, D, and E. $\quad\square$

LEMMA 11.10

Let T be a syntax tree. There exists a program to compute T using m LOAD's if and only if T has no more than m minor nodes.

Proof. If we examine procedure **code**(n, i) of Algorithm 11.2, we find that only step (2) introduces a LOAD statement. Since step (2) applies only to minor nodes, the "if" portion is immediate.

The "only if" portion is proved by an argument similar to that of Theorem 11.6, making use of the facts that the only way the value of a leaf can appear in an accumulator is for it to be "LOADed" and that the left argument of any operator must be in an accumulator. $\quad\square$

LEMMA 11.11

Let T be a syntax tree. There exists a program P to compute T using M STORE's if and only if T has no more than M major nodes.

Proof.

If: Again referring to procedure **code**(n, i), only step (7) introduces a STORE, and it applies only to major nodes.

Only if: This portion is by induction on the number of nodes in T. The basis, a tree with one node, is trivial, as the label of the root is 1, and there are thus no major nodes. Assume the result for syntax trees of up to $k - 1$ nodes, and let T have k nodes.

Consider a program P which computes T, and let M be the number of major nodes of T. We can assume without loss of generality that P has as few STORE's as any program computing T. If $M = 0$, the desired result is immediate, and so assume that $M \geq 1$. Then P has at least one STORE, because the label of a major node is at least $N + 1$, and if no STORE's were present in P, a violation of Theorem 11.6 would occur.

The value stored by the first STORE instruction of P must be the value of some node n of T, or else a program with fewer STORE's than P but computing T could easily be found. Moreover, we may assume that n is not a leaf for the same reason. Let T' be the syntax tree formed from T by making node n a leaf and giving it some new name X as value. Then T' has fewer nodes than T, and so the inductive hypothesis applies to it. We can find a program P' which evaluates T' using exactly one fewer STORE than P. P' is constructed from P by deleting exactly those statements needed to compute the first value stored and replacing subsequent references in P to the location used for that STORE by the name X until a new value is stored there.

If we can show that T' has at least $M - 1$ major nodes, we are done, since by the inductive hypothesis, we can then conclude that P' has at least $M - 1$ STORE's and thus that P has at least M STORE's.

We observe that no descendant of n in T can be major, since a violation of Theorem 11.6 would occur. Consider a major node n' of T. If n is not a descendant of n', then n' will be a major node in T'. Thus, it suffices to consider those major nodes $n_1, n_2, \ldots$ on the path from n to the root of T. By the argument of case 3 of Theorem 11.6, n cannot itself be major. The first node, n_1, if it exists, may no longer be major in T'. However, the label of n_1 in T' is at least N, because the direct descendant of n_1 that is not an ancestor of n must have a label at least N in T and T'. Thus, $n_2, n_3, \ldots$ are still major nodes in T'. We conclude that T' has at least $M - 1$ major nodes. The induction is now complete. $\square$

THEOREM 11.7

Algorithm 11.2 always produces a shortest-length program to compute a given expression.

Proof. By Lemmas 11.10 and 11.11, Algorithm 11.2 generates a program with the fewest LOAD's and STORE's possible. Since the minimum number of operation instructions is clearly equal to the number of interior nodes of the tree and Algorithm 11.2 yields one such instruction for each interior node, the theorem follows.   □

Example 11.20

As pointed out in Example 11.19, the arithmetic expression of Fig. 11.9 has one major and four minor nodes (assuming that $N = 2$). It also has five interior nodes. Thus, at least ten statements are necessary to compute it. The program of Example 11.18 has ten statements. Note that one of these is STORE, four are LOAD's, and the rest operations.   □

11.2.4. Effect of Some Algebraic Laws

We can define *the cost of a syntax tree* as the sum of

(1) The number of interior nodes,
(2) The number of major nodes, and
(3) The number of minor nodes.

The results of the previous section indicate that this cost is a reasonable measure of the "complexity" of a syntax tree, in that the number of instructions needed to compute a syntax tree is equal to the cost of the tree.

Often, algebraic laws may apply to certain operators, and making use of these identities can reduce the cost of a given syntax tree. From Section 11.1.6 we know that each algebraic law induces a corresponding transformation on syntax trees. For example, if n is an interior node of a syntax tree associated with a commutative operator, then the commutative transformation reverses the order of the direct descendants of n.

Likewise if θ is an associative operator [i.e., $\alpha\,\theta\,(\beta\,\theta\,\gamma) = (\alpha\,\theta\,\beta)\,\theta\,\gamma$], then using the corresponding associative transformation on trees we can transform two syntax trees as shown in Fig. 11.11. The associative transformation depicted in Fig. 11.11 corresponds to the transformation

$$\begin{matrix} X \longleftarrow B\,\theta\,C \\ Y \longleftarrow A\,\theta\,X \end{matrix} \quad \underset{\longrightarrow}{\longleftarrow} \quad \begin{matrix} X' \longleftarrow A\,\theta\,B \\ Y \longleftarrow X'\,\theta\,C \end{matrix}$$

on blocks. In Section 11.1.6 we retained the statement $X \longleftarrow B\,\theta\,C$ after the transformation from left to right. However, in our present discussion this statement will always be useless after the transformation, and so it can be safely removed without changing the value of the block.

DEFINITION

Given a set $\mathcal{A}$ of algebraic laws, we say that two syntax trees T_1 and T_2 are *equivalent under* $\mathcal{A}$, written $T_1 \equiv_{\mathcal{A}} T_2$, if there exists a sequence of transformations derived from these laws which will transform T_1 into T_2. We shall write $[T]_{\mathcal{A}}$ to denote the equivalence class of trees $\{T' \mid T \equiv_{\mathcal{A}} T'\}$.

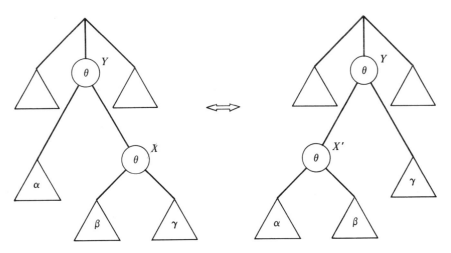

Fig. 11.11   Associative transformation on syntax trees.

Thus, if we are given a syntax tree T and we know that a certain set $\mathfrak{a}$ of algebraic laws prevails, then to find an optimal program for T we might want to search $[T]_{\mathfrak{a}}$ for an expression tree with the minimum cost. Once we have found a minimum cost tree, we can apply Algorithm 11.2 to find the optimal program. Theorem 11.7 guarantees that the resulting program will be optimal.

If each law preserves the number of operators, as do the commutative and associative laws, then we need only minimize the sum of major and minor nodes. As an example, we shall give algorithms to do this minimization, first in the case that some operators are commutative and second in the case that some commutative operators are also associative.

Given a syntax tree T and a set $\mathfrak{a}$ of algebraic laws, the next algorithm will find a syntax tree T' in $[T]_{\mathfrak{a}}$ of minimal cost provided that $\mathfrak{a}$ contains only commutative laws applying to certain operators. Algorithm 11.2 can then be applied to T' to find the optimal program for the original tree T.

ALGORITHM 11.3

Minimal cost syntax tree assuming some commutative operators.

Input. A syntax tree T (with three or more nodes) and a set of commutative laws $\mathfrak{a}$.

Output. A syntax tree in $[T]_{\mathfrak{a}}$ of minimal cost.

Method. The heart of the algorithm is a recursive procedure **commute**(n) which takes a node n of the syntax tree as argument and returns as output a modified subtree with node n as root. Initially, **commute**(n_0) is called, where n_0 is the root of the given tree T.

Procedure **commute(*n*)**.

(1) If node *n* is a leaf, **commute(*n*)** = *n*.
(2) If node *n* is an interior node, there are two cases to consider:
    (a) Suppose that node *n* has two direct descendants n_1 and n_2 (in this order) and that the operator attached to *n* is commutative. If n_1 is a leaf and n_2 is not, then the output of **commute(*n*)** is the tree of Fig. 11.12(a).
    (b) In all other cases the output of **commute(*n*)** is the tree of Fig. 11.12(b). ☐

Example 11.21

Consider Fig. 11.9 (p. 883) and assume only * is commutative. Then the result of applying Algorithm 11.3 to that tree is shown in Fig. 11.13. Note that the label of the root of Fig. 11.13 is 2 and that there are two minor nodes.

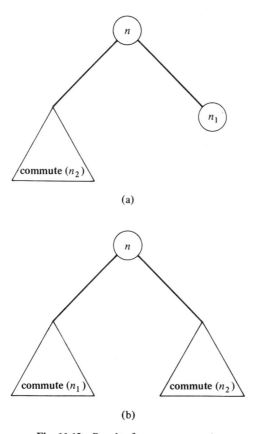

(a)

(b)

Fig. 11.12 Result of **commute** procedure.

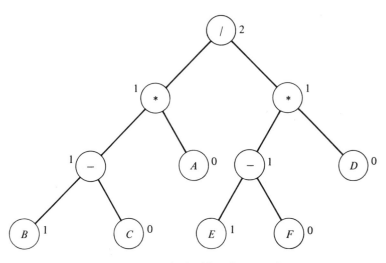

Fig. 11.13   Revised arithmetic expression.

Thus, if two accumulators are available, only seven statements are needed to compute this tree, compared with ten for Fig. 11.9.   ☐

THEOREM 11.8

If the only algebraic law permitted is the commutative law of certain operators, then Algorithm 11.3 produces that syntax tree in the equivalence class of the given tree with the least cost.

Proof. It is easy to see that the commutative law cannot change the number of interior nodes. A simple induction on the height of a node shows that Algorithm 11.3 minimizes the number of minor nodes and the label that would be associated with each node after applying Algorithm 11.1. Hence, the number of major nodes is also minimized.   ☐

The situation is more complex when certain operators are both commutative and associative. In this case we can often transform the tree extensively to reduce the number of major nodes.

DEFINITION

Let T be a syntax tree. A set S of two or more nodes of T is a *cluster* if

(1) Each node of S is an interior node with the same associative and commutative operator.

(2) The nodes of S, together with their connecting edges, form a tree.

(3) No proper superset of S has properties (1) and (2).

The *root of the cluster* is the root of the tree formed as in (2) above. The *direct descendants* of a cluster S are those nodes of T which are not in S but are direct descendants of a node in S.

Example 11.22

Consider the syntax tree of Fig. 11.14, where $+$ and $*$ are considered associative and commutative, while no other algebraic laws pertain.

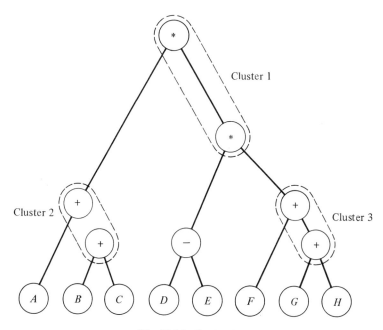

Fig. 11.14   Syntax tree.

The three clusters are circled. The cluster which includes the root of the tree has as direct descendants, in order from the left, the root of cluster 2, the node to which the $-$ operator is attached, and the root of cluster 3. ☐

We observe that the clusters in a syntax tree T can be uniquely found and that the clusters are disjoint. To find a tree of minimal cost in $[T]_\alpha$, when α contains laws reflecting that some operators are associative and commutative while others may be only commutative, the concept of an associative tree, which condenses clusters into a single node, is introduced.

DEFINITION

Let T be a syntax tree. Then T', the *associative tree* for T, is formed by replacing each cluster S of T by a single node n having the same associative and commutative operator as the nodes of the cluster S. The direct descendants of the cluster in T are made direct descendants of n in T'.

Example 11.23

Consider the syntax tree T in Fig. 11.15. Assuming that $+$ and $*$ are both associative and commutative, we obtain the clusters which are circled in Fig. 11.15. The associative tree for T is shown in Fig. 11.16. Note that the associative tree is not necessarily a binary tree. □

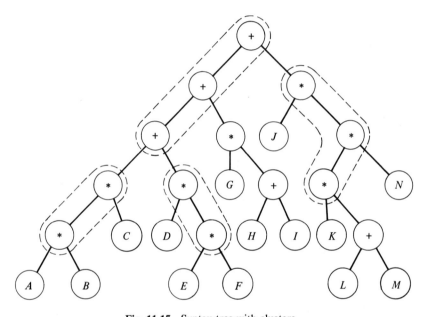

Fig. 11.15   Syntax tree with clusters.

We can *label* the nodes of an associative tree with integers from the bottom up as follows:

(1) A leaf which is the leftmost direct descendant of its ancestor is labeled 1. All other leaves are labeled 0.

(2) Let n be an interior node having nodes $n_1, n_2, \ldots, n_m$ with labels $l_1, l_2, \ldots, l_m$ as direct descendants, $m \geq 2$.

   (a) If one of $l_1, l_2, \ldots, l_m$ is larger than the others, let that integer be the label of node n.

   (b) If node n has a commutative operator and n_i is an interior node with $l_i = 1$ and the rest of $n_1, \ldots, n_{i-1}, n_{i+1}, \ldots, n_m$ are leaves, then label node n by 1.

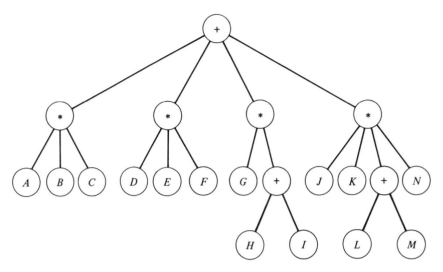

Fig. 11.16 Associative tree.

(c) Provided that (b) does not apply, if $l_i = l_j$ for some $i \neq j$ and l_i is greater than or equal to all other l_k's, let the label of node n be $l_i + 1$.

Example 11.24

Consider the associative tree in Fig. 11.16. The labeled associative tree is shown in Fig. 11.17.

Note that condition (2b) of the labeling procedure applies to the third and fourth direct descendants of the root, since $*$ is a commutative operator. $\square$

We now give an algorithm which takes a given syntax tree and produces that tree in its equivalence class with the smallest cost.

ALGORITHM 11.4

Minimal cost syntax tree, assuming that certain operators are commutative and that certain operators are both associative and commutative but that no other algebraic laws pertain.

Input. A syntax tree T and a set $\mathcal{C}$ of commutative and associative-commutative laws.

Output. A syntax tree in $[T]_\mathcal{C}$ of minimal cost.

Method. First create T', the labeled associative tree for T. Then compute **acommute**(n_0), where **acommute** is the procedure defined below and n_0 is

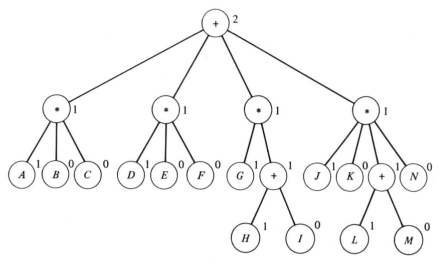

Fig. 11.17 Labeled associative tree.

the root of T'. The output of **acommute**(n_0) is a syntax tree in $[T]_\alpha$ of minimal cost.

Procedure **acommute**(n).

The argument n is a node of the labeled associative tree. If n is a leaf, **acommute**(n) is n itself. If n is an interior node, there are three cases to consider:

(1) Suppose that node n has two direct descendants n_1 and n_2 (in this order) and that the operator attached to n is commutative (and possibly associative).

  (a) If n_1 is a leaf and n_2 is not, then the output **acommute**(n) is the tree of Fig. 11.18(a).

  (b) Otherwise, **acommute**(n) is the tree of Fig. 11.18(b).

(2) Suppose that θ, the operator attached to n, is commutative and associative and that n has direct descendants $n_1, n_2, \ldots, n_m, m \geq 3$, in order from the left.

Let $n_{\max}$ be a node among $n_1, \ldots, n_m$ having the largest label. If two or more nodes have the same largest label, then choose $n_{\max}$ be be an interior node. Let $p_1, p_2, \ldots, p_{m-1}$ be, in any order, the remaining nodes in $\{n_1, \ldots, n_m\} - \{n_{\max}\}$.

Then the output of **acommute**(n) is the binary tree of Fig. 11.19, where each r_i, $1 \leq i \leq m - 1$, is a new node with the associative and commutative operator θ of n attached.

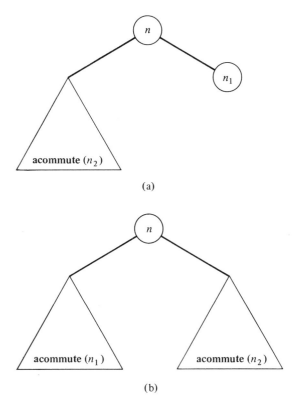

(a)

(b)

Fig. 11.18   Result of **acommute** procedure.

(3) If the operator attached to n is neither commutative nor associative, then the output of **acommute**(n) is as in Fig. 11.18(b).   ☐

Example 11.25

Let us apply Algorithm 11.4 to the labeled associative tree in Fig. 11.17. Applying **acommute** to the root, case (2) applies, and we choose to treat the first direct descendant from the left as n_{max}. The binary tree which is the output of Algorithm 11.4 is shown in Fig. 11.20.   ☐

We shall conclude this section by proving that Algorithm 11.4 finds a tree in $[T]_\alpha$ with the least cost. The following lemma is central to the proof.

LEMMA 11.12

Let T be a labeled syntax tree and S a cluster of T. Suppose that r of the direct descendants of S have labels $\geq N$, where N is the number of accumulators. Then at least $r - 1$ of the nodes of S are major.

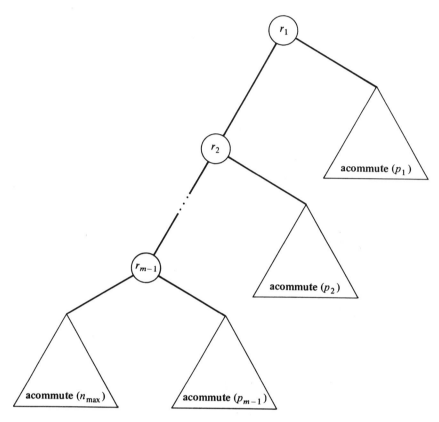

Fig. 11.19   Result of **acommute** procedure.

Proof. We prove the result by induction on the number of nodes in T. The basis, one node, is trivial. Thus, assume that the result is true for all trees with fewer nodes than T. Let node n be the root of S and let n have direct descendants n_1 and n_2 with labels l_1 and l_2. Let T_1 and T_2 be the names of the subtrees with roots n_1 and n_2, respectively.

Case 1: Neither n_1 nor n_2 is in S. Then the result is trivially true.

Case 2: n_1 is in S, but n_2 is not. Since T_1 has fewer nodes than T, the inductive hypothesis applies to it. Thus, in T_1, $S - \{n\}$ has at least $r - 2$ major nodes if $l_2 \geq N$ and at least $r - 1$ major nodes if $l_2 < N$. In the latter case, the conclusion is trivial. In both cases, the result is trivial if $r \leq 1$. Thus, consider the case $r > 1$ and $l_2 \geq N$. Then $S - \{n\}$ has at least one direct descendant with label $\geq N$, so $l_1 \geq N$. Thus, n is a major node, and S contains at least $r - 1$ major nodes.

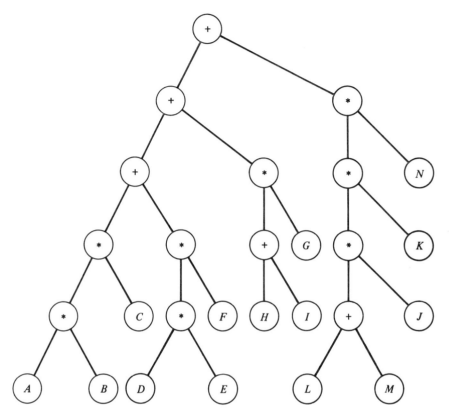

Fig. 11.20   Output of Algorithm 11.4.

Case 3: n_2 is in S, but n_1 is not. This case is similar to case 2.

Case 4: Both n_1 and n_2 are in S. Let r_1 of the direct descendants of S with labels at least N be descendants of n_1 and r_2 of them be descendants of n_2. Then $r_1 + r_2 = r$. By the inductive hypothesis, the portions of S in T_1 and T_2 have, respectively, at least $r_1 - 1$ and at least $r_2 - 1$ major nodes. If neither r_1 nor r_2 is zero, then $l_1 \geq N$ and $l_2 \geq N$, and so n is major. Thus, S has at least $(r_1 - 1) + (r_2 - 1) + 1 = r - 1$ major nodes. If $r_1 = 0$, then $r_2 = r$, and so the portion of S in T_2 has at least $r - 1$ major nodes. The case $r_2 = 0$ is analogous. $\square$

THEOREM 11.9

Algorithm 11.4 produces a tree in $[T]_a$, that has the least cost.

Proof. A straightforward induction on the number of nodes in an associative tree A shows that the result of applying procedure **acommute** to its root is a syntax tree T whose root after applying the labeling Algorithm 11.1 has the same label as the root of A. No tree in $[T]_\alpha$ has a root with label smaller than the label of the root of A, and no tree in $[T]_\alpha$ has fewer major or minor nodes.

Suppose otherwise. Then let T be a smallest tree violating one of those conditions. Let θ be the operator at the root of T.

Case 1: θ is neither associative nor commutative. Every associative or commutative transformation on T must take place wholly within the subtree dominated by one of the two direct descendants of the root of T. Thus, whether the violation is on the label, the number of major nodes, or the number of minor nodes, the same violation must occur in one of these subtrees, contradicting the minimality of T.

Case 2: θ is commutative but not associative. This case is similar to case 1, except that now the commutative transformation may be applied to the root. Since step (1) of procedure **acommute** takes full advantage of this transformation, any violation by T again implies a violation in one of its subtrees.

Case 3: θ is commutative and associative. Let S be the cluster containing the root. We may assume that no violation occurs in any of the subtrees whose roots are the direct descendants of S. Any application of an associative or commutative transformation must take place wholly within one of these subtrees, or wholly within S. Inspection of the result of step (2) of procedure **acommute** assures us that the number of minor nodes resulting from cluster S is minimized. By Lemma 11.12, the number of major nodes resulting from S is as small as possible (inspection of the result of procedure **acommute** is necessary to see this), and hence the label of the root is as small as possible.

Finally we observe that the alterations made by Algorithm 11.4 can always be accomplished by applications of the associative and commutative transformations. $\quad\square$

EXERCISES

11.2.1. Assuming that no algebraic laws prevail, find an optimal assembly program with the number of accumulators $N = 1, 2$, and 3 for each of the following expressions:
(a) $A - B * C - D * (E + F)$.
(b) $A + (B + (C * (D + E / F + G) * H)) + (I + J)$.
(c) $(A * (B - C)) * (D * (E * F)) + ((G + (H + I)) + (J + (K + L)))$.
Determine the cost of each program found.

11.2.2. Repeat Exercise 11.2.1 assuming that $+$ and $*$ are commutative.

11.2.3. Repeat Exercise 11.2.1 assuming that $+$ and $*$ are both associative and commutative.

11.2.4. Let E be a binary expression with k operators. What is the maximum number of parentheses required to express E without using any unnecessary parentheses?

*11.2.5. Let T be a binary syntax tree whose root is labeled $N \geq 2$ after applying Algorithm 11.1. Show that T contains at least $3 \times 2^{N-2} - 1$ interior nodes.

11.2.6. Let T be a binary expression tree with k interior nodes. Show that T can have at most k minor nodes.

*11.2.7. Given $N \geq 2$, show that a tree with M major nodes has at least $3(M + 1)2^{N-2} - 1$ interior nodes.

*11.2.8. What is the maximum cost of a binary syntax tree with k nodes?

*11.2.9. What is the maximum saving in the cost of a binary syntax tree of k nodes in going from a machine with N accumulators to one with $N + 1$ accumulators?

**11.2.10. Let $\mathcal{C}$ be an arbitrary set of algebraic identities. Is it decidable whether two binary syntax trees are equivalent under $\mathcal{C}$?

11.2.11. For Algorithm 11.2 define the procedure **code**$(n, [i_1, i_2, \ldots, i_k])$ to compute the value of node n with accumulators $A_{i_1}, A_{i_2}, \ldots, A_{i_k}$, leaving the result in accumulator A_{i_1}. Show that by making step (5) to be

$$\mathbf{code}(n, [i_1, i_2, \ldots, i_k]) =$$
$$\mathbf{code}(n_2, [i_2, i_1, i_3, \ldots, i_k])$$
$$\mathbf{code}(n_1, [i_1, i_3, i_4, \ldots, i_k])$$
$$\text{`OP } \theta \quad A_{i_1}, A_{i_2}, A_{i_1} \text{'}$$

Algorithm 11.2 can be modified so that assembly language instructions of types (3) and (4) are only of the form

$$\text{OP } \theta \quad A, B, A$$

11.2.12. Let

$$\mathbf{sign}(a, b) = \begin{cases} |a| & \text{if } b > 0 \\ 0 & \text{if } b = 0 \\ -|a| & \text{if } b < 0 \end{cases}$$

Show that **sign** is associative but not commutative. Give examples of other operators which are associative but not commutative.

*11.2.13. The instructions

$$\text{LOAD} \quad M, A$$
$$\text{STORE} \quad A, M$$
$$\text{OP } \theta \quad A, M, B$$

each use one memory reference. If B is an accumulator, then OP θ A, B, C uses none. Find the minimum number of storage references generated by a program that computes a binary syntax tree with k nodes.

*11.2.14. Show that Algorithm 11.2 produces a program which requires the fewest number of memory references to compute a given expression.

*11.2.15. Taking G_0 as the underlying grammar, construct a syntax-directed translation scheme which translates infix expressions into optimal assembly language programs, assuming N accumulators and that

(a) No algebraic identities hold,
(b) $+$ and $*$ are commutative, and
(c) $+$ and $*$ are associative and commutative.

11.2.16. Give algorithms to implement the procedures **code, commute,** and **acommute** in linear time.

*11.2.17. Certain operators may require extra accumulators (e.g., subroutine calls or multiple precision arithmetic). Modify Algorithms 11.1 and 11.2 to take into account the possible need for extra accumulators by operators.

11.2.18. Algorithms 11.1–11.4 can also be applied to arbitrary binary dags if we first convert a dag into a tree by duplicating nodes. Show that now Algorithm 11.2 will not always generate an optimal program. Estimate how bad Algorithm 11.2 can be under these conditions.

11.2.19. Generalize Algorithms 11.1–11.4 to work on expressions involving operators with arbitrary numbers of arguments.

*11.2.20. Arithmetic expressions can have unary $+$ and unary $-$ operators. Construct an algorithm to generate optimal code for arithmetic expressions with unary $+$ and $-$. [Assume that all operands are distinct and that the usual algebraic laws relating unary $+$ and $-$ to the four binary arithmetic operators apply.]

*11.2.21. Construct an algorithm to generate optimal code for a single arithmetic expression in which each operand is a distinct variable or an integer constant. Assume the associative and commutative laws for $+$ and $*$ as well as the following identities:

(1) $\alpha + 0 = 0 + \alpha = 0$.
(2) $\alpha * 1 = 1 * \alpha = \alpha$.
(3) $c_1 \theta c_2 = c_3$, where c_3 is the integer that is the result of applying the operator θ to integers c_1 and c_2.

11.2.22. Find an algorithm to generate optimal code for a single Boolean expression in which each operand is a distinct variable or a Boolean constant (0 or 1). Assume that Boolean expressions involve the operators **and, or,** and **not** and that these operators satisfy the laws of Boolean algebra. (See p. 23 of Volume I.)

**11.2.23. In certain situations two or more operations can be executed in parallel. The algorithms in Sections 11.1 and 11.2 assume serial execution. However, if we have a machine capable of performing parallel operations, then we might attempt to arrange the order of execution to create as many simultaneous parallel computations as possible. For example, suppose that we have a four-register machine in which four operators can be simultaneously executed. Then the expression $A_1 + A_2 + A_3 + A_4 + A_5 + A_6 + A_7 + A_8$ can be done as shown in Fig. 11.21. In the first step we would load A_1 into the first register,

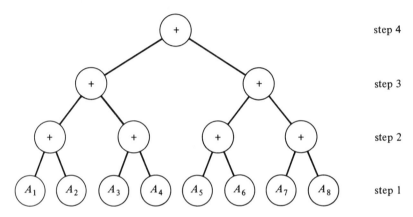

Fig. 11.21   Tree for parallel computation.

A_3 into the second, A_5 into the third, and A_7 into the fourth. In the second step we would add A_2 to register 1, A_4 to register 2, A_6 to register 3, and A_8 to register 4. After this step register 1 would contain $A_1 + A_2$, register 2 would contain $A_3 + A_4$, and so forth. At the third step we would add register 2 to register 1 and register 4 to register 3. At the fourth step we would add register 2 to register 1. Define an N-register machine in which up to N parallel operations can be executed in one step. Assuming this machine, modify Algorithm 11.1 to generate optimal code (in the sense of fewest steps) for single arithmetic expressions with distinct operands.

Research Problem

11.2.24. Find an efficient algorithm that will generate optimal code of the type mentioned in this section for an arbitrary block.

Programming Exercise

11.2.25. Write programs to implement Algorithms 11.1–11.4.

BIBLIOGRAPHIC NOTES

Many papers have been written on the generation of good code for arithmetic expressions for a specific machine or class of machines. Floyd [1961a] discusses a number of optimizations involving arithmetic expressions including detection of common subexpressions. He also suggested that the second operand of a noncommutative binary operator be evaluated first. Anderson [1964] gives an algorithm for generating code for a one-register machine that is essentially the same as the code produced by Algorithm 11.1 when $N = 1$. Nakata [1967] and Meyers [1965] give similar results.

The number of registers required to compute an expression tree has been investigated by Nakata [1967], Redziejowski [1969], and Sethi and Ullman [1970]. Algorithms 11.1–11.4 as presented here were developed by Sethi and Ullman [1970]. Exercise 11.2.11 was suggested by P. Stockhausen. Beatty [1972] and Frailey [1970] discuss extensions involving the unary minus operator. An extension of Algorithm 11.2 to certain dags was made by Chen [1972].

There are no known efficient algorithms for generating optimal code for arbitrary expressions. One heuristic technique for making register assignments in a sequence of expression evaluations is to use the following algorithm.

Suppose that expression α is to be computed next and its value stored in a fast register (accumulator).

(1) If the value of α is already stored in some register i, then do not recompute α. Register i is now "in use."

(2) If the value of α is not in any register, store the value of α in the next unused register, say register j. Register j is now in use. If there is no unused register available, store the contents of some register k in main memory, and store the value of α in register k. Choose register k to be that register whose value will be unreferenced for the longest time.

Belady [1966] has shown that this algorithm is optimal in some situations. However, the model assumed by this algorithm (which was designed for paging) does not exactly model straight line code. In particlar, it assumes the order of computation to be fixed, while as we have seen in Sections 11.1 and 11.2, there is often much advantage to be had by reordering computations.

A similar register allocation problem is discussed by Horwitz et al. [1966]. They assume that we are given a sequence of operations which reference and change values. The problem is to assign these values to fast registers so that the number of loads and stores from the fast registers to main memory is minimized. Their solution is to select a least-cost path in a dag of possible solutions. Techniques for reducing the size of the dag are given. Further investigation of register allocation where order of computation is not fixed has been done by Kennedy [1972] and Sethi [1972].

Translating arithmetic expressions into code for parallel computers is discussed by Allard et al. [1964], Hellerman [1966], Stone [1967], and Baer and Bovet [1968].

The general problem of assigning tasks optimally to parallel processors is very difficult. Some interesting aspects of this problem are discussed by Graham [1972].

11.3. PROGRAMS WITH LOOPS

When we consider programs that contain loops, it becomes literally impossible to mechanically optimize such programs. Most of the difficulty stems from undecidability results. Given two arbitrary programs there is no algorithm to determine whether they are equivalent in any worthwhile sense. As a consequence there is no algorithm which will find an optimal program equivalent to given program under an arbitrary cost criterion.

These results are understandable when we realize that, in general, there are arbitrarily many ways to compute the same function. Thus, there is an infinity of algorithms that can be used to implement the function defined by the source program. If we want true optimization, a compiler would have to determine the most efficient algorithm for the function computed by the source program, and then it would have to generate the most efficient code for this algorithm. Needless to say, from both a theoretical and a practical point of view, optimizing compilers of this nature do not exist.

However, in many situations there are a number of transformations that can be applied to a program to reduce the size and/or increase the speed of the resulting object language program. In this section we shall investigate several such transformations. Through popular usage, transformations of this nature have become known as "optimizing" transformations. A more accurate term would be "code-improving" transformations. However, we shall bow to tradition and use the more popular, but less accurate term "optimizing transformation" for the remainder of this book. Our primary goal will be to reduce the running time of the object language program.

We begin by defining intermediate programs with loops. These programs will be very primitive, so that we can present the essential concepts without going into a tremendous amount of detail. Then we define a flow graph for a program. The flow graph is a two-dimensional representation of a program that displays the flow of control between the basic blocks of a program. A two-dimensional structure usually gives a more accurate representation of a program than a linear sequence of statements.

In the remainder of this section we shall describe some important transformations that can be applied to a program in an attempt to reduce the running time of the object program. In the next section we shall look at ways of collecting the information needed to apply some of the transformations presented in this section.

11.3.1. The Program Model

We shall use a representation for programs that is intermediate between source language and assembly language. A program consists of a sequence of statements. Each statement may be labeled by an identifier followed by a colon. There will be five basic types of statements: assignment, goto, conditional, input–output, and halt.

(1) An *assignment statement* is a string of the form $A \leftarrow \theta\, B_1 \cdots B_r$, where A is a variable, $B_1, \ldots, B_r$ are variables or constants, and θ is an r-ary operator. As in the previous sections, we shall usually use infix notation for binary operators. We also allow a statement of the form $A \leftarrow B$ in this category.

(2) A *goto statement* is a string of the form

$$\textbf{goto} \ \langle \text{label} \rangle$$

where $\langle\text{label}\rangle$ is a string of letters. We shall assume that if a goto statement is used in a program, then the label following the word **goto** appears as the label of a unique statement in the program.

(3) A *conditional statement* is of the form

$$\textbf{if } A \ \langle\text{relation}\rangle \ B \textbf{ goto } \langle\text{label}\rangle$$

where A and B are variables or constants and $\langle\text{relation}\rangle$ is a binary relation such as $<$, $\leq$, $=$, and $\neq$.

(4) An *input–output statement* is either a *read statement* of the form

$$\textbf{read} \quad A$$

where A is a variable, or a *write statement* of the form

$$\textbf{write} \quad B$$

where B is a variable or a constant. For convenience we shall use the statement

$$\textbf{read} \quad A_1, A_2, \ldots, A_n$$

to denote the sequence of statements

$$\textbf{read} \quad A_1$$
$$\textbf{read} \quad A_2$$
$$\vdots$$
$$\textbf{read} \quad A_n$$

We shall use a similar convention for write statements.

(5) Finally, a *halt statement* is the instruction **halt**.

The intuitive meaning of each type of statement should be evident. For example, a conditional statement of the form

$$\text{if } A \ r \ B \text{ goto } L$$

means that if the relation r holds between the current values of A and B, then control is to be transferred to statement labeled L. Otherwise, control passes to the following statement.

A *definition statement* (or *definition* for short) is a statement of the form **read** A or of the form $A \leftarrow \theta B_1 \cdots B_r$. Both statements are said to *define* the variable A.

We shall make some further assumptions about programs. Variables are simple variables, e.g., $A, B, C, \ldots$, or simple variables indexed by one simple variable or constant, e.g., $A(1)$, $A(2)$, $A(I)$, or $A(J)$. Further, we shall assume that all variables referenced in a program must be either input variables (i.e., appear in a previous read statement) or have been previously defined by an assignment statement. Finally, we shall assume that each program has at least one halt statement and that if a program terminates, then the last statement executed is a halt statement.

Execution of a program begins with the first statement of the program and continues until a halt statement is encountered. We suppose that each variable is of known type (e.g., integer, real) and that its *value* at any time during the execution is either undefined or is a quantity of the appropriate type. (It will be assumed that all operators used are appropriate to the types of the variables to which they apply and that conversion of types occurs when appropriate.)

In general the input variables of a program are those variables associated with read statements and the output variables are the variables associated with write statements. An assignment of a value to each input variable each time it is read is called an *input setting*. The *value of a program* under an input setting is the sequence of values written by the output variables during the execution of the program. We say that two programs are *equivalent* if for each input setting the two programs have the same value.†

This definition of equivalence is a generalization of the definition of equivalent blocks used in Section 11.1. To see this, suppose that two blocks $\mathscr{B}_1 = (P_1, I_1, U_1)$ and $\mathscr{B}_2 = (P_2, I_2, U_2)$ are equivalent in the sense of Section 11.1. We convert $\mathscr{B}_1$ and $\mathscr{B}_2$ into programs $\mathcal{P}_1$ and $\mathcal{P}_2$ in the obvious way

---

†We are assuming that the meaning of each operator and relational symbol, as well as the data type of each variable, is established. Thus, our notion of equivalence differs from that of the schematologists (see for example, Paterson [1968] or Luckham et al. [1970]), in that they require two programs to give the same value not only for each input setting, but for each data type for the variables and for each set of functions and relations that we substitute for the operators and relational symbols.

That is, we place read statements for the variables in I_1 and I_2 in front of P_1 and P_2, respectively, and place write statements for the variables in U_1 and U_2 after P_1 and P_2. Then we append a halt statement to each program. However, we must add the write statements to P_1 and P_2 in such a fashion that each output variable is printed at least once and that the sequences of values printed will be the same for both $\mathcal{P}_1$ and $\mathcal{P}_2$. Since $\mathcal{B}_1$ is equivalent to $\mathcal{B}_2$, we can always do this.

The programs $\mathcal{P}_1$ and $\mathcal{P}_2$ are easily seen to be equivalent no matter what the space of input settings is and no matter what interpretation is placed on the functions represented by the operators appearing in $\mathcal{P}_1$ and $\mathcal{P}_2$. For example, we could choose the set of prefix expressions for the input space and interpret an application of operator θ to expressions $\epsilon_1, \ldots, \epsilon_r$ to yield $\theta\epsilon_1 \cdots \epsilon_r$.

However, if $\mathcal{B}_1$ and $\mathcal{B}_2$ are not equivalent and $\mathcal{P}_1$ and $\mathcal{P}_2$ are programs that correspond to $\mathcal{B}_1$ and $\mathcal{B}_2$, respectively, then there will always be a set of data types for the variables and interpretations for the operators that causes $\mathcal{P}_1$ and $\mathcal{P}_2$ to produce different output sequences. In particular, let the variables have prefix expressions as a "type" and let the effect of operator θ on prefix expressions $\epsilon_1, \epsilon_2, \ldots, \epsilon_k$ be the prefix expression $\theta\epsilon_1\epsilon_2 \cdots \epsilon_k$.

Of course, we may make assumptions about data types and the algebra connected with the function and relation symbols that will cause $\mathcal{P}_1$ and $\mathcal{P}_2$ to be equivalent. In that case $\mathcal{B}_1$ and $\mathcal{B}_2$ will be equivalent under the corresponding set of algebraic laws.

Example 11.26

Consider the following program for the Euclidean algorithm described on p. 26 (Volume I). The output is to be the greatest common divisor of two positive integers p and q.

$$
\begin{array}{ll}
& \textbf{read} \quad p \\
& \textbf{read} \quad q \\
loop: & r \longleftarrow \textbf{remainder}(p, q) \\
& \textbf{if} \quad r = 0 \ \textbf{goto} \ done \\
& p \longleftarrow q \\
& q \longleftarrow r \\
& \textbf{goto} \ loop \\
done: & \textbf{write} \quad q \\
& \textbf{halt}
\end{array}
$$

If, for example, we assign the input variables p and q the values 72 and 56, respectively, then the output variable q in the write statement will have value

8 when that statement is executed with the normal interpretation of the operators. Thus, the value of this program for the input setting $p \leftarrow 72$, $q \leftarrow 56$ is the "sequence" 8 which is generated by the output variable q.

If we replace the statement **goto** *loop* by **if** $q \neq 0$ **goto** *loop*, we have an equivalent program. This follows because the statement **goto** *loop* cannot be reached unless the fourth statement finds $r \neq 0$. Since q is given the value of r at the sixth statement, it is not possible that $q = 0$ when the seventh statement is executed. ☐

It should be observed that the transformations which we may apply are to a large extent determined by the algebraic laws which we assume hold.

Example 11.27

For some types of data we might assume that $a * a = 0$ if and only if $a = 0$. If we assume such a law, then the following program is equivalent to the one in Example 11.26:

$$
\begin{array}{ll}
 & \textbf{read} \quad p \\
 & \textbf{read} \quad q \\
loop: & r \longleftarrow \textbf{remainder}(p, q) \\
 & t \longleftarrow r * r \\
 & \textbf{if} \quad t = 0 \quad \textbf{goto} \quad done \\
 & p \longleftarrow q \\
 & q \longleftarrow r \\
 & \textbf{goto} \quad loop \\
done: & \textbf{write} \quad q \\
 & \textbf{halt}
\end{array}
$$

Of course, this program would not be more desirable in any circumstance we can think of. However, without the law stated above, this program and the one in Example 11.26 might not be equivalent. ☐

Given a program P, our goal is to find an equivalent program P' such that the expected running time of the machine language version of P' is less than that of the machine language version of P. A reasonable approximation of this goal is to find an equivalent program P'' such that the expected number of machine language instructions to be executed by P'' is less than the number of instructions executed by P. The latter goal is an approximation in that not every machine instruction requires the same amount of machine time to be executed. For example, an operation such as multiplication or division usually requires more time than an addition or subtraction. However, initially we shall concentrate on reducing the number of machine language instructions that need to be executed.

Most programs contain certain sequences of statements which are executed considerably more often than the remaining statements in the program. Knuth [1971] found that in a large sample of FORTRAN programs, a typical program spent over one-half of its execution time in less than 4% of the program. Thus, in practice it is often sufficient to apply the optimization procedures only to these heavily traveled regions of a program. Part of the optimization may involve moving statements from heavily traveled regions to lightly traveled ones even though the actual number of statements in the program itself remains the same or even increases.

We can often deduce what the most frequently executed parts of a source program will be and pass this information along to the optimizing compiler along with the source program. In other cases it is relatively easy to write a routine that will count the number of times a given statement in a program is executed as the program is run. With these counts we can obtain the "frequency profile" of a program to determine those parts of the program in which we should concentrate our optimization effort.

11.3.2. Flow Analysis

Our first step in optimizing a program is to determine the flow of control within the program. To do this, we partition a program into groups of statements such that no transfer occurs into a group except to the first statement in that group, and once the first statement is executed, all statements in the group are executed sequentially. We shall call such a group of statements a *basic block*, or *block* if no confusion with the term "block" in the sense of Section 11.1 arises.

DEFINITION

A statement S in a program P is a *basic block entry* if

(1) S is the first statement in P, or

(2) S is labeled by an identifier which appears after **goto** in a goto or conditional statement, or

(3) S is a statement immediately following a conditional statement.

The *basic block belonging to a block entry* S consists of S and all statements following S

(1) Up to and including a halt statement or

(2) Up to but not including the next block entry.

Notice that the program constructed from a block in the sense of Section 11.1 will be a basic block in the sense of this section.

Example 11.28

Consider the program of Example 11.26. There are four block entries, namely the first statement in the program, the statement labeled *loop*, the assignment statement $p \leftarrow q$, and the statement labeled *done*.

Thus, there are four basic blocks in the program. These blocks are given below:

Block 1		**read** p
		read q
Block 2	*loop*:	$r \longleftarrow$ **remainder**(p, q)
		if $r = 0$ **goto** *done*
Block 3		$p \longleftarrow q$
		$q \longleftarrow r$
		goto *loop*
Block 4	*done*:	**write** q
		halt

From the blocks of a program we can construct a graph that resembles the familiar flow chart for the program.

DEFINITION

A *flow graph* is a labeled directed graph G containing a distinguished node n such that every node in G is accessible from n. Node n is called the *begin node*.

A *flow graph of a program* is a flow graph in which each node of the graph corresponds to a block of the program. Suppose that nodes i and j of the flow graph correspond to blocks i and j of the program. Then an edge is drawn from node i to node j if

(1) The last statement in block i is not a goto or halt statement and block j follows block i in the program, or

(2) The last statement in block i is **goto** L or **if** $\cdots$ **goto** L and L is the label of the first statement of block j.

The node corresponding to the block containing the first statement of the program is the begin node.

Clearly, any block that is not accessible from the begin node can be removed from a given program without changing its value. From now on we shall assume that all such blocks have been removed from each program under consideration.

Example 11.29

The flow graph for the program of Example 11.26 is given in Fig. 11.22. Block 1 is the begin node.   □

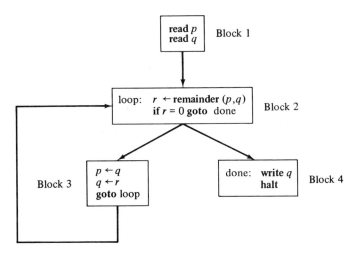

Fig. 11.22   Flow graph.

Many optimizing transformations on programs require knowing the places in a program at which a variable is defined and where that definition is subsequently referenced. These definition–reference relationships are determined by the sequences of blocks that can actually be executed. The first block in such a sequence is the begin node, and each subsequent block must have an edge from the previous block. Sometimes the predicates used in the conditional statements may preclude some paths in the flow graph from being executed. However, there is no algorithm to detect all such situations, and we shall assume that no paths are precluded from execution.

It is also convenient to know for a block ℬ whether there is another block ℬ′ such that each time ℬ is executed, ℬ′ was previously executed. One application of this knowledge is that if the same value is computed in both ℬ and ℬ′, then we can store this value after it is computed in ℬ′ and thus avoid recomputing the same value in ℬ. We now develop these ideas formally.

DEFINITION

Let F be a flow graph whose blocks have names chosen from set Δ. A sequence of blocks $\mathcal{B}_1 \cdots \mathcal{B}_n$ in Δ^* is a *(block) computation path* of F if

(1) $\mathcal{B}_1$ is the begin node of F.

(2) For $1 < i \leq n$, there is an edge from block $\mathcal{B}_{i-1}$ to $\mathcal{B}_i$.

In other words, a computation path $\mathfrak{B}_1 \cdots \mathfrak{B}_n$ is a path from $\mathfrak{B}_1$ to $\mathfrak{B}_n$ in F such that $\mathfrak{B}_1$ is the begin node.

We say that block $\mathfrak{B}'$ *dominates* $\mathfrak{B}$ if $\mathfrak{B}' \neq \mathfrak{B}$ and every path from the begin node to $\mathfrak{B}$ contains $\mathfrak{B}'$. We say that $\mathfrak{B}'$ *directly dominates* $\mathfrak{B}$ if

(1) $\mathfrak{B}'$ dominates $\mathfrak{B}$, and
(2) If $\mathfrak{B}''$ dominates $\mathfrak{B}$ and $\mathfrak{B}'' \neq \mathfrak{B}'$, then $\mathfrak{B}''$ dominates $\mathfrak{B}'$.

Thus, block $\mathfrak{B}'$ directly dominates $\mathfrak{B}$ if $\mathfrak{B}'$ is the block "closest" to $\mathfrak{B}$ which dominates $\mathfrak{B}$.

Example 11.30

Referring to Fig. 11.22, the sequence 1232324 is a computation path. Block 1 directly dominates block 2 and dominates blocks 3 and 4. Block 2 directly dominates blocks 3 and 4.   □

Here are some algebraic properties of the dominance relation.

LEMMA 11.13

(1) If $\mathfrak{B}_1$ dominates $\mathfrak{B}_2$ and $\mathfrak{B}_2$ dominates $\mathfrak{B}_3$, then $\mathfrak{B}_1$ dominates $\mathfrak{B}_3$ (transitivity).
(2) If $\mathfrak{B}_1$ dominates $\mathfrak{B}_2$, then $\mathfrak{B}_2$ does not dominate $\mathfrak{B}_1$ (asymmetry).
(3) If $\mathfrak{B}_1$ and $\mathfrak{B}_2$ dominate $\mathfrak{B}_3$, then either $\mathfrak{B}_1$ dominates $\mathfrak{B}_2$ or conversely.

Proof. (1) and (2) are Exercises. We shall prove (3). Let $\mathfrak{C}_1 \cdots \mathfrak{C}_n \mathfrak{B}_3$ be any computation path with no cycles (i.e., $\mathfrak{C}_i \neq \mathfrak{B}_3$, and $\mathfrak{C}_i \neq \mathfrak{C}_j$ if $i \neq j$). One such path exists since we assume that all nodes are accessible from the begin node. By hypothesis, $\mathfrak{C}_i = \mathfrak{B}_1$ and $\mathfrak{C}_j = \mathfrak{B}_2$ for some i and j. Assume without loss of generality that $i < j$. Then we claim that $\mathfrak{B}_1$ dominates $\mathfrak{B}_2$.

In proof, suppose that $\mathfrak{B}_1$ did not dominate $\mathfrak{B}_2$. Then there is a computation path $\mathfrak{D}_1 \cdots \mathfrak{D}_m \mathfrak{B}_2$, where none of $\mathfrak{D}_1, \ldots, \mathfrak{D}_m$ are $\mathfrak{B}_1$. It follows that $\mathfrak{D}_1 \cdots \mathfrak{D}_m \mathfrak{B}_2 \mathfrak{C}_{j+1} \cdots \mathfrak{C}_n \mathfrak{B}_3$ is also a computation path. But none of the symbols preceding $\mathfrak{B}_3$ are $\mathfrak{B}_1$, contradicting the hypothesis that $\mathfrak{B}_1$ dominates $\mathfrak{B}_3$.   □

LEMMA 11.14

Every block except the begin node (which has no dominators), has a unique direct dominator.

Proof. Let $\mathfrak{S}$ be the set of blocks that dominate some block $\mathfrak{B}$. By Lemma 11.13 the dominance relation is a (strict) linear order on $\mathfrak{S}$. Thus, $\mathfrak{S}$ has a minimal element, which must be the direct dominator of $\mathfrak{B}$. (See Exercise 0.1.23.)

□

We now give an algorithm to compute the direct dominance relation for a flow graph.

ALGORITHM 11.5

Computation of direct dominance.

Input. A flow graph F with $\Delta = \{\mathcal{B}_1, \mathcal{B}_2, \ldots, \mathcal{B}_n\}$, the set of blocks in F. We assume that $\mathcal{B}_1$ is the begin node.

Output. DOM($\mathcal{B}$), the block that is the direct dominator of block $\mathcal{B}$, for each $\mathcal{B}$ in Δ, other than the begin node.

Method. We compute DOM($\mathcal{B}$) recursively for each $\mathcal{B}$ in $\Delta - \{\mathcal{B}_1\}$. At any time, DOM($\mathcal{B}$) will be the block closest to $\mathcal{B}$ found to dominate $\mathcal{B}$. Ultimately, DOM($\mathcal{B}$) will be the direct dominator of $\mathcal{B}$. Initially, DOM($\mathcal{B}$) is $\mathcal{B}_1$ for all $\mathcal{B}$ in $\Delta - \{\mathcal{B}_1\}$. For $i = 2, 3, \ldots, n$, do the following two steps:

(1) Delete block $\mathcal{B}_i$ from F. Using Algorithm 0.3, find each block $\mathcal{B}$ which is now inaccessible from the begin node of F. Block $\mathcal{B}_i$ dominates $\mathcal{B}$ if and only if $\mathcal{B}$ is no longer accessible from the begin node when $\mathcal{B}_i$ is deleted from F. Restore $\mathcal{B}_i$ to F.

(2) Suppose that it has been determined that $\mathcal{B}_i$ dominates $\mathcal{B}$ in step (1). If DOM($\mathcal{B}$) = DOM($\mathcal{B}_i$), set DOM($\mathcal{B}$) to $\mathcal{B}_i$. Otherwise, leave DOM($\mathcal{B}$) unchanged. $\square$

Example 11.31

Let us compute the direct dominators for the flow graph of Fig. 11.22 using Algorithm 11.5. Here $\Delta = \{\mathcal{B}_1, \mathcal{B}_2, \mathcal{B}_3, \mathcal{B}_4\}$. The successive values of DOM($\mathcal{B}$) after considering $\mathcal{B}_i$, $2 \leq i \leq 4$, are given below:

i	DOM($\mathcal{B}_2$)	DOM($\mathcal{B}_3$)	DOM($\mathcal{B}_4$)
Initial	$\mathcal{B}_1$	$\mathcal{B}_1$	$\mathcal{B}_1$
2	$\mathcal{B}_1$	$\mathcal{B}_2$	$\mathcal{B}_2$
3	$\mathcal{B}_1$	$\mathcal{B}_2$	$\mathcal{B}_2$
4	$\mathcal{B}_1$	$\mathcal{B}_2$	$\mathcal{B}_2$

Let us compute line 2. Deleting block $\mathcal{B}_2$ makes blocks $\mathcal{B}_3$ and $\mathcal{B}_4$ inaccessible. We have thus determined that $\mathcal{B}_2$ dominates $\mathcal{B}_3$ and $\mathcal{B}_4$. Prior to this point, DOM($\mathcal{B}_2$) = DOM($\mathcal{B}_3$) = $\mathcal{B}_1$, and so by step (2) of Algorithm 11.5 we set DOM($\mathcal{B}_3$) to $\mathcal{B}_2$. Likewise, DOM($\mathcal{B}_4$) is set to $\mathcal{B}_2$. Deleting block $\mathcal{B}_3$ or $\mathcal{B}_4$ does not make any block inaccessible, so no further changes occur. $\square$

THEOREM 11.10

When Algorithm 11.5 terminates, DOM($\mathcal{B}$) is the direct dominator of $\mathcal{B}$.

Proof. We first observe that step (1) correctly determines those $\mathcal{B}$'s dominated by $\mathcal{B}_i$, for $\mathcal{B}_i$ dominates $\mathcal{B}$ if and only if every path to $\mathcal{B}$ from the begin node of F goes through $\mathcal{B}_i$.

We show by induction on i that after step (2) is executed, DOM($\mathcal{B}$) is that block $\mathcal{B}_h$, $1 \leq h \leq i$, which dominates $\mathcal{B}$ but which, in turn, is dominated by all $\mathcal{B}_j$'s, $1 \leq j \leq i$, which also dominate $\mathcal{B}$. That such a $\mathcal{B}_h$ must exist follows directly from Lemma 11.13. The basis, $i = 2$, is trivial.

Let us turn to the inductive step. If $\mathcal{B}_{i+1}$ does not dominate $\mathcal{B}$, the conclusion is immediate from the inductive hypothesis. If $\mathcal{B}_{i+1}$ does dominate $\mathcal{B}$, but there is some $\mathcal{B}_j$, $1 \leq j \leq i$, such that $\mathcal{B}_j$ dominates $\mathcal{B}$ and $\mathcal{B}_{i+1}$ dominates $\mathcal{B}_j$, then DOM($\mathcal{B}$) $\neq$ DOM($\mathcal{B}_{i+1}$). Thus, DOM($\mathcal{B}$) does not change, which correctly fulfills the inductive hypothesis. If $\mathcal{B}_{i+1}$ dominates $\mathcal{B}$ but is dominated by all $\mathcal{B}_j$'s which dominate $\mathcal{B}$, $1 \leq j \leq i$, we claim that prior to this step, DOM($\mathcal{B}$) = DOM($\mathcal{B}_{i+1}$). For if not, there must be some $\mathcal{B}_k$, $1 \leq k \leq i$, which dominates $\mathcal{B}_{i+1}$ but not $\mathcal{B}$, which is impossible by Lemma 11.13(1). Thus DOM($\mathcal{B}$) is correctly set to $\mathcal{B}_{i+1}$, completing the induction. $\square$

We observe that if F is constructed from a program, then the number of edges is at most twice the number of blocks. Thus, step (1) of Algorithm 11.5 takes time proportional to the square of the number of blocks. The space taken is proportional to the number of blocks.

If $\mathcal{B}_1, \mathcal{B}_2, \ldots, \mathcal{B}_n$ are the blocks of a program (except for the begin block), then we can store the direct dominators of these blocks as the sequence $\mathcal{C}_1, \mathcal{C}_2, \ldots, \mathcal{C}_n$, where $\mathcal{C}_i$ is the direct dominator of $\mathcal{B}_i$, for $1 \leq i \leq n$. All dominators for block $\mathcal{B}_i$ can be recovered from this sequence easily by finding DOM($\mathcal{B}_i$), DOM(DOM($\mathcal{B}_i$)), and so forth until we reach the begin block.

11.3.3. Examples of Transformations on Programs

Let us now turn our attention to transformations that can be applied to a program, or its flow graph, in an attempt to reduce the running time of the object language program that is ultimately produced. In this section we shall consider examples of such transformations. Although there does not exist a complete catalog of optimizing transformations for programs with loops, the transformations considered here are useful for a wide class of programs.

1. Removal of Useless Statements

This is a generalization of transformation T_1 of Section 11.1. A statement that does not affect the value of a program is unnecessary in a program and can be removed. Basic blocks that are not accessible from the begin node are clearly useless and can be removed when the flow graph is constructed. Statements which compute values that are not ultimately used in computing an output variable also fall into this category. In Section 11.4, we shall provide a tool for implementing this transformation in a program with loops.

2. Elimination of Redundant Computations

This transformation is a generalization of transformation T_2 of Section 11.1. Suppose that we have a program in which block $\mathcal{B}$ dominates block $\mathcal{B}'$ and that $\mathcal{B}$ and $\mathcal{B}'$ have statements $A \leftarrow B + C$ and $A' \leftarrow B + C$, respectively. If neither B nor C are redefined in any (not necessarily cycle free) path from $\mathcal{B}$ to $\mathcal{B}'$ (it is not hard to detect this; see Exercise 11.3.5), then the values computed by the two expressions are the same. We may insert the statement $X \leftarrow A$ after $A \leftarrow B + C$ in $\mathcal{B}$, where X is a new variable. We then replace $A' \leftarrow B + C$ by $A' \leftarrow X$. Moreover, if A is never redefined going from $\mathcal{B}$ to $\mathcal{B}'$, then we do not need $X \leftarrow A$, and $A' \leftarrow A$ serves for $A' \leftarrow B + C$.

In this transformation we assume that it is cheaper to do the two assignments $X \leftarrow A$ and $A \leftarrow X$ than to evaluate $A' \leftarrow B + C$, an assumption which is realistic for many reasonable machine models.

Example 11.32

Consider the flow graph shown in Fig. 11.23. In this flow graph block $\mathcal{B}_1$ dominates blocks $\mathcal{B}_2$, $\mathcal{B}_3$, and $\mathcal{B}_4$. Suppose that all assignment statements involving the variables A, B, C, and D are as shown in Fig. 11.23. Then the expression $B + C$ has the same value when it is computed in blocks $\mathcal{B}_1$, $\mathcal{B}_3$, and $\mathcal{B}_4$. Thus, it is unnecessary to recompute the expression $B + C$ in blocks $\mathcal{B}_3$ and $\mathcal{B}_4$. In block $\mathcal{B}_1$ we can insert the assignment statement $X \leftarrow A$ after the statement $A \leftarrow B + C$. Here X is a new variable name. Then in blocks $\mathcal{B}_3$ and $\mathcal{B}_4$ we can replace the statement $A \leftarrow B + C$ and $G \leftarrow B + C$ by the simple assignment statements $A \leftarrow X$ and $G \leftarrow X$, respectively, without affecting the value of the program. Note that since A is computed in block $\mathcal{B}_2$, we cannot use A in place of X. The resulting flow graph is shown in Fig. 11.24.

The assignment $A \leftarrow X$ now in $\mathcal{B}_3$ is redundant and can be eliminated. Also note that if the statement $F \leftarrow A + G$ in block $\mathcal{B}_2$ is changed to $B \leftarrow A + G$, then we can no longer replace $G \leftarrow B + C$ by $G \leftarrow X$ in block $\mathcal{B}_4$. $\square$

Eliminating redundant computations (common subexpressions) from a program requires the detection of computations that are common to two or more blocks of a program. While we have shown a redundant computation occurring at a block and one of its dominators, an expression such as $A + B$ might be computed in several blocks, none of which dominate a given

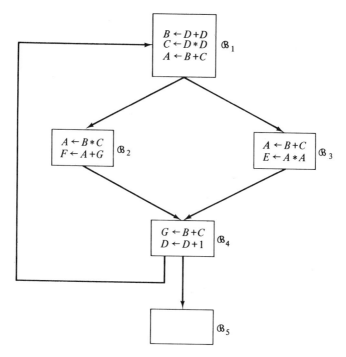

Fig. 11.23   Flow graph.

block $\mathcal{B}$ (which also needs expression $A + B$). In general, a computation of $A + B$ is *redundant* in a block $\mathcal{B}$ if

(1) Every path from the begin block to $\mathcal{B}$ (including those which pass several times through $\mathcal{B}$) passes through a computation of $A + B$, and

(2) Along any such path, no definition of A or B occurs between the last computation of $A + B$ and the use of $A + B$ in $\mathcal{B}$.

In Section 11.4 we shall provide some tools for the detection of this more general situation.

We should note that as in the straight-line case, algebraic laws can increase the number of common subexpressions.

3. Replacing Run Time Computations by Compile Time Computations

It makes sense, if possible, to perform a computation once when a program is being compiled, rather than repeatedly when the object program is being executed. A simple instance of this is *constant propagation*, the replacement of a variable by a constant when the constant value of that variable is known.

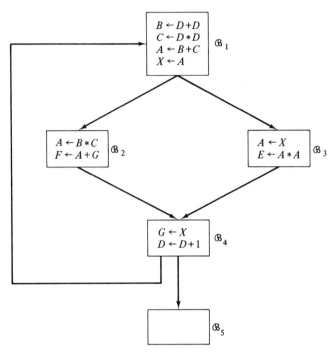

Fig. 11.24 Transformed flow graph.

Example 11.33

Suppose that we have the block

$$\textbf{read} \quad R$$
$$\text{PI} \longleftarrow 3.14159$$
$$A \longleftarrow 4/3$$
$$B \longleftarrow A * \text{PI}$$
$$C \longleftarrow R \uparrow 3$$
$$V \longleftarrow B * C$$
$$\textbf{write} \quad V$$

We can substitute the value 3.14159 for PI in the fourth statement to obtain the statement $B \longleftarrow A * 3.14159$. We can also compute 4/3 and substitute the resulting value in $B \longleftarrow A * 3.14159$ to obtain $B \longleftarrow 1.33333 * 3.14159$. We can compute $1.33333 * 3.14159 = 4.18878$ and substitute 4.18878 in the statement $V \longleftarrow B * C$ to obtain $V \longleftarrow 4.18878 * C$. Finally, we can eliminate the resulting useless statements to obtain the following shorter equivalent program:

$$\begin{aligned}
&\textbf{read} \quad R \\
&C \longleftarrow R \uparrow 3 \\
&V \longleftarrow 4.18878 * C \\
&\textbf{write} \quad V
\end{aligned}$$ □

4. Reduction in Strength

Reduction in strength involves the replacement of one operator, requiring a substantial amount of machine time for execution, by a less costly computation. For example, suppose that a PL/I source program contains the statement

$$I = \text{LENGTH}(S1 \parallel S2)$$

where $S1$ and $S2$ are strings of variable length. The operator $\parallel$ denotes string concatenation. String concatenation is relatively expensive to implement. However, suppose we replace this statement by the equivalent statement

$$I = \text{LENGTH}(S1) + \text{LENGTH}(S2)$$

We would now have to perform the length operation twice and perform one addition. But these operations are substantially less expensive than string concatenation.

Other examples of this type of optimization are the replacement of certain multiplications by additions and the replacement of certain exponentiations by repeated multiplication. For example, we might replace the statement $C \leftarrow R \uparrow 3$ by the sequence

$$\begin{aligned}
&C \longleftarrow R * R \\
&C \longleftarrow C * R
\end{aligned}$$

assuming that it is cheaper to compute $R * R * R$ rather than calling subroutines to evaluate R^3 as ANTILOG(3 * LOG(R)).

In the next section we shall consider a more interesting form of reduction in strength within loops, where it is possible to replace certain multiplications by additions.

11.3.4. Loop Optimization

Roughly speaking, a loop in a program is a sequence of blocks that can be executed repeatedly. Loops are an integral feature of most programs, and many programs have loops that are executed a large number of times. Many programming languages have constructs whose explicit purpose is the establishment of a loop. Often substantial improvements in the running time of a program can be made by taking advantage of transformations that only reduce the cost of loops. The general transformations we just discussed—removal of useless statements, elimination of redundant computation, constant propagation, and reduction in strength—are particularly beneficial when applied to loops. However, there are certain transformations that are specifically directed at loops. These are the movement of computations out of loops, the replacement of expensive computations in a loop by cheaper ones, and the unrolling of loops.

To apply these transformations, we must first isolate the loops in a given program. In the case of FORTRAN DO loops, or the intermediate code arising from a DO loop, the identification of a loop is easy. However, the concept of a loop in a flow graph is more general than the loops that result from DO statements in FORTRAN. These generalized loops in flow graphs are called "strongly connected regions." Every cycle in a flow graph with a single entry point is an example of a strongly connected region. However, more general loop structures are also strongly connected regions. We define a strongly connected region as follows.

DEFINITION

Let F be a flow graph and S a subset of blocks of F. We say that S is a *strongly connected region* (*region*, for short) of F if

(1) There is a unique block $\mathcal{B}$ of S (the *entry*) such that there is a path from the begin node of F to $\mathcal{B}$ which does not pass through any other block in S.

(2) There is a path (of nonzero length) that is wholly within S from every block in S to every other block in S.

Example 11.34

Consider the abstract flow graph of Fig. 11.25. $\{2, 3, 4, 5\}$ is a strongly connected region with entry 2. $\{4\}$ is a strongly connected region with entry 4. $\{3, 4, 5, 6\}$ is a region with entry 3. $\{2, 3, 7\}$ is a region with entry 2. Another region with entry 2 is $\{2, 3, 4, 5, 6, 7\}$. The latter region is *maximal* in that every other region with entry 2 is contained in this region.   □

The important feature of a strongly connected region that makes it amenable to code improvement is the single identifiable entry block. For example, one optimization that we can perform on flow graphs is to move a computation that is invariant within a region into the predecessors of the entry block of the region (or we may construct a new block preceding the entry, to hold the invariant computations).

We can characterize the entry blocks of a flow graph in terms of the dominance relation.

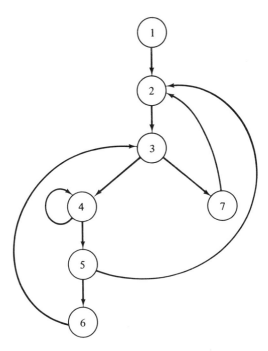

Fig. 11.25   Flow graph.

THEOREM 11.11

Let F be a flow graph. Block $\mathcal{B}$ in F is an entry block of a region if and only if there is some block $\mathcal{B}'$ such that there is an edge from $\mathcal{B}'$ to $\mathcal{B}$ and $\mathcal{B}$ either dominates $\mathcal{B}'$ or is $\mathcal{B}'$.

Proof.

Only if: Suppose that $\mathcal{B}$ is the entry block of region $\mathcal{S}$. If $\mathcal{S} = \{\mathcal{B}\}$, the result is trivial. Otherwise, let $\mathcal{B}'$ be in $\mathcal{S}$, $\mathcal{B}' \neq \mathcal{B}$. Then $\mathcal{B}$ dominates $\mathcal{B}'$, for if not, then there is a path from the begin node to $\mathcal{B}'$ that does not pass through $\mathcal{B}$, violating the assumption that $\mathcal{B}$ is the unique entry block. Thus, the entry block of a region dominates every other block in the region. Since there is a path from every member of $\mathcal{S}$ to $\mathcal{B}$, there must be at least one $\mathcal{B}'$ in $\mathcal{S} - \{\mathcal{B}\}$ which links directly to $\mathcal{B}$.

If: The case in which $\mathcal{B} = \mathcal{B}'$ is trivial, and so assume that $\mathcal{B} \neq \mathcal{B}'$. Define $\mathcal{S}$ to be $\mathcal{B}$ together with those blocks $\mathcal{B}''$ such that $\mathcal{B}$ dominates $\mathcal{B}''$ and there is a path from $\mathcal{B}''$ to $\mathcal{B}$ which passes only through nodes dominated by $\mathcal{B}$. By hypothesis, $\mathcal{B}$ and $\mathcal{B}'$ are in $\mathcal{S}$. We must show that $\mathcal{S}$ is a region with entry $\mathcal{B}$. Clearly, condition (2) of the region definition is satisfied, and so we must show that there is a path from the begin node to $\mathcal{B}$ that does not pass through any other block in $\mathcal{S}$. Let $\mathcal{C}_1 \cdots \mathcal{C}_n \mathcal{B}$ be a shortest computation path leading to $\mathcal{B}$. If $\mathcal{C}_j$ is in $\mathcal{S}$, then there is some i, $1 \leq i \leq j$, such that $\mathcal{C}_i = \mathcal{B}$, because $\mathcal{B}$ dominates $\mathcal{C}_j$. Then $\mathcal{C}_1 \cdots \mathcal{C}_n \mathcal{B}$ is not a shortest computation path leading to $\mathcal{B}$, a contradiction. Thus, condition (1) of the definition of a strongly connected region holds. $\square$

The set $\mathcal{S}$ constructed in the "if" portion of Theorem 11.11 is clearly the maximal region with entry $\mathcal{B}$. It would be nice if there were a unique region with entry $\mathcal{B}$, but unfortunately this is not always the case. In Example 11.34, there are three regions with entry 2. Nevertheless, Theorem 11.11 is useful in constructing an efficient algorithm to compute maximal regions, which are unique.

Unless a region is maximal, the entry block may dominate blocks not in the region, and blocks in the region may be accessible from these blocks. In Example 11.34, e.g., region {2, 3, 7} can be reached via block 6. We therefore say that a region is *single-entry* if every edge entering a block of the region, other than the entry block, comes from a block inside the region. In Example 11.34, region {2, 3, 4, 5, 6, 7} is a single-entry region. In what follows, we assume regions to be single-entry, although generalization to all regions is not difficult.

1. Code Motion

There are several transformations in which knowledge of regions can be used to improve code. A principal one is *code motion*. We can move a region-independent computation outside the region. Let us say that within some single-entry region variables Y and Z are not changed but that the statement $X \leftarrow Y + Z$ appears. We may move the computation of $Y + Z$ to a newly created block which links only to the entry block of the region.† All links from outside the region that formerly went to the entry now go to the new block.

Example 11.35

It may appear that region-invariant computations would not appear except in the most carelessly written programs. However, let us consider the following inner DO loop of a FORTRAN source program, where J is defined outside the loop:

$$K = 0$$
$$DO \ 3 \quad I = 1,1000$$
$$3 \quad K = J + 1 + I + K$$

The intermediate program for this portion of the source program might

---

†The addition of such a block may make the flow graph unconstructable from any program. However, the property of constructability from a program is never used here.

look like this:

$$K \leftarrow 0$$
$$I \leftarrow 1$$
loop: $T \leftarrow J + 1$
$$S \leftarrow T + I$$
$$K \leftarrow S + K$$
if $I = 1000$ **goto** *done*
$$I \leftarrow I + 1$$
goto *loop*
done: **halt**

The corresponding flow graph is shown in Fig. 11.26.

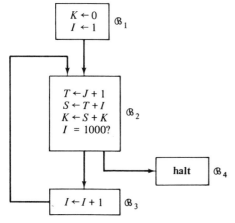

Fig. 11.26   Flow graph.

We observe that $\{\mathcal{B}_2, \mathcal{B}_3\}$ in Fig. 11.26 is a region with entry $\mathcal{B}_2$. The statement $T \leftarrow J + 1$ is invariant in the region, so it may be moved to a new block, as shown in Fig. 11.27.

While the number of statements in the flow graphs of Figs. 11.26 and 11.27 is the same, the presumption is that statements in a region will tend to be executed frequently, so that the expected time of execution has been decreased. □

2. Induction Variables

Another useful transformation concerns the elimination of what we shall call induction variables.

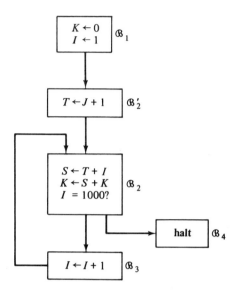

Fig. 11.27   Revised flow graph.

DEFINITION

Let $\S$ be a single entry region with entry $\Re$ and let X be some variable appearing in a statement of the blocks of $\S$. Let $\Re_1 \cdots \Re_n \Re \mathcal{C}_1 \cdots \mathcal{C}_m$ be any computation path such that $\mathcal{C}_i$ is in $\S$, $1 \leq i \leq m$, and $\Re_n$, if it exists, is not in $\S$. Define $X_1, X_2, \ldots$ to be the sequence of values of X each time X is assigned in the sequence $\Re \mathcal{C}_1 \cdots \mathcal{C}_m$. If $X_1, X_2, \ldots$ forms an arithmetic progression (with positive or negative difference) for arbitrary computation paths as above, then we say that X is an *induction variable* of $\S$.

We shall also consider X to be an induction variable if it is undefined the first time through $\Re$ and forms an arithmetic progression otherwise. In this case, it may be necessary to initialize it appropriately on entry to the region from outside, in order that the optimizations to be discussed here may be performed.

Note that it is not trivial to find all the induction variables in a region. In fact, it can be proven that no such algorithm exists. Nevertheless, we can detect enough induction variables in common situations to make the concept worth considering.

Example 11.36

In Fig. 11.27, the region $\{\Re_2, \Re_3\}$ has entry $\Re_2$. If $\Re_2$ is entered from $\Re_2'$ and the flow of control passes repeatedly from $\Re_2$ to $\Re_3$ and then back to $\Re_2$, the variable I takes on the values $1, 2, 3, \ldots$. Thus, I is an induction variable. Less obviously, S is an induction variable, since it takes on values $T + 1, T + 2, T + 3, \cdots$. However, K is not an induction variable, because it takes values $T + 1, 2T + 3, 3T + 6, \cdots$. $\square$

The important feature of induction variables is that they are linearly related to each other as long as control is within their region. For example, in Fig. 11.27, the relations $S = T + I$ and $I = S - T$ hold every time we leave $\mathcal{B}_2$.

If, as in Fig. 11.27, one induction variable is used only to control the region (indicated by the fact that its value is not needed outside the region and that it is always set to the same constant immediately before entering the region), it is possible to eliminate that variable. Even if all induction variables are needed outside the region, we may use only one inside the region and compute the remaining ones when we leave the region.

Example 11.37

Consider Fig. 11.27. We shall eliminate the induction variable I, which qualifies under the criteria listed above. Its role will be played by S. We observe that after executing $\mathcal{B}_2$, S has the value $T + I$, so when control passes from $\mathcal{B}_3$ back to $\mathcal{B}_2$, the relation $S = T + I - 1$ must hold. We can thus replace the statement $S \leftarrow T + I$ by $S \leftarrow S + 1$. But we must then initialize S correctly in $\mathcal{B}_2'$, so that when control goes from $\mathcal{B}_2'$ to $\mathcal{B}_2$, the value of S after executing the statement $S \leftarrow S + 1$ is $T + I$. Clearly, in block $\mathcal{B}_2'$, we must introduce the new statement $S \leftarrow T$ after the statement $T \leftarrow J + 1$.

We must then revise the test $I = 1000$? so that it is an equivalent test on S. When the test is executed, S has the value $T + I$. Consequently, an equivalent test is

$$R \longleftarrow T + 1000$$

$$S = R?$$

Since R is region-independent, the calculation $R \leftarrow T + 1000$ can be moved to block $\mathcal{B}_2'$. It is then possible to dispense with I entirely. The resulting flow graph is shown in Fig. 11.28.

We observe from Fig. 11.28 that block $\mathcal{B}_3$ has been entirely eliminated and that the region has been shortened by one statement. Of course, $\mathcal{B}_2'$ has been increased in size, but we are presuming that regions are executed more frequently than blocks outside the region. Thus, Fig. 11.28 represents a speeding up of Fig. 11.27.

We observe that the step $S \leftarrow T$ in $\mathcal{B}_2'$ can be eliminated if we identify S and T. This is possible only because at no time will the values of S and T be different, yet both will be "active" in the sense that they may both be used later in the computation. That is, only S is active in $\mathcal{B}_2$, neither is active in $\mathcal{B}_1$, and in $\mathcal{B}_2'$ both are active only between the statements $S \leftarrow T$ and $R \leftarrow T + 1000$. At that time they certainly have the same value. If we replace T by S, the result is Fig. 11.29.

To see the improvement between Figs. 11.26 and 11.29, let us convert

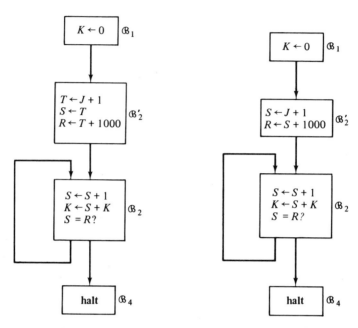

Fig. 11.28   Further revised flow graph.   **Fig. 11.29**   Final flow graph.

each into assembly language programs for a crude one-accumulator machine. The operation codes should be transparent. (JZERO stands for "jump if accumulator is zero" and JNZ for "jump if accumulator is not zero.") The two programs are shown in Fig. 11.30.

```
            LOAD   = 0                    LOAD   = 0
            STORE  K                      STORE  K
            LOAD   = 1                    LOAD   J
    LOOP:   STORE  I                      ADD    = 1
            LOAD   J                      STORE  S
            ADD    = 1                    ADD    = 1000
            ADD    I                      STORE  R
            ADD    K              LOOP:    LOAD   S
            STORE  K                      ADD    = 1
            LOAD   I                      STORE  S
            SUBTR  = 1000                 ADD    K
            JZERO  DONE                   STORE  K
            LOAD   I                      LOAD   S
            ADD    = 1                    SUBTR  R
            JUMP   LOOP                   JNZ    LOOP
    DONE:   END                          END
             (a)                          (b)
    Program from Fig. 11.26        Program from Fig. 11.29
```

Fig. 11.30   Equivalent programs.

Observe that the length of the program in Fig. 11.30(b) is the same as that of Fig. 11.30(a). However, the loop in Fig. 11.30(b) is shorter than in Fig. 11.30(a) (8 instructions vs. 12), which is the important factor when time is considered. $\square$

3. Reduction in Strength

An interesting form of reduction in strength is possible within regions. If within a region there is a statement of the form $A \leftarrow B * I$, where the value of B is region-independent and the values of I at that statement form an arithmetic progression, we can replace the multiplication by addition or subtraction of a quantity, which is the product of the region-independent value and the difference in the arithmetic progression of the induction variable. It is necessary to properly initialize the quantity computed by the former multiplication statement.

Example 11.38

Consider the following portion of a source program,

$$\text{DO} \quad 5 \quad J = 1, N$$
$$\text{DO} \quad 5 \quad I = 1, M$$
$$5 \quad A(I, J) = B(I, J)$$

which sets array A equal to array B assuming that both A and B are M by N arrays. Suppose element $A(I, J)$ is stored in location $A + M * (J - 1) + I - 1$ for $1 \leq I \leq M$, $1 \leq J \leq N$. Let us make a similar assumption about $B(I, J)$. For convenience, let us denote location $A + L$ by $A(L)$. Then the following partially optimized intermediate program might be created from this source program:

$$M' \leftarrow M - 1$$
$$N' \leftarrow N - 1$$
$$J \leftarrow -1$$
$$outer: \quad J \leftarrow J + 1$$
$$I \leftarrow -1$$
$$K \leftarrow M * J$$
$$loop: \quad I \leftarrow I + 1$$
$$L \leftarrow K + I$$
$$A(L) \leftarrow B(L)$$
$$\textbf{if } I < M' \textbf{ goto } loop$$
$$\textbf{if } J < N' \textbf{ goto } outer$$
$$\textbf{halt}$$

The flow graph for this program is shown in Fig. 11.31. In this flow

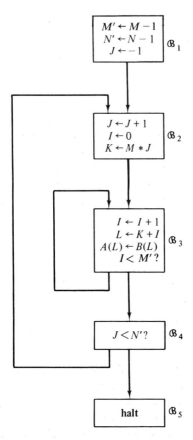

Fig. 11.31   Flow graph.

graph $\{\mathcal{B}_2, \mathcal{B}_3, \mathcal{B}_4\}$ is a region in which M is invariant and J is an induction variable with increment 1. We can therefore replace statement $K \leftarrow M * J$ by statement $K \leftarrow K + M$ provided K is initialized to $-M$ outside the region. The flow graph that results is shown in Fig. 11.32. The program represented by this new flow graph is longer than before, but the region represented by blocks $\mathcal{B}_2''$, $\mathcal{B}_3$ and $\mathcal{B}_4$ can be executed more quickly, because a multiplication has been replaced by an addition. Moreover, additional time can be saved by eliminating the induction variable J in favor of L.

It is interesting to note that we can obtain a far more economical program by replacing the entire region $\{\mathcal{B}_2'', \mathcal{B}_3, \mathcal{B}_4\}$ by a single block in which $A(L)$ is set to $B(L)$ for $1 \leq K \leq M * N$. The resulting flow graph is shown in Fig. 11.33. $\square$

4. Loop Unrolling

The final code-improving transformation which we shall consider is exceedingly simple but often overlooked. It is *loop unrolling*. Consider the

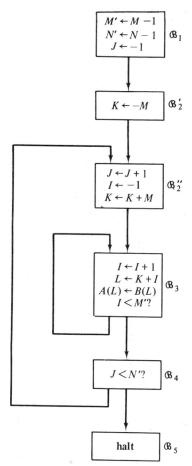

Fig. 11.32 New flow graph.

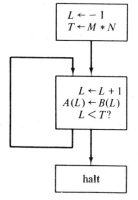

Fig. 11.33 Final flow graph.

flow graph in Fig. 11.34. Blocks $\mathcal{B}_2$ and $\mathcal{B}_3$ are executed 100 times. Thus 100 test instructions are executed. We could dispense with all 100 test instructions by "unrolling" the loop. That is, the loop could be unfolded into a straight-line block consisting of 100 assignment statements:

$$A(1) \longleftarrow B(1)$$
$$A(2) \longleftarrow B(2)$$
$$.$$
$$.$$
$$.$$
$$A(100) \longleftarrow B(100)$$

A less frivolous approach would be to unroll the loop "once" to obtain the flow graph in Fig. 11.35. The program in Fig. 11.35 is longer, but fewer instructions are executed. In Fig. 11.35 only 50 test instructions are used, versus 100 for the program in Fig. 11.34.

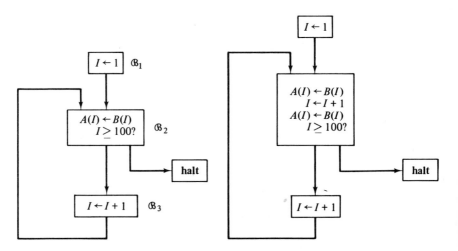

Fig. 11.34   Flow graph.   Fig. 11.35   Unrolled flow graph.

EXERCISES

11.3.1.   Construct intermediate programs equivalent to the following source programs:
   (a) $S = (A + B + C) * .5$
        $D = S * (S - A) * (S - B) * (S - C)$
        $\text{AREA} = \text{SQRT}(D)$

(b) **for** $I := 1$ **step** 1 **until** N **do**
    begin
        $A[I] := B[I] + C[I * 2];$
        if $(A[I] = 0)$ **then halt**
            else $A[I] := I$
    end

(c)   DO 5 $I = 1, N$
    5 $A(I, I) = C * A(I, I)$

11.3.2. What functions are computed by the following two intermediate language programs?

(a)   **read** N
              $S \leftarrow 0$
              $I \leftarrow 1$
  loop: $S \leftarrow S + I$
              if $I \geq N$ **goto** *done*
              $I = I + 1$
              goto *loop*
  done: **write** S
              halt

(b)   **read** N
              $T \leftarrow N + 1$
              $T \leftarrow T * N$
              $T \leftarrow T * .5$
              write T
              halt

Are the two programs equivalent, if N and I represent integers and S and I represent reals?

11.3.3. Consider the following program P:

                    read A, B
                    $R \leftarrow 1$
                    $C \leftarrow A * A$
                    $D \leftarrow B * B$
                    if $C < D$ **goto** X
                    $E \leftarrow A * A$
                    $R \leftarrow R + 1$
                    $E \leftarrow E + R$
                    write E
                    halt
        X: $E \leftarrow B * B$
                    $R \leftarrow R + 2$
                    $E \leftarrow E + R$
                    write E
                    if $E > 100$ **goto** Y
                    halt

$$Y: \quad R \longleftarrow R - 1$$
$$\textbf{goto } X$$

Construct a flow graph for P.

11.3.4. Find the dominators and direct dominators of each node in the flow graph of Fig. 11.36.

11.3.5. Let $ON(\mathcal{B}_1, \mathcal{B}_2)$ be the set of blocks that can appear on a path from block $\mathcal{B}_1$ to block $\mathcal{B}_2$ (without going through $\mathcal{B}_1$ again, although the path may go through $\mathcal{B}_2$ more than once) in a flow graph. Show that if $\mathcal{B}_1$ dominates $\mathcal{B}_2$, then

$ON(\mathcal{B}_1, \mathcal{B}_2) = \{\mathcal{B} \mid$ there is a path from $\mathcal{B}$ to $\mathcal{B}_2$
when $\mathcal{B}_1$ is deleted from the flow graph}.

What is the time required to compute $ON(\mathcal{B}_1, \mathcal{B}_2)$?

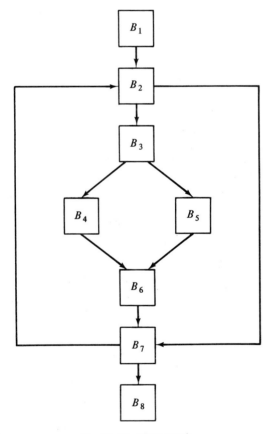

Fig. 11.36 Flow graph.

11.3.6. Prove assertions (1) and (2) of Lemma 11.13.

11.3.7. We can define a postdominance relation as follows. Let F be a flow graph and $\mathcal{B}$ a node of F. A node $\mathcal{B}'$ is a *postdominator* of $\mathcal{B}$ if every path from $\mathcal{B}$ to a **halt** statement passes through $\mathcal{B}'$. An *immediate postdominator* of $\mathcal{B}$ is postdominated by every other postdominator of $\mathcal{B}$. Show that if a node in a flow graph has a postdominator, then it has an immediate postdominator.

11.3.8. Devise an algorithm to construct the immediate postdominators of all nodes in a flow graph.

11.3.9. Find all strongly connected regions in Fig. 11.36. Which regions are maximal?

11.3.10. Let P be the program in Exercise 11.3.3.
  (a) Eliminate all common subexpressions from P.
  (b) Eliminate all unnecessary constant computations from P.
  (c) Remove all invariant computations from the loop in P.

11.3.11. Find all induction variables in the following program. Eliminate as many as you can and replace as many multiplications by additions as possible.

$$I \longleftarrow 1$$
$$\textbf{read } J, K$$
$$X: \quad A \longleftarrow K * I$$
$$B \longleftarrow J * I$$
$$C \longleftarrow A + B$$
$$\textbf{write } C$$
$$I \longleftarrow I + 1$$
$$\textbf{if } I < 100 \textbf{ goto } X$$
$$\textbf{halt}$$

11.3.12. Give algorithms to find all (a) regions (b) single-entry regions and (c) maximal regions in a flow graph.

*11.3.13. Give an algorithm to detect some of the induction variables in a single-entry region.

*11.3.14. Generalize the algorithm in Exercise 11.3.13 to handle regions that are not single-entry.

11.3.15. Give an algorithm to move region-independent computations out of a (not necessarily single-entry) region. *Hint:* Blocks outside the region that can reach the region other than by the region entry are permitted to change variables involved in the region-invariant computation.

We may need to place new blocks between blocks outside the region and blocks within the region.

**11.3.16. Show that it is undecidable whether two programs are equivalent. *Hint:* Choose appropriate data types and interpretations for the operators.

**11.3.17. Show that it is undecidable whether a variable is an induction variable.

11.3.18. Generalize the notion of scope of variables and statements to programs with loops. Give an algorithm to compute the scope of a variable in a program with loops.

*11.3.19. Extend transformations T_1-T_4 of Section 11.1 to apply to programs with no backward loops (programs with assignment statements and conditional statements of the form **if** $x \, R \, y$ **goto** L, where L refers to a statement after this conditional statement).

*11.3.20. Show that it is undecidable whether a program will ever terminate.

Research Questions

11.3.21. Characterize the machine models for which the transformations we have described will result in faster-running programs.

11.3.22. Develop algorithms that will detect large classes of the phenomena with which we have been dealing in this section, e.g., loop-invariant computations or induction variables. Note that, for most of these phenomena, there is no algorithm to detect all such instances.

Open Question

11.3.23. Is it possible to compute direct dominators of an n-node flow graph in less than $0(n^2)$ steps? It is reasonable to suppose that $0(n^2)$ is the best we can do for the entire dominance relation, since it takes that long just to print the answer in matrix form.

BIBLIOGRAPHIC NOTES

There are several papers that have proposed various optimizing transformations for programs. Nievergelt [1965], Marill [1962], McKeeman [1965], and Clark [1967] list a number of machine independent transformations. Gear [1965] proposes an optimizer capable of some common subexpression elimination, the propagation of constants, and loop optimizations such as strength reduction and removal of invariant computations. Busam and Englund [1969] discuss similar optimizations in the context of FORTRAN. Allen and Cocke [1972] provide a good survey of these techniques. Allen [1969] discusses a global optimization scheme based on finding the strongly connected regions of a program.

The dominator approach to code optimization was pioneered by Lowry and Medlock [1969], although the idea of the dominance relation comes from Prosser [1959].

There has been a great deal of theoretical work on program schemas, which are similar to our flow graphs, but with unspecified spaces for the values of variables and unspecified functions for operators. Two fundamental papers regarding equivalence between such schemas independent of the actual spaces and functions are Ianov [1958] and Luckham et al. [1970]. Kaplan [1970] and Manna [1973] survey the area.

11.4. DATA FLOW ANALYSIS

In the previous section, we used certain information about the computations in the blocks of a program without describing how this information could be efficiently computed. In particular, we have used

(1) The "available" expressions upon entering a block. An expression $A + B$ is said to *be available* on entering a block if $A + B$ is always computed before reaching the block but not before a definition of A or B.

(2) The set of blocks in which a variable could have last been defined before the flow of control reaches the current block. This information is useful for propagating constants and detecting useless computations. Another application is in detecting possible programmer errors in which a variable is referenced before being defined.

A third type of information that can be computed using the techniques of this section is the computation of active variables, those whose value must be retained on exit from a block. This information is useful when blocks are converted to machine code, as it indicates those variables which must either be stored or retained in a fast register on exit from the block. In terms of Section 11.1, this information is needed to determine which variables are output variables. Note that a variable might not be computed in the block in question (but rather in a previous block) and still be an input and output variable of the block.

Of these three problems, we shall here discuss only question (2)—the determination of where a variable could have been defined previous to reaching a given block. Our technique, called "interval analysis," partitions a flow graph into larger and larger sets of nodes, placing a hierarchical structure on the entire graph. This structure is used to give an efficient algorithm for a class of flow graphs, called "reducible" graphs, that occurs with surprising frequency in flow graphs derived from actual programs. We then show the extension necessary to handle irreducible graphs.

In the Exercises, we shall discuss some of the changes necessary to gather the other two types of information using interval analysis.

11.4.1. Intervals

We begin with the definition of a type of subgraph that is useful in data flow analysis.

Definition

If h is a node of a flow graph F, we define $I(h)$, the *interval with header* h, as the set of nodes of F constructed as follows:

(1) h is in $I(h)$.
(2) If n is a node not yet in $I(h)$, n is not the begin node, and all edges entering n leave nodes in $I(h)$, then add n to $I(h)$.
(3) Repeat step (2) until no more nodes can be added to $I(h)$.

Example 11.39

Consider the flow graph of Fig. 11.37.
Let us consider the interval with header n_1, the begin node. By step (1), $I(n_1)$ includes n_1. Since the only edge to enter node n_2 leaves n_1, we add n_2 to $I(n_1)$. Node n_3 cannot be added to $I(n_1)$, since n_3 can be entered from node

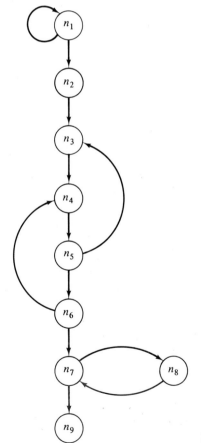

Fig. 11.37   Flow graph.

n_5 as well as n_2. No other nodes can be added to $I(n_1)$. Thus, $I(n_1) = \{n_1, n_2\}$.
Now let us consider $I(n_3)$. By step (1), n_3 is in $I(n_3)$. However, we cannot
add n_4 to $I(n_3)$, since n_4 may be entered via n_6 (as well as n_3) and n_6 is not in
$I(n_3)$. No other nodes can be added to $I(n_3)$, and so $I(n_3) = \{n_3\}$.

Continuing in this fashion, we can partition this flow graph into the following intervals:

$$I(n_1) = \{n_1, n_2\}$$
$$I(n_3) = \{n_3\}$$
$$I(n_4) = \{n_4, n_5, n_6\}$$
$$I(n_7) = \{n_7, n_8, n_9\} \qquad\qquad \square$$

We shall provide an algorithm for selecting interval headers and constructing the associated intervals so that a flow graph is partitioned into disjoint intervals. However, we shall first make three observations concerning
intervals.

THEOREM 11.12

(1) The header h dominates every other node in $I(h)$ [although not every
node dominated by h need be in $I(h)$].

(2) For each node h of a flow graph F, the interval $I(h)$ is unique and
independent of the order in which candidates for n in step (2) of the definition of interval are chosen.

(3) Every cycle in an interval $I(h)$ includes the interval header h.

Proof. We shall leave (1) and (2) for the Exercises and prove (3). Suppose
that $I(h)$ has a cycle $n_1, \ldots, n_k$ which excludes h. That is, there is an edge
from n_i to n_{i+1}, $1 \leq i < k$, and an edge from n_k to n_1. Let n_i be the first of
$n_1, \ldots, n_k$ added to $I(h)$. Then n_{i-1} (or n_k, if $i = 1$) must have been in $I(h)$
at that time, in contradiction. $\square$

One of the interesting aspects of interval analysis is that flow graphs
can be partitioned uniquely into intervals, and the intervals of one flow
graph can be considered to be the nodes of another flow graph, in which
an edge is drawn from interval I_1 to a distinct interval I_2 if there is any edge
from a node of I_1 to the header of I_2. (There clearly cannot be an edge from
I_1 to a node of I_2 other than the header.) This new graph can then be broken
into intervals in the same way, and this process can be continued. For this
reason, we shall subsequently consider a flow graph to be composed of nodes
of unspecified type, rather than blocks. The nodes may thus represent structures of arbitrary complexity.

We shall now give the algorithm that partitions a flow graph into a set of
disjoint intervals.

ALGORITHM 11.6

Partitioning a flow graph into disjoint intervals.

Input. A flow graph *F*.

Output. A set of disjoint intervals whose union is all the nodes of *F*.

Method.

(1) We shall associate with each node of *F* two parameters, a *count* and a *reach*. The count of a node *n* is a number which is initially the number of edges entering *n*. While executing the algorithm, the count of *n* is the number of these edges which have not yet been traversed. The reach of *n* is either undefined or some node of *F*. Initially, the reach of each node is undefined, except for the begin node, whose reach is itself. Eventually, the reach of a node *n* will be the first interval header *h* found such that there is an edge from some node in *I*(*h*) to *n*.

(2) We create a list of nodes called the *header list*. Initially, the header list contains only the begin node of *F*.

(3) If the header list is empty, halt. Otherwise, let *n* be the next node on the header list. Remove *n* from the header list.

(4) Then use steps (5)–(7) to construct the interval *I*(*n*). In these steps the direct successors of *I*(*n*) are added to the header list.

(5) *I*(*n*) is constructed as a list of nodes. Initially, *I*(*n*) contains only node *n* and *n* is "unmarked."

(6) Select an unmarked node *n′* on *I*(*n*), mark *n′*, and for each node *n″* such that there is an edge from *n′* to *n″* perform the following operations:

(a) Decrease the count of *n″* by 1.

(b) (i) If the reach of *n″* is undefined, set it to *n* and do the following. If the count of *n* is now 0 (having been 1), then add *n″* to *I*(*n*) and go to step (7); otherwise, add *n″* to the header list if not already there and go to step (7).

(ii) If the reach of *n″* is *n* and the count of *n″* is 0, add *n″* to *I*(*n*) and remove *n″* from the header list, if it is there. Go to step (7).

If neither (i) nor (ii) applies, do nothing in part(b).

(7) If an unmarked node remains in *I*(*n*), return to step (6). Otherwise, *I*(*n*) is complete, and we return to step (3).   □

DEFINITION

From the intervals of a flow graph *F*, we can construct another flow graph *I*(*F*) which we call the *derived graph* of *F*. *I*(*F*) is defined as follows:

(1) *I*(*F*) has one node for each interval constructed in Algorithm 11.6.

(2) The begin node of *I*(*F*) is the interval containing the begin node of *F*.

(3) There is an edge from interval *I* to interval *J* if and only if *I* ≠ *J* and there is an edge from a node of *I* to the header of *J*.

$I(F)$, the derived graph of a flow graph F, shows the flow of control among the intervals of F. Since $I(F)$ is a flow graph itself, we can also construct $I(I(F))$, the derived graph of $I(F)$. Thus, given a flow graph F_0 we can construct a sequence of flow graphs $F_0, F_1, \ldots, F_n$, which we call the *derived sequence* of F, in which F_{i+1} is the derived graph of F_i, for $0 \leq i < n$, and F_n is its own derived graph [i.e., $I(F_n) = F_n$]. We say that F_i is the ith *derived graph* of F_0. F_n is called the *limit* of F_0. It is not hard to show that F_n always exists and is unique.

If F_n is a single node, then F is said to be *reducible*.

It is interesting to note that if F_0 is constructed from an actual program, there is a high probability that F_0 will be reducible. In Section 11.4.3, we shall discuss a node-splitting technique whereby every irreducible flow graph can be transformed into one that is reducible.

Example 11.40

Let us use Algorithm 11.6 to construct the intervals for the flow graph of Fig. 11.38.

The begin node is n_1. Initially, the header list contains only n_1. To construct $I(n_1)$, we add n_1 to $I(n_1)$ as an unmarked node. We make n_1 marked by considering n_2, the direct successor of n_1. In doing so, we decrease the count of n_2 from its initial value of 2 to 1, set the reach of n_2 to n_1, and add n_2 to the header list. At this point no unmarked nodes remain in $I(n_1)$, so $I(n_1) = \{n_1\}$ is complete.

The header list now contains n_2, the successor of $I(n_1)$. To compute $I(n_2)$, we add n_2 to $I(n_2)$ and then consider n_3, whose count is 2. We decrease the count of n_3 by 1, set the reach of n_3 to n_2, and add n_3 to the header list. Thus, we find that $I(n_2) = \{n_2\}$.

The header list now contains n_3, the successor of $I(n_2)$. To compute $I(n_3)$, we begin by placing n_3 in $I(n_3)$. We then consider nodes n_4 and n_5, decreasing their counts from 1 to 0, making their reach n_3, and adding both n_4 and n_5 as unmarked nodes to $I(n_3)$. We mark n_4 by decreasing the count of n_6 from its initial value of 2 to 1, making n_3 the reach of n_6 and adding n_6 to the header list. When we mark n_5 on $I(n_3)$, we change the count of n_6 from 1 to 0, remove n_6 from the header list, and add n_6 to $I(n_3)$.

To mark n_6 on $I(n_3)$, we make the count of n_7 0, set the reach of n_7 to n_3, and add n_7 to $I(n_3)$. Node n_3 is considered next, since there is an edge from n_6 to n_3. Since its reach is n_2, n_3 does not affect $I(n_3)$ or the header list at this point. To mark n_7, we make the count of n_8 0, set the reach of n_8 to n_3, and add n_8 to $I(n_3)$. Node n_2 is also a successor of n_7, but since the reach of n_2 is n_1, n_2 is not added to $I(n_3)$ or the header list. Finally, to mark n_8, no operations are needed, since n_8 has no successors. At this point no unmarked nodes remain in $I(n_3)$, and so $I(n_3) = \{n_3, n_4, n_5, n_6, n_7, n_8\}$.

The header list is now empty, and so the algorithm terminates. In summary, we have partitioned the flow graph into three disjoint intervals:

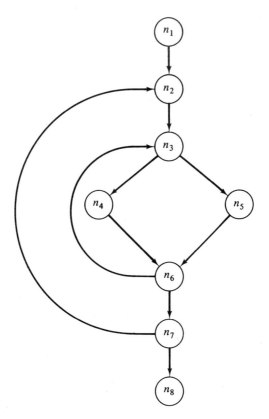

Fig. 11.38 Flow graph.

$$I(n_1) = \{n_1\}$$
$$I(n_2) = \{n_2\}$$
$$I(n_3) = \{n_3, n_4, n_5, n_6, n_7, n_8\}$$

From these intervals we can construct the first derived flow graph F_1. We can then apply Algorithm 11.6 to F_1 to obtain its intervals. Repeating this entire process, we construct the sequence of derived flow graphs shown in Fig. 11.39. □

Example 11.41

Consider the flow graph F in Fig. 11.40. The intervals for F are

$$I(n_1) = \{n_1\}$$
$$I(n_2) = \{n_2\}$$
$$I(n_3) = \{n_3\}$$

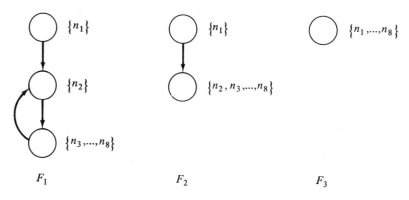

F_1 F_2 F_3

Fig. 11.39   Sequence of flow graphs.

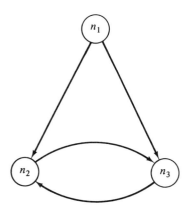

Fig. 11.40   Flow graph F.

We find that $I(F) = F$. Thus, F is not a reducible flow graph.   ☐

THEOREM 11.13

Algorithm 11.6 constructs a set of disjoint intervals whose union is the entire graph.

Proof. Disjointness is obvious. If a node is added to an interval in step (6bi) of Algorithm 11.6, that node will not be added to the header list. If a node is added to an interval in step (6bii), that node is removed from the header list. Likewise, it is easy to show that the union of all $I(n)$ constructed is the set of nodes of F. Assuming that F is a flow graph, every node is accessible from the begin node of F and so is placed either on the header list or in an interval. Unless a node is added to an interval, it will become the header of its own interval.

Finally, we must show that each $I(n)$ constructed is an interval. In step (6), n'' is added to $I(n)$ if and only if its reach is n and its count has been reduced to 0. Thus, every edge entering n'' comes from a node already in $I(n)$, and n'' can be added to $I(n)$ according to the definition of an interval. $\square$

We observe that Algorithm 11.6 can be executed in time proportional to the number of edges in the flow graph on a random access computer. Since a flow graph whose nodes are blocks of a program has no more than two edges leaving any node, this is tantamount to saying that Algorithm 11.6 is linear in the number of blocks in the program. It is left for the Exercises to show that each derived graph constructed from a program of n blocks by repeated application of Algorithm 11.6 has no more than $2n$ edges.

11.4.2. Data Flow Analysis Using Intervals

We shall show how interval analysis can be used to determine the data flow within a reducible graph. The particular problem that we shall discuss is that of determining for each block $\mathcal{B}$ and for each variable A of a reducible flow graph at which statements of the program A could have last been defined when control reaches $\mathcal{B}$. Subsequently, we shall extend the basic interval analysis algorithm to irreducible flow graphs.

It is worthwhile pointing out that part of the merit in the interval approach to data flow analysis lies in treating sets as packed bit vectors. The logical AND, OR, and NOT operations on bit vectors serve to compute set intersections, unions, and complements in a way that is quite efficient on most computers.

We shall now construct tables that give, for each block $\mathcal{B}$ in a program, all locations l at which a given variable A is defined, such that there is a path from l to $\mathcal{B}$ along which A is not redefined. This information can be used to determine the possible values of A upon entering $\mathcal{B}$.

We begin by defining four set-valued functions on blocks.

DEFINITION

A *computation path from statement s_1 to statement s_2* is a sequence of statements beginning with s_1 and ending with s_2 that may be executed in that order during the execution of a program.

Let $\mathcal{B}$ be a block of P. We define four sets of definition statements as follows:

(1) $\text{IN}(\mathcal{B}) = \{d \text{ in } P \mid$ there is a computation path from definition statement d to the first statement of $\mathcal{B}$, such that no statement in this path, except possibly the first statement of $\mathcal{B}$, redefines the variable defined by $d\}$.

(2) $\text{OUT}(\mathcal{B}) = \{d \text{ in } P \mid$ there is a computation path from d to the last

statement of ⊛, such that no statement in this path redefines the variable defined by d}.

(3) TRANS(⊛) = {d in P | the variable defined by d is not defined by any statement in ⊛}.

(4) GEN(⊛) = {d in ⊛ | the variable defined by d is not subsequently defined in ⊛}.

Informally, IN(⊛) contains those definitions that can be active going into ⊛. OUT(⊛) contains those definitions that can be active coming out of ⊛. TRANS(⊛) contains the definitions transmitted through ⊛ without redefinition in ⊛. GEN(⊛) contains those definitions generated in ⊛ that are active on leaving ⊛. It is easy to show that

$$\text{OUT}(⊛) = (\text{IN}(⊛) \cap \text{TRANS}(⊛)) \cup \text{GEN}(⊛)$$

Example 11.42

Consider the following program:

$$
\begin{aligned}
&S1: && I \longleftarrow 1 \\
&S2: && J \longleftarrow 0 \\
&S3: && J \longleftarrow J + I \\
&S4: && \textbf{read } I \\
&S5: && \textbf{if } I < 100 \textbf{ goto } S8 \\
&S6: && \textbf{write } J \\
&S7: && \textbf{halt} \\
&S8: && I \longleftarrow I * I \\
&S9: && \textbf{goto } S3
\end{aligned}
$$

We have labeled each statement for convenience. The flow graph for this program is shown in Fig. 11.41. Each block has been explicitly labeled. Let us determine IN, OUT, TRANS, and GEN for block ⊛$_2$.

Statement $S1$ defines I, and $S1$, $S2$, $S3$ is a computation path that does not define I (except at $S1$). Since this path goes from $S1$ to the first statement of ⊛$_2$, we see that $S1 \in \text{IN}(⊛_2)$. In this manner we can show that

$$\text{IN}(⊛_2) = \{S1, S2, S3, S8\}$$

Note that $S4$ is not in IN(⊛$_2$), because there is no computation path from $S4$ to $S3$ that does not redefine I after $S4$.

OUT(⊛$_2$) does not include $S1$, since all computation paths from $S1$ to $S5$ redefine I. The reader should verify that

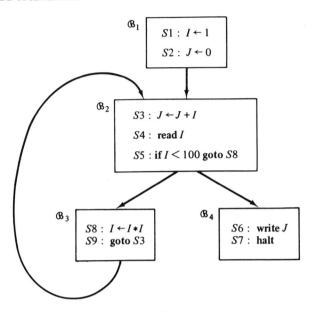

Fig. 11.41   Flow graph.

$$\text{OUT}(\mathcal{B}_2) = \{S3, S4\}$$
$$\text{TRANS}(\mathcal{B}_2) = \varnothing$$
$$\text{GEN}(\mathcal{B}_2) = \{S3, S4\} \qquad\qquad \square$$

The remainder of this section is concerned with the development of an algorithm to compute IN($\mathcal{B}$) for all blocks of a program. Suppose that $\mathcal{B}_1, \ldots, \mathcal{B}_k$ are all the direct predecessors of a block $\mathcal{B}$ in P. (One of these direct predecessors may be $\mathcal{B}$ itself.) Clearly,

$$\text{IN}(\mathcal{B}) = \bigcup_{i=1}^{k} \text{OUT}(\mathcal{B}_i)$$
$$= \bigcup_{i=1}^{k} [(\text{IN}(\mathcal{B}_i) \cap \text{TRANS}(\mathcal{B}_i)) \cup \text{GEN}(\mathcal{B}_i)]$$

To compute IN($\mathcal{B}$), we could write this set equation for each block in the program along with IN($\mathcal{B}_0$) = $\varnothing$, where $\mathcal{B}_0$ is the begin block, and then attempt to solve the collection of simultaneous equations.† However, we shall give an alternative method of solution that takes advantage of the interval structure of flow graphs. We first define what we mean by an entrance and exit of an interval.

---

†As with the regular expression equations of Section 2.2, the solution may not be unique. Here we want the smallest solution.

DEFINITION

Let P be a program and F_0 its flow graph. Let $F_0, F_1, \ldots, F_n$ be the derived sequence of F_0. Each node in F_i, $i \geq 1$, is an interval of F_{i-1} and is called an *interval of order i*.

The *entrance* of an interval of order 1 is the interval header. (Note that this header is a block of the program.) The *entrance* of an interval of order $i > 1$ is the entrance of the header of that interval. Thus, the entrance of any interval is a basic block of the underlying program P.

An *exit* of $I(n)$, an interval of order 1, is the last statement of a block $\mathfrak{B}$ in $I(n)$ such that $\mathfrak{B}$ has a direct descendant which is either the interval header n or a block not in $I(n)$. An *exit* of an interval $I(n)$ of order $i > 1$ is the last statement of a block $\mathfrak{B}$ contained within $I(n)$† such that there is an edge in F_0 from $\mathfrak{B}$ either to the header of interval n or to a block outside $I(n)$.

Note that each interval has one entrance and zero or more exits.

Example 11.43

Let F_0 be the flow graph in Fig. 11.41. Using Algorithm 11.6, we obtain

$$I_1 = I(\mathfrak{B}_1) = \{\mathfrak{B}_1\}$$
$$I_2 = I(\mathfrak{B}_2) = \{\mathfrak{B}_2, \mathfrak{B}_3, \mathfrak{B}_4\}$$

as the partition of F_0 into intervals. From these intervals we can construct the first derived graph F_1 shown in Fig. 11.42. From F_1 we can construct its intervals (there is only one),

$$I_3 = I(I_1) = \{I_1, I_2\} = \{\mathfrak{B}_1, \mathfrak{B}_2, \mathfrak{B}_3, \mathfrak{B}_4\}$$

and obtain the limit flow graph F_2, also shown in Fig. 11.42.

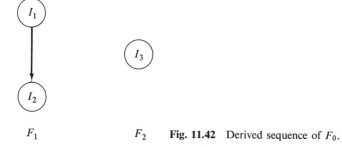

$F_1 \qquad\qquad F_2 \qquad$ **Fig. 11.42** Derived sequence of F_0.

†Strictly speaking, an interval I of order $i > 1$ has intervals of order $i - 1$ as members. We shall informally say that a block $\mathfrak{B}$ is in I if it is in one of I's members. Thus, the set of blocks comprising an interval of arbitrary order is defined as we would intuitively expect.

I_1 and I_2 are intervals of order 1. The entrance of I_2 is $\mathcal{B}_2$. The entrance of I_3 is $\mathcal{B}_1$. The only exit of I_1 is statement $S2$. The only exit of I_2 is statement $S9$. I_3 is an interval of order 2 with entrance $\mathcal{B}_1$. I_3 has no exits.   □

We now extend the functions IN, OUT, TRANS, and GEN to intervals. Let $F_0, F_1, \ldots, F_n$ be the derived sequence of F_0, where F_0 is the flow graph of a program P. Let $\mathcal{B}$ be a block of P and I an interval of some F_i, $i \geq 1$. We make the following recursive definitions:

(1) $\text{IN}(I) = \begin{cases} \text{IN}(\mathcal{B}) \text{ if } I \text{ is of order 1 and } \mathcal{B} \text{ is the header of } I. \\ \text{IN}(I') \text{ if } I \text{ is of order } i > 1 \text{ and } I' \text{ is the header of } I. \end{cases}$

In (2), (3), and (4) below, s is an exit of I.

(2) $\text{OUT}(I, s) = \text{OUT}(\mathcal{B})$ if s is the last statement in $\mathcal{B}$ and $\mathcal{B}$ is in I.

(3) (a) $\text{TRANS}(\mathcal{B}, s) = \text{TRANS}(\mathcal{B})$ if s is the last statement in $\mathcal{B}$.

(b) $\text{TRANS}(I, s)$ is the set of statements d in P such that there exists a cycle-free path $I_1, I_2, \ldots, I_k$ consisting solely of nodes in I and a sequence of exits $s_1, \ldots, s_k$ of $I_1, \ldots, I_k$, respectively, such that

(i) I_1 is the header of I.

(ii) In F_0, s_j is in a block that is a direct predecessor of the entrance of I_{j+1} for $1 \leq j < k$.

(iii) d is in $\text{TRANS}(I_j, s_j)$ for $1 \leq j \leq k$.

(iv) $s_k = s$.

These conditions are illustrated in Fig. 11.43.

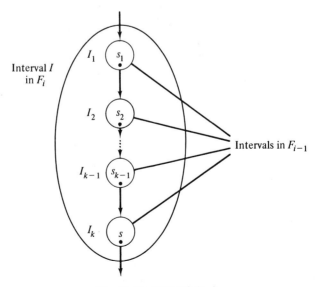

Interval I in F_i

Intervals in F_{i-1}

I_1 $\;$ s_1

I_2 $\;$ s_2

I_{k-1} $\;$ s_{k-1}

I_k $\;$ s

Fig. 11.43 TRANS (I, s).

(4) (a) GEN($\mathcal{B}$, s) = GEN($\mathcal{B}$) if s is the last statement of $\mathcal{B}$.
  (b) GEN(I, s) is the set of d in P such that there is a cycle-free path $I_1, \ldots, I_k$ consisting solely of nodes in I and a sequence of exits $s_1, \ldots, s_k$ of $I_1, \ldots, I_k$, respectively, such that
    (i) d is in GEN(I_1, s_1).
    (ii) In F_0, s_j is in a block that is a direct predecessor of the entrance of I_{j+1}, $1 \leq j < k$.
    (iii) d is in TRANS(I_j, s_j) for $2 \leq j \leq k$.
    (iv) $s_k = s$.
  Note that I_1 need not be the header of I here.

Thus, TRANS(I, s) is the set of definitions that can pass from the entrance of I to exit s without being redefined in I. GEN(I, s) is the set of definitions in I which can reach s without being redefined.

Example 11.44

Let us consider F_0 of Fig. 11.41 and F_1 and F_2 of Fig. 11.42. In F_1, interval I_2 is $\{\mathcal{B}_2, \mathcal{B}_3, \mathcal{B}_4\}$ and has exit $S9$. Thus, IN(I_2) = IN($\mathcal{B}_2$) = $\{S1, S2, S3, S8\}$, and OUT($I_2, S9$) = OUT($\mathcal{B}_3$) = $\{S3, S8\}$.
TRANS($I_2, S9$) = $\varnothing$, since TRANS($\mathcal{B}_2$) = $\varnothing$.
GEN($I_2, S9$) contains $S8$, since there is a sequence of blocks consisting of $\mathcal{B}_3$ alone, with $S8$ in GEN($\mathcal{B}_3, S9$). Also, $S3$ is in GEN($I_2, S9$), because of the sequence of blocks $\mathcal{B}_2, \mathcal{B}_3$, with exits $S5$ and $S9$. That is, $S3$ is in GEN($\mathcal{B}_2, S5$), $\mathcal{B}_2$ is a direct predecessor of $\mathcal{B}_3$, and $S3$ is in TRANS($\mathcal{B}_3, S9$). $\square$

We shall now give an algorithm to compute IN($\mathcal{B}$) for all blocks of a program P. The following algorithm works for only those programs that have a reducible flow graph. Modifications necessary to do the computation for irreducible flow graphs are given in the next section.

ALGORITHM 11.7

Computation of the IN function.

Input. A reducible flow graph F_0 for a program P.

Output. IN($\mathcal{B}$) for each block $\mathcal{B}$ of P.

Method.

(1) Let $F_0, F_1, \ldots, F_k$ be the derived sequence of F_0. Compute TRANS($\mathcal{B}$) and GEN($\mathcal{B}$) for all blocks $\mathcal{B}$ of F_0.
(2) For $i = 1, \ldots, k$, in turn, compute TRANS(I, s) and GEN(I, s) for all intervals of order i and exits s of I. The recursive definition of these functions assures that this can be done.
(3) Define IN(I) = $\varnothing$, where I is the lone interval of order k. Set $i = k$.
(4) Do the following for all intervals of order i. Let $I = \{I_1, \ldots, I_n\}$ be

an interval of order i. $(I_1, \ldots, I_n$ are intervals of order $i - 1$, or blocks, if $i = 1$.) We may assume that the ordering of these subintervals is the order in which they were added to I in Algorithm 11.6. That is, I_1 is the header, and for each $j > 1$, $\{I_1, \ldots, I_{j-1}\}$ contains all nodes of F_{i-1} that are direct predecessors of I_j.

(a) Let $s_1, s_2, \ldots, s_r$ be the exits of I such that each s_i is in a block of F_0 that is a direct predecessor of the entrance of I. Set

$$\text{IN}(I_1) = \text{IN}(I) \cup \bigcup_{i=1}^{r} \text{GEN}(I, s_i)$$

(b) For all exits s of I_1,† set

$$\text{OUT}(I_1, s) = (\text{IN}(I_1) \cap \text{TRANS}(I_1, s)) \cup \text{GEN}(I_1, s)$$

(c) For $j = 2, \ldots, n$, let $s_{r1}, s_{r2}, \ldots, s_{rk_r}$ be the exits of I_r, $1 \leq r < j$, such that each exit is in a block of F_0 that is a direct predecessor of the entrance of I_j. Set

$$\text{IN}(I_j) = \bigcup_{r,l} \text{OUT}(I_r, s_{rl})$$

$$\text{OUT}(I_j, s) = (\text{IN}(I_j) \cap \text{TRANS}(I_j, s)) \cup \text{GEN}(I_j, s)$$

for all exits s of I_j.

(5) If $i = 1$, halt. Otherwise, decrease i by 1 and return to step (4).   □

Example 11.45

Let us apply Algorithm 11.7 to the flow graph of Fig. 11.41.

It is straightforward to compute GEN and TRANS for the four blocks of F_0. These results are summarized below:

Block	GEN	TRANS
$\mathcal{B}_1$	$\{S1, S2\}$	$\varnothing$
$\mathcal{B}_2$	$\{S3, S4\}$	$\varnothing$
$\mathcal{B}_3$	$\{S8\}$	$\{S2, S3\}$
$\mathcal{B}_4$	$\varnothing$	$\{S1, S2, S3, S4, S8\}$

For example, since $\mathcal{B}_3$ defines only the variable I, $\mathcal{B}_3$ "kills" the previous definitions of I but transmits the definitions of J, namely $S2$ and $S3$. Since no block defines a variable twice, all definition statements within a block are in GEN of that block.

We observe that I_1, consisting of $\mathcal{B}_1$ alone, has one exit, the statement $S2$.

---

†If an interval has two exits connecting to the same next interval, they can be "merged" for efficiency of implementation. The "merger" consists of taking the union of the GEN and TRANS functions.

Since paths in I_1 are trivial, $\text{GEN}(I_1, S2) = \{S1, S2\}$ and $\text{TRANS}(I_1, S2)$ is the empty set.

I_2 has exit $S9$. We saw in Example 11.44 that $\text{GEN}(I_2, S9) = \{S3, S8\}$ and $\text{TRANS}(I_2, S9) = \varnothing$.

We can thus begin to compute the IN function. As required, $\text{IN}(I_3) = \varnothing$. Then we can apply step (4) of Algorithm 11.7 to the two subintervals of I_3. The only permissible order for these is I_1, I_2. We compute in step (4a), $\text{IN}(I_1) = \text{IN}(I_3) = \varnothing$, and in step (4b),

$$\text{OUT}(I_1, S2) = (\text{IN}(I_1) \cap \text{TRANS}(I_1, S2)) \cup \text{GEN}(I_1, S2) = \{S1, S2\}.$$

Then, in step (4c),

$$\text{IN}(I_2) = \text{OUT}(I_1, S2) = \{S1, S2\}$$

Going to intervals of order 1, we must consider the constituents of I_1 and I_2. I_1 consists only of $\mathfrak{B}_1$, and so we compute $\text{IN}(\mathfrak{B}_1) = \varnothing$. I_2 consists of $\mathfrak{B}_2, \mathfrak{B}_3$, and $\mathfrak{B}_4$, which we may consider in that order. In step (4a), we have $\text{IN}(\mathfrak{B}_2) = \text{IN}(I_2) \cup \text{GEN}(I_2, S9) = \{S1, S2, S3, S8\}$. In step (4b)

$$\text{OUT}(\mathfrak{B}_2, S5) = (\text{IN}(\mathfrak{B}_2) \cap \text{TRANS}(\mathfrak{B}_2, S5)) \cup \text{GEN}(\mathfrak{B}_2, S5) = \{S3, S4\}$$

Since $S5$ leads to $\mathfrak{B}_3$, we find that $\text{IN}(\mathfrak{B}_3) = \text{OUT}(\mathfrak{B}_2, S5) = \{S3, S4\}$. Then, since $S5$ also leads to $\mathfrak{B}_4$, we find that

$$\text{IN}(\mathfrak{B}_4) = \text{OUT}(\mathfrak{B}_2, S5) = \{S3, S4\}$$

Summarizing, we have

$$\text{IN}(\mathfrak{B}_1) = \varnothing$$
$$\text{IN}(\mathfrak{B}_2) = \{S1, S2, S3, S8\}$$
$$\text{IN}(\mathfrak{B}_3) = \{S3, S4\}$$
$$\text{IN}(\mathfrak{B}_4) = \{S3, S4\} \qquad \square$$

We can prove by induction on the order of I that:

(1) $\text{TRANS}(I, s)$ is the set of definition statements d in P such that there is a path from the first statement of the header of I up to s along which no statement redefines the variable defined by d.

(2) $\text{GEN}(I, s)$ is the set of definitions d such that there is a path from d to s along which no statement redefines the variable defined by d.

Then we can prove the following statement by induction on the number of applications of step (4) of Algorithm 11.7.

(11.4.1)   If step (4) is applied to compute $\text{IN}(I_j)$, then $\text{IN}(I_j)$ is the set of definitions such that there is a path from d to the entrance of I_j along which no statement redefines the variable defined by d, and $\text{OUT}(I_j, s)$ is the set of d such that there is a path from d to s along which no statement redefines the variable defined by d.

The special case of (11.4.1), where I_j is a block, is the following theorem.

THEOREM 11.14

In Algorithm 11.7, for all basic blocks $\mathscr{B}$ in P, $IN(\mathscr{B})$ is the set of definitions d such that there is a path in F_0 from d to the first statement of $\mathscr{B}$ along which no statement redefines the variable defined by d.   □

11.4.3. Irreducible Flow Graphs

While not every flow graph is reducible, there is an additional concept, called node splitting, which allows us to generalize Algorithm 11.7 to all flow graphs. A node n with more than one edge entering is "split" into several identical copies, one for each entering edge. Each copy of n thus has a single edge entering and becomes part of the interval of the node from whence this edge comes. Thus, an application of node splitting followed by interval construction will reduce the number of nodes in the graph by at least 1. Repeating this process if necessary, we can transform any irreducible flow graph into a reducible one.

Example 11.46

Consider the irreducible flow graph in Fig. 11.40 (p. 943). We can split node n_3 into two copies, n_3' and n_3'', to obtain the flow graph F', shown in Fig. 11.44. The intervals for F' are

$$I_1 = I(n_1) = \{n_1, n_3'\}$$
$$I_2 = I(n_2) = \{n_2, n_3''\}$$

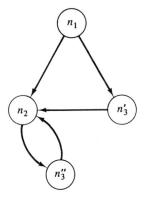

Fig. 11.44   Split flow graph.

F_1', the first derived graph of F' will have two nodes, as shown in Fig. 11.45. The second derived graph of F' consists of a single node. Thus by node splitting we have transformed F into a reducible flow graph F'.   □

Fig. 11.45 First derived graph.

We shall give a modified version of Algorithm 11.7 to take this new technique into account. First, a simple observation is useful.

LEMMA 11.15

If G is a flow graph and $I(G) = G$, then every node n other than the begin node has at least two entering edges; neither edge comes from n.

Proof. Each edge from a node to itself disappears in an application of the interval instruction. Thus, assume that node n has only one entering edge, from another node m. Then n is in $I(m)$. If $I(G) = G$, then node m eventually appears on the header list in Algorithm 11.6. But then n is placed in $I(m)$, and so $I(G)$ cannot be G. $\square$

ALGORITHM 11.8

General computation of the IN function.

Input. An arbitrary flow graph F for a program P.

Output. IN($\mathcal{B}$), for each block $\mathcal{B}$ of P.

Method.

(1) Compute GEN($\mathcal{B}$) and TRANS($\mathcal{B}$) for each block $\mathcal{B}$ of F. Then apply step (2) recursively to F. The input to step (2) is a flow graph G with GEN(I, s) and TRANS(I, s) known for each node I of G and each exit s of I. The output of step (2) is IN(I) for each node I of G.

(2) (a) Let G be the input to this step and let $G, G_1, \ldots, G_k$ be the derived sequence of G. If G_k is a single node, proceed exactly as in Algorithm 11.7. If G_k is not a single node, we may compute GEN and TRANS for all the nodes of $G_1, \ldots, G_k$ as in Algorithm 11.7. Then, by Lemma 11.15, G_k has some node other than the begin node with more than one entering edge. Select one such node I. If I has j entering edges, replace I by new nodes $I_1, \ldots, I_j$. One edge enters each of $I_1, \ldots, I_j$, each from a different node from which an edge previously entered I.

    (b) For each exit s of I, create an exit s_i of I_i, $1 \leq i \leq j$, and imagine that in F there is an edge from each s_i to the entrance of every node to which s connected in G_k. Define GEN(I_i, s_i) = GEN(I, s)

and $\text{TRANS}(I_i, s_i) = \text{TRANS}(I, s)$ for $1 \leq i \leq j$. Call the resulting graph G'.

(c) Apply step (2) to G'. Recursively, the IN function will be computed for G'. Then, compute the IN function for the nodes of G_k by letting $\text{IN}(I) = \bigcup_{i=1}^{j} \text{IN}(I_i)$. No other changes to the IN function are made.

(d) Compute IN for G from the IN function for G_k as in Algorithm 11.7.

(3) After step (2) is complete, the IN function will have been computed for each block of F. This information forms the output of the algorithm. □

Example 11.47

Consider the flow graph F_0 of Fig. 11.46(a). We can compute $F_1 = I(F_0)$, which is shown in Fig. 11.46(b). However, $I(F_1) = F_1$, so we must apply the

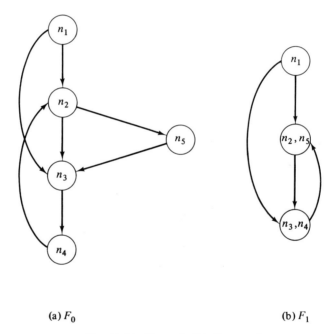

(a) F_0 (b) F_1

Fig. 11.46 Non-reducible flow graphs.

node splitting procedure of step (2). Let node $\{n_2, n_5\}$ be I, and split I into I_1 and I_2. The result is shown in Fig. 11.47. We have chosen to connect n_1 to I_1 and $\{n_3, n_4\}$ to I_2. Edges from I_1 and I_2 to $\{n_3, n_4\}$ have been drawn. Actually, each exit of I is duplicated, one for I_1 and one for I_2. It is the duplicated

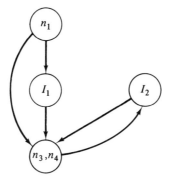

Fig. 11.47 Flow graph.

exits which connect to the entrance of $\{n_3, n_4\}$, a fact which is represented by the two edges in Fig. 11.47. Note that the graph of Fig. 11.47 is reducible.

□

THEOREM 11.15

Algorithm 11.8 always terminates.

Proof. By Lemma 11.15, each call of step (2) is either on a reducible graph, in which case the call surely terminates, or there is a node I which can be split. We observe that each of $I_1, \ldots, I_j$ created in step (2) has a single entering edge. Thus, when the interval construction is applied, they will each find themselves in an interval with another node as header. We conclude that the next call of step (2) will be on graphs with at least one fewer node, so Algorithm 11.8 must terminate.   □

THEOREM 11.16

Algorithm 11.8 correctly computes the IN function.

Proof. It suffices to observe that GEN and TRANS for $I_1, \ldots, I_j$ in step (2) are the same as for I. Moreover, IN(I) is clearly $\bigcup_{i=1}^{j}$ IN(I_i) and OUT(I) is $\bigcup_{i=1}^{j}$ OUT(I_i). Since each I_i connects wherever I connects, the IN function for nodes other than I in G_k is the same as in G'. Thus, a simple induction on the number of calls of step (2) shows that IN is correctly computed.   □

11.4.4. Chapter Summary

If we are going to construct an optimizing compiler, we must first decide what optimizations are worthwhile. This decision should be based on the characteristics of the class of programs the compiler is expected to compile. Unfortunately, these characteristics are often hard to determine and little has been published on this subject.

In this chapter we have approached code optimization from a rather general point of view and it would be wise to ask how the various aspects of code optimization that we have discussed relate to each other.

The techniques of Section 11.2, on arithmetic expressions, can be used at the time the final object program is constructed. However, some aspects of the algorithms in Section 11.2 can also be incorporated into the generation of intermediate code. That is, portions of the algorithms of that section can be built into the output of the syntax analyzer. This will lead to straight-line blocks that tend to make efficient use of registers.

At the code generation phase of the compiler, we have an intermediate program which we may suppose looks something like the "programs" of Section 11.3. Our first task is to construct the flow graph in the manner described in that section. A possible next step is to perform loop optimizations as described in Section 11.3, starting with inner loops and proceeding outward.

Having done this, we can compute global data flow information, e.g., as suggested by Algorithm 11.8 and/or Exercises 11.4.19 and 11.4.20. With this information, we can perform the "global" optimizations of Section 11.3, e.g., constant propagation and common subexpression elimination. At this stage, however, we must be careful not to add steps to inner loops. To do this, we could flag blocks in inner loops and in such blocks avoid an additional store of an expression, even if that expression were used later on in a block outside the loop. If the machine for which we are generating code has more than one register, we can use active variable determination (Exercise 11.4.20) to determine which variables should occupy registers on exit from blocks.

Finally, we can treat the basic blocks by the methods of Section 11.1 or an analogous method, depending on the exact form of the intermediate language. Also at this stage, we allocate registers within the block, subject to the constraints imposed by the global register assignment mentioned above. Some heuristic techniques are usually needed here.

EXERCISES

11.4.1. Construct the derived sequence of flow graphs for the flow graphs in Fig. 11.32 (p. 931) and Fig. 11.36 (p. 934). Are the flow graphs reducible?

11.4.2. Give additional examples of irreducible flow graphs.

11.4.3. Prove Theorem 11.12(1) and (2).

*11.4.4. Show that Algorithm 11.6 can be implemented to run in time proportional to the number of edges in flow graph F.

11.4.5. Prove Theorem 11.14.

11.4.6. Complete the proof of Theorem 11.16.

11.4.7. Use interval analysis (Algorithm 11.7) as the basis of an algorithm that determines, given a statement which references variable A, whether A was explicitly defined to have the same constant value at each execution of the statement. *Hint:* It is necessary to determine which definition statements defining A could have been the previous definition of A before the current execution of the statement in question. It is easy to determine this if there is a previous statement defining A in the block of the statement in question. If not, we need $IN(\mathcal{B})$ for the block of the statement. In the latter case, we say that A has a constant value if and only if all definition statements in $IN(\mathcal{B})$ which define A give A the same constant value.

11.4.8. Give an algorithm using interval analysis as a basis to determine whether a statement S is useless, i.e., whether there is some statement which might use the value defined by S.

11.4.9. Let $\mathcal{B}$ be a block of a flow graph with edges to $\mathcal{B}_1$ and $\mathcal{B}_2$. Let d be a definition statement in $\mathcal{B}$ whose value is not used by $\mathcal{B}$. If no block accessible from $\mathcal{B}_2$ uses the value defined by d, then d may be moved to $\mathcal{B}_1$. Use interval analysis as the basis of an algorithm to detect such situations.

11.4.10. Compute IN for each block of the following program:

$$N \longleftarrow 2$$
$$Y: \quad I \longleftarrow 2$$
$$W: \quad \textbf{if } I < N \textbf{ goto } X$$
$$\textbf{write } N^{.}$$
$$Z: \quad N \longleftarrow N + 1$$
$$\textbf{goto } Y$$
$$X: \quad J \longleftarrow \textbf{remainder}(N, I)$$
$$\textbf{if } J = 0 \textbf{ goto } Z$$
$$I \longleftarrow I + 1$$
$$\textbf{goto } W$$

11.4.11. Compute IN for each block of the following program:

$$\textbf{read } I$$
$$\textbf{if } I = 1 \textbf{ goto } X$$
$$Z: \quad \textbf{if } I > 10 \textbf{ goto } Y$$
$$X: \quad J \longleftarrow I + 3$$
$$\textbf{write } J$$

$$W: \quad I \longleftarrow I + 1$$

goto Z

$$Y: \quad I \longleftarrow I - 1$$

if $I > 15$ **goto** W

halt

*11.4.12. Let T_1 and T_2 be two transformations defined on flow graphs as follows:

T_1: If node n has an edge to itself, remove that edge.

T_2: If node n has a single entering edge, from node m, and n is not the begin node, merge m and n by replacing the edge from m to n by edges from m to each node n' which was formerly entered by an edge from n. Then delete n.

Show that if T_1 and T_2 are applied to a flow graph F until they can no longer be applied, then the result is the limit of F.

*11.4.13. Use the transformations T_1 and T_2 to give an alternative way of computing the IN function without using interval analysis.

**11.4.14. Let G be a flow graph with initial node n_0. Show that G is irreducible if and only if it has nodes n_1, n_2, and n_3 such that there are paths from n_0 to n_1, from n_1 to n_2 and n_3, from n_2 to n_3, and from n_3 to n_2 (See Fig. 11.48) which do not coincide except at their end points. All of n_0, n_1, n_2 and n_3 must be distinct, with the exception that n_1 may be n_0.

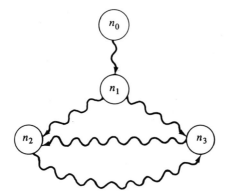

Fig. 11.48 Pattern in every irreducible flow graph.

11.4.15. Show that every d-chart (See Section 1.3.2) is reducible. *Hint:* Use Exercise 11.4.14.

11.4.16. Show that every FORTRAN program in which every transfer to a previous statement of the program is caused by a DO loop has a reducible flow graph.

**11.4.17.   Show that one can determine in time $O(n \log n)$ whether a program flow graph is reducible. *Hint:* Use Exercise 11.4.12.

*11.4.18.   What is the relation between the concepts of intervals and single-entry regions?

*11.4.19.   Give an interval-based algorithm that determines for each expression (say $A + B$) and each block $\mathcal{B}$ whether every execution of the program must reach a statement which computes $A + B$ (i.e., there is a statement of the form $C \leftarrow A + B$) and which does not subsequently redefine A or B. *Hint:* If $\mathcal{B}$ is not the begin block, let $\text{IN}(\mathcal{B}) = \cap_i \text{OUT}(\mathcal{B}_i)$, where the $\mathcal{B}_i$'s are all the direct predecessors of $\mathcal{B}$. Let $\text{OUT}(\mathcal{B})$ be

$$(\text{IN}(\mathcal{B}) \cap X) \cup Y$$

where X is the set of expressions "killed" in $\mathcal{B}$ (we "kill" $A + B$ by redefining A or B) and Y is the set of expressions computed by the block and not killed. For each interval I of the various derived graphs and each exit s of I, compute $\text{GEN}'(I, S)$ to be the set of expressions which are computed and not subsequently killed in every path from the entrance of I to exit s. Also, compute $\text{TRANS}'(I, s)$ to be the set of expressions which if killed, are subsequently generated in every such path. Note that $\text{GEN}'(I, s) \subseteq \text{TRANS}' (I, s)$.

*11.4.20.   Give an algorithm, based on interval analysis, that determines for each variable A and each block $\mathcal{B}$ whether there is an execution which after passing through $\mathcal{B}$ will reference A before redefining it.

11.4.21.   Let F be an n node flow graph with e edges. Show that the ith-derived graph of F has no more than $e - i$ edges.

*11.4.22.   Give an example of an n node flow graph with $2n$ edges whose derived sequence is of length n.

*11.4.23.   Show that Algorithm 11.7 and the algorithms of Exercises 11.4.19 and 11.4.20 take at most $O(n^2)$ bit vector steps on flow graphs of n nodes and at most $2n$ edges.

There is another approach to data flow analysis which is tabular in nature. For example, in analogy with Algorithm 11.8, we could compute a table $\text{IN}(d, \mathcal{B})$ which had value 1 if definition d was in $\text{IN}(\mathcal{B})$ and 0 otherwise. Initially, let $\text{IN}(d, \mathcal{B}) = 1$ if and only if there is a node $\mathcal{B}'$ with an edge to $\mathcal{B}$ and d is in $\text{GEN}(\mathcal{B}')$. For each 1 added to the table, say at entry $(d, \mathcal{B})$, place a 1 in entry $(d, \mathcal{B}'')$ if there is an edge from $\mathcal{B}$ to $\mathcal{B}''$ and $\mathcal{B}$ does not kill d.

*11.4.24.   Show that the above algorithm correctly computes $\text{IN}(\mathcal{B})$ and that it operates in time $O(mn)$ on an n node flow graph with at most $2n$ edges and m definitions.

*11.4.25.   Give algorithms similar to the above performing the tasks of Exercises 11.4.19 and 11.4.20. How fast do they run?

**11.4.26.   Give algorithms requiring $0(n \log n)$ bit vector steps to compute the IN functions of Algorithm 11.7 or Exercise 11.4.19 for flow graphs of n nodes.

**11.4.27.   Show that a flow graph is reducible if and only if its edge set can be partitioned into two sets E_1 and E_2, where (1) E_1 forms a dag, and (2) If (m, n) is in E_2, then $m = n$, or n dominates m.

**11.4.28.   Give an $0(n \log n)$ algorithm to compute direct dominators for an n node reducible graph.

Research Problems

11.4.29.   Suggest some additional data flow information (other than that mentioned in Algorithm 11.7 and Exercises 11.4.19 and 11.4.20) which would be useful for code optimization purposes. Give algorithms to compute these, both for reducible and for irreducible flow graphs.

11.4.30.   Are there techniques to compute the IN function of Algorithm 11.8 or other data flow functions that are superior to node splitting for irreducible graphs? By "superior," we are assuming that bit vector operations are permissible, or else the algorithms of Exercises 11.4.24 and 11.4.25 are clearly optimal.

BIBLIOGRAPHIC NOTES

The interval analysis approach to code optimization was developed by Cocke [1970] and further elaborated by Cocke and Schwartz [1970] and Allen [1970]. Kennedy [1971] discusses a global algorithm that uses interval analysis to recognize active variables in a program (Exercise 11.4.20).

The solutions to Exercises 11.4.12–11.4.16 can be found in Hecht and Ullman [1972a]. Exercise 11.4.17 is from Hopcroft and Ullman [1972b]. An answer to Exercise 11.4.19 can be found in Cocke [1970] or Schaefer [1973]. Exercises 11.4.24 and 11.4.26 are from Ullman [1972b]. Exercise 11.4.27 is from Hecht and Ullman [1972b]. Exercise 11.4.28 is from Aho, Hopcroft and Ullman [1972].

There are several papers that discuss the implementation of optimizing compilers. Lowry and Medlock [1969] discuss some optimizations used in the OS/360 FORTRAN H compiler. Busam and Englund [1969] present techniques for the recognition of common subexpressions, the removal of invariant computations from loops, and register allocation in another FORTRAN compiler.

Knuth [1971] collected a large sample of FORTRAN programs and analyzed some of their characteristics.

BIBLIOGRAPHY FOR VOLUMES I AND II

AHO, A. V. [1968]
Indexed grammars—an extension of context-free grammars.
J. ACM **15**:4, 647–671.

AHO, A. V. (ed.) [1973]
Currents in the Theory of Computing.
Prentice-Hall, Englewood Cliffs, N.J.

AHO, A. V., P. J. DENNING, and J. D. ULLMAN [1972]
Weak and mixed strategy precedence parsing.
J. ACM **19**:2, 225–243.

AHO, A. V., J. E. HOPCROFT, and J. D. ULLMAN [1968]
Time and tape complexity of pushdown automaton languages.
Information and Control **13**:3, 186–206.

AHO A. V., J. E. HOPCROFT, and J. D. ULLMAN [1972]
On finding lowest common ancestors in trees.
Proc. Fifth Annual ACM Symposium on Theory of Computing, (May, 1973), 253–265.

AHO, A. V., S. C. JOHNSON, and J.D. ULLMAN [1972]
Deterministic parsing of ambiguous grammars.
Unpublished manuscript, Bell Laboratories, Murray Hill, N.J.

AHO, A. V., R. SETHI, and J. D. ULLMAN [1972]
Code optimization and finite Church–Rosser systems.
In *Design and Optimization of Compilers*
(R. Rustin, ed.). Prentice-Hall, Englewood
Cliffs, N.J., pp. 89–106.

AHO, A. V., and J. D. ULLMAN [1969a]
Syntax directed translations and the pushdown assembler.
J. Computer and System Sciences **3**:1, 37–56.

AHO, A. V., and J. D. ULLMAN [1969b]
Properties of syntax directed translations.
J. Computer and System Sciences 3:3, 319–334.

AHO, A. V., and J. D. ULLMAN [1971]
Translations on a context-free grammar.
Information and Control 19:5, 439–475.

AHO, A. V., and J. D. ULLMAN [1972a]
Linear precedence functions for weak precedence grammars.
International J. Computer Mathematics, Section A, 3, 149–155.

AHO, A. V., and J. D. ULLMAN [1972b]
Error detection in precedence parsers.
Mathematical Systems Theory, 7:2 (February 1973), 97–113.

AHO, A. V., and J. D. ULLMAN [1972c]
Optimization of LR(k) parsers.
J. Computer and System Sciences, 6:6, 573–602.

AHO, A. V., and J. D. ULLMAN [1972d]
A technique for speeding up LR(k) parsers.
Proc. Fourth Annual ACM Symposium on Theory of Computing, pp. 251–263.

AHO, A. V., and J. D. ULLMAN [1972e]
Optimization of straight line code.
SIAM J. on Computing 1:1, 1–19.

AHO, A. V., and J. D. ULLMAN [1972f]
Equivalence of programs with structured variables.
J. Computer and System Sciences 6:2, 125–137.

AHO, A. V., and J. D. ULLMAN [1972g]
LR(k) syntax directed translation.
Unpublished manuscript, Bell Laboratories, Murray Hill, N.J.

ALLARD, R. W., K. A. WOLF, and R. A. ZEMLIN [1964]
Some effects of the 6600 computer on language structures.
Comm. ACM 7:2, 112–127.

ALLEN, F. E. [1969]
Program optimization.
Annual Review in Automatic Programming, Vol. 5., Pergamon, Elmsford, N.Y.

ALLEN, F. E. [1970]
Control flow analysis.
ACM SIGPLAN Notices 5:7, 1–19.

ALLEN, F. E., and J. COCKE [1972]
A catalogue of optimizing transformations.
In *Design and Optimization of Compilers*
(R. Rustin, ed.). Prentice-Hall, Englewood Cliffs, N.J., pp. 1–30.

ANDERSON, J. P. [1964]
A note on some compiling algorithms.
Comm. ACM 7:3, 149–150.

ANS X.3.9 [1966]
American National Standard FORTRAN.
American National Standards Institute, New York.

ANSI SUBCOMMITTEE X3J3 [1971]
Clarification of FORTRAN standards—second report.
Comm. ACM **14**:10, 628–642.

ARBIB, M. A. [1969]
Theories of Abstract Automata.
Prentice-Hall, Englewood Cliffs, N.J.

BACKUS, J. W., et al. [1957]
The FORTRAN Automatic Coding System.
Proc. Western Joint Computer Conference, Vol. 11, pp. 188–198.

BAER, J. L., and D. P. BOVET [1968]
Compilation of arithmetic expressions for parallel computations.
Proc. IFIP Congress 68, B4–B10.

BAGWELL, J. T. [1970]
Local optimizations.
ACM SIGPLAN Notices **5**:7, 52–66.

BAR-HILLEL, Y. [1964]
Language and Information.
Addison-Wesley, Reading, Mass.

BAR-HILLEL Y., M. PERLES, and E. SHAMIR [1961]
On formal properties of simple phrase structure grammars.
Z. Phonetik, Sprachwissenschaft und Kommunikationsforschung **14**, 143–172.
Also in Bar-Hillel [1964], pp. 116–150.

BARNETT, M. P., and R. P. FUTRELLE [1962]
Syntactic analysis by digital computer.
Comm. ACM **5**:10, 515–526.

BAUER, H., S. BECKER, and S. GRAHAM [1968]
ALGOL W implementation.
CS98, Computer Science Department, Stanford University, Stanford, Cal.

BEALS, A. J. [1969]
The generation of a deterministic parsing algorithm.
Report No. 304, Department of Computer Science,
University of Illinois, Urbana.

BEALS, A. J., J. E. LAFRANCE, and R. S. NORTHCOTE [1969]
The automatic generation of Floyd production syntactic analyzers.
Report No. 350. Department of Computer Science,
University of Illinois, Urbana.

BEATTY, J. C. [1972]
An axiomatic approach to code optimization for expressions.
J. ACM, **19**:4.

BELADY, L. A. [1966]
A study of replacement algorithms for a virtual storage computer.
IBM Systems J. **5**, 78–82.

BELL, J. R. [1969]
A new method for determining linear precedence functions for precedence grammars.
Comm. ACM **12**:10, 316–333.

BELL, J. R. [1970]
The quadratic quotient method: a hash code eliminating secondary clustering.
Comm. ACM **13**:2, 107–109.

BERGE, C. [1958]
The Theory of Graphs and Its Applications.
Wiley, New York.

BIRMAN, A., and J. D. ULLMAN [1970]
Parsing algorithms with backtrack.
IEEE Conference Record of 11th Annual Symposium on Switching and Automata Theory, pp. 153–174.

BLATTNER, M. [1972]
The unsolvability of the equality problem for sentential forms of context-free languages.
Unpublished Memorandum, UCLA, Los Angeles, Calif. To appear in *JCSS*.

BOBROW, D. G. [1963]
Syntactic analysis of English by computer—a survey.
Proc. AFIPS Fall Joint Computer Conference, Vol. 24.
Spartan, New York, pp. 365–387.

BOOK, R. V. [1970]
Problems in formal language theory.
Proc. Fourth Annual Princeton Conference on Information Sciences and Systems, pp. 253–256. Also see Aho [1973].

BOOTH, T. L. [1967]
Sequential Machines and Automata Theory.
Wiley, New York.

BORODIN, A. [1970]
Computational complexity—a survey.
Proc. Fourth Annual Princeton Conference on Information Sciences and Systems, pp. 257–262. Also see Aho [1973].

BRACHA, N. [1972]
Transformations on loop-free program schemata.
Report No. UIUCDCS-R-72-516, Department of Computer Science, University of Illinois, Urbana

BRAFFORT, P., and D. HIRSCHBERG (eds.) [1963]
Computer Programming and Formal Systems.
North-Holland, Amsterdam.

BREUER, M. A. [1969]
Generation of optimal code for expressions via factorization.
Comm. ACM **12**:6, 333–340.

BROOKER, R. A., and D. MORRIS [1963]
The compiler-compiler.
Annual Review in Automatic Programming, Vol. 3.
Pergamon, Elmsford, N.Y., pp. 229–275.

BRUNO, J. L., and W. A. BURKHARD [1970]
A circularity test for interpreted grammars.
Technical Report 88. Computer Sciences Laboratory, Department of Electrical
Engineering, Princeton University, Princeton, N.J.

BRZOZOWSKI, J. A. [1962]
A survey of regular expressions and their applications.
IRE Trans. on Electronic Computers **11**:3, 324–335.

BRZOZOWSKI, J. A. [1964]
Derivatives of regular expressions.
J. ACM **11**:4, 481–494.

BUSAM, V. A., and D. E. ENGLUND [1969]
Optimization of expressions in Fortran.
Comm. ACM **12**:12, 666–674.

CANTOR, D. G. [1962]
On the ambiguity problem of Backus systems.
J. ACM **9**:4, 477–479.

CAVINESS, B. F. [1970]
On canonical forms and simplification.
J. ACM **17**:2, 385–396.

CHEATHAM, T. E., [1965]
The TGS-II translator-generator system.
Proc. IFIP Congress 65. Spartan, New York, pp. 592–593.

CHEATHAM, T. E. [1966]
The introduction of definitional facilities into higher level programming
languages.
Proc. AFIPS Fall Joint Computer Conference. Vol. 30.
Spartan, New York, pp. 623–637.

CHEATHAM, T. E. [1967]
The Theory and Construction of Compilers (2nd ed.).
Computer Associates, Inc., Wakefield, Mass.

CHEATHAM, T. E., and K. SATTLEY [1964]
Syntax directed compiling.
Proc. AFIPS Spring Joint Computer Conference, Vol. 25. Spartan, New York,
pp. 31–57.

CHEATHAM, T. E., and T. STANDISH [1970]
Optimization aspects of compiler-compilers.
ACM SIGPLAN Notices 5:10, 10–17.

CHEN, S. [1972]
On the Sethi–Ullman algorithm.
Unpublished memorandum, Bell Laboratories, Holmdel, N.J.

CHOMSKY, N. [1965]
Three models for the description of language.
IEEE Trans. on Information Theory 2:3, 113–124.

CHOMSKY, N. [1957]
Syntactic Structures.
Mouton and Co., The Hague.

CHOMSKY, N. [1959a]
On certain formal properties of grammars.
Information and Control 2:2, 137–167.

CHOMSKY, N. [1959b]
A note on phrase structure grammars.
Information and Control 2:4, 393–395.

CHOMSKY, N. [1962]
Context-free grammars and pushdown storage.
Quarterly Progress Report No. 65. Research Laboratory of Electronics, Massachusetts Institute of Technology, Cambridge, Mass.

CHOMSKY, N. [1963]
Formal properties of grammars.
In *Handbook of Mathematical Psychology*, Vol. 2, R. D. Luce, R. R. Bush, and E. Galanter (eds.). Wiley, New York, pp. 323–418.

CHOMSKY, N. [1965]
Aspects of the Theory of Syntax.
M.I.T. Press, Cambridge, Mass.

CHOMSKY, N., and G. A. MILLER [1958]
Finite state languages.
Information and Control 1:2, 91–112.

CHOMSKY, N., and M. P. SCHUTZENBERGER [1963]
The algebraic theory of context-free languages.
In Braffort and Hirschberg [1963], pp. 118–161.

CHRISTENSEN, C., and J. C. SHAW (eds.) [1969]
Proc. of the extensible languages symposium.
ACM SIGPLAN Notices 4:8.

CHURCH, A. [1941]
The Calculi of Lambda-Conversion.
Annals of Mathematics Studies, Vol. 6.
Princeton University Press, Princeton, N.J.

CHURCH, A. [1956]
Introduction to Mathematical Logic.
Princeton University Press, Princeton, N.J.

CLARK, E. R. [1967]
On the automatic simplification of source language programs.
Comm. ACM **10**:3, 160–164.

COCKE, J. [1970]
Global common subexpression elimination.
ACM SIGPLAN Notices **5**:7, 20–24.

COCKE, J., and J. T. SCHWARTZ [1970]
Programming Languages and Their Compilers (2nd ed.).
Courant Institute of Mathematical Sciences, New York University, New York.

COHEN, D. J., and C. C. GOTLIEB [1970]
A list structure form of grammars for syntactic analysis.
Computing Surveys **2**: 1, 65–82.

COHEN, R. S., and K. CULIK, II [1971]
LR-regular grammars—an extension of LR(k) grammars.
IEEE Conference Record of 12th Annual Symposium on Switching and Automata Theory, pp. 153–165.

COLMERAUER, A. [1970]
Total precedence relations.
J. ACM **17**:1, 14–30.

CONWAY, M. E. [1963]
Design of a separable transition-diagram compiler.
Comm. ACM **6**:7, 396–408.

CONWAY, R. W., and W. L. MAXWELL [1963]
CORC: the Cornell computing language.
Comm. ACM **6**:6, 317–321.

CONWAY, R. W., and W. L. MAXWELL [1968]
CUPL—an approach to introductory computing instruction.
Technical Report No. 68–4. Department of Computer Science,
Cornell University, Ithaca, N.Y.

CONWAY, R. W., et al. [1970]
PL/C. A high performance subset of PL/I.
Technical Report 70–55. Department of Computer Science,
Cornell University, Ithaca, N.Y.

COOK, S. A. [1971]
Linear time simulation of deterministic two-way pushdown automata.
Proc. IFIP Congress 71, TA–2. North-Holland, Amsterdam. pp. 174–179.

COOK, S. A., and S. D. AANDERAA [1969]
On the minimum computation time of functions.
Trans. American Math. Soc. **142**, 291–314.

CULIK, K., II [1968]
Contribution to deterministic top-down analysis of context-free languages.
Kybernetika **4**:5, 422–431.

CULIK, K., II [1970]
n-ary grammars and the description of mapping of languages.
Kybernetika **6**, 99–117.

DAVIS, M. [1958]
Computability and Unsolvability.
McGraw-Hill, New York.

DAVIS, M. (ed.) [1965]
The Undecidable. Basic papers in undecidable propositions, unsolvable problems and computable functions.
Raven Press, New York.

DE BAKKER, J. W. [1971]
Axiom systems for simple assignment statements.
In Engeler [1971], pp. 1–22.

DEREMER, F. L. [1968]
On the generation of parsers for BNF grammars: an algorithm.
Report No. 276. Department of Computer Science,
University of Illinois, Urbana.

DEREMER, F. L. [1969]
Practical translators for LR(*k*) languages.
Ph. D. Thesis, Massachusetts Institute of Technology, Cambridge, Mass.

DEREMER, F. L. [1971]
Simple LR(*k*) grammars.
Comm. ACM **14**:7, 453–460.

DEWAR, R. B. K., R. R. HOCHSPRUNG, and W. S. WORLEY [1969]
The IITRAN programming language.
Comm. ACM **12**:10, 569–575.

EARLEY, J. [1966]
Generating a recognizer for a BNF grammar.
Computation Center Report, Carnegie-Mellon University, Pittsburgh.

EARLEY, J. [1968]
An efficient context-free parsing algorithm.
Ph. D. Thesis, Carnegie-Mellon University, Pittsburgh.
Also see *Comm. ACM* (February, 1970) **13**:2, 94–102.

EICKEL, J., M. PAUL, F. L. BAUER, and K. SAMELSON [1963]
A syntax-controlled generator of formal language processors.
Comm. ACM **6**:8, 451–455.

ELSON, M., and S. T. RAKE [1970]
Code-generation technique for large-language compilers.
IBM Systems J. **9**:3, 166–188.

ELSPAS, B., M. W. GREEN, and K. N. LEVITT [1971]
Software reliability.
Computer 1, 21–27.

ENGELER, E. (ed.) [1971]
Symposium on Semantics of Algorithmic Languages.
Lecture Notes in Mathematics. Springer, Berlin.

EVANS, A., JR. [1964]
An ALGOL 60 compiler.
Annual Review in Automatic Programming, Vol. 4.
Pergamon, Elmsford, N.Y., pp. 87–124.

EVEY, R. J. [1963]
Applications of pushdown-store machines.
Proc. AFIPS Fall Joint Computer Conference, Vol. 24.
Spartan, New York, pp. 215–227.

FELDMAN, J. A. [1966]
A formal semantics for computer languages and its application in a compiler-compiler.
Comm. ACM 9:1, 3–9.

FELDMAN, J. A., and D. GRIES [1968]
Translator writing systems.
Comm. ACM 11:2, 77–113.

FISCHER, M. J. [1968]
Grammars with macro-like productions.
IEEE Conference Record of 9th Annual Symposium on Switching and Automata Theory, pp. 131–142.

FISCHER, M. J. [1969]
Some properties of precedence languages.
Proc. ACM Symposium on Theory of Computing, pp. 181–190.

FISCHER, M. J. [1972]
Efficiency of equivalence algorithms.
Memo No. 256, Artificial Intelligence Laboratory, Massachusetts Institute of Technology, Cambridge, Mass.

FLOYD, R. W. [1961a]
An algorithm for coding efficient arithmetic operations.
Comm. ACM 4:1, 42–51.

FLOYD, R. W. [1961b]
A descriptive language for symbol manipulation.
J. ACM 8:4, 579–584.

FLOYD, R. W. [1962a]
Algorithm 97: shortest path.
Comm. ACM 5:6, 345.

FLOYD, R. W. [1962b]
On ambiguity in phrase structure languages.
Comm. ACM **5**: 10, 526–534.

FLOYD, R. W. [1963]
Syntactic analysis and operator precedence.
J. ACM **10**: 3, 316–333.

FLOYD, R. W. [1964a]
Bounded context syntactic analysis.
Comm. ACM **7**: 2, 62–67.

FLOYD, R. W. [1964b]
The syntax of programming languages—a survey.
IEEE Trans. on Electronic Computers **EC–13**: 4, 346–353.

FLOYD, R. W. [1967a]
Assigning meanings to programs.
In Schwartz [1967], pp. 19–32.

FLOYD, R. W. [1967b]
Nondeterministic algorithms.
J. ACM **14**: 4, 636–644.

FRAILEY, D. J. [1970]
Expression optimization using unary complement operators.
ACM SIGPLAN Notices **5**: 7, 67–85.

FREEMAN, D. N. [1964]
Error correction in CORC, the Cornell computing language.
Proc. AFIPS Fall Joint Computer Conference, Vol. 26.
Spartan, New York, pp. 15–34.

GALLER, B. A., and A. J. PERLIS [1967]
A proposal for definitions in ALGOL.
Comm. ACM **10**: 4, 204–219.

GARWICK, J. V. [1964]
GARGOYLE, a language for compiler writing.
Comm. ACM **7**: 1, 16–20.

GARWICK, J. V. [1968]
GPL, a truly general purpose language.
Comm. ACM **11**: 9, 634–638.

GEAR, C. W. [1965]
High speed compilation of efficient object code.
Comm. ACM **8**: 8, 483–487.

GENTLEMAN, W. M. [1971]
A portable coroutine system.
Proc. IFIP Congress 71, TA-3. North-Holland, Amsterdam, pp. 94–98.

GILL, A. [1962]
Introduction to the Theory of Finite State Machines.
McGraw-Hill, New York.

GINSBURG, S. [1962]
An Introduction to Mathematical Machine Theory.
Addison-Wesley, Reading, Mass.

GINSBURG, S. [1966]
The Mathematical Theory of Context-Free Languages.
McGraw-Hill, New York.

GINSBURG, S., and S. A. GREIBACH [1966]
Deterministic context-free languages.
Information and Control **9**: 6, 620–648.

GINSBURG, S., and S. A. GREIBACH [1969]
Abstract families of languages.
Memoir American Math. Soc. No. 87, 1–32.

GINSBURG, S., and H. G. RICE [1962]
Two families of languages related to ALGOL.
J. ACM **9**: 3, 350–371.

GINZBURG, A. [1968]
Algebraic Theory of Automata.
Academic Press, New York.

GLENNIE, A. [1960]
On the syntax machine and the construction of a universal compiler.
Technical Report No. 2. Computation Center,
Carnegie-Mellon University, Pittsburg, Pa.

GRAHAM, R. L. [1972]
Bounds on multiprocessing anomalies and related packing algorithms.
Proc. AFIPS Spring Joint Computer Conference, Vol. 40
AFIPS Press, Montvale, N.J. pp. 205–217.

GRAHAM, R. M. [1964]
Bounded context translation.
Proc. AFIPS Spring Joint Computer Conference, Vol. 25.
Spartan, New York, pp. 17–29.

GRAHAM, S. L. [1970]
Extended precedence languages, bounded right context languages and deterministic languages.
IEEE Conference Record of 11th Annual Symposium on Switching and Automata Theory, pp. 175–180.

GRAU, A. A., U. HILL, and H. LANGMAACK [1967]
Translation of ALGOL 60.
Springer-Verlag, New York

GRAY, J. N. [1969]
Precedence parsers for programming languages.
Ph. D. Thesis, Department of Computer Science, University of California, Berkeley.

GRAY, J. N., and M. A. HARRISON [1969]
Single pass precedence analysis.
IEEE Conference Record of 10th Annual Symposium on Switching and Automata Theory, pp. 106–117.

GRAY, J. N., M. A. HARRISON, and O. IBARRA [1967]
Two way pushdown automata.
Information and Control 11:1, 30–70.

GREIBACH, S. A. [1965]
A new normal form theorem for context-free phrase structure grammars.
J. ACM 12:1, 42–52.

GREIBACH S. A., and J. E. HOPCROFT [1969]
Scattered context grammars.
J. Computer and System Sciences 3:3, 233–247.

GRIES, D. [1971]
Compiler Construction for Digital Computers.
Wiley, New York.

GRIFFITHS, T. V. [1968]
The unsolvability of the equivalence problem for Λ-free nondeterministic generalized machines.
J. ACM 15:3, 409–413.

GRIFFITHS, T. V., and S. R. PETRICK [1965]
On the relative efficiencies of context-free grammar recognizers.
Comm. ACM 8:5, 289–300.

GRISWOLD, R. E., J. F. POAGE, and I. P. POLONSKY [1971]
The SNOBOL4 Programming Language (2nd ed.).
Prentice-Hall, Englewood Cliffs, N.J.

GROSS, M., and A. LENTIN [1970]
Introduction to Formal Grammars.
Springer-Verlag, New York.

HAINES, L. H. [1970]
Representation theorems for context-sensitive languages.
Department of Electrical Engineering and Computer Sciences, University of California, Berkeley.

HALMOS, P. R. [1960]
Naive Set Theory.
Van Nostrand Reinhold, New York.

HALMOS, P. R. [1963]
Lectures on Boolean Algebras.
Van Nostrand Reinhold, New York.

HARARY, E. [1969]
Graph Theory.
Addison-Wesley, Reading, Mass.

HARRISON, M. A. [1965]
Introduction to Switching and Automata Theory.
McGraw-Hill, New York.

HARTMANIS, J., and J. E. HOPCROFT [1970]
An overview of the theory of computational complexity.
J. ACM **18**:3, 444–475.

HARTMANIS, J., P. M. LEWIS, II, and R. E. STEARNS [1965]
Classifications of computations by time and memory requirements.
Proc. IFIP Congress 65. Spartan, New York, pp. 31–35.

HAYNES, H. R., and L. J. SCHUTTE [1970]
Compilation of optimized syntactic recognizers from Floyd-Evans productions.
ACM SIGPLAN Notices **5**:7, 38–51.

HAYS, D. G. [1967]
Introduction to Computational Linguistics.
American Elsevier, New York.

HECHT, M. S., and J. D. ULLMAN [1972a]
Flow graph reducibility.
SIAM J. on Computing **1**:2, 188–202.

HECHT, M. S., and J. D. ULLMAN [1972b]
Unpublished memorandum,
Department of Electrical Engineering, Princeton University

HELLERMAN, H. [1966]
Parallel processing of algebraic expressions.
IEEE Trans. on Electronic Computers **EC-15**:1, 82–91.

HEXT, J. B., and P. S. ROBERTS [1970]
Syntax analysis by Domolki's algorithm.
Computer J. **13**:3, 263–271.

HOPCROFT, J. E. [1971]
An $n \log n$ algorithm for minimizing states in a finite automaton.
CS71-190. Computer Science Department, Stanford University, Stanford, Cal.
Also in *Theory of Machines and Computations,* Z. Kohavi and A. Paz (eds).
Academic Press, New York, pp. 189–196.

HOPCROFT, J. E., and J. D. ULLMAN [1967]
An approach to a unified theory of automata.
Bell System Tech. J. **46**:8, 1763–1829.

HOPCROFT, J. E., and J. D. ULLMAN [1969]
Formal Languages and Their Relation to Automata.
Addison-Wesley, Reading, Mass.

HOPCROFT, J. E., and J. D. ULLMAN [1972a]
Set merging algorithms.
Unpublished memorandum. Department of Computer Science,
Cornell University, Ithaca, N.Y.

HOPCROFT, J.E., and J. D. ULLMAN [1972b]
An $n \log n$ algorithm to detect reducible graphs
Proc. Sixth Annual Princeton Conference on Information Sciences and Systems,
pp. 119–122.

HOPGOOD, F. R. A. [1969]
Compiling Techniques.
American Elsevier, New York.

HOPKINS, M. E. [1971]
An optimizing compiler design.
Proc. IFIP Congress 71, TA-3. North-Holland, Amsterdam, pp. 69–73.

HORWITZ, L. P., R. M. KARP, R. E. MILLER, and S. WINOGRAD [1966]
Index register allocation.
J. ACM **13**:1, 43–61.

HUFFMAN, D. A. [1954]
The synthesis of sequential switching circuits.
J. Franklin Institute **257**, 3–4, 161, 190, and 275–303.

HUXTABLE, D. H. R. [1964]
On writing an optimizing translator for ALGOL 60.
In *Introduction to System Programming*, Academic Press, New York.

IANOV, I. I. [1958]
On the equivalence and transformation of program schemes.
Translation in *Comm. ACM* **1**:10, 8–11.

IBM [1969]
System 360 Operating System PL/I (F) Compiler Program Logic Manual.
Publ. No. Y286800, IBM, Hursley, Winchester, England.

ICHBIAH, J. D., and S. P. MORSE [1970]
A technique for generating almost optimal Floyd-Evans productions for
precedence grammars.
Comm. ACM **13**:8, 501–508.

IGARISHI, S. [1968]
On the equivalence of programs represented by Algol-like statements.
Report of the Computer Centre, University of Tokyo **1**, pp. 103–118.

INGERMAN, P. Z. [1966]
A Syntax Oriented Translator.
Academic Press, New York.

IRLAND, M. I., and P. C. FISCHER [1970]
A bibliography on computational complexity.
CSRR 2028. Department of Applied Analysis and Computer Science,
University of Waterloo, Ontario.

IRONS, E. T. [1961]
A syntax directed compiler for ALGOL 60.
Comm. ACM **4**:1, 51–55.

IRONS, E. T. [1963a]
An error correcting parse algorithm.
Comm. ACM **6**:11, 669–673.

IRONS, E. T. [1963b]
The structure and use of the syntax directed compiler.
Annual Review in Automatic Programming, Vol. 3.
Pergamon, Elmsford, N.Y., pp. 207–227.

IRONS, E. T. [1964]
Structural connections in formal languages.
Comm. ACM **7**:2, 62–67.

JOHNSON, W. L., J. H. PORTER, S. I. ACKLEY, and D. T. ROSS [1968]
Automatic generation of efficient lexical processors using finite state techniques.
Comm. ACM **11**:12, 805–813.

KAMEDA, T., and P. WEINER [1968]
On the reduction of nondeterministic automata.
Proc. Second Annual Princeton Conference on Information Sciences and Systems,
pp. 348–352.

KAPLAN, D. M. [1970]
Proving things about programs.
Proc. 4th Annual Princeton Conference on Information Sciences and Systems,
pp. 244–251.

KASAMI, T. [1965]
An efficient recognition and syntax analysis algorithm for context-free languages.
Scientific Report AFCRL-65-758. Air Force Cambridge Research Laboratory,
Bedford, Mass.

KASAMI, T., and K. TORII [1969]
A syntax analysis procedure for unambiguous context-free grammars.
J. ACM **16**:3, 423–431.

KENNEDY, K. [1971]
A global flow analysis algorithm.
International J. Computer Mathematics **3**:1, 5–16

KENNEDY, K. [1972]
Index register allocation in straight line code and simple loops.
In *Design and Optimization of Compilers* (R. Rustin, ed.).
Prentice-Hall, Englewood Cliffs, N.J., pp. 51–64.

KLEENE, S. C. [1952]
Introduction to Metamathematics.
Van Nostrand Reinhold, New York.

KLEENE, S. C. [1956]
Representation of events in nerve nets.
In Shannon and McCarthy [1956], pp. 3–40.

KNUTH, D. E. [1965]
On the translation of languages from left to right.
Information and Control **8**:6, 607–639.

KNUTH, D. E. [1967]
Top-down syntax analysis.
Lecture Notes.
International Summer School on Computer Programming, Copenhagen.
Also in *Acta Informatica* **1**:2, (1971), 79–110.

KNUTH, D. E. [1968a]
The Art of Computer Programming, Vol. 1: *Fundamental Algorithms.*
Addison-Wesley, Reading, Mass.

KNUTH, D. E. [1968b]
Semantics of context-free languages.
Math. Systems Theory **2**:2, 127–146.
Also see *Math. Systems Theory* **5**: 1, 95–95.

KNUTH, D. E. [1971]
An empirical study of FORTRAN programs.
Software-Practice and Experience **1**:2, 105–134.

KNUTH, D. E. [1973]
The Art of Computer Programming, Vol. 3: *Sorting and Searching.*
Addison-Wesley, Reading, Mass.

KORENJAK, A. J. [1969]
A practical method for constructing LR(k) processors.
Comm. ACM **12**:11, 613–623.

KORENJAK, A. J., and J. E. HOPCROFT [1966]
Simple deterministic languages.
IEEE Conference Record of 7th Annual Symposium on Switching and Automata Theory, pp. 36–46.

KOSARAJU, S. R. [1970]
Finite state automata with markers.
Proc. Fourth Annual Princeton Conference on Information Sciences and Systems, p. 380.

KUNO, S., and A. G. OETTINGER [1962]
Multiple-path syntactic analyzer.
Information Processing 62 (IFIP Congress), Popplewell (ed.).
North-Holland, Amsterdam, pp. 306–311.

KURKI-SUONIO, R. [1969]
Notes on top-down languages.
BIT **9**, 225–238.

LAFRANCE, J. [1970]
Optimization of error recovery in syntax directed parsing algorithms.
ACM SIGPLAN Notices **5**:12, 2–17.

LALONDE, W. R., E. S. LEE, and J. J. HORNING [1971]
An LALR(k) parser generator.
Proc. IFIF Congress 71, TA–3. North-Holland, Amsterdam, pp. 153–157.

LEAVENWORTH, B. M. [1966]
Syntax macros and extended translation.
Comm. ACM **9**:11, 790–793.

LEDLEY, R. S., and J. B. WILSON [1960]
Automatic programming language translation through syntactical analysis.
Comm. ACM **3**, 213–214.

LEE, J. A. N. [1967]
Anatomy of a Compiler.
Van Nostrand Reinhold, New York.

LEINIUS, R. P. [1970]
Error detection and recovery for syntax directed compiler systems.
Ph. D. Thesis, University of Wisconsin, Madison.

LEWIS, P. M., II, and D. J. ROSENKRANTZ [1971]
An ALGOL compiler designed using automata theory.
Proc. Symposium on Computers and Automata, Microwave Research Institute
Symposia Series, Vol. 21. Polytechnic Institute of Brooklyn., New York.,
pp. 75–88.

LEWIS, P. M., II, and R. E. STEARNS [1968]
Syntax directed transduction.
J. ACM **15**:3, 464–488.

LOECKX, J. [1970]
An algorithm for the construction of bounded-context parsers.
Comm. ACM **13**:5, 297–307.

LOWRY, E. S., and C. W. MEDLOCK [1969]
Object code optimization.
Comm. ACM **12**:1, 13–22.

LUCAS, P., and K. WALK [1969]
On the formal description of PL/I.
Annual Review in Automatic Programming, Vol. 6, No. 3.
Pergamon, Elmsford, N.Y., pp. 105–182.

LUCKHAM, D. C., D. M. R. PARK, and M. S. PATERSON [1970]
On formalized computer programs.
J. Computer and System Sciences **4**:3, 220–249.

MANNA, Z. [1973]
Program schemas.
In Aho [1973].

MARKOV, A. A. [1951]
The theory of algorithms (in Russian).
Trudi Mathematicheskova Instituta imeni V. A. Steklova **38**, 176–189. (English
translation, *American Math. Soc. Trans.* **2**:15 (1960), 1–14.)

MARILL, M. [1962]
Computational chains and the size of computer programs.
IRE Trans. on Electronic Computers, **EC-11**: 2, 173–180.

MARTIN, D. F. [1972]
A Boolean matrix method for the computation of linear precedence functions.
Comm. ACM **15**: 6, 448–454.

MAURER, W. D. [1968]
An improved hash code for scatter storage.
Comm. ACM **11**: 1, 35–38.

MCCARTHY, J. [1963]
A basis for the mathematical theory of computation.
In Braffort and Hirschberg [1963], pp. 33–71.

MCCARTHY, J., and J. A. PAINTER [1967]
Correctness of a compiler for arithmetic expressions.
In Schwartz [1967], pp. 33–41.

MCCLURE, R. M. [1965]
TMG—a syntax directed compiler.
Proc. ACM National Conference, Vol. 20, pp. 262–274.

MCCULLOCH, W. S., and W. PITTS [1943]
A logical calculus of the ideas immanent in nervous activity.
Bulletin of Math. Biophysics **5**, 115–133.

MCILROY, M. D. [1960]
Macro instruction extensions of compiler languages.
Comm. ACM **3**: 4, 414–220.

MCILROY, M. D. [1968]
Coroutines.
Unpublished manuscript, Bell Laboratories, Murray Hill, N.J.

MCILROY, M. D. [1972]
A manual for the TMG compiler writing language.
Unpublished memorandum, Bell Laboratories, Murray Hill, N.J.

MCKEEMAN, W. M. [1965]
Peephole optimization.
Comm. ACM **8**: 7, 443–444.

MCKEEMAN, W. M. [1966]
An approach to computer language design.
CS48. Computer Science Department, Stanford University, Stanford, Cal.

MCKEEMAN, W. M., J. J. HORNING, and D. B. WORTMAN [1970]
A Compiler Generator.
Prentice-Hall, Englewood Cliffs, N.J.

MCNAUGHTON, R. [1967]
Parenthesis grammars.
J. ACM **14**: 3, 490–500.

McNaughton, R., and H. Yamada [1960]
Regular expressions and state graphs for automata.
IRE Trans. on Electronic Computers **9**: 1, 39–47.
Reprinted in Moore [1964], pp. 157–174.

Mendelson, E. [1968]
Introduction to Mathematical Logic.
Van Nostrand Reinhold, New York.

Meyers, W. J. [1965]
Optimization of computer code.
Unpublished memorandum. G. E. Research Center, Schenectady, N.Y.

Miller, W. F., and A. C. Shaw [1968]
Linguistic methods in picture processing—a survey.
Proc. AFIPS Fall Joint Computer Conference, Vol. 33.
The Thompson Book Co., Washington, D.C., pp. 279–290.

Minsky, M. [1967]
Computation: Finite and Infinite Machines.
Prentice-Hall, Englewoods Cliffs, N.J.

Montanari, U. G. [1970]
Separable graphs, planar graphs and web grammars.
Information and Control **16**: 3, 243–267.

Moore, E. F. [1965]
Gedanken experiments on sequential machines.
In Shannon and McCarthy [1956], pp. 129–153.

Moore, E. F. [1964]
Sequential Machines: Selected Papers.
Addison-Wesley, Reading, Mass.

Morgan, H. L. [1970]
Spelling correction in systems programs.
Comm. ACM **13**: 2, 90–93.

Morris, Robert [1968]
Scatter storage techniques.
Comm. ACM **11**: 1, 35–44.

Moulton, P. G., and M. E. Muller [1967]
A compiler emphasizing diagnostics.
Comm. ACM **10**: 1, 45–52.

Munro, I. [1971]
Efficient determination of the transitive closure of a directed graph.
Information Processing Letters **1**: 2, 56–58.

Nakata, I. [1967]
On compiling algorithms for arithmetic expressions.
Comm. ACM **12**: 2, 81–84.

NAUR, P. (ed.) [1963]
Revised report on the algorithmic language ALGOL 60.
Comm. ACM **6**:1, 1–17.

NIEVERGELT, J. [1965]
On the automatic simplification of computer programs.
Comm. ACM **8**:6, 366–370.

OETTINGER, A. [1961]
Automatic syntactic analysis and the pushdown store.
In *Structure of Language and its Mathematical Concepts, Proc. 12th Symposium on Applied Mathematics.* American Mathematical Society, Providence, pp. 104–129.

OGDEN, W. [1968]
A helpful result for proving inherent ambiguity.
Mathematical Systems Theory **2**:3, 191–194.

ORE, O. [1962]
Theory of Graphs.
American Mathematical Society Colloquium Publications, Vol. 38, Providence.

PAGER, D. [1970]
A solution to an open problem by Knuth.
Information and Control **17**:5, 462–473.

PAINTER, J. A. [1970]
Effectiveness of an optimizing compiler for arithmetic expressions.
ACM SIGPLAN Notices **5**:7, 101–126.

PAIR, C. [1964]
Trees, pushdown stores and compilation.
RFTI—Chiffres **7**:3, 199–216.

PARIKH, R. J. [1966]
On context-free languages.
J. ACM **13**:4, 570–581.

PATERSON, M. S. [1968]
Program schemata.
Machine Intelligence, Vol. 3 (Michie, ed.).
Edinburgh University Press, Edinburgh, pp. 19–31.

PAUL, M. [1962]
A general processor for certain formal languages.
Proc. ICC Symposium on Symbolic Language Data Processing.
Gordon & Breach, New York, pp. 65–74.

PAULL, M. C., and S. H. UNGER [1968a]
Structural equivalence of context-free grammars.
J. Computer and System Sciences **2**:1, 427–463.

PAULL, M. C., and S. H. UNGER [1968b]
Structural equivalence and LL-k grammars.

IEEE Conference Record of Ninth Annual Symposium on Switching and Automata Theory, pp. 176–186.

PAVLIDIS, T. [1972]
Linear and context-free graph grammars.
J. ACM **19**:1, 11–23.

PETERSON, W. W. [1957]
Addressing for random access storage.
IBM J. Research and Development **1**:2, 130–146.

PETRONE, L. [1968]
Syntax directed mapping of context-free languages.
IEEE Conference Record of 9th Annual Symposium on Switching and Automata Theory, pp. 160–175.

PFALTZ, J. L., and A. ROSENFELD [1969]
Web grammars.
Proc. International Joint Conference on Artificial Intelligence, Washington, D. C., pp. 609–619.

POST, E. L. [1943]
Formal reductions of the general combinatorial decision problem.
American J. of Math. **65**, 197–215.

POST, E. L. [1947]
Recursive unsolvability of a problem of Thue.
J. Symbolic Logic, **12**, 1–11. Reprinted in Davis [1965], pp. 292–303.

POST, E. L. [1965]
Absolutely unsolvable problems and relatively undecidable propositions—account of an anticipation.
In Davis [1965], pp. 338–433.

PRATHER, R. E. [1969]
Minimal solutions of Paull-Unger problems.
Math. System Theory **3**:1, 76–85.

PRICE, C. E. [1971]
Table lookup techniques.
ACM Computing Surveys, **3**:2, 49–66.

PROSSER, R. T. [1959]
Applications of Boolean matrices to the analysis of flow diagrams.
Proc. Eastern J. Computer Conference, Spartan Books, N.Y., pp. 133–138.

RABIN, M. O. [1967]
Mathematical theory of automata.
In Schwartz [1967], pp. 173–175.

RABIN, M. O., and D. SCOTT [1959]
Finite automata and their decision problems.
IBM J. Research and Development **3**, 114–125.
Reprinted in Moore [1964], pp. 63–91.

RADKE, C. E. [1970]
The use of quadratic residue search.
Comm. ACM **13**:2, 103–109.

RANDELL, B., and L. J. RUSSELL [1964]
ALGOL 60 Implementation.
Academic Press, New York.

REDZIEJOWSKI, R. R. [1969]
On arithmetic expressions and trees.
Comm. ACM **12**:2, 81–84.

REYNOLDS, J. C. [1965]
An introduction to the COGENT programming system.
Proc. ACM National Conference, Vol. 20, p. 422.

REYNOLDS, J. C., and R. HASKELL [1970]
Grammatical coverings.
Unpublished memorandum, Syracuse University.

RICHARDSON, D. [1968]
Some unsolvable problems involving elementary functions of a real variable.
J. Symbolic Logic **33**, 514–520.

ROGERS, H., JR. [1967]
Theory of Recursive Functions and Effective Computability.
McGraw-Hill, New York.

ROSEN S. (ed.) [1967a]
Programming Systems and Languages.
McGraw-Hill, New York.

ROSEN, S. [1967b]
A compiler-building system developed by Brooker and Morris.
In Rosen [1967a], pp. 306–331.

ROSENKRANTZ, D. J. [1967]
Matrix equations and normal forms for context-free grammars.
J. ACM **14**: 3, 501–507.

ROSENKRANTZ, D. J. [1968]
Programmed grammars and classes of formal languages.
J. ACM **16**:1, 107–131.

ROSENKRANTZ, D. J., and P. M. LEWIS, II [1970]
Deterministic left corner parsing.
IEEE Conference Record of 11th Annual Symposium on Switching and Automata Theory, pp. 139–152.

ROSENKRANTZ, D. J., and R. E. STEARNS [1970]
Properties of deterministic top-down grammars.
Information and Control **17**:3, 226–256.

SALOMAA, A. [1966]
Two complete axiom systems for the algebra of regular events.
J. ACM **13**: 1, 158–169.

SALOMAA, A. [1969a]
Theory of Automata.
Pergamon, Elmsford, N.Y.

SALOMAA, A. [1969b]
On the index of a context-free grammar and language.
Information and Control 14:5, 474–477.

SAMELSON, K., and F. L. BAUER [1960]
Sequential formula translation.
Comm. ACM 3:2, 76–83.

SAMMET, J. E. [1969]
Programming Languages: History and Fundamentals.
Prentice-Hall, Englewood Cliffs, N.J.

SCHAEFER, M. [1973]
A Mathematical Theory of Global Program Optimization
Prentice-Hall, Englewood Cliffs, N.J., to appear.

SCHORRE, D. V. [1964]
META II, a syntax oriented compiler writing language.
Proc. ACM National Conference, Vol. 19, pp. D1.3-1–D1.3-11.

SCHUTZENBERGER, M. P. [1963]
On context-free languages and pushdown automata.
Information and Control 6:3, 246–264.

SCHWARTZ, J. T. (ed.) [1967]
Mathematical Aspects of Computer Science.
Proc. Symposia in Applied Mathematics, Vol. 19.
American Mathematical Society, Providence.

SCOTT, D., and C. STRACHEY [1971]
Towards a mathematical semantics for computer languages.
Proc. Symposium on Computers and Automata, Microwave Research Institute
Symposia Series, Vol. 21. Polytechnic Institute of Brooklyn, New York, pp.
19–46.

SETHI, R. [1973]
Validating register allocations for straight line programs.
Ph. D. Thesis, Department of Electrical Engineering, Princeton University.

SETHI, R., and J. D. ULLMAN [1970]
The generation of optimal code for arithmetic expressions.
J. ACM 17:4, 715–728.

SHANNON, C. E., and J. MCCARTHY (eds.) [1956]
Automata Studies.
Princeton University Press, Princeton, N.J.

SHAW, A. C. [1970]
Parsing of graph-representable pictures.
J. ACM 17:3, 453–481.

SHEPHERDSON, J. C. [1959]
The reduction of two-way automata to one-way automata.
IBM J. Research **3**, 198–200. Reprinted in Moore [1964], pp. 92–97.

STEARNS, R. E. [1967]
A regularity test for pushdown machines.
Information and Control **11**:3, 323–340.

STEARNS, R. E. [1971]
Deterministic top-down parsing.
Proc. Fifth Annual Princeton Conference on Information Sciences and Systems,
pp. 182–188.

STEARNS, R. E., and P. M. LEWIS, II [1969]
Property grammars and table machines.
Information and Control **14**:6, 524–549.

STEARNS, R. E., and D. J. ROSENKRANTZ [1969]
Table machine simulation.
*IEEE Conference Record of 10th Annual Symposium on Switching and Automata
Theory*, pp. 118–128.

STEEL, T. B. (ed.) [1966]
Formal Language Description Languages for Computer Programming.
North-Holland, Amsterdam.

STONE, H. S. [1967]
One-pass compilation of arithmetic expressions for a parallel processor.
Comm. ACM **10**:4, 220–223.

STRASSEN, V. [1969]
Gaussian elimination is not optimal.
Numerische Mathematik **13**, 354–356.

SUPPES, P. [1960]
Axiomatic Set Theory.
Van Nostrand Reinhold, New York.

TARJAN, R. [1972]
Depth first search and linear graph algorithms.
SIAM J. on Computing **1**:2, 146–160.

THOMPSON, K. [1968]
Regular expression search algorithm.
Comm. ACM **11**:6, 419–422.

TURING, A. M. [1936]
On computable numbers, with an application to the *Entscheidungsproblem.*
Proc. London Mathematical Soc. Ser. 2, **42**, 230–265. Corrections, *Ibid.*, **43**
(1937), 544–546.

ULLMAN, J. D. [1972a]
A note on hashing functions.
J. ACM **19**:3, 569–575.

ULLMAN, J. D. [1972b]
Fast Algorithms for the Elimination of Common Subexpressions.
Technical Report TR-106, Dept. of Electrical Engineering, Princeton University, Princeton, N.J.

UNGER, S. H. [1968]
A global parser for context-free phrase structure grammars.
Comm. ACM **11**:4, 240–246, and **11**:6, 427.

VAN WIJNGAARDEN, A. (ed.) [1969]
Report on the algorithmic language ALGOL 68.
Numerische Mathematik **14**, 79–218.

WALTERS, D. A. [1970]
Deterministic context-sensitive languages.
Information and Control **17**:1, 14–61.

WARSHALL, S. [1962]
A theorem on Boolean matrices.
J. ACM **9**:1, 11–12.

WARSHALL, S., and R. M. SHAPIRO [1964]
A general purpose table driven compiler.
Proc. AFIPS Spring Joint Computer Conference, Vol. 25.
Spartan, New York, pp. 59–65.

WEGBREIT, B. [1970]
Studies in extensible programming languages.
Ph. D. Thesis, Harvard University, Cambridge, Mass.

WILCOX, T. R. [1971]
Generating machine code for high-level programming languages.
Technical Report 71-103. Department of Computer Science, Cornell University, Ithaca, N.Y.

WINOGRAD, S. [1965]
On the time required to perform addition.
J. ACM **12**:2, 277–285.

WINOGRAD, S. [1967]
On the time required to perform multiplication.
J. ACM **14**:4, 793–802.

WIRTH, N. [1965]
Algorithm 265: Find precedence functions.
Comm. ACM **8**:10, 604–605.

WIRTH, N. [1968]
PL 360—a programming language for the 360 computers.
J. ACM **15**:1, 37–34.

WIRTH, N., and H. WEBER [1966]
EULER—a generalization of ALGOL and its formal definition, Parts 1 and 2.
Comm. ACM **9**: 1–2, 13–23, and 89–99.

WISE, D. S. [1971]
Domolki's algorithm applied to generalized overlap resolvable grammars.
Proc. Third Annual ACM Symposium on Theory of Computing, pp. 171–184.

WOOD, D. [1969a]
The theory of left factored languages.
Computer J. **12**:4, 349–356, and *13*:1, 55–62.

WOOD, D. [1969b]
A note on top on top-down deterministic languages.
BIT **9**:4, 387–399.

WOOD, D. [1970]
Bibliography 23: Formal language theory and automata theory.
Computing Reviews **11**:7, 417–430.

WOZENCRAFT, J. M., and A. EVANS, JR. [1969]
Notes on Programming Languages.
Department of Electrical Engineering, Massachusetts Institute of Technology,
Cambridge, Mass.

YERSHOV, A. P. [1966]
ALPHA—an automatic programming system of high efficiency.
J. ACM **13**:1, 17–24.

YOUNGER, D. H. [1967]
Recognition and parsing of context-free languages in time n^3.
Information and Control **10**:2, 189–208.

INDEX TO LEMMAS, THEOREMS, AND ALGORITHMS

INDEX TO VOLUMES I AND II